INDIA

INDIA

A Guide for the
Quality-Conscious Traveller

by Louise Nicholson

The Atlantic Monthly Press

BOSTON / NEW YORK

FIRST AMERICAN EDITION

LIBRARY OF CONGRESS CATALOGING IN PUBLICATION DATA

Nicholson, Louise, 1954–
    India, a guide for the quality-conscious traveller.

    Includes bibliographies and index.
    1. India—Description and travel—1981—   —Guide-
books. I. Title.
DS414.2.N52   1985   915.4'0452   85-71410
ISBN 0-87113-047-5

M V

PRINTED IN THE UNITED STATES OF AMERICA

For my parents

Contents

Acknowledgements

I am abashed by the enthusiasm and generosity with which friends in Britain and India have greeted the idea of this book. Everyone I have spoken to has eagerly responded with tips and advice based on their experience and knowledge of India. They, like myself, want other people to enjoy this fascinating and stimulating land and to avoid the potential pitfalls. Their contribution to the following chapters has been invaluable and I am deeply grateful.

In Britain, I would like to thank especially Air India for flying me to India to do research and the staff of the Government of India Tourist Office and the High Commission for India for their constant support. British Airways carried home all my extra luggage and assisted me on an earlier visit to India. I am indebted to many individuals including Robert Alderman, Sarah Anderson, John Bethell, Anthony Blond, Paddy Bowring, Idrone and Roger Brittain, Andrew Brock, Tina Brown, Sandeep Chatterjee, Julia Clarke, Bruce Cleghorn, Shona Crawford Poole, Mitch Crites, Teresa de Chair, Niranjan Desai, Simon Digby, Josceline Dimbleby, Margaret Erskine, Harry Evans, Lillian Fonseca, Jack Franses, Sarah Giles, Christoph Goodhart, Nicholas Grace, Joss Graham, Germaine Greer, Sarah Gristwood, Kenneth Griffiths, Michael and Claire Hamlyn, Derek Healey, Laura and Sarah Hesketh, Niall Hobhouse, Yasmin and Shahid Hosain, Anthony Hutt, Gour Kanjilal, Shashi Kapoor, Peter Kaufeler, M. M. Kaye, Philip Knightley, Bernard Levin, Andrew Logan, Joanna Lumley, Victoria Mather, Gita Mehta, Malcolm and Kitty Muggeridge, Dr and Mrs Seyid Mohammed, Veronica Murphy, Prince Ali Murza and Princess Ara Murshidabad, Christina Noble, Pepita Noble, Amy Osborne, Camellia Panjabi, Indar and Aruna Pasricha, Emma Playfair, Shubita Punja, Frances and Richard Rice, Carol Robertson, Jancis Robinson, Phyllis Rogers, Lady Jane Sheldon, Kranti Singh, Robert Skelton, Gavin Stamp, Cob Stenham, Edwin Taylor, Andrew Topsfield, Dr Anthony Turner, Lucia van der Post, Nick van Gruisen, Jay Visva-Deva, John Warrington, Brian Witham, Carol Wood and Mark Zebrowski. My husband, Nick, and my brother-in-law, Tim, have been constant supports.

In India, my thanks go first to the Welcomgroup of hotels who hosted me in their hotels and also provided me with my invaluable research aid, a car and driver for six weeks. I am grateful to the Taj group of hotels and to Cox & Kings travel agent for their assistance on this and a previous extended visit to India. My thanks also go to Indian Airlines and to the Ashok, Clarks, Palace, Sheraton and Spencer hotel groups; to the Cama and Ritz hotels in Ahmedabad, the Malabar Hotel at Cochin. Throughout India, staff of the Government of India Tourist Offices and state

INDIA

Tourist Offices have been generous with their time and knowledge.

However, it is the extraordinary friendship and immediate help from individuals that I would like to acknowledge most of all. To name them all is impossible but I would particularly like to thank Anand who was my driver for many days, Arun and Rupam Bahl, Baiji, Anil Bajaj, Anoop Banerjee, S. K. Beri, G. D. Brara, D. K. Burman, Sreelata Bhatia, Dr T. K. Biswas, D. S. Chauda, Veena Chawla, Malti Chopra, Sarla Chopra, Dr Das, Sudir and Meena Deshpande, Ravi Dube, Allan Fernandes, Trevor and Penny Fishlock, Sanjay Ganguli, Feroz Gimi, Harish Gorsia, Mr and Mrs Guhan, B. S. Gupta, Kushru Irani, Jaya Jaitley, Guli and Vihar Juneja, S. K. Kandhari, Kanoul Kapoor, Sanjay and Zareen Khan, Prem Kumar, V. Lakshminarayanan, Lakshmi Lal, Zelma Lazarus, Ena Malhotra, Nutan Malhotra, Gulam Mohammad Major, Mr Mangalick, K. M. Mathew, Mario Miranda, Naomi Meadows, S. K. Mukherjee, Umaima Mulla-Feroze, Shanka Sheela Nai, Aman Nath, Mrs Vibha Pandhi, Girish Patel, Naveen Patnaik, Primo Pereira, Dileep Rao, Ratna Sahai, Babla Senapati, Rabindra Seth, Arun Sharma, R. K. Sharma, Dr Maurice Shellim, K. G. Shenoy, Indu Shridhar, Toby Sinclair, Brijendra Singh, I. V. Singh, Malvika and Tajbir Singh, Moyna Singh, Partha Talukdar and Bob and Anne Wright.

John Grimwade created the very fine maps from my tangle of references. Margaret Cornell undertook the mammoth tasks of editing, proof-reading and indexing.

Preface

My husband introduced me to India for our honeymoon. He gave me a month in paradise. Our days were entirely free from the disasters faced by many first-time visitors to India. This was largely thanks to the generosity of our friends who know India well and gave us the benefit of their experiences. This book, the product of subsequent visits to India and more tips from friends, aims to give everyone the opportunity to explore and enjoy all that India has to offer unhampered by practical problems.

The criteria for luxury are not the same in India as in the West. India is ablaze with exotic traditions, crafts, peoples, food, wildlife, buildings and colours. These are the luxuries on which visitors get hooked. These are what they return for again and again. If you find yourself dreaming of your next visit to India on the plane home, then you, too, have been caught by this fascinating and stimulating land.

So that future visitors can benefit from your experiences, too, please write to me with any advice and tips you feel would be useful to them.

Transliteration note

As far as possible, the English transliteration of Indian words follows the common usage in India today. Thus, Pune rather than Poona, Varanasi rather than Banaras and sati rather than suttee.

INDIA

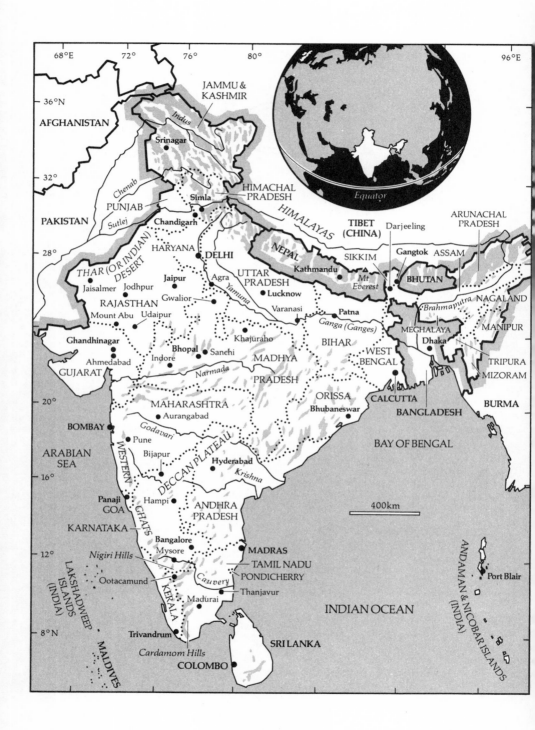

Dreams to departure:
Pre-India preparation

The map

The first step towards realising the dream of going to India is to buy Bartholomew's World Travel Map no. 15: Indian subcontinent, India, Pakistan, Bangladesh, Sri Lanka (see bookshop lists, p. 15). The vastness of India is quickly apparent. The browns and greens of deserts, mountains and fertile areas stretch from 8 to 37 degrees latitude and from 68 to 97 degrees longitude. The size is baffling. Indians living near the southern tip are as far away from their capital, Delhi, as Athens is from London. Hopping from Delhi to Bombay or Calcutta is much the same as going from London to Madrid or Rome.

Clearly, a visit to India must be selective – unless you have a few years on your hands to explore it all. But there really is little point in going to India for less than three weeks. Those who think that two weeks will be enough for the first visit do not understand the complications of travelling inside the country and the mental adjustment needed to make sense of it all. It takes at least three or four days to throw off jet lag and get used to the climate, pace and rhythms of India. Conversely, it is unlikely that a first-time visitor will be able to concentrate and absorb the onslaught of visual and mental stimulations which the country provides for more than about four weeks.

From the second visit onwards, you will be able to judge how much of India you can take in at a time. Some people, equipped with their first experiences, will be able to tackle a long stay. Similarly, they will be able to go to selected parts of India for as short as two weeks.

After buying the map, the next step is to decide which parts of India to visit. This is the most crucial decision for a successful and happy trip, and depends upon numerous personal likes and dislikes and a few salient truths and tips.

When to go where

CLIMATE   It is quite possible to go to India the year round, avoiding blistering heat and monsoons, provided you choose your area. While it is roasting in the South, it can be mild in Delhi and the Himalayan peaks will be covered in snow. Whatever climate suits you, it can be found somewhere in India throughout the year.

The plains of India are at their freshest and best during the winter. The optimum season to travel in northern India, to Rajasthan and around Delhi, is between September and March, although it can be quite chilly in December and January. To the east, the more extreme combination of heat, humidity and monsoon leaves only November to February fairly comfortable. Southern India is hot all the time but again best between November and February. Even then, some people will

1

find the heat disagreeable. The green strip of Kerala down the Malabar Coast is more temperate, with a much gentler climate.

The scorching pre-monsoon heat, the monsoon deluge and the post-monsoon humidity strike almost everywhere some time between May and September. All aspects of the monsoon are to be avoided if at all possible, although many places are particularly lush and beautiful immediately after the rains.

Monsoon is the time to go up into the Himalayas, choosing any spot from Srinagar right across to Darjeeling, or even nipping out of India to Nepal or Bhutan. The weather

in the hills intensifies as the slopes get high and the air thinner, bringing winter snov spring and summer blossoms under soft su shine, and rich autumn colours. The rair months in the hills are quite localised ar should be checked out carefully.

Other cool spots are the southern Nilg and Cardamom hills which divide the state Tamil Nadu from Kerala, the hilltop haun inland from Bombay, and Mount Abu, on tl Rajasthan-Gujarat border. See under Whe to Go and Hard Facts chapter headings f more guidelines. See also weather chart b low.

Weather Chart

T = Temperature (°
R = Rainfall (mm.)

City			Jan	Feb	Mar	Apr	May	Jun	Jul	Aug	Sep	Oct	Nov	D
Ahmedabad	T	max.	29	31	36	40	41	38	33	32	33	36	33	
		min.	12	15	19	23	26	27	26	25	24	21	16	
	R	avg.	4	0	1	2	5	100	316	213	163	13	5	
Aurangabad	T	max.	29	32	36	38	40	35	29	29	30	31	30	
		min.	14	16	20	24	25	23	22	21	21	20	16	
	R	avg.	3	3	4	7	17	141	189	146	179	62	32	
Bangalore	T	max.	28	31	33	34	33	30	28	29	28	28	27	
		min.	15	16	19	21	21	20	19	19	19	19	17	
	R	avg.	4	14	6	37	119	65	93	95	129	195	46	
Bhopal	T	max.	26	29	34	38	41	37	30	29	30	31	29	
		min.	10	13	17	21	26	25	23	23	22	18	13	
	R	avg.	17	5	10	3	11	137	429	308	232	37	15	
Bombay	T	max.	31	32	33	33	33	32	30	29	30	32	33	
		min.	16	17	20	24	26	26	25	24	24	23	20	
	R	avg.	0	1	0	0	20	647	945	660	309	117	7	
Calcutta	T	max.	26	29	34	36	36	34	32	32	32	31	29	
		min.	12	15	20	24	26	26	26	26	26	24	18	
	R	avg.	13	22	30	50	135	263	320	318	253	134	29	
Cochin	T	max.	31	31	31	31	31	29	28	28	28	29	30	
		min.	23	24	26	26	26	24	24	24	24	24	24	
	R	avg.	9	34	50	139	364	756	572	386	235	333	184	
Coimbatore	T	max.	30	33	35	35	34	31	30	31	32	31	29	
		min.	19	19	21	23	23	22	22	22	22	22	21	
	R	avg.	7	4	5	70	76	35	37	18	42	127	127	
Darjeeling	T	max.	9	11	15	18	19	19	20	20	20	19	15	
		min.	3	4	8	11	13	15	15	15	15	11	7	
	R	avg.	22	27	52	109	187	522	713	573	419	116	14	

eather Chart

T = Temperature (°C)
R = Rainfall (mm.)

y			Jan	Feb	Mar	Apr	May	Jun	Jul	Aug	Sep	Oct	Nov	Dec
elhi	T	max.	21	24	30	36	41	40	35	34	34	35	29	23
		min.	7	10	15	21	27	29	27	26	25	19	12	8
	R	avg.	25	22	17	7	8	65	211	173	150	31	1	5
yderabad	T	max.	29	31	35	37	39	34	30	29	30	30	29	28
		min.	15	17	20	24	26	24	22	22	22	20	16	13
	R	avg.	2	11	13	24	30	107	165	147	163	71	25	5
pur	T	max.	22	25	31	37	41	39	34	32	33	33	29	24
		min.	8	11	15	21	26	27	26	24	23	18	12	9
	R	avg.	14	8	9	4	10	54	193	239	90	19	3	4
nmu	T	max.	18	21	26	33	39	40	35	33	33	31	26	21
		min.	8	11	15	21	26	28	26	25	24	19	13	9
	R	avg.	71	54	57	25	17	61	321	319	151	29	8	29
dhpur	T	max.	25	28	33	38	42	40	36	33	35	36	31	27
		min.	9	12	17	22	27	29	27	25	24	20	14	11
	R	avg.	7	5	2	2	6	31	122	145	47	7	3	1
cknow	T	max.	23	26	33	38	41	39	34	33	33	33	29	25
		min.	9	11	16	22	27	28	27	26	25	20	13	9
	R	avg.	24	17	9	6	12	94	299	302	182	40	1	6
adras	T	max.	29	31	33	35	38	37	35	35	34	32	29	28
		min.	20	21	23	26	28	28	26	26	25	24	23	21
	R	avg.	24	7	15	25	52	53	83	124	118	267	309	139
adurai	T	max.	30	32	35	36	37	37	36	35	35	33	31	30
		min.	21	22	23	25	26	26	26	25	25	24	23	22
	R	avg.	26	16	21	81	59	31	48	117	123	179	161	43
naji (Goa)	T	max.	31	32	32	33	33	31	29	29	29	31	33	33
		min.	19	20	23	25	27	25	24	24	24	23	22	21
	R	avg.	2	0	4	17	18	580	892	341	277	122	20	37
rt Blair	T	max.	29	30	31	32	31	29	29	29	29	29	29	29
		min.	23	22	23	26	24	24	24	24	24	24	24	23
	R	avg.	29	26	23	71	363	589	435	436	516	329	205	157
ne	T	max.	31	33	36	38	37	32	28	28	29	32	31	30
		min.	12	13	17	21	23	23	22	21	21	19	15	12
	R	avg.	2	0	3	18	35	103	187	106	127	92	37	5
ri	T	max.	27	28	30	31	32	31	31	31	31	31	29	27
		min.	18	21	25	27	27	27	27	27	27	25	21	18
	R	avg.	9	20	14	12	63	187	296	256	258	242	75	8
mla	T	max.	9	10	14	19	23	24	21	20	20	18	15	11
		min.	2	3	7	11	15	16	16	15	14	10	7	4
	R	avg.	65	48	58	38	54	147	415	385	195	45	7	24
inagar	T	max.	4	8	13	19	25	29	31	30	28	23	15	9
		min.	−2	−1	3	7	11	14	18	18	13	6	0	−2
	R	avg.	73	72	104	78	63	36	61	63	32	29	17	36
ivandrum	T	max.	31	32	33	32	31	29	29	29	30	30	30	31
		min.	22	23	24	25	25	24	23	23	23	23	23	23
	R	avg.	20	20	43	122	249	331	215	164	123	271	207	73
aranasi	T	max.	23	27	33	39	41	39	33	32	32	32	29	25
		min.	9	11	17	22	27	28	26	26	25	21	13	9
	R	avg.	23	8	14	1	8	102	346	240	261	38	15	2

3

INDIAN FESTIVALS Bursts of colour, song, drums, trumpets, dance, elephants in fancy dress, banners, fireworks, processions and ecstatic enjoyment punctuate the Indian calendar. Indians are quite blasé about their constant stream of glorious festivals, so much so that one Calcuttan even suggested that tourists might wish to avoid Durga Puja, Calcutta's most spectacular major festival. But, for Westerners, the Indian art of celebration outshines any Easter Parade, Christmas, Bastille Day or Thanksgiving.

There is a festival for everything, from weddings and elections to the all-important harvest and the arrival of the rains – even festivals to honour bullocks and snakes. There are Muslim, Christian, Sikh, Buddhist and Jain festivals. But the vast plethora of Hindu gods and goddesses have the most. Every temple deity has its own special festival, as well as various extras. A deity may visit a fellow deity in another temple, take a bath, change her clothes or collect his wife. It may be the god's wedding anniversary or annual holiday. Or a festival may celebrate the past triumphs of a hero god, as recounted in the great Indian epics. Hindu gods have very worldly emotions and life-styles and are an integral part of Hindu life. Hindu and Muslim festivals, as well as the big markets and fairs, attract the quality performers of classical and folk dance, music and singing. And some festivals attract pilgrims, itinerant entertainers and visitors from all over India, and last for up to ten days.

Although you are bound to bump into small festivals, to coincide with one of the major festivals is a memorable experience. However, it is not very straightforward to find one. Only four festivals have absolute fixed dates, and they are not the best. They are Republic Day (January 26), Independence Day (August 15), Mahatma Gandhi's Birthday (October 2) and Christmas Day (December 25). Hindu religious festivals are calculated according to the lunar calendar, roughly keeping within a four-week span. The final decisions are made annually by the pundits for the following year. Muslim festivals move right around the year. By November, the worldwide Indian tourist offices can supply a list of the following year's major festival dates.

The next trick is to be in the right place for the right festival. For instance, the September–October festival of Dussehra is best seen at Varanasi (Banaras) and Delhi, where it is called Ram Lila; at Calcutta, where it is called Durga Puja; and at Mysore, where it is Dassehra. Holi is best in Rajasthan, Pongal in Tamil Nadu and Muharram Lucknow. See pp. 251–3, for a list of the bigg festivals and see under When To Go and Ha Facts chapter headings for details about them. O or two travel agents organise package tours spec cally to coincide with big festivals and fairs.

Where to go

THE SELECTION PROCESS India has eve thing. Only you can decide what you want to s and how you want to see it. Your idea of a drea holiday in India may be rushing up mountai palace-hopping in Rajasthan, drooling ov Dravidian temple architecture, making long tra journeys, watching the local craftsmen or spotti wildlife from an elephant's back.

The following chapters try to give an idea of t range on offer. But one man's fascination another's absolute boredom. Recently, o Indophile recommended Bijapur, one of I favourite cities, to a friend. His friend dro through the night from Bombay and arrived to fi an unsympathetic atmosphere, no accommodati and buildings not to his taste at all.

There is far more to India than the golden t angle of Delhi, Agra and Jaipur and, although t Taj and Fatehpur Sikri are magical, there is compulsion to visit them first. They will still there next time. Many people see the Cote d'Az before Paris, Tuscan villages before Rome a Disney World before New York or Washington. addition, the Indian golden triangle is much mo enjoyable outside the tourist rush of November January. There is so much else to see and do tha seems a shame to follow the Western throng.

It is best to select one or two areas of the coun and combine visits to monuments with wanders town bazaars and outings to nearby villages by and train. This way, you can see how people liv work and celebrate their festivals. This is far mo rewarding than taking a plane every other day t new set of isolated monuments. And a few days a game park, walking the hills or soaking in the s always happily tags on to the front or back of two three weeks of sightseeing and travelling.

ARCHITECTURE India is full of sublin architecture, despite the ravages of countle marauders. There are Buddhist, Hindu, Musli Jain and colonial monuments of the highest quali throughout the country. But some are much eas to get to and better equipped for tourists th thers. The more isolated sites suggested in this ook will, I hope, repay the longish journeys to get them and the more modest accommodation.

Old Delhi, Agra and Fatehpur Sikri have the reat Mughal monuments. Rajasthan is covered in illtop forts and sumptuous, wedding-cake alaces, many of which are now converted into otels. All these are very easy to visit. So are the ck temples of Ajanta and Ellora, the Hindu temles of Orissa and Khajuraho, the sacred city of aranasi and nearby Buddhist Sarnath. All of these e served with airports and comfortable hotels.

The rewards of the more hardy and intrepid aveller are sensational. In Karnataka, the agnificent ruined city of Hampi and the Hoysala mples are a bit of an effort to reach, as are some of e temple cities of Tamil Nadu. Karnataka's other easures are hardly ever visited – Bidar, Bijapur nd the early Hindu temples in and around adami. Nor do many visitors reach the central idian monuments at Sanchi, Mandu and Bhopal the ruined palace forts of Datia and Orchha, uth of Gwalior. Accommodation may not be xurious in these places, but the quality of the iildings most certainly is.

ILDLIFE SANCTUARIES   The parks of India id Nepal cover thousands of square kilometres id give sanctuary to a wide range of threatened ecies of mammal, reptile and bird, as well as wers and trees. India is an important area for imal conservation work (see p. 106 on Project ger). Visitors explore the parks by jeep and on ephant. However, few are yet as well run as the frican parks and accommodation may be quite mple. One exception is the Royal Chitwan ational Park in Nepal. See Wildlife Sanctuaries ction at the end of each chapter for which ones ould fit in with your itinerary.

EACHES   Considering the length and beauty of coastline, India has few good beach resorts. Goa best, followed by the coast south of Madras. But e choice extends to the smart beaches of Sri inka, the escapist islands of the Maldives and the mote Andaman and Nicobar Islands. All are very autiful and perfect places for switching off (see hapter 9).

LUBS AND SPORTS   The network of thriving cial clubs with good sports facilities is a legacy of e Raj days, when they were developed to their eight. India is sports-crazy. Cricket is not only played on every available patch of green (or brown), but on a bigger pitch several games can be played simultaneously. Some fielders take part in two matches at once. Apparently there is never an accident. Golf and tennis are just as popular.

The clubs are often in the city centre. The better ones have excellent facilities (golf, tennis, swimming, indoor games, libraries, etc.) and charming buildings set in acres of immaculate gardens and lawns. Some are more exclusive than others. Temporary membership is usually granted to foreigners. A few have reciprocal arrangements with European clubs. A few have rooms to stay in. The relevant Secretary is the person to approach for details. Useful clubs are listed in the chapters below.

BIG CITIES   India's big cities are much more difficult to visit than their equivalents in Europe and America. They are huge, sprawling and over-populated. But Delhi, Bombay, Calcutta and Madras have fine colonial buildings and offer rare opportunities to see India's great musicians and dancers. Delhi and Bombay have the best restaurants in the country and something almost approaching the Western idea of a night life. Both cities are essential for stocking up on information, bookings and literature on the way into India and have the best shopping on the way out. A full two days in either city at the beginning and end of the trip makes things run much more smoothly in between. See pp. 43 and 116.

MOVING AROUND   Just as important and amusing as deciding which places to visit is deciding how best to get to them. For instance, few journeys are as enjoyable as the flight up from Srinagar to Leh, the boat from Goa to Bombay, the train from near Coimbatore to Ooty, the ferry from Kottayam to Alleppey or the drive from Jammu to Srinagar. See p. 24 and the Getting There: Getting Away and The Hard Facts sections of the following chapters.

Package holidays: the pros and cons

Booking flights and hotels in India from home can be a slog, particularly if you are not sticking to the big hotel chains. And booking trains and planes, hiring cars and generally getting around is quite hard work in India. The overwhelming advantage

5

of a package holiday is that someone else does the hard work and the worrying.

Package holidays have come a long way in recent years, particularly the more unusual holidays for small groups. There are trips which specialise in wildlife, flowers, trekking, Rajasthan palaces, trains and there is even a gourmet tour.

The good firms have been ferrying travellers around for some years and have developed their own character and reputation. They have representatives throughout India who meet and look after clients. They inspect their hotels carefully and switch allegiance if necessary. They have good guides for monuments and expert sherpas for trekking. They apply for all the necessary visas. Furthermore, because they can do good deals with air carriers and hotels, the prices they offer can often be substantially less than arranging the same trip oneself. The most successful example of this is Kuoni's 8-night Taj tour to Delhi, Agra and Jaipur, currently selling for £498 all in.

Tour operators are increasingly sensitive to the tourist who cannot abide group living. They take great care and trouble over planning and booking tailor-made trips for individuals. They run tours where the flight and hotel room are the only fixed items – all meals, sight-seeing and trips are optional. The larger firms offer optional extra weeks for individual tour members to go on a houseboat in Kashmir, to a Goa beach or to visit Nepal. These are hitched on to the front or back of the main sight-seeing tour. Again, they do all the booking and worrying, you just pay a flat fee. And some firms can also offer clients the option of going off on their own after the tour, so long as they fly out of India with one of their tour groups. In the high season, there are plenty of flights.

Having avoided most of the old phobias of being part of a travelling circus and of not being able to stay in one place long enough, the only big disadvantage of a package deal is that, even with tailor-made trips, it is not that easy to change the programme. So, if you decide you want to visit Khajuraho instead of Varanasi or to spend extra days in Udaipur and skip Jodhpur, it can be difficult to arrange. And it is maddening to discover that there is a major festival coming up two days after you leave town. This flexibility is crucial to many travellers and is why, for them, it is better to go solo. Outside the high season, getting into the recommended hotels is usually quite easy, except where indicated in the chapters below.

The worldwide Indian Tourist Offices supply a full and impartial list of tour operators who go India from any country. Below are a few of the many British operators to give an idea of the range of tours available. All of these firms have a constantly high reputation for quality and service both in Britain and in India and do tailor-made trips.

BRITISH TOUR OPERATORS

Kuoni Travel Ltd, Kuoni House, Dorking, Surrey (tel: 0306 885044). Currently the largest tour operator from the UK to India. Quality tours to the principal sights throughout India, divided into two groups: the cheaper Kuoni 3 range (including the £498 Taj trip) and Kuoni Worldwide, their more expensive, in-depth visits.

Cox & Kings Travel Ltd, 46 Marshall Street, London W1 (tel: 439 8292). Have been ferrying the British and their baggage to and from India for two centuries. With Kuoni, the best reputation for solid, quality tours throughout India and expert client attention. Now widening their range to include eastern and southern India and the Maldives.

Abercrombie & Kent, 42 Sloane Street, London SW1 (tel: 235 9761/4). In addition to regular sights their off-beat trips include a Goa tour with visits the splendid private Portugese mansions.

Speedbird Holidays, 152 King Street, London W6 (tel: 741 8041). A subsidiary of British Airways Slightly less smart than those listed above, but solid range of good trips covering areas from the Himalayas down to the Maldives and Sri Lanka.

Bales Tours Ltd, Bales House, Barrington Road Dorking, Surrey (tel: 0306 885991). Trips range from a Top Market Tour of leisurely comfort Rajasthan to mountain treks, wildlife tours and exploring South India.

Fairways & Swinford Ltd, 37 Abbey Road, London NW8 (tel: 624 9352). The aim of 'stimulating but not exhausting' is put into practice with such details as including an overnight stop at Bharatpur on the Rajasthan tour and ending a trip to Orissa and Karnataka with Goan beaches.

Serenissima Travel Ltd, 2 Lower Sloane Street London SW1 (tel: 730 9841/7281). Immensely grand and exclusive tours led by the grand, even titled, for their fellows. Sir Hugh Casson led the 1984 Taj trip (six days for £880, compared Kuoni's £498). Their clients' reports are mixed.

ExplorAsia Ltd, Blenheim House, Burnsall Street, London SW3 (tel: 630 7102). The umbrella for Tiger Tops, Mountain Travel, Himalayan River xploration and Jungle Lodges and Resorts. They ⅃n the best camps in the wildlife parks, and have tffices in Delhi, Srinagar, Bangalore and Kathman-⅃ (in Nepal). Experts lead specialised tours on ⅃ildlife safaris, climbing mountains, river-rafting, ꞁododendron treks, to Ladakh, trout fishing in ⅃ashmir and south India, and explorations of Nep-⅃, Rajasthan and south India.

West Himalayan Holidays Ltd, 66 Hungerford ⅃oad, London N1 (tel: 607 4809). Christina Noble ⅃as been organising walks for over a decade and ⅃ves in the Kulu valley for six months of the year. ⅃roups benefit from her intimate knowledge of the ⅃ea and peoples.

Andrew Brock Travel Ltd, 10 Barley Mow ⅃assage, London W4 (tel: 994 6477). Wide range of ⅃ff-beat tours include a textiles study tour to ⅃ajasthan and Gujarat, tours entirely by car, trips ⅃hrough Kashmir by boat and on foot, camel treks ⅃ Rajasthan, botanical trips, crossing the ⅃imalayas from Kathmandu to Darjeeling, a trip ⅃p to Bhutan and Sikkim, and beach holidays to ⅃e Maldives.

Other specialist operators include The Curry ⅃lub, PO Box 7, Haslemere, Surrey (tel: 0428 2452): ⅃ourmet food tours; Butterfield's Indian Railway ⅃our, Burton Fleming, Driffield, North Humber-⅃ide (tel: 026 287 230): puff-puff your way around ⅃dia for 18–32 days, wonderful sights, simple ⅃omforts; Twickers World, 22 Church Street, ⅃wickenham, Surrey (tel: 892 7606): good tours, ⅃nd Cygnus Wildlife Holidays, 96 Fore Street, ⅃ingsbridge, Devon (tel: 0548 6178): bird-watching ⅃ips led by ornithologists.

Trailfinder, 46–48 Earls Court Road, London W8 ⅃el: 937 9631/5400). A complete travel centre to ⅃erve every pocket from budget traveller to the big ⅃plurge. Their pride is in being able to 'find the best ⅃alue tickets that prevailing regulations and man's ⅃genuity allow'. The highly trained and compu-⅃er-equipped staff book anything from a single ⅃ight to package tours run by all operators. There is ⅃ full travel insurance desk, immunisation centre ⅃homas Cook are the only other agency in the UK ⅃ith one), worldwide hotel discount arrangement, ⅃ank for travellers cheques and currency, visa and ⅃ermit service and a bookshop for maps and ⅃uides.

ꞁECOMMENDED TOUR OPERATORS OUTSIDE ⅃RITAIN:

⅃RANCE The French are much more intrepid ⅃avellers than the British. A French traveller will

happily take a 21-day tour of South Indian temples that a British tourist would deem an assault course. Both the firms suggested offer a variety of unusual tours, expertly run. Naturally, it is possible for anyone to book on these tours, provided they join them from Paris and can understand French.

Carrefour de l'Inde, 15 rue des Ecoles, 75005 Paris (tel: 634.03.20). Exemplary travel operator already including Shekhavati, Jaisalmer and Chittaugarh in Rajasthan tours; Gwalior, Mandu and Bhubaneswar in Central India tours, and running special tours focusing on the music and dance of Kerala.

Voyages Kuoni SA, 95 rue d'Amsterdam, 75008 Paris (tel: 285.71.22). Their Fetes du Monde brochure includes Pushkar fair in a tour of Western Rajasthan and Gujarat, the Hemis festival in a Ladakh tour, Onam in Kerala and the Puri car festival in Orissa.

UNITED STATES It is well worth comparing American prices with European equivalents. Even after adding on the price of a cheap flight to London, British tours are very often substantially cheaper than American ones.

Journeyworld International Ltd, 155 East 55th Street, New York NY 10022 (tel: 212.752.8303)

Maupintour, 1515 St Andrew's Drive, Lawrence, Kansas 66044 (tel: 913.843.1211)

Mountain Travel Inc., 1398 Solano Avenue, Albany, CA 94706 (tel: 415.527.8100)

Olson-Travelworld Ltd, 5855 Green Valley Circle, Culver City, CA 90230 (tel: 213.670.7100)

Tours of Distinction, 141 East 44th Street, New York, NY 10017 (tel: 212.661.4680)

Travcoa, Koll Center Suite 650E, 4000 MacArthur Boulevard, Newport Beach, CA 92660 (tel: 714.975.1152)

Abercrombie and Kent Int. Inc., 1000 Oak Brook Road, Oak Brook, Ill. 60521 (tel: 312.887.7766)

Four Winds Travel, 175 Fifth Avenue, New York, NY 10010 (tel: 212.777.0260)

General Tours, 711 Third Avenue, New York, NY 10017 (tel: 212.687.7400)

INDIA A few good Indian operators, with branches throughout India, have offices abroad (see Survival Code, p. 24, for more on their Indian offices):

Mercury Travels Ltd, 300 East 42nd Street, New York, NY 10017 (tel: 212.661.0380)

SITA World Travel, Indrama, 527 Madison Avenue, Suite 1206, New York, NY 10022 (tel:

212.753.5884); c/o Miss Ince, Hotel and Travel Consultants, 26 York Street, London W1 (tel: 486 3582)
TCI Ltd, 20 East 53rd Street, New York, NY 10022 (tel: 212.371.8080); Suite 235, High Holborn House, 52/54 High Holborn, London WC1 (tel: 242.9930/3131)
Trade Wings Ltd, 25 West 43rd Street, Suite 1400, New York, NY 10036 (tel: 212.354.8328/9)

Going solo: Booking up yourself

THE FLIGHT TO INDIA It is much better to take a direct flight. This gives a certain guarantee of arriving on time. Once a plane lands to re-fuel or collect or dump passengers, any amount of delay can begin.

When booking the international flight, seats on internal Indian Airlines flights can also be booked and paid for (see below). International flights usually arrive at Delhi or Bombay. Each connects with the rest of India on the internal flights. See Getting There: Getting Away sections for both cities, pp. 39 and 112 below.

THE FARE At the time of going to press, the current London–India–London air fares range from the incredibly low £280 (maximum of 6 kilos of luggage) to a hefty £1,854. Trailfinder (see p. 7) will find some of the cheapest fares, although there are countless bucket shops to hunt around. Bucket shops advertise in the newspapers and in magazines.

There is even a big price range for the two national carriers, Air India and British Airways. To give an idea, their current rates are listed below. Other airlines which have good, regular and reliable services to India include Air France, Lufthansa, PanAm, SAS, Swissair, Singapore Airlines, Thai Airways and Japan Airlines.

Air India, 17–18 New Bond Street, London W1 (reservations tel: 491 7979; flight information at Heathrow tel: 897 6311). Daily non-stop flights between London and Bombay or Delhi. Their New York flights stop at London. Their Paris flights usually stop at Rome and enter India at Delhi before continuing to Bombay. The ticket structure is as follows: Tourist class (GN10 ticket – a group ticket, the airline may help to make up the group) £425, for a minimum of 14 days stay, entering and leaving India from the same airport; Excursion (YE120 ticket) £570, for stays between 14 and 120 days; Excursion (YE90 ticket) £662, for stays of 28–90 days; Full economy/club £1,044; First class £1,854.

British Airways, 421 Oxford Street, London W and 65/75 Regent Street, London W1 (reservation tel: 897 4000; flight information at Heathrow te 759 2525). Some non-stop flights to Delhi and Bom bay. The ticket structure is as follows: Group far (minimum of 10 people, the airline may help yo make up the group) £425, for stays between 14 day and one year; Excursion fare £570, for stays 14–120 days; Tourist fare £662, for stays of 28–9 days; Full economy/club fare £1,044; Super-clu fare £1,202; First class £1,854.

BAGGAGE WEIGHT LIMITS Both the abov airlines restrict baggage to 20 kilos except for supe club and first class who may take 30 kilos. Ove weight charges are calculated at one per cent of th first class fare.

FLIGHTS WITHIN INDIA Indian Airlines ru an extensive network of internal flights (see di gram opposite) Their timetable undergoes mode revision once or twice a year. It is wise to book a internal flights when booking the internation flight, whichever carrier you use, particularly the high season. It is important that the seats a 'confirmed' and that you re-confirm each one India. On arriving at a city where a flight is to l taken, re-confirm your ticket as soon as possibl (Your hotel will do this for a few rupees.)

DISCOUNT INTERNAL FLIGHTS Indian Ai lines offer several discount schemes, called S India Travel Schemes, all good value. The You Fare, restricted to 12–30 year olds, gives 25% di count off the US dollar fare prices for any intern flights for up to 90 days. The Discover India tick costs a flat US$375, is valid for 21 days and permi flights all over India but no repeats (except in ord to get from one destination to another). Sou India Excursion gives a 30% discount on US doll fares for up to 21 days. All the above must be pa for in a non-Indian currency. They can be boug at airline offices and travel agents outside Ind and at any Indian Airlines office within t country.

INTERNAL TRAINS A train journey is as mu part of a visit to India as seeing a festival or strolli round a bazaar. A single journey is easier to bo on arrival. The hotel travel desk will do it mo quickly than you can. The chapters below gi suggestions for some of the more interesting tri (see Getting There: Getting Away sections).

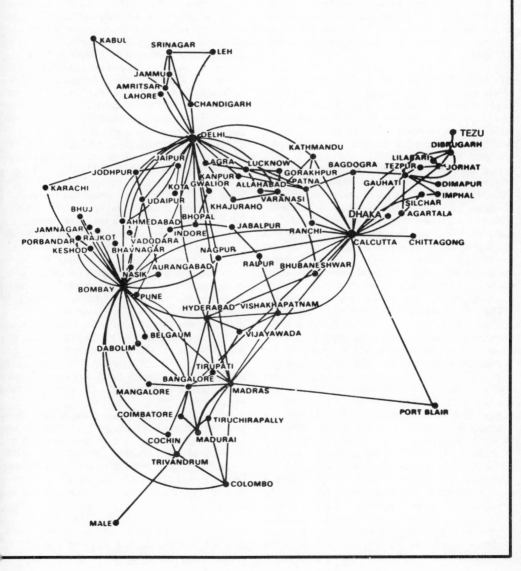

INDRAIL PASSES If you want to take several journeys by train – and it is certainly a good way of seeing the countryside – there are a variety of rover tickets, called Indrail Passes. In Britain, they can be bought at some travel agents, such as Cox & Kings and Trailfinders (see pp. 6 and 7 for addresses). In India, they are bought at the large stations (see Information and Reservations sections of Delhi, Bombay and Calcutta chapters).

Indrail Passes must always be paid for in foreign currency. Rates are cheap and it is certainly best to buy the Air-Conditioned First Class ticket. Validity ranges from 7 days (US$160) up to 90 days (US$600).

HOTELS There are some exceedingly luxurious hotels in India, both modern and old, with hundreds of smiling Indians rushing around to spoil you. They often serve the best food in town and offer excellent facilities, such as swimming pools, health clubs, travel desks and extensive room service.

The top hotels divide into two types: modern and efficient but lacking in character; old and slightly less efficient but with bundles of character. There are a few rare exceptions that combine both, such as the Taj, Bombay, the Oberoi Grand, Calcutta, the West End, Bangalore, and one or two of the palace hotels in Rajasthan. Of the new hotels, the Mughal Sheraton at Agra is by far the most successful: beautiful, very good and with a distinct character. Most British people tend to go for character, but businessmen would need the efficiency.

The palace hotels are unique to India. Rajasthan is littered with palaces. It was at Jaipur that the lucrative trade of turning the Rambagh Palace into a hotel was initiated by the Maharaja. Many saw his success and jumped on the band-wagon. Today, a tourist can live like a maharaja in these wildly extravagant, romantic piles. The better ones are run either by the Taj or Welcomgroup hotel chains. The more relaxed ones are still under the management of the now ex-maharajas, often with their charming old retainers. Palace hotels are not restricted to Rajasthan. There are some in Gujarat and some around Mysore in Karnataka.

Outside the tourist towns, accommodation tends to be simple, with mediocre food. It is the price you pay for seeing some of the wonders of India that the general tourist has yet to discover. The places suggested in the following chapters are the best available – or the only ones available. Old Raj hotels are full of atmosphere, such as the South

Eastern Railway Hotel (known as the BNR) at Pur in Orissa.

The government-run accommodation falls in several categories. There are Guest Houses, Circu Houses, Rest Houses, Forest Rest Houses, Da Bungalows, Tourist Bungalows, etc. The be grade is a Circuit House, but Indian governmen officials take precedence in the allocation of room The lowest grade is a Dak Bungalow. All grades ar usually clean and simple. They often do not pro vide food unless it is ordered in advance. They ma have fans rather than built-in air-conditioning Many do not accept credit cards. All are ver cheap. Some of the older buildings have gre charm, such as Hampi Power Station Guest Hous in Karnataka and the Tourist Bungalow at Quilo in Kerala which was built as the British Residency

There are also the Indian clubs which, as note earlier, have excellent facilities, spacious build ings, extensive grounds and are often right in th city centre. If introduction through a member required, you will find that most businessmen both Western and Indian, will belong to the goo clubs of their city, since they are the social centre Some Indian clubs have reciprocal membershi with overseas clubs. If you are a club member home, it is worth checking with your secretary fo reciprocal membership before setting off. See als p. 5 above.

Unlike Europe, where a tiny hotel in Paris o Rome is family run and delightful, most tiny hote in big Indian cities are pretty awful. Furthermor there are not enough top hotels to service th ever-itinerant Indian businessmen. Thus, fo Delhi, Bombay and Calcutta, as many good an central hotels as possible have been listed, togeth with their prices, which are higher than elsewher in India but well worth paying. The prices quote for these and for beach hotels are aimed to serv as a guideline. They will, of course, increas annually.

The Indian system of awarding stars to hote has very strange criteria, best ignored. As els where in the world, the management team crucial to a hotel's success. Last year, a dismal hot in the South was transformed into a very good on by the arrival of a new manager. The recommer dations below are almost all based on person experience.

HOTEL FACILITIES Of the hotels recom mended below, all the large ones have ai conditioning unless otherwise noted. It can b dividually controlled by a switch in your room. nderstandably, the Indians are very keen on tting cool, so hotel staff turn it up to full when-er they can, making the room like a refrigerator.

modest places, where there is no air-nditioning there are fans. Almost every hotel has om service and all the bigger ones operate it und the clock. Except for the very tiny places – here you would probably only stay overnight yway – all hotels and clubs have a good laundry rvice. There is often something called four-annel music in your room. Rarely do four chan-ls work and those that do usually have fuzzy ception and blare out repetitive music, Indian or estern. A few hotels boast televisions. This only s significance if the hotel runs a video program-e, which can be quite good, as in the Oberoi ter-Continental in Delhi. In all but remote places, ls can be settled with credit cards.

Some of your hotels will be very much part of ur trip to India, especially the palace ones, so an ea of their character and history is given in the commendations below. As palace hotels are con-rted private residences, rooms vary enormously. metimes a particular room or view is significant d this is indicated too. In bigger cities, the hotels e social centres for the smart locals, offering aces to meet and some of the best restaurants, ops, bookstalls, beauty salons and health clubs. e clubs are social centres for sports and relaxa-n, particularly at week-ends. This is especially e of Calcutta.

OTEL BOOKING Whether booking by letter, lex or telegram, it is essential to ask for confir-ation of the booking – and in some cases of the ecise room or view. It is also essential to take the ritten confirmation (letter, telex or cable) with u. Even the best hotels have been known to deny at their guest has made a reservation. It is also orth asking to be met at the airport or railway ation.

To make booking easier, the big hotel chains ve a central reservations system. The main oups are:

beroi Hotels Hotels at Bombay, Calcutta, Dar-ling, Delhi (2), Goa, Gopalpur-on-Sea, Kath-andu, Khajuraho, Simla (2) and Srinagar. Central servations at Oberoi Maidens, New Delhi (tel: 1591; telex 2703; cable AHI). London representa-n: L. R. I. Lawson, 30 Old Bond Street, London 1 (information tel: 491 7431; reservations tel: 1 1199, telex: 21237). New York office: Oberoi

Hotels (I) Pvt Ltd, 7th Floor, 300 East 42nd Street, New York, NY 10017 (tel: 800.223.1474/ 212.661.0380; telex: 225069 MERCUR; cable: MER-CINDIA).

Taj Group of Hotels Hotels at Bangalore, Bom-bay (2), Delhi (2), Covelong, Goa, Jaipur, Madras, Madurai, Maldives (2), Udaipur and Varanasi. Central reservations at Taj Mahal, Bombay (tel: 2023366; telex: 113791 TAJB IN; cable: PALACE). London representative is Utell, Banda House, Cambridge Grove, London W6 (tel: 741 1588; telex: 27817). New York office: c/o Inter-Continental Hotels, 200 Park Avenue, New York, NY 10017 (tel: 212.880.1564).

Welcomgroup Hotels at Agra, Andamans, Au-rangabad, Bangalore, Bhutan, Bombay, Delhi, Goa, Gwalior, Hyderabad, Jaipur, Jammu, Jodh-pur, Khimsar, Madras, and in Sri Lanka. Central reservations at Maurya-Sheraton, Diplomatic En-clave, New Delhi (tel: 674366/374127; telex: 3147/ 4911). New York office: ITC Ltd, 342 Madison Avenue, New York (tel: 212.986.3724; telex: 426083 ITCL UI). Reservations for Sheraton hotels within the Welcomgroup (Delhi, Agra, Madras; additions of Aurangabad, Hyderabad and Jaipur are in line to join Sheraton in 1985) can be made through Sheraton Reservations System in London (tel: 636 6411; telex: 851 261534) and in the United States (toll-free tel: 800.325.3535).

Spencer Hotels Hotels at Bangalore, Madras and Ooty. Central reservations at Connemara Hotel, Madras (tel: 810051/83161; telex: 041 486 CH IN; cable: CONNEMARA).

Clarks Group of Hotels Hotels at Agra, Jaipur, Lucknow, Patna and Varanasi. Central res-ervations: UP Hotels Ltd, 1101/2 Surya Kiran, 19 Kasturba Gandhi Marg, New Delhi (tel: 351467; telex: 2447; cable: UPHOTEL).

The extensive Ashok Group of government-run hotels are, on the whole, disappointing, although they might be useful at Bangalore, Bharatpur, Bhubaneswar (an exceptionally good one), Delhi, Kovalam (sensational building, badly run), Mysore (beautiful palace, badly run), Udaipur and, if des-perate, Bijapur. Central reservations: Ashok Res-ervation Service, Hotel Janpath, New Delhi (tel: 350070; telex: 2468; cable: CENTRES).

Visas and permits

All foreigners entering India must hold a valid visa. They are quite easy to obtain. Your nearest Indian mission (embassy, consulate or high commission)

supplies the form. The completed form, together with three passport photos and the fee, is then either delivered back in person or sent by post. In London, the fee is £3.35; delivery times are 9.30am–1pm; collection times are 4.30–5.30pm the same or following day; applications by post should allow ten days.

Permits are needed for restricted and protected areas. They are much easier to get at home than in India. Again, apply to your Indian mission. It is better to go equipped with all the permits you may need. They often take several weeks to be issued, so it is best to apply for them as soon as dates are fixed and certainly six to eight weeks ahead of departure. If an area is sensitive, such as the north-eastern states, then the permit may not be issued. Permits are needed for Darjeeling (but not if flying up for less than 15 days), Jaldapara (West Bengal), Kasiranga and Manas (Assam), Shillong (Meghalaya); Rumtek, Phodang and Dzongri (Sikkim); some of the Andaman and Nicobar Islands. In addition, there may sometimes be temporary restricted areas.

Should you not have a permit before leaving, it is possible to obtain one in India. See relevant chapters, below especially pp. 150 and 163.

A visa is also necessary for Bhutan, available from the Royal Bhutan Government or their missions abroad, and for Nepal, available at Kathmandu airport or from the Nepalese missions abroad. A visa is not necessary for the Maldives nor for visits of less than 30 days to Sri Lanka.

PROHIBITION Laws against consuming and possessing alcohol vary from state to state, and are changed according to the government in power. Currently, the only state with total prohibition is Gujarat, where there is no alcohol served, even in hotels. Other states have partial prohibition, which can mean anything from one dry day a week to one a month. On dry days, most hotels will serve alcohol on room service. On all other days, hotels serve alcohol without demanding to see a permit. Your hotel and the local tourist office will tell you what the current restrictions are in that particular state.

Where prohibition is in force, to go to a drink shop, to transport alcohol and to consume alcohol requires an All India Liquor Permit, issued by the Indian missions abroad and by the Government of India Tourist Offices at Delhi, Bombay, Calcutta and Madras.

Health

Having the right injections at the right time essential. Everyone going to India should have full course against typhoid, be up to date with pol and tetanus, and have a gamma globulin injecti immediately before departure. This last is again hepatitis, and surveys done on the US Peace Cor and the Voluntary Service Overseas voluntee both concluded that, provided you accept the tir limitations, it is very effective. There are two do types: the smaller for two months, the larger f five to six months.

There are three good immunisation clinics London. They are specialists whose sole job is ensure that everyone sets out with the corre protection for the country to which they are goir Sometimes a cholera jab is required, and the clin will know whether it is or not. The centres are British Airways, 65/75 Regent Street, London \ (tel: 439 9584), Trailfinder, 46–48 Earls Court Roa London W8 (tel: 937 9631), and Thomas Cook, Berkeley Street, London W1 (tel: 499 4000). T Department of Health and Social Security (DHS publishes a leaflet called *Protect Your Health Abr* (SA35) giving information and a list of count wide clinics.

Insurance

It is a good idea to make a small payment agai the possibility of all kinds of disasters. Packa holidays often include insurance but it may not enough for you. Most banks and insurance co panies have their own holiday and business tra insurance schemes. The form can be complet when you pick up your travellers cheques.

For illness, the policy should cover all medi costs, hospital benefits, permanent disabilities a the full flight home – all four seats if you unfortunately lying flat out. There should also clauses for personal liability; cancellation and c tailment, travel delay and loss of baggage a possessions, including money. If you are takin package tour, the travel trade indemnity clau protects you against the tour company going bu

Money

The big hotels, shops, restaurants and Indian A lines take credit cards. However, although they accept a wide range, they are not consistent as precisely which ones they do accept. There

n discrepancies within one hotel chain. It is best
refore to take all those you possess.

'ravellers cheques are the safest form of money
l can also be used directly to settle bills. The best
rencies to take are US dollars and pounds ster-
5. The maximum cash allowance to be taken into
ia is $1,000 or the equivalent.

t is forbidden to take Indian rupees into or out of
ia.

hat to pack

rinciple, the less the better. It is impossible not
buy things in India. The most reluctant and
erly shoppers succumb within the first few
rs unless they are held back. The trick seems to
o take as little as possible in the first place and
n allow for some of that to be used up (creams,
mpoo, etc.) or thrown out at the end.

ND LUGGAGE It is much safer to keep all
uments in your hand luggage: passports,
ets, confirmations of bookings, insurance pol-
s, travellers cheques, permits, visas, immunis-
n certificates, etc. Despite the claims at air-
ts, it is also safer to keep all film and breakable
tles with you.

OTHES Essentials are a subsistence supply
loose cotton clothes – man-made fibres are
emely uncomfortable and sweaty. Winter
ellers from Britain can pick up bargain summer
hes in the January sales. Hotel laundries are
and good, if a bit brutal. If the supply proves to
nadequate, European designs are substantially
aper in India than elsewhere and are sold in the
el shopping arcades. In addition, clothes can be
ied and tailored in one day, using fabric bought
he metre – not everything is sold in sari lengths.
art from the big cities, where suits and silk are
pant, people do not dress up very grandly in
evenings.

ther essential clothes are a pair of socks for
ting temples and mosques, otherwise there is
tic scurrying from shadow to shadow to avoid
ning the soles of the feet. A jumper is useful for
hills and cool desert evenings; trousers for
llife parks; a hat for sunny sight-seeing; bath-
costume or trunks for hotel pools and beaches
less and bottomless are not yet the done thing
India). If forgotten, all these are available in
ia. There is an inexhaustible choice of comfort-
, good-looking, cheap sandals in India (see

Delhi, Bombay and Madras shopping sections), so
two pairs would be enough to be going on with.
For temple and mosque visits, it is better if shoes
can be slipped on and off easily.

MEDICINES It is tempting to take a medicine
trunk loaded with every possible preventive and
curative potion. In fact, just a few tubes, pots and
pills with save most disasters. Dr A. C. Turner, the
authority on tropical travelling and author of *The
Traveller's Health Guide* (London, Roger Lascelles
1985, 3rd edition) has the latest advice for that
hardy perennial of tropical travelling, jippy tummy, also known as Delhi Belly in India.

To lessen the risk of learning more about Indian
lavatories (on the whole, not pretty) than Hindu
monuments, take the preventive tablet Streptotriad, an antibiotic available on prescription (not to
be taken by sulphonamide-sensitive people). The
dose is one tablet twice daily while in India, then
for two days afterwards, to be taken over a maximum total of four weeks. As Dr Turner says: 'I am
certain this cuts down incidence of diarrhoea'.

When, despite Streptotriad, Delhi Belly strikes,
Imodium is the best cure. It is more effective than
Lomatil. It was developed by the Belgian firm,
Janssens, who previously developed Lomatil and
then sold the formula to the United States. Dr
Turner does not advise taking Entero-vioform,
because of its toxic properties.

The other pills to take are those to prevent ma-
laria. Dr Turner recommends taking two different
pills: Maloprim, one pill weekly, starting a week
before departure; and Paludrine (proguanal), one
pill daily, starting the day before departure. Both
pills should be continued for four weeks after your
return.

A tube of antiseptic cream and some simple
dressings do not take up much room. Steritabs,
Puritabs or other water purifying pills are generally
good if used in the strengths recommended and
enable you to drink the so-called boiled water put
in the hotel room with greater confidence. Be sure
to pack a full supply of any regular medicines you
take as many drugs will not be available in India.

Lipsalve guards against damage from both the
dry heat and the thinner mountain air. A very good
anti-mosquito stick or aerosol, such as Autan, is
essential, as is a soothing cream for when the little
horrors get biting before the anti-mosquito potion
is on. They seem at their hungriest during the early
evening and when you are asleep. Indians suffer as
much as Westerners. On the BBC radio pro-

gramme, 'Desert Island Discs', the Maharani of Jaipur chose a never-ending supply of anti-mosquito potions as her single permitted luxury on the island!

Very few Western cosmetics of any quality are available in India. Where they are, the prices are high. As one regular visitor put it: 'Everything available in Boots is not available in India'. It is worth taking a generous supply of pre and post sun lotions; razors, razor blades (although Wilkinson sell a blade called Wiltek in India) and shaving cream; make-up, perfume, shampoo and toothpaste. If you run out of Tampax, they can be bought in general household stores and hotel chemists of big cities. A universal basin plug can ease washing in more modest hotels.

For daily travelling about, there is an invaluable kit: a hand towel and a small bar of soap for washing before and after eating or to freshen up in the heat; a roll of soft lavatory paper for its original purpose and also for handkerchiefs – the roll keeps much cleaner than boxes of paper handkerchiefs; and a plastic bottle for drinking water.

SIGHT-SEEING EQUIPMENT The Bartholomew's map of India helps you locate what you are driving through, passing by in a train or flying over. State maps give more detail. For guide books, the most exhaustive on history and monuments is Murray's *Handbook for India* and the best on practical, modern travelling in India is Lonely Planet's *India* . . . (see p. 15 below for details and bookshops). Depending on your itinerary, there are other invaluable guides, such as bird books (see bibliographies at the end of the appropriate chapters).

Quality camera film is a much sought-after commodity in India so stock up before you set off. If you take too much, it makes a perfect thank-you present for the embarrassing kindnesses shown by Indians in museums, hotels and socially. By numbering the films as they are used, and even jotting down subjects in a notebook, the record of the trip stays in order; it is surprising how quickly the memory can muddle up views and monuments. A pair of binoculars helps with looking closer at birds, wildlife and detailed carving on buildings.

READING MATTER Now is your chance to read the great tomes you have been eyeing for years. In general, night life in India is non-existent, airport lounges are grim (planes are prone to de-

lays) and there is a limit to how long watch Indian life from a train carriage remains fascinat on a long journey. To get in the mood, there plenty of very good fiction set in India and so superb travel accounts and biographies. Some late to specific parts of India, such as Paul Sco *Raj Quartet* (hill stations) and R. K. Narayan's M gudi novels (based on Mysore); E. M. Forster's *Hill of Devi* is letters from Central India, and Gay Devi's *A Princess Remembers* is the Maharani Jaipur's memoirs. John Keay's *Into India* and Tre Fishlock's *India File* are both excellent introducti to India. See pp. 15–18 and the more spec chapter bibliographies for more suggestions.

If you intend to pick up any of the glorious a extremely cheap furnishing fabrics or to orde carpet or dhurrie, it is a good idea to take necessary measurements and colour matches w you. The brightness of the Indian sunlight fuddles the memory for precise tones.

GADGETS Electricity works most of the tim most parts of India. And that is as firm as it g Contrary to popular belief, candles and matc are brought to even the most modest hotel roo the moment the lights go out. But the big ho have their own generators. Voltage is 220, with occasional 230. It is best to take your own trans mer. A travelling iron is often quicker than send garments to be ironed. The Sanyo steam travell iron is very light. A penknife is useful for open bottles and peeling fruit.

A small, short-wave radio is usually far be than the channels of dreadful piped music in hotel room. All India Radio is clear everywh in India and has regional stations whose p grammes are listed in the local paper. BBC W Service is on short wave at 25.82, 31.04 41.35 metre bands and is broadcast from 18.45 u 22.30GMT. It can also be received on Medi Wave, 140KHz, at 16.00GMT. A Sony Walkr and some favourite tapes can supplement risks of radio reception and will make a cha from the latest film music on the local statio Supplies of batteries for flash, radio, Walkr and anything else have to be packed too.

PRESENTS Very important. The kindn generosity and hospitality of Indians know bounds. If you arrive in India with just address, or none at all, you are bound to leave v many. In essence, anything foreign is fashiona Half bottles of duty-free Scotch whisky go d

ry well for men (it is extremely expensive in
dia). Videos are all the rage among successful
dians and blank tapes for VHS machines are
tremely popular. A recorded tape must be VHS
the PAL system. European table mats, drinks
asters, soap and pretty floral porcelain pots are
ht in weight but always welcome. Indians are
dly delighted by things with a royal connotation
a crest. Children love the latest small toy cars.
d all Indians seem to be crazy about gadgets.
used film makes a good leaving present. It is
rth buying a carton of duty-free cigarettes to
e packets as extra thanks to a good driver or
m boy.

seful Addresses

DIAN MISSIONS ABROAD
ese issue visas and permits.
gh Commission for India, India House,
dwych, London WC2 (tel: 836 8484)
abassy of India, 2107 Massachusettes Avenue,
V, Washington, DC 20008 (tel: 202.939.7070/
9)
nsulate General of India, 3 East 64th Street, New
rk, NY 10021 (tel: 212.879.7888)
abassade de l'Inde, 15 rue Alfed Dehodencq,
16 Paris (tel: 520.39.30)

VERNMENT OF INDIA TOURIST OFFICES
ROAD
ually extremely helpful and knowledgeable
ff. Offices packed with literature on every area
d aspect of India. Supply lists of following year's
tival dates; Indian Airlines timetable; basic
ps; information on trains; and lists of govern-
nt and state tourist offices and their services and
rs.
ork Street, London W1 (tel: 437.3677)
Rockefeller Plaza, Room 15, North Mezzanine,
w York, NY 10020 (tel: 212.586.4901)
Boulevard de la Madeleine, 75009 Paris (tel:
.83.86)

nd out more

bulk of books written about India have been
blished in India or London. They fall into two
ad categories: those published before the 1930s
those published since the 1960s, when the
aissance of interest in India's history and cul-
began and India opened up as a general travel

destination. The recent publications range from
huge coffee-table tomes with magnificent photographs to very readable general histories and highly practical guides on tropical health or what to
pack. Nevertheless, few of the old or new books
are printed in long runs and many of them are
either out of print, very expensive or difficult to
locate. The following reference libraries and bookshops should help in locating titles mentioned
in the bibliographies below and at the end of
chapters. All will answer enquiries or orders. The
bookshops mail worldwide.

London

LIBRARIES
The National Art Library, Victoria and Albert
Museum, London SW7 (tel: 589 6371). Open
Mon.–Thurs., 10am–5.45pm; Sat., 10am–1pm,
2–5.30pm. Open to the public for reference.

Commonwealth Institute, Kensington High
Street, London W8 (tel: 603 4535). Library open to
the public for reference Mon.–Sat., 10am–5.30pm.

India Office Library and Records (British Library
Reference Division), 197 Blackfriars Road, London
SE1 (tel: 928 9531). Open Mon.–Fri., 9.30am–6pm;
Sat., 9.30am–1.30pm. Open to the public for reference. Open to members to borrow books that are
up to 25 years old. Membership is by recommendation by a sponsor who belongs to a reputable
firm or institution. All enquiries should be addressed to The Superintendent of Reading Rooms.

The London Library, 14 St James's Square,
London SW1 (tel: 930 7705). Open to members
only, Mon.–Sat., 9.30am–5.30pm, Thurs. until
7.30pm. Membership, open to residents anywhere
in the world, costs £70 per annum. Members living
in London may borrow 10 books at a time; members living outside London may borrow 15 books.
All enquiries should be addressed to The Librarian.

School of Oriental and African Studies, Malet
Street, London WC1 (tel: 637 2388). Open Mon.–
Fri., 9am–5pm; Sat., 9.30am–12.30pm (later clos-
ings during term time). Day reference ticket available on proof of identity; annual membership for
reference and lending £5 (and £50 deposit against
borrowing books). Application forms from the
Issue Desk, SOAS Library.

BOOKSHOPS
Hatchards Ltd, 187 Piccadilly, London W1 (tel:
437 3924), covers all subjects, with a very helpful
travel section on the ground floor.

15

Maggs Bros Ltd, Booksellers, 50 Berkeley Square, London W1 (tel: 493 7160). Excellent stock of second-hand books on all aspects of India and new books on Indian art.

St George's Gallery Books Ltd, Art Booksellers, 8 Duke Street, London SW1 (tel: 930 0935). Adept at obtaining any book in print, not just on art.

Travel Bookshop, 13 Blenheim Crescent, London W11 (tel: 229 5260). Stocks guides, maps, history and fiction currently in print, plus out of print titles. Supplies an Indian list.

Books from India, 45 Museum Street, London WC1 (tel: 405 7226). The biggest stock of books and maps printed in and out of India to be found outside India. All subjects; supplies booklists by subject; can order titles from India.

Edward Stanford Ltd, 12 Long Acre, London WC2 (tel: 836 1321). Stocks maps, guides and travel writing. Booklist available.

Paris

LIBRARIES

Centre national des langues orientales, 1 rue de Lille, 75007 Paris (tel: 260.34.58)

Centre d'Etudes indiennes, 54 boulevard Raspail, 75007 Paris (tel: 544.39.79)

Musée de l'Homme, Palais de Chaillot, place de Trocadéro, 75016 Paris (tel: 553.70.60), library and photograph collection open to the public

Musée Guimet, 6 Place Iena, Paris (tel: 723.61.65), library open to the public

La Bibliothèque Publique d'Information, Centre national d'art et de culture George Pompidou, Plateau Beaubourg, 75191 Paris Cedex 04 (tel: 227.13.33)

BOOKSHOPS

Ulysse, 35 rue St-Louis en l'Ile, 75004 Paris (tel: 325.17.35)

L'Asiathèque, 6 rue Christine, 75006 Paris (tel: 325.34.57)

Libraire Sudestasie, 18 rue du Cardinal-Lemoine, 75005 Paris (tel: 326.27.78)

Libraire Orientaliste Paul Geuthner, 12 rue Vavin, 75006 Paris (tel: 634.71.30)

Libraire Orientale H. Samuelian, 51 rue Monsieur-Le-Prince, 75006 Paris (tel: 326.88.65)

Maison neuve, 11 rue Saint-Suopice, 75006, Paris (tel: 326.86.35)

United States of America

LIBRARIES

New York Public Library, Fifth Avenue and 42 Street, New York, NY 10018 (tel: 212.340 084 Open Mon.–Thurs., 9am–9pm; Fri. and Sa 10am–8pm.

Library of Congress, First Street, between E Capitol and Independence Avenue, SE, Washi ton DC (tel: 202.287.5000). Open Mon.–F 8.30am–9.30pm; Sat., 8.30am–5pm; Sun., 1–5p

BOOKSHOPS

The Advent Bookshop Inc., 141 East 44th Stre New York, NY 10017 (tel: 212.697.0887)

Paragon Book Gallery, 2130 Broadway, corner 75th Street, New York, NY 10023 (tel: 212.496.23

Select background bibliograph

For titles on more specific or local topics, see F Out More section at the end of each chapter.

PRACTICAL HELP

Hatt, J: *The Tropical Traveller: An Essential Guid Travel in Hot Climates*, London, 1982

Turner, Dr A. C.: *The Traveller's Health Gu* London, 1985 (3rd edition)

GUIDE BOOKS

Fodor's India, Nepal and Sri Lanka, Hodder a Stoughton, New York and London, publish annually. Surprisingly dull about the wonderfu rich land it is concerned with.

India – a travel survival kit, Lonely Planet, So Yarra, Australia, 1981, 2nd edition 1984. Ja packed with essential factual information – hotel, restaurant, bus route or train connectio left unturned. The best available for practical he *Nagel's Guide to India and Nepal,* Gene Switzerland, 1980. Laboriously comprehensive

A Handbook for Travellers in India, Pakist Nepal, Bangladesh and Sri Lanka (Ceylon), L. F. Rushbrook Williams, 22nd edition, Jo Murray, London, 1978. The classic Victorian tra book, originally published in three gloriously tailed volumes between 1859 and 1882 (well wo getting out of a library), now reduced and reas ably updated but still by far the best for architect and history.

NOVELS, TRAVEL WRITING AND PERSONAL VIEWS:

Ackerley, J. R.: *Hindoo Holiday*, London, 1931, 1983
Allen, C., ed.: *Plain Tales from the Raj*, London, 1975
Bannerjee, B.: *Pather Panchali*, London, 1968
Biardeau, M.: *India*, London, 1960
Cameron, J.: *An Indian Summer*, London, 1974
Collins, L. and Lapierre, D.: *Freedom at Midnight*, India, 1976
Eden, Emily: *Up the Country: Letters from India*, London, 1972
Fishlock, T.: *India File: Inside the Subcontinent*, London, 1983
Forster, E. M.: *Passage to India*, London, 1924, 1983
Foster, W. ed.: *Early Travels in India*, London, 1921
Galbraith, J. K.: *John Kenneth Galbraith introduces India*, London, 1974
Gandhi, I., and Nou, J.-L.: *Eternal India*, New Delhi, 1980
Godden, J. and R.: *Shiva's Pigeons – An Experience of India*, London, 1972, 1983
Gurliman, M.: *India*, London, 1966
Huber, W. and Boesch, H.: *India*, New Delhi, nd
Jhabvala, R. P.: *To Whom She Will*, the first of many novels and volumes of short stories set in India
Kaye, M. M.: *The Far Pavilions*, London, 1978
Keay, J.: *Into India*, London, 1973
Levi, P.: *The Light Garden of the Angel King*, London, 1972
Lloyd, S.: *An Indian Attachment*, London, 1984
Longford, E., intro.: *A Viceroy's India: leaves from Lord Curzon's notebook*, London, 1984
Mahajan, J.: *The Ganga Trail*, Delhi, 1984
Mehta, G.: *Karma Cola*, Glasgow, 1981
Mehta, Ved: *Walking the Indian Streets*, London, 1961. His many other books about India include 'Portrait of India', 'The New India' and 'A Family Affair: India under Three Prime Ministers'
Morris, Jan: *The Pax Britannica Trilogy*, London, 1968–78
Morris, John: *Eating the Indian Air*, London, 1968
Murphy, D.: *Full Tilt*, London, 1965
Naipaul, V. S.: *Area of Darkness* (London, 1964) and *A Wounded Civilisation* (London, 1977) are just two of many works on the subject of India
Nehru, J.: *Discovery of India*, Bombay, 1946; London, 1947, 1983
Pandey, B. N.: *A Book of India*, Delhi, 1982
Pommaret-Imaeda, F., Imaeda, Y. and van Strynck, G.: *Bhutan*, London, 1984
Premchand: *Godan*, Bombay, 1979
Rao, Raja: *The Serpent and the Rope*, London, 1960

Rushdie, S.: *Midnight's Children*, London, 1981
Singh, K.: *I Shall Not Hear the Nightingale*, Bombay, 1983, one of many books on India
Theroux, P.: *Great Railway Bazaar*, London, 1980
Wilson, Lady: *Letters from India*, London, 1984
Wood, M.: *Third Class Ticket*, London, 1983

THE HINDU EPICS:

So much of Indian life, religion, festivals, painting and sculpture and art relates to the two long epics, the Mahabharata and the Ramayana (see p. 259), that curiosity might be roused to find out more about them. Of the several translations, these are both very readable: Rajagopalachari, C.: *Mahabharata*, Bharatiya Vidya Bhavan, Bombay, 1979, Rajagopalachari, C.: *Ramayana*, Bharatiya Vidya Bhavan, Bombay, 1978. If these are too long, there are amusing cartoon comics, each with a short episode from one of the epics, available worldwide and on every Indian news-stand.

HISTORY AND RELIGION:

The Cambridge History of India, vols I–VI
Dowson, J.: *A Classical Dictionary of Hindu Mythology and Religion*, Calcutta, 1982. Of the several dictionaries of the gods, this is one of the clearest to follow.
Gandhi, M. K.: *An Autobiography or The Story of My Experiments with Truth*, first published 1927–9, London, 1982
Hibbert, C.: *History of the Indian Mutiny*, London, 1978
Humphreys, Christmas: *Buddhism*, London, 1951
Hutheesing, K. N.: *Dear to Behold*, Bombay, 1969
Kincaid, D.: *British Social Life in India (1608–1937)*, London, 1958
Macaro J., trans: *The Bhagavad Gita*, London, 1962
Mehta, Ved: *Mahatma Gandhi and His Apostles*, London, 1982
Moraes, Dom: *Mrs Gandhi*, London, 1980
Moorhouse, G.: *India Britannica*, London, 1983
Pouchepadas, J. and Nou, J.-L.: *The Last Majarajas*, Delhi, 1981
Sen, K. M.: *Hinduism*, London, 1961
Spear, P. and Thapar, R.: *A History of India*, vols. 1 & 2, London, 1978
Watson, F.: *A Concise History of India*, London, 1974
Woodford, Peggy: *Rise of the Raj*, London, 1978
Yule, H. and Burnell, A. C.: *Hobson-Jobson: A Glossary of Colloquial Anglo-Indian Words and Phrases . . .*, first published 1903, new edition edited by W. Crooke, Delhi, 1984

ART, ARCHITECTURE AND PERFORMING ARTS

Aditi, Festival of India Exhibition Catalogue for the Handicrafts and Handlooms Exports Corporation of India, New Delhi, 1982

'*Aspects of the Performing Arts of India*', Marg, Vol. XXXIV, No. 3, Bombay

Barnouew, E., and Krishnaswamy, S.: *Indian Film*, New York and London, 1963

Barrett, D. and Gray, B.: *Painting of India*, Lausanne, 1963

Binney, E.: *The Mughal and Deccani schools from the collection of Edwin Binney, 3rd*, Portland, Oregon, 1973

Binney, E. and Archer, W. G.: *Rajput miniatures from the collection of Edwin Binney, 3rd*, Portland, Oregon, 1968

Brown, P.: *Indian Architecture*, vols. I & II, Bombay, 1942, later reprints

Devi, B. C.: *An Introduction to Indian Music*, Delhi, 1981

Fabri, C. L.: *An Introduction to Indian Architecture*, New Delhi, 1963

Fabri, C. L.: *Discovering Indian Sculpture*, New Delhi, 1970

Falk, T. and Archer, M.: *Indian miniatures in the India Office Library*, London, 1981

Grover, S.: *Indian Architecture*, vols. I & II, Delhi, 1981

In the Image of Man, Festival of India exhibition Catalogue, Arts Council of Great Britain, Londo[n] 1982

Jayakar, P.: *The Earthen Drum: An introduction to t*[*he*] *Ritual Arts of India*, New Delhi, 1980

Keay, J.: *India Discovered; The Achievement of t*[*he*] *British Raj*, London, 1981

Khokar, M.: *Traditions of Indian Classical Dan*[*ce*] Delhi, 1979

Martin, F. R.: *The miniature painting and painters* [*of*] *Persia, India and Turkey*, London, 1912, 1968

Marg: Periodical concentrating on the arts a[nd] culture of India, often devoting an issue to a sing[le] topic, published in Bombay, back copies often so[ld] in bookshops

The Master Weavers, Festival of India Exhibiti[on] Catalogue, Bombay, 1982

Morris, Jan and Winchester, S.: *Stones of Empi*[*re:*] *The Buildings of the Raj*, Oxford and New York, 198[?]

Nilsson, Sten: *European Architecture in Ind*[*ia*] *1750–1850*, London, 1968

'*Pageant of Indian Art*', an appreciation of the Festi[v]al of India exhibitions, Marg, Bombay, 1983

Rangoonwalla, F.: *Indian Cinema*, Delhi, 1982

Rowland, B.: *The Art and Architecture of Ind*[*ia:*] *Buddhist, Hindu, Jain*, London, 1953

Schechner, R.: *Performative Circumstances, from t*[*he*] *Avant Garde to Ramlila*, Calcutta, 1983

Stoukine, I.: *La peinture Indienne*, Paris, 1929

Welch, S. C.: *A flower from every meadow*, New Yor[k] 1973

India survival code

Finding your kind of luxury in India

Everyone has their own idea of luxury. If it is pressing buttons, eating green salads, having a clockwork time-table and painting the town red every night, then India is not for you. India's luxury lies elsewhere, among its landscape, colour, peoples, traditions and its extraordinary service. It is a country accustomed to pampering. In Europe, good service has almost disappeared except for a large fee. In the United States, good service is more common – but also at a price. However, India overflows with people willing to serve at very small cost. And they all do it with a smile and good grace. But it is important to reward their willing service with a suitable fee (see tipping and bargaining, below).

The luxury is sometimes topsy-turvy. For instance, a hired car always comes with a chauffeur, costing a total of up to Rs400 per day, but the roads are often a single track of bumpy, dusty tarmac. You can stay in a four-roomed suite of a palace, but there might not be sufficient electric light to read by.

For visitors used to the way things work in Europe and America, there are a string of potential disasters, but they can be easily averted. For instance, in the West a train ticket is often bought 30 seconds before the train departs. In India, it can take hours of queuing, first for the ticket, then to reserve the berth. The process is best done the day before, preferably hiring someone else, for a tiny percentage fee, to do it for you.

Below are some tips to help you find the luxury and avoid the disasters.

Manners

Indian hospitality is so indulgent to Western habits that it is easy to forget that there is a strong Indian code of politeness.

LANGUAGE   Because Indians speak a very colloquial English, with plenty of idioms ('hop in the back', 'just a tick', etc.), it is easy to assume you are understanding one another perfectly. This is not necessarily the case. Misunderstandings are as easy between a Westerner and an Indian as be-tween an American and an Englishman. The most common difficulty for a Westerner is to understand when an Indian means yes and when he means no. A smile and a curious movement of the head as if it is about to drop off means yes. The problem is that it can also mean 'I don't know'.

GETTING YOUR OWN WAY   Almost certainly, there will be a moment when you will no longer find the incomprehensible Indian ways deliciously mysterious but very annoying. At these moments, to repeat your needs slowly and with an enormous smile is likely to get results far more speedily than bursting into a tirade, which will bring incomprehension from the very people you are trying to communicate with. If stronger action is needed to remedy the problem, the best policy is to go straight to the top, be it to the director of a travel firm or to the manager of a hotel.

SPEED   The all-pervading bureaucracy in India covers up a great deal of laziness. With a bit of persuasion, information that you have been assured cannot be discovered will somehow be found out, and jobs that have been declared impossible will be done. The best policy is to persist and never take no for an answer.

DOING BUSINESS   Many Indian businessmen are extremely hard-working and dynamic. An Indian is often happy to make appointments from dawn through until midnight. However, he is also liable to arrive at your hotel at any hour and to ring you from the lobby, expecting to hold a meeting in your room immediately. Alternatively, he will patiently await your return to the hotel for several hours. Conversely, as the telephones are unreliable, it is quite acceptable for you to arrive and introduce yourself without prior notice.

PESTERING   In the cities and at tourist sites, you will be offered all sorts of services. You may be invited to see a shop or factory, which you may wish to accept. But beware of buying anything until you compare prices in other places. You may be offered a guided tour of a monument. But, unless the guide is hired from the Tourist Office and has taken the full government training, he is unlikely to enlighten you very much. A lad offering to find you a hotel is likely to be a professional tout who receives payment from the hotel for every guest he brings in. You can be sure that he will not have your interests at heart. To reject any of these offers only requires a very firm 'No, thank you'. Pesterers have a knack of knowing those who mean it.

BEGGING   Begging is part of Indian life, despite being officially illegal. Beggars around the big hotels are not going to starve that night if you fail to empty your purse. These beggars are professionals, and each group has its own beat. The serious poverty of India lies off the regular tourist routes. If and when you wish to give money to a beggar, it is best to give a small amount (well under

a rupee). But beware. News travels fast among beggars and you will get no more peace until you leave that place, so be generous only shortly before leaving an area for good.

BARGAINING   Also part of Indian life. From the moment you arrive at the airport, you begin to bargain, unless you are being met. A taxi fare that might appear very cheap to you may well be four times the going rate. It should be as much a matter of pride for you to play the game of haggling as it is for the taxi driver. He will still end up with a good deal and you will pay less. Both parties will be happy with the outcome. The same principle applies to bargaining for all other human services and to all shopping. You may be absolutely sure an Indian will never under-sell his labour or his wares.

TIPPING   Lavish tipping is not as common in India as in the West, although the habit and expectancy is growing. The usual tip for carrying luggage, at the airport or anywhere else, is Rs2 per bag. (Where the airport has a baggage charge per piece, you do not have to tip the porter further.) Hotels will add various taxes and sometimes a service charge to your bill. You may feel that that is enough. But, if you have had a regular room boy or maid, it is customary to give him or her a tip of about Rs2 per day handed over personally. Be sure to ignore all those who arrive to witness your departure and claim to have served you. If you hire a car and driver, a good driver should be given a tip, usually about Rs10–20 for a full day. A taxi driver need not be tipped. The extent of a guide's service varies greatly but, if you feel pleased, a tip of Rs10–20 for a day's work is appropriate. You do not have to tip any form of taxi or rickshaw transport, nor any grade of restaurant.

DRESS   Transparent and low-cut dresses do not go down well with older or more traditional people. And they are absolutely disapproved of in holy places. Leather (belts, shoes, bags, etc.) will also offend in holy places.

INDIAN HOMES   If invited to dinner at someone's home, it is usual to arrive a little after the time invited, except where it is an official event. A present of flowers, European chocolates or anything brought from abroad goes down well. Otherwise, a box of good Indian sweetmeats is most appropriate. Indian evening timetables follow

egular pattern. Hours of drinking end with dinner
t around midnight, eaten very fast before every-
ne disappears. Westerners quite often miss out
ntirely. It is certainly a good idea to have a snack
efore going out. In more traditional homes, the
women will probably not appear.

'HOTOGRAPHY In addition to removing
hoes at temples and mosques, many of the faithful
vill not wish to be photographed. Throughout
ndia, women and all Muslims may well not like
he camera. The safest thing is to ask if in doubt. It
s far safer to take film home to be developed.
Quality in India is disappointingly low.

Money

'he Indian rupee is divided into 100 paise. A good
upply of smaller coins pays for all the things that
re constantly being done for you to maintain your
uxurious life. As in Italy, there is a constant small-
hange problem.

CHANGING MONEY There is a choice be-
ween your hotel, which is quicker and open all
ours, and the bank, which usually has a better
ate but is slow and generally open only during the
norning. Unless you are counting every paise, the
otel is better. Be sure to keep all certificates of
ransactions. And ensure that you are not given
ny torn notes as they may be refused in shops.

COUNTING India does not count in thousands
nd millions but in lakhs and crores. A lakh is a
undred thousand and a crore is ten million. Thus,
he official population of India at the 1981 census is
vritten 68,51,84,692.

PENDING YOUR MONEY Large hotels,
hops, restaurants, and Indian Airlines take credit
ards (see p. 12). And, mercifully, the bills usually
ake several weeks to get back home. It is tempting
o spend now and pay much later. However, you
vill need cash at the very small hotels, rest houses,
tc., and for transport, for buying in bazaars and
or tipping.

Arrival in India

'IME Indian Standard Time is 5½ hours ahead
f Greenwich Mean Time and 9½ hours ahead of
JS EST.

CUSTOMS It is as well to have your inoculation
certificates with your passport. You may also be
asked how much money, in cash and travellers
cheques, you are bringing into the country.

AIRPORT TO HOTEL Once through customs,
you may be faced with a crowd of porters jostling
very close to you, all offering to carry your bags or
find you a taxi or a hotel. The best policy is to
choose one person very firmly. The rest will dis-
appear immediately.

If you are being met by your hotel, someone
should make themselves known to you if you just
stand around and look as if you are waiting to be
met. A few hotels have cars at the airport as a
matter of course, so it is worth enquiring at the
Tourist Office or Hotels Reservations Desk.

If you are not being met, you can go to the bank,
keeping a watchful eye on your porter (he will lead
the way), to buy rupees. The queue may be long
and will certainly be very slow-moving. You can
also go to the Tourist Office desk, again with your
porter beside you, to find out the going rate for a
taxi to your hotel. (The airport police also have this
information and in some airports the prices are
pinned up on the wall.) The desk can also book
hotels and provide tourist literature and usually
has a good map of the city.

Armed with the knowledge of the going rate,
you can bargain with the taxi driver until he comes
down to the right price. If you do not come to an
agreement, there is always another taxi driver who
will. Once the price is agreed, it is important to see
your luggage is all safely put in the taxi. Only then
should you pay off your porter. If a fellow passenger is travelling your way, it is perfectly acceptable
to share a taxi into town and each be delivered to a
different address. Alternatively, you can go
straight to the taxi rank, ask the driver to pay off
your porter and, on arrival at your hotel, ask the
driver to wait while you change money (which is
far quicker than at the airport).

Throughout India, meters on taxis and auto rickshaws are liable to be broken – or drivers will claim
they are broken. Occasionally, there is a meter that
works. If so, it is important to ensure that it is
started only when you begin your journey.

Hotels

CHECKING IN Even the plusher hotels give
off-season discounts, so it is a good idea to enquire
when checking in whether any are available. It is

quite common to be told: 'I am very sorry but we can only offer you 25% discount.' Occasionally the Front Manager will look blank when you arrive, denying all knowledge of your booking. Producing the written confirmation helps him find the booking after all.

It is always worth asking for a room overlooking the sea, the hills or the town, whatever is appropriate, and then going to look at your room before the luggage goes up. If you are shown one over the staff quarters, ask to see another until you find one you like. If you requested a particular room when you booked, producing the written confirmation of this works wonders. If you do not ask for one of the best rooms, somebody else certainly will.

SECURITY It is wise to keep a close eye on your luggage to ensure it arrives at your room and not somebody else's. At night, you should always lock your room from the inside. And be wary of balcony windows and ground floor windows, too. If in doubt, close them and use the air-conditioning. Most hotels have a safe for valuables such as jewellery, tickets, passport and money. It is very unwise to leave any valuables in your room.

USING THE HOTEL All the big hotels are well equipped with services, leaving you free to enjoy yourself. You need never do any drudgery. In the first place, no matter whether you arrive in town by train, boat, plane or bus, the hotel can meet you. If you will be leaving town by air, your first and most essential job is to ask the hotel to have your seat re-confirmed. This should be done as far in advance as possible (the fee is Rs10–25) and then once more the day before your departure. If you need train tickets bought and train seats reserved (often two separate operations), the hotel will do that, too. Many hotels have in-house travel agents who will advise and book everything (see travel agents, 24).

LAUNDRY SERVICE Usually very quick and efficient, although the prices have increased considerably in recent years. There is often a full dry cleaning service, too. The laundry tariff is usually two-tiered: normal, sent in the morning and returned the same evening or following morning, and express, which can be as little as three hours and costs at least double the normal price.

ILLNESS Big hotels have a good doctor o call. He can be summoned very quickly. Ther may also be a chemist in the hotel shoppin arcade.

ROOM SERVICE Often very extensive, wit elaborate six-page menus in your room. It operate all day long or, as in many city hotels, right aroun the clock.

The hotel Bell Captain (Head Porter) keep stamps and wraps and sends parcels. He gets yo taxis and, in Delhi, keeps copies of the usefu publication, *Delhi Diary*. If you are keen on ex periencing Indian post office queues, then allow several hours and ensure that you are the perso who sticks on the stamps, otherwise stamp an parcel may never meet. The Bell Captain als orders and delivers newspapers to the room.

HOTEL BOOKSTALLS They stock news papers including the *International Herald Tribun* quite regularly and other foreign papers les regularly. They also have magazines, maps novels, books on India and the best printed pos cards. Cheap post cards often have very strang and blotched colours. Both hotel and city bool shops stock guide books. Those published by th Archaeological Survey of India are the best but ne always easy to find.

TELEPHONE AND BUSINESS FACILITIES Some hotels have direct dial telephones for loca calls. In Delhi, Bombay, Hyderabad and Madras they often work. Elsewhere they rarely work, bu the operator will help. It is often quicker, an expected, to simply arrive at the destination an announce yourself. Telephone directories are confusing delight. Subscribers are often liste under their employers (who have supplied th telephone) rather than under their own surnames There are often several numbers, some marke residence, dining-room, etc. They are all to be use at any time. It is part of the Indian passion fc public accessibility.

Long-distance calls within India are graded. To grade is called lightning, is the fastest and costs th most. Other grades take hours, if not days, to ge through. International calls have to be booked and again, it can take hours to get through. The hote mark-up on telephone charges can be very high, s it is wise to check their terms before telephoning Cables can be urgent or ordinary. Urgent get ther ordinary may not. Hotel secretarial services ar sually excellent. Telexes have a variable success ate in reaching their destination.

The hotel will also help with sport, leisure, eauty, fitness, culture and it often has extremely ood shops, patronised by locals who know what's vhat. Where there is any night life, it is usually at ne hotel. See below.

nformation

NEWSPAPERS The Indian newspaper industry ourishes, providing a range of English-language apers in every area. They provide all-India and cal news, views and gossip as well as an enter- ainments section listing cultural performances nd film and radio broadcasting programmes. Television is barely worth watching.) Advertise- nents are a treat to read, particularly the match- naking marriage columns of Sunday's *The Times of ndia*. Currently the big press barons include the irlas, who own *The Hindustan Times*, and the Goenkas of Madras, who own *The Indian Express*.

MAGAZINES Big business, too. They include *ndia Today*, *The Week* (published in Kerala), *Sunday* nd *The Illustrated Weekly of India*. *The India Maga- ine*, published monthly, is the best general cultu- al magazine. There is a deluge of film magazines, ull of bitchy gossip and interviews. And, for chil- ren, delightful strip-cartoon comics recount epi- odes from the great Hindu epics – a good way of rushing up on who's who in the gods.

TOURIST INFORMATION Found in two sep- rate organisations. There are 22 Government of ndia Tourist Offices spread over the country. Each as an excellent and well-trained staff; many are right young sparks with more than one degree nd dreams of going to work in America. They arry information on the area they serve as well as n everywhere else in India. The two best are in Delhi and Bombay, where a team of India experts nanages to answer almost any question and the helves of their offices are piled high with informa- ive brochures and city maps. The Government of ndia Tourist Offices often take bookings for ITDC ours (see below).

The second organisation is the network of State 'ourist Offices, again often staffed by very knowl- dgeable people. However, they only hold in- ormation on their own state and are remarkably linkered about their neighbours, however near. 'he most extreme example is Agra, in Uttar

Pradesh, on the borders of Madhya Pradesh and Rajasthan, where you have to skip between three state tourist offices to get a full idea of the sights in the area.

In cities where there are central and state tourist offices, each usually keeps different information, so both are worth visiting. As they are govern- ment-run bodies, their advice may sometimes be biased, such as in giving a blanket recommenda- tion to government emporia for shopping or state- run hotels. But their sightseeing tours are often extremely good value and led by good quality guides. In the main, you get a far better introduc- tion with a morning's tour than you would on your own, even if you hire a car and driver (see p. 24).

ITDC AND STATE TDC Both central and state tourist organisations have long-winded titles. In their literature and in the following pages, they are frequently abbreviated from Government of India Tourism Development Corporation to ITDC and from, say, Kerala Tourism Development Corpor- ation to KTDC.

While the tourist offices carry certain informa- tion, the hotel management often know the city's sports, restaurant and shopping facilities better. Where membership is required for, say, golf or tennis, someone on the hotel staff can often intro- duce a guest. People in the hotel business in- variably know where the best haunts are to find good local food. And the many smart women now working in the hotel trade certainly know the best and cleverest places to shop. Furthermore, the really big hotels have a hospitality desk devoted to helping guests find what they want in town.

BOOKSHOPS The big cities are well-equipped. These are the places to get stocked up with in- formation for the rest of the trip. All too often the guardian of a fantastic site says cheerily: 'Sorry, no guide books here, madam. But you can get one in Delhi.' This is not much use if you are in Karna- taka. In addition to its bookshops, Delhi has a tourist office for every state and the central office of the Archaeological Survey, a gold-mine of superb publications.

NAMES, ADDRESSES AND INITIALS Many streets have two names – pre-Independence and post-Independence. Locals usually refer to the for- mer; most town plans are printed using the latter. For instance, the main street of Madras is known to all as Mount Road but is officially Anna Salai. Few

23

people, even taxi-drivers, know precise addresses and some quite important buildings include 'behind' or 'near' or 'opposite' in theirs. Furthermore, the Indians have a penchant for bestowing very long names on streets and states but referring to them always by initials, for example, Benoy-Badal-Dinesh Bagh in Calcutta is known as BBD Bagh. Almost every town has an MG Road, standing for Mahatma Gandhi. The first question one Indian asks of another when they meet is where he comes from. The answer may well be MP, UP or HP (meaning Madhya, Uttar or Hamachal Pradesh). The cult of initials extends even to people. A man may be known by all his friends and work colleagues as VJ or SK without anyone ever asking what the letters stand for.

Directions are often given by the most familiar landmarks, cinemas, just as pubs are used in Britain. A building will be 'just by The Majestic' or 'near The Paradise'.

Travel Reservations

TRAVEL AGENTS   As in all countries, some are better than others. The good Indian travel agents are efficient, reliable and still very cheap. And they save you endless bother. Some have offices inside hotels and keep very long hours. They will meet you from the airport, make hotel reservations, organise transport and car hire, buy tickets, arrange cultural programmes, wildlife safaris and have their own package tours. Their regional offices are spread throughout India. Among the biggest and best are:

Mercury Travels, founded in 1951 by M. S. Oberoi who also began the big hotel chain. 8 branches. Head office: Jeevan Tara Building, Parliament Street, New Delhi (tel: 321403/321411; telex: 3207/3423; cable: MERCTRAVEL).

SITA, begun by an American in 1933 as Student International Travel Association. In India since 1954 and claims the highest turnover. 13 branches. Head office: F-12 Connaught Place, New Delhi (tel: 43103; telex: 2343; cable: SITATRAVEL)

TCI (Travel Corporation (India)) claims to be the biggest Indian travel agency conglomerate. 18 branches and associated with Tourist Guide Service in Rajasthan. Head office: Travel Corporation (India) Ltd, Chander Mukhi, Nariman Point, Bombay (tel: 231881/232245; telex: 112366/113983)

Trade Wings, founded 1949, now covers India and boasts the greatest number of tickets sold through any agency. 16 branches. Head office: 30 K Dubash

Marg, Bombay (tel: 244334/242429; telex: 011.249 TWBB IN)

INTERNAL FLIGHTS   The golden rule is to re confirm your seat as soon as you arrive in the tow where you are to take a plane. This way, you a assured of your seat. At the moment, it is impo sible to confirm from another city. For instance, the flight is from Jaipur, it must be confirmed i Jaipur. Therefore, if your journey requires two o three flights, you cannot confirm right throug You just have to hope all will run smoothly. Som times it does not and you may have to wait for second flight or, more usually, stay overnight. Th is one reason why a timetable in India must b flexible. Indian Airlines have ambitious plans remedy this problem with a computer.

If you want to get on a flight and do not have confirmed seat, it is usually quite easy, except o the main tourist routes in high season and on th week-end flights out from and back to the b cities. It is best to arrive at the airport in good tim as seat allocation is on the first come, first serve basis. Each would-be passenger is told his place the cancellation queue. Even very high numbe usually get a seat.

CAR HIRE   A car always comes with a driver ar costs up to Rs400 for an eight-hour day. Price measured according to hours and distance. Petr is very expensive in India. A hired car is an abs lute luxury: you can drive where you want, whe you want, stop when you want and look out of th window non-stop without having an accident. keep a driver for a few days, you can strike a har bargain for a round sum that works out well belo the local daily rate. On tour, he should be give overnight money (about Rs20). If the car is hire through an agency, it is best to tip a good driv direct as his share of the fee is very little (abo Rs20). If the driver is clearly hopeless, or the c unlikely to make the journey, it is best to return the agency and ask for another. The manager w provide a replacement without embarrassme and will respect you for knowing what you wa and for issuing clear instructions.

COACHES AND BUSES   There are various ve good air-conditioned coaches, particularly co necting the Rajasthan cities. Some have becon very smart and show videos on the journey. Tou ist offices have the coach timetables and routes ar will tell you where to catch the bus. It is alwa vorth taking the most expensive coach available, ot only for the added comfort but also to avoid the rowded cheaper buses. It takes very little time to earn to avoid the crammed facilities of everyday ndia. Local buses are very slow, extremely rowded and, for some people, uncomfortable. But short trip on one is worth experiencing once.

RAINS A train journey is an essential part of ny trip to India. There are 60,666 kilometres of ailway in the country, often passing through glo ous countryside and right beside rural villages. ome of the Victorian stations are magnificent, ubbling with Indians on the move. As they are ocated in the centre of big cities, they are quicker to each than airports and infinitely nicer to arrive in. ravelling by train has strong Raj overtones. Meals re ordered at one station, messages sent up the ne, trays of piping hot dishes picked up at the ext and delivered to your seat. There is every ning from early morning tea, known as bed tea, nd full breakfast to afternoon tea and a three ourse dinner, always washed down with a hot, ilky, sweet and strong cuppa, delivered with all ne ingredients already added.

Some of the best train journeys are suggested in ne Getting There: Getting away sections of the hapters below. An Indrail pass is excellent value, ven the seven-day one (see above, p. 10). There re several classes of ticket. The best is Air onditioned First Class. Again, queuing may be voided by using a travel agent. Alternatively, the rain reservation offices in the big cities have Tour st Guide Assistants who are excellent. They hold ckets reserved for tourists for some popular trains nat will be booked out at the normal ticket coun ers. They give advice and help with bookings nroughout India.

Out and about

ORGANISED TOURS The government and tate tourist offices run city tours, usually covering lmost identical ground. Although many travellers ate the idea of a coach tour, these are often xtremely good as an introduction to the city or own. Favourite monuments can always be visited gain later. The tours tend to be quite exhausting, isting five hours or so, with an expert guide. here are also longer, full-day trips to surrounding ights, again cheap and well-run. For both types, ne coach picks up and delivers back to the main otels of the town (except in the big cities). Booking

is through the hotel front desk or travel desk, or by telephone or in person to the local tourist office. The Government of India Tourist Office publishes the useful booklet, *Conducted Sightseeing Tours*.

The tickets for a tour often have seat numbers. These are rigidly enforced by the tour leader, even when there are only a dozen people on the tour. The leader is also strict about timing at each place, in order to keep to his schedule. So, if you are late back on to the bus, he may rebuke you strongly. At big tourist sights, such as Agra and Fatehpur Sikri, it is worth noting the registration number of the bus so that you can find the right one. It is wise to take lavatory paper as places where the bus stops are unlikely to be well-equipped. You can buy fizzy drinks at all big tourist sites but, for a longer trip, you can ask your hotel to make up a picnic lunch (and you can specify what you would like it to contain).

GUIDES The government and state tourist offices hire out properly trained guides for half and full days. Rates for a party of up to four are about Rs35 for a half-day (four hours), Rs65 for a full day (eight hours). However, a large number of the 700 million or so Indians have become self-taught guides. They pop up everywhere, behind the most remote temple or in a hillside rock temple. Usually they are awful, reeling off a few facts, identifying a few gods and generally intruding upon any enjoy ment of the sight. And when you try to get rid of them, they threaten you with a calamity, such as being attacked by monkeys or eaten by a tiger.

SOLO SIGHT-SEEING All the bother of finding transport is easily avoided. In a town with scattered monuments, you can hire a bicycle rick shaw or three-wheeler auto rickshaw for several hours. Just agree a flat fee (the going rate will vary from town to town) with the driver, and he will wait for you at each monument. You then pay at the end. Smart hotels do not allow bicycle or auto rickshaws up to their front doors but there are usually some lingering at the gates. Sensitive visi tors from the West may balk at the idea of a scrawny, bare-foot child pedalling them around in a comfortable rickshaw. First-time visitors have been known to pay up and walk the rest. More seasoned travellers can argue to themselves that it is better to generously exploit them – being sure to pay a decent amount at the end of the journey – than not to employ them in favour of an auto rickshaw. Auto rickshaws should have a working meter. If the meter does not work, it is best to agree a price before setting off.

For longer distances, a hired car is better. If you take a taxi to a residential area or a place where taxis are scarce, the driver will wait and then take you to your next destination. The taxi waiting charge is a few rupees an hour; the going rate needs to be checked locally. In more out-of-the-way places, there are delightful tongas, two-wheeled carriages drawn by a pony or horse.

MONUMENTS   To visit a mosque, the head and legs should be covered, the shoes removed – some Muslims are more particular than others about women's legs being covered. To visit a Hindu temple, the shoes should be removed. At both, it is customary to give a tiny coin, say a 10 paise piece, to the shoe guardian. Some Hindu gods have a special day each week devoted to them. On these days there are likely to be processions and music in temples dedicated to the god. For instance, Hanuman, the monkey god, is worshipped on Tuesdays. Shiva's day is Monday.

Food and drink

These are the biggest worries for most visitors. Although there are one or two golden rules, the dreaded diarrhoea, fondly known as Delhi Belly, can strike anywhere, anytime. One woman who had travelled throughout India over seventeen trips remained unaffected until the night following a smart diplomatic cocktail party in Delhi.

However, to discourage any disease, it is vital to take the preventive measures before leaving home, to take the daily and weekly doses during and after a visit to India and to be careful while there. At first, such details as washing your teeth in sterilised or boiled water are a nuisance, but they quickly become a habit. If Delhi Belly hits you, in addition to taking Imodium, the stomach will welcome plenty of liquid and plenty of settling foods such as curd (yoghurt), lemon juice, bananas, rice and eggs. Hotels in cities have good in-house doctors. Remote areas do not.

FOOD

India has so many different cuisines, each of great sophistication, that it is a pity not to try the local dishes. In the following chapters, the local specialities and where to find them are given where possible. However, the best Indian food is most certainly served in the home. Indians are dis-

armingly hospitable, so you are very likely to b invited to eat in someone's home.

Restaurant menus often boast three cuisine Indian, Chinese and Continental. The Indian foo varies; the Chinese can be very good; the Cor tinental is usually awful. Such a variety is terme tri-cuisine in the following chapters.

The only two cities with a wide range of res taurants are Delhi and Bombay. Elsewhere, yo often need to impress upon the head waiter tha you want the real local dish, not a watered-dow version. Continental food tends to be bad, inst tutional, overcooked and tasteless.

DANGERS   In general, eating off the street i madness and eating fried food, salads, unpeele fruits and ice-cream is risky in most places. Hov ever, some people cannot resist the occasiona deviation, which is less risky in some parts of Indi than others. For instance, everyone, quite rightly warns against ice-cream because it may be froze and thawed several times before it reaches you And, in any case, freezing does not kill the typhoi bug. But in Gujarat, a relatively clean state wit substantial dairy farming, ice-cream is so deliciou and so much a part of Gujarat life that suppl seems only just to keep up with demand, reducin the risk. Both local street snacks and ice-cream ar listed below, where they are good, leaving you t weigh up temptation against risk. The best rule t follow is: if in doubt, don't eat it.

If your stomach feels delicate, south India vegetable dishes with plenty of curd (yoghurt) an rice will soon settle it. You can just ask for a tha and the whole meal comes on a tray (see p. 179). may be tempting to eat familiar European food bu it is not necessarily going to be very settling. Mea is less likely to be fresh than vegetables and it i much heavier to digest in a hot climate. Too muc rich Mughlai food is like a constant blow-out o French classic dishes washed down with crea and claret. It really should be eaten in small dose with plenty of the many delicious breads.

THE EATING PROCESS   Dishes tend to b served all at once instead of a long string courses. From a huge menu, you select suc goodies as something cooked in the tandoor over some meat, fish and vegetable dishes, a variety rice and breads, a dhal (pulse) and a curd to coc down the spices. When it all arrives, quite th nicest way of eating is with the fingers, pulling o pieces of freshly baked bread and wrapping ther around a piece of meat or mixing the spicy juices into rice. As breads are best hot, you can order more as you go. It is important only to eat with the right hand. There is always somewhere to wash and many restaurants bring bowls of hot water to the table afterwards.

FISH Delicious and very fresh all around the coast. The tandoor-cooked pomfret is in a class of its own. In the south, there are plenty of lobster, crab and giant prawns. Where there is inland fresh-water fish, that is very good too. But it is not such a good idea to eat fish where it has had to be trans-ported, such as in Delhi.

PUDDINGS Usually very sweet and often rice-based. Otherwise, there is kulfi (Indian ice-cream with pistachio nuts) and fresh fruit. You only find hard cheese in the hills; cream cheese is added to vegetable dishes.

FRUIT A fantastic variety throughout the coun-try, from Kashmiri apples to the delicious pink bananas of the south. Bazaars have piles of fruit and often a better selection than the hotels. The absolute rule is to eat peeled fruit only. If grapes and tomatoes are irresistible, they should be washed in sterilised water first.

SWEETMEATS Developed to a high culinary art in India, much as great pastries in the West. Diffe-rent towns have their own special sweetmeats. Religious festivals, marriages and other celebra-tions have theirs. They are given as temple offer-ings and presents. Women who do no other cook-ing will make the important family sweetmeats, whose quality is dictated by both how long they take to make (the longer the better) and what they taste like. The smartest have a thin sheet of real silver paper on top. (You can buy boxes of the silver papers in grocery shops and impress friends back home.) Although they are rarely served in res-taurants, every town has good sweetmeat shops. Local specialities are mentioned in the chapters below.

PAAN This is the digestive taken after an Indian meal. It is also the cause of all those red-stained lips and teeth. Paan is a mixture of spices, slaked lime and the mildly addictive betel nut wrapped up in a leaf. It is chewed. When you have had enough, you do not swallow it but spit it out. All sorts of potions can be added to make the paan mixture sweet or sour, a little intoxicating or very intoxicating. The contents dictate the huge price range. In smart restaurants, the paan is made up from a beautiful paan box of ingredients. On the street, the paan seller sits amidst a collection of tins and trays. An Indian has his regular paan seller who makes up his particular mixture.

DRINK

WATER To be strictly avoided unless you are absolutely sure it has been boiled, however parched with thirst you are. The rule is: if in doubt, don't drink. Indians have an equally wary attitude to their water and carry thermosflasks when on the move. And, remember, ice is just frozen water.

HOT DRINKS To avoid being served instant coffee, you need to ask for freshly brewed Mysore coffee. It is delicious and served throughout the South and in good hotels in the North. However, it is almost never available in moderate hotels. In small restaurants, it is served with milk and sugar already added. Chai (tea) served in a simple res-taurant or on a train is made by boiling up water, milk, sugar and tea leaves together to produce a reviving army-style brew.

COLD DRINKS A huge variety of fizzy drinks can be bought anywhere with relative safety. They include bottled soda water, Limca and Sprint (lem-onades), Campa Cola and Thums Up (India's own versions of Coca Cola), Fanta and Gold Spot (orangeades), tonic waters, etc. However sweet, they are better than nothing. You should always witness the top being taken off, otherwise the flies may have been buzzing about.

Still draughts are best taken where the hygiene is reasonably dependable. A nimbu soda (or nimbu pani) is the most thirst-quenching. It is fresh lime juice diluted with soda water and served either straight or with sugar or salt. Whatever fruit is in season can be pressed for a fruit juice, from mango and sweet lime to papaya and orange. In the South, coconut milk is very refreshing. The top is slashed off and the whole coconut served with a straw. In dairy areas, the milk is delicious. It is served straight, as exotic milk shakes or as lassi, usually a thin yoghurt but in western Rajasthan and Gujarat a rich, creamy concoction.

ALCOHOL Almost all hotels, except in Gujarat state, currently serve beer and spirits in their bars and restaurants, which is part of their attraction for

27

locals. Outside hotels, the prohibition laws of each state are different and are strictly enforced, with the major exception of Gujarat state, which is completely dry. State dry days even hit the hotels and alcohol is then only available on room service. On prohibition, see above, p. 12 and individual chapters below. Check current restrictions with your hotel or local tourist office.

INDIAN BEER   Similar to lager and quite gassy. It is both thirst-quenching and suitable to drink with spiced food. Favourite brands are Kingfisher and Haywards, especially in Bombay and the South, and Rosy Pelican in the North. London Pilsner is also made in India.

WINE   Not the best drink in India. Imported wine has often suffered en route; home-grown wine is very variable. Both are expensive. French film crews are known to bring their daily supplies with them. There are three principal Indian labels: Bosca, Anjou and Golconda. Anjou is made in Goa. Bosca grapes are grown in Maharashtra. Golconda uses grapes grown on the hot Deccan Plateau of Andhra Pradesh and Karnataka. Jancis Robinson, a Master of Wine, was surprised by the quality of Golconda Ruby; she described it as 'clean and balanced. It looks and smells quite mature and, although it is very sweet, there is enough acidity to balance it. Considering the heat, it is quite impressive.'

SPIRITS   There are various types. Imported liquor is available in hotels and very expensive, which is why it makes a good present. Indian liquor is cheaper and confusingly known as Indian Made Foreign Liquor, or Foreign Liquor for short. For whisky, imported Scotch concentrate may be blended with home-grown malt; the preferred labels are Peter Scott, Diplomat, McDowell No 1 and Dunhill. Indian gin is not very good and best drunk as a Tom Collins cocktail, a sort of alcoholic nimbu soda; good labels are Booth's and Carew's Blue Ribbon. Indian rum is excellent and cheap. It is made in most states, using the Indian-grown sugar-cane. Khoday dark rum is a good brand; Old Monk is matured in a cask; White rum from Sikkim is very good. Vodka is excellent too, especially Hayward's.

LIQUEURS AND LOCAL DRINKS   There are numerous local potions, often very powerful. Feni, made from the cashew tree or coconut palm, comes from Goa. Toddy is the coconut spirit of the South. In Sikkim they make tea- and paan-based liqueurs.

Keeping fit

OUTDOOR ACTIVITIES   These really are luxurious. Walkers and trekkers have their food and luggage carried, their tents carried and pitched – some with a separate washroom – and delicious meals cooked for them over the fire. If a walker tires, there is often a spare horse to ride. Fishermen have their tackle carried, the bait put on the fly and even the rod cast if they wish. And, of course, the catch is cooked for them on the spot.

GOLF   At most courses, visitors are welcome and given temporary club membership. Caddies, clubs and shoes can be hired. The clubhouse will advise on caddy payments. In some places, drinks and snacks are brought to golfers on the course. Hotels will assist with necessary introductions.

TENNIS   Where hotels have tennis courts, they usually have both balls and ball boys. Some provide a marker (partner) for a single player. Rackets and balls supplied by hotels have rarely stood up to the Indian climate, so keen players should bring their own. Where a hotel does not have a tennis court, the management can usually make arrangements for guests to use one nearby.

SWIMMING POOLS   Pools in hotel grounds are usually very well chlorinated, making them entirely safe. A cool plunge after a day of sweaty sightseeing or business dealing is a joy. In the big cities, the daily dip is an almost essential treat when the weather is hot. But beware: some hotels decide to empty and clean their pools sometime between November and February – just when a European is likely to be wanting them – as this is, of course, winter time in India. Also, some pools close at 7pm, the very time you are likely to return from a steamy day of sightseeing. Poolside barbecues are excellent at most hotels, showing off the north Indian tradition of meat and fish cooking at its best.

SEA SWIMMING AND BEACHES   The balmy waters are deceptive. There is often an undertow, especially on the east coast. Hotels have life guards who advise on when and where to swim. On other beaches, the local fishermen should be consulted. Scanty bikinis are OK at tourist beaches and around hotel pools, but in less Westernised places it is more tactful to wear a teeshirt as well, to avoid upsetting the locals. To go topless, let alone totally naked, is frowned upon in India, except at one or two hippy beaches. Either a group of people will arrive and stare, or someone will bluntly ask you to cover up.

BOATING   A hired boat comes with a rower and is always very cheap. In Kashmir, if it is 4 o'clock on a shikara (floating double sofa), the servant brews up tea and serves it with fresh macaroons, scones and lotus-blossom honey.

Health and beauty

HEALTH CLUBS AND BEAUTY SALONS Found in the top hotels of the Taj, Oberoi and Welcomgroup chains, these are some of the most luxurious in the world, with low prices. In their labyrinth of marble-lined rooms, trained masseurs give body, head and back massages, using a variety of oils. There are masseurs for men and masseuses for women. As men have stronger hands, a woman can ask to have a masseur. There are gymnasiums, saunas, jacuzzis, yoga lessons and every sort of beauty treatment from hair coiffeuring to pedicures for tired tourists' feet. As hygiene is particularly important, it is best to keep to the hotel parlours which are used by all the locals, too, unless you have a personal recommendation.

Respecting and caring for the body is part of the Indian tradition. And massage is part of family life, whether rich or poor. A wife will often give her husband a massage. A mother massages her children from when they are babies right into adulthood. There are special women who come to the house to massage babies. Girls use oil and a mixture of turmeric and gramflour paste to remove body hair. Massage after childbirth is used to restore the body's shape. It is not unusual for a busy working woman in her thirties to have a massage from her mother as part of her week-end relaxation. Massage is sometimes part of the ritual of a festival or a religious occasion. The oil varies according to what is available locally. In the South, it is coconut oil; in the North, mustard oil. These are absorbed better than the thicker almond oil which is used on the feet.

ARYAVAIDYA MASSAGE   Of the three main types of massage in India, this is the most common. The other two are siddha and unani, but elements of each overlap. Herbs collected by student masseurs are boiled, pressed or ground, then mixed with oil. Different combinations are used according to the purpose of the massage, such as to relax an athlete's muscles, keep a dancer's hands and feet supple or to soothe the whole body.

The principles of a massage are to open the skin pores so that the oil enters and lubricates the skin tissues, veins and muscles. The pressure of the massage promotes blood circulation and removes congestion, thus easing digestion and circulation and eliminating toxins. Even a general massage is good for the skin, joints, veins and nerves.

Most big towns have an Aryavaidya College where you can go for advice and treatment. Full treatment consists of a controlled diet, oral medicines and various oil applications, such as oil baths and warm oil pressed on the body. As with the increasingly popular homeopathic medicine in the West, both Western and Indian people have found aryavaidyia medicine to be the cure for migraines, headaches, depression, low blood pressure, poor circulation, arthritis, rheumatism, asthma and even diabetes. The local colleges are always listed in the telephone directory.

HEADS AND HAIR   With the heat and humidity, hair needs more attention. Again, women wash, comb and massage one another's heads. The massage is with oil, yoghurt or egg, or with lime and salt to get rid of dandruff. When it also includes the neck and back, it is the best of all massages, as it works on the nerves of the spinal cord to relax the whole body. Beauty salons are, on the whole, good and very experienced at taking care of Western perms.

FEET   Open sandals or no sandals at all mean the feet need regular attention. Pedicure and foot massage are a wonderful treat after a day's sightseeing. Some of the Bata shoe shops in big cities give good pedicures for about Rs10.

COSMETICS   Herbal oils and creams, often home-made, are also a part of Indian life. There is an endless variety of potions. Dried and ground orange peel is used as a face pack cleanser, as are honey, milk and gramflour. Of the herbal cosmetics bottled up and put on the market, Cheriss Products and Shahnaz Hussein's range are the best. They are available in health clubs, beauty salons and some chemists.

YOGA Fitness, mental calm and beauty at the same time. As people increasingly take up yoga in the West, more visitors to India are keen to start or keep up their lessons. Yoga institutions are everywhere, even inside hotels and on beaches. (The Kovalam Hotel in Kerala has a particularly good one.) The exercises bring physical, mental and emotional relaxation. It is not at all a waste of time to take one or two lessons, as you feel the difference very quickly. You learn a few simple postures and exercises for breathing and for flexing body joints and organs. As you repeat them daily, the relaxation increases; and the yoga clinic gives advice on how to continue. The important thing is to stick to one system.

Yoga is often used medicinally in conjunction with massage to maintain energy, improve sleep and relieve high blood pressure, asthma and other ailments. Ashrams, in or near every town, are the best places in which to follow intensive courses. Many Indians look forward to unwinding for an annual two weeks at their favourite ashram in the same way as Westerners long for their fortnight's skiing, sailing or lying on a beach. The Bihar School of Yoga at Monghyr, Bihar, is currently one of the foremost systems. The school has many publications available by post and is extremely reliable to visit.

If you want to go to an ashram, it is best to go to one frequented by Indians rather than one full of tourists. Since the sixties, several ashrams have sprung up in India aimed to entice Westerners and fleece them of considerable amounts of money. Many Indians believe that these are fraudulent and betray the principles of the true ashram, so beware. To get reliable advice, consult your hotel management or the local Tourist Office.

Night life

Night life is not great in India. However, the day tends to start early for everyone and the early morning light is magical everywhere. And, during the hot months, the hours between dawn and mid-morning are the best of the day. Where there is any night life, it tends to be early evening.

CINEMA Almost as essential a part of a trip to India as taking a train or seeing a festival. There are film shows all day, the last one usually between 8 and 9pm. See pp. 124, 157, 181 for more on the massive Indian film industry.

DANCE, THEATRE AND MUSIC India is very rich in high quality contemporary performers, but they are not easy to find in their places of origin. Delhi, Bombay and Calcutta have plenty of halls with constant programmes during the winter months. Down in the South, there are regular performances of Kathakali dance-drama at Cochin and Trivandrum and of Bharata Natyam classical dance at Madras. Other cities have sporadic festivals: Varanasi, Lucknow, Gwalior, etc. (see following chapters and p. 251). Performances are advertised in the daily paper and usually start between 6 and 7pm. If you are particularly interested in attending the smaller, often private concerts, the hotel can usually help. Top hotels stage 'Dances of India' programmes, usually of poor quality. Some restaurants have Indian dancers and musicians. Despite it being considered very detrimental to a serious career, there are some good performers. But a proper concert in a hall is best of all.

NIGHT CLUBS AND DISCOTHEQUES The former, also called supper clubs, are usually restaurants serving Continental or Chinese food (occasionally Indian) to the Western music of a live and raucous band. The latter, also called night spots, are very thin on the ground, so exclusive they are empty half the time, and mostly equipped with archaic lighting and music. At the moment Bombay, Delhi and Calcutta each have one good discotheque. Discotheques in hotels change a nominal entrance fee to residents but a very high membership fee to restrict local patronage to high society.

Shopping

WHEN TO SHOP There are two schools of thought on shopping in India. One says, when you see something you like, buy it as you may not find it again. The other says, save up your shopping until the end. A combination of the two gets the best results. Rare local craftsmanship certainly needs to be snapped up when it is found. On the other hand, most people leave India through Delhi or Bombay, and both cities have excellent shopping for goods produced throughout the country. Wherever you shop, be sure to keep all bills in case customs want to see them on your return home.

INDIAN CRAFTSMANSHIP In all fields this can be of very high quality. The craftsmen serve an ndian public who still keep their money in gold, ems and silk. It is worth buying the best and voiding the junk produced for tourists and sold rom stalls beside monuments. Top-quality silk, otton, jewellery, leather and carving can be as nuch as five times the cost when bought abroad. And there is much more choice in India. Also, tems can easily be made to order on the spot, or ent on later. As Malcolm Muggeridge observed of n Indian woman in 1934: 'She loves money in an Oriental way, not as money but translated into xpensive jewels and exquisite silks.'

Whatever skill you want, it is available. Tailors vill run up a dress, shirt or suit almost overnight and can copy any design expertly. Dhurries (flat-veave rugs) cost little and can be made to specific lesigns, colours and sizes, then shipped home and they do arrive). Furnishing and dress abrics of the highest quality cotton and silk are cheap, come in an endless variety and can also be woven to order. If you buy curtain fabric, he curtains can be made up and sent on by ship. Craftsmen will make up the fine pearls and Indian gems into any design in a week, or less. You can even have your favourite shoes copied.

GOVERNMENT EMPORIA   Every state has its own chain of shops, called emporia. They are stocked with a good variety of crafts produced in that state, the quality depending upon the ability of the buyers. For instance, the Gurjari emporia of Gujarat are superb. The buyers do the hard slog, going around the villages to get supplies and commissioning craftsmen to make pieces. The expanding chain of the Central Cottage Industries Emporia at Delhi (see p. 59), Bombay, Calcutta, Jaipur (and soon Bangalore) stocks pieces from all over India. If you prefer to shop in the bazaars, a quick recky in the emporia gives an idea of a price to aim for when bargaining. By doing this research you can sometimes strike a better deal in a bazaar than in an emporium where prices are, supposedly, fixed – but you need to inspect goods carefully for quality.

Although prices at both types of shop may be slightly higher than in the market place, the quality can be very high and they enable you to shop quickly. In addition, the assistants usually know all about their stocks and can direct you to see the craftsmen at work. The emporia shipping services are usually reliable and not expensive. The price depends upon a combination of volume and weight. A huge crate arrives back home after about three months.

HOTEL SHOPS   Unlike their counterparts in the West, they are often of high quality and yet reasonable prices. Significantly, they are heavily patronised by locals. Their clothes, leather and jewellery shops stock copies of the latest European designs. And there are quality Indian crafts. Clothes shops have tailors on call who can whip up garments overnight.

JEWELLERY   Hotel stores are the safest places to buy big items, although the price might be slightly higher. Gems can usually be authenticated by a government office. Jewellers will give a certificate of authenticity and usually offer to buy back the gems when you next come, should you wish to exchange them or change their setting.

FABRICS   The wealth of handloom fabrics throughout the country is impossible to resist, from the woollen shawls of Kashmir to the heavy silks of Kanchipuram. The bazaars have a good selection of cheaper pieces, but the more special weaves are found in some of the shops suggested below. A sari length varies around the country, so it is worth checking the local length if you are thinking of having it cut and made up. Cotton, wool and silk are also woven in long pieces. When fabric is cut from a long, continuous piece, it is sold by the metre length, but the width is still described in inches.

ANTIQUES   Not always as old as they look. Ageing help is sometimes given to newly made objects sold in shops and bazaars, so beware. A reputable antique shop will give a guarantee; in the big cities, this opinion can be endorsed by officials (see p. 32 below). On the whole, antiques are very expensive, and nice things take time to find. There is a larger range of quality old paintings, bronzes, textiles and sculptures to be found at the dealers and auction houses of London, New York and Paris. Run-of-the-mill art has a high premium within India and is expensive. If in doubt, stick to buying new crafts.

Packing to come home

As it is highly likely you will have picked up things along the way and also had a shopping blitz at the end, packing is an event.

If you make a list of what you have bought and ensure that all the bills and currency exchange receipts are in your hand luggage, customs clearance both out of India and into your home country is quicker.

There are several restrictions on what can be taken out of India, including large pieces of ivory, snake-skin, peacock feathers, animal skin and objects more than 100 years old. For instance, the current restriction on gold jewellery applies to pieces worth up to a maximum total of Rs10,000. The restriction on precious stones is the same amount. The local tourist office or government emporium should have the most up-to-date list. If in doubt, the local Customs Office will help. To ascertain whether your treasures are 100 years old or not, the following authorities can be consulted:

Director, Antiquities, Archaeological Survey of India, Janpath, New Delhi
Superintending Archaeologist, Antiquities, Archaeological Survey of India, Sion Fort, Bombay
Superintending Archaeologist, Eastern Circle, Archaeological Survey of India, Narayani Building, Brabourne Road, Calcutta
Superintending Archaeologist, Southern Circle, Archaeological Survey of India, Fort St George, Madras
Superintending Archaeologist, Frontier Circle, Archaeological Survey of India, Minto Bridge, Srinagar.

If still in doubt, the best policy is to declare your goods at the airports both when leaving India and entering back home.

So that you can roughly gauge the overweight charges and dispose your packing as well as possible, the hotel will weigh your baggage for you. You may need rupees to pay for overweight baggage (see p. 8). You will need Rs100 per person for Airport Tax.

The disarming thing about the luxurious life in India is that you need not lift your luggage until you reach your home airport. Only then will you realise the enormous weight of all the treasures and memories packed inside.

Delhi and Agra:
Power and politics

Delhi lives, breathes, eats and sleeps politics; politics hits every facet of life. The difference between Delhi and Bombay is India's version of that between Washington and New York. Indeed, one Delhi gentleman looked down his knowledgeable nose, dismissing Bombay as a 'cheap imitation Manhattan'. As the saying goes: Delhi is structured red tape, Bombay is money – to which Calcuttans add, optimistically, Calcutta is living.

Social rank in Delhi is measured solely by political power. A new-boy politician is several rungs above an eminent lawyer, and certainly above any out-dated nonsense like maharajas. Indeed, Delhi is the only city where the former princes are most definitely former. In provincial towns, citizens doff their caps to His Highness and parade him on elephants at festivals; even in up-to-the-minute Bombay, the titled certainly retain their panache. But in Delhi they have had to go where the power goes, following fellow Jaipur, Gwalior and Jodhpur royals into Parliament. Indian film stars do not fare much better here, a unique experience for them; in a magazine article on the dining haunts of ten Delhi celebrities, four were politicians and six were writers, painters or performing artists – but not a single film star.

Delhi's day-to-day social life-style is controlled by politics. The scheming and gossiping is non-stop, round the clock, often behind the white walls of those peaceful-looking bungalows of New Delhi; and sharp Delhi gossip can truly break a man. It is for chosen ears only. So, political Delhi, which one way or another includes almost everyone of means, has less use for Bombay's hotel-culture, developed for the moneyed to see and be seen.

Even night life is politically determined. Delhi may bulge with museums, hum with performing arts and positively groan with history and monuments. But, for the capital city of what amounts to a continent, night-time Delhi is depressingly dead unless you get into the private social scene. Then you are off, thrown into a succession of jolly evenings, samosa titbits spiced up with the latest scandals. A dinner of MPs is a caricature of Delhi life, the men standing drinking whisky, the women sitting chattering in a corner, food gobbled down in two seconds long after midnight. Then everyone goes straight home.

Lunch times, long light evenings and week-ends, when club-life might blossom, are similarly hit. Whereas Pall Mall lunches and Sunday golf are part of British politics, they have little place in Delhi's scheme of things. Clubs here are either open to all and sundry, like pleasure parks, or stiflingly elite. And none has the welcome warmth and social style of the Bombay Willingdon or the Calcutta Tollygunge, which bubble with families and friends at week-ends. It is not

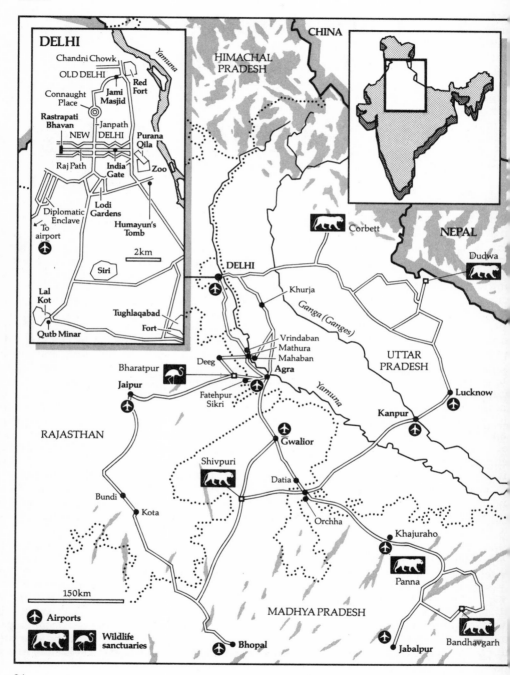

DELHI

Chandni Chowk
OLD DELHI
Red Fort
Connaught Place
Jami Masjid
Rastrapati Bhavan
Janpath
NEW DELHI
Purana Qila
Raj Path
India Gate
Zoo
Diplomatic Enclave
To airport
Lodi Gardens
Humayun's Tomb
2km
Siri
Lal Kot
Tughlaqabad
Qutb Minar
Fort

CHINA

HIMACHAL PRADESH

NEPAL

Yamuna

Corbett
Dudwa

DELHI

Khurja
Ganga (Ganges)

UTTAR PRADESH

Vrindaban
Mathura
Mahaban
Deeg
Agra
Bharatpur
Jaipur
Fatehpur Sikri
Yamuna
Lucknow
Kanpur

RAJASTHAN

Gwalior

Shivpuri
Datia

Bundi
Kota
Orchha
Khajuraho
Panna
Jabalpur
Bandhavgarh

MADHYA PRADESH

150km

Bhopal

Airports

Wildlife sanctuaries

at Delhi is deserted. Far from it. Few people
are leave in case they miss a move in the
olitical game, be they big shot or acolyte.
st a few – the Gandhis and hotel millionaire
. S. Oberoi included – have 'farms' outside
e city. A farm has nothing to do with col-
cting warm hens' eggs for breakfast; it is
ore like a country house set in several acres
(possibly) tilled land, carrying immense
ob value just as a dacha does in Russia.

In industry, political influence is every-
ing to any firm, determining whether or
ot a factory is built, goods imported or li-
nces granted. Influence can speed up the
untless hops, skips and jumps through
ops needed to penetrate successfully the
ngled, overgrown labyrinth of govern-
ent bureaucracy which baffles even its
lministrators.

Each process demands more signatures,
athorisations, forms and written permis-
ons than the last – and each one extracted
om a different office. As job creation goes, it
brilliant. But for those on the other side, it
emands powers of persuasion, intrigue,
ame-dropping and baksheesh (present-
ving) that would have impressed the
ughal court. This is why most big firms
ased in Bombay, Calcutta, Ahmedabad,
[adras or Bangalaore have a Delhi office
ith on-site Men of Influence. And it is why
any MPs constantly have to desert their
ates to be always on call and to be seen in
elhi. For those not seen are not heard. And
is why a Hindu businessman will be found
sacred Tirupati fulfilling an outstanding
ow he made six years before to go on a
ecial pilgrimage when his business was
entually set up.

The basic workings of this all-pervading
olitical machine were set down in the Con-
itution of 1950. India became Independent
1947. The official transfer of power was
ade by the last Viceroy, Lord Louis Mount-
atten, to India's first Prime Minister, Pundit
waharlal Nehru, on August 15. That day is
ow celebrated as Independence Day, when
e Prime Minster delivers an address from
e ramparts of Lal Qila (Red Fort). In 1947,
ehru made an optimistic speech, the Union

Jack came down, the star of India went up.
Nehru then went to Viceroy House (now
called Rastrapati Bhavan) where the two
leaders merrily toasted each other in port, the
Englishman with 'To India', the Indian
with 'To King George VI'. Meanwhile, the
Mahatma, who had fought so hard for this
moment, was saying his prayers in Calcutta;
he was to be assassinated in Delhi the following year.

The previous day, August 14, Mount-
batten had attended the creation of a new
neighbouring country, Pakistan. All this happened just sixteen years after Lord Irwin had
inaugurated Lutyens's New Delhi, designed
and built (at vast cost) as the new British
capital of her Eastern Empire. While the British packed their trunks to go home, some five
million Hindus and Sikhs uprooted themselves to move east out of Muslim Pakistan,
to be replaced by Muslims from India, amid
horrendous bloodshed.

In 1950 the Constitution of India, adopted
in 1949, came into force. It outlined a democ-
racy with a President as Head of State, a
Prime Minister as Head of Government and a
two-house parliament (Lok Sabha and Rajya
Sabha) elected by universal suffrage of the
then 170 million Indians. (The figure is now
700 million and rising.) The official residence
for the head of this pyramid is Viceroy
House, re-named Rastrapati Bhavan. Its first
occupant was Dr Rajentra Prasad (1950–
1962); its current occupant is Gyani Zail Singh
(since July 1982). The Constitution was loosely based on Westminster, but also drew on
the 1935 Government of India Act and looked
to the United States by incorporating a Bill of
Rights spelling out basic liberties.

The system of law and administration, the
civil service, the railways, roads and irrigation systems, all left by the British, provided a basic infrastructure – as did the
English language which, despite all efforts, is
still the main lingua franca throughout India.
Added to which, India had abundant raw
materials and, as Francis Watson observed,
'human resources incalculable in their potential, administrative and managerial experience awaiting only the opportunity of expan-

sion'. This was the equipment to transform an agricultural country in debt into, hopefully, a modern dynamic economy.

On January 26, 1950 the Republic of India was inaugurated. The event is celebrated annually with ironically British-style parades in Delhi, then Beating Retreat three days later (see below). The whole city is spruced up like the preparations for the King and Queen in *Alice In Wonderland*. Fairy lights are tested; blossoming trees are trimmed or coaxed.

With all the former princely states incorporated into the 3,280,483 sq km of Independent India, from huge Hyderabad to pockethandkerchief dominions like Devas Senior in Madhya Pradesh, boundaries were rejigged to create reasonably balanced states. There are now 22 states and nine Union Territories and Special Areas (of which Delhi is one). The princes were allowed to keep their titles and were given privy purses and privileges, but all these were abolished in 1971 to make every citizen equal before the law. (Although you would not think so in most areas; feudalism dies hard.)

Language was always a problem, and still is. Hindi was proclaimed the national language in 1965, but resentment to it was especially strong in the South. Disturbances in Madras threatened national unity. And today's traveller still finds English more useful than Hindi. Classical Hindi, spoken by the cultured, is a Sanskrit-based language. The official Hindi used for administration is the everyday language spoken in the North, with some simplifications. As a means of expression, this version is proving inadequate. When the erudite All-India Radio staff were told to broadcast in this more cockney Hindi, they were not pleased. And, despite government backing, there is little quality modern literature in official Hindi.

To ease the problem, both Hindi and English are official languages today. Of the remaining 3,000 or so languages and dialects, 15 are recognised as national regional languages. To promote the use of Hindi at government level, the law has had to dictate that an officially Hindi-speaking state must communicate with a non-Hindi-speaking state in Hindi – but with a full English translation. 1983, the eminent lawyer Nani Palkhiva described India as 'the largest experime ever undertaken in the art of democratic li ing. Never before, and nowhere else, has or seventh of the human race lived together freedom as a single political entity.'

Today there are about 700 million equ citizens in India. (North and South America total population is around 623 million whi Europe's, excluding the USSR, is a mere 4 million.) Each citizen votes for his state Members of Parliament who then have tricky job of keeping in touch with local nee and fighting for them in far-away Delhi. I adequate state taxes force them to go cap hand to the centre for funds; for instanc while the state is responsible for educatio most of the funds for higher education ha to be extracted from the centre.

Where the state does rake in the rupees from lotteries. The one-rupee tickets are so on the street and bought regularly by ever citizen who can, if only just, afford it. For th weekly prizes are dreamworthy – oft Rs100,000. Even the rich buy tickets, sin the prize money carries a flat 30 per cent t and is not added to earnings. But both centr and state governments fleece the tourist. Th state Sales Tax (10–15%) and Luxury T (which varies enormously, soaring to 30% some Gujarat hotels) are levied by hotels ar restaurants on top of a central tax on tot annual profits. In modest restaurants, or wonders if there is any part of the bill left f the chef.

Electioneering is as colourful as a religiou festival, and as much show-business as it is America. To reach India's illiterate – ov 60% in the 1981 Census – each political par has a symbol. Congress (I), the party of M Gandhi, has a hand. (Nehru's Congre Party split in 1969 into Congress (I), f Indira, and several other smaller Congre parties). These symbols, which may include pair of yoked bullocks, a sickle, a flower or rising sun, are chosen by the Election Con mittees of the parties and are painted c walls throughout the country. In the run u to an election, politicians roar around th untry addressing meetings.

Film stars are wheeled out to support ndidates, drawing vast crowds – although eir intervention in politics is not always flected in the votes. A film director's charis- a once drew 40,000 to a rally, but the candi- ate lost his deposit at the election. In the uth, actors stand themselves, with suc- ss: Tamil Nadu, Andhra Pradesh and Kar- ataka have all had big movie stars as Heads State.

On polling day, an electorate of about 400 illion sallies forth, often en famille, to one the 429,912 polling stations, singing along e way. The women dress in their Sunday st. Bullocks and cows are garlanded, carts ecorated. There are fairs, entertainers and enty of dancing and music. And after the sults, there is more fun for the celebrations.

Indira Gandhi, Prime Minister from Janu- y 1966 to March 1977 and again from Janu- y 1980 until her assassination on October , 1984 has been the dominant figure in cent Indian politics. Her image was surreal r many of her electorate. She was no film ar, yet she received superstar treatment. er picture was in almost every office and staurant and daily on newspaper front ages. Crowds would chant 'Indira is India; dia is Indira'. Her family life, her likes and islikes were reported as minutely as her olitical life, and lapped up by supporters d detractors alike. She was known to make detour to a tiny village outside Varanasi for er favourite sweetmeats; she had a pen- ant for Italian food; she slept little, woke arly and was a devout Hindu; she wore andloom saris but no make-up or perfumes; e did not drink or smoke and, like her ther, she took a keen interest in the garden her official residence, no. 1 Safdarjung oad.

She travelled widely and was remarkably ccessible to her people and to visitors. Re- ote villagers hailed her as 'Mother'. In De- i, she held a morning open audience in her arden, when teachers took pupils to meet er. Supporters took garlands and had their hotograph taken with her. She was an ar- ent and active supporter of wildlife con-

servation, helping to set up and improve the National Parks, backing laws to protect en- dangered species. She was crucial to the suc- cess of wildlife protection in India. There is now a government department devoted ex- clusively to conservation. She had an inti- mate knowledge of all aspects of her country and, in her coffee-table tome, *Eternal India*, wrote of 'this extraordinary land' where 'ev- ery journey brings to light some new fact, local legend or contemporary develop- ment'.

Foreigners granted interviews never failed to be impressed. The former *Times* (of Lon- don) correspondent to India, Trevor Fish- lock, wrote of her 'considerable charm' and 'incandescent smile' as 'she sits in dignified, straight-backed repose, listens and does not fidget, and fills in pauses with good small talk about flowers and theatre'. Some other jour- nalists referred to her as the Empress. She hated the term, preferring to describe herself as having become 'one of the monuments of Delhi'.

This remarkable woman was groomed for her career from an early age. Shrimati Indira Gandhi was born on November 19, 1917 at Allahabad, the daughter of Jawaharlal Nehru, a Kashmiri of the Brahmin caste. Af- ter a thoroughly international schooling— Allahabad (Uttar Pradesh), Santiniketan (West Bengal, see p. 160), Badminton (Eng- land), Switzerland, Pune, Bombay and Somerville College, Oxford (where Margaret Thatcher also studied)—she was imprisoned with her Parsee husband, Feroze, during the Quit India Movement of 1942. Her marriage, though not always happy, had the incalcul- able advantage of the Gandhi surname. Even in India many people had no idea she was not the daughter or grand-daughter of the Mahatma. When her father was Prime Minis- ter, she was first his hostess, courting a pub- lic image of domestic femininity, and then his political aide from 1957 to his death in 1964. In 1959 she was the third Nehru to be elected president of the Congress Party. The follow- ing year her husband died after a heart attack.

In January 1966, aged 48, she became the

second woman ever to be elected Prime Minister of an entire country. Eleven years later, in 1977, her authoritarian ways and her unpopularity (and that of her son, Sanjay) forced her to take the country to the polls. She lost, but remained constantly in the public eye, achieving a landslide victory back to power in January, 1980. The same year, Sanjay was killed in an aeroplane accident.

Her elder son, Rajiv, who was quite content with his career as a pilot, was reluctantly dragged into political limelight. It took his mother a whole year to lure him to stand for parliament for Uttar Pradesh, his home state. Less than four years later his mother was assassinated in her beloved New Delhi garden. And, while India mourned and world leaders arrived to pay their respects, Congress (I) Party leaders met and President Zail Singh swore in the 40-year-old son as her successor at Rastrapati Bhavan.

Even if Mrs Gandhi liked to think of herself as one of the capital's newer monuments, she

was also responsible for several new lan. marks: a vast and superb sports complex f the Asiad in 1982, a plethora of hotels ar fly-overs for the meeting of the Non-align Movement (known as NAM), and still mo for the Commonwealth Heads of Gover ment Meeting (known as CHOGM), bo held in 1983. The overdose of concrete tarmac was compensated by the clearing ar cleaning up of the capital. Delhi is now unusually well cared for, airy and gree capital, a particular incongruity in India. the political pace is too much, residents ar visitors can lose themselves in the Islam monuments, built by empires from Slaves Mughal's and surrounded by beautiful kept parks; or they can wander along t blossoming boulevards of New Delhi. For taste of the old Muslim city, there are t alleys of Old Delhi and Nizamuddin. As t painter, Edward Ardizzone, noted in 195 Delhi is a 'combination of extreme newne and age, with nothing in between'.

When to go

After the frantic cleaning up for NAM and CHOGM, Delhi's prettiest months are now February and March. Flowers and trees blossom in Lutyens's spacious city amid the fresh air and sunshine of an English summer (despite growing pollution). October–November are also green and pleasant but other months bring the extremes of the plains. The debilitating post-monsoon mugginess lifts during September; December–January are distinctly chilly – adored by locals who throw open every window while unprepared tourists shiver. With the intense heat of May–June come dust storms and the hot 'loo' winds, and then the July–August downpours.

FESTIVALS There are festivals to head for and festivals to avoid. People celebrating Holi (March) in Delhi have recently taken to throwing stones instead of harmless pink powder and water. *Republic Day*, January 26, is a matter of choice. Politicians and tourist offices make a big fuss of it. Everything closes across the country. In Delhi anyone of interest disappears to his country farm or to Bombay

for some fun, leaving the capital socially dead. T morning parade is led by the President in ceremonial coach, escorted by the President's Bo Guard, founded as his personal body guard Warren Hastings in 1773, the most senior unit the Indian Army. Then follow the impressive floa from each state, folk dancing, quantities of gai caparisoned elephants and camels, and even helicopter in full elephant fancy-dress showerir rose petals. But it continues with a massive ar seemingly endless display of guns, tanks and mi tary strength. Each evening that week the strin; of lights outlining the Rastrapati Bhavan a switched on (as they are for Independence Da August 15), best seen from the rooftop restaura of the Taj hotel. The Folk Dance Festival fills eve hall for the next two days, followed by *Beati Retreat*, on January 29, a picturesque sunset para of massed bands of the armed forces which end strangely, with Gandhi's favourite hymn, 'Abi With Me'. For the British, accustomed to excelle parades without guns, it is not worth planning itinerary around. Every second is televised ar television should be country-wide very soon. Se ckets can be obtained from travel agencies and ourist offices.

But, if you are in the area, stay in Delhi for *ussehra* (October). It is celebrated in different ways throughout India, and in Delhi as Ram Lila (Rama play). Plays, classical dance, contemporary ance and music recitals fill every hall. Each eve-ing an episode from the Ramayana epic is re-ounted to commemorate Rama's victory over the emon Ravana and thus the freedom of his captive rife, Sita. Ornate chariot processions daily pass rough Old Delhi. On the tenth day, there is a rand procession of huge, firework-stuffed, ainted paper effigies of ten-headed wicked avana and his relatives which proceeds to the am Lila maidan (the open ground between Old nd New Delhi). Amid the seething masses of eople, the battle of Lanka is re-enacted, Sita is eed and the effigies are burned with bangs, racks, whoops and a jolly fair. *Diwali*, also nation-ride, follows three to four weeks later (October–ovember). Oil lamps in every spring-cleaned ouse welcome Lakshmi, the goddess of prosper-y, wealth and pleasure, to the start of a new lindu financial year. (Official New Year is April 3, a public holiday with fairs.) People put on new othes, eat special sweetmeats and, for nine days r so, the Diwali Mela (fair) is alive with stalls, ntertainment and fireworks.

Delhi and Lucknow, both great Mughal centres, elebrate Muslim festivals with feasts and jollity: *fuharram*, commemorating the martyrdom of nam Hussain, grandson of the Prophet Moham-ad; Id-ul-Fitr, celebrating the end of Ramadan, ne ninth month of the Muslim calendar when here must be rigid fasting during all daylight ours; and Id-ul-Zuha, when the sacrifice of Abra-am is remembered with prayers, presents for hildren and new clothes. At Muharram, for nine ays the huge tazias (tinsel, silver or brass replicas f Husains's tomb) are paraded by mourning men, ccompanied by drummers. There are passion lays; men lash themselves in sorrow; Ulema (re-gious scholars) read from pulpits in the mosques. is seen at its most spectacular at Lucknow. See p. 251–3 for more festivals.

RTS Delhi is very lively around Republic Day, am Lila and Diwali. In addition, there are the angeet Sammelan music festival in November nd four important festivals in February: Tansen nusic, named after Akbar's court composer); hrupad (strictly orthodox music); Maharaj Kalka

Bindadi Kathak Mahotsave (classical Kathak dance); and the Shankar Lal Festival (music).

SOCIAL CALENDAR Reaches its height in February–March too. There is the Horse Show, polo, the vintage car rally and the Northern India Golf Championship. India's answer to the Chelsea Flower Show is the Delhi Flower Show, when the air around Purana Qila is heavy and sweet with the scent of thousands of blooms. Of course, being India, there are entertainers as well. The Rose Show is in January; the Chrysanthemum Show in December. The January International Film Fes-tival, run from Delhi, is held here in alternate years (Delhi 1987). In Delhi it is competitive; when it visits Bombay, Calcutta and elsewhere it is non-competitive.

Getting there: getting away

Hitting and quitting Delhi is very easy by air or train. The airport, Palam, lies a quick 15 minutes south-west of New Delhi. However, crossing the city to a central or northern hotel is another story and can take an hour in the daytime. The airport is full of the usual queues for banks, tickets, reserva-tions, baggage and bureaucratic nonsense, swarm-ing day and night with travellers and locals, car-peted with sleeping bodies. But for the inevitable delays there is a good, clean, air-conditioned and quite peaceful restaurant upstairs, much nicer than any of the waiting areas.

Train is even easier. New Delhi Railway Station lies between Old and New Delhi; the older Delhi Railway Station is in the middle of the old city. Short hops are quicker by train than plane. If the holiday is short, this is a good place to slip in the essential Indian train journey, perhaps to Agra on the wonderfully named Taj Express or to Jaipur on the Pink City Express. The classic inter-city trains – with names like Frontier Mail and Rajdhani Ex-press – take longer than a flight but give an oppor-tunity to see rural life and the landscape and to feel the vastness of the country.

Most international airlines serve Delhi. Indian Airlines then feeds passengers into the rest of the country, especially the surrounding states, major cities and the hills. The daily early morning Rajas-than shuttle stops at Jaipur, Jodhpur and Udaipur. Other daily services include Agra, Ahmedabad, Aurangabad, Bangalore, Bhopal, Bombay, Cal-cutta, Gwalior, Hyderabad, Khajuraho, Lucknow, Madras, Nagpur, Vadodara, Varanasi. For the hills, daily flights go to Amritsar, Chandigarh (for the narrow gauge railway to Simla), Jammu and Srinagar as they do up to Kathmandu in Nepal. The weather in Leh determines all flights there (from Delhi or Srinagar). For other places, connections may or may not fly out the same day. And if two flights are necessary, these too may be staggered. Go via Bombay, Madras, Bangalore and Hyderabad for southern cities; via Bombay for Gujarat (except Ahmedabad) and Goa (Dabolim airport, daily); via Madras or Bombay for Sri Lanka (Colombo). The Maldives (Male) are three hops away, via Madras or Bombay, then Trivandrum, (Mon., Thurs.).

Short train journeys mostly leave early and serve an excellent breakfast of scrambled eggs on toast, bananas and tea. Go to Agra (3 hours) and Gwalior (5 hours) on the Taj Express (New Delhi station); Jaipur (5 hours) and Ajmer (8 hours) on the Pink City Express (Delhi station). Lucknow railway station should be experienced: arrive overnight (10 hours) on the Lucknow Mail or by day (10 hours) on the Gomti Express (both from New Delhi station). Reach the hill cities via Jammu on the overnight (12 hours) Jammu Tawi Mail (Delhi station). For a longer, inter-city journey with excellent arm-chair sightseeing and formidable but safe meals, go on the Rajdhani Express II to Bombay (17 hours) and the Rajdhani Express I – the fastest train in India, hitting 120kph – to Calcutta (16 hours), and on the Tamil Nadu to Madras (32 hours).

Where to stay

Hotels mushroomed in Delhi when it played host to world politicians and sportsmen. Most are ghastly, some are unfinished. Of the older hotels, only Claridges combines character and modern facilities, but it does not compete with the Taj in Bombay, or the Oberoi Grand in Calcutta. Nevertheless, Delhi is the best equipped of all the big cities. In such a sprawling capital, location is as important as quality of hotel. Top modern hotels (Taj, Maurya Sheraton, Oberoi Intercontinental, Taj Palace) are sited south of the New Delhi government buildings: all right for the airport and diplomatic area; lousy for inner New Delhi and Shahjahanabad, which are impossible to reach without transport. In addition, auto-rickshaws are not always waiting at the gates of grand hotels (they are not allowed inside), so taxi bills soar. Older hotels with good character and varying facilities are scattered: Claridges and Ashok south,

Oberoi Maidens north and Imperial bang in th middle.

Another important criterion is food and night li since the best are found in the newer hotel Delhi's night-life is centred on what locals ca 'hotel culture', and it is much better in some hote than others. (It very much depends what you wa out of Delhi as to where you stay.) To help gau how a hotel relates to the city, its distance bo from Connaught Place and from the airport a given below. Book early for October–March (mar tourists are not deterred by the cold), especially there is also some big international event. Hot swimming pools are usually emptied in the wint so, if a daily plunge is essential, check that the po is in action. Even in Delhi, where electric power reasonably constant, all good hotels have the own generators, 'otherwise', as the manager of th Imperial pointed out, 'guests would first get stuc in the lift, then check out'.

Taj Mahal Hotel, 1 Mansingh Road, New Del 100011
Telephone: 386162
Telex: 31-3604/31-4758 TAJD IN
Cable: TAJDEL
Airport 13km; Connaught Place 3km
350 rooms, including 26 suites, attached bat
Single Rs750; double Rs850.

Every service including travel counter, c rental, bank, business services, pool, healt club, beauty salon, chemist, baby sitter, Khazar shopping arcade.

Often referred to as Taj Man Singh, this impo ing, 21-storey white mountain opened in 1978 an scores points on most tests except character. Eve then, the bold brashness of the dazzling whi marble lobby with fountain and miniature pain ings makes up for the exterior and safe-but-sma room decor. It is the most central of all the moder luxury hotels, the most fashionable to be seen i Standards and most services meet the Taj Group high reputation. Go for a high floor: excelle views over the city plus (in east-facing room stunning sunrises, the ball of fire rising above th misty Delhi plains. Sumptuous health club wit separate facilities for men and women, from gy to jacuzzi; large swimming pool; a heavily teste and recommended travel counter; and an exemp lary shopping arcade praised by discerning local Also on the plus side are the Chinese and India restaurants – some of the best in town – poolsid barbeque and sunny coffee shop.

Then come the minuses: room service can be low; the bar is dreary; enjoying the wonderful views of the rooftop restaurant means suffering bad Italian food and live European music; and Number One discotheque is going down the charts. The flashy Taj is a favourite with Delhi society, so be prepared: to eat well, reserve a table at House of Ming and Haveli restaurants – otherwise it's bad pasta or taxi ride time. See below for more on restaurants, health and shopping.

Claridges, 12 Aurangzeb Road, New Delhi 110011
Telephone: 370211
Telex: 031 2518
Cable: CLARIDGES
Airport 12km. Connaught Place 4km
140 rooms, including 9 suites, bath attached. Single Rs450; double Rs550; suites Rs850–1300.
Mod. cons include car rental, business services, swimming pool, health club, beauty parlour.

The only central, period hotel combining character with modern facilities, smiling staff and some degree of efficiency. Colonial courtyard form, with much wood and some original furnishings; friendly but quiet atmosphere, food passable. A hotel where guests still take afternoon tea around the courtyard pool with a certain formality. One high-powered World Bank employee living in Delhi finds it 'the nicest of all Delhi hotels. I'd stay there myself. I book all my friends in there.' Plenty of young guests include actor Nicholas Grace ('Heat and Dust') who finds it 'fun without being expensive. A good place to meet like-minded people.' Some areas are far from the kitchens; so, if room service and hot breakfast are important, check the geography of your room.

Maurya Sheraton, Sardar Patel Marg, Diplomatic Enclave, New Delhi 110021
Telephone: 370271
Telex: 031-3247/4911 WELC IN
Cable: WELCOTEL, NEW DELHI
As headquarters of the Welcomgroup chain, Central Reservation Service is here (see p. 11).
Airport 6km; Connaught Place 7km
510 rooms, including 12 suites, attached bath. Single Rs775; double Rs875; triple Rs975; suites Rs1100–4000+.
Every mod. con. includes travel counter, car rental, bank, business services, Cable TV in each room, baby sitter, heated swimming pool, health club, yoga centre, beauty salon, discotheque, shopping arcade with tailoring and astrologer.

Built and run by the Welcomgroup, owned by India Tobacco Company (ITC). Huge, 7-storey,

stepped building, the lobbies and suites adorned with quality contemporary Indian art. The pieces, on the theme of the Mauryan Empire, were commissioned from prominent painters and sculptors. J. Swaminathan, Akbar Padamsee, M. F. Husain and Tyeb Mehta added others. Krishna Khanna directed the project and contributed his own painting. Sculptors include Ramachandran and Meera Mookerjee (her statue of Ashoka is in front of the hotel). All the public area and the main structure have strong contemporary designs inspired by Indian traditions and avoid the anonymity and brashness of most modern Indian hotels.

Its major disadvantage is being out on a limb in a rather barren area, but efficient services and excellent facilities, lively atmosphere. Rooms in both main building and adjoining executive tower all smart. Suites, some with terraced gardens, verge on the bizarre – one has its own sauna. Health club good, pool too small for size of hotel, shopping arcade excellent. (In-house astrologer, Mohinda Chowpra, will 'reveal the heights to which you may rise'.) Indian, North-West Frontier and Chinese restaurants praised and patronised by locals, so book. Pleasant coffee shop and cocktail bar. Best discotheque in town. See below for more on restaurants and health.

Oberoi Intercontinental, Dr Zakir Hussain Road, New Delhi 110003
Telephone: 699571
Telex: 2372/3829 OBDL
Cable: INHOTELCOR/OBHOTEL
Airport 16km, Connaught Place 5km
330 rooms, including 17 suites, bath attached. Single Rs850; double Rs950; suites Rs2500–4000.
All facilities, including travel agency, car rental, bank, business services, pool, health club, yoga classes, beauty parlour, baby sitter, shopping arcade.

The pioneer Indian high-rise luxury hotel, opened in 1965 when the Oberoi chain was already well-established. Stunning efficiency in a building void of all character – service directory so comprehensive it is a hard-back book for bed-time browsing.

Excellent site, all rooms overlooking lush golf course or zoological gardens and Mughal and Lodi monuments, the nicest location of all the up-market hotels. But this functional, businessman's machine is now showing signs of wear and tear and is undergoing a total refurbishment. So far, the redecorated rooms have a heavy, European, repro stuffiness: buttoned, salmon pink upholstery, dark

41

wood, vast televisions, walls hung with prints, masses of light switches, sumptuous chestnut-brown granite bathrooms with baths to take the largest body. Plus the latest Indian toys: press button telephone (that works), Cable TV with full film programme – and one suite even has a jacuzzi. The many restaurants, lobby and discotheque, currently not on a par with competitors, are to be tackled next and include a rooftop Chinese restaurant (without the dreaded live European music) and rooftop bar-discotheque with huge open terrace. Sounds promising. Good pool area. The health club has kindly staff, separate extensive equipment for men and women and is considered by some local globe-trotters to be the best in Delhi, if not anywhere in the world. Food does not match service; coffee is undrinkable.

Oberoi Maidens, 7 Sham Marg, Delhi 110054
Telephone: 250078/252611/255464
Telex: 2703 OMDL
Cable: OBMAIDENS
As headquarters of the Oberoi chain, Central Reservation Service is here (see p. 11).
Airport 24km; Connaught Place 7km
75 rooms, including 18 suites. Single Rs350–395; double Rs450–495; suites Rs500–1050.
Facilities include fridge in every room, car rental, beauty salon, baby sitter, tennis court, pool, garden.

Built just north of Old Delhi (Shahjahanabad), in 1900 by Mr Maiden, this is one of the oldest hotels in Delhi and one of the nicest. Lutyens stayed here while his new city was going up. Colonial building with spacious rooms ('double suites' particularly good) and wide verandahs set in eight acres of garden. Well-placed for wandering in Shahjahanabad and for picking up rickshaws to go further afield. Not so good for nipping to a business meeting or the airport. Gentle and peaceful atmosphere of a private house; for relaxation, not business. Hard double tennis court, badminton court and pool with separate children's area set in well-tended gardens shaded by banyan tree and bougainvillea. Rather drab restaurant and coffee shop but amusing 1960s discotheque, the only one in Old Delhi and popular with local university students.

Imperial, Janpath, New Delhi 110001
Telephone: 311511
Telex: 3303 HTL IMP
Cable: COMFORT
Airport 18km; Connaught Place ½km.
160 rooms, including 16 suites, bath attached.

Single Rs400; double Rs500; suites Rs900–1100.
Facilities include bank, car rental, beauty salo[n] tennis, pool, garden, shopping arcade.

The most central of all recommended hote[l] with reasonable facilities. Built 1933–35 in the late style on an 8-acre site facing on to Queensw[ay] (Janpath), the north-south nerve of New Delh[i] Italian marble, London silver and crockery a[nd] European chandeliers were piled into the whi[te] building ready for the grand banquet and openi[ng] by Vicereine Lady Willingdon (Lord Willingd[on] was Viceroy 1931–36), which launched it as a soc[ial] and political focus. Half a century later the hug[e] stuccoed and mirrored ballroom is still used f[or] parties. The rooms have their original hardwo[od] writing desks and beds, hideous floral carp[et] (more woven as it wears out), marble baths a[nd] Daniells prints. (Avoid 1960s furnished secon[d] floor rooms.) Reluctant air-conditioning, stored [in] vast trunks, blows hot air in winter and cold [in] summer 'eventually', says the smiling manage[r]. Every meal, from breakfast onwards, can be tak[en] on the extensive lawns shaded by soaring roy[al] palms. The mature garden is supplied by its ow[n] on-site nursery. Behind a hedge lies the large p[ool] and hard tennis court. A haven of peace and rel[ax]ation amid city bustle.

Ashok, 50-B Chanakyapuri, New Delhi 110021
Telephone: 370101
Telex: 031-2567
Cable: ASHOKA HOTEL
As headquarters of the Ashok chain, Central R[e]servation Service is here (see p. 11).
Airport 10km; Connaught Place 5km
589 rooms, including 106 suites, bath attache[d]
Single Rs700; double Rs800; suites Rs1100–5000.
All mod. cons include travel agent, car rent[al] bank, health club, beauty salon, baby sitter, tenn[is] pool, shopping arcade. Federica Fellini swears [by] the in-house astrologer.

ITDC's showpiece hotel of their vast, and usua[l]ly very disappointing, chain. Extensively, expen[s]ively and controversially renovated for the rece[nt] Delhi events under the auspices of dynamic ITD[C] whizz-kid, 34-year-old Rajan Jatley (who was [at] school with Rajiv Gandhi). What upset locals mo[st] has been changing the huge, 1954 landmark fro[m] pink to white (now peeling back to pink). Few ha[ve] gone inside to see the other improvements. I[n]terior designer Dale Keller has beautifully refu[r]bished a dozen suites, each with the crafts of a[n] individual state. The Kashmir one has crewel-wo[rk] curtains, carved walnut wood tables, papier mac[hé]

riting paper holders, etc. And his restaurants are
me of the prettiest in Delhi – a tented French one,
oriously fresh green and white garden bar, a
acious and sunny coffee shop. The luxury of
ace is everywhere: wide corridors, big rooms,
wns. In all, a refreshing break from the usual
otel stuffiness. But reports of slow service and
aly fair food.

aj *Palace,* Sardar Patel Marg, Diplomatic Enclave,
ew Delhi 110021
elephone: 323500
elex: 031-5151 TAJD IN
able: TAJ PALACE, DELHI
irport 6km; Connaught Place 7km
0 rooms, including 37 suites, bath attached.
ngle Rs650; double Rs750.
l mod. cons including travel agency, car rental,
nk, extensive business services, airlines offices,
ealth club, beauty parlour, pool, shopping
cade.

With a honey-coloured marble lobby big enough
play elephant polo, this hotel is for the athletic
uest. Every part is smart, highly efficient, gleam-
g and miles from anywhere else. Perhaps that is
hy the escalator is necessary – the only one in
elhi, so terrifying to local ladies that there is a
otice warning of its dangers and a parallel stair-
se. Perhaps that is also why the specially im-
orted electronic telephone exchange is necessary
it would take an hour to drop round to a col-
ague. The fresh rooms are decorated in cream,
ey and blue and the suites, some with terraces,
e furnished with nice art.

Opened for NAM in 1983, this newest and
ishiest of Delhi's hotels is located next to the
aurya (with those location pros and cons) and
ared to conference businessmen, complete with
slightly down-market version of the sister hotel's
hazana shopping arcade and an assortment of
staurants including one verging on the gim-
icky: a replica carriage from the Orient Express
iin serving over-priced Continental food. The
tchens are presided over by a woman head chef,
haina Jayal. And the health club is sensational, a
ever-ending warren of moss-green marble rooms.
oodness knows what happens when 500 people
ll out of a convention and all want a swim in the
oderate-sized pool.

Information and reservations

If you enter India through Delhi, this is the moment to acquire countrywide information and to
book as much as possible. It is maddening to arrive
at Sanchi, in central India, and be told the guide-
book is only available in Delhi. There are offices
representing everyone and everything here. The
capital's obsession with bureaucracy is catching,
however, resulting in slowness and inefficiency,
the notable exception being the Janpath Tourist
Office. But whatever you need is here somewhere,
fortunately often to be hunted down in a private
shop or travel agent.

The usual government office opening hours are
Mon.–Sat., 10am–5pm; closed every Sun. and the
second Sat. of each month.

Delhi Tourism Development Corporation, N
Block, Connaught Place (tel: 46356). Also desks at
New Delhi Railway Station, Delhi Railway Station
and airport. All open 7am–9pm, except the airport
one, which is open 24 hours.

Government of India Tourist Office, 88 Janpath
(tel: 320005/320008), known to many as the Janpath
Tourist Office. Extremely good. Knowledgeable
assistants on Delhi and every part of India. Issues
permits to visit Rastrapati Bhavan and Gardens.
Also has desk at airport. Mon.–Sat., 9am–6pm;
summer 8am–6pm.

Each state has a tourist office in Delhi, usually
very ungrand but with helpful staff. They have lots
of information, plus the state map. They are conveniently bunched together in two big groups. At
Chanderlok Building, 36 Janpath, go upstairs at the
far end to find Haryana (tel: 344911), Himachal
Pradesh (tel: 345320), Jammu & Kashmir (tel:
345373), Rajasthan (tel: 322332) and Uttar Pradesh
(tel: 322251). At the State Emporia Complex, Baba
Kharak Singh Marg, go round to the back of the
building to find the office corresponding to each
shop at the front, usually on the first or second
floor: Andhra Pradesh (tel: 343894), Assam (tel:
321967), Bihar (tel: 370147), Gujarat (tel: 343173,
piles of literature), Karnataka (tel: 343862), Madhya
Pradesh (tel: 351187), Maharashtra (tel: 343281),
Orissa (tel: 345880), Punjab (tel: 343055), Tamil
Nadu (tel: 343913, particularly good) and West
Bengal (tel: 343775). The Andaman & Nicobar
Liaison Office is at Curzon Road Apartments,
Kasturba Gandhi road (tel: 387015).

While getting organised for the rest of the trip,
visit the Archaeological Survey of India, next to the
National Museum, which has the most authori-

tative area maps and guides to all the major archaeological sights (usually sold out on site). The Archaeological Survey has another office upstairs in the Cottage Industries Emporium, Janpath. The Indian headquarters of the World Wildlife Fund are at C-570 Defence Colony. The special Project Tiger office is at Shastri Bhavan.

There are plenty of newspapers in the capital. *The Times of India, The Indian Express, The Hindustan Times* and *The Statesman* are the principal ones, full of news of the Government's doings, plus daily lists of main events. *The Times of India* runs 'The Week That Will Be' on Fridays, an exhaustive list of forthcoming cultural events. *The Indian Express* also has a preview cultural section and probably has the biggest circulation of all Indian English-language newspapers. *India Today*, published fortnightly in Delhi, provides spunky political, economic and social commentary. *Delhi Diary* is packed with arbitrary lists of cultural events, exhibitions, restaurants and shops, lacking any criticism (free from hotel bell captains). The tourist office's fortnightly *Programme of Events* gives skeleton information.

Best of the several guide-books is *Guide to Delhi*, 2nd edition published 1982 by ITDC. Ensure the free map from the Janpath Tourist Office is the 1984 edition, as there has been a lot of building recently. See bibliography for a selection of the many books on Delhi. See shopping section for bookshops.

Delhi has several excellent libraries including the American Library, 24 Kasturba Gandhi Marg (tel: 44251), the British Council Library, All India Fine Arts and Crafts Society, Rafi Marg (tel: 381401); Max Mueller Bhavan, Kasturba Gandhi Marg (tel: 384956/382792); Delhi Public Library in Old Delhi; the excellent Rama Krishna Mission Library in New Delhi and the three government-funded cultural academies: Lalit Kala Akademi (tel: 387243), Sahitaya Akademi (tel: 388667) and Sangeet Natak Akademi (tel: 387248), all in Rabindra Bhavan, Feroz Shah Road.

TRAVEL AGENTS
American Express, Wenger House, A Block, Connaught Place (tel: 344119/344485); Cox & Kings, Indra Palace, Connaught Circus (tel: 321428/320067); Indtravels, Hotel Imperial, Janpath (tel: 312887); Mackinnon Travel Service, Bank of Baroda Building, 16 Parliament Street (tel: 310840); Mercury Travels, 4A Ground Fl, Jeevan Tara Building, Parliament Street (tel: 321403/321411) and at Oberoi Intercontinental (tel: 69571); SITA World Travel, F12 Connaught Place (tel: 43103/45564); Thomas

Cook, Hotel Imperial, Janpath (tel: 312468/31151: Tiger Tops Mountain Travel, 1/1 Rani Jhansi Roa (tel: 523057), especially for wildlife parks and f Nepal; Trade Wings, 60 Janpath (tel: 321322); TC Hotel Metro, N-49 Connaught Circus (tel: 4518) Less grand but reliable are United Travel Servic 802 Nirmal Tower, Barakhamba Road, (tel: 64101 and Paradise Tour Co, 2526 Asaf Ali Road (t 261076).

AIRLINE OFFICES
Indian Airlines, Kanchenjunga, Barakhamba Roa (on the first floor, reached via steps at the back the building; when found at last, huge queues elbowing and shouting people that do not move f hours. Conclusion: pay a travel agent to do t work, particularly for several bookings on a row ticket, and go off and enjoy Delhi.

The major international airlines offices, stru along and around Janpath, are easier to handle. C Janpath are Air India (tel: 344225) and Air Fran (tel: 374775) in Scindia House, Japan Airlines (t 322122) and Pan Am (tel: 322356) at no.36, bo Lufthansa (321133) and Swissair (322877) at no.5 and Royal Nepal Airlines (tel: 320817/321572) no.44. Aeroflot (tel: 42843) is with Indian Airlin on Barakhamba Road; British Airways (tel: 34342 and Cathay Pacific (tel: 351286) are at 1A Co naught Place; SAS and Thai International (t 343608) are at 12A Connaught Place. Others are the telephone directory.

TRAIN RESERVATIONS
Foreigners go to Baroda House, Kasturba Gand Marg (tel: 387889), where Tourist Guide Assistar advise and help book trains for anywhere in Inc and sell Indrail Passes. They also have a spec tourist quota of seats. Northern Railway Reserv tion Office, opposite K Block, Connaught Circ (tel: 344877) for air-conditioned and first cla tickets on trains from New Delhi and De stations, plus Indrail Passes. Much queuing. Op Mon.–Sat. 8am–8pm; Sun. 8am–1pm.

CONSULATES AND EMBASSIES
Concentrated in Chanakyapuri (Diplomatic E clave), including UK (tel: 690371), USA (t 690351) and West Germany (tel: 694361), all Shantipath. France is at 2 Aurangzeb Road (t 374682). For neighbouring countries, Bhutan is Chandragupta Marg (tel: 699227), Burma at 3/5 Nyaya Marg, Chanakyapuri (tel: 619461), Nepal 1 Barakhamba Road (tel: 381484) and Sri Lanka

Kautilya Marg, Chanakyapuri (tel: 370201). For
ers, see telephone directory. Foreigners Reg-
ation Department is at Hans Bhavan (first
or), Tilak Bridge (tel: 272790).

RMITS FOR RESTRICTED AREAS

ry much better obtained before leaving home.
wever, it is possible to try to get them in Delhi in
son or through a recommended travel agent
o will plough through the forest of paperwork.
ose longing to experience Indian bureaucracy
first hand get permits for Darjeeling from
eigners' Registration Office (see above). But
y go to the Ministry of Home Affairs, Lok Nayak
avan, Khan Market for Sikkim and other rested north-eastern areas, and the Ministry of
me Affairs, North Block for Andaman and Nico-
islands. Nepal, Bhutan and Burma consulates
ue their visas. Janpath Tourist Office issues All
dia Liquor Permits.

ere is a big General Post Office and inland
egraph Office at Eastern Court, Janpath. Over-
s Communications Service, Bangla Sahib Road,
ds cables abroad. But both telephone and cable
more easily tackled through the hotel. If you are
the recommended hotels have good in-house
ctors or can call one quickly. Kemp & Co., Radial
ad no.6, E Block, Connaught Circus, is a good
mist, open Mon.–Sat. 24 hours. The new luxury
tels also have chemists.

e city by day

hi is made up of about fifteen cities, spanning
period from the 11th to the 20th centuries.
ere is little left of the early cities. They litter
plains, some still living, some deserted ruins.
lers tended to drastically build over the city they
erited or abandon it for a fresh power-house on
gin soil. This luxury of space, unknown to any
er historic capital, continues to be explored for
using and industry. In the smart residential
as, often called colonies, houses are surrounded
large, leafy gardens, far different from cramped
mbay. Thus Old Delhi (Shahjahanabad) and
w Delhi, the two most recent cities and the heart
modern Delhi, are relatively intact – although
M. Kaye, author of *The Far Pavilions*, remem-
s well the open vistas of the 1940s, dotted with
ughal buildings that are now destroyed or clut-
ed up with concrete.
he capital is best seen city by city, outdoors.

There are few opening and closing times, lots of
parks to pause in, and only the very centre gets
jammed up with traffic. Compared to Bombay and
Calcutta, it is a spacious dream. Furthermore, most
roads are known by a single name, unusually
straightforward for an Indian city. Explore Mughal
Shahjahanabad's tiny streets, market and fort on
foot; expansive Imperial New Delhi, now India's
government headquarters, by car or auto-
rickshaw, stopping here and there (drivers wait
quite happily). Ruins of Purana Qila and Feroz
Shah Kotla cities are just to the east, a rickshaw ride
away. But first take a car out south to the remains of
the oldest cities, glorious for a sunny ramble
among the monuments and hillocks and a picnic.
Delhi's many indoor museums and museum
houses are excellent; most close on Mondays.

ITDC and DTDC (Delhi Transport Development
Corporation) do morning tours to New Delhi (but
not inside Rastrapati Bhavan) and out to the Qtub
Minar etc. (see p. 46); afternoon tours to Old Delhi
(Shahjahanabad) include the Red Fort. Taking both
gives a good idea of the overall layout, even if the
chronology is thrown out of gear. Prices are cheap,
guides good and pauses at monuments not too
short – to cover that ground costs ten times as
much by taxi and takes far longer by any other
transport. Book ITDC tours at L Block, Connaught
Place (tel: 350331), 6.30am–10pm; DTDC tours at
Scindia House, opposite N Block, Connaught
Circus.

The Janpath Tourist Office rents out guides for a
half or full day. The recommended travel agents
can arrange a car and a good driver. A taxi can take
five people before there is a surcharge. Auto-
rickshaws weave through in-town traffic quickest
of all. As Delhi is so spread out, it is worth paying
the small charge to keep your transport waiting to
avoid being stranded and having a long walk.

Early cities, Lal Kot to Jahanpanah Quite the
nicest introduction to Delhi is a mini-rural trip, a
visual history of early Delhi seen through the cities
and monuments set in fields, villages and park-
land. On the way to the site of the first cities lie the
ruins of prosperous *Siri*, which followed them.
Built by Ala-ud-din, Afghan Turk and Sultan of the
second Delhi dynasty, the Khiljis (1290–1320), its
water came from Haus Khan. The huge haus
(reservoir) was later surrounded by a university
(1354, with fine two-storeyed colonnade), mosque
and various Lodi monuments (see especially the
early 16th century Moth ki Masjid, possibly

45

surpassing those in the Lodi Gardens). The rather insubstantial ruins of Mohammad Tughlaq's *Jahanpanah* city (begun 1325) adjoin Siri to the south, but it is worth seeking out Begampur Mosque (1387) and Kirki Mosque (1375), a fort-like structure with kirkis (perforated windows) built by a Tughlaq prime minister.

Out at *Lal Kot*, very little remains of the first citadel of Delhi, built about 1060 and won from the Tomar Rajputs by the Chauhan Rajputs. (The Tomars' city of Dillika was founded in 736.) Their 12th century ruler, Prithviraj III, extended the city and renamed it after himself, Qila (citadel) Rai Pithora. Then came the Turks. In 1206, the great builder and former slave Qutb-ud-din Aibak proclaimed himself the first Sultan of Delhi – he had been governor since 1191. This Sultanate period, under various dynasties, lasted until 1526. Aibak's Slave dynasty (1191–1246) marked the start of the all-pervading Islamic influence in India and laid the foundations of the future Imperial style of Islamic architecture.

Already, in 1193, having demolished 27 or so richly and delicately carved temples in Qila Rai Pithora, he built the first mosque in India, Quwwat-ul-Islam Masjid (Might of Islam Mosque). But although the structure is Islamic and the carving restricted to floral and geometric patterns, it feels very Hindu. Hardly surprising as most of the stonework, including the beautiful columns, is second-hand, taken from the demolished Hindu temples. But the grand, five-arched maqsura (screen) covered with verses from the Qur'an in deep, tracery-fine carving was entirely new and marks the start of a happy combination: Islamic design and Indian labour. How the Gupta iron pillar with its 4th or 5th century Sanskrit inscription arrived in the courtyard – let alone the technical feat of casting it – is a complete mystery, thick with legends. One is its ability to grant the wish of anyone who can encircle it with his arms behind his back.

Aibak also built the exquisitely carved, red sandstone, five-storey tower, the *Qutb Minar* (begun 1199). One of the symbols of Delhi, it is in fact modelled on the tower at Ghazni. The Qutb (pole, axis) signified the pivot of justice, sovereignty and, of course, the Islamic faith – a highly symbolic tower of victory. Originally more than its current 72.55m in height, it was also a handy minaret for the muezzin to call the faithful to the mosque. The great art historian Percy Brown expounds on it: 'unique . . . made possible by the inspired vision

of Qutb-ud-din Aibak, and realized through t creative genius of the Indian workmen'.

The British sketched it endlessly, the India rushed up and down it until there was a tra accident with many killed in 1981, since when t stairs have been temporarily closed. See also t very richly carved tomb of Aibak's son-in-law a successor, Iltutish, built by himself in 1235, and t buildings put up under Ala-ud-din of Siri fame cloister around the mosque, the Alai-Darwa (south gateway), his unfinished rival tower and l tomb (in the ruins of his college for Islamic studie More monuments are scattered along the ro south to Mehrauli and in the village itself.

East of the Qutb Minar lie the rampart ruins the city after Siri, *Tughlaqabad*. This massive, gate, fort was built by Ghiyasuddin Tughlaq (ru 1320–25), first of the Tughlaq dynasty (1320–141 but abandoned five years later after his eccen son, Sultan Mohammad, committed patrici Mohammad first built a new city, Jahanapana between Siri and Lal Kot. Then, like the grand Duke of York, he marched the whole populat down to the new capital of Daulatabad in Ma rashtra and, several years later, marched th back again (see p. 130). Opposite Tughlaqaba Ghiyasuddin's simple tomb and Adilabad Fi possibly built by Mohammad, who presump ously called himself Al-Adil (The Just).

Suraj Kund, a vast amphitheatre possibly built the Tomar Rajputs in the 10th century, is 2 south. On the road back into town are the recei discovered rock edicts of a Mauryan king (century BC), probably aimed at travellers pass along the trade route. Do this trip in the ea morning for fresh sunlight and peace before tour buses arrive at Qutb Minar, or in the afterno after they have gone; avoid Sunday picnicke Haus Khas and Qutb Minar complex have open hours: sunrise to sunset. Ensure your drive briefed, as not everything is obvious tourist stu **Ferozabad** The rather more stable Feroz S Tughlaq – builder, intellectual and antique coll tor – succeeded mad-cap Mohammad in 1351 f long reign of 37 years. The city of palaces, mosq and gardens he founded on the banks of the Ya una River stretched right to Haus Khas where built the college. It was the richest city in the wo and a magnet to scholars. Only ruins of his pala the Kushk-i-Feroz (with tank (man-made lake) mosque), and the Ashoka Pillar he brought fr Ambala survive. The 3rd century BC inscription the pillar was the first of the Mauryan empere

any edicts for peace to be deciphered. James
rincep cracked the ancient Brahmi script, fore-
nner of modern devnagari, in 1937.

North of Ferozabad are memorials to Mahatma
andhi and India's prime ministers. Raj Ghat is
here Gandhi was cremated the day after his
sassination (January 30, 1948); Gandhi Museum
earby (open Tues.–Sun., 9.30am–5.30pm). Shan-
Vana (Forest of Peace) is where Jawaharlal Nehru
ied May 27, 1964) and his daughter Indira Gan-
i (assassinated October 31, 1984) were cremated
dira's son, Sanjay is remembered too). Vijay
hat is dedicated to Lal Bahadur Shastri (died
nuary 11, 1966). West of Ferozabad is Khuni
arwaza, one of Sher Shah's gateways; south is the
ternational Dolls Museum (5,000 of them), open
es.–Sun., 10am–6pm).

di Gardens   After the Tughlaqs, the Sayyids
414–51) and Lodis (1451–1526) were only in-
rested in building for the dead. Delhi turned into
necropolis with over 50 large octagonal and
uare memorials and dozens of smaller ones.
me of the most majestic are here, set amid the
wns, ponds, flowers and trees formerly called
dy Willingdon Park. There are the Bara Gumbad
rge dome) and Sheesh Gumbad (dome of glass),
ll with blue enamelled tiles and painted floral
signs; the tombs of Mubarak Shah (died 1434),
ohammad Sayyid (died 1444), and Sikandar Lodi
ied 1517).

The last has the newly imported Persian double
me; excellent views from the roof (up steps at
ght-hand corner of courtyard). It was Sikandar
di who moved his court to Agra in 1502, initiat-
g 146 years of royal oscillation between Agra and
lhi that ended with the building of Shahjahana-
d. Especially pleasant at sunset, Aashiana café in
rdens (open 10am–10pm).

fdarjang Tomb   Off-track historically but just
ross the road from Lodi Gardens. The last of the
and Mughal garden tombs, built 1753–74 for
fdar Jang, Nawab of Oudh and prime minister to
ohammad Shah. The standard Humayun de-
gn, materials pinched from Khan-i-Khanan's
mb; fountains splashing in the gardens. More
od   views   from   the   roof.   Just   south
Safdarjang Airport, where Mrs Gandhi's son,
njay, was killed in a plane accident in 1980.

zamuddin   Medieval Sufi village, the oldest
ing area of Delhi, full of atmosphere. Described
archaeologist Mitch Crites as having 'the most
portant concentration of Indo-Islamic archi-
ture in India'. It evolved around the dargah

(shrine) of the Sufi saint Sheikh Nizamuddin Chisti
(Hazrat Nizamuddin Aulia) who died in 1325. The
court poet Amir Khusrau (died 1325), whom the
saint enticed there to write his Urdu verse, the poet
Ghalib (died 1893), Shah Jahan's daughter and
Mohammad Shah are all buried here. Today, a
hereditary family of priests runs the Jamat Khana
Masjid, built by Ala-ud-din Khilji, which is crammed with worshippers for Friday noon prayers.

In the narrow lanes little Muslim buildings survive; women still live in purdah; boys attend daily
scripture lessons; women wash in the sacred water
of the large baoli (step well); stalls sell typically
Muslim items of rose petals, incense sticks, embroidered verses from the Qur'an. On Thursdays
qawwalis, Khusrau's creation of choral songs to
heighten religious experience, are sung around his
and Nizamuddin's graves, the air scented with the
spices of delicious biryani (rice and meat dishes)
sold from steaming cauldrons.

At Urs festival there are qawwalis, poetry readings and fairs. Qawwalis are mystical poems set to
the classical raga modes. It was Khusrau who
introduced many of the innovations into the
modes and established the first and truest synthesis of the Indo-Islamic music culture. He was
certainly an inspiration for the mass Hindu conversion to Islam that began in the 14th century.
Today, qawwalis still follow Khusrau's pattern
and often use his words.

Do not give money to the shrine – it reaches
other pockets; a project for the desperately needed
conservation is under way. To get there, take the
narrow lane by the police station on Mathura Road.
Purana Qila   Final cities before the big stuff of Old
Delhi (Shahjahanabad). Babur (The Tiger), a Barlas
Turk descended from both Timur-i-Leng (Tambur-
laine) and Jenghiz Khan, defeated Ibrahim Lodi at
the battle of Panipat in 1526. (Timur had made a
brief visit to Delhi in 1398, conquering the city and
then walking out the next year with a tidy ransom
of 120 elephants, sacks of gold and Delhi's renowned stonemasons.) The Delhi Sultanate ended; the Mughal empire began. Babur died four
years later, leaving a few gardens in Agra, nothing
in Delhi.

His son, Humayun, erected the first buildings of
the budding empire. Danpanah (Shelter of the
Faith) Fort was constructed on the sacred site believed to have been the Pandavas' city of Indra-
prastha (city of the God Indra), founded and fought
over by Arjuna, hero of the epic Mahabharata, and
replacing the totally mythical first city of Delhi,

Khandavipuri. (Not such a mad idea if you see the excavations on the southern slope which reveal stratified levels dating back to 1000 BC, the period of the epic; see also site museum.) The massive walls and three double-storeyed gateways survive, Indian pavilions perched on the Islamic arches.

But Humayun preferred designing carpets, writing poetry, commissioning astrological treatises and feasting to consolidating his inheritance. Thus, in 1540, the Afghan, Sher Shah Suri, was able to drive Humayun out and ran a highly efficient city for five years before his death. Having made the Purana Qila (old fort) bigger and stronger, he naturally renamed it Shergarh. Two of his gateways stand, Kuni (or Kabul) Darwaza (opposite Ferozabad) and Lal Darwaza (just outside Purana Qila).

Inside, his mosque (1541), the Qila-i-Kuhna Masjid, survives as a landmark in Indo-Islamic architecture: fine arches, elaborate decoration inside and outside, and introducing the favourite Mughal facade of black and white marble on red sandstone. Nearby is his Sher Mandal, a two-storeyed octagonal building more famous for its association with Humayun than Sher Shah.

After defeat, Humayun had wandered around India before going to Shah Tahmasp's court in Persia. He stayed for ten years, paying for his keep with, among other jewels, the Koh-i-Nur diamond. With an army supplied by Shah Tahmasp, Humayan won back Delhi in 1555. He converted the Sher Mandal into his library but a year later tripped on the steps as he answered the muezzin's call to prayer, dying from his wounds three days later. Open daily, 8am–6.30pm.

Khairu'l Manzil Masjid Built in 1561 by Akbar's formidable and influential wet-nurse, Mahem Anga. Once decorated with enamel tiles like those on buildings in early Mughal miniature paintings. Sher Shar Road, opposite the Purana Qila. Also in this area are the Zoo and the Crafts Museum.

Zoo The most important zoo in India, founded 1959, 1,500 occupants. Open-plan (water channels instead of bars), verdant, superb views of soaring Purana Qila and Humayun's tomb. Contents hit both extremes: rare white tigers of Rewa (first one bred in captivity here) and an elephant that plays the harmonica. Plus tigers, lions, bears and monkeys and flocks of autumnal migratory birds. Mathura Road. Open Sat.–Thurs., 9am–5pm; summer 8am–5pm.

Crafts Museum Vast collection of traditional crafts displayed in regional buildings of India. Old and new examples of wood, terra cotta and bra crafts plus textiles; techniques explained and d monstrated, although not always well organise Excellent thematic temporary exhibitions. P vides a good peephole into rural India. Aditi Co plex, Pragati Maidan. Open daily, 9.30ar 4.30pm; special shows on Sunday, 11am and 3p

Tombs of Humayun and Khan-i-Khanan N years after his death, the most important ea Mughal monument in Delhi was built to Humay by his senior widow, Haji Begum. Percy Bro rhapsodises over it: 'Not only one of the m arresting examples of the building art in India, an outstanding landmark in the development the Mughal style . . . The exceptionally satisfyi appearance . . . and the lucidity of its compositi have been obtained by the skilful realisation of those qualities essential in a great work of a And there is more: 'In spirit and in structu Humayun's tomb stands as an example of synthesis of two of the great building styles of A – the Persian and the Indian.'

The red sandstone and marble garden tomb the pattern for Mughal memorials that culminat in the Taj at Agra: an ornamental gateway pierci a high wall leads to a formal garden where domed memorial is set on a broad podium. It v constructed 1565–71 to designs by the Pers architect Mirak Mirza Ghiyas (probably one of spoils of Humayun's exile), who applied the spa concepts of Timurid and Safavid architecture local architectural forms and materials. He a introduced the important Mughal double do whose two skins resolve the problem of achievin lofty exterior while keeping the internal p portions in balance.

Among the other Mughal royals buried her Dara Sikoh, Shah Jahan's favourite son. A here, in 1857, the last Mughal Emperor, Baha Shah Zafar, hid and then surrendered to the B ish. Outside the gateway are nobleman Isa Kha octagonal Lodi-style tomb (1547), and a row dormitories, probably the living quarters of Persian craftsmen working on the mausoleum. heavy tomb of Khan-i-Khanan (1627), a dist guished poet and military man under Akt follows the Humayun blue-print. Although exterior facing was carried off for Safdarjan tomb, the interior still preserves its finely inci and painted plaster work. To the left of the e ance are the beautiful gardens of Sundar Nurse

Old Delhi (still known as **Shahjahanabad**, its o inal name, by some): Agra, not Delhi, benefit om the creative genius of Humayun's son, kbar. Akbar's son, Jehangir, and grandson, Shah han, further embellished it. But, after ten years of le, while the Taj Mahal was being built for his eloved wife, Shah Jahan got itchy feet and moved e capital back to Delhi. Here, between 1638 and 648 he built the splendid capital that is still the robbing heart of Delhi. The empire's top masons nd craftsmen worked on stone brought from gra, obliterating most of Ferozabad and Sherarh. And, on completion, the empire's adminisation and the gold, jewel-encrusted Peacock hrone, made for Shah Jahan and a symbol of his henomenal wealth, were ceremoniously brought the Red Fort.

Whereas in the previous cities an overdose of nagination is needed to back up accounts of the any mosques, palaces, markets and gardens, in hahjahanabad it is all here – and all alive and cking, apart from the pristine and lifeless Lal Qila Red Fort). For Shah Jahan's palace of white arble, once encrusted with silver ceilings and recious stones, is cold and desolate. As one elhi connoisseur puts it: 'They've picked out verything, but one has to go there'. And as rently as the 1940s, M. M. Kaye saw many more arkles on the walls.

It is traditional to go the Red Fort first, but far tter to start at Shah Jahan's last building, the *Jami asjid*, which is full of life. The faithful stream in d out from the surrounding bazaars and the resent Imam is directly descended from Shah han's Imam. The red sandstone mosque, with ld marble and brass inlay, is the largest mosque India, built 1644–58 to designs by Ustad Khlil. om the courtyard there is a memorable first view the Red Fort through the arcade, especially der early morning sunlight. And from the inaret the whole city plan is clear. (Women on eir own must enlist an escort before being lowed up.) The broad Chandni Chowk, the comercial nerve-centre, runs from Fatehpuri Masjid stwards to the moated and isolated Red Fort, the urt and political centre. The old city walls are tlined by the present Gokhale, Shradha Nand, saf Ali and Mahatma Gandhi roads. Delhi, rkman and Ajmeri Gates are south entrances; ashmiri Gate in the north saw some of the oodiest fighting when the British retook Delhi in 57.

For action, the best time to visit the Jami Masjid is Fridays and during Muslim festivals. Through-t *Ramadan* all Muslims over the age of twelve do not eat or drink during the day. As the Qur'an decrees, they must 'strictly observe the fast from dawn until nightfall and touch them (wines) not but be at (their) devotions in the mosque'.

In addition to praying five times a day during Ramadan, Muslims attend tarawih (congregational prayers). A pole is put high up on the mosque with a light on the end which blazes red for fasting, green for eating and drinking. When the green light shows, it is time for iftari (breakfast). There is a mad rush to carts of food lined up along the walls of the Jami Masjid – special dishes include malpuva (sweet egg pancake) and, in Delhi and Lucknow, kebabs, breads, pakoras and sweetmeats. Nights are lively, right until sehri, the pre-dawn meal. But the climax of gourmandising and celebrating is at Id, the end of Ramadan.

Lal Qila (Red Fort) entirely reflects the grand but stultifying court etiquette of Shah Jahan. His income was treble that of Akbar and Jehangir, but he managed to spend four times as much. Edward Terry (chaplain to the sixteenth-century English ambassador to India, Sir Thomas Roe) observed he was the 'greatest and richest master of precious stones that inhabits the whole earth'. From the moment he woke, the whole palace revolved around a minutely strict programme of pomp, ceremony and ritual.

Entry is through the Lahore Gate, built by Aurangzeb. Immediately beyond is the Chatta Chowk, the princes' private Burlington Arcade of court jewellers, goldsmiths and weavers, somewhat lower grade today (beware). Across the courtyard is the Naqqar Khana (Royal Drum House), the official gateway to the palace, with musicians playing above. Immediately inside is the Diwan-i-Am (public audience hall), a high colonnaded plinth for the emperor so that his subjects could see him from the large courtyard. Behind, across gardens, are the six mahals (palaces) overlooking the river. (Look out for excellent views; musicians and acrobats are often down below.)

From the right, the palaces start with Mumtaz Mahal (now a small museum, open Sat.–Thurs. 9am–5pm) and Rang Mahal (the painted palace), whose silver ceiling was put to use when the coffers ran low. The cooling Naher-i-Bahisht (Stream of Paradise) used to start here, from the marble lotus-shaped pool. It flowed through the palaces and reflected their dazzling interiors; sadly, it never flows now. Next door is Khas Mahal, the emperor's three private marble apartments for eating, sleeping and worship, still richly decorated – at sunrise he appeared before his people on the balcony.

The Diwan-i-Khas (private audience hall) was the inner and luxurious sanctum for the highest princes. The most important decisions, the best parties and the most tragic events happened here. Listening to music, the candlelight playing on the jewel-inlaid silver ceiling and silk brocades, Shah Jahan is reported as cooing: 'If on earth there be a paradise of bliss, It is this, Oh! It is this! It is this!' (inscribed in gold above the arches). Less happy events include Mohammad Shah's surrender to Nadir Shah in 1739. Nadir Shah took the Peacock Throne kept here off to Iran, together with the Koh-i-Nur diamond which had somehow got back into the Mughal treasury after its previous trip to Persia. In 1857, the British exiled Bahadur Shah to Rangoon from here.

Next come the hamams (baths) where merry hours were passed and affairs of state discussed in the stained-glass-windowed dressing room with rose-scented fountain and the hot steam room. The tiny, white marble Moti Masjid (Pearl Mosque) was built by pious Aurangzeb (1659) so that he could pray five times daily without that long trek to the Jami Masjid. Beyond was the Hayat Baksh Bagh (life-bestowing garden) which had saffron, crimson and purple blooms surrounding the Zafar Mahal, and pavilions around the edges.

All are open sunrise to sunset; avoid free-lance guides; buildings prettily lit for sound and light shows, twice daily after sunset (English and Hindi); times, which language and bookings from Fort booking office, Tourist Office or ITDC (tel: 350331). Delhi's flea market, the Kabari Bazaar, is held every Sunday on the river side of the fort.

Chandni Chowk Literally, moonlit crossroads. One of the most vibrating and interesting areas of Delhi. Shopkeepers squat in cubicle shops with green and blue painted doors and carved projecting balconies above. Between the houses, whose topmost floors almost meet, are squeezed polychrome temples where the faithful drop in throughout the day. Easy to lose hours wandering in the maze of alleys off the main thoroughfare, thronged with people, bullocks, cows and horses, air scented with fresh breads, cauldrons of thickening sweet milk, spices, perfumes and curries, tame pigeons fluttering down from old havelis (courtyard mansions), cries of shopkeepers, coolies and rickshaw wallahs, clatters and whirrs of furious industry.

The fair has gone on non-stop since 1648 whe Jahanara Begum, Shah Jahan's favourite daughte laid out the 21-metre wide street (not a crossroad at all), lined with lofty old town-houses for me chants and noblemen, with a refreshing wat channel down the middle. In 1663 Francois Berni reckoned it was the biggest commercial centre the East. At the top of the chowk, opposite the Re Fort entrance, is Digambar Jain Mandir (1656), t Jain temple whose inmates wear mouth masks ar sweep the ground before them lest they harm insect, and whose adjoining hospital is exclusive for birds – complete with Out Patients section.

Moving down, past the much reduced Pul-k Mandi (flower market) that used to spread over t whole street, you find Dariba Kalan on the le This is a lane of very old shops good for huntin down old and new silver and gold (sold by weigh from jewellers whose forefathers served t emperors; for buying Lotus and Moonlight att (perfume, see p. 73 for more) from Gulab Singh (also has a newer, wood-panelled shop on the ma chowk); and for chewing exceptional jaleb (sweets) from the shop on the corner of the ma street.

Gurudwara Sisganj (open to all), on the sam side, is dedicated to Tegh Bahadur, a Sikh gu beheaded by intolerant Aurangzeb, who also d posed his brother, Dara Sikoh, paraded hi around Chandni Chowk dressed as a beggar, mu dered him and exhibited his corpse here. Furthe on the same side, are two gruesome sites: t kotwali (police station) where nationalists we hanged and the Mughal princes exhibited after t British retook Delhi in 1857; and Sonehri Masj (1722) where Nadir Shah stood in 1739 watchin his soldiers massacre 30,000 Delhi inhabitant Ghate Wala sweetmeat shop, established in 179 is on the same side.

Then comes another treat: Paratha Wali G (Alley of Unleavened Bread), where the lofty o houses leave just enough room for two people pass, and where cross-legged cooks sit in tin restaurants and prepare fresh stuffed paratha served with yoghurt to cool the spices. Furth along the same alley are the sweetmeat shop selling the Mughal favorite, halwa, and then Kinari Galli, branching to the left, are all the pagd (bridegroom turbans), plumes and tinsel a Hind boy needs for his wedding day. At the junction, t glittering shops sell gold-threaded saris for h bride.

Back on Chandni Chowk and off again down N

Sarak (by the taxi stand), the air is sickly sweet from shops selling perfumes, incense and tobacco. Other shops specialise in hand-made paper, and Moti Lal Benarsi Das Keeps his books on indology here. Return once more to see Fatehpuri Masjid marking the end of the chowk, built in 1650 by Fatehpuri Begum, one of Shah Jahan's queens.

Civil Lines For the British, Delhi was a backwater until 1911. Calcutta and Bombay were where the action was, the power wielded, the fortunes made. Thomas Metcalfe, Agent and Commissioner 1835–53, lived in Ludlow Castle (restored after a fashion) on Mahatma Gandhi Road. He filled it with antiques and devoted an entire room to his hero, Napoleon.

His friends living around him in huge Victorian bungalows included Colonel James Skinner (c. 1778–1841), son of a Scotsman and a Rajput lady, who created Skinner's Horse regiment and later built Delhi's first church, the well-kept Greek Revival, St James's, consecrated in 1836. It stands just outside Kashmiri Gate. Inside are monuments to Colonel George Fraser, Skinner and Metcalfe. Skinner's preserved home is found nearby, through the middle gate of Sultan Singh. Not far away is the thoroughly Raj Nicholson Cemetery (recently cleaned up), where Brigadier-General Nicholson was buried after his heroic death during the retaking of Delhi in 1857.

The beautifully kept Mughal Qudsia Gardens are in this area, laid out in 1748 by Qudsia Begum, whose path from slave rags to riches led to marriage with Emperor Mohammad Shah. And, in complete contrast, up in the Cantonment lurks an escaped New Delhi building, St Martin's church (built 1928–30), designed by A. G. Shoosmith, who was Lutyens's full-time India representative 1920–31. Built of 3½ million red bricks, Gavin Stamp describes it as 'one of the most remarkable of 20th century churches: a sublime mass of brick', but Penelope Chetwode remembers it by its nickname, 'The Cubist Church'.

Jantar Mantar Giant, abstract, salmon-pink sculptures that look newer than New Delhi but were actually built back in 1724 by mad keen astrologer Maharaja Jai Singh II of Jaipur as masonry versions of brass astronomical instruments. Built when he was revising the calendar and astronomical tables for Emperor Mohammad Shah, this is the first of his five brick and plaster observatories. (See p. 87 for more). Sansad Marg, open sunrise to 10pm.

New Delhi The British contribution to Delhi's string of cities is the most successful 20th century planned city yet built. Designed by Edwin Lutyens to administer an empire, it is now government headquarters for a single country of about 700 million people who speak over 1,650 dialects. The whole city is full of trees, air and space. Politicians plan their schemes from elegant bungalows set in large gardens behind avenues lined with lemon- and flame-blossomed trees. Very grand and, for the visitor, very anonymous; the antithesis to the bustling honeycomb lanes of Old Delhi. And quite the opposite of throbbing Bombay, which Robert Byron described in 1931 as 'that architectural Sodom', reserving the word 'magnificence' to describe New Delhi.

On December 12, 1911, George V, King and Emperor, announced at the Delhi Durbar that the capital of India was to move from Calcutta back to Delhi – a Durbar where each of the 562 maharajas had an average of 9.2 elephants, 11 titles, 5.8 wives, 12.6 children, 2.8 railway carriages, 3.4 Rolls Royces, and a bag of 22.9 tigers. And, in true Delhi tradition, nothing existing was good enough. A new city was to be built from scratch. The whole project was either the blindest act of pomposity by the soon-to-dwindle British Empire or its greatest gift to future independent India. Perhaps both.

A northern site was selected and George V and Queen Mary happily laid the foundation stone. However, when the Planning Commission of Edwin Lutyens, J. A. Brodie and G. S. C. Swinton arrived from England, it rode around on an elephant in the boiling heat and chose another site. So, in the middle of one night in 1913, the foundation stone was put in a gunny bag and trundled on a bullock cart to Raisina Hill. Countless similar incidents, much argument and quantities of building later, this 'Anglo-Indian Rome' was inaugurated on February 9, 1931.

Lutyens, assisted by Herbert Baker, had designed a city to reflect the power and size of the British Empire, to accommodate 70,000 people and to have endless options for future expansion. Viceroy Lord Hardinge, who had been behind the transfer, took a keen interest in the plan; his successors Lord Chelmsford and Lord Reading watched it being realised; Lord Irwin, who became Viceroy in 1926, saw the completion and inauguration, just sixteen years before Independence. To level the land, build roads, bring water and electricity, transport stone from Dholpur, employ 30,000 unskilled labourers and sangtarashs (stone cutters) from Agra, Mirzapur and Bharatpur, and plant 10,000 trees, the bill was a cool £15 million. And that was just for putting the official buildings up. If the move from Calcutta had been a subject for hot debate, the phenomenal and ever-spiralling costs did not last long. The rest of the plan was firmly modified.

Volatile arguments included the fundamental question of architectural style: should the city be Indian, Western classical with Indian elements, straight Calcutta classical or Bombay gothic? The second style won. Lutyens did not think much of Hindu architecture – apart from Datia Palace (see below, p. 70), which he thought one of the finest buildings in India. But he admired and was influenced by the Buddhist monuments of Sanchi – as the Rastrapati Bhavan dome shows.

One gaffe that messed up Lutyens's concept had been the steep gradient of Baker's hill which effectively ruined the view from India Gate up to Lutyens's Rastrapati Bhavan (Viceroy's house), digging deeper the rift between the two architects and causing Lutyens to wail that he had met his 'Bakerloo'.

Rastrapati Bhavan, the Prime Minister's official residence, built as the Viceroy's regal home, covers the 330 acres of Raisina Hill and dominates the city. It looks down over the administrative buildings along the broad green vista of Raj Path (road of those who govern) to India Gate and, originally, beyond to Purana Qila – a view wrecked by the next Viceroy, Lord Willingdon, and his 'interfering philistine' wife who allowed a stadium to block out the Purana Qila view. A road either end of Raj Path and one in the centre (Janpath, road of the people) run north to the brick and (peeling) plaster colonnades of Connaught Place, designed to link Old and New Delhi. This area, full of shops and restaurants, has caught some of the liveliness of Old Delhi (Shahjahanabad). It is the focus for the jean-clad young Delhi crowd who follow any Western habit. The latest craze is for hamburgers.

Lutyens and other architects filled the triangle whose points are Rastrapati Bhavan, India Gate and Connaught Circus with bungalows (he called Baker's designs 'bungle oh!s'). Of the projected houses for the important independent Indian princes, only five were built. The excellent 10-acre Rastrapati Bhavan Mughal garden was the brainwave of Lady Hardinge after a trip to Srinagar. Lutyens designed it with the help of discussions over breakfast about plants with William Robertson Mustoe (ex-Kew Gardens and Punjab Horti-

cultural Department). Mustoe and W. S. George landscaped the rest of the city, Mustoe choosing and supplying the trees. He planted the big trees called rai haman, on Raj Path, and the blossoming laburnum and gulmohur.

There is a good overall view from Baker's unfortunate slope (and the rooftop restaurant of the Taj hotel). Arrange a visit to the superb Rastrapati Bhavan (every crisp detail and Lutyens's architectural witticisms a treat) and Lutyens/Baker surrounding buildings (especially Baker's Secretariat) through the Tourist Office; visit the Mughal garden, open February–March; passes obtainable from the Tourist Office.

With a handful of exceptions, other buildings are tricky to get into, often because they are government- or diplomat-occupied and sensitive to prowlers. However, see the exteriors of Lutyens' Staff Quarters, the large bungalows on Willingdon Crescent (Lutyens stayed at no.1 for his 1923–28 visits); the Imperial Record Office and War Museum along Raj Path; the War Memorial at India Gate and nearby Hyderabad House; and the 'stripped and rather brutal' Baroda House (now the Railway Booking Office, so open to the public).

Buildings by other architects worth looking at include Sansad Bhavan (by Baker, see below) Jaipur House (by C. G. Blomfield, now the National Gallery of Modern Art, see below); No. Janpath, built for one of the main contractors for the city, Sirdar Sir Sobha Singh, and St Stephen' College, which fosters some of the most successful and high-powered brains in India (both by W. S George); and Teen Murti House (now the Nehru Museum, see below).

Sansad Bhavan (Parliament House) Lutyens' idea but designed by Baker. Circular, colonnaded building with domed central hall and three semi-circular halls designed to house the Chamber of Princes, the Council of State and the Legislative Assembly. Now houses the Rajya Sabha (Upper House) and Lok Sabha (House of the People), with offices for MPs along the corridors and a very fine library (former meeting hall for the princes). Parliament sits eight months of the year. Sessions can be as heated and entertaining as at Westminster (see below, p. 61). South end of Sansad Marg; visit easily arranged through any Embassy or MP.

Nehru Memorial Museum One of the nicest museums in Delhi. One of the few New Delhi houses open to the public. Fine building, with many of the original fittings; lawns, shrubberies and rose-walks maintained by an army of gar-

eners. Built for the British Commander-in-Chief
f India. Occupied by Jawaharlal Nehru, first Prime
Minister of India, from 1948 until 1964 and now a
museum devoted to him: library, bedroom, draw-
ng room exactly as he left them. Vases of fresh
oses – Nehru wore a rose in his button-hole every
ay.

Galleries of photographs recounting his life pro-
ide an excellent introductory guide to the history
f 20th century India. There are records of the
vealthy Nehrus of Kashmir standing by one of the
rst cars to be imported into India; handsome
awaharlal having a ball at Harrow and Cambridge;
Gandhi's Salt March, etc. Celebrations here and at
ndia Gate on November 14, Nehru's birthday,
vhich is also National Children's Day. Teen Murti
House, Teen Murti Marg. Open Tues.–Sun., 10am
5pm. Sound and light show in the garden daily at
pm (English), mid-September to mid-July, tickets
nd information from the house (tel: 375333) or
Cottage Industries Emporium (tel: 311931/311506).

National Museum Devastatingly rich for a collec-
on founded only around 1950. Its nucleus is the
abulous Indian art exhibition held in London 1947
48 which drew on public and private collections
throughout India. Sir Marc Aurel Stein's magnifi-
ent collection of booty found at the close of the
9th century along the Silk Road, whose golden
ge was the 7th and 8th centuries, is divided be-
ween this museum and the British Museum:
aintings on silk and paper, textiles, stucco
gures, religious items – poorly displayed (his
aurals from Miran and Bezeklik are in the
rchaeological museum, next door). Find both of
hese collections on the first floor; also very in-
eresting are the Harappan, Mauryan, Sunga and
Gupta finds (ground floor) and the Heeramaneck
ollection of Pre-Colombian art (second floor). The
ew wing houses Sharan Rani Backliwal's extraor-
inary collection of over 300 classical, folk and
ribal musical instruments – Sharan Rani was her-
elf a great sarod player. Good publications. 11
anpath. Open Tues.–Sun., 10am–5pm.

National Gallery of Modern Art Built by
lomfield as the Maharaja of Jaipur's town house.
ike many other 'modern' galleries, a misnomer
hat increases annually. In fact, its real treasures
irst floor) are the prints and lithographs by the
rothers Thomas and William Daniell and other
9th century European artists working in India
nd, amongst Indian painters, the strong Bengali
chool exponents Abanindranath Tagore, Jamini
oy, Amrita Shergil and Nandalal Bose (the gallery

owns 6,000 of his paintings). There are also the
bizarre Europeanised portraits by Raja Ravi Varma
and examples of post-Independence movements
in Baroda, Calcutta, Bombay, Delhi and Madras.
But recent Indian art is depressing in the light of
the heights of the 16th to 19th centuries and modern Western developments – best to save your eyes
for the National Museum. Sculptures in the verdant garden. Jaipur House, India Gate. Open
Tues.–Sun. 10am–5pm.

Museum Round-up There are as many museums
as there are parks in Delhi. In addition to the three
general ones listed above, these below have collections of interest for specialists.

Air Force Museum, Palam, open Wed.–Mon.,
10am–1.30pm. *Crafts Museum*, Exhibition Ground,
Pragati Maidan, open daily, 9.30am–4.30pm. *Gandhi Memorial Museum*, Raj Ghat, open Tues.–Sun.,
9.30am–5.30pm. *Hall of the Nation Buildings* (portraits plus museum to Gandhi who was assassinated here on January 30, 1948), Birla House, Tees
January Road, open Tues.–Sun., 9.30am–5.30pm.
Both Gandhi museums attract flocks of pilgrims
daily, bearing garlands. *International Dolls Museum*,
Nehru House, Bahadur Shah Zafar Marg, open
Tues.–Sun., 10am–6pm. *National Museum of Natu-
ral History*, FICCI Building, Barakhamba Road,
open Tues.–Sun., 10am–5pm, Sat. until 7pm.
National Philatelic Museum (rich collection), Dark
Tar Bhavan, Sardar Patel Square, Sansad Marg,
open Mon.–Sat., 10.30am–12.30pm; 2.30–4.30pm.
Rail Transport Museum (new but excellent), Shanti
Path, open Tues.–Sun., 9.30am–7.30pm in winter;
8.30–11.30am and 4–7.30pm in summer. *Tibet
House* (Tibetan art), 1 Institutional Area, Lodi
Road, open Mon.–Sat., 9–5pm.

Exhibitions of contemporary art are found in the
performing arts centres grouped on Delhi's cultural campus at the south end of Barakhamba Road
(Sri Ram Centre, Triveni Kala Sangram), the Lalit
Kala Gallery, Rabindra Bhavan, Feroz Shah Road,
open daily 10am–1pm and 3–7.30pm; and Kunika
Chemould Arts Centre, Cottage Industries Emporium, Janpath, open Mon.–Sat., 9.30am–6pm.

Space and peace

In Delhi there is a luxury of green open space found
in few other capital cities. If you cannot stand the
bustle another minute, it is never far to a park or
garden. And, even more surprising for India,
peace is plentiful too. Many of the best places
surround the monuments described above. And as

53

coach tours stick rigidly to their well-worn track and schedules, even the standard sights are havens for most of the day.

Especially refreshing in the south are the zoo and the Mughal gardens of Humayun's Tomb (Sundar Nursery next door) and Safdarjang's Tomb (National Rose Garden opposite). There are quiet strolls in the back lanes of Nizamuddin. Moving west, Nehru Park and Buddha Jayanti Park are both pleasant, with good views from the second which was laid out on a ridge by the Japanese (women should not go to either alone). Go further out to Haus Khas or on to the plains around Lal Kot for assured calm, except Sunday when Delhi goes picnicking. The Mughal Qudsia Garden, to the north, is a forgotten gem.

Right in the centre, there are always people sleeping, relaxing, eating ice creams and chatting on the two kilometres of lawns beside Raj Path and India Gate, favourite meeting places for locals. Rastrapati Bhavan gardens, when open, are very beautiful but also very popular. But surpassing all these is a sunset stroll in Lodi Gardens.

Keeping fit and beautiful

With all its gardens, parks and leafy avenues, the best exercise is walking – fanatics can jog. Smart club life in Delhi is more exclusive than in Bombay or Calcutta and does not welcome foreigners with such open arms. Nor are clubs the social focus, since Delhi residents prefer the privacy of their own gardens for gossip and scheming. A visitor who wants serious exercise must select a hotel with a good pool and gýmnasium and the ability to arrange outside sports. For example, the Maurya can fix golf, riding, archery and tennis; the Oberoi is bang next door to the Golf Club and will book a game; the Maidens and Ashok have their own tennis courts. Alternatively, you can use the Delhi sports clubs which are open to everyone (see below). Long-stay visitors should apply to the club Secretaries.

Swimming pools In Delhi, pools are often emptied in December–January, so check when booking. The Maurya's is solar-heated and open all the year round. The Taj Man Singh, Oberoi and Imperial have the biggest and best pools; the Imperial's is nicely secluded from the social life of the lawn. Pools at the Maurya and Taj Palace are good but smaller; Claridges courtyard pool is so-so and very public, quite the opposite of the prettiest pool of all at the back of the Maidens garden. The

Ashok, Claridges, Imperial and Maurya open the pools to non-residents for a nominal charg (Rs10–25).

For controlled relaxation, there are several goo yoga centres, including Delhi Yoga Sabha, Bham shah Marg (tel: 222997) and Shri Vaidyana Yogashram, 172 Tagore Park, Model Town (te 715401).

Health clubs The sumptuous, marble-lined con plexes in the top hotels can indulge and beauti every part of the body with oils, creams, jacuzz and steams, by massage, pummelling, pedicur manicure and coiffeuring – top quality, top to tc titivation. The best equipped health clubs, beaut salons and gymnasiums are at the two Taj hote and the Oberoi, all with separate equipment fe men and women and instructors for gym and yog The Maurya has only one set, which is annoyir (women 8.30am–3pm; men 3–10pm). The Ashok rebuilding its clubs.

CLUB CHECKLIST
Chelmsford Club, Raisina Road (tel: 384693).
Delhi Flying and Gliding Clubs, Safdarjang Ai port (tel: 618271/611298). Temporary membersh available. Open 1–6pm. Sanjay Gandhi did h ill-fated flying here. Gliding season March–Jun September–November.
Delhi Golf Club, Dr Zakir Hussain Marg (te 699236). Temporary membership available. Clu for hire. The North India Championship is held Delhi. The amateur Golf Championship (est. 1892 the most important Golf event in the East, alte nates between Calcutta, Bombay and Delhi (19 Bombay, 1986 Delhi). There is also an 18-hc course as well as fishing and boating at Suraj Kun near Tughlaqabad.
Delhi Gymkhana Club, Safdarjang Road (T 375531). Membership mostly for government ar defence services. Very exclusive compared with i friendly Bombay brother but excellent faciliti (squash, tennis, etc.) and nice bar and restaurant crumbling period buildings.
Delhi Polo Club, President's Estate, Rastrapa Bhavan (tel: 375604). Temporary membersh available from The Secretary c/o The Presiden Body Guard. Wooded and open land, high seaso mid-December to end-January when matches a played on Jaipur Polo Grounds, inside the rac course.
Delhi Riding Club, Safdarjang Road (tel: 37189 Open to all. Information from the Club Secretar Book the previous day for early mornir

5.30–9.30am) or late afternoon (4–7pm) riding – so hot in between.

Roshanara Club, Roshanara Road (tel: 712715). Old colonial cricket club with cricket ground. Pretty enough to be a set for the film 'Gandhi'. Delhi test matches are held at Feroz Shah Cricket Ground.

Good Eats: Night lights

Delhi entertains at home in spacious bungalows and gardens where no-one eavesdrops on the political gossip. So the capital of India lacks the expected riot of restaurants and night spots – go to Bombay for that. In brief, Delhi is pretty dead socially unless you have contacts. However, the cultural scene is more lively. Here is the greatest concentration of performing arts in north India, attracting all the great Indian exponents, so this may be the moment to catch some good Kathak dancing. For lighter entertainment, there are the mega-stars, psychedelic colours and sing-along intervals of a block-buster Hindi movie followed by a good hotel nightclub.

Prohibition in Delhi reflects the government's half-hearted commitment to eventual total prohibition in India. Currently, the first and seventh day of every month and national holidays are dry but these should be confirmed with your hotel or at the Tourist Office. Liquor stores are closed and hotels serve alcohol only through room service. Otherwise, hotel bars and restaurants serve spirits and wines. Other places do not.

RESTAURANTS

There is some very good food to be had in Delhi, particularly the Mughal- (and thus Persian-) influenced north Indian food and the classic Mughlai court cuisine: meat and vegetable dishes cooked in exotic combinations of gentle spices and thick cream, equal in richness to any classic French dish. To eat a variety of freshly-cooked, layered and stuffed paratha and kulchai breads to avoid over-taxing the digestive juices.

Mughlai meat dishes include the classic biryani, meat cooked with spices and then put in a sealed pot with rice which cooks slowly in the meat juices. Then there is murg methi (chicken with fenugreek, cashewnuts, coriander, chilli, etc.) and Patharka Gosht (marinated mutton cooked on a stone). Some Mughlai vegetable dishes date back to Akbar's time, when doctors advised the 42-year-old emperor to become vegetarian, but royal chefs still had

to produce an array of tempting and succulent dishes. Try baingan mumtaz (stuffed aubergine), khatte alloo (potato) or goochi pulao (mushrooms and rice).

North India also produces kebabs of every kind, the meat tenderised in spiced yoghurt and papaya paste. Tandoor cooking is at its best in Delhi. A clay oven is used to cook marinated chicken, mutton or fish (pomfret is best) and spiced or stuffed breads.

You will find good cooking in the top hotels and in tiny restaurants that amply reward a spirit of adventure. Restaurants in between are disappointing. A deluge of bad, live Continental music tends to accompany Continental food. Be sure to reserve a table at the hotel restaurants; the city-wise Delhi socialites leave tourists queuing and hungry.

Local savoury snacks are sold from roadside stalls and in some hotels. They include chole bhatura (fermented fried bread and chick-peas) and puri bhaji (fried bread with tomatoes and potatoes). Chaat (savoury snack) stalls and restaurants are found wherever there are shops. They serve snacks such as pakoras, dosas, samosas and thirst-quenching lassi (thin yoghurt).

RESTAURANT SUGGESTIONS

North Indian *Bukhara. Maurya*; sensational North West Frontier food eaten with the fingers, seated on the most uncomfortable stools at low tables (awkward even for someone small) in Pathan-style surroundings. However, it is worth every discomfort for the magnificent Rashmi (silken) chicken kebab, Burra mutton kebab, Afghan-style lamb – and what breads! There is a glass-walled kitchen for watching chefs throw romolai (handkerchief) roti. Praised by Shashi Kapoor (and many other world-weary eaters) for 'the best north Indian food in India'.

Handi: Taj Palace; also ethnic, with very good food, 'delicious, just like it is in north Indian villages' (Kapoor again) but in comfortable Gujarat surroundings of carved wood and patola canopies. There is a buffet of a dozen north and west Indian dishes cooked in the traditional handis (brass cooking pots with a tight-fitting lid, so food cooks slowly in its own steam). Also tandoor food and a wide range of exotic, stuffed breads.

The *Frontier Restaurant* of the *Ashok* does not compare with these two but the *Tandor, Hotel President*, Asaf Ali Road, is of a consistently high standard and remains a firm favourite among journalists and diplomats who eat mostly tandoor cooked chicken to the sound of Indian musicians.

55

The following have much less swish surroundings but very good food. *Degchi*, 13 Regal Building, Connaught Place; run by the grandson of Shobha Singh, principal contractor for New Delhi. Tandoor and dishes cooked in a degchi, similar to a handi. *Kaka's Restaurant*, Plaza Building, Connaught Place; modest upstairs dining room serves good handi dishes and delicious green masala fish. *Gaylord*, 7 Regal Building, Connaught Circus; the original restaurant, started 1952, followed by Bombay 1956, now has two branches in London and one in Hong Kong (the one in New York is closed). Would-be classy mirrors and chandeliers, solid Indian (and Western) menu. *Khyber*, Kashmir Gate; excellent Peshawari dishes, often cooked in a kadhai (Indian wok). Well patronised by *The Times* (London) correspondent, Michael Hamlyn. *Maseeta*, Jami Masjid (tricky to find; ask); definitely for the adventurous. Feels as if it started when Shahjahanabad was built. Kebabs and romalai roti mouth-watering. The formerly good *Moti Mahal*, Darya Ganj, set in an old courtyard and well-patronised by tourists, has gone downhill.

Mughlai *Haveli, Taj Man Singh*; top for food and social scene, but lighting dim to obscurity and abominable live Indian classical dancing (apparently to be rectified). Try tandoor-cooked kebabs, rich murgh shabnam (chicken cooked in cashewnut and cream), korma and gosht dishes such as Achar gosht, a very Mughlai biryani (meat tenderised in herbs, spices, nuts, raisins, coconut and cream, then cooked with rice), a selection of breads and, to finish, a Mughlai sherbet (like a sorbet water-ice) flavoured with gulab (rose) or chandan (sandalwood).

Mayur, Maurya; also excellent Mughlai and Hindustan cooking, tables well spaced in fresh, Mughlai-ish decor, with live Indian music and ghazels (light songs) good enough to entice local patrons to linger longer, listen in silence and applaud. Try murg gulmar (chicken and lamb's brain, fenugreek, egg and cream), malai kofta vegetables and bhawan kulcha (a bread). They also serve the special raan-e-mirza, supposedly reserved for royalty: leg of lamb cooked very slowly in curd, cardamoms and cumin, garnished with almonds. The recipe is said to come from Bahadur Shah Zafar, the last Mughal emperor.

Karim's has two branches, both popular: Nemat Kada, Nizamuddin West, near Police Station, and in Gulli Kababian (Alley of Kebabs), behind the Jami Masjid. Some of the best Mughlai and tandoor food in Delhi for the ambitious eater. Especially good kalmi chicken kebab, burra mutton keba▌ biryani and bhakar khani (a very rich brea▌ kneaded with ghi and dried fruits); quite h▌ spices, so order some curd (yoghurt). Very mode▌ but extremely atmospheric restaurants, packed o▌ at lunch and supper, merit every effort to visit ▌ combine well with a wander in Nizamuddin (as ▌ prelude to Thursday songs) or exploring in Chan▌ ni Chowk – if Paratha Wali Gali (see p. 50) has n▌ proved irresistible. The *Moghul Room, Oberoi*, an▌ the *Peacock, Ashok* (Indian musicians), also serv▌ Mughlai cuisine, but their reputations are not ▌ high. However, *Gulnar, Janpath Hotel* is popula▌ with locals; good atmosphere from live qawwa▌ and ghazels (check performance is on). *Jawaha▌ Matia Mahal*, near Jami Masjid; like Karim's this ▌ unpretentious, full of locals.

On no menu does one find Shah Jahani pulao, ▌ truly royal biryani of spiced saffron rice steame▌ with mutton or chicken, garnished with boile▌ eggs wrapped in silver foil. But, if ordered ▌ advance, a good chef will prepare any dish.

South Indian Many, all very clean, very veget▌ rian, very good for delicate stomachs newly arrive▌ in India. Here are four good ones. *Dasaprakas▌ Ambassador Hotel*, Sujan Singh Park; described as ▌ 'cross between a film set and a church', wid▌ menu, especially delicious fresh grape-juice, butt▌ dosa and honey and fig ice-cream. The *South Indi▌ Boarding House*, opposite Shanker Market; fille▌ with south Indians who say it's the best. *Sona Ru▌ Janpath; south Indian and Bengali. *Woodlands, Lo▌ Hotel*, Lala Rajpat Lai Marg; order a thali. See p. 17▌ for more on south Indian food.

Chinese Several excellent places, all wide▌ praised, usually Chinese chefs. *House of Ming, T▌ Man Singh*; Ming vases, the smartest. *Bali H▌ Maurya Sheraton*; Chinese and Polynesian wit▌ rooftop views but European band. *Café Chinoi▌ Oberoi*; superb rooftop views (book one of the fe▌ window tables), redecoration should be complete▌ by now and band ousted. *Mandarin Room. Janpat▌ Hotel*; good decor. *Chinese Room, Nirula's*, Co▌ naught Place; oldest Chinese restaurant in Delh▌ very fresh. Try also *Tea House of the August Moo▌ Taj Palace*: recently opened Chinese dim sum te▌ house and restaurant serving Cantonese, Szech▌ wan and regional dishes in pretty Chinese garde▌

Continental Not often good. Best in India is ▌ the Taj Palace, Delhi and the Taj, Bombay, chefs ▌ both trained at Les Trois Frères, London. *Orien▌ Express, Taj Palace*: bit of a gimmick, the bar ▌ station waiting room, the tables in a railway ca▌

iage, the prices high, menu spans the London–Constantinople journey. *Williamsburg Room, Qutub Hotel*, off Sri Aurobindo Marg; more American than Continental, good steaks. *Captain's Cabin, Taj Man Singh*; basically a bar, with good fish dishes. *Takshila, Maurya*; rooftop views go with Mediterranean paté and pasta. *The Taj, Oberoi*; worldwide menu, quails, crepes 'n' all.

Lebanese *El Arab*, 13 Regal Buildings, Connaught Place; enjoyed by the young. Full menu from hummus to dolmas.

Lunch specials Around Connaught Place, head straight for the *Imperial* and have chicken tikka, nan (soft bread) and a nimbu soda on the expansive lawn sheltered from the bustle, with the band playing gently. (Their garden room is pretty for breakfast, too, but the dining room is dowdy.) In Old Delhi (Shahjahanabad), go to one of the suggested modest Indian restaurants, or Paratha Wali Gali, a lane in Chandni Chowk, for a memorable paratha or the lanes behind Jami Masjid for an excellent kebab. Back at the hotel, either have a barbecue around the pool (huge prawns, lobster, tandoor chicken) or taste an array of dishes at the lunchtime buffet served in most hotels.

Sweetmeat shops Mughlai sweets are very, very sweet and equally sticky and heavy. Bengali sweets, the aristocrats of sweetmeats, made of milk and cheese, are easier to handle (see p. 156 for more). Best shops are *Nathu's*, Bengali Market; *Malik*, Connaught Place; and *Bengali Sweet House*, Gole Market, Connaught Place.

Tea Delhi lacks the colonial and club tradition necessary for good teas. Those who know go to *Claridges* courtyard or the lawns of the *Imperial*.

Cocktails With few high-rise buildings, sunset-over-city cocktails are restricted to the *Oberoi Skylark Bar* (soon to have big terraces). Sadly, the top of the Taj is devoted to a mediocre Italian restaurant. Next best is the *Imperial*, non-alcoholic cocktails on the lawn, boozy ones in the Garden Restaurant/Bar. The *Maurya* has a nice ground floor bar. The beauty of Lodi Gardens compensates for the non-alcoholic cocktails at the outdoor café there, the *Aashiana* (also serves food, 10am–10pm).

Drink Chaas is special to Delhi and very refreshing. It is thin lassi (yoghurt) flavoured with ginger, coriander, green chillies and roasted cumin powder.

24-hour coffee shops The Oberoi, Maurya, Ashok and both Taj hotels have splendid round-the-clock cafes. These are excellent meeting places, good for a cup of tea, a quick bite or a full-blown meal at any time. They usually serve European and Indian food; most are cheerful and overlook the hotel pool or garden; they are frequently quicker than room service or restaurants.

NIGHT LIFE

Discotheques Without question the best is *Ghungroo* in the *Maurya*: well designed, good lighting and music, and excellent atmosphere – more like a private party than a public disco – hardly surprising since membership is so exclusive that most people know one another. *Taj Man Singh's Number One* is considered smarter and more exclusive but tends to resemble a morgue except on Friday and Saturday. The *Sensation* at the *Maidens* (amusingly dated decor) is popular with students. All are open to residents for a nominal charge, to other visitors by arrangement – membership fee tends to be hefty.

CULTURE

Delhi and Bombay are the places to catch good classical dance, drama and music and regional folk dance. See Information section p. 44 for how to find out what is going on where. Performances usually start 6–6.30pm. Central ticket office at Cottage Industries Emporium, Janpath.

Venues The cultural campus is at the south end of Barakhamba Road. Here are the Sri Ram Centre for Art and Culture (theatre, art gallery, cafe, art book shop and Sutra Dar Puppet Theatre, shows Saturday evening and Sunday morning); the trendy Triveni Kala Sangram (three art galleries, theatre for plays and dance, café-theatre); FICCI Auditorium (major concerts); Sapru House (theatre); Kathak Kendra (dance); Rabindra Bhavan (National School of Drama theatres, Lalit Kala and Yavanika Sangeet Natak galleries); Kamani Theatre (plays, dance, music); Bhartiya Kala Kendra (theatre, cafe).

Not far away are Gandharva Mahavidyalay (music and dance) and Max Muller Bhavan, Janpath. Elsewhere there are the India International Centre, by Lodi Tombs, on Lodi Estate Road No.2, some ticketed shows (i.e. open to the public) very good for catching opening performances in all arts; Gopal Sherman's Akshara Theatre, 11 Baba Kharak Singh Marg (two auditoria) the only theatre with an all-year resident company; and the Fine Arts and Crafts Society, Rafi Marg (amateur theatre, galleries, British Council Library on top floor).

The Exhibition Grounds are also worth checking out. They produce a monthly list of events and several free shows (two cinemas, performance venues). Peak season November. Entrance to grounds Rs1.

Rabindra Bhavan In the mid-1950s, the government set up various academies to encourage the somewhat imperilled Indian arts. They included the Lalit Kala Akademi (1954), to encourage contemporary visual art and the study of art history – its two journals concentrate on these two aspects; Sangeet Natak Akademi (1953), to survey and stimulate performing art forms throughout India (auditoria plus galleries of musical instruments, puppets, masks); and Sahitya Akademi (1954), to encourage literature in Indian languages. The National School of Drama, established at the same time, is affiliated to the Sangeet Natak Akademi. All these came under the umbrella of Rabindra Bhavan when the government initiated a string of art centres througout India in the centenary year of Rabindranath Tagore's birth, 1961.

Dance venues There are regular 'Dances of India' programmes (classical, tribal, folk) at Taj Man Singh and Taj Palace hotels, cheap and with explanatory commentary, but of mediocre quality. Similar show daily at Parsee Anjuman Hall, Bahadur Shah Zafar Marg, 7pm. For Kathak, see below. A lighter form of Kathak, the ras lila, recounts the Krishna legend in song, dance, mime and words. It is performed at the Natya Ballet Centre but is best seen in temple courtyards around Mathura at Janmashtami (Krishna's birthday) (see p. 68).

Theatre Before Independence Delhi was a cultural backwater, staging only amateur adaptations of Broadway and London West End productions. Bombay and Calcutta led the way (see pp. 156 and 123). After Independence Sapru House (inaugurated by Nehru in 1955) and Rabindra Bhavan became the main cultural hiring halls, stimulated by the lively Bengalis. When the dynamic Ebrahim Alkazi came up from Bombay to run the National School of Drama, things changed. He injected a sense of professionalism and had many plays translated into Hindi, even if 90% were still adaptations. But official language Hindi theatre acquired the reputation of being sarkari (government) theatre and the NSD has had a chequered reputation since Alkazi.

Look out for Bengali and Punjabi plays at Sapru House. Dramatists to catch: Vijay Tendulkar (Mahrathi, see p. 124), Badal Sircar (Bengali) and Mohan Rakesh (Hindi). Gopal Sherman is attempting to achieve something else. His Akshara Company was formed in 1966 and opened its theatre in

1971, helped by gifts of lighting from Yehudi Menuhin, J. B. Priestley, John Schlesinger and others. Productions range from contemporary plays, musicals and political satires to classical texts such as the Sanskrit Upanishads. There are no adaptations from other cultures but, as with other new theatre movements, Sherman draws on India's rich classical and folk heritage. Plays have included an English interpretation of the epic Ramayana, commissioned by the Royal Shakespeare Company and taken on tour around India as well as to New York and London.

Kathak dance Kathakaras, story-tellers attached to temples in the Braj region in Uttar Pradesh (east of Delhi), were probably behind the emergence of a northern classical dance form. Their devotional recitations used mime and music. The dance that evolved at the Mughal court lays equal emphasis on mime and dance, although now radically refined and secularised. The solo dancer, a man or woman, usually recounts an episode from Krishna's life with a feat of mime, supple twirling and dazzlingly speedy footwork (layakari) whose frenetic rhythms compete with the percussion music. The two main schools are: Bhatkhande Sangeet Vidyapath, Lucknow, and the Jaipur Gharana. It is the Lucknow-school style that is practised in Delhi, at Kathak Kendra (whose dancers also perform at the Kamani Theatre).

In particular, look out for performances by Birju Maharaj, a spell-binding male dancer whose Lucknow family have practised Kathak for centuries who directed both dance sequences in Satyajit Ray's film 'The Chess Players'. Saswati Sen, a woman and one of the foremost of his many disciples, did the actual dancing. Other dancers to notice are Sitara Devi, Damayanti Joshi, Roshan Kumari and Uma Sherma.

What to buy where

Delhi and Bombay have the best shopping for goods from all over India. But while the Delhi cognoscenti are prepared to give Bombay precedence for restaurants, they claim supremacy for shopping, substantiated by Calcuttans and Bombayites who come to Delhi for their shopping sprees. Mala Singh, editor of the Delhi-based *India Magazine*, only goes to Bombay for restaurants and to buy books, dismissing all else there as 'tatty mock-western junk'. Indeed, Delhi has thousands of good shops, often tidily grouped together by subject – antiques, crafts emporia, European shions, etc. Spending is so easy it is almost mpossible to avoid.

The biggest centre is Connaught Place, where ue fixed price government emporia jostle with memists, bookshops and the Shankar Market, ue Palika Bazaar (underground, 300 shops), anchuian Road Market (lamps, brass, wood) and ue Super Bazaar. Chandni Chowk is much more un, but needs hard bargaining. Sundar Nagar (see elow) has good art and antique shops.

Then there are hundreds of markets, a shopping entre for each residential area and the big hotel mopping arcades. Taj Man Singh's Khazana reasury) has a single buyer rather than being let ut to various shopkeepers and is considered by iscerning locals the best shop in town, even for ntiques. Taj Palace's The Collection, on the same rinciple, is less good. Maurya has excellent rcades, and those at Oberoi and Imperial are ood. Look out also for the permanent trade fair at ue Exhibition Grounds: since crafts are a serious idustry, there are often state craft pavilions idvertised in the daily papers).

Shops tend to be open Mon.–Sat., 9am–7pm, osed 1.30–2.30pm for lunch. Markets are more ften areas of firmly established shops rather than d hoc stalls put up on the street once a week. Veekly markets include Chow Bazaar, behind Red ort (Sun.) and the bazaar by Hanuman Temple, aba Kharak Singh Marg (Tues.). As elsewhere in idia, fixed prices are only truly fixed in govern-nent-run shops – and these do not include 'gov-rnment approved' shops. Almost nothing opens n Sunday.

The following are just a tiny selection of what is n offer. See also Chandni Chowk above, p. 50.

rafts in general To get some idea of the range, op into the Crafts Museum (see p. 48) which has xamples of old and new crafts in various media rom all over India. Then see what is on offer in the overnment-run emporia around Connaught lace. After that, equipped with a fair idea of what hould be what in quality and price, the city is ours for tracking down the best. Central Cottage idustries Emporium, Janpath is a craft depart-nent store par excellence. The quality and range is ood enough to furnish a complete home, from ny brass trays to furniture. Highly knowledge-ble and helpful assistants run a section for each tate, bursting with fair-priced crafts and fabrics often better than the individual state emporia). Goods can be made to order and then shipped (e.g. urtains made up for an amazing Rs12 per length

including lining). Gift-wrapping, packing and shipping are quickly arranged. There is a book-shop, restaurant, booking counter for theatre/dance and an office of the Archaeological Survey of India upstairs for maps. See shopping sections of other chapters for suggestions of what to find it each department.

The row of state emporia is on Baba Kharak Singh Marg, two roads round Connaught Place from Cottage Industries, going clockwise. Quality varies. Almost everything from Gujarat is superb; the manageress, Jaya Jaitly, is dedicated to main-taining quality of crafts. Glorious carved and lacquered swing seats (Rs5,900) and children's cradles (Rs2,000–3,000) dismantle for shipping. Bihar (silk), Andra Pradesh (bidri ware), Orissa (crafts and fabrics) and Tamil Nadu also have good buyers; Rajasthan, with its rich traditions, could outdo Gujarat but does not. Opposite the complex is Hanuman Temple where there are special pujas (worshipping) on Tuesday afternoons and a bazaar (toys, bangles). Almost next door, Man Singh's makes the best lassi in town. Round in Bara-khamba Road is the Central Cottage Export House at G6, New Delhi House, a general emporium plus gallery.

Fabrics For the broadest selection, it is back to the large emporia. Handloom House, 9–A Connaught Place, is disappointing. Cottage Industries is well stocked. The first floor is an Aladdin's cave de-voted to fabrics of every kind from every region, from block-printed cotton to fine silk wedding saris; cotton, silk and wool by the metre; braiding up to 15cm wide embroidered with dancing elephants; and the special Orissa double ikat, Gujarat patola, Murshidabad shot and Varanasi brocades. There is silk of every quality including shot, in a rainbow of colours (about Rs90 per metre; dry clean only), also plain fine wool by the metre and every sort of sari.

Downstairs, Kashmiri crewel-work furnishing fabric (Rs80–120 per metre). Go to Bihar Emporium for fine raw silk; to Benares Silk, Connaught Place, for brocades.

Khadi Gramodyog Bhawan, 24 Regal Building, Connaught Place, is heavily subsidised by the gov-ernment to promote rural industry, so prices are low. Khadi is cloth that is spun, dyed, woven and printed by hand as opposed to handloom cloth which is mill-spun, then hand-woven. Good khadi buys include Kashmiri tweeds made from merino sheepswool (Rs70–75 per metre), or mixed with Rajasthan wool (Rs45–50 per metre). There is no tailoring service, but assistants know how much would be needed, such as 7 metres for a 6-foot tall man with a 44-inch chest (a typical Indian mixture of measuring systems).

There are also brightly coloured, checked car rugs from Harayana (Rs62–225 depending on wool quality), and cosy old-fashioned dressing gowns of striped or checked wool (Rs200–400). Punjab and Himachal Pradesh emporia also stock good tweed; that from Kashmir emporium is over-priced.

Lavish, sparkly Hindu wedding saris, silks and tinsels come from Kinari Galli, an alley off Chandni Chowk (see p. 50). FabIndia, N-Block, Greater Kailash, has some of the highest quality and most imaginative weaves. Worth the detour. It also stocks ready-made clothes, takes orders and ships reliably.

Linen White cotton sheets and towels are a quarter of their London price, although not the finest of fine. Pandit Bros., Connaught Place, has good stock. Bombay Dying is a quality brand name. Smart Bombayites buy their European design, hand-printed table and bed linen with matching lampshades, towels and bedspreads at Xquisite in South Extension Market (closed on Mondays). For the best traditional table linens, go to FabIndia (see above).

Books Moti Lal Benarsi Das, Nai Sarak, off Chandni Chowk, for indology old and new. Both Oxford Book and Stationery Co, Scindia House, Connaught Circus and The Bookshop, Khan Market, for a wide choice of new books; the second often has export editions of paperbacks printed in England before the English publication date. Shops and pavements around Regal Building on Connaught Circus south side are piled with old and new volumes, especially novels. Urdu Bazaar, behind Jami Masjid, for Urdu books, journals and manuscripts, old and new. Also behind Jami Masjid are the fireworks shops, stocking huge Catherine wheels and enormous rockets which fire into clouds of twinkling stars and then parachute plastic images of Hindu gods down to earth. For contemporary arts, the Sri Ram Centre is good (see p. 57). The best second-hand bookshop is Prabhu Service at Gurgaon village, a few kilometres beyond the airport, owned by Vijay Kumar Jain – a book collector's dream.

Art, jewellery and antiques If in doubt or if big money is involved, have art objects authenticated at the National Museum or the Archaeological Survey of India, on Janpath; jewels and stones at the Government Gem Laboratory in Barakhamba

Road (open 10am–3pm). Objects over 100 years old cannot be exported (see Survival Guide, p. 32). The best group of antique shops fills the square of Sundar Nagar, beside the Zoo – wood, paintings, jewellery, bronzes and especially brass from near by Moradabad. Bharany's, La Boutique (high quality goods, but barter a bit) and Kumar Gallery (also branches in the Ashok and Maurya hotels) are all good. All will supply a certificate for objects less than 100 years old. Chawri bazaar, leading west from Jami Masjid, and alleys off it operate more in the Portobello Road tradition of rummaging among old and new, good and bad. Ask for Ivory Mart, an 18th century shop with showroom basement and craftsmen working upstairs. Good Tibetan jewellery and curios are found at stalls outside the Imperial hotel.

Western clothes Ever-entrepreneurial, Indians do not waste any time. Either side of Central Cottage Industries Emporium, the shops of Janpath Market have the latest European styles, either export rejects (so inspect for faults) or identikit copies of exports. (The clothes that are exported go to smart stores such as Harrods or Bloomingdales. The shops are in big competition with each other, so barter hard for simple summer dresses, pretty shirts and grander stuff. Jain Bros at shop number 70M have very jazzy high evening fashion with acres of sequins and beadwork.

Lots more in the hotel shopping arcades, at higher prices and sometimes higher standards. Upstairs in Cottage Industries Emporium are very pucka tweed jackets (Rs370) being bought by classy Indians off to the hills, and glorious kids clothes made of dazzling plain silk (skirt and top Rs 170–300).

Tailors Find the fastest and most clued up for European styles in the hotel shopping arcades – if the plane leaves, they lose. For instance, the Maharani of India in the Maurya has a 24-hour turn-around: choose the pattern (Vogue and Simplicity books), modify it if necessary, choose the fabric or buy it elsewhere, and the garment is made up for a very small charge. Men's clothes are even faster. In one day, for around Rs55 plus material, a shirt can be copied from ready-made stock (with stylistic or fabric amendments) or copied from one of the client's own shirts. Jackets, trousers and safari suits cost more.

Leather The latest designs are copied and made up in Madras, centre of the leather trade, Kashmir (jackets) or Agra (shoes). At Khan Market in Delhi (also good for books) find the latest Italian shoes at a fraction of their Milan prices, and have shoes made to order. There is more variety (and higher prices) in the superb leather shops at the Maurya, Taj and Cottage Industries Emporium and at Bharat Leather Shop, opposite Nirula's, Connaught Circus. Smooth smart briefcases in cobra skin or analine (a small goat) leather are priced according to their lock; Indian ones are cheap, German and Swiss best and most expensive (Rs500–1000). There are handbags (Rs100–450), hold-all bags (Rs200–600), belts (Rs100), shoes (very soft men's pair Rs300–350; women's sandals Rs100–200), wallets (Rs50–100). At Cottage Industries, the Kashmir sheepskin leather shop uses north Kashmiri artisans living in Delhi to make the latest off-the-peg European designs in leather and suede, special styles made up in four days (jacket Rs575; full-length coat Rs850, sales tax of 15% exempt if goods shipped). See p. 229 for furs, which are excellent buys.

Rugs and carpets Daunting for the uninitiated, but tempting as prices are considerably less than in Europe or America. However, at Central Cottage Industries no customer should be taken for a ride. Carpets range from all-wool to all-silk and come in every size and pattern. To help, each one should have a descriptive label on the back providing a list of information. One such reads: item (where made): Kashmir; size (in feet): 6 × 4; (knots per square inch): 18 × 18 (=324); contents: 10% silk, 70% wool, 20% cotton (called silk touch); design (each traditional pattern has a name): Kirman; price: 5,500. And assistants will help further.

Dhurries, (the Hindi name for flat-weave floor covering). Mostly made at Agra, Mirzapur (near Varanasi) and in Rajasthan. Come in all sizes, with current European pastel colours and designs as found at Habitat and Conran (e.g. Rs1,300–1,800 for 6 × 4 foot rug plus Rs250 shipping). Prices are the same for cotton and wool since a cotton dhurrie takes more work. The more light-weight rugs, known as shuffles, are very cheap, all colours, often striped – from Andra Pradesh for loose weave but smooth finish, from Rajasthan for tight weave but rougher finish. All may run disastrously if not dry-cleaned. Khadi house has jolly, striped Gujarat shuffles, mini-dhurries with narrow stripes of turquoise, red, yellow and black from Punjab, and jazzy dhurries with a bobbled texture from Uttar Pradesh – all very cheap. See also p. 66.

Tea Indian tea gardens grow some of the best leaves of all. Good fresh teas are sold at Aap ki Pasand Tea Taster's Centre, 15 Netaji Subhash Marg.

Pottery Delhi blue-glazed pottery, mostly made at nearby Kurja, can be found at the Central Cottage Industries. (See also p. 62.)

See how it's done: Politics and Crafts

Parliament The major industry of Delhi is politics. To see the machinery of Indian government at work, always lively and generally good value entertainment, sit in on a session at Sansad Bhavan, arranged through an Embassy, High Commission or an MP. Debates and cross-banter are in English and the Indian Constitution is loosely based on the Westminster model. India has a President, who is Head of State, and a Prime Minister, who is Head of Government. The two houses of Parliament are Lok Sabha (House of the People, Lower Chamber) and Rajya Sabha (Council of States, Upper Chamber). Lok Sabha, composed of 525 elected members from the States, 17 Union Territories members and 2 Anglo-Indian representatives, sits eight months in the year and elects its own Speaker. The ruling party draws its Prime Minister and Cabinet from this house. Like the American Senate, membership of Rajya Sabha is not for life, as with the House of Lords, but by election (except for a dozen appointments by the President). A third of the 244 members retire every two years. It lacks a Speaker but has the Vice-President as Chairman. Parliament legislates, approves all government spending, amends the Constitution, elects the President and Vice-President (and can oust them) and must approve a Proclamation of Emergency.

Ivory carving The skilled craftsmen can be seen working at Ivory Mart in Chawri Bazaar behind Jami Masjid; their finished work is for sale downstairs.

Water-pots The pretty, unglazed earthenware khumba matkas (water-pots) piled high around New Delhi Station are made locally. According to Hindu legend, the first pot was made to store amrit (the water of immortality) thrown up while Vishnu was cleaning out the oceans. Thus the khumbas, the name also given to the potting community, were held in high esteem. But, as plastic and tin are the last word in India today, few khumbas survive. However, there is a thriving workshop opposite the station, tucked behind the main road. Here, smoking hookahs and dressed in dhotis, khumbas throw the matkas (basic pots). After drying in the

61

sun, the women dip them in red slip, fire them in the communal kiln, then sell them across the road. Quality depends upon no cracks, proved by a deep resonant bong when tapped.

Glazed pottery It was probably the Pathan potters from Afghanistan who introduced their glazing techniques to the Muslim court. Kurja, an old town about 80km from Delhi, is still full of Muslim potters living in the tiny alleys of the old town. They use the inky Persian blue known as Jaipur blue (it is used there too), as background for floral designs on Muslim shapes. They also make tiles, use mould casts and do pottery cut-work. It is well worth the journey for pottery enthusiasts. For contemporary ceramics, stay in Delhi. Gouri Khosla, who did the huge peacock mural at Palam Airport, and Nirmala Patwardhan, who has worked with Bernard Leach, both pot at Lalit Kala Akademi studios which are built in a large medieval fortress at Garhi, East of Kailash in south Delhi. Two other lively potteries are Purush Potteries, 4 Vail Lane and Delhi Blue Art Pottery, 1 Factory Road.

Awaydays

Fortunately, Delhi is a pleasant, open city and the need to escape should not prove too acute. Although it is feasible to go to Agra or Lucknow for the day – even Khajuraho for a four-hour flip around the temples – all three deserve far longer. For instance, the Taj works a different magic by moonlight, dawn light and every other light and each phase should not be missed. Nearer Delhi, the most enjoyable days are passed ambling around the early cities on the plains, mentioned above. And there really is nothing much in between these two extremes. When it gets hot and you have to be in Delhi – the temperature hits 47 degrees in early June – do as one jet-set English businessman does: holds meetings and receives clients sitting in the hotel pool, with a nimbu soda in his hand.

TIME CAPSULE TAJ TRIPS
Round trip 394km. However short a visit to Delhi, it is incomplete without setting eyes on the Taj. For those high flyers who cannot spare a few days in Agra, there are several solutions, all bookable through the travel agents recommended above. (Do try to avoid full moon, when coach-loads of would-be romantics make the Taj garden look like a rally in Hyde Park.)

BY CAR Rent a car and driver to go by road, enjoying yet more early monuments strung along the very direct route (3hrs either way, faster at dawn). If there is no release from daytime Delhi, drive down at sunset, see the Taj by moonlight, stay at the Mughal Sheraton and eat a delicious dinner of Mughlai food, possibly return to the Taj after dinner and once more at purple dawn before sleeping on the drive back.

BY TRAIN The Taj Express leaves New Delhi station at 7.05am. There are much the same monuments to see along the way. After scrambled eggs for breakfast and a short snooze, be sure to sign up with the Agra guide who does his rounds during the journey. His tour is cheap and good. (By coach to Fatehpur Sikri for the morning, Fort and Taj for the afternoon.) If the trip does not appeal, rent a car or use bicycle rickshaws to spend the day alternating between the Taj, the Fort, more Taj, taking sustenance from the rooftop restaurant of Clarks hotel (brilliant views), yet more Taj, then the evening train back at 6.55pm (3hrs 10 mins each way).

BY AIR This is the most expensive method and, if delayed, no faster. Planes take off at 7.30am and 12.30pm (allowing time to squeeze in a Delhi morning meeting). On arrival, rent a car and driver through extremely charming tourist desk at airport; return by the 4.10pm or the 6.55pm (35min flight each way, plus check-in 40mins in advance).

Note: The Taj is open from dawn until 10pm except on full moon nights and four nights either side when it remains open until midnight.

Forays further afield

Delhi is a good springboard for leaping off in every direction. Agra, to the south, is not only a magnet drawing thousands to the Taj but a good base for surrounding Mughal, Hindu and nature sights. For total escape, Khajuraho's temples are isolated on a peaceful, rural plain. To the east, Lucknow preserves its Muslim grandeur, bazaars and atmosphere. All three have good hotels and make perfect breaks. Further south lies Central India whose treasures more than compensate for simpler accommodation (see p. 132).

Leaping up north into the cool Himalayas there is every sort of sport, from drifting on lotus lakes to scaling mountains and spotting Bengal tigers (see

). 221). And, in the west, the collection of princely states that make up Rajasthan are a succession of palace-filled desert cities, each more beautiful than he last (see p. 77). Shekhavati, an area of villages and deserted forts crammed with painted houses, ies just inside Rajasthan, 150km west of Delhi (see). 90).

There are some very good flight deals. For instance, Delhi–Agra Khajuraho–Varanasi–Kathmandu costs round about the same as Delhi–Kathmandu. A good travel agent will seek out the best deals.

Agra, Uttar Pradesh

The complement to Delhi. Agra fills the gaps in Delhi's Muslim history that begin with Sultan Sikandar Lodi taking a fancy to Agra in 1502 and end with Shah Jahan's preparations to return in 1648. Indeed, the principal monuments – the Taj, Fort and Fatehpur Sikri – were built when the Mughal Empire reached its peak in wealth, power and enlightenment, and Agra was the capital and focus of attention. The rulers fulfilled its Mahabharata name, Agrabana – paradise. Akbar (ruled 1556–1605) built extensively, Jehangir (ruled 1605–27) continued, and Shah Jahan (ruled 1627 -58) lifted court lavishness to new heights before moving it lock, stock and barrels of jewels when he spanking new city of Delhi was ready in 1648. Agra today is a bustling town as thoroughly geared to tourism as Jaipur. The legacy of the British Cantonment dominates its spacious character.

And there are not only Mughal monuments. Lying at the meeting point of three states, Madhya Pradesh, Rajasthan and Uttar Pradesh (which it is just inside), other nearby sights include Bharatpur bird sanctuary, Deeg Hindu palace, Mathura and Gwalior Fort. Datia and Orchha, just beyond Gwalior, are even more stunning. Agra is by no means a one-night stop.

THE HARD FACTS   197km from Delhi. Season mid-September to mid-March (beautiful gardens blossom January–March), then it gets very hot until the deluge starts at the end of June. There is colourful and serious kite-flying every Sunday, with local betting. From Delhi, go by car, train or plane (see p. 62 Time capsule Taj trips). There are also daily direct flights from Khajuraho, Varanasi and Lucknow. Connect with Jaipur direct by train or via Delhi by plane; this is decoit country and it is unwise to go by road.

Choose between two unusually good hotels, bursting with facilities: both have travel counters, car rental, pool, garden and can arrange golf (Agra has three golf courses) and tennis. Lots of other hotels, all pretty ghastly, so book early. The old British favourite, Laurie's, is in total decay.

Mughal Sheraton, Tajganj (tel: 64701; telex: 0565–210; cable: POWHATTAN AGRA). One of the best designed, furnished and maintained modern hotels in India. Magnificent showpiece of the Welcomgroup of hotels, opened in 1976, designed by Ramesh Khosla in the Mughal tradition, using brick and marble for low-lying buildings around garden courtyards with Mughal water channels. It is all set in huge, secluded, mature gardens immaculately maintained by an army of gardeners who stock both it and parts of the kitchen larders from the on-site nursery. A winner of the Aga Khan Award for architecture in 1980. 200 rooms plus Raja Man Singh and Tansen suites (one with swing seat). Extensive facilities with health club, beauty salon, baby sitting, croquet, mini-golf, archery, elephant on call for rides and, weather permitting, afternoon gliding over the Taj. In keeping with Agra, there is top quality Mughlai food accompanied by Indian musicians in the Nauratna restaurant. Also a tri-cuisine restaurant.

Clarks Shiraz, 54 Taj Road (tel: 72421; telex: 0565–211; cable: SHIRAZ). By comparison, an unexciting pink building on two sides of a large but flat and rather public-feeling garden (comes second after the Mughal in the annual Agra garden competition). 145 rooms, dreary decor, good facilities (see above) plus pool-side kebabs, badminton, croquet, huge shopping arcade and, most of all, stunning views over Agra from 4th-floor rooms and rooftop restaurant (tri-cuisine, live Western band with dinner) and cocktail bar (outdoor terrace).

Tourist information is tricky since each state is autonomous and denies the existence of other states. For Agra and Mathura, go to Uttar Pradesh Tourist Office, 64 Taj Road, charming but vague. For Bharatpur and Deeg, go to Rajasthan Emporium in Taj Precinct; for Gwalior, in Madhya Pradesh, go to Usha Kirin Hotel. ITDC, 191 The Mall (tel: 72377), has a broader view on life and rents out guides. But it is best to get equipped in Delhi. TCI travel agency is at Clarks hotel (tel: 64111). There is a large selection of books on the monuments in both hotels, plus Modern Book Depot, Sadar Bazaar. UP State Road Transport Corporation runs the good tour to Fatehpur Sikri,

Fort and Taj, leaving Agra Railway Station daily at 10.30am. Excellent guides allow sufficient time at each place. Bookable at 96 Gwalior Road (tel: 72206), Platform no.1 at the station, or on the Taj Express. Move around Agra by bicycle rickshaw. Currently, there is no prohibition in UP or MP.

OUT AND ABOUT   **The Fort:** For a sensational first view of the Taj, across the bend of the Yamuna River, start here. The fort is also associated with all three emperors who erected Agra's important buildings. Ramble all over this *Boy's Own*, unkempt fort city with high walls and wide moat; on to roofs, up and down stairs, in and out of palace rooms – all of it in dire need of conservation.

Its Mughal history began the day of the battle of Panipat in 1526, when Babur immediately sent his son Humayun off to guard the Lodi treasury at Agra. There Humayun found the Maharaja of Gwalior's family, who placated him with a golf-ball-sized diamond, now believed to have been the Koh-i-Nur (mountain of light) which Humayun later gave to Shah Tahmasp of Persia. Two years later Babur held a grand feast where guests heaped piles of gold and silver on to a carpet laid before him. Mughal splendour in Agra had begun. And when Akbar, aged 14 but virtually illiterate, succeeded Humayun (who did little to improve Agra) the real building and embellishment began.

Akbar's rule was marked by religious tolerance for which he set the example. By marrying a Rajput princess from Amber (now the ever so grand Jaipurs) in 1562, he began to turn the warrior Rajputs into allies, killing two birds with one stone. To curry favour, the Rajas of Bikaner and Jaisalmer, and rulers as far off as Tibet, presented pretty relations to Akbar's harem. He eventually had 300 wives living in a harem of about 5,000 women.

Luckily, Akbar enjoyed building. By 1565 he had pulled down the Lodi brick fort and five years later his new fort of dressed red sandstone was built. His rooms remain, the spacious Jahangiri Mahal, overlooking the Yamuna where he would watch elephant fights on the shore. While it was being built, he lived in a pleasure city 10 kilometres to the south where, among other games, he played polo at night using a ball of wood embers. Then, just as the fort was finished, Akbar began his new capital, Fatehpur Sikri.

Next, it was the turn of Jehangir (literally Seizer of the World, although he was in reality politically unambitious). Edwin Binney III, who has formed one of the finest contemporary collections of Indian miniature paintings, describes him as: 'The greatest of art patrons of this highly distinguished family'. His eye was trained in the royal atelier at Fatehpur Sikri. He encouraged greater realism single-artist paintings rather than shared works, and the signing and dating of pictures. He employed the brilliant artists Bichitr, Abu'l Hassan, Mansur and many others. However, he was happy to adopt for himself the symbolic nimbus found on saints in European paintings which were highly fashionable at the Mughal court since the Jesuits gave some to Akbar. When Sir Thomas Roe, England's first ambassador to India, visited Jehangir the only diplomatic gifts to truly impress the emperor were English paintings, especially portrait miniatures. These inspired the many miniature portraits of Jehangir at a window – in some he even holds an icon of the Virgin.

Jehangir lived in the fort, bound by the rigid daily royal programme maintained from Akbar to Shah Jahan and described by Roe as: 'Regular as a clock that stricks at sett howers'. His contribution to Agra's buildings was his father's tomb at Sikandra and, indirectly, his marriage. For his wife he laid out Shalimar Bagh, the finest Mughal garden at Srinagar in Kashmir.

This love-marriage to the clever daughter of a self-made courtier had a bearing on the two near-perfect Mughal tombs in Agra. The woman was a Persian widow, Mihr-an-Nisa, later known as Nur Jahan (Light of the World). She strengthened the power of her father, chief minister Itimad-ud-Daulah (Pillar of the Government); and married her niece, Mumtaz, to the next emperor, Shah Jahan. Itimad-ud-Daulah's equally influential son and grandson were the next two chief ministers. Nur Jahan added to her family's strength by discovering how to preserve attar (perfume) from roses, much to the delight of Jehangir. (For more on attar, see p. 73.)

Shah Jahan (Ruler of the World) spent like mad and built like mad in Lahore, Delhi and Agra. Here, in the fort at Agra, he added a rich cluster of pietra dura marble palace rooms along the river front (1628–37) and the exquisite Moti Masjid (Pearl Mosque), begun in 1646, just two years before his new city at Delhi was ready. There is a Diwan-i-Am (public audience hall), Diwan-i-Khas (private audience hall), the emperor's private Khas Mahal with vineyard in front, the Shish Mahal (Mirror Palace) and the Musamman Burj (octagonal tower). This last, exceptionally fine and pervaded with romance, is the best place from which view the Taj. Shah Jahan built it for his beloved Mumtaz-Mahal (Chosen One of the Palace – real name Arjumand Banu), who went with him on all his campaigns. Then, when he was deposed by his son Aurangzeb, he lived the last eight years of his life here, gazing across to the mausoleum he built for Mumtaz.

Of the few missing details of his buildings, the inlaid colonnade of his bathroom, behind the Diwan-i-Khas, has recently been identified in the Victoria and Albert Museum, London. It has had a remarkable history. It was torn out by the Marquis of Hastings (Governor-General 1813–23) to be given to the Prince Regent (later George IV). However, it failed to be despatched and was sold at auction by a successor, Lord Bentinck, to be presented to the V&A by Sir Alfred Lyall after the Royal Colonial and Indian Exhibition of 1886. The Fort is open daily, sunrise to sunset. No sound and light show.

Taj Mahal The greatest monument to love and the strongest magnet to any visitor to India. Irresistible to see on each trip, and more lovely each time. The white marble reflects every change in the light, so go as many times as possible – and it really is worth being there when it floats in soft mauves and pinks at dawn. (Book up with a rickshaw boy the day before. Much nicer than a taxi.) Mumtaz died giving birth to her fourteenth child (of which seven survived) in 1631, after 17 years of blissful marriage to Shah Jahan. He was heartbroken. For the rest of his life, his only other love was architecture.

The following year he began building her mausoleum, the masterpiece among all his buildings, the design probably masterminded by himself. It is the ultimate refinement of the Mughal tomb design first seen at Humayun's Tomb in Delhi (see p. 48). It took 21 years to complete and employed 20,000 labourers and craftsmen (including one Veronio from Venice and a Monsieur Austin de Bordeaux). From the gateway across the garden, the overall shape is perfect; close up, the pietra dura, marble screens and all the craftsmanship are of astounding precision.

The tombs of both Mumtaz and Shah Jahan are in the basement. (The macabre theory that Shah Jahan planned a black version of the Taj for himself was put about by the not entirely reliable traveller, Jean-Baptiste Tavernier, but has no firm substance.) Good views of the Fort from the platform. In the garden, the left-hand pavilion houses the worthwhile Taj Museum. Open daily, sunrise to

10pm, remaining open until midnight on full moon and four days either side.

The Taj is particularly beautiful at dawn and dusk. Coach trips arrive for hard afternoon light when the dazzling marble hurts the eyes. Try to avoid the crowds on Fridays (this is a monument to a Mughal queen) and full moon nights.

Akbar's Mausoleum At Sikandra, 10km from the Agra Fort. Tomb and lush garden built over the Lodi city of Sultan Sikandar (ruled 1488–1517) – one or two Lodi remains in the corner. Designed by Akbar in 1602, it reflects his din-i-Ilani (religion of God), his mixture of Hindu, Muslim, Sikh and Christian thought. Slightly gawky because when Jehangir took over after Akbar's death in 1605, he made the half-built design more lavish and swapped sandstone for white marble. Beautiful polychrome mosaic designs on the south gateway, with Jehangir's delicate floral painted vaults inside, nicely restored. Climb right to the top for good views through finely carved windows of Jehangir's white marble courtyard – a taste of Agra building to come. Open daily, sunrise to sunset.

Itimad-ud-Daulah's Tomb The jewel of Agra, with fewer visitors and greater serenity than the Taj. Like a large reliquary, it is the first Agra building entirely coated with white marble and smothered in pietra dura inlay. The craftsmanship is more refined, delicate and precise than even that on the Taj. It was built by his powerful daughter, de facto empress Nur Jahan and completed in six years flat, in 1628. Not to be missed. Reached through the old town and over a rickety bridge or, when the post-monsoon water is high, by boat from behind the Taj. 3km north is Ram Bagh, the earliest Mughal garden, built by Babur in 1528, still maintained. Both open daily, sunrise to sunset.

See also the old British buildings, such as those flanking Sardar Patel Park, and the two Christian cemeteries, both well-maintained and historically very interesting. Episodes of family histories are carved on tombs built in the latest architectural styles to reach India. In the Roman Catholic cemetery (land given by Akbar), among the Islamic-style mausolea and classic cenotaphs are the earliest Christian tomb in north India, that of John Mildenhall (1614), and the mini sandstone Taj of Colonel John Hessing (1803). In the Protestant cemetery the tombs date back to three 17th century factors.

SHOPPING AND CRAFTS Hundreds of shops, every other one confusingly professing to be 'official approved' or 'approved Emporium'. They are all highly competitive, so barter everywhere. No price is fixed here. Most open every day, 10am–7pm. Agra is the worst place for rickshaw boys/taxi drivers/guides offering to show you the best shops. Invariably you pay more and they get a rake-off. For treasures and junk, explore the bazaars in the area west of the Fort. One whole street is devoted to selling glorious kites. The doyen kite-maker is Hosain Ali. Kites made to order in one day.

Good marble shops are Oswal Emporium, 30 Munro Road and Subhash Emporium, 18/1 Gwalior Road. Shop for the local Agra rugs and dhurries at Mangalick and Co, 5 Taj Road, Sadar Bazaar; totally reliable, big stock and takes orders for designs, colours and sizes, then ships them when woven. Mangalick is in a good cluster of shops. His neighbours are Jaiwal (brass), Modern Book Depot, Singh and Sons (chemist) and Agra's Kwality Restaurant. Opposite is Madhu sweetmeat shop which sells the Agra speciality, meshur pak, and Mathura specialities, barfi kulchen and barfi kaisha. (Sadar Bazaar closes Tuesday.)

For jewellery, go to the well-established Munshi Ganeshi Lal and Sons, who have shops on MG Road and 194 Fatehabad Road, or to Kohinoor Jewellers, MG Road. Jewel House, Taj Ganj, has good dhurries, carpets and embroidery. The Handicraft Emporium, 16 Gen. Carriapa Road, has good quality local marble, brass, copper and jewellery, simple dhurries, made by local prisoners, and brightly coloured bed-covers woven by local women. Other state emporia – UP, Rajasthan, Kerala, Haryana – are in the Taj precinct.

Marble pietra dura Some 500 families in Agra – about 5,000 craftsmen – work the hard, durable and non-porous (so non-staining) marble from Macrana, near Jaipur. The process is the same now as in the 17th century. Apprenticeship begins at the age of 8 and takes 15 years, each student learning all the processes. He then specialises, choosing between being a marble-cutter, gem cutter, gem setter (with secret adhesive recipe) or chiseller, and he makes his own tools.

The shop owner buys the marble and brings it to the craftsmen. A design is agreed on paper and the marble is cut. Using a pointed tool, the design is drawn through a coat of red powder paint covering the marble; stones are selected and placed; the holes are chiselled (slow, precise work); stones are fitted, the final adjustment done with an emery paste wheel; stones are glued and, finally, polished with increasingly fine emery.

Dhurrie weaving Dhurrie in Hindi, kilim in Persian. Whereas it seems pile carpet weaving was introduced into India by Akbar, the flat dhurri weaving seems to have been an indigenous craft. In the 19th century, it was introduced into prisons to relieve the boredom of inmates who also took up silk-weaving, cobbling, tie-dye, basket-work and horticulture. Prison officers kept a tight control on standards; the prisoners hardly needed to turn out slap-dash work for a quick return. Finished dhurries were sold in bazaars or presented to local maharajas, any proceeds going to the prisoner and his family. They reached a peak of technical skill, sophistication and design between 1880 and 1920. Today, the quality work is done in villages, not jails, although for some time young village women have woven their dreams into the panja (wedding dhurrie).

The women of a dhurrie-weaving family work at a horizontal bamboo loom set a few inches off the ground, inside or outside their home. As they chat and gossip, a senior aunt or grandmother, in the centre, keeps a fierce eye on each team member's work. Materials and designs are supplied by an agent employing up to 100 families in widely scattered villages. But while his designs are just variants of the traditional stars, diamonds, crosses, chevrons and diagonal patterns, he has introduced new materials and modified the palette. Formerly dhurries were of cotton; now wool and even silk are woven. The strong indigo, red and saffron are often supplanted by soft blue, ice-cream pink and peppermint green.

Both changes pander to the European market but old and new can be found. The traditional Agra design of stripes going to a point at either end, leaving a plain surrounding field, is woven with a shuttle, whereas the complex Jaipur designs need a lot of finger work. To see weaving around Agra, contact Mr Mangalick (see above), whose nearest weaving families are only 5km away. There is no obligation. As he says: 'You are a guest of my city and my country.'

Forays out of Agra

These suggestions include day trips. Some link up well to make a longer day or a mini-break, stopping overnight.

TEHPUR SIKRI, UTTAR PRADESH
km. Essential to visit. The most perfectly pre-
ved and complete Mughal palace city of all, built
Akbar using the highest quality workmanship,
n totally abandoned by him 14 years later (prob-
y because of inadequate water supply), to be a
ost town for ever.

Aged 26, Akbar had no heir, despite all those
ves. After the defeat of Chittor in 1568, he made
annual pilgrimage to Ajmer – notice the kos
nars (brick tower milestones) still standing en
te. He also visited the holy man Shaikh Salim
ishti at Sikri who told him he would have three
s. The prediction came true. The next year his
st Rajput wife, the Amber princess Jodhbai, bore
im (later Jehangir). After a pilgrimage of thanks
Ajmer a second son was born and, in 1572, the
rd son. This was impressive. By 1571 Akbar had
cided to build a totally new capital at Sikri and
ved his masons there.

Of the town, only the ruined walls remain. But
e magnificent palace complex stands, the elabor-
ely carved red sandstone and marble as crisp as it
s 400 years ago, still carrying the atmosphere of
kbar's cultured and enlightened court. The build-
g style is closer to the pure Indian of Gwalior
rt, keeping to the column and slab principle,
an to the Mughal Persian-Indian mélange. But
e complex motifs of Gwalior decoration fuse
ppily with Persian jali work and decorative
otifs such as the vase of flowers.

Shaikh Salim's white marble tomb with delicate
is (finely carved screens) is up to the standard of
medabad's Siddi Sayyid Mosque (1515), and is
ll visited by childless women. The fine marble
d decoration of the surrounding mosque was
ded by Shah Jahan.

The palace buildings are alive with a mirage of
lace life. There is the Diwan-i-Khas where Akbar
t above the central pillar, his ministers on the
lconies, spectators standing below. The so-
lled Jodhbai Palace has a refined salon for a
een's elegant relaxation. The entirely gilded so-
lled Miriam's House nearby was in fact occupied
Jodhbai. The even tinier Turki Sultana's carved
lace is also nearby, as is the casket-like private
me of Raja Birbal. The Panj Mahal (the harem) is
e a five-layered wedding cake of spun sugar. The
nkh Michauli (hide and seek) was used for stor-
g records – and finding them – rather than play-
g games. Adjoining the Diwan-i-Am is the
chesi Courtyard, where Akbar used his ladies as
eces to play pachesi (a game similar to chess) on

the outsized board built into the marble ground.
Best seen with a good guide. Open daily, sunrise to
sunset.

KEOLADEO NATIONAL PARK, BHARATPUR, RAJASTHAN

54km from Agra, 17km from Fatehpur Sikri. One of
the finest bird sanctuaries in the world, established
1956. 29 sq km of fresh water swamp developed
by the Maharaja of Bharatpur for his famous
duck shoots where enormous bags were taken;
Kitchener and Curzon were at the first shoot in
1902, Viceroy Lord Linlithgow was the guest
of honour for the biggest bag of all, 4,273, in 1938.

Today, there are more than 360 species of birds;
spot breeding September–October, spot migratory
birds November–February. Best time dawn or
dusk. It is best to take a jersey and a pair of
binoculars. As the mist lifts at sunrise, take a
rowing boat around the islands on the still water.
Morning bird songs and flapping, yawning wings
are the only sounds. There are water-dancing
Chinese coots, gliding eagles, large painted and
black-necked storks on treetops, electric-blue
kingfishers on low branches. The rare Siberian
crane visits here (December–January only), its only
known winter home. There are hunchbacked
herons, dazzling white egrets and many more.
Then take a hot breakfast at the Forest Lodge. At
dusk, there are non-water birds, pythons and
animals – sambhar, chital, nilgai, pig. Worth hiring
a bicycle in town to bike around the sanctuary.

To enjoy both dusk and dawn, stay at *Bharatpur
Forest Lodge* in the sanctuary (tel: 2260/2232; cable:
FORESTOUR). 18 rooms, some with a view over
sanctuary. Pleasant staff, some publications but
best to arrive with Salim Ali's *Book of Indian Birds*.
See also the stern early 18th century Lohagarh fort
(open daily, 9am–5pm), palace and museum (Sat.–
Thurs.) in Bharatpur.

DEEG, RAJASTHAN

90km from Agra (via Bharatpur or Mathura).
Krishna's gopies (milkmaids) had their clothes
woven and embroidered here. Walled summer
palace of the Maharaja of Bharatpur, completed
1750, a grand complex of buildings with slightly
overgrown Mughal gardens set between two huge
tanks (artificial lakes). One of the few Rajasthan
palaces open to the public yet not tarted up for
visitors. Furniture and the occasional aged servant
give a feeling that the family has gone for an
extended holiday.

67

The facade of Gopal Bhavan (main palace) looking out over the tank has carved and painted balconies. Inside, there is European furniture on the ground floor and a vast black marble bed and a built-in horse-shoe dining table upstairs. The marble swing outside is booty from Delhi. Find frescoes in Nand Bhavan. The marble-lined Suraj Bhavan and Sawan and Bhadon pavilions are islands amid the surrounding ponds and fountains in the gardens. Keshav Bhavan, the open pavilion, is across the central garden, Purana Mahal, the old palace, along the south side. The huge exercise room opposite would have had its floor dust mixed with perfume.

The 500 fountains, which used to splash coloured water as a backdrop to lavish fireworks displays and mock thunder storms with full sound, are now turned on for the August festival. M. C. Joshi's excellent guide book available on site. Open daily, 8am–noon; 1–7pm.

MATHURA, UTTAR PRADESH

On the Delhi-Agra Road, 147km from Delhi, 56km from Agra, 34km from Deeg. Krishna country. Birthplace of the mischievous, blue-skinned, human 7th incarnation of the god Vishnu who subsequently moved to Dwarka in Western Gujarat (see p. 140). As Krishna scholar P. Banerjee has written: 'The love and adoration of Krishna sank deep into the heart of India . . . He is so fundamentally the God who is human in everything.' Thus, a major centre of Hindu pilgrimage and Krishna worship at least since the 4th century BC. Subsequently a prosperous trading centre under the Shaka and Kushana dynasties. Then, a Buddhist centre developed under the Guptas (350BC–465AD) with 3,000 monks furnishing 20 monasteries.

There is a superb museum, packed with sculptures, terracottas, bronzes and coins (open Tues.– Sun., 10.30am–4.30pm; April 16–June 30 7.30am– 12.30pm). Also in town: bathing ghats on the Yamuna River, especially Vishram Ghat where Krishna rested after killing the tyrant king of Mathura. (Morning and evening riverside puja by pilgrims); Sati Burj (1570), a tower commemorating a Jaipur royal's sati (a widow's self-immolation); Raja Man Singh of Amber's ruined Kans Qila fort; Aurangzeb's Jami Masjid (1661), built with his usual aggressiveness right on the spot where Krishna was believed to have been born; and the fun Dwarkadheesh Temple (1914), built by Seth Gokuldass of Gwalior, dedicated to Krishna and decorated like a Christmas tree for the big festiva (open 6–10.30am; 4–6pm).

Near the town are several sacred villages. Vri daban (10km) is where Krishna flirted with th milkmaids. The many temples here include th exceptional Gobind Deo (Divine Cowherd, 159 (all temples open 8–11am; 5–9pm). Other villag are Mahaban (11km) where Nanda, Krishna's fo ter-father, tended the young god; Gokul (10km where Krishna was brought up in secrecy; Barsa (47km) where Radha, Krishna's consort, was bor Goverdhan (26km), the hillock Krishna lifted on h finger for a week to protect the cowherds of Br from the god Indra's storms.

It is well worth coinciding with a big Hind festival such as Holi, Diwali, Janmashtar (Krishna's birthday, a time for the Krishna ras li dances in the temples) or Annakut, when Mathu and all these Braj villages take turns in the ce ebrations. For instance, at Holi in Vrindaba Krishna's life is daily enacted by young, painte and tinselled Brahmin boys at Ashram Sri Caitan Prema Sansthan for 14 days before Holi night. Th Holi water is made by steeping flowers in vats, n by chemicals. Those who visit Banki Bihari temp are pelted with rose petals. People get merry on concoction of clotted cream, nuts, rosewater an bhang (hashish). Cows are dressed up in heav brocades. There is ritual bathing in the Yamun Women chase men in a mock battle, throwir dung and brandishing sticks. Surrounding villag take their turn during the following days. At Bars na, likened by artist Andrew Logan to Bethlehem men from the neighbouring village lie down und shields to be thwacked with huge sticks by veile women. As well as mounting plays, the Ashram Vrindahan is making important music recordin including the old masters of the classic dhrupa form. It is possible to stay overnight.

GWALIOR, MADHYA PRADESH

118km by road from Agra; direct daily flights co nect Delhi and Bhopal (in central India, see p. 132 Spectacular fort built on sheer rock that 'qui stunned' India connoisseur Mark Zebrowski wl puts it 'far ahead of Lucknow' in his priorities places to visit. Cunningham praised it as: 'th noblest specimen of Hindu domestic architectu in northern India'. No wonder in its heyday influenced Akbar's Fatehpur Sikri. Since a Rajp built the first fortress in the 8th century, it has bee contested by various powers – Tomars, Sikand odi, Babur, the Mahrathas and the British. he Tomar family rose in 1398. Man Singh, the trongest Tomar, ruled 1486–1517. Today a royal 1other and son of the Scindias of Gwalior Marathas) are prominent in the Indian govern-1ent. She has been the Vice-President of the Janata arty since 1980 and twice Vice-President of the .ll-India Women's Conference. He, educated at Vinchester and Oxford, is another ex-Maharaja to e voted to the Lok Sabha on the Congress (I) cket.

Visit the *fort* first, if possible picking up as a uide Yashwant Singh who lives at the Hindola ateway below the museum and whose charm, loquent English and knowledge about every pect of the fort transform a visit. Approach by the 2uth-west road, passing the colossal Jain statues 1 the rock (found indecent by Babur who obliter-ted the faces), through the 10 metre high and very 1ick walls.

Inside is Man Singh's palace, still embellished 'ith lapis blue tiles of ducks, elephants and pal-1yra palms. Dancers are carved into the lattice 'ork of the music room. Brackets are stone eacocks and fabulous beasts. The natural air-onditioning system passes over perfumed water 1 the summer rooms. The dark, cool basements vhere Aurangzeb hanged his brother) are in 1yers below the waiting room where the women 2uld watch for the flag of victory or defeat. If ecessary, they could immediately commit sati on 1e fire already prepared.

Still in the fort, see also the Karan, Jehangir and hah Jahan palaces, the two 11th century Sasbahu ?mples (currently being well restored) – the most pectacular of all the views is from here – and the :h century Teli-ka-Mandir, a marriage temple 'ith delicate sculptures on the exterior which ?ach brides-to-be how to love their husbands. The .rchaeological Survey office, adjoining the Man ingh Palace, has padlocked trunks full of guide 2oks to various parts of India but only occasion-lly to Gwalior.

The good museum is found inside the Hindola ate and housed in the Gujari Palace (*c.* 1500), built y Man Singh for his favourite wife Mringanaya om Gujarat: established 1913, fine collection of 1scriptions, carvings, Gupta sculptures and mini-ture paintings. Good guide book. (Open Tues.–un., 8–11am, 2–5pm; April 1–September 30, 7–0am, 3–6pm).

Down in the *town*, amid huge three-wheeler 1xis that lumber and lurch along the road, pump-ing their squeezy horns, there is the tomb of the great musician Tansen (b.1506), whom Akbar made Master of Music at his court in 1562. He is the focus of an annual music festival in December when India's greatest living musicians play round the clock for several days and nights in huge, brightly coloured tents (the Delhi Tansen festival is in February). The stately dhrupad form of Hindustani classical vocal and instrumental music, of which there are few practitioners today, was developed by Raja Man Singh Tomar, then elaborated by Swami Haridas and his disciple, Tansen. Tansen was also crucial to the development of the open-throated simple Gwalior gharana singing (easier on Western ears). Agra, Jaipur and other cities each have distinctive gharana schools but Gwalior's is the oldest and the fountainhead.

When the Gwalior family squabbles have concluded, the Scindias' *Jai Vilas* pile of a palace will be open again. The ornate, Italianate design was prepared by Lieut.-Col. Sir Michael Filose of the Indian Army for the sly Maharaja Jayaji Rao, who borrowed money from the British but died leaving wealth, precious stones and treasure valued at 62 million rupees. It was completed in three years flat, 1872–4, to be ready for the Prince of Wales's visit. Before the two vast chandeliers were hung in the Durbar hall – claimed to be the biggest in the world, 248 candles each – three elephants were hoisted on to the roof to test its strength. The rest of the interior continues in the same vein, with imaginative details such as a silver train set that circulated cigars and port round the dining-room table, added by the next ruler, Madhav Rao. He drove his full-sized train himself, 'in a dashing fashion' according to E. M. Forster, who also noted in 1921 that this 'shrewd man of business' but 'vigorous and vulgar prince' nicknamed his children George and Mary, the ultimate compliment to the British.

If Gwalior fort impressed you, then don't turn back, for south lie Datia and, just beyond Jhansi, Orchha. Stay overnight in Gwalior at *Usha Kiran Palace*, Jayendragunj (tel: 23453/22049; telex: 566 –225 GARG; cable: USHAKIRAN); a modest Jai Vilas guest house in the palace grounds, run by the Welcomgroup but maintaining all the Maharaja's 1930s high-style furniture: standard lamps, geometric rugs in pastel shades, coloured glass wall-lights, even his curtains. 22 rooms, some more air-conditioned than others; pleasant, relaxed atmosphere, not grand. Garden being restored. Tennis, riding and badminton on palace estate; golf by arrangement.

DATIA-ORCHHA, MADHYA PRADESH

A memorable day-trip from Gwalior to Datia (69km) and Orchha (120km) – and hardly a tourist in sight. Leave at the crack of dawn. At Datia, the fine, seven-storey hilltop Gobinda Palace (1614) is one of the few Indian buildings Lutyens admitted to admiring. More recently, John Keay compared it to Delhi and Agra as 'more integrated and imposing than either'. Above the cool, dark first two storeys, behind the pierced screens, there are sun-dappled verandahs, pavilions and pillared corridors, and lofty rooms, their walls still holding mosaics and paintings. This and Orchha palace were built by Raja Bir Singh Deo, a Rajput ruler based at Jhansi, whose wealth and influence, as a firm favourite of Jehangir, leapt after he did him the favour of assassinating Akbar's personal friend and close adviser, the high-powered Abul Fazl (author of the Akbar-nama and Ain-i-Akbari), while Jehangir was still Prince Salim.

Speed on to Orchha, the perfect medieval city, if crumbling a bit, extolled by an India buff as 'very special; by far the least changed and most unspoilt Rajput city I've seen in India', and by another as 'rather like Jaisalmer used to be' (and Jaisalmer is pretty good even now). A village survives beside the wooded island fort which was deserted in the 18th century. Inside the fort, find several palaces: the tiered Jehangir Mahal (built for Jehangir; good views); the Raj Mahal, and Sheesh Mahal. There are silver-framed mirrors and more wall-paintings in their huge rooms, fine carved brackets and jali (pierced) screens. Also paintings in Lakshmi Narayan Temple and several other temples and chhatris (cenotaphs). Perfect for a long wander and a picnic.

To have more time, stay at the charming *Hotel Sheesh Mahal*, 3 rooms, in a corner of the palace – the Maharaja would stay overnight in the large one with Victorian furniture. Now run by MP Tourism. Book in writing or through MP Tourist Office, 19 Ashok Road, New Delhi (tel: 351187). Also Motel Tansen, Gandhi Road, Gwalior (tel: 21568). Otherwise, return to Gwalior. Avoid night driving: dangerous decoit country.

Khajuraho, Madhya Pradesh

The temple sculptures, inspired by the ecstatic pleasure of life and deep admiration of female beauty, are famous in the West merely as an A to Z of erotic naughtiness, to be ogled and sniggered at. Nothing could be further from the aims of the builders, as is apparent the moment the carvings are seen. On a rural plain, with birds singing and fields of wheat swaying in the breeze, stand the 2 survivors of a temple city built by the rich and powerful Chandella rulers in the 10th and 11th centuries. The sculptures covering the temples celebrate with human warmth and utter frankness the sublime joy of life and love, reflecting an entirely open society, free from all prudishness of Western sexual neurosis. They express the highest spiritual experience open to man: the Hindu theory that when all the senses give fully, there is total union physically and mentally, arrived at through love-making. The Hindus of Khajuraho love without shame, uninhibited by the Western concept of original sin. Their sculptures celebrate woman in all her sensuality and vanity, from yawning at daybreak to laughing with her lover at a playful monkey. They could not be further from voyeuristic pornography. They are vivacious and optimistic. Just a plane-hop away, they should not be missed. And the peace: few hawkers, no false guides, no beggars, and bicycle rickshaws instead of cars.

THE HARD FACTS Central India plains get very hot indeed. Avoid April–September and the July–August downpour. Essential to stay overnight as the eyes get cultural indigestion coping with solid temples in a five-hour spin. The Western Group are gloriously serene at sunset and sunrise. In fact, it is tempting to stay several nights for complete relaxation.

The seven-day dance festival falls in early March. It has a good reputation. Top dancers perform classical dance-drama against temple back-drops. Although it disturbs the peace of the temples, this is a chance to see dance in its original setting. Apart from the temples, a tiny village and two classy hotels, there is an airstrip. Daily flights from Delhi, Agra and Varanasi; connections to Calcutta and Kathmandu. The two very good, new hotels each have full facilities and a clean pool, garden, good food, good atmosphere and, between them (they are back-to-back), two well stocked bookshops (other shops are touristy).

Jass Oberoi (tel: 66; cable: OBHOTEL); sparkling 1980s new, quite small, beautifully designed with huge white marble lobby and central sweeping staircase. 54 rooms, each with balcony, all mod cons, baby sitter; meals served inside or outside; peaceful atmosphere; service good but lacks the usual Oberoi polish.

?handela (tel: 54; cable: CHANDELA); got here
?st, built in 1969 by Shyam Poddar, who also
?ganised the airstrip; managed by his sixth son;
?gger than Jass with the same pros and cons; more
?hite marble and huge lobby. 102 rooms, each
?th verandah, dreary decor; all mod. cons and big
?opping arcade, health club, very good herbal
?auty parlour, hair-dresser (all open to non-
?sidents); tennis court, mini-golf – even a temple;
?ficient and sensitive service (delicious fresh
?ffee).

The Tourist Office is not useful. The Khajuraho
?oklet by Krishna Deva, sold at the Western
?oup gateway, is essential. Opposite, at Raja's
?fé, there are excellent guides, especially
?ijendra Singh whose world revolves around the
?mples: half-day Rs35; full day Rs65. Beware of
?ying 'old' brass, much of it made in Delhi the
?evious week.

?UT AND ABOUT See the two main groups of
?mples, Western and Eastern, and a few to the
?uth. Linger on the green lawns surrounding the
?estern Group. The Rajput Chandellas' rise to
?ower in Central India at the beginning of the 10th
?ntury led to a vigorous literary and architectural
?owering, patronised by the rulers and focused on
?eir capital, Khajuraho. The belief was that to
?ild a temple was to reserve a suite in heaven. But
?e temple city may also have been planned as a
?n-monastic centre of learning and religion.

The 85 temples erected by them reached the peak
? Central Indian temple architecture and sculp-
?re, comparable to – if not surpassing – the
?rissan temples at Bhubaneswar (see p. 169).
?svanatha and Parsvanastha, two of the finest,
?ere constructed under Dhanga (c. 950–1002).
?handella power, built on diamonds and booty
?om conquests, waned from the mid-11th century,
?t the religious centre thrived for another 200
?ars. Fortunately, their remoteness protected
?em from Muslim destruction. They were redisco-
?red in the mid-19th century by the intrepid Brit-
?n.

As at Bhubaneswar, the temples follow a distinct
?ttern. Each is a compact mass of porch, hall,
?stibule and sanctum, the walls surmounted by
?ehive spires (sikharas) which, seen from the
?de, make a rhythmic pattern up to the highest,
?er the sanctum. The whole temple stands on a
?gh platform, facing east. One explanation for the
?atforms suggests that the land was flooded to
?ake a lake of temples.

Exuberant sculpture rampages over every surface, inside and outside, modulated to become
surprisingly easy to read. Thus, large figures in full
light are offset by flat stones or geometric patterns
set back in shadow. Friezes of continuous narrative
run around the platform but the sikharas have
lace-fine geometric cutting to give them feathery
lightness.

The technological feat of constructing such marvels, mostly between 950 and 1050, is mind-
boggling. Although the flat granite land, birthplace
of the first Chandella king, was an ideal site, the
sandstone was dug from the Ken River, 20km
away. This explains the crispness, for river sandstone is harder than quarried. Notice the women's
flesh creases, their delicate finger nails, the drop-
lets of water on the skin, even the mark where she
is scratching herself. The system was to cut and
carve every stone for the temple, then assemble it
in a mathematical triumph of dry-stone interlocking; a 3-D puzzle that makes frivolity of those 5,000
piece cardboard jigsaw puzzles.

It is a short rickshaw ride to the Eastern Group to
see *Parsvanatha Jain temple*, an architectural masterpiece. Charming sculptures include a woman applying eye make-up, another removing a thorn
from her foot. Also see the rest of the enclosure and
the temples in and around tiny Khajuraho village.

In the Western Group, every temple is worth
looking at, especially the early *Lakshmana* (c. 930
–950), the most complete, retaining its corner
shrines, *Visvanatha* (c. 950–1002) and the magnificent *Kandariya Mahadev* (1025–50), the most sublime of all both in architecture and sculpture, the
zenith of Chandella art. There are friezes of
elephants, horses and soldiers on campaign,
fighting and having a ball on their return home;
upsaras (seductive women) stretching, squeezing
out water from their hair after a bath, preening in
the mirror, awaiting their lovers, swaying inviting-
ly and coyly; mithunas (couples love-making) in
dalliance, embracing and fondling. All temples
open sunrise to sunset.

For yet more, see the southern group and visit
the museum (open Sat.–Thurs., 9am–5pm, entrance by ticket to Western Group enclosure). It
seems impossible but, if boredom strikes, there are
diamond mines, the Panna National Park and the
Rajka Falls to visit. Keen archaeologists will find
the plain littered with interesting sites.

Lucknow, Uttar Pradesh

Capital of Uttar Pradesh, yet a quiet Muslim city whose grand decaying monuments and busy bazaars still carry touches of 18th century decadent courtliness. Unlike Ahmedabad, Lucknow has not been gobbled up by the 20th century. It seems that a servant could easily trot past, carrying his master's hookah to prepare it at the house where he is dining, wondering if he will offer a puff to some fellow guest, the ultimate gesture of friendship. The very Muslim Amindabad market, originally run by women exclusively for women, still thrives, but now admits men. Here, the huge gardens of the carved palaces are being restored, the Muslim arts of attar (perfume) preparation and chikankari (white-on-white embroidery) are alive and well, and festivals celebrate the fine musical tradition.

The population is Shi'ite, rather than Sunni as found in Delhi, Agra, Gujarat and Hyderabad. The Shi'ite Nawabs of Oudh (today Avadh, in Bihar) rose to power in the 18th century as the Mughals declined. So, whereas Safdar Jang, son of Sa'adat Khan (who rose from rags to nawabhood), was stylishly buried in Delhi (see p. 47), his successors made first Farrukhabad, then Fyzabad and then Lucknow (from 1775) their capital.

Asaf-ud-Daula (1775–97) and Sa'adat Ali Khan (1798–1814) were the best of the ten lazy, plump, pleasure-loving and debauched Nawabs. But Muslim culture benefitted. To enjoy themselves, they built with aplomb, employed Mughal artists and craftsmen, encouraged Hindustani music and Urdu poetry, and, of course, led the legendary cult of the Lucknow courtesan-dancing girls to its peak of sophistication. Two good films depict the height and deterioration of Lucknow court life. One is Muzaffa Ali's 'Umrao Jaan', adapted from a 19th century Urdu novel about a contemporary courtesan's abduction as a child, her training and rise to fame, and then her attempts to get free; set during Lucknow's cultural and nawabi zenith. The other is Satyajit Ray's 'The Chess Players'.

Quite the most head-in-the-sand Nawab was the last, music-loving Wajid Ali Shah (1847–56), whose blind extravagance and indolence led the British to exile him to Calcutta, one of many contributions to the Bengal Uprising of 1857 (which the British on their side, call the Mutiny) which staged some of its bloodiest scenes at Lucknow. But Wajid Ali Shah should be remembered rather for his music. Sitting in his marble palace, he composed and patronised the light-weight thumri love songs,

inspired by the Krishna-Radha romance. Music like courtesans, was crucial to all the Nawab After eating, ghazels, light songs of Urdu poetry were sung.

The courtesan, or tawaef, was quite differe from the basic prostitute, or takaiyan. She was a integral part of Nawabi society. She entertaine the Nawabs with dance and song for substanti gold rewards. She could write tolerable Urd poetry. And she was famed for her guftagoo (art conversation). The accomplished Bacchua sar ghazels at royal weddings, Addha Biggam w known for poetry, Mushtari for her wit. Althoug often born into a humble family and amusing h patrons with a good romp as well as a song, th courtesan would become so cultured that the nob ity sent their children to be educated by her. B education and pleasure were kept quite separat The son of a big Lucknow family recently educate by a tawaef was scolded by her when he returne to enjoy other amusements. At the height of tawa culture and influence in the 19th century, a Nawa gave enormous gifts for the exclusive use of tawaef's pleasures – jewellery, gold, mang groves, whole estates and a grand town haveli.

THE HARD FACTS   Extremes again. Avoid th April–September scorching heat, but beware chilly winter days. Colourful celebrations of th Muslim festivals (see p. 39 and p. 49). The for night-long *Lucknow Festival* (February) attrac India's top musicians and dancers who perfor qawwalis (group songs), ghazels, thumris (ligh classical song), kathak dance (see p. 58) and class dramas; there is also the All-India Kite Flyin Tournament, fireworks and a film festival. *Bha kande* festival (September) is pure music. Some India's many great artists take part in these: Usta Amjad Ali Khan (plays sarod), Birju Maharaj (fro a Lucknow dancing family of many generations Ustad Ali Akbar (plays sarod) and Ustan Vilay Khan (plays sitar). Great Varanasi musicians mig include Bismila Khan (plays shahnai, a wind i strument) and Pandit Kishan Maharaj (plays ta la). Ravi Shankar now performs as much outside inside India, introducing his sitar skills to Wester ears.

Go by train or plane. Arrive from Delhi on th Lucknow Mail (departs 9.25pm, arrives 7.25am) the Gomti Express (departs 2.55pm, arriv 10.22pm) at the overpoweringly gigantic Charbag railway station. Planes connect with Delhi an Calcutta (daily) and with Agra (Tues., Thurs., Sat ın.). Possible to go for the day; far better to stay ıe or two nights. For a bed, go for concrete and ficiency, or character; both have car rental, ʔauty parlours and business services.

ʼotel Clarks Avadh, 8 Mahatma Gandhi Marg (tel:)131; telex: 0535–243; cable: AVADH); part of the ·liable Clarks chain; 98 beds, all mod. cons plus ˈrary, golf and restaurant serving good Lucknow ·od, the richest Mughlai cuisine of all, with lots of ˌeam, almonds and pistachios. Try Lucknowi ·ecialities such as murg nawabi (chicken), mali ˌutney wala (fish), noormahal biryani (mutton ˈd rice), baingan mumtaz (stuffed aubergine) and ˌcknow dahl. Seviyan (vermicelli cooked in veetened milk) and firni (also milk-based) are the ˈassic puddings.

arlton Hotel, Shahnajaf Road (tel: 44021-5; telex: 535-217; cable: CARLTON); lots of character; old, ˌmbling, former palace with columns, pillars, ˌooden staircase and a wonderful garden; 51 ˈoms, mediocre food – eat at Clarks.

The good UP Tourist Office is at 21 Vidhan Sabha ˌarg (tel: 29214). Monuments tend to open 6am to ˈm.

UT AND ABOUT Wander in the Nawab's ˌonuments and lavish gardens. Asaf-ud-Daula ˌılt the great Imambara mosque (1748) as a famine ˌlief project, designed by architect of the day, ˌıfayatullah. The Nawab and his wife are buried in ˌe central hall, claimed by locals to be the largest ˈom in the world unsupported by pillars. Up an ˌternal staircase adjoining the central hall can be ˌund the bhul bhulaiyan, a labyrinth of galleries, ˈrridors and rooms. There are excellent views ˈom the top. Asaf also built the splendid Ram ˌarwaza gate next door to try to upstage those at ˌtanbul. The Husainabad Imambara (1837, silver ˌrone inside), the Picture Gallery (former summer ˈuse, portraits of the Nawabs) and the exterior of ˌe fine Jami Masjid – all built by Mohammad Shah ˌ837–42) – are worth seeing.

There is a good Archaeological Museum in ˌaisarbagh palace and a State Museum on Barnarsi ˌgh (both open 10am–4.30pm, Tues.–Sun.). The ˌesidency (1800) is a frozen reminder of the Bengal ˌprising, untouched since the two sieges and the ˌrrible British retribution led by Gen. Sir James ˌeill, which, as Geoffrey Moorhouse writes, 'was ˌle when it came'.

On the outskirts of the city, don't miss the ˈench-Indian pile of La Martinière school. Orig-ˌally called Costantia, it was built as a country

residence by French adventurer Major-Gen. Claude Martin (1735–1800), who made a tidy for-tune working concurrently for the Nawab and the East India Company as well as playing the indigo business. It is huge ('too big for the camera lens'), partly designed by Martin who threw in every-thing that tickled his fancy: semi-circular wings, bastions, statues, gargoyles. He died before its completion, but endowed it as a school; Kipling's Kim was sent here.

SHOPPING AND CRAFTS Chowk is the old market area, a maze of alleys full of the aroma of spices and paan ingredients. In small upper rooms aged ex-Nawabs pensioned off by the British live stylishly. Here lived some tawaefs, but many more takaiyans. If a man casts his eye up today, a pimp may well beckon. Find good bidri work (see p. 183 Hyderabad), silver and gold jewellery, fine embroidery – and poke into doorways to see crafts-men at work.

For **attar**, go to Asgar Ali Mohammad Ali in Chowk. Nearby Kannauj is the centre of the exotic Indian perfume industry, but some of the finest are sold here. They are distilled in the traditional way, as introduced by Akbar, who built a perfumery where potions containing pearls, opium, gold and amber were concocted. Basically, essential oils are distilled out of sandlewood, lemongrass, ginger, cintronella, deodar wood, etc. They are then used as carriers for the aroma. This is first distilled from the flowers, or whatever, then its vapours are absorbed by the oil.

Attar is a vital part of Indian life: rose-water is used in cooking and sprinkled at festivals, and attardans (boxes of perfume bottles) are circulated at weddings. A good rose-water uses petals picked before sunrise (for the strongest oil) from the Damascene, Bulgarian or Indica bushes. But a smart lady gives off the expensive musk, saffron or agarwood attar.

Lal Behari Tandon, also in Chowk, has very good **chikankari**, the dying art of extremely skilled and delicate white embroidery on fine white mus-lin practised by Muslim women and children in their mud-floor homes. (Some can be seen at work.) Merchants supply the cloth; men cut, make up the article and block print the design; women and children work it; the merchant has it washed and ironed and sells it.

The spider's-web fine work, adored by the Nawabs who attracted master craftsmen to Luck-now, can be bought as saris or clothes or table

73

linen. Alternatively, choose a design in the shop, decide what is to be made and where the embroidery is to be worked – wide border, dotted flowers, etc. – and have it sent on. Totally reliable, it is even possible to send specific orders from abroad.

At Aminabad market, you can find everything from saris to fruit. In Nakhas, one of the oldest areas, live more than 5,000 bird-sellers. It is the centre for collectors to buy, sell and exchange parrots, doves, pigeons, budgerigars and cocks, a legacy from the nawabi addiction to kabootabaazi (pigeon flying) and game bird fighting (using quail and cocks).

Akbar was so keen on kabootabaazi that he renamed it ishq-baazi (love-play). He owned some 20,000 pigeons, took some on campaign and taught them mid-air acrobatics. The 19th century Gaekwad of Baroda, Khanderao, gave his pet pigeons a sensational wedding party, attended by princes and nobles, caparisoned elephants, with presents of jewels for the happy couple.

Wildlife sanctuaries

There are some good sanctuaries in north and central India, although they are not always easy to reach or well-organised. However, the fine bird sanctuary at Bharatpur is right by Agra and has reasonable accommodation (see p. 67). Royal Chitwan Park in Nepal, one of the best-run Asian parks, is very accessible, if expensive (see p. 235.) Deep in Madhya Pradesh is Kanha National Park, with the well-run Kipling Camp (see p. 141.) The selection below are the most accessible and/or interesting.

CORBETT, UTTAR PRADESH
Season November–May, best January–March; closed during monsoon. Go by good road, 297km (about 6hrs). Of several places to stay at Dhikala, the best three have confusingly similar names: *New Forest Rest House* (rooms with attached bath), *Old Forest Rest House* and *Forest Rest House Annex*, all bookable through UP Tourist Office, Chandralok Bhavan, 36 Janpath, New Delhi (tel: 322251), which also runs week-end package tours; or through the Chief Wild Life Warden, 17 Rana Pratap Marg, Lucknow (tel: 32). Good guides and many machans (watch towers). Explore by elephant or jeep.

With one of the best tourist infrastructures of the Indian sanctuaries, the park is particularly beautiful and well worth visiting. 520sqkm of sub-

Himalayan foothills, covering the Patlidun Vall of the Ramganga River and the lower slopes of th Shivalik range. Established in 1935, it is India oldest wildlife sanctuary and is named after India wildlife champion Jim Corbett, who grew up her In 1944, he was already concerned about the thre to India's wildlife and championed the conse vation awareness of Indians. Explore miles of op country by car or elephant. From the machans sp the many tigers. This is a Project Tiger park, successful, according to the director, Mr Sing that the territorially possessive tigers are no fighting each other to the death (9 tigers killed 1983), so more land must be found for the increa ing tiger population (a tiger needs up to 80 sq km Also plenty of elephant, Himalayan black bea leopard, ugly hog deer and handsomely antler chital. In the Ramganga river see the large riv tortoise and, in spring, fish for fat mahseer a goonch (permit from Dhikala Game Warden). Ri bird life (over 500 species).

DUDHWA NATIONAL PARK, UTTAR PRADESH
Season November–May, best January–March. (by road, 430km from Delhi (about 10hrs), 215k from Lucknow (or daily train). Stay at *Tiger Have* the home of wildlife expert Arjan (Billy) Sing where all charges go towards the wildlife work; at *Forest Rest House*. Both bookable through Wil life Warden (Kheri Region), Dudhwa Nation Park, Lakhimpur Kheri District, UP. Explore elephant or jeep.

490 sqkm lying on the India-Nepal border, r by Arjan Singh who was one of the first committe wildlife conservationists to attempt to re-introdu the tiger and other big cats into the wild. Esta lished in 1977, it was awarded the World Wildli Gold Medal for rehabilitation of captive-bred tig and leopard into the wild. In addition to big ca the park forests hold sambhar, various de (swamp, hog, barking, spotted), sloth bear, nilga elephant, hyena, jackal and porcupine. Also ri bird life and reptiles. Some fishing.

BANDHAVGARH, MADHYA PRADESH
November–June; closed July 1–October 31 for mo soon. Fly to Khajuraho, then 210km by road; Jabalpur, then 175km by road; or overnight train Satna, met by park jeep. Stay at *Bandhavgarh Jung Camp*, run by naturalist Mr K. K. Singh with Tig Tops India, bookable through Tiger Tops Mou tain Travel, 1/1 Ravi Jhansi Road, New Delhi (te 523057/771055). If full, stay at *White Tiger Fore*

odge; 8 rooms, bookable through Tours Manager, MP State Tourism Development Corporation, Gangotri, T. T. Nagar, Bhopal (tel: 62173; telex: 705-275) or, if less than 10 days in advance, through MPSTDC, Railway Station, Jabalpur (tel: 1111).

Established 1968. Currently harbours one of the highest density tiger populations of any Indian park (22 counted in 1982), so a good place to spot them. And there is a camp good enough for up-market package tours to use. The first white tiger was found just outside the park in 1951. The park stretches across the heart of the Vidhayan mountain range of central India, with sal forest and valleys, pre-historic caves and 14th century Bandhavgarh fort. By elephant and jeep see plenty of tiger, langur, sloth bear, wild boar and gaur (Indian bison); deer such as chital, sambhar, barking deer and chausingha (antelope). Find leopards on the east side of the park.

SHIVPURI, MADHYA PRADESH

Season February–June. Fly or drive to Gwalior, then 112km. Stay at *Sakhya Sagar Boat Club* in the park or *Shivpuri Hotel Circuit House*, both bookable through The Collector, Shivpuri.

160 sq km of deciduous plains forest, former summer capital of the Scindias of Gwalior who went on tiger chikar (hunting). Spot the occasional tiger, leopard and bear today, and many sambhar, chital, nilgai, chinkara and chowsingha pig. Good lake birdlife includes flocks of demoiselle cranes.

PANNA, MADHYA PRADESH

Season October–April. 48km by road from Khajuraho. Stay in Khajuraho.

543 sq km of 'incredible wilderness' of valleys and gorges bordering the Ken River; countless post-monsoon waterfalls. One of India's newest National Parks, dotted with living temples of a bizarre Spanish style that amused the Maharaja of Panna. Formerly some of the best, but highly controlled, shooting for the local rulers; then, after independence, indiscriminate shooting had a devastating effect. Teak forest harbours tiger, leopard, blue bulls, sambhar and chinkara. The rare gharial and maggar crocodiles can be found in the Ken. There is a profusion of paradise flycatchers, MP's state bird. Ken Crocodile Sanctuary nearby.

Find out more

Countless books have been written on Delhi and on the Mughals. The few included below are highly readable and have good bibliographies. The contemporary diaries and accounts, stocked by good libraries (see p. 15), are fascinating and bring the whole period alive.

Ali, Salim: *The Book of Indian Birds*, Bombay, 1979
Anand, M.: 'Khajuraho', *Marg*, Bombay, 1958
Ansari, M. A.: *Social Life of the Mughal Emperors*, Allahabad, 1974
Ardizzone, Edward: *Indian Diary 1952–53*, London, 1984
Beach, M. C.: *The Grand Mogul, imperial painting in India 1600–1660*, Williamstown, 1978
Beach, M. C.: *The Imperial Image, Paintings for the Mughal Court*, Washington, 1981
Binyon, L.: *The Court Painters of the Grand Moguls*, London, 1921
Brown, P.: *Indian Painting under the Mughals*, Oxford, 1924
Carroll, D.: *The Taj Mahal*, New York, 1972
Corbett, J.: *Man Eaters of Kumaon*, Oxford, 1948
'Delhi Agra, Sikri', *Marg*, Bombay, nd
Deva, K.: *Khajuraho*, Delhi, 1978
Fazl, Abul: *Akbar-nama*, trans. H. Beveridge, 3 vols, Calcutta, 1907–39
Fazl, Abul: *Ani-i-Akbari*, trans. H. Blochmann and H. S. Jarrett, 3 vols, Calcutta, 1873–94
Foster, W., ed.: *Early Travels in India, 1583–1619*, London 1921
Foster, W. ed.: *The Embassy of Sir Thomas Roe to India, 1615–19*, London, 1926
Gascoigne, B: *The Great Moghuls*, London 1979
Godden, R.: *Gulbadan*, based on the Humayun-nama written by Babur's daughter, London, 1980
Hambly, G.: *Cities of Mughal India*, London, 1968
Hutchins, F. G.: *Young Krishna*, New Hampshire, 1980
The Indian Heritage: Court Life & Arts under Mughal Rule, Festival of India exhibition catalogue, Victoria and Albert Museum, London, 1982
Irving, R. G.: *Indian Summer: Lutyens, Baker and Imperial Delhi*, Oxford, 1981
Jehangir: *Tuzuk-i-Jahangiri*, trans. Alexander Rogers, ed. H. Beveridge, 2 vols, London, 1909–14
'Khajuraho', *Marg*, vol. X, no. 3, Bombay, 1957
Lall, J: *Taj Mahal and the Glory of Mughal Agra*, India, 1982
Marshall, D. N.: *Mughals in India: a Bibliographical Survey*, London, 1967
Moraes, Dom: *Madhya Pradesh*, India, 1983

Moraes, Dom; *Mrs Gandhi*, London, 1980

Palkhivala, Nani, A: *We, the People*, Bombay, 1984

Sharma, R. C.: *Mathura Museum of Art*, Mathura, 1967

Sharma, Y. D.: *Delhi and its Neighbourhood*, Delhi, 1964

Singh, B. A.: *Tiger Haven*, London, 1973

Singh, K. and Rai, R: *Delhi: A Portrait*, Delhi and Oxford, 1983

Spear, P.: *Twilight of the Moghuls*, London, 1951

Welch, Stuart C.: *The Art of Mughal India*, New York, 1963

Welch, Stuart C: *Imperial Mughal Painting*, New York and London, 1978

Woodcock, M: *Collins Handguide to the Birds of Indian Sub-Continent*, London, 1980

Rajasthan:
Pleasure palaces and desert villages

jasthan is classic fantasy India at its best.
laces built on dreams glow in the fiery
sert setting sun. Fortress cities conceal
·asure-trove bazaars of jewellery, precious
ones, enamelling, embroidery and mirror-
ork. Piles of spices sweeten the air. Women
ing colour and sparkle to every city alley
d village well: shy, smiling girls and
ighing ladies draped in splashes of rasp-
rry pink, lapis blue, saffron, pillarbox red
d tangerine, weighed down with silver
ıgs on their noses, ears and toes, bangles
ound their arms and ankles. Snooty camels
ul cartloads of fire-wood along the road
d jam up the city alleys. Bhopas (folk bal-
liers) and their families, swathed in long,
nato-red tunics and turbans, sing ballads
out Rajasthani heroes and lovers. And the
lo-playing maharajas are alive and well,
ning with their citizens in the constant
und of festive gaiety.

The princes of India may have lost their
es, land and revenues since Indepen-
nce, but feudalism lives on. Their former
tes maintain their individuality. Both rural
d city people, on the whole, have a pro-
ınd sense of belonging to the old order and
ow love and respect to their maharaja –
1om they call just that. Some even elect him
their member of parliament, endorsing his
mer position as their protector.

3ut gone are the days of pomp and cer-
ıony that outshone Croesus in their mad
extravagances. When the ship from England
carrying furniture for the new 347-room
1930s Jodhpur palace sank, the Maharaja
merely ordered replica sets to be made.

When Maharaja Madho Singh of Jaipur
went to England for Edward VII's coronation, in 1902, he had a temple built in the
P&O liner he chartered. He threw bags of
gold, silver and silk into Bombay harbour to
invoke a safe journey from the oceans. In
England, he drank nothing but Ganga water,
stored in gigantic silver pots, and he and his
retinue filled three large Kensington houses.

Each prince now lives in just one or two of
his several palaces. His other past pleasure
houses lie decaying across his state. But the
canny Rajput often puts his luxurious legacy
to commercial work to replenish his revenue-
starved coffers. His product is his homes,
households and sometimes himself. His market is the delighted tourist, who can, for a few
days, live like a maharaja or his maharani,
enjoying their amusements, pampered to
distraction.

The palaces, like real-life Piranesi capriccii,
dominate each city and boggle the mind with
their massive size, their hotchpotch styles
and their splendid interiors. But they are just
a recent amusement of the Rajput princes,
the majority built in the 19th or even 20th
centuries. Before then, war was their game.
The tall, proud, moustachioed, Rajput warriors, all excellent horsemen, make no bones

77

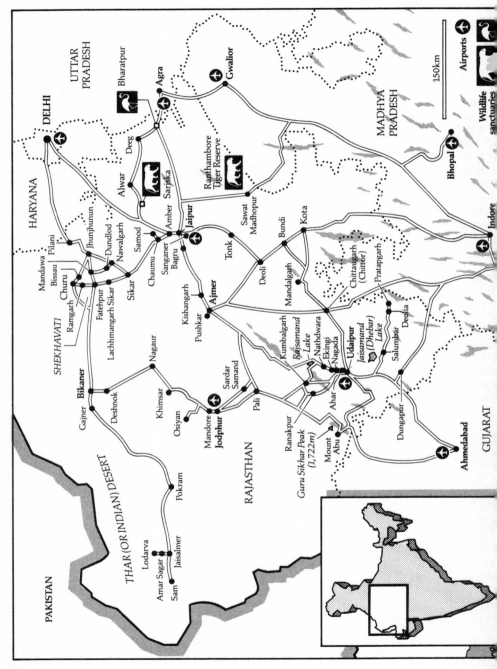

Airports

Wildlife sanctuaries

150km

UTTAR PRADESH

Bharatpur

Agra

Gwalior

MADHYA PRADESH

Bhopal

Indore

DELHI

Deeg

HARYANA

Alwar

Sariska

Ranthambore Tiger Reserve

Jhunjhunun

Dundlod

Nawalgarh

Samod

Amber

Jaipur

Sawat
Madhopur

Kota

Bundi

Pilani

Mandawa

Bissau

Churu

Fatehpur

Ramgarh

Lachhmangarh Sikar

Sikar

Chaumu

Sanganer

Bagru

Tonk

Deoli

Mandalgarh

Chittangarh
(Chittor)

Pratapgarh

SHEKHAVATI

Kishangarh

Ajmer

Pushkar

Kumbalgarh

Rajsamand
Lake

Nathdwara

Ekingi

Nagada

Udaipur

Jaisamand
(Dhebar)
Lake

Salumbar

Deolia

Nagaur

Bikaner

Khimsar

Sardar
Samand

Pali

Ahar

Deshnok

Osiyan

Mandore

Jodhpur

Ranakpur

Guru Sikhar Peak
(1,722m)

Mount
Abu

Dungapur

Ahmedabad

GUJARAT

Gajner

RAJASTHAN

Pokram

THAR (OR INDIAN) DESERT

Lodarva

Amar Sagar

Sam

Jaisalmer

PAKISTAN

out their pedigree: they claim descent from
e sun and moon via the hero gods of the
amayana and Mahabharata epics.

On a more mundane level, they were prob-
ly descended from the Huns who settled
north-west India, rising to power in the
h and 10th centuries. After Mahmud of
hazni's Muslim expansions of the 11th cen-
ry, those in the west built clifftop forts and
ed dacoits' lives, raiding valleys for food
d booty. They fought hard; they drank
rd. When a battle was clearly a loser, they
nned saffron and fought to the death, nev-
fleeing. Their women were equally heroic.
hen Chittaugarh was lost in 1533, the
ueen Mother led 13,000 women to the pyre
commit johar, mass ritual suicide by burn-
g. Finally, they gained supremacy over
e area that became known as Rajwarra,
jputana and now Rajasthan, land of
inces.

It took Akbar to subdue them, one by one,
th countless marriages to Rajput prin-
sses (see p. 64) but even then he gained
ly alliances, not subjugation. Under this
aky Mughal security, the Rajput rulers gra-
ally descended from their hilltop forts to
ild lakeside palaces, go hunting and pat-
nise exquisite miniature paintings.

Stability ended when Mahrathas, Sikhs
d others rebelled against Mughal suprema-
and this state of affairs continued until the
itish rewarded the princes for their support
ring the Bengal Uprising of 1857. When
itish India came under Crown rule in 1858,
e Rajput princes remained independent,
ng with about half the country which be-
me known as Princely India – the other big
cts were Hyderabad and Mysore.

To encourage loyalty, the British heaped
ivileges on the princes: titles, medals, hon-
rs and their own special military units.
ey encouraged them to modernise their
tes and to play them at polo and cricket.
e British also set up Indian versions of
itish public schools for their sons, like
ayo College at Ajmer. Founded in 1875 by
litical agent Colonel Walter who wished
e sons of the aristocracy' to have an 'Eton
India', it quickly followed the British public

school tradition of gaining most renown for
its sportsmen, in this case polo players.

But the young princes maintained their
Indian standards. Officially, boys were
allowed three personal servants, but many
pupils kept separate households with quantities of servants and stables with dozens of
horses. Photographs of the Maharaja of
Jaipur, a Mayo College product, holding polo
trophies at Windsor Great Park line the walls
of the cocktail bar of the Rambagh Palace
hotel. Other public schools, still thriving,
included the Doon School at Dehra Dun,
where Rajiv and Sanjay Gandhi were educated and Sherwood College, in the hills at
Naini Tal.

The British ploy worked well. The princes
forsook war for peace. To live in peace was to
build and live as ostentatiously as possible,
which they did with a crazed fervour. The
Maharaja of Baroda hails the palaces as 'a
testament to the princes' power, wealth and
capacity for self-indulgence'.

The benefit for the rest of us is that visitors
to Rajasthan can now stay in fairytale
palaces. There are rooms with murals of
dancing girls and black marble bathrooms.
Those with a large family or retinue can take a
suite of seven rooms surrounding a tinkling
fountain. It is possible to take a swing across a
palatial indoor swimming pool. There are
dazzling gold and gems set in the walls of city
palaces. There are chances to ride velvet-
caparisoned elephants and to wander among
princesses' gardens amid peacocks and cooling fountains. Rajasthan offers a glorious
variety of luxurious pursuits: to go out to a
royal game park dotted with pretty pavilions;
to explore the painted Marwari havelis; or to
visit desert villages by jeep and camel, sleeping under the stars. If the time is right, there
is the Pushkar Camel Fair, or the Holi festival
in jewel-like Jaisalmer or the Muslim festival
of Urs at Ajmer.

But Rajasthan is not just palaces. There is a
different, but equally exotic, luxury in its
bazaars, villages, even along the roads. Here
the rich diversity and colour of the traditional
charm are really found. Monuments and
museums cannot be missed, but it is also

worth poking around the back alleys and getting out on the road to the tiny surrounding villages. As the artists Tim Lovejoy and Christian Peltenburg-Brechneff recently found: 'We felt the remote isolation of rural India 10 minutes out of any town or city, like travelling back 100 years or more; the road is like a tunnel, your car zooming through not just the past but a whole other time zone.'

When to go

Season September–March, beginning with post-monsoon stickiness and clouds, ending with desert dryness. Best months visually are September–October when trees blossom and pleasure lakes are full; actual monsoon, July–August, can be stunning, even if wet. Flowers blossom November–March. November–January evenings are cold and the locals wrap themselves in brightly coloured woollen shawls. February–March are sunny and clear, with fewer package tours – an important consideration in Rajasthan tourist traps.

FESTIVALS   The best of the Hindu religious festivals to see in Rajasthan are Dussehra (September–October), Diwali (20 days later) and Holi (March–April), all public holidays when everything closes. There are big fairs and often huge firework displays. At *Dussehra*, 10 days of plays, processions and firework effigies celebrate Rama's victory over the demon Ravana and coincide with the harvest (but it is best of all in Delhi and Varanasi). At *Diwali*, women don black veils edged with gold tinsel. Oil lamps (clay pots holding lighted wicks in oil) are lit in every home to show Rama the way home from exile and to welcome Lakshmi, the goddess of wealth. Five days of jollity begin with the new year. It is a big time for gamblers – those favoured by Lakshmi to win at Diwali should keep a lucky hand for the whole year. For trading communities, such as the Marwaris of Shekhavati, this is business new year as well. Many put coins, an earthenware lamp, a weapon, a book and other objects before the youngest child who selects one, indicating the course of the following year. The next three days are devoted to Krishna, Shiva and the demon Bali, a monkey king son of the temperamental god Indra. On the fifth day, sisters put the red tika mark on their brothers' foreheads.

Holi celebrates the arrival of spring. Rajasthan is the place to be, with pure enjoyment for everyone in every city, best of all Jaisalmer. In the days running up to Holi, children get deliriously excited. On the eve, bonfires of unwanted or dirty possessions symbolise the end of the year and fresh start for the new one. On Holi itself, laws and social conventions are suspended from dawn until noon. Men and women flirt, playing holi by squirting pink water at one another or throwing clouds of pink, mauve, green and saffron powder. The men often a bit merry on alcohol, sing and dance through the streets, banging the dramatic, repetitive rhythm out on a chang (huge drum).

Holi celebrations at Nathdwara are unique but unlike those at Mathura (see p. 000) have little to offer the visitor as they centre on the temple, which is closed to non-Hindus. Here, the black Krishna icon, called Srinath, is dressed in turmuric yellow, a diamond natha on his forehead. On Holi and other days the pichwai (cloth-painting) is drawn back so that hundreds of pilgrims can worship him. Srinath images and pichwais fill the markets of Nathdwara and Udaipur.

Then there are Rajasthan specialities. *Gangaur* (March–April, about two weeks after Holi) is the most important. Gauri (another name for Shiva's wife, Parvati) is the goddess of abundance and fertility. Gauri also means yellow, the colour of ripened wheat. After a fortnight of light-hearted prayer for married bliss and faithfulness to paint wooden images of Gauri, a singing procession takes the Gauri image from her temple for a ceremonial bath in the nearest lake. Shiva then arrives to collect his bride in a pageant of caparisoned horses and elephants. There used to be a big water pageant on Pichola Lake at Udaipur.

Teej (July–August), when there is singing and dancing and women (wearing striped green veils) and children play on flower-bedecked swings hung from trees, is a double celebration: the onset of the monsoon and the reunion of Shiva and his wife, Parvati. This is best at Jaipur, where gaily caparisoned elephants escort the Parvati image from her parents' home to her husband's. The kite festival on January 14th is also spectacular, although kites are flown to a lesser extent at other festivals too. Men and boys expertly fill the sky with bobbing splashes of vibrant colour.

Head for Ajmer for the Muslim festival of *Urs*; nearby Pushkar for the cattle fair (November–ecember); India's biggest livestock fair at Nagaur the Thar Desert, 130km from Jodhpur (January–bruary); and Nag Panchami, in honour of Naga, e serpent king, at Jodhpur (July–August), when omen worship the visiting snake charmers. The cently established Desert Festival at Jaisalmer anuary–February), with camel polo, camel races d desert music and dance, has had a mixed ception.

ietting there: Getting away

ajasthan has three airports: Jaipur, Jodhpur and daipur. The daily early morning shuttle runs lhi – Jaipur – Jodhpur – Udaipur – Aurangabad – mbay (and vice versa) plus a lunchtime flight to daipur and evening flight to Jaipur (which stops Jodhpur, Mon., Wed., Fri.). Be sure to book at gh season, November–January. Otherwise, it is st to travel between cities by car, train or speedy -conditioned buses. All three airport cities make od bases for touring. Alternatively, it is a good ea to arrive at one and leave from another. Car re gives the most freedom and is not exorbitantly iced. Distances are not huge, roads are quite od, and the rural daily life is packed with colour d tradition. Unless the luxurious Palace on heels train, consisting of ex-maharajas' car-ges, improves its programme (which rumour ys it may), it does not stop long enough any-here. Passengers enjoy superficial glimpses of jasthan on a memorable train journey, but to see jasthan properly, they must come again. Far tter, on a short holiday, to take one or two dinary trains. For instance, the Pink City Express m Delhi to Jaipur (departs 5.55am, arrives am); the overnight train from Jodhpur to Jaisal-r; the overnight Super-Fast Express from Delhi Jodhpur (departs 6.10pm, arrives 6.55am); and e morning express from Agra to Jaipur (about rs).

iformation and reservations

set up a trip after arrival in India, go to the ommended Delhi and Bombay travel agents, e pp. 44 and 116. Rajasthan has various chains of od agents. Tourist Guide Service run a string of icient offices and are agents for the big TCI ency; Mirza Ismail Road, Jaipur (tel: 61062); xman Bhawan, Fort Jalmer, Jaisalmer (tel: 150);

Bungalow 15, Old Public Park, Raikabagh, Jodh-pur (tel: 25454); Rajendra Marg, Sharma Sadan, Mount Abu (tel: 201); Chetak Circle, Udaipur (tel: 3526). Mayur Travels, Mirza Ismail Road, Jaipur (tel: 77284), has offices throughout Rajasthan and is efficient. Rajasthan Tours specialise in the area and have a string of offices (Udaipur, Bikaner, Jodhpur), with their headquarters in Jaipur, at the Rambagh Hotel (tel: 76041). A travel agent can book trains, cars, hotels and find out precise cur-rent bus times. His fee is small. It saves hours of effort, or the disappointment of arriving at a full hotel.

Two tours can fill up the biggest palace hotels, so for November–January travellers should book well in advance. On the whole, the government and state tours in each city are good: quality guides give thorough introductions to scattered palaces and forts. Food is not wildly exciting in Rajasthan, except in one or two hotels (see below); it is rarely up to Delhi standards. Several Indians even say they stick to vegetarian food in Rajasthan. If you are in any doubt about hygiene, head for a town's South Indian restaurant. Rajasthan has partial pro-hibition, in this case meaning that national and religious holidays are dry. Nightlife apart from what a hotel organises is usually pretty poor, but the English fortnightly, *Rajasthan Echo*, carries de-tails of what there is. Local tourist offices help find folk dancing and music. Uma Anand's *Guide to Rajasthan* is excellent, as is the *Guide to Rajasthan*, published by the ITDC. Jaipur, the state's capital, has the best shopping for all Rajasthani crafts, but beware of the prices which are geared to unsus-pecting tourists. By bargaining, it is possible to bring the prices right down.

See – and hear – how it's done

Despite the onslaught of tourism into Rajasthan, heavier than anywhere else in India, the vast fund of traditional music, folklore, ritual and crafts thrives across the state. Communities add their own idiosyncrasies to general Rajasthani tra-ditions. It is important to stress that the way to encounter them is to explore the backstreets of cities and, even more so, to go out to the villages, keeping a beady eye on the roadside and not being afraid to ask the car driver to stop if there is something interesting. Here are just a few things to look out for. (Those special to one city are men-tioned with that city's attractions.)

To find a particular sort of musician, dancer or

craftsman, just ask. Tour guides, museum keepers and tourist offices should know what's what. Shopkeepers are especially helpful about where their stock is made and will give precise directions and even sometimes play escort in their spontaneous kindness.

Bhopas The most familiar musician is the itinerant bhopa (balladier), originating from Marwar. Clad in vermilion with matching or saffron turban, he sings and dances with his heavily veiled wife and often his young son, playing his rawanhatta stringed instrument with a short bow tinkling with bells. They perform ad lib, proud to be able to produce the right song for the moment, a birthday, honeymoon, wedding anniversary, etc. They are delighted by requests. Pabuji ka bhopas are a special class (found everywhere except Alwar and Bharatpur), who use the prop of the 13-metre-long cotton Pabuji Ki Phad (scroll-painting ballad) to elaborate upon each scene as they sing heroic poetry and mime-dance, holding an oil lamp up to each intricately painted scene as the story of Pabuja unfolds. The subject is a 13th century hero from Rathore and performances of his deeds are supposed to remove evil influences from homes. Phads, densely illustrated in dominant red, yellow and green, are produced in Chittaugarh and by the joshis of Shahpur. It is best to avoid the smaller panels produced for the tourist in poster colours.

Folk dance In the days leading up to Holi, Gangaur, Teej and marriages, wealthier women dance the ghoomar in streets and villages, moving round in circles and twirling their ghongras (very full skirts). And during the fortnight before Holi, everyone, irrespective of caste, dances the gingad. Men dance the gair to the beat of the chang drum. The ghoomar-gair dance is much faster, the dancers twisting and turning as they strike each others' sticks. The Garasias tribe love dancing, often after a day's work and for days and nights together before Holi. Teratal is closer to ritual acrobatics than dancing. The men sing while the women dance and accompany them simultaneously, playing the 13 cymbals (teratal) tied all over their bodies.

Itinerant entertainers These ply their trade at any wayside hamlet, fair or festival. A man with a dummy silk horse fitted to his waist dances the lok nritaka to the beat of his partner's huge drum. A folk musician plays the morchang (like a Jew's harp). A man dressed up as a monkey amuses passers by; another as the monkey god, Hanuman, howls and chatters and mimics his audience. Acro-

bats walk the tightrope or bend an iron bar with their foreheads.

The nomadic Kalvelias tribe of snake charmers, the women heavily bejewelled, sing, dance and play the been (or punji, made of a gourd) to entice the snake to rise and sway. There are different tunes for different snakes. The Kalvelias have milked the snakes' poison sacs and return them to the wild when the sac refills.

The Kangujri wears a tight pyjama, flowing skirt and conical hat, and calls himself both Radha and Krishna at once, singing songs about them as he travels from door to door. And there are puppeteers and all sorts of bhopas, some with bells, others playing the mashak (a bit like Scottish bag pipes) and others performing feats like piercing a needle through the tongue.

Mendhi The leaves of mendhi (myrtle) have an astonishing array of properties. Dried, crushed and dissolved in sugary water, they are painted on women's hands and feet. The fine, lacey design are highly symbolic, usually related to prosperity and happiness, and are an essential part of Hindu ritual at ceremonies and festivals. Woe betide the woman who forgets her mendhi. It can bring sterility. Failure before Teej festival by a wife whose husband is abroad means he may not return. The mendhi paste put between the palms of a bride and groom at their wedding must turn crimson, or the marriage will be a disaster. A good design on a woman's hand improves her luck and is essential to avert tragedy: the satiya, a reverse swastika motif, is applied just before a mother gives birth. After birth, she will only recover if mendhi applied to her nails. (It does not stop at humans, when a cow gives birth, both cow and calf are painted.) Who applies the mendhi is vital: a barber's wife brings prosperity, especially if five married women sing menhadi songs at the same time. A widow is such bad luck that she cannot even paint herself, let alone others. And so it continues, touching every corner of life. Each motif has a meaning: the scorpion for love; the parrot for separated lovers (it carries their messages); the peacock to be a companion to lonely love; lotus and fish for women's eyes. It is used as a perfume, a medicinal cure for headaches, a dye for cloth or to prevent hair turning grey, and is drunk by singers to improve the voice. It is quite obviously the wonder drug for which the West has been searching.

Kathputli Puppeteering, one of the oldest entertainment forms and possibly the source of India's drama. Formerly entirely nomadic, the puppeteers now spend the monsoon at their homes – villages in the eastern desert areas, where their yajmans (patrons) are. They spend eight months of the year on the road. The cot, or stage, for the performance has an embroidered curtain, gloriously known as Taj Mahal. The shows are at night, about two hours long, performed by the kathputliwala (puppeteer) and his wife. He pulls the strings, she plays a drum and sings the story. Puppeteers carve their own big, wooden puppets (a metre or more tall), then paint and costume them beautifully. Old and new puppets can be found in the bazaars, especially in Jodhpur. Some puppeteers will sell their surplus.

Kavad Brightly painted, wooden, mobile temples of all sizes, with lots of little compartments closed with doors, are carried from village to village by the itinerant kavadia bhat to perform kavad. As he narrates the Ramayana, he opens each door to reveal little paintings of the gods in the story, the finale being, of course, Rama, Lakshmana and Sita. There is a coin slit in the temple for offerings. Old temples are found in antique shops; new ones in Udaipur, Jodhpur and Jaipur.

Barbers Shaving is a public activity, as is dentistry which draws good crowds for tooth extraction. The barber sharpens his knife on a stone (which also cleans it), rubs water on the beard, shaves it off to a silken finish, tidies up the eyebrows and avoids at all costs the carefully nurtured, thick, drooping Rajasthani moustache. As he shaves he wipes the hairs off the knife on to his leg. In former days the hairs would be weighed and the barber would exact an equivalent fee in gold from a rich man, in kind from a poor man. Barbers give a luxuriously smooth shave, almost never breaking the skin. To be shaved is a luxurious treat for a Westerner, and quite safe.

Teeth beauticians An equally public activity. For 50 paise, the beautician will rub ointment on to a patient's teeth and gums, then clean and improve the teeth, shaping them with a strange assortment of files. If necessary, he replaces a missing tooth.

Meenakari The art of enamelling. The highest quality and quantity crafted is to be found at Jaipur, the meenakari centre. Delicate patterns of birds and flowers in ruby red, deep green and peacock blue on a brilliant white ground are fired on to elaborate gold earrings, pendants, cosmetic boxes, attardans (perfume holders) and other objets d'art. The grander ones are then made more glittering with white sapphires and dangling natural pearls;

the cheaper ones use silver or copper in place of gold.

The art is also practised in other Rajasthani cities, such as Amber and Nathdwara, and in Delhi and Varanasi. Indian meenakari, similar to European champ-levé work, was introduced by the Mughals – although Queen Aahhotep of Egypt was adorning herself with enamel jewellery in 1700BC. Heights of perfection were reached in the Mughal court ateliers, the envy of all. Towards the end of the 16th century, Raja Man Singh lured five meenakaars (enamelwork craftsmen) from Lahore to his capital at Amber. Their descendants still work in the new capital, Jaipur.

The method is painstakingly slow, precise and demands top quality materials – a master meenakaar takes 15 days just to enamel both sides of a pendant. First, the goldsmith copies old designs to make the object. He uses 23½ carat gold and a touch of copper, so that it does not melt during firing. On to the surface he solders tiny moulds for the gems. Then the meenakaar takes over. His aim is to achieve the most glowing colours, mixing secret potions of metal oxides (cobalt for blue, iron for green) in a vitreous base. He used to use finely ground precious stones. Each enamel colour is pulverised, then made into a paste. The meenakaar engraves his miniature arabesques and birds on to the gold, chisels out tiny flat fields and fills them with the enamel paste, applying it dot by dot with a stylus. As each colour is completed, the piece is fired, starting with red, which sustains heat best, and ending with white, which is liable to run. The firing is extremely tricky: too hot and the gold will melt; too cool and the enamel will not melt enough to fuse. After the kiln, a bath of water and acid reveals the success of the colour.

When all the colours are done, they are buffed with a corrundum stone (like a sapphire) to smooth the surfaces. Then to the gem setter for kundan (gem setting) in pure gold leaf. After several months and considerable skill, the object is complete.

Craftsmen can be found most easily in Jaipur back streets. Master meenakaar Deen Dayalji works with his sons and pupils in his haveli, Gopalji ka Rasta in Memiyon ki Gali, a very narrow alley. Kudrat Singh is another Jaipur master meenakaar. Nathdwara work tends to use silver, making it cheaper. Cheaper meenakari can be found in the bazaars. A jeweller is best for bigger buys.

Lacquered brassware A combination of applied

lacquer and engraving to decorate brass trays, bowls, dishes and vases, the grander pieces of which are silver or gold plated. To make the object, shapes are cut from brass sheets, soldered together and refined with tools. For the complicated patterns (the more refined and intricate the better), the engraver first sketches the scheme on the brass. With his tools he chases the pattern, raising parts by repoussée, indenting parts by embossing, engraving fine arabesques and details. The craftsman makes his own sticks of lac for colour and, after applying them, buffs them up to a metallic shimmer.

Leatherwork Mojadis (slippers), often made of camelskin, are decorated with embroidered designs, the cobbler working in his bazaar shop. Shoes can be made to order, with special designs, as can water bottles and handbags.

Pottery In the villages, potters make the big storage and water pots. The clay is a rough mixture of earth, water and dung (for fibre and strength), pounded by a woman of the household. The potter throws the clay on a huge stone, perhaps a metre in diameter, whirling on just a wooden peg. The stone's weight maintains the momentum for a good long spin, sped with a stick if necessary. He then roughly shapes about 30 pots in the early morning, leaving them to dry for about eight hours before beating them into exact shape, using a hammer on the outside and a pummel inside. After more drying, the women decorate them with simple designs, using mineral paints. When the kiln is full, they are fired, then distributed around the village. The surplus are taken to market.

Bandhana The very ancient Indian technique of tie-dyeing fabrics, seen throughout Rajasthan and Gujarat. Rajasthani women wear bandhana or wood-block patterned odhnis or pilos (head veils) over their cholas (short-sleeved, tight-fitting blouses) and ghongras (very full skirts), some ten metres round. Every community has its own designs, the man drawing the patterns, the women and children tightly binding all his dots, some pinhead small, before dying the fabric. The strings are then untied to reveal the pattern. The more complex the design, the tinier the dots and the more precisely tie-dyed, the more the article is worth. But the colours have universal significance: yellow for spring and fertility; nila (indigo) for Krishna; hari nila (a paler blue) for water; gerua (saffron) for the wise man and poet who renounces worldly things.

In towns, the merchants supply the fabric and

designs to families. Women and children as youn as six work them, their nimble fingers tying whole veil in one day for about Rs2. The fabric the goes to the dyer before the merchant sells the veil at Rs60 a piece – a tidy profit. There is an enormou variety of patterns and quality: cheap bandhan work can be found in markets; top quality in shop

Block-printing Fabric printed with carve wooden blocks on borders, in circles or all ove Practised in Gujarat, Rajasthan and neighbourin states, and in the South, but most lively in Raja than. In its heyday, the tiny village of Sangane outside Jaipur, was known as the 'Metropolis Calico-Printing'. The colours of the design ar separated on to tracing paper, then pricked on t the wood by the block-maker. He then cuts it o with hammer and chisel. Precision is essential: on mistake and a new block must be cut. The cheepa (hand block printers) really prefer vegetable an mineral colours and boil up their evil-smellin witches' brews. To make black, they take iror charcoal, molasses and flour and boil the together for 15 days – one feels they might we throw in a frog and chant a spell for good measure

Printing is often done in a long, barn-like buil ing with high windows and built-in niches to sto the blocks. The whole length of fabric – fine musli to heavy cotton – is pinned on to long, spong padded table tops. The first colour is printed rig along, by which time the beginning is dry enoug for the second colour, then a third, fourth, eve fifth shade. The printer depends entirely on his ey and a steady hand to get the flowers, trees, an mals, houses, birds and stripes clear and accurat After boiling to make the design fast, the fabric sometimes khari printed.

Khari-printing Embossed printing in gold or si ver, usually in delicate floral designs, each mot individually printed by the chipa (khari-printer) o to plain or printed fabric. The process is usuall done in a special room, the air twinkling with gol like dust caught in a sunray. In bazaar lanes, th khari printers will emboss borders on people skirts, blouses and dresses very quickly for a tir charge.

Screen-printing The modern, speedy version block-printing. Whereas it takes four people block-print eight four-coloured saris in a day, thos same four can screen-print 160 similar saris in day, increasing output 20-fold. In addition, wooden block wears out fast and even on day on has a fuzzy outline compared to a screen-print. Th practical set-up is much the same as for block rinting but the printer just hooks the printing ames on to alignment pegs on either side of the ng tables to ensure a precise match.

hurrie-weaving see p. 66.

he cities: Where to stay; ut and about

possible, it is nicer to stay at least three days referably longer) in the bigger cities to really see eir old fortresses, museums, palaces, bazaars, rrounding forts and villages. And it is important leave time for amusement and relaxation staying the dream palaces of princes and the homes of bles.

astern Rajasthan

IPUR

59km from Delhi, 228km from Agra. Bustling, onkey-filled, oleander pink, toytown capital of ajasthan. A perfect piece of humanist town lanning laid out in 1728 by Maharaja Jai ngh II (1699–1744) and his architect, Vidyadhar hakravarti. A grid system of very wide tree-ned avenues, and a surrounding crenolated wall ith seven gates, follow the principles of the Hin-u architectural treatise, Shilpa-Shastra. Airy, flat nd ordered, it is a complete contrast to the old lltop fort capital, Amber, where the rulers had ccumulated vast wealth and influence, substan-ally increased from the moment the wily Mughal onqueror Akbar created his first Rajput alliance by arrying the charming Amber princess in 1562.

Jai Singh II marked the Jaipur rulers' switch from arring to cultural living. Enthroned at the age of , he was a precocious and shrewd politician ho, within the year, had won from Emperor urangzeb the hereditary title Sawai, meaning ne and a quarter, to indicate his superiority over s contemporaries. He was an aesthete, architect, ngineer, astronomer, inventor, mathematician nd patron of art and music. In his new city, aders and craftsmen had their own areas and stinctive architecture, painted a variety of col-rs. The city's coat of warm pink is a 19th century decoration job.

In addition to its monuments, several floodlit at ght, Jaipur is the Rajasthan city best equipped ith hotels, restaurants, information and shops. It also the final point of the fly-by-night tourist's olden Triangle, Delhi-Agra-Jaipur, of which the

local citizens can take undue advantage. Beware of over-pricing and over-booking. Hotels are best booked in advance and it is advisable to arrive clutching the written confirmation.

THE HARD FACTS There are two top-notch places to stay, one for playing princes, the other for central location.

The Rambagh Palace, Bhawani Singh Road (tel: 75141; telex: 36254 RBAG IN; cable: RAMBAGH); former main palace of Maharaja Man Singh II (1911–1970, known as Jai to his friends) who, in 1957, was the first to enter the palace hotel game; run by the Taj chain since 1972. Maharaja Ram Singh (1835–80) developed a small hunting lodge out of some pleasure pavilions outside the city walls, embellished by Madho Singh II (1880–1922). Besotted with England after attending Edward VII's coronation in 1902 (see p. 77), he added the deep herbaceous borders (glorious January–March), squash and tennis courts, indoor swim-ming pool with trapeze swing and, being a polo fanatic, a private polo field next door. (After break-ing an arm, he turned to flying and built his own aerodrome.)

His adopted son and successor, Jai, lived here and, while he was at Woolwich Training Academy in 1931, had it enlarged and modernised to be his official residence, with further up-datings when he married his third wife in 1940, Gayatri Devi (Ayesha to friends).

A beautiful princess from Cooch Behar in North-East India, she shot her first leopard at the age of 12, enjoyed London society as a teenager and returned to marry the Maharaja. After Indepen-dence, she was elected MP in 1962 for the oppo-sition Swatantra Party with a majority of 175,000, the largest ever in a democratic country, and now lives at Lillypool, a house in the Rambagh gardens. In her autobiography, she recalls being vastly im-pressed when she visited the Maharaja's first two wives there in the winter of 1932, not expecting 'the furnishings . . . would be so modern and have such an air of sophistication; they could have been anywhere, in England or Europe or Calcutta'. Many rooms are exactly the same today: the latest and most boldly stylish rugs, lamps, built-in elec-tric fires and chaises-longues that high 1930s de-sign could produce. Unfortunately, the delightful period atmosphere has been destroyed in the re-cently refurbished rooms (new fitted carpets, etc.), and they are to be avoided.

104 large rooms, plus modest health club, beauty

salon, business services, good travel agent, car rental, shopping arcade, the above sports facilities and camel riding and golf on request, and magnificent, well-maintained gardens with Lalique fountains, folk dancers and musicians performing during the day and evening. It is best to go for a room overlooking the gardens; and it is worth splashing out on one of the 16 suites, especially the Maharaja's, with superb fittings and black marble bathroom, and the Maharani's, both decorated in honour of his 1940 wedding. Service can be sleepy. Avoid the new Garden Wing and back rooms. Try samosas on the lawns, pucka tea and cakes on deep verandahs, and cocktails in the Polo Bar. Lofty dining room with Indian musicians (lunch and dinner) accompanying variable food (Indian and Continental).

Mansingh, Sansar Chandra Road (tel: 78771; telex: 036344 WLCO IN; cable: WELCOMOTEL). Central (just off Agra Road, good for shops), opened 1978, very well designed and decorated by Welcomgroup (Rajasthani tie-dye and embroidered mirror work, etc.); 100 rooms, all mod. cons include travel agent, car rental, beauty salon, shopping arcade, golf/tennis/riding/polo by arrangement; good ground floor restaurant, excellent rooftop Shiver restaurant, bar and terrace with stunning views, top quality Mughlai and vegetarian food enjoyed with equally good Indian ghazals (light songs) at lunch and dinner. Locals' requests keep the musicians and singer going into the early hours. Efficient service; swimming pool and health club being built for 1985; sadly, no garden.

Others: **Rajmahal Palace**, off Hawa Sarak Road (tel: 61257/8/9; telex 036 313 JAI IN; cable: RAJMAHAL); Used as the British Residency from 1921; later used by the Maharaja after leaving the Rambagh. Here, handsome Jai and glamorous Ayesha entertained such fellow celebrities as John and Jackie Kennedy and the Queen and Prince Philip. The Jaipur royals' furnishings, trophies, paintings, knick-knacks and photographs throughout provide a very good atmosphere; 14 spacious rooms, ground floor deluxe suite recommended. Deep verandahs and extensive gardens, nice pool, tennis and squash courts. Rather shambolically run. The food and dining room are dull (formerly excellent).

The thakurs (nobles) of the Jaipur court lived in fine houses built on land given by the maharajas to their concubines. Some of their descendants are now hard-up and, having sold land and pos-

sessions, run their family homes as small hotel Great charm, original furnishings, painted wall libraries and gardens. All rooms have fans (a fe have air-cooling systems) and bathrooms (usual just shower, not tub). A few of the especial pleasant ones are listed below.

Narain Niwas, Kanota Bagh, Narain Singh Roa (tel: 65448; cable: NARAINIWAS). Rajput have built in 1881 by Narain Singh Ji, now run by M Mohan Singh. Rich fin de siècle interior with fou poster beds, chandeliers, Afghan carpets, pair ings and East India Company furniture. 17 room (one with wall-paintings of fantasy colonnade and two garden cottages (with plans to expand), rooms air-cooled, clean throughout, terraces ar garden. Good food cooked as and when requeste

Achrol Lodge, Civil Lines Road (tel: 72254). Gent Mr Mahandra Singh runs his handsome, simp furnished, peaceful family home with big lawn shady trees. 8 rooms, all with fans, some wi delicate tracery wall-painting. They only ser breakfast and Indian dinner.

Bissau Palace, Chandpole Gate (tel: 74191/6772 cable: HOBI). Excellent location for walled cit Run by Mr and Mrs Sanjay Singh, descended fro the Bissaus, a Rajput family from Shekhava Beautifully maintained library and drawing roon (family trophies, silver, swords), with a garde and small swimming pool. Lively atmosphere. rooms, all with fans, 24-hour refreshments. Goo food includes Rajasthani dishes.

Khetri House, Chandpole Gate (tel: 69183; cabl KHETRIHOUSE). Next to Bissau Palace, Ra Bahadur Sardar Singhji-Khetri's 1930s haveli in huge secluded garden. Drawing room with hig 1930s plaster relief of elephants. Run by Mr N bhaya Singh. 13 very simple, clean rooms, all wi fans. Food not great.

Tourist information from the Government of Raja than Tourist Office, C Scheme (tel: 74857/7387. and at the Railway Station (tel: 69714); and Saw Ram Singh Road (tel: 72345). Government of Ind Tourist Office at Rajasthan State Hotel (tel: 6545 72200). Both RTDC and ITDC run good five-ho tours with the focus on Amber Fort and then th City Palace, Observatory and City Museum. R commended. RTDC also do a full day tour. Bo offer inexpensive guides. Rajasthan Tours at th Rambagh will help with specialist guiding, such to nobles' houses, or around the back streets or see crafts. Cultural programmes are held in Rave dra Manch, near Albert Hall. To find out what ing on, read the *Rajasthan Echo* or ask at a tourist fice. Several good bookshops on the west side of haura Rasta (Usha, Arvind, Best Book).

Sports facilities are the best in Rajasthan. All otels can arrange tennis/squash/riding/polo. Polo especially important in Jaipur: the season is nuary–March, when five big tournaments are eld. There is also elephant polo (the day before oli), camel polo and bicycle polo. Fishing at amgarh Lake (30km, used for the Asian Games chting competitions), permit from Gangaur ourist Bungalow (tel: 74373) or Fisheries Project ffice, Tonk Road (tel: 76253). Jaipur Flying Club ffiliated to Delhi Flying Club). Swimming at ambagh Palace open to non-residents for Rs20.

Rajasthan Mounted Sports Association, undlod House, Civil Lines (tel: 66276/66147), run y young locals, can set up a wide range of sports d safaris: polo, riding, horse safaris through ajasthan (7–12 days) and to Pushkar Fair (3 days). ey can also set up re-creations of Holi, Diwali, en a complete 'Princely Wedding' for up to 50 ople to attend, with caparisoned elephant and orse procession, 14-man band, fireworks display, actors in the full dress and jewellery of princes d princesses, the wedding ceremony performed y a Brahmin, and a dinner – yours for only $4,000. at there is no restriction on numbers for their ephant spectacle: a procession of 20 caparisoned ephants, 9 camels and much more, followed by ephant racing and elephant polo. It costs $2,400.

UT AND ABOUT   There is a lot to see in and ound Jaipur but it is nicest to start by going out of wn up to the old fort city of Amber (11km, see low), the capital before Jaipur was built. On turn, start with Jai Singh's model palace.

ity Palace complex   Described by the Maharaja Baroda as 'the most daring and successful synesis of Moghul and Rajput styles'. Begin on the utside with the Hawa Mahal (Palace of the inds), a lace-like five-storey building in the alace wall, one room deep, built in 1799 so that the yal women in purdah could watch the world utside from its 593 niches and windows without e world watching them. Open daily, 10am–5pm, imb to the top for views.

Inside, there are the palace rooms, museum, ntar Mantar (Observatory) and Govind Devi emple, set in gardens and courtyards – part still cupied by the Maharaja. White marble elephants ard the private apartments. A silver urn that

stored Ganga water for Madho Singh's trip to England stands inside. The two-tiered doorways of the main courtyard are totally encrusted with coloured stones. Rooms of the seven-storeyed Changra Mahal (Moon Palace, good view from top), are decorated with wall-paintings of flowers and figures, pachikari-kakam and kanch work (see Amber, p. 89). In the Maharaja Sawai Man Singh II Museum, founded 1959 and housed in palace rooms and recently enlarged, do not miss the textiles and musical instruments in the Zenana, the carpets in the Diwan-i-Am, the Mughal and Rajasthani paintings, the transport collection, the changing exhibitions from the vast and fascinating collection of royal photographs and, of course, the armour, probably the finest in India. Good publications. Open daily, 9.30am–4.30pm, except public holidays and festivals.

Outside the large gateway is the strangely contemporary-looking *Jantar Mantar* Instrument Formula. Jai Singh II was the first Indian astronomer to depart from the Hindu emphasis on theory in preference to observation; the first to build an observatory in India; and the first to make contact with European astronomers. (The Jesuit expedition Jai Singh II sent to Europe in 1730 returned with the latest astronomical gadget, the telescope.) Mohammad Shah entrusted him to revise the lunar calendar and correct the astrological tables, for the smoother working of religion and empire alike. He made daily observations, sent astronomers abroad on research, consulted with his guru Pandit Jagannath, and translated Euclid and read Ptolomy before he began building five sets of outsized astronomical instruments resembling cubist sculptures for a children's playground.

The first was at Delhi (1724–27). The one at Jaipur (1728–34) is the largest and best preserved, because of its marble lining. Ujjain, Varanasi and Mathura (destroyed) followed, being the ancient centres of religion and learning. Jaipur's device has recently been restored to look even more like cubist toys. Each structure has a different purpose: the large, circular Ram Yatras are for reading altitudes and azimuths (distances in the sky); the 12 Rashivilayas for calculating celestial latitudes and longitudes; the Samrat Yantra (Supreme Instrument) is a vast gnomon (right-angle triangle) that acts as a sundial for measuring solar time by reading its shadow on the quadrants either side (accurate to within 15 seconds). Open daily, 9am–5pm.

At the *Govind Devi Temple*, it is possible to see puja (worship) being performed: devout local ladies wait for the temple doors to open, then witness the images of Krishna and Radha enacting their daily lives, such as waking up (5.15am) or having their clothes changed (10.30am), followed by jolly music and processions. Ceremonies, lasting about 30 minutes, are daily at 5.15am, 8.15am, 10.30am, 12 noon, 5.15pm, 6.30pm, 8pm.

Central Museum The collection begun in 1833 and housed in the gloriously named Albert Hall, founded by one baronet in 1887, designed by another, Sir Swinton Jacob. It is as educational in its aims as its namesake in South Kensington, London. It houses examples of everything connected with Rajasthani life, from puppets and costumes to brasswork, woodwork, jewellery and models showing how a horse works, all very well labelled. Ask to see the Carpet Museum, housed in the detached Durbar Hall at the front of Albert Hall and kept under lock and key. Fabulous carpets include the huge persian Garden Carpet of c. 1632, the design a bird's eye view of a garden, with water, ducks, birds feeding their young in trees and sporting animals. (Ask for the good booklet on it, by H. P. Vaish.) In Ram Niwas Gardens, open Sat.–Thurs., 10am–5pm, packed on Sunday.

There are other Jaipur palaces and forts to see. The *Nahargah (Tiger) Fort* was mainly built by Jai Singh II in 1734 as a retreat from his maharanis. It is reached by jeep (6.5km) or, for a nice evening stroll, up a short-cut paved route north-west of the City Palace, past goat-herds descending at sunset. Superb views (small café).

En route to Amber, the impressive *Jaipur chhatris* (cenotaphs) are at Gaitor (8km). Jai Singh II's has a dome, pillars and peacock carvings. Just beyond is Jalmahal, a ruined pleasure palace built in Man Sagar Lake, best seen from another ruined palace on the lake edge, along with the buffalos lounging among the waterweed. The charming little *Sisodia Rani Palace* (8km), murals on the exterior, terraced gardens below, with fountains and pools, was built in 1774 by Maaji Chundawt Sisodia. *Ramgarh* (25km) hilltop fort was the stronghold before Amber. There is also a temple, Art Deco villa and boating. (And there are rumours that it is to be developed as a health resort.)

RESTAURANTS The *Mansingh's Shiver* is without doubt the best for Mughlai food, with the bonus of good music and view. The *Rambagh* is lovely for a snack or tea. In the dining hall, ask for Rajasthani sulla (barbecued mutton). If in Johari bazaar, go to *LMB* for excellent vegetarian food

and the best sweetmeats in Jaipur (local specialitie are firni, misri mawa and, in winter, halwa) and selection of home-made ice creams big enough t impress queues of discerning American travellers In Mirza Ishmail Marg (known as MI Marg), which flanks the south wall of the city, *Niro's* an *Chanayka* (formerly Kohinoor) have good reputations for north Indian food – kebabs, tandoors etc. – and *Kwality* is safe, clean, run-off-the-mill.

SHOPPING AND CRAFTS Crafts still thriv from the days of Jai Singh's patronage, when h designed special areas for the bandhanas, cheepa and meenakari workers. The bazaars are concen trated to the south of the walled city. Other shop are on M I Marg and Agra Road. It is best to avoi the vastly over-priced shops opposite the Haw Mahal (except for charming raconteur Pritan Singh, who sits on the pavement selling handful of agate and moonstone for a twentieth of the pric in the shops behind him). Do beware of antiqu shops in Jaipur. As one shopkeeper said, a twinkl in his blue eyes: 'Some of my things are really old But what I do is make new pieces with old design and then treat them to give them the antiqu touch.'

At Sanganer Gate, there are the kite shops. To b the patang-undane wala guru (master kite-flyer o the community) is a big thing in Rajasthan. Nearb Bapu Bazaar (closed Monday) has cheap, fu meenakari jewellery (see above) plus some of th more expensive pieces; and bandhani, block an screen print fabric shops, including work from Sanganer, sold by sari length and by the metre Colour ranges are both the traditional sombre eart reds, oranges and browns as well as shockin stripes and large polka dots in citrus yellow, har red and bright green. Good selections at Yashdev no. 7, and Mona Prints, no. 28 – shop owners wil direct you to craftsmen. There are embroidere mojadis (leather slippers) in Nehru bazaar (close Wednesday).

In the wide Johari bazaar plain cotton, in daz zling peacock blue, sunshine yellow, April gree and magenta, and bandhani work are sold b weight in various qualities of cloth. On the sam street and in two tiny alleys off it, Gopalji Ka Rast and Haldiyon Ka Rasta, there are silversmiths an semi-precious stones (bargain hard). It is interest ing to watch the lapidary turning stones with a bov attached to the grinding wheel, using metal disc and abrasives to cut the facets.

In the back streets, poke into the courtyards t

ind leather-workers and sweet-makers, look up to see women's co-operatives printing on roof-tops, and notice the pretty facades, with delicate designs on the pink plasterwork and overhanging balconies. Chaura Rasta and Tripolia bazaars stock fabrics and quantities of tin for jolly costume jewellery bangles.

On M I Marg, serious jewellery and stone buying can be done at Gem Palace, established for generations, or Lall Gems and Jewels, from Agra, both reliable, helpful and charming. Fair prices (about 10% of London prices) for semi-precious stones; and a smoky topaz as big as a pigeon's egg for a few rupees, cut and polished garnets, yellow topaz, amethyst, black stars, most of them brought down from Kashmir. Bhuram Rajamah Surana, a jeweller in Johari Bazaar, is all right too. Locals shop at the Central Cottage Industries Emporium and the Rajasthan Handicrafts Emporium, where quality is high but there is none of the fun of seeking out a treasure for oneself.

To see dhurrie-weaving (see p. 66), ask at the emporia or go to Art Age, C-34 Lajpat Marg, Bhagwandas Road (tel: 75726) and Mr Vijaivargia will take you to some of his weaving families working in Jaipur. His weavers will make dhurries to order using traditional or modern designs drawn out full size on squared paper and painted in watercolours; any mistake and the rug is completed and sold off cheaper. Modern designs include harlequin squares, like an American patchwork, tigers and elephants and floral motifs.

SANGANER

6km south from Jaipur on the Tonk road.

In addition to the different fabric printing techniques, the meenakari work, brasswork and leatherwork, all practised in Jaipur, anyone interested in crafts should nip out here. The ruined palace can be found through the triple gateways. The small, sandy, camel-filled town is fascinating for seeing block, screen and khari printing (see above), block cutting in the bazaar shops, papermaking (ask at A L Paper House, Sanganer bazaar) and Jaipur blue pottery being turned (ask at Jaipur India Blue Art Potteries, Laxmi Colony, Sanganer). **Paper-making** Practised in the kagazi mohulla area), mainly by Muslims. Paper-making complements the cotton and silk rag trade as it uses its waste (some comes from work for the European shops Monsoon and Anokhi). The stone machinery is in rooms off family homes whose courtyards are reminiscent of the Merchant-Ivory film, 'The

Householder', with chickens pecking, children playing, women cooking and weaving straw jalis (mats). The rags are churned with water and bleached in a circular stone vat until they are pulp; strained, sieved and dried; then moved to square vats for dying and rinsing. Then a wooden ladder and a jali are floated on the liquid surface while the slurry is stirred furiously with a wooden stick. It settles between the wood and the mat which are removed, the slurry clinging to the mat. The mat is then placed on a thin muslin sheet and drawn away with a quick twitch. When the pile of wet sheets between the muslin is high enough, it is pressed. The sheets are then pegged up to dry, perhaps dyed, then painted with starch, trimmed and finished (in many grades from silky to rough). The beautiful gold and silver speckling, seen on the album leaves of Mughal paintings in museums, is done last.

Jaipur blue pottery Superficially like the Delhi blue pottery (see p. 62) and sharing the Persian influence of elegant shapes decorated with lapis, turquoise and ultramarine floral designs on a white ground. But the pottery material is different and the designs are much richer, incorporating birds, animals and faces into the floral patterns, using a fine, squirrel-hair brush.

AMBER

11km from Jaipur on the Jaipur–Delhi road, past Gaitor, past hills whose every peak is fortified, between cliffs of wild bouganvillea to the magnificent *fortress-palace* which seems to grow out of the rocky hill rising above Maota Lake, where cranes, ducks, buffalo and farmers cool off. Former capital of the entensive Jaipur state until Jai Singh II moved down to the plains, the site was won by the Rajputs in 1037. But the fort was not built until 1592, by Raja Man Singh I, commander in Akbar's army, and completed by his successor, Jai Singh I.

The stern exterior of ramparts and terraces belies the jewelled interior whose richness increases as the small rooms get higher, up to the Sheesh Mahal (Hall of Mirrors). There are taks (niches) for gold and silver ornaments; walls painted with floral dadoes, floor borders and cornices; distemper wall-paintings of hunting and battle scenes.

To make the walls shine, powdered marble, egg shells and even pearls were added to the last coat of paint. More lavish apartments have ceilings and walls encrusted with pachikari-kakam, convex pieces of coloured mirror glass set in patterns in the plaster, and with kanch work, larger pieces of mirror outlined with vermilion, gold and silver. This mirror work is found also at Jaipur and Jodhpur, but the finest is here, outlining cyprus trees and delicate arabesques.

The doors of the old zenana are elaborately carved with arabesques inlaid with ivory. There are latticed galleries, mosaics, stained glass windows, a rooftop garden and fine views (best from Jai Mandir, the Hall of Victory). Everything is star-spangled and shimmering.

At the white marble Sila Devi Temple, puja is regularly performed with clanging bells and beating drums. Beyond the square where people take elephant rides, through an arch, there is a path down to the pretty village. Open daily, 9.30am–5.30pm, best to go up to the fort by jeep rather than elephant – save that for the top.

ALWAR

143km from Jaipur or Delhi. Driving between the two cities, Alwar is a stop on the slightly longer and prettier route. Crowned by another hilltop fort, Alwar only became free from Jaipur in 1776, forming one of the last Rajput states. Alliance with the British considerably helped its dynastically unstable life during which, somehow, a cluster of fine palaces were constructed at the foot of the hill, extravagant tiger shoots were held on hunting elephants, and elaborate pageantry filled the streets.

Vinai Vilas, the City Palace, (1840), is a sensitive marriage of Mughal proportions with Rajput decoration; stables could hold 3,000 thoroughbreds from India and England, and the treasury housed state jewels that included a cup cut out of a single diamond. Now it is a fine museum of more than 7,000 manuscripts and good Mughal and Rajasthani miniature paintings, many from the outstanding royal library, and good armour, textiles and musical instruments. (Open Sat.–Thurs., 10am–4.30pm). The House of the Elephant carriage, to the right of the palace, was designed to carry 50 people and be hauled by four elephants. There is a splendid view from the top of the ruined fort. See the Purjan Vihar garden and summer house, the royal chhatris, the temples and pavilions beside the tanks.

Worth seeing also is Yeshwant Niwas, an Italianate palace built by Maharaja Jey Singh. Disliking it on completion, he never lived there but instead built in 1927 Vijay Mandir, a 105-room palace beside Vijay Sagar (Lake of Victory), where the ex-royals still live (partly open to the public). Nearby

is Siliserh Lake, 'full of crocodiles' according to Murray's Handbook, huge and pretty, with waterside chhatris and a palace (open to the public), just right for a picnic. The palace is now a hotel, with facilities for boating and fishing.

Bharatpur: 174km from Jaipur, 100km from Alwar, see p. 67.
Deeg: 192km from Jaipur, 89km from Alwar, see p. 67.

SHEKHAVATI

Literally, Garden of Shekha, a 15th century ruler of this area in north-east Rajasthan which lies within the triangle of Delhi, Bikaner and Jaipur. Recent pioneer work by Francis Wacziarg and Aman Nath has put the area on the map (see bibliography p. 107). Here, in more than 360 villages, lived the wealthy Marwaris who, in the 19th century, built themselves grand havelis and covered them inside and out with lively frescos, like life-size miniature paintings. They are a catalogue of their lives, fashions, habits and the latest news. They show the camel as a means of transport forsaken for the horse carriage, a car, a train and finally the 'flying ship' of the Wright brothers. Queen Victoria in mourning is recorded, as is the visit of King George V and Queen Mary to India.

The Marwaris, originally from Marwar further west, were the merchant communities who prospered on the caravan trade routes between Delhi and the coast and between central Asia and China. Their name later became synonymous with the Rajasthan merchant class. With their money they financed and served the princely courts which in turn protected them, so there was mutual benefit. They were also extravagant patrons and had an in-built philanthropic sense, building not only immensely grand painted havelis to impress their friends and amuse their women, who were not permitted to go outside, but also schools, wells and reservoirs.

Then, in the mid-19th century, came problems. The British, who had overshadowed the princely courts, created customs barriers to cut off the entrepot markets and introduced new British goods to compete with Indian products. At the same time came the Opium Wars (1839–42), decline in indigo trading because of German synthetic dyes and the replacement of overland trade routes by water and rail.

So the canny Marwaris upped sticks and went

f to the ports, where the money was. They did
ot make for Bombay, where competition in the
370s was stiff, but east, taking with them their
rong business traits of financial conservatism,
cial orthodoxy and generous willingness to
romote others in their community.

And they prospered. So, when the British began
elling out in Calcutta, the buyer was often a
Marwari. G. D. Birla was one who left his family in
lani to go to live in Calcutta; his descendants are
ow one of the richest families in India. The
odars and Goenkas are two other powerful
Marwari families. Indeed, Thomas A. Timberg
stimated that 'more than half the assets in the
odern sector of the Indian economy are control-
d by the trading castes originating in the northern
alf of Rajasthan'.

However successful a Marwari is, he often feels
hekhavati is still his home, so many havelis are
aintained there – or at least have guardians.
hese walled town mansions have rooms facing
wards to two or more courtyards, the mardana
r the men, the zenana for the women. The main
oorway may be fortress-like, of heavy carved
ood embellished with brass and iron fittings.
here was not much furniture, but the facades,
ateways, courtyard walls, parapets and ceilings
ere covered with paintings worked in a quality
esco technique similar to the Italian method, that
as kept many remarkably well preserved.

The paintings date from the 18th century but the
ajority were produced 1830–1900, often by men
ho had followed their fortune to the ports but left
eir hearts – and, initially, their families – in
hekhavati where they continued to build and
ecorate. Early images of local legends and religion
ature portraits of Krishna and Radha, Hanuman,
akshmi – all Rajput favourites – and always
anesh above the entrance. The Birla ancestral
ome, Shiv Narayan Birla (now a small museum),
t Pilani, built in 1864, has a parade of elephants on
e facade. The paintings of the later Goenka haveli
Mandawa, about 1870, show the development
more ornamental designs, every inch covered
ith polychrome floral patterns, tromp l'oeil
rchitecture and pictures.

HE HARD FACTS Drive around the area for
wo or three days, looking at havelis and forts,
taying at a choice of three places: Castle Mandawa,
ved by Delhi diplomats, built 1755, beautiful
ooms, original furnishings (bolsters, striped dhur-
ies), fine views over Mandawa's havelis, 15
rooms, all with bath, hot water arranged during
winter months; Dundlod Fort, same period, slightly
less grand but comfortable; Roop Niwas Haveli,
Nawalgarh, built early 20th century, less character
but a wonderful town. Booking by cable or letter;
the two forts get busy at week-ends. Take picnic
lunches. Winter nights get cold. Be sure to rent a
good car with a driver who knows the area and
how his car works; garages are scarce.

OUT AND ABOUT A trip from Jaipur could
include some of the following. Day one, take a
picnic and set off for Fatehpur, 160km away. Just
out of Jaipur spot Chaumu fort, then take a detour
right to Samod, through the narrow lanes to the
remarkable palace with its elaborately painted
rooms, gilding, meenakari work and louvred windows so that the women could listen without being
seen.

Then pause at Sikar to find the old quarter near
the Clock Tower, with the Biyani havelis of Wedg-
wood blue, the Jubilee Hall, the temple converted
from a palace and the fort (with a portrait of Queen
Victoria as Empress of India). Stop at Lachhmangarh
for a picnic inside the hilltop fort – asking the
chaukidar (keeper) to close the gates for peace;
glorious views over town below and Shekhavati
beyond.

To Fatehpur. Lively, many painted havelis include superb Devra and Singhania havelis, with
mirrorwork and Japanese tiles. Then backtrack via
Lachhmangarh to Mukundgarh, built around the
temple square, local handicrafts in market.
Then to Mandawa: to stay in the huge fort (c.1755).
Stunning views and old frescoes, havelis in the
bazaar, more havelis of Chokhanis, Goenkas and
Sarafs.

Day two, to Ramgarh (the Podar chhatri) via
Fatehpur; to Mahansar for the best haveli of all –
Soni Chandi Ki Haveli, the showroom of the gold
and silversmiths; to Bissau (painted chhatris, havelis plus fort); and to Jhunjhunun to see Modi and
Tibdiwala havelis, the Chhe (six) Haveli complex
and the Rani Sati Temple where the Marwaris
gather for the annual fair. (North-east of here is
Pilani, the Birla haveli museum, about 80km; Delhi
is 180km beyond.) Nawalgarh has hundreds of
havelis. Catch the frescoed telephone exchange
and the aerial view of Jaipur painted in the fort
dome (ask for it to be unlocked) and finally to
Dundlod (another Goenka haveli).

Bissau connects with Bikaner (205km); from
Nawalgarh, the road returns to Jaipur via Sikar

(138km) or to Delhi (230–260km, depending on the route chosen).

Central and southern Rajasthan

AJMER

131km from Jaipur; 198km from Jodhpur; 302km from Udaipur. Sacred Muslim shrine in a crowded, walled, lakeside town beneath Taragarh Hill, an important Muslim pilgrimage centre in Hindu-dominated Rajasthan. Mahmud of Ghazni may have sacked it in 1024 and Mohammed Gori in 1193, but for the Mughal emperors it was a religious and strategic centre. Akbar, who annexed it in 1556 and built a palace, came annually, often partly on foot (see p. 67). Sir Thomas Roe presented his credentials to Jehangir here in 1616, marking, according to some, the foundation of the British Empire in India. From 1818 it was a small area of Rajasthan controlled directly by the British and not via the princes.

THE HARD FACTS Best place to witness the Muslim festival of Urs. Travel by car, stopping at Bagru (20km from Jaipur) to see vegetable dying and printing, and at Kishangarh, 27km outside Ajmer, for a picnic beside the deserted lakeside palaces. There are good trains from Jaipur, Delhi, Jodhpur and Udaipur. Tourist Office at Khadim Tourist Bungalow (tel: 20490). Stay at *Pushkar* (11km, see p. below); alternatively, in Ajmer at the government *Circuit House* overlooking Ana Sagar Lake or *Ajaymeru Hotel*, near the lake (tel: 20089). New, all mod. cons.

OUT AND ABOUT See Akbar's fort-palace (1570), housing the excellent museum's collection of Mughal and Rajput armour (open Sat.–Thurs., 10am–5pm); the Adhai-Din-Ka-Jhopra (The Hut of Two and a Half Days), a fine mosque said to have been built in that amount of time by Mohammad Ghori in 1193 after he had blindly destroyed 30 Hindu temples and a Sanskrit College (best in late sunlight, full of the faithful on Fridays); beyond is the path up to Taragarh (Star) fort (views). There is a Disneyland-style 19th century Nasiyan (Red) Jain temple; beyond are Shah Jahan's white marble pavilions in a delightful park on the east banks of the man-made Ana Sagar Lake (1135–50), overlooked by the old Residency. South-east of the town lies the famous Mayo College, school-time home of boy princes.

Urs mela (festival, dates vary) is even better here than at Nizamuddin in Delhi. It is held in the old town in the Dargah, built by Humayun and known as Dargah Sharif (Holy Shrine) or Dargah Khwaj Sahib (remove shoes before entering). It is the tomb of the Sufi saint, Khwaja Muin-ud-din Chishti, who came to India in 1192, and later to Ajmer. Wealthy first-time pilgrims pay for a sumptuous feast to be cooked in the huge iron deg (cauldrons) in the courtyard, eaten by them and afterwards gorged by the locals.

The festival, commemorating the saint's death is six days of continuous music and fairs attended by Muslims from all over India and the Middle East: qawwalis are sung through the night, while dervishes elect their king. Rare opportunities to hear quality Urdu music that was born in the court and shrines. Roses cover the tomb, washed on the final day by women rubbing rose water over it with their hair, then squeezing it out into bottles, to be taken as medicine by the sick.

PUSHKAR

11km north-west of Ajmer, over Nag Pahar (Snake Mountain); 149km from Jaipur. A quite extraordinary and magical quality of light hovers over the lake, bouncing off the surrounding ghats and temples. The music of bells, drums and worship from some of the thousands of tiny lakeside temples softly reverberates across the water. The faithful quietly perform their ablutions in the holy water said to have sprung from a lotus blossom carelessly dropped by Brahma as he was contemplating where to perform a Vedic yagna (sacrifice); other versions are more complex (pushkar seems to be Sanskrit for both lotus and full to the brim). Certainly, the lake is second only to Mansarovar in the Himalayas in sanctity. From the hills above, the eye sees only desert. The deep fiery red sunsets are sensational.

This gentle village is peaceful and soothing for most of the year, but thrown into raucous and colourful confusion for the annual cattle and camel fair at Kartik Poornima (November–December full moon), amplified by equally colourful pilgrims who believe that to wash in the holy waters on these days is to be cleansed of sin. In both moods, it is worth visiting.

THE HARD FACTS Normally, go by car from Ajmer or Jaipur. Stay at *Sarovar Tourist Bungalow* (tel: 40; cable: SAROVAR), another of the Maharaja of Jaipur's palaces, with internal courtyard air-cooled rooms. Ask for one of the five rooms overlooking the lake. Essential to book. During Pushkar fair, stay in the glorious and highly civilised tented village erected for tourists: double tents with shower and lavatory, communal dining tents, food included in tent price. Take woollen sweaters. Surprisingly, there is no smell of camel.

Pushkar Fair 10-day hubbub of colour, noise, commerce and faith as the desert tribes and camel caravans meet to trade cattle, camels, goats, sheep, cloth, shoes, jewellery and spices beside the sacred lake and to perform their rituals in its waters. 500,000 or so attend, with their 120,000 camels, horses and cattle.

Best are the last five days. There are camel races to show off and encourage buyers – and gamblers. The Ladhu Unt (loading the camel) race has whole teams (up to 10 men) clambering on to each camel before a chaotic race. Camels for sale are groomed, then examined, prodded and probed before the long negotiations over price begin. There is splashing in the ghats, folk dancing, bazaars selling every kind of adornment for humans and camels (beautiful wool rugs), magicians and a circus.

Temple music wafts through the night, as the fires die down and the Rajasthani melodies played on the stringed ek-tara come to a close. On the night of the full moon, the pilgrims bathe by moonlight, then send marigold and rose petals floating across the lake on green plate-like leaves. It is worth getting up early to see the camels and tribes rousing themselves in the pink of the dawn desert light.

BUNDI
200km from Jaipur, via Deoli; 142km from Ajmer; 156km from Chittaugarh. In 1820, even 19th century palace know-all, Lieut.-Col. James Tod, who knew Rajasthan inside out, was vastly impressed by the romance and prettiness of it all. In 1983, India buff Shalini Saran wrote on approaching the city: 'I had known that Bundi would be beautiful, but I hadn't imagined anything quite as beautiful as what now lay before me.'

Rarely visited by tourists, this lively backwater town nestles in the narrow valley of Bandoo beneath its protective fort and within massive, castellated walls, looking just like one of the delicate miniature paintings produced at its court. Inside the walls, tiny shops like window ledges pierce the maze of narrow street walls at eye level. They sell traditional Rajput wares, such as green and brown

afion (opium) pellets symmetrically arranged on a thali (platter). A sprawling pile of palaces growing out of the hillside have their interior walls covered in astonishing murals, although some are in dire need of restoration. And the terraced palace gardens crawl right up the hillside, complete with spy-holes and trap doors.

Backward Bundi reluctantly changed its method of marking time from a bowl of water and a gong to the new-fangled clock at the beginning of this century. And the modern palace, constructed to entertain British guests with British customs such as balls, and built in most other states at the turn of the century, was only begun in 1945, just two years before the British left – and is still unfinished. As the thoroughly modern (ex-)Maharaja of Baroda writes: 'Bundi is deliciously behind the times.'

THE HARD FACTS   It takes about six hours to drive to Bundi, but the route is pretty, especially after Deoli, and the arrival breath-taking. Leave early, taking a picnic to enjoy on arrival at Bundi. Stay in *Ranjit Niwas*, the former Maharaja's guesthouse, being sure to book by letter or cable in advance. Or, stay at the *Circuit House* (government officials take precedence over tourists); again, book in advance. Alternatively, stay in Kota (see below). All three should be able to organise permission for the palace murals to be unlocked; if not, use lashings of charm on the chaukidar. Move about town in tongas (pony carriages).

OUT AND ABOUT   Go up to the ruined Taragarh (Star) Fort, built 1372, for fine views. Visit the *palace* below and its terraced gardens, really a conglomeration of palaces built by successive rulers and named after them. Rao Chattar Sal (1631–59), a warrior hero and Governor of Delhi under Shah Jahan, made the last addition, the Chattar Mahal. In keeping with Bundi's backwater tradition, it is all pure Rajput with few of the Mughal touches of order, proportion, arches and columns but plenty of romantic-looking drooping roofs, richly carved brackets supporting projecting balconies, and an abundance of lotus flower and elephant motifs.

In the mid-18th century, after a spot of territorial warring, Maharaja Umed Singh (1744–71) was a great art patron. It was he who had the splendid murals painted in the Chitra Shala, a cloister-like courtyard. They coat the walls and ceilings, depicting in the bold and fresh Bundi-school style: Krishna dancing with the cowgirls; enthroned rulers; tiger chikar in the local forests; ladies swinging at

Teej festival; military triumphs; elephants giving a princess a shower; and much more. It is all enlivened with ducks, symbolising lovers, dabbling in lotus-filled lakes, and is painted in a cool palette of blue, cream and shades of green. See also the magnificent views, the very deep Sabirna-Dha-Ka-Kund (square, stepped water tank (reservoir)) built in 1654 to cope with the considerable changes in water level, and another well, the Nathawatji-Ki-Baoli, outside the east gate.

Then hie off to explore out of town: to the new but traditional *Phool Sagar* (3km) with fine gardens and lake and interiors described as 'near-Deco', where the Durbar (the title by which the ex-ruler is still known) lives (permission from his Secretary, telephone number 1, of course); Shikar Burj, a royal hunting lodge; the chhatri in the well-kept Kohak Bagh (gardens) nearby; and to *Baroli* (16km), a deserted city with crumbling fort and three of the hundred 9th century carved temples that formed one of the earliest temple complexes in Rajasthan.

KOTA

38km south of Bundi. Not quite such a time-warp as Bundi. Kota is Rajasthan's fastest growing industrial city, with an Atomic Power Station, India's largest fertiliser plant, etc. The old part is not polluted, but full of glorious buildings, an even more grandly decorated palace and two museums, reflecting the time when in 1579 Rao Ratan Singh, ruler of Bundi, gave his son, Madho Singh, the tiny principality of Kota that blossomed into a powerful, cultured city.

THE HARD FACTS Kota is a short drive from Bundi, so it is possible to stay here in the 1930s waterside **Brij Raj Bhavan Palace** (tel: 3071). Not the swishest of palace hotels but air-cooled and full of atmosphere, with furnishings of royal photographs and chikar trophies. Comfortable, with good food. Guests are tended by aged family retainers who also look after the former royals living in another part of the palace. Tourist Office at Chambal Tourist Bungalow (tel: 6527), should be able to help with unlocking the city palaces.

OUT AND ABOUT The excellent Maharao Madho Singh Museum is housed in the equally brilliant and very Rajput *palace*, entered through a Hathi Pol (Elephant Gate), flanked by a mural of a wedding procession. There are armour, textiles, miniatures dating from the height of the Kota

school of painting (18th–19th centuries) and sculptures – and the rich and busy decoration that covers every surface of the palace rooms. See especially the 18th century decoration in the Durbar Hall, including lamp niches; a chequer-board of Kota miniature portraits of equestrian, enthroned and standing nobles, the doors inlaid with precision mirrorwork and black and white inlay using ebony, ivory and elephants' teeth. Also in the palace is the Government Museum of coins, manuscripts and sculptures rescued from Baroli. (Open all Sat.–Thurs., 11am–5pm).

Apart from the palace, have a look at the Umed Bhavan, designed for Umed Singh II at the beginning of this century by Sir Swinton Jacob (who also designed the Central Museum, Jaipur and the bigger Bikaner palace), with its beautiful garden; see the royal chhatri outside the northern city walls; take a stroll in Chambal Gardens; go boating here or on Kishor Sagar.

Outside the city, visit *Mandalgarh fort* (with Chittaugarh and Kumbhalgarh, the third great Mewar fort built by Rana Kumbha); Tod's Bridge (8km), built by the Colonel. If you are driving on to Chittaugarh from Bundi or Kota, Baroli and Mandalgarh lie on the route.

CHITTAUGARH (CHITTOR)

156km from Bundi; 115km from Udaipur; 187km from Ajmer. One of the most stunning forts in Rajasthan, former capital of Mewar. It has everything a Rajput fort should have: legend, historical drama, courage, romance and desolation. The legend is that the fort was built on the precipice by Bhim, one of the Pandava hero brothers in the great epic, the Mahabharata. The historical fact, here almost better than legend, is that the capital of the Sisodias, the number one family in the Rajput hierarchy of 36, was sacked three times, and three times the warriors donned saffron robes and rode into battle to die while their wives performed mass suicide by fire, known as johar, to preserve themselves from the conquerors.

In the second sack, in 1533, 32,000 warriors and 13,000 of their women died. There is romance in that the first sack, in 1303, was by Ala-ud-din, the Kilji Sultan of Delhi, to win the beautiful Padmini who, when defeat was imminent, followed her women on to the burning pyre, dressed up in their wedding finery and singing merrily.

After the third sack, by Akbar in 1568, 8,000 warriors rode out to their death. Maharana Udai Singh, forgoing Rajput tradition, fled to Udaipur where he established his capital, never to return to Chittaugarh. Meanwhile, Akbar did the Muslim conqueror's act and devastated almost all the buildings, leaving it a ghost city.

THE HARD FACTS Excellent mid-way stop between Bundi or Kota and Udaipur, or a day trip from either, taking a picnic. If necessary, stay overnight at the *Panna Tourist Bungalow* (tel: 273), modern, modest and clean. Ensure a room with fort view. (Their restaurant is OK for lunch.) Tourist Information at Janta Tourist Rest House, by the railway station (tel: 9); runs 3-hour conducted tours, starting at 7.30am and 2.30pm. Archaeological Survey of India Office in the Fort (tel: 14), opposite Rana Kumbha's palace, supplies approved guides (can be good) and, sometimes, publications. Move around by tonga.

OUT AND ABOUT The romantic remains of temples, palaces and towers date from the 7th to 15th centuries and are scattered through the walled city of five square km, jutting up 180m above the surrounding plain. See the seven pols (gates); the huge palace ruins of Rana Kumbha, 15th-century enlightened ruler who built 32 fortresses to further defend his kingdom (the women are said to have performed johar in a vault here); the palace of the heirs apparent, opposite (together with museum and Archaeological Survey office); the Jain and Hindu temples; the Stambha (Tower of Victory) to the south, an architectural feat built to commemorate Kumbha's victory over the Sultan of Malwa in 1440 (you can climb to the top); and the smaller Kirti Stambha (Pillar of Fame). Then there are other palaces: Patta of Kelwa's delicate balconies; Padmini's palace and water pavilion; Ratan Singh's and Falla's palaces – every building drenched in Rajput romance.

UDAIPUR

115km from Chittaugarh; 264km from Ajmer; 275km from Jodhpur; 185km from Mount Abu; 262km from Ahmedabad (for launching into Gujarat, see p. 133). As romantic as Chittaugarh but this time very much alive: a thriving provincial city with bustling bazaars, fountains playing in princesses' gardens, royalty – albeit officially former royalty – living in the City Palace, two excellent museums and a string of lakes throwing off an exquisite light. There is even an island dream palace to stay in. A warm, friendly atmosphere pervades all, unspoilt by the deluge of tourists, far

less commercially aggressive than Jaipur. And Udaipur has pedigree splendour too. When Udai Singh made this his Mewar capital in 1567, he brought with him the honour and pride of the top Rajput family clan, the Sisodias, descended directly from the sun via the god Rama (see Chittaugarh, above). His oasis town of lakes and streams set in the Girwa Valley of the Aravalli mountains had a good water supply and excellent natural defences. On the advice of a sage, Udai Singh built a temple above Lake Pichola, then his palace around it.

Successive rulers added more rooms to make it the biggest of all Rajasthan palaces, yet it is harmonious in its overall Rajput character, with jharokahs (projecting balconies), inlaid walls and coloured glass windows. Above it all rises the gold kalash (pinnacle), the privilege of only the gods or independent kingdoms.

There is a story that superior pride led one heir apparent, Maharana Pratap, to display the height of chivalrous one-upmanship. Disapproving of the Jaipur subservience to conqueror Akbar through a marriage alliance, he invited Raja Man Singh of Jaipur to a picnic beside Udai Sagar Lake, then left his son to play host. Afterwards he had the ground Man Singh had trod on washed with Ganga water and insisted his generals take purification baths, for which insult Man Singh (himself a general under Akbar) reaped appropriate revenge and Pratap never came to the throne.

A later ruler, Amar Singh, bowed to Jehangir's Mughal might in 1612 before abdicating for this shameful act. But intrigue continued and Maharana Karan Singh gave refuge to Jehangir's rebellious son on Jagmandir Island in Pichola Lake where he proclaimed himself Emperor when his father died. Royal chivalry raised its head again when Aurangzeb threatened to marry the neighbouring Princess of Roopnagar: the Mewar hero, Raj Singh, swooped down to marry her, and then had to face the emperor's fury and his revival of the jizya (tax on all non-Muslims) which led, of course, to war. In 1818, like so many other Rajasthan states, Mewar came under the British yoke but managed to avoid almost all British cultural influence.

THE HARD FACTS Arrive by air (see p. 81, airport about 25km out of town, so share taxi), train (for instance, Chittaugarh-Udaipur trains leaving at 5.50am arrive 9.10am and at 3.40pm arrive 8.30pm), or car. Three royal palaces to stay in, of varying grandeur.

Lake Palace Hotel, PO Box 5, Pichola Lake (tel: 3241; telex: 033 203 LPAL IN; cable: LAKE-PALACE); a dazzling, white marble fantasy island in the deep azure Pichola Lake, built about 1740 (some earlier and later bits) as a summer palace for the Maharana to frolic with his ladies. Crocodiles in the surrounding water deterred fellow courtiers from sampling his pleasures when he was away. Wall-paintings of dancing girls and hunting scenes and crystal and silk furnishings typical of Indian royal taste decorate rooms surrounding courtyards of lotus pools and terraces (now suitable for stunning sunset cocktails). Built for pleasure; now run as a pleasure hotel since 1962. Under the auspices of the Taj Group since 1971, whose recent refurbishment is criticised by artist Andrew Logan as 'Trust House Forte Motorway Style'. But they are having the coloured glass and mirrorwork in other parts of the building beautifully restored. Known as 'the James Bond hotel' after location shooting for the 007 movie, 'Octopussy'. Reach it by tiny, bobbing, rowing boat.

82 rooms, including 10 suites, 62 of them centrally air-conditioned, all mod. cons include travel desk, car rental, bank, doctor on call, baby sitter, marble swimming pool, painted and inlaid bar, boating. The suites have the swing and the murals: dancing gopis (Krishna's cow-girls) in the Sajjan (Lotus) Nivas, huge coloured glass windows and double swing in the Khush (Happiness) Mahal. Otherwise go for any non-refurbished room looking out across the lake, to the City Palace for morning sun, the beautiful Jagmandir Island, or west for sunsets. Sports are swimming, boating and watching sunsets.

The disadvantages: pigeon mess takes the gleam off the central pool and courtyards; the food is improved but still dreary; if there is a group tour the atmosphere is wrecked and there is much queuing for boats, removing all spontaneity. So, it is at its best early or late in the season.

Shiv Niwas (tel: 3236/3203; use Lake Palace telex and cable service). Josceline Dimbleby found it 'swish beyond anything', 'terribly grand', with 'the best views of any hotel anywhere'. Here guests stay in the royal guest house of the top-notch Udaipurs, part of the vast and rambling city palace overlooking Pichola Lake. Built by Maharana Fateh Singh early last century, with carved pillars, mosaics, ponds, delicate wall-paintings, carved balconies and lavish space, it has been given a dusting (lack of royalty these days) and furnished with Udaipur surplus treasures such as Persian carpets, coloured chandeliers, Chinese lamps, brass bedsteads, Mewar School miniature paintings, ivory inlaid furniture, massive mirrors and big family portraits. The result is royal opulence (and royal prices, for India), with perfectly blending modern additions and facilities.

18 suites (at Rs1,500–3,000); all mod. cons; masses of servants, as many towels, courtyard, swimming pool with marble lining, circular turret bar, stunning banquet lounge and crystal room (only for looking), food reasonable.

If those do not match your wishes or your purse, try the *Laxmi Vilas Palace Hotel* (tel: 4411/2/3; cable: TOURISM). Rather stern building, with unexciting 1960s-style interiors and food but stunning views over Lake Fateh Sagar and swimming pool; the *Rang Niwas Hotel* (tel: 3611), actually a modest, simple and charming guest house built around a courtyard, on Lake Palace Road, underneath the City Palace.

Tourist Office at railway station (tel: 3605) supplies guides. RTDC (tel: 3509) run excellent five-hour morning tours of scattered monuments, gardens and museums, recommended; and afternoon tours to Nathdwara, Eklingi and Halidghati. Good travel agents are Tourist Guide Service, Chetak Circle (tel: 3526); Rajasthan Tours at Garden Hotel (tel: 3030) and Lake Palace (tel. 5533) and the wonderful Mr Hiram, opposite the pier for the Lake Palace, who is reported by a London globe-trotter to be efficient and able to book anything for anywhere. For sport, the hotel can organise horses, ('rotten old nags' according to one rider) for a 6.30am ride around the lake à la 'Jewel in the Crown' – you go on your own, following the banks, through a rustic village on the far side with wonderful views across to the city, and back into Udaipur through the old gates, feeling superb but likely to get saddle-sore.

OUT AND ABOUT There is plenty of the City Palace left after the former royals and the paying would-be royals have taken their chunks. It houses the museum and, like other palaces, is itself a museum, every wall and ceiling decorated (some by Hindu craftsmen who had worked under Shah Jahan but were booted out by bigoted Aurangzeb). Visitors enter through the Tripolia Gate (1725), under which the ruler would be weighed in gold on his birthday, the pieces distributed to his people, a practice followed by Mughal emperors too.

See the wonderful Indian miniatures in the

Krishna Vilas and Zenana Mahal; porcelain and glass in the Manak (Ruby) Mahal; 3-D peacock mosaics in the Mor Chowk, the garden of Bari Mahal; the mirrorwork of Moti Mahal; the Chinese tiles lining the Chini Mahal; narrative wall-paintings, royal cradles – and do not forget to peek out over Pichola Lake. Open daily, 9.30am–5.30pm. Enter a separate museum through the Rai Angam (Royal Courtyard): very fine miniature paintings, toys and views, open daily, 9.30am–5.30pm.

The **lakes and gardens** are the joy of Udaipur. Rent a boat opposite the Lake Palace (with or without rower; motor boat not so nice) and go round Pichola Lake, enlarged by Maharana Udai Singh, past the merchants' havelis, women singing and washing on the ghats, temples, a royal hunting lodge, the exquisitely beautiful and romantic Gul Mahal pavilion (1621–28) on Jagmandir Island whose stone elephants greet visitors (if possible, take picnic here, island currently under threat of development into another hotel), ending with a nimbu soda or cocktail at the Lake Palace which forms Jagniwas Island.

The lakes to the north are also lovely: see them all from the Pratap Memorial on high Moti Magri (Pearl Hill), open daily 9am–6pm; then boat on Lake Fateh Sagar (dug out by Fateh Singh), stopping off at Nehru Island, a garden with restaurant; and drive around the lake edge, dotted with parks.

Visit Saheliyon ki Bari, Garden of the Maids of Honour (in fact, a clutch of Delhi damsels sent by the emperor as a peace offering), where boys were turfed out after they reached eight years of age. Fountains play over the lotus pools, marble kiosks and life-size marble elephants – one of the few gardens in India where the water, so essential to the total effect, is switched on; open daily, 9am–5pm. The views from Sajjan Garh (Monsoon Palace) over the whole city are sensational, especially at sunset; Gulab Bagh (Rose Garden), Sajjan Niwas Gardens and Samor Bagh are all within the old city walls.

Anyone interested in Rajasthan folk arts, crafts and traditions should visit the exemplary **Bhartiya Lok Kala Mandal**, a museum housing puppets, masks, costumes, instruments, kavads (mobile temples), Pabuji Ki Phads (scroll-painting ballads) and much more, with daily shows using the treasures, and workshops around the back where craftsmen carve and rasp puppet heads, paint kavads or tailor clothes for puppets. Good publications. Open daily, 9am–6pm.

RESTAURANTS Not many, in keeping with Udaipur's provincial atmosphere. Best food in town is at *Park View*, a small restaurant in the town centre near Chetak Circle (recommended by Lake Palace hotel management, who can give directions) or *Berry's*, nearby. Go to *Lake Palace* for courtyard tea and terrace/bar cocktails, to *Laxmi Vilas* for view – and moonlight boat rides back to Lake Palace are heavenly.

SHOPPING AND CRAFTS Bapu Bazaar is delightful. Explore its side alleys to find carpenters making wooden toys (sets of military bands, birds, animals). And there are puppet-makers, sweetmeats bubbling in iron cauldrons, bookshops, jewellers, pawn shops, Lover's Paradise restaurant, old coins, wood carving, musicians, khari printing (have a dress decorated on the spot, see p. 84), bandhansa prints, meenakari and brasswork, and plain woollen shawls for slashes of vivid colour. Plus dark images of Sri Nathji and pichwais (cloth paintings, usually bad quality), both from nearby Nathdwara (see below). Avoid the paintings on ivory and bone.

Out of town, visit *Shikarbadi* in the hills, a turn of the century hunting lodge; fun to stay overnight and to ride (low-grade horses again). Arrange through Lake Palace, go by car (10 minutes) or elephant (40 minutes). For sunset peace, go to Ahar (3km) where the Mewar chhatris stand amid a ruined city. For a beautiful picnic, go to *Jaisamand Lake* (48km), built by Maharana Jai Sing in the 17th century (and still the second largest artificial lake in Asia), surrounded by chhatris guarded by marble elephants, with summer palaces for Udaipur queens on either side. At *Dungapur* (another 50km, south-west of Salumba) are two stunningly decorative and lavishly decorated palaces, perfectly preserved (private, but try writing in advance). The painted palace of *Deolia* (Deogarh) is 60km east of Salumba, just before Pratapgarh.

NATHDWARA
48km from Udaipur, via temples at Nagada and Ekingi (22km), battle site of Pratap versus Akbar (1576, Pratap won) at Haldighati (40km). A black stone image of Vishnu, called Sri Nathji, was brought here from Mathura in 1669. It is kept in the temple of Sri Nathji and is an object of pilgrimage for many Hindus. Although non-Hindus are forbidden entry, the bazaar around the temple is interesting.

97

See pichwais (cloth paintings hung in front of the Sri Nathji image when he is sleeping or being washed) being made, images of Sri Nathji, and the extraordinary temple sweets: about 20 varieties of sweeter-than-sweet prasaad made in the temple, blessed, sold to pilgrims who take them home to those who could not go on the pilgrimage – so delicious that Indians have them sent to far-flung addresses. Rajsamand Lake beyond (18km) has pretty chhatris and arches.

RANAKPUR

98km from Udaipur; 197km from Mount Abu; 160km from Jodhpur. An exceptionally beautiful drive through mountain, desert and farmland to a cluster of Jain temples at one of the five most sacred Jain sites (see Mount Abu, below), this time in a remote valley surrounded by the wooded Aravalli hills instead of the hilltop Palitana, Girnar and Abu.

The central, enormous temple, built in 1439 and dedicated to Tirthankara (Jain saint) Rishabdeo, contains a three-storey chaumukha (four-faced shrine) dedicated to Adinath, 29 halls supported by 1,444 pillars, a riot of carving on every surface, the whole capped with quantities of domes and spires. See also the subsidiary temples. Eat a thali at the dharamsala or, much nicer, have a picnic in the surrounding hills. Open daily, noon-5pm. Return to Jaipur via the impressive 15th century *Kumbhalgarh Fort* (rated second after Chittaugarh by Rajputs), then via Rajsamand Lake and Nathdwara (see above).

MOUNT ABU

185km from Udaipur; 197km from Ranakpur; 222km from Ahmedabad; 264km from Jodhpur. The only escape from the dusty, desert heat of Rajasthan and eastern Gujarat. Here, on a large, 1200m-high plateau, are lungfulls of fresh air, a feast of green trees, viewpoints by the dozen and lakes and lush gardens.

Very fashionable with Indian honeymoon couples who take rolls of photographs of each other and dutifully go to the Honeymoon Point at sunset – which is indeed very pretty. Important to Hindus because Nakki Lake was dug by the gods, using only their nakks (nails); because the serpent Arbunda, son of the Himalayas, rescued Shiva's bull, Nandi, from a chasm here – hence Abu. Important to Rajput Hindus because the sage Vasishta lived here, from whose fire Brahmin priests performed Yajna and created a race of war-

riors, the four primary Rajput clans. But it is mo⟨re⟩ important to Jains for its group of temples, ⟨of⟩ which Vimal Vasahi (1031) and Tejpal (1230) di⟨s⟩play some of the finest architecture and carving ⟨of⟩ all Jain art.

THE HARD FACTS Season March–June (aft⟨er⟩ that, rain) and September–November (after tha⟨t⟩ cold). Stay at one of the small hotels, run lik⟨e⟩ provincial English guest-houses, with nurture⟨d⟩ gardens and smiling welcomes for guests and the⟨ir⟩ dogs, all rooms with bath:
Mount Hotel, Dilwara Road (tel: 55; cabl⟨e⟩ MOUNTHOTEL), 7 rooms, boasts India⟨n⟩ Continental, Parsee and Gujarat cuisines.
Palace Hotel, Bikaner House (tel 21/33; cabl⟨e⟩ PALACE), 27 rooms.
Hotel Hilltone (tel: 137/237; cable: HILLTONE), ⟨4⟩ rooms.

Tourist Office (tel: 51), opposite bus stand, ca⟨n⟩ supply approved guides. The RTDC runs identica⟨l⟩ five-hour morning and afternoon tours, bookab⟨le⟩ at the Youth Hostel. Sightsee by car or on foo⟨t⟩. Mount Hotel's food is about the best; otherwis⟨e⟩ stick to Gujarati fare of vegetarian thalis and de⟨-⟩licious ice-cream found at a string of modest bu⟨t⟩ very clean restaurants on the road to Nakki Lake.

OUT AND ABOUT Head out of town up to th⟨e⟩ five Dilwara *Jain Temples* (5km). See especiall⟨y⟩ Vimal Vasahi and Tejpal temples, both built b⟨y⟩ ministers to Gujarat rulers, the first dedicated t⟨o⟩ Adinath (first Tirthankara) and built of Makran⟨a⟩ marble, entered through 48 carved pillars, past ⟨a⟩ procession of carved elephants, to a courtyard of 5⟨2⟩ cells, the central shrine and an octagonal dome, al⟨l⟩ richly carved; the second dedicated to Neminat⟨h⟩ (22nd Tirthankara), every facet of the marbl⟨e⟩ carved with delicate, lace-like figures and patterns. Do not miss the huge, almost transparent lotu⟨s⟩ suspended from the dome.

For views, go to *Guru Shikhar* (15km), at the en⟨d⟩ of the plateau and, at 1,725m, the highest point i⟨n⟩ Rajasthan; to the *Durga Temple* (3km), up 200 stee⟨p⟩ steps; *Achalgarh* (11km) to see a Shiva temple; an⟨d,⟩ nearer town, Robert's Spur and, of course, Honey⟨-⟩moon Point and Sunset Point. In town, there ar⟨e⟩ pretty strolls around Nakki Lake, boating on th⟨e⟩ lake, the public gardens, and a small museum o⟨n⟩ Raj Bhavan Road (open Sat.–Thurs., 10am–5pm⟨).⟩ Apart from that, go for hillside strolls and relax.

'estern Rajasthan

DHPUR

5km from Udaipur; 264km from Mount Abu;
)km from Jaipur; 290km from Jaisalmer; 240km
m Bikaner. Lying on the edge of the Thar Desert
lthough locals will say firmly it does not start for
other 100km – the flat, sandy, colourful, slow-
ced city is dominated by two massively huge
laces, totally out of proportion, one a city-fort
onghold built on a high natural bluff, the other,
e of the finest large buildings of the 1930s,
ected by a remarkably unimaginative ruler as
s solution to unemployment during famine.
dhpur does not seem very grand now, but it
rtainly was. As capital of Marwar, on both the
ding routes and the strategic Delhi–Gujarat
ute, the Marwaris reaped fortunes from the pas-
ig camel caravans and their loads of copper,
tes, silks, sandalwood, dyes, opium, spices, cof-
e and much more. These were the trading Mar-
aris who later moved east to Shekhavati (see p.
) and who now dominate Indian commerce.
Jodhpur was founded in 1459 by Rao Jodha,
hough the 35,000 square mile territory was won
the Rathores back in 1211. Jodha was chief of the
thore Rajput clan, firmly descended from the
n god, Surya, and the most powerful prince in
jasthan.
The rock must have been an irresistible site,
hough the sati buffs testify to the usual Rajput
male valour at moments of defeat. By the time
kbar was suing for peace with the Rajput clans,
10 Udai Singh (died 1581) was able to win wealth
helping him begin to add Gujarat to his con-
lests. (His son completed the job and moved on
tackle the Deccan.) He then gained influence at
urt in 1580 by marrying first his sister to the
nperor, then his daughter to Akbar's son. Finally
kbar pronounced him King of the Desert.
Maharaja Jaswant Singh (died 1678) led Shah
han's armies and, unfortunately, Dara Sikoh's
ainst Aurangzeb, the winner. Hot on the heels of
feat came disaster, murder and patricide, lead-
g to endless internal feuds. It was not until the
rong personality of progressive Pratap Singh
nerged in the 1870s that Jodhpur regained credi-
lity. A younger royal son but three times regent,
e was a fanatical royalist (he went to London to
eet Queen Victoria in 1885), a fervent huntsman
bught hand to hand with jungle boars), had
peccable manners and tried to toughen up the

royal heirs by making them wrestle with muzzled
leopards.

Maharaja Umaid Singh (died 1947) had a topsy-
turvy understanding of Pratap's progressiveness.
When in 1929 the monsoon failed for the third year,
famine struck and Jodhpur was living up to its
name of Land of Death, he buried his head in the
plentiful sand and served his people by employing
3,000 of them each day to build him a vast palace to
the latest designs and with all mod. cons, completed in 1945, on the eve of Independence. Today's former ruler has turned it, contents and all,
into another of Rajasthan's fantasy hotels.

THE HARD FACTS   This is desert country, so
expect much dry dustiness and heat after mid-
March. The hot Thar Desert, divided between the
Jodhpur, Bikaner and Jaisalmer Rajputs, is known
by a contraction of marust'hali, meaning abode of
death. It is no joke forgetting to take a water bottle
or some cold drinks on trips out into the villages.
Jodhpur's airport is just 4km from the city; excellent time-saving overnight trains connect with
Delhi, Ahmedabad and Jaisalmer. Choose between two princely homes: the vast and wondrous
Umaid Bhawan and the relaxed, friendly home of
royal cousins – each offers something entirely
different and there is a good case for staying two
nights at each. Each is a fundamental part of Jodhpur and each gives a completely different aspect to
the city.
Umaid Bhawan Palace (tel: 22316; telex: 0352 202
UBP IN; cable: PALACE); exemplary use of a
palace as a hotel, total period feeling maintained by
careful restoration where necessary, such as re-
upholstering sofas with the correct fabric. Run by
the Welcomgroup. Looks over the town from
Chittar Hill, a site dictated by the astrologers but as
ridiculous as the whole project. It lacked any water
supply and, even today, the deep wells mean that
the alkaline water sometimes tastes very odd. A
12-mile railway had to be built to carry the sandstone from the quarry at Sursagar. An estimated
half a million donkey loads of earth had to be
carried up for the foundations alone. And rock had
to be blasted so that trees could take root. The
sandstone was cut and interlocked, without using
mortar.

Goodness knows what the starving labourers
thought of the finished project in 1945, when the
family moved in. The 195 × 103 metre rose sandstone palace was designed by British architect
H. V. Lanchester, president of the Royal Institute

of British Architects, its massiveness bearing the mark of his Delhi work under Lutyens and his experience in town hall architecture. His other India work included planning in Lucknow, Madras and Calcutta.

The design was symmetrical, in the beaux-arts tradition, each section with its own courtyard for privacy. Modernity had to compromise with strict purdah, so the pillared corridors were hung with bamboo curtains to allow the women to move around the palace.

The interior was also high European 1930s tempered with local Indian traditions and a royal taste for gilt. Massive brass front doors, good enough to rival contemporary ones in New York or Paris, led to courtyards and 347 rooms which included eight dining rooms and a banquet hall to seat 300. Carved big cats race up the sweeping marble staircase to suites for Their Highnesses and visiting princes. The furniture was fated. The ship bringing the first set from England sank. A second order was placed but the factory was bombed. Finally some imitation European furniture was made locally and mixed with what had been obtained elsewhere.

Then there were all the latest toys for the progressive prince. The double dome (the outer skin 24m above the inner) of the huge central courtyard uses reinforced concrete. Inside the dome is a whispering gallery. Below it lies a marble floor and gilt furniture. 40m below the courtyard is the magnificent swimming pool, the walls painted with fish and a continuous seabed for an underwater rather than underground feeling. Air-conditioning throughout is part of the original plan. There is a billiard room and a cinema/theatre. During the Second World War, vast Christmas balls were given for all the troops, when dancers overflowed from the ballroom into the gardens. The Maharaja gave each guest an embossed pewter mug one year, a leather wallet another.

The palace is now divided into three: the hotel takes the lion's share; the present Maharaja Gaj Singh II has a part; and the main halls are a museum well worth visiting. The museum includes the fine Durbar Hall with 1940s murals by a palace-hopping Polish painter who forgot to seal his plaster, so that it peels. There are good miniature paintings (a fraction of the huge collection – ask to see more) and armour, and a fine clock collection (clock catalogue recently published). Open daily, 9am–5pm.

The hotel part has 55 very spacious rooms, in-cluding 6 suites of up to 7 rooms apiece, ful decorated with original furnishings and furnitu giving an entirely period feeling. Facilities inclu all the mod. cons noted above plus travel count (including booking the Jodhpur royal carriage Jaisalmer), car rental, doctor on call, badminto squash and tennis courts; golf on request. Peacoc screech in the gardens. Worth taking a suite as it relatively cheap and enormous fun, with hi 1930s lighting and decor. The suite Peter O'To stayed in while filming 'Kim' is designed like ship. The two enormous royal suites have fi views, beds big enough for a zenana, glorious deco mirrors, paintings, bathtubs and a tinkli Belgian crystal fountain in their courtyard. The G Singh suite has a completely subsidiary bathroo suite (with a choice of squat or sitting lavatory).

Service slowish, especially room service; it mu be half a mile to the kitchens (worth orderi breakfast the previous evening). Food varies fro awful – one guest claimed it was 'the worst food India, without a doubt, but that must be what t maharajas ate' – to excellent, especially the d licious western Rajasthani dishes, so talk to t chef. Moonlit courtyard barbecues are a roman delight. Local bhopas and their families sing a make merry music every evening. Try to take te thick milkshakes or cocktails on the verandah ga ing at the stunning sunsets. For sightseeing, co sult with Baiji, the knowledgeable public relatio lady whose grandfather was Pratap Singh and wl knows everything about Jodhpur.

The disadvantages: it could simply be too hu and impersonal for some. Forty years on, son would prefer new light fittings and curtains; othe comforts like new mattresses. For others, it is pure period piece and should not be missed.

Ajit Bhawan, near Circuit House (tel: 2040S Delightful family house built for Umaid Singh younger brother, Maharaja Dhiraj Ajit Singl crammed with furniture, hunting trophies, fami mementoes and warm atmosphere. About 50% the palace rates. Run in the guest-house traditic by two of Ajit's descendants, Maharaj Sobha Singh and Maharaj Swaroop Singh, who are ded cated to giving visitors a chance to see somethir other than forts, palaces and bazaars. They ho their guests as if they were private friends, givir them home-made chilli chutney, fussing over the if they do not eat breakfast, advising them wit care on their sightseeing and even taking them o into the surrounding villages themselves – a gre treat.

25 rooms scattered around the house, all double with bath and air-cooling; some around the central courtyard, others in charming, purpose-built cottages in the gardens. Each cottage is a room and bathroom, designed like a traditional villager's home, the furniture and fabrics made locally to complement the old family pieces (note: quite small for two big people). An exemplary use of India's wealth of traditional craftsmen for modern needs. Room price includes food, good home cooking, usually local Rajasthani dishes cooked in degchies (big pots) in the courtyard or pretty garden. Golf, squash and camel riding by arrangement. The owners play golf, using a mat to tee off because of the sandiness. The disadvantages: Ajit's could be a little claustrophobic and lack privacy.

Tourist Office at the Tourist Bungalow, High Court Road (tel: 21900), open daily, 9am–7pm; Information Centre, Government of Rajasthan, High Court Road (tel 20493), neither very good. Better to use the in-house knowledge of Umaid and Ajit's. Universal Book Depot, at Jalori Gate, is good. The charmingly written and useful *Jodhpur, a traveller's guide*, is available from the bookshop and the shops inside the fort gateways. Move around by tonga and bicycle rickshaw but take a taxi up to the fort. To find out more about the rich music and dance traditions, contact Rajasthan Sangeet Natak Academy, B-Road, Paota Area, open Mon.–Sat., 10am–5pm. Asha Medical Hall, Sojati Gate, is a good chemist.

OUT AND ABOUT **Meherangarh** *(Majestic)* **Fort** is magnificent. It is really a fort city inside a 10km wall. Local musicians serenade visitors' arrival up the winding road. The handprints made by devoted and proud women before committing sati mark the wall beside Lohapol (Iron) Gate. Well worth the surprising Rs10 entrance fee. 18 sections, guided by charming old retainers with impeccable English and memories. The maharajas' paraphernalia is laid out by subject: howdahs, including a huge glass one to be carried by 12 men, booty from a Gujarat defeat; cradles including the present maharaja's, with a portrait of his father on top – early training in respect; festive tents; very fine miniature paintings, especially Jodhpur rulers such as Man Singh, who built the fort; exceptional armour; Durbar Hall; temple; dazzling white inner courtyard for Holi celebrations; painted playroom with swing, coloured balls hanging from the ceiling, pachesi boards; and everywhere the most delicate jali work (pierced screens), each with a

different pattern. From the ramparts you can see the city beneath the sheer drop, with blue-painted houses belong to Brahmins and the gurgling of life, music and shouting wafting up. The musicians strike up again as visitors leave, earning their baksheesh. Open daily, 9am–5pm. Of the shops, Sunderam Art Emporium is definitely OK, see below. The blinding white Jaswant Thada cenotaph, built 1899, is on the route down to the town.

Day trips to villages in family jeeps Meet and talk to villagers. Be the guest of handsome Jhats for lunch. Witness the weekly barber's visit. See potting and weaving and discuss marital customs. Take tea with smiling Bisnoi tribeswomen, brightly clad, heavy bangles up the whole length of their arms; their men wear pure white. All Bisnois believe in the sanctity of animal and plant life, as laid down by the 15th century Guru Jambeshwar in the form of 29 basic tenets, hence Bis (twenty) noi (nine). They further believe their ancestors are reincarnated as deer, so there are usually herds of deer found near Bisnoi villages. Spot the wildlife and, if very lucky, a white buck in the scrub.

And sample a draught of afion (opium). It used to be given to Rajput runners and to warriors before battle. It is still taken as an umlpano (infused in water), to be drunk by a guest from the cupped hand of his host. But, in the 19th century, Tod observed of the Rajputs that 'the hookah is the dessert to the umlpano; the panacea for all the ills . . . and with which he can at any time enjoy a paradise of his own creation'. He found the Bhatti Rajputs of Jaisalmer 'as addicted as any of his brethren to the immoderate use of opium . . . inhaling mechanically the smoke long after they are insensible to all that is passing around them'. (Trips organised by Ajit Bhawan cost Rs250 per person, well worth it.)

If staying at Ajit Bhawan, it is worth visiting the Umaid Bhawan palace museum and having a swim (very welcome amid the sand) and a verandah drink, and the courtyard barbecue, if it is on that night. If staying at the Umaid Bhawan, it is a good idea to telephone the Ajit Bhawan to arrange to go on the jeep trip for the day, ending with dinner at Ajit's, if they are not too full with guests. Jodhpur really is a two-horse or, rather, two-camel town.

RESTAURANTS AND FOOD In addition to the two hotels, try *Kalinga*, near the railway station, and the vegetarian *Pankaj* at Jalori Gate. West Rajasthani cooking uses the locally grown millet, so dishes are quite heavy. Sogra is a thick, millet chapati served with plenty of ghi (clarified butter) Sohita is mutton cooked with millet. Sulla is another mutton dish, the pieces marinated then cooked on skewers over charcoal. Khud khar (rabbit) gosh is whole rabbit cooked very slowly. Krer kumidai saliria is three desert beans cooked with cumin, chillies and other spices.

Local food to buy in the markets includes mirchibada, a large chilli whose centre is scooped out and mixed with potato and spices, then put back and deep fried, eaten with the very necessary cooling dahi (curd) and known locally as dynamite. Local sweetmeat specialities include mawaki-kachori, an immobilising meal of pastry stuffed with a mixture of nuts and coconut, with a syrup poured through the hole at the top when it is bought. It is best found at Misthra Bhander, an old establishment quite near the clock tower in Sardar bazaar. And do not fail to drink SPL (=special) Makania Lassi at Sri Mishri Lal Hotel at the main Sardar bazaar gateway, the thickest, richest, creamiest in India – the spoon stands up in it. And, if asked, they will grind up bhang (local hashish) and stir that in, too, turning the lassi green.

SHOPPING AND CRAFTS Jodhpur is rich in both. There are nice wooden boxes, speckled ones made at Jaisalmer, plain ones here, circular for cosmetics, small for opium, rectangular for money and jewels. And there are huge puppets – this is a big centre for puppet-making; painted horses, originally made as toys for the horse-crazy maharajas; ink-wells; silver pipes, where the tobacco is smoked through hot coals; and, of course, bandhana-printed textiles. Within Meherangarh Fort, Sunderam Art Emporium has some nice boxes and the manager, Mr Pathan, will tell – even show – visitors where the craftsmen are, such as the Muslim bandhana families in Bambamola area and other bandhana workers around Siwanchi and Jalori Gates; the shoe-makers of Udaimandel and around Mochi (shoe) Bazaar; the wood-turners; the ivory workers; wooden horse-makers (one made a life-size horse for a rupee-millionaire Bombay wallah); and the delightfully honest Gujarat furniture-maker who ages his lovely carvings to make them 'duplicate antiques – the French and Germans do not like new carving'.

Lalji, on Umaid Bhawan Palace Road (tel: 22472) is the Aladdin's cave for anything old, from small pieces of silver, wood, brass or ivory to huge appliqué wall-hangings, all stocked from the surrounding villages, with very knowledgeable staff,

entirely fair prices and reliable shipping. Many treasure in a smart Delhi home was found here The Rajasthan Emporium is good too. Avoi Albani Handicraft Emporium, which is ove priced.

The best bandhana is found at the big shop outside Sojati Gate, at Bhagatram Ishwarlal, Luck Silk Shop and Prakash Silk Stores. To see dhurri weaving, go to Salavas village (18km); and for mor bandhana, and leather and woodwork, go to Pipa (70km).

The central Sardar Bazaar is full of colour, witl no cars and almost no begging. Enter by Sojati Gat and head directly for Sri Mishri Lal Hotel, in th right-hand part of the main market gateway, fo some milk-of-the-gods lassi. Then on, into th market: street barbers and dentists by the cloc tower landmark; past piles of earthenware pot beyond and through a gateway. Here is th Krishna temple, Gulab Sagar Tank and an ol palace (now a girls school).

Back to the clock tower and turn right to find maze of alleys, each with its own theme, so th shops are highly competitive and shout agains each other to vie for custom, be it flowers, sweet meats, shoes, wool, silver or bandhana. The crafts men work behind. Just outside Sojati gate, wome sell bangles and there is a gold and silver market and Maharaja Handicrafts, which is good.

Out of town, to the east, are desert villages. It best to visit these with advice from Ajit Bhawan o with some of the family – it will be much mor rewarding (see above p. 101). South-east, throug several other interesting villages, lies *Sarda Samand* (55km), summer palace of the Maharaj with a wildlife sanctuary. To the north is firs *Balsamand* (7km), whose lake and garden wer constructed in 1159. The modern palace dates from 1936 (open daily, 8am–6pm, nice for picnics). *Man dore* (2km beyond), is the old capital of Marwar where the fine chhatris of the Jodhpurs are set i lush, terraced gardens outside the ruined city. Se especially the 15 rock-cut figures in the Hall o Heroes and Ek Thamba Mahal, a delicately carved circular, three-storeyed palace. Take the stee winding path to the right, cross the reservoir t find about 60 chhatris of the Ranis.

KHIMSAR

100km north of Jodhpur, or 130km via Osiyar 150km south of Bikaner. A remote 15th century Rajput stronghold in the Thar Desert, its castle th otel. Excellent for a quiet escape or a night or two etween Jodhpur and Bikaner.

It is a good journey from Jodhpur or Bikaner. rom Jodhpur, go by car via Balsamand and Man- ore (see above), making a detour to Osiyan to see 5 fine 8th–11th century Hindu and Jain temples. rom Bikaner, stop off first to see Karni Mata emple at *Deshnok* (32km), where holy rats frolic reely, and are fed and cared for by the faithful who elieve they will be reincarnated one day as holy nen. If your stomach cannot take the rats, the next top is *Nagaur* (110km), another medieval desert wn with a very fine fort. It also has a mosque built y Akbar, the shrine of the disciple of Khwaja luin-ud-din Chisti of Ajmer (see p. 92). There are cluster of chhatri outside the town gates. And a uge, colourful four-day cattle fair takes place in anuary/February with camel races, cock fights, orse and bullock competitions and lots of pup- eteers, folk dancing and singing.

At Khimsar, it is best to stay at the moated *Royal astle* (tel: 72314, or book through Umaid Bhawan alace, Jodhpur, see p. 99). Built as a fortified iikana (home of a local thakur, ruler), by Karam ingh, fifth son of Rao Jodha, founder of Jodhpur. : was named Fateh Mahal after a Sufi saint buried iere. Repairs over the centuries mean the present hakur Saheb, Onkar Singh, lives in the 18th cen- iry part. Watchmen still guard the heavy gates. he hotel run by the Welcomgroup; 10 rooms in the 920s wing, all with bath and hot and cold water; ilk dancing, music, West Rajasthan food, barbe- ues in the Maharaja's tent, 6-seater jeep for sight- eeing. A good idea is to drive out into the desert)r sunset, to spot antelope, blue bull and quan- ties of peacocks and deer. (The nearby villagers re Bisnois.)

IKANER

40km from Jodhpur; 280km from Jaisalmer; 150 om Khimsar; 205km from Bissau (Shekhavati). ight out in the desert, the principal town of orth-west Rajasthan is a heavily fortified, pink andstone city famous for its camels and colourful iihabitants, set amid the arid sand and scrub, nder scorching, relentless sun. Founded by Rao ikaji in 1488, it has a superb fort. It derived its vealth from being sited on the trade route and its ecurity from an effective team of military camels. he rulers could safely lounge about smoking pium and drinking their favourite aphrodisiac pple, asha, made from gold, silver, pearls and heeps' and goats' brains. When these pleasures

were threatened, they gave the British 200 camels for their Afghan warring in 1842 and acquired political standing.

Then along came the inventive and progressive Maharaja Ganga Singh (ruled 1887–1943) – quite a different type from his would-be progressive fellow prince in Jodhpur. With a combination of military, industrial and sporting entre- preneurship, he lifted backward, filthy Bikaner into the 20th century and became the most pukka prince of all. In 1898 he founded the colourful Bikaner Camel Corps, called the Ganga Rissala (seen at Delhi Republic Day Parade). He built a railway and encouraged coal-mining, a combina- tion that trebled the state's income and resulted in a spate of public building and his own spectacular pink pile of a palace, built outside the walls to Sir Swinton Jacob's design.

Then he instigated an essential event in the social calendar: the annual shoot for imperial sand- grouse, followed by roaring about in a Rolls Royce after black buck, a military tattoo by camels in black chainmail and a huge banquet, attended by the Prince of Wales in 1905. The day's bag for 40 guests could be 10,000–12,000 birds, the highest count being achieved by the guest of honour, of course, sometimes surreptitiously ensured by tucking two good marksmen behind him.

THE HARD FACTS Arrive by road or take a train from Jodhpur, Jaipur or Delhi. It is best to stay at the **Lallgarh Palace** (tel: 312; cable: LALLGARH PALACE); begun in 1881 to designs by Sir Swinton Jacob and smothered in the results of both his work at Jaipur, where he had published a catalogue of Rajput architectural decoration, and his study of Bikaner fort. There is delicate jali work, friezes cover every surface, archways are scalloped, romantic cupolas break the skyline. Building and gardens are a bit run-down now. As at Jodhpur, the royal family still live in a wing and run the hotel. The main rooms are a museum (much gilt, vast carpet made by Bikaner prisoners, a zoo of stuffed animals, bronzes and shooting photo- graphs galore, open 9am–6pm) and the remainder is hotel. 14 rooms, meals included in the room price; golf and squash by arrangement.

Alternatively, stay out at **Gajner Palace** (32km, book through Lallgarh); a royal summer palace of the 1890s in delicate Art Nouveau style, with orig- inal Waring and Gillows furniture and fittings. The Maharaja and his family pass Sundays there, en- joying the lake and the wildlife park where the imperial sand-grouse migrate – now in greater safety. 18 rooms, a converted royal hunting lodge, out of town but quiet. Good for spotting wildlife. Both have bundles of charm but slow service and bad food served by local lads. Tourist Office in Tourist Bungalow, Pooram Singh Circle.

OUT AND ABOUT The glorious **Junagarh Fort**, entered between two life-sized elephants, was built 1588–93 by Raja Rai Singh, one of Akbar's generals. It can compare with Jodhpur's fort. The emperor made one of his many Rajput marriage alliances with a Bikaner princess. The fort has a magnificent Mughal Durbar Hall. Its pretty surrounding palaces – Har Mandir (for royal weddings), Karan Mahal, Durgar Nivas, Chandra Mahal (Moon Palace), Phool Mahal (Flower Palace), Anup Mahal – with exteriors of pavilions and balconies and interiors of carved marble, wall-paintings (including fake pietra dura), lacquer work and mirrorwork, and a small, choice museum (manuscripts, armour), open Thurs.–Tues., 9.30am–5pm.

It is worth exploring the Lallgarh palace and museum, wandering through the dazzlingly colourful bazaars (spotting the nomads visiting from the desert) and visiting the Ganga Golden Jubilee Museum which houses a fine collection of archaeological stone carvings (pre-Harrapan, Gupta and Kahsan), quality Bikaner school miniature paintings, local crafts and, of course, armour, open Sat.–Thurs., 10am–5pm.

The best trip out of Bikaner is to the local *camel-breeding farm* (10km), run by the government. Go at about 5pm, ride camels, then watch hundreds of the proud beasts being brought in. Notice their eye lashes which breeders try to make grow longer to keep the dust out of their eyes. The beautiful royal chhatris at Devi Kund (8km) are also worth visiting.

JAISALMER
280km from Bikaner; 290km from Jodhpur. The most western city in Rajasthan, and the most perfect Rajput walled desert city, is a golden jewel shimmering above the hard sand, like a fairytale mirage. Satyajit Ray called his film set there 'Sonar Kella' (Fortress of Gold). Consistent wealth from lying on the trade route – the city had five camel caravanserais to cope with the through traffic – was lavished on domestic architecture. Every building is a joy. The ethereal havelis have astonishing carving of the highest quality – as the

Keeper of the Palace of Westminster put it: 'No t here. The rest of India is full of tat.' The women ar children, dressed in vivid Rajasthan brightnes smile and giggle in the narrow streets. Others car water jugs with the grace of classical ballet dancer There is extraordinary elegance and style ever where, all bathed in a desert light that starts eac day at dawn with membrane-pale mauve and en the day at sunset, hot and livid red.

THE HARD FACTS During the much-laude Desert festival (first held in 1979), when pric soar, accommodation and train seats are difficult find. But Holi (February/March) is nicer here tha anywhere else. In addition, there are the big Ran deo fairs in August–September and November December and the other big Rajasthan festivals Dussehra, Diwali and Gangaur, all celebrated wi traditional jollity. From Jodhpur, the train is bes (The railway line was built when the city becam strategically important during the Indo-Pakista wars of 1965 and 1971.) The road is unexcitir unless miles of hot empty desert bring a thrill. A c is superfluous in Jaisalmer.

Take a sleeper to Jaisalmer, either the regular or or the Maharaja's two dazzling white carriages, h coat of arms painted on the side: one has 7 coup and 2 baths, for 14 people (Rs50,000), the other ha 3 coupés, a sitting room and bath, for 6 peop (Rs9,000). Prices include cooks, butlers and esco from Umaid Bhawan Palace (see p. 99) and 2 nigh (there and back) plus breakfast, lunch and dinn in Jaisalmer. Book well ahead. Taking the regul sleeper, the Umaid Bhawan will lend pillow an blanket, to be put in the left luggage office Jaisalmer station when confirming the retur sleeper on arrival, then used for the return jou ney. A jeep bus service runs between the statio and city. There is no train between Jaisalmer an Bikaner, but there is car or camel (see below). E car, Pokram makes a nice stop to see anoth superb fortress town with carved houses.

To stay in Jaisalmer – and it certainly deserv more than one day – go to *Jaisal Castle* (tel: 62; cabl JAISAL CASTLE), an old courtyard house at th top of the city, run in the guest-house tradition b Mahendra Singh who lives there too. 11 sma rooms, simply furnished, cold water only, nir with views over the desert, two over the tow Glorious sunsets from the flat roof, wonderf atmosphere. Second best is *Narayan Nivas Hot* (tel: 108; cable: NARAYAN NIVAS), a converte caravanserai at the bottom of the town, run by th

me family. 24 rooms, each with shower. No
rden but a deep open hall, like a giant verandah,
here the camels used to sleep – the men slept on
e cooler roof. Local Langas, Mangniyars and
holis play and sing music in both hotels each
ening. Local food can be good, but ask for it.
Tourist Office at the Tourist Bungalow on the
ad into the city from the station. The guide book
isalmer, The Golden City, by K. N. Sharma, is
aarming. Jaisal Tours operates from Jawahar
alace (tel: 97).
Both hotels can arrange camel and jeep tours,
n by Mohendra Singh, whose family also breed
d own about 100 camels. To go on a camel tour
r a few hours, go directly to Narayan hotel on
rival by train and they can be ready in one hour.
r a longer tour, sleeping overnight in the desert,
e party consists of camels (one each plus one for
ggage), cook, bedding, tent, onions to keep the
akes away, night watchman and wireless contact
ith the police (this is well-guarded territory
rdering on Pakistan), all for Rs250 per person per
y. It takes 11 days to reach Bikaner; seven to
kram. A camel covers 20–30km a day. Beware of
eap camel marketeers: their beasts will not be
ained, the saddles will not be good. And their
eks will not be safe. For faster exploring, take a
y's jeep safari and visit 10–12 villages, possibly
eeping out overnight.

UT AND ABOUT   On arrival by train, go to
disar Tank, the large natural oasis that attracted
awal Jaisal to the site. See early morning light on
e Jain temples, women with chaori (rings of
ory) up the length of their arms collecting water;
ft of the beautiful archway (supposedly built by a
ostitute), climb on to temple roofs for views.
en off up to the fort on Trikuta (three-peak) hill.
ilt in 1156 by Rawal Jaisal, of the Bhatti Rajput
an, it is the second oldest fort in Rajasthan, after
ittaugarh. Its chivalry is rather second-best too.
e women managed to perform johar (mass
icide) two and a half times. The half was when
e 16th century ruler, Rawal Loon Karan, had to
ll the women himself because the enemy had
ready entered the city secretly and there was no
ne to prepare the fire.
Within the fort, see the seven-storey palace just
side the thick gateway, and the four other mahals
alaces); the highly decorative Jain temples are
ar the entrance (open daily until noon).
But the nicest thing to do is wander through the
eys seeking out the magnificent havelis. These
are quite different from the Shekhavati havelis:
they are very tall to catch the breeze; very thick-
walled to keep cool; their jali screens are still used
today because Jaisalmer women still observe purdah; and instead of paintings, their exterior walls
have been carved to honeycomb delicacy with a
feverish energy; and several of the interiors are
painted and decorated too.

See especially Nathamal ki Haveli (1885), a prime
minister's home. It was carved by two Muslim
brothers, Hati and Laloo. There are sandstone
elephants at the door. Inside is the beautifully
painted first floor. The five Patwa havelis stand in a
row, built 1800–60 by five brothers on the proceeds
of opium-dealing and smuggling and gold and
silver trading. Now two are owned by the government (open daily, 10.30am–5pm), one is rented to
a shopkeeper who encourages people to ramble
over it, one is lived in by some Patwa descendants,
one by another family. Salim Singh ki Haveli, built
by Salim Singh in the 17th century when he was
prime minister, has a superb facade but there is
almost nothing left inside. And do not miss the
time-warp Mandir palace, a giant carved reliquary
built at the end of the 19th century in Rajput style
with Islamic elements brought by passing traders,
furnished entirely with silver – for only that can
reflect the moon, the Jaisalmer ancestor (small area
open daily).

Shopping around the bazaars and alleys can turn
up constant treasures, since this is the central
market place for all the surrounding villages. Find
the local bandhana (made at Kadi Bundar), including very lovely wool-work. There are also silk
shawls, wool jackets, camel leather mojadis (slippers), camel-hair carpets, goat-hair weaving,
jewellery, the huge Rajasthan gathered skirts (up
to 7 metres), and some nice old clothes with good
embroidery. The shop in one of the Patwa havelis
has some particularly nice things, if it is still there.
(The future use of the house is uncertain.)

Out of town, take a camel to the Jaisalmer chhatris for sunset – the view back to the city is un-
forgettable. Further afield lie Amar Sagar (6km), for
pretty Jain temple and ruined garden, and Lodarva
beyond (another 7km), more Jain temples amid the
ruins of the pre-Jaisalmer ancient capital. Heading
west from Amar Sagar, find first Mool Sagar
(another 3km), a garden and tank, then Sam sand
dunes, as seriously desert as Rajasthan gets.

Wildlife Sanctuaries

Despite the arid land, the princes nurtured their forests to ensure lavish, status symbol chikars (hunts). The three main sanctuaries in Rajasthan evolved from this tradition.

KEOLADEO NATIONAL PARK, BHARATPUR, RAJASTHAN see p. 67.

RANTHAMBORE TIGER RESERVE, RAJASTHAN
November–May; best March and even better April–May but very hot. 160km from Jaipur by car or train, nearest station Sawai Madhopur. Directly accessible on the Delhi–Bombay train. Enquire if the *Maharaja's Lodge* is re-opened (it is to be under the Taj group management, who run the Rambagh Palace hotel, Jaipur). Otherwise, accommodation can be booked through Rajasthan Tours (see p. 81).

400 sq km of dry deciduous forest, perfect natural habitat for tigers. Set in the Aravalli and Vindhyan hills, dotted with pavilions and dominated by the hilltop Ranthambore fort. Plenty of tigers and other game to be seen in a very picturesque landscape. Favourite hunting haunt of the late Maharaja of Jaipur, who built the lodge and entertained, among many others, the Mountbattens and the Queen and Prince Philip. Other guests were given elaborate tents. Tiger, leopard, hyena, bear, blue bull, sambhar and other deer were spotted or shot from elephants. When the royal party was there in 1961, the Maharani recalls that Prince Philip 'bagged a large tiger with a beautiful shot'.

Today the tigers are being saved, not shot, and Prince Philip is an ardent conservationist. Since Project Tiger was launched by the World Wildlife Fund in 1973, the estimated Indian population of tigers has risen from a disastrous 2,400 to about 3,300, and national parks and sanctuaries (including 11 tiger reserves) cover 75,763 sq km – 2.3% of all India and 19% of India's forest. But it is a misconception to blame India's wildlife problems on the princes and the Raj. They observed strict sporting rules and guarded their wildlife preserves ruthlessly, even if they did occasionally dull tigers' senses with opium-laced water and hold big chikars to impress visiting Viceroys and fellow royals. The real damage came after Independence when sporting rules were ignored, villagers had guns, there was widespread poaching and, worst of all, colossal deforestation. A tiger population of around 30,000 in 1947 (unchanged since 1930) dropped to 2,400 in 23 years.

The 900 increase during the first decade of Project Tiger was described by Guy Mountfort, Vice President of the World Wildlife Fund, as 'probably the most successful conservation project for wildlife ever launched'. The tigers are breeding well. Their food of pigs and deer are also multiplying. Protected forest areas are increasing. The problem is the competition for space between tiger and man – a tiger needs up to 80 sq km and defends it to the death. Fellow tigers are thereby endangered and, occasionally, so are humans. Not all conservationists are optimistic about the big cats' future.

SARISKA, RAJASTHAN
February–June; April best for tiger. On the Delhi–Jaipur road, 200km from Delhi, 96km from Jaipur. Stay at the modest *Tourist Rest House* (tel: Alwar 2348); booking and information from Wildlife Warden, Sariska (tel: Alwar 2348).

210 sq km of deciduous forest near Alwar, a sanctuary since 1958. Formerly enjoyed by the Maharajas who held highly organised tiger chikars when VIP guests mounted their well-trained hunting elephants while the Alwar soldiers and cavalry acted as beaters with military precision. See tiger, leopard, sloth bear, pig, nilgai and chital from jeeps and two machans (watch towers) overlooking water-holes, especially at dusk. During the monsoon, the sanctuary is very lush, beautiful and full of birds.

Find out more

Allen, C. and Dwirendi, S.: *Lives of the Indian Princes*, London, 1984
Archer, W. G.: *Indian paintings from Rajasthan*, London, 1957; rev. ed. Calcutta, 1962
Baroda, Maharaja of: *The Palaces of India*, London, 1980
Beach, M. C.: *Rajput Painting at Bundi and Kota*, Askona, Switzerland, 1975
Beny, R.: *Rajasthan*, London, 1981
Brunel, F.: *Rajasthan*, London, 1985
Devi, G. and Rau, S. R.: *A Princess Remembers. The Memoirs of the Maharani of Jaipur*, London, 1976 reprinted 1984
Hendley, T. H.: *Rulers of India and Chiefs of Rajputana*, London, 1897
Mountfort, G.: *Saving the Tiger*, London, 1981

al, P.: *The Classical Tradition in Rajput Painting from he Paul F. Walter Collection*, New York, 1978

ingh, R.: *Rajasthan, India's Enchanted Land*, Hong .ong, 1981

'od, J.: *Annals and Antiquities of Rajasthan*, ed. W. Crooke, 3 vols, Oxford, 1920

Topsfield, A.: *Paintings from Rajasthan in the National Gallery of Victoria*, Melbourne, 1980

Wacziarg, F., and Nath, A.: *Rajasthan: the painted walls of Shekhavati*, Delhi, 1982

Bombay:
Business and bustle

Bombay has vitality. It throbs with action and money. It is positive and forward-looking. It is India's only modern international city. A single Indian working woman can lead a more liberated life here than elsewhere in the country, even in Delhi. The top Indian businessmen, merchants, dealers, actors and all those who make their worlds go round are here. Even if the politics of commerce and industry is dealt with in Delhi, the activity is here. Gujaratis, Parsees and Goans contribute to the immigrant population of 8 million, swollen by a floating population of other Indians and foreigners, some working, some just having a good time. The coffers of rupees are emptied and replenished quickly and with panache.

Bombay is the country's financial, industrial, commercial and trading centre. It has about 15% of India's factories, 45% of her textile mills, handles 50% of her foreign port traffic and is responsible for a third of her income-tax receipts. The cash economy, known as 'black money', thrives here like nowhere else. As one Malabar Hill resident remarked: 'There are two economies in India, white and black. Nothing happens without the black. We could not sit here having tea and cakes without it. And when the tax man swoops, you do a deal with him, too.'

Bombay has by far the highest cost of living in India, the largest film industry in the world, and property values on a par with New York. It is the centre of the Indian gold and diamond markets, has excellent, quality shopping and the best night life, and is the only Indian city to have an extensive network of good restaurants.

It all grew on seven boggy, malarial islands acquired by the British for next to nothing. Mumbadevi, the largest, was part of Catherine of Braganza's dowry when she married Charles II in 1661. But London was neither impressed nor aware of what it had acquired. Pepys termed it 'that poor little island'. Lord Clarendon believed it had 'towns and castles therein which are very little distance from Brazil'. Four years later the British took possession of the remaining islands and in 1668 leased the lot to the East India Company for £10 in gold per annum. The 'Company', which had received its trading Charter from Queen Elizabeth 1 in 1600 and had a base on the coast at Surat, knew just what a good deal it had got. It could collect all Bombay's revenue (then estimated at £2,833 per annum), make the laws and, when its headquarters were moved there in 1687, the city soon became the centre for the west coast trade.

Trade fed Bombay's progress from seven island swamp to single-island city, as it did that of Calcutta. Both grew and prospered to become great cities and centres of British administration. Both were – and still are – magnets for immigrants. But whereas Bombay continues to absorb newcomers and t

eate wealth, Calcutta, formerly so much
ander and flashier, can offer its floods of
migrants little today. In Bombay things get
one, telephones work and appointments
e kept (almost) on time.

But this wealth came slowly to Bombay.
erald Aungier, known as father of Bombay
d Governor 1672–77, established the
ourts of Justice, began the Company militia
nich became the East India Company
my, and started the practice of encourag-
g all religions and nationalities to settle in
mbay. He welcomed Parsees, merchants
m Gujarat, Banians (Hindu traders)
eing Jesuit oppression in Goa, and Arab
ders. But, for the British, life was pretty
im. There was little amusement, few
men, a bit of racing but plenty of corrup-
n, and often too much Bombay punch.
is consoling concoction was a mixture of
al toddy (coconut-based spirit), sugar,
e-juice, spice and water, the five ingredi-
ts called punch from the Mahratti word for
e, panch. Even by the end of the 18th
ntury, when the population had grown to
out 120,000, there were probably barely
00 Europeans and life was not bright.

Then, at the beginning of the 19th century,
ings began to hot up. In 1813 trade restric-
ns relaxed when the Company lost its
onopoly of trade between Britain and
dia. The new P & O steamers brought
men out to India. Later on, batches of
ung women arriving in search of husbands
ere known as 'the Fishing Fleet'. The rail-
ay came in 1853 (the first east of Suez), the
egraph in 1865, the first cotton mill opened
1857. The vast docks were begun that
uld take decades to complete.

Under Sir Bartle Frere, Governor 1862–7,
w streets were laid out and the great Vic-
ian Gothic public buildings rose which still
minate the city centre. Bombay needed
ace so, once the islands were joined
gether, projects were begun to reclaim land
m the sea by throwing in Bombay's hills
d much else. By the 1950s, the city's total
ea had increased by a third.

Reclamation continues today – so maps are
nstantly out of date, with buildings where

the sea is painted. But it is insufficient and
now there is to be a new twin city across the
harbour, designed by India's 44-year-old
architect king, Charles Correa. Correa's recent buildings include Bharat Bhavan, an arts
complex at Bhopal in central India (see p.
132), and the Cidade de Goa beach hotel in
Goa. He also designed the stunning Kovalam
Beach Resort in Kerala, part of the government's Ashok hotel group (see p. 244). In
1984, the Royal Institute of British Architects
awarded him their Gold Medal for his
architectural work.

The wealth and expansion of Bombay were
the fruit of trade that had begun to blossom in
the early 1800s. After a famine in China in the
1770s, much cotton-growing land was given
over to grain. India began to supply cotton as
well as opium to China, exchanging them for
tea, which was catching on in Britain with the
reduction in import duty. In 1859, opium
took 42% and cotton 30% of Bombay's total
trade. In 1863 the railway linked the city to
the cotton-growing Deccan. Six years later
the Suez Canal opened, making Bombay the
uncontested premier Western port of India,
vying with Calcutta on the east coast.

The early 1860s were a period of enormous
prosperity. The American Civil War boosted
an already surging cotton trade when the
Confederacy ports were blocked, halting cotton exports to Manchester. India immediately stepped in, cotton prices soared for four
years – nothing but pint mugs of champagne
were drunk – and then crashed in March 1865
when news reached Bombay that the war had
ended and American trading would resume.

Small communities and strong individuals
have built Bombay. They brought with them
their own food, customs, architecture and
languages which, to an extent, they still retain. The so-called 'cages' of the red-light
district around Falkland Road are considered
by some to be traditional Gujarati houses
whose box-like rooms have slatted facades on
the ground floor. Bombay still has no common language and is full of variety, making it
truly cosmopolitan.

One such strong individual was David
Sassoon, whose family later spread to Europe

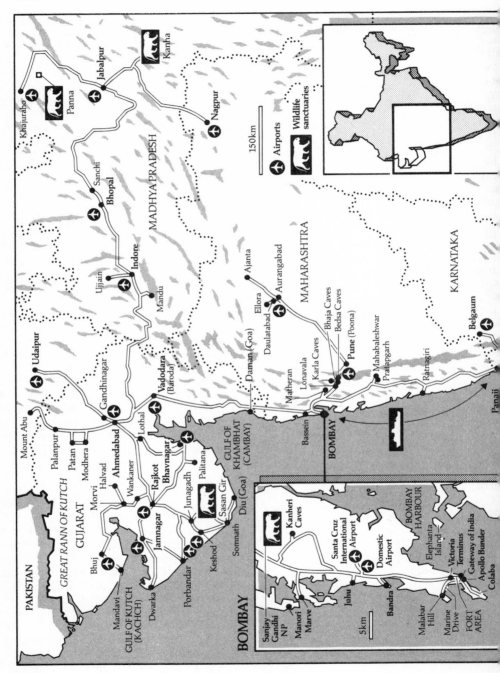

d America. He was a Sephardic Jew from a
ghdad family of bankers and community
ders. He arrived in Bombay in 1833 and
thin 25 years had built up an empire that
vered every aspect of trading, from the
ods to the docks. He put his eight sons in
y world trading cities, took British
izenship in 1853 and, the final symbol of
cial success, in 1872 his son was created a
ronet, Sir Albert Sassoon of Kensington
ore.

But the best-known group of immigrants
e the *Parsees* who arrived in the 1670s. This
enomenally successful but tiny com-
unity of Zoroastrans (fire-worshippers) mi-
ated from Persia when the Muslims came
power, finally landing at Sanjan in Gujarat
745 AD. The story goes that their emissaries
the king of Surat returned with a full glass
milk, indicating that Gujarat was a land of
osperity but full up. The Parsee captain
opped a teaspoonful of sugar into the milk
d sent it back, indicating they would add
e sweetness of life. (Less romantic variants
ve a coin dropped in and claims of greater
osperity.) Whatever the truth, the Parsees
re accepted.

They remain a very tight-knit community.
eir scriptures are in Persian, they speak
ajarati, and the bodies of their dead are laid
towers of silence for vultures to eat rather
an be allowed to pollute the sacred fire or
rth. They seldom marry outsiders because
e children would not be true Parsees. In a
all and elite community this means inter-
arriage and so, whilst the sane tend to be
elligent and successful, there is a certain
aount of battiness about.

The Parsees came to Bombay as traders,
ipbuilders and bankers. Both at work and
play, they made instant friends with the
tish, on whom they increasingly modelled
eir lives, from learning Shakespeare and
earing top hats to playing cricket and golf.
me of the first Indian undergraduates at
:ford and Cambridge were Parsee. There
re the shipbuilding Wadias, the Camas,
stonjis, Readymoneys and Jeejeebhoys.

Jamshetji Jeejeebhoy (1783–1859) was the
first Indian to be created a baronet. Streets,
statues and institutions named after the
families litter the city.

The most talked about Parsee family today
is the Tatas. Jamshetji Nusserwanji Tata
(1839–1904), father of the dynasty, first
reaped his rupees from the cotton trade.
Although his fingers were severely burned
when the cotton bubble burst in 1865 and he
was stuck on a ship bound for London, he
recovered to build mills, a hydro-electric
works, a steel works, open iron-ore mines,
start a shipping line – and build a huge
memorial to himself, the Taj Mahal Hotel.

His descendants have pushed out the feel-
ers of the House of Tata even further: into tea,
trucks, scientific research. It was Tata Airlines, founded in 1932, that went public as
Air India in 1946, and two years later became
Air India International, the first joint under-
taking between the government and the private sector. Like Value Added Tax in Britain,
Tata is impossible to avoid. Today's leading
Parsees are often lawyers, writers or doctors.
One is Nani Palkhivala, one of India's leading
lawyers, who served as Ambassador to the
United States from 1977 to 1979.

Bombay's gleaming sky-scrapers on the
newly claimed land at Nariman Point have a
Manhattan air about them. Their symbol of
wealth is in harsh contrast to the crowded old
bazaars and seedy suburbs that constitute
most of Bombay. As Correa says: 'Every day
it gets worse and worse as physical environment . . . and yet better and better as city . . .
every day it offers more skills, activities,
opportunities on every level.' Nevertheless,
there is a rising trend to opt for the spacious-
ness of Delhi. For the Westerner arriving in
India, Bombay is an easy, welcoming city. It
is a painless introduction with the rough
corners smoothed off. Real India lies beyond,
in the cities of Calcutta, Madras, Delhi and
Ahmedabad, in the Kashmir hills and Tamil
Nadu temples, in lush Kerala and desert
Rajasthan.

When to go

Between October and February the air is fresh, the skies blue. Bombayites rival the British in their talk about the weather, praising the 'glorious cold winter' (which resembles a Continental summer). But in March, heat and humidity start rising and their previous banter makes sense. By June it is boiling hot. Then comes the drenching monsoon until September – known as 'three-shirts-a-day-weather'. After that, the stickiness decreases slowly.

FESTIVALS *Ganesh* (or Ganapati), the benign elephant-headed deity, is the subject of the biggest festival, celebrated on his birthday in September. Ganesh's abilities to smooth the path to success in anything from writing a letter to starting up a business or going on a journey is eminently suited to money-making Bombay. The city is filled with gaudy, pink, garlanded clay images of the fat, sweet-toothed god of prosperity and wisdom – each with a morsel of last year's figure added to this year's clay mixture. More than 6,000 images are made annually, the largest ones by factory workers who compete fiercely, collecting funds months in advance. Traditional idols are sometimes jazzed up with flickering multi-coloured lights or electric fountains, like a Hindi film prop. There is even a society entirely devoted to Ganesh Utsav (festival).

The ten-day celebrations begin with much puja performed to the images set up in homes and on street corners. Women buy new saris and bangles, prepare kheer (a special rice pudding) and spruce up the home. On the tenth day, full-moon day, half the city parade their idols down to Chowpatty beach, which is already adorned with multi-coloured Ganesh sand sculptures. The images are carried on high – the huge ones on trucks – amid clouds of pink gulal (powder), music and dancing, and then finally immersed in the water to bob out into the Arabian Sea. In 1894, when the British banned crowd assemblies, Lokmanya Bal Gangadhar Tilak successfully claimed that this was a religious festival and his political messages, disguised in dance and drama, stirred Bombayites to fight for independence.

There are good celebrations for Diwali, Dussehra, Holi, Gokulashtami and Coconut Day, as well as the big non-Hindu festivals (see p. 251).

SOCIAL CALENDAR Keeps to the cool months, October–March. It revolves around racing which culminates in the Derby in February–March, cricket which peters out in March, gloriously vulga weddings which peak in December–January, an the big festivals from Ganesh until Christmas an New Year. Grand Hindi film premières are in th winter too. (The government funds the Indian Fil Festival, keeping it on a short rein in Delhi, an lengthening the leash for other cities to act as ho on alternate years.)

Getting there: Getting away

Arriving at Bombay's new International airport Sahar is not the joy it should be – nor is leavir through it. If India is keen to attract tourism (an thus foreign currency), this method fails. Bagga is unbelievably slow to arrive, the lavatories reser ble paddling pools, there are few chairs and queu for the bank never move. (Officially, all rupees a in India, so it may be essential to change mon before taking a taxi into town.) To depart, th airport charges R100 (for precious little service). takes over an hour to check in, and then a five-fo boarding card check implies that one is the chi suspect of some dirty deed.

Arriving on domestic flights at Santa Cruz a port is better. But to connect a domestic with international flight means taking a taxi for the 5k between airports as the bus service is erratic.

There are two roads from the airports ov Mahim Creek on to the central Bombay isthmu both unattractive and jammed with traffic except the middle of the night. It takes ruthless fare ba gaining and then at least an hour by taxi (see p. of Survival Code).

Internally the nicest way to arrive or leave Bor bay is by train at the majestic Victoria Termin (but some arrive at the other station, Bomb Central). The exception is travelling up from G when it is essential to try to leave time for th steamer. The more adventurous could drive up car.

Most international airlines serve Bombay. Ma of them have late night departures, allowing pa sengers to avoid the traffic and hanging arou in the airport amid crowds and heat. Internall Indian Airlines makes excellent connections, e pecially to Gujarat, Rajasthan, and central a southern India. Daily direct flights go to all maj cities including Ahmedabad, Aurangabad, Bang lore, Belgaum, Bhavnagar, Calcutta, Cochi Dabolim (for Goa), Delhi, Hyderabad, Jamnag Keshod, Madras, Mangalore, Nagpur, Pune, F

t, Trivandrum and Vadodara (Baroda). The dai-
morning Rajasthan shuttle stops at Udaipur,
lhpur and Jaipur. Daily flights go north to Srina-
r via Delhi. Colombo (Sri Lanka) is accessible
ily except Fridays, either direct or via Trivan-
um or Madras. Male (the Maldives) is reached
Trivandrum on Mondays or Thursdays.

The best train to and from Delhi, the Rajdhani
press (17hrs), runs five times a week but uses
mbay Central, whereas the Punjab Mail arriving
Victoria Terminus takes 29 hours. For Calcutta
 Gitanjali Express and the Calcutta Mail both
 Victoria Terminus. But the Madras Express
hrs) and Madras Mail (31 hours) and trains for
ne (3½hrs) and Hyderabad (18 hours) leave
m a third station, Dadar.

The steamer is better taken from Goa to Bombay,
 vice versa. This way the stops to collect passen-
's are during the day, the final stop just as the
ows are silhouetted against the sunset over the
abian Sea. Next morning's arrival at Bombay
gests pre-aircraft days, gliding past the Taj
tel and India Gate to Goa Docks, Ferry wharf,
ere armies of coolies shout and jostle. The
amer has several berths, all fairly basic, plus one
ch larger double berth, with its own washing
ilities, called the Owner's Cabin, and two first-
ss deluxe A cabins. Food in the galley is simple,
l European unless Indian is ordered. A bottle of
i might be handy. Tea and beer are served
istantly. Book tickets and the essential berths
ough the Government of Maharashtra Tourism
velopment Corporation.

here to stay

'tune seekers and fortune spenders, with all
ir hangers-on, have been passing through rich
l fashionable Bombay in large numbers for over
entury. And they continue to do so. It should be
ffed with good hotels, both the bright 'n' brassy
l the comfy colonial. But it is not. In downtown
nbay – and there is little point in staying else-
ere – the choice is between the Taj and Oberoi,
h top services and matching prices. The Wel-
ngroup's SeaRock, technically in the same
gue, is too far out (at Bandra) and fails to fully
loit its superb location. However, it is perfect
an airport stop-over.

)ther hotels are a dozen rungs down the ladder,
 the top two are constantly heavily booked.
ch less chic and expensive but pleasant and

central are – in descending order of price and
sophistication – the President, Ambassador,
Fariyas, Natraj, Ritz and Grand. For more privacy,
the Royal Bombay Yacht Club and the Cricket Club
of India have rooms but require a little pre-
planning. There are no rooms at the Willingdon
Club or the Bombay Gymkhana.

If the hotel is just for an overnight stop between
flights, avoid the swish-looking Centaur hard by
the airport, with its petrol-smelling air, and head
for the sea. It is a 15 minute taxi ride to the SeaRock,
with good restaurants, pools and views. Next best
is the Holiday Inn at Juhu.

In the commercial and trading capital of India,
with the best links to the rest of the country and the
world beyond, hotel beds are hot property and
rights to reservations can be contested. So book
well in advance and arrive clutching the hotel's
letter of confirmation.

CENTRAL HOTELS
Taj Mahal and Taj Mahal Intercontinental Apol-
lo Bunder, Bombay 400039
Telephone: 2023366
Telex: 112442/116175 TAJB IN.
As headquarters of the Taj Group of Hotels, the
Central Reservation System is here (see p. 11).
Cable: PALACE
Airports 30km
650 rooms, including 42 suites, attached bath.
Single Rs700; double Rs800; suites Rs1,050–3,500.
Every service including travel agency, bank, airline
offices, business services, pool, health club, hair-
dresser, florist, chemist, babysitter, shopping
arcade.

Quite justifiably an institution and a thriving
memorial to the father of the Tata clan. But the
difference in the two hotel titles is crucial. The
red-domed Taj Mahal Hotel was built in 1903 by
Jamshetji Nusserwanji Tata, designed by a local
English architect named Chambers, constructed
the right way round, contrary to popular myth,
cost £500,000, has its own Turkish baths and electric laundry and is the one to stay in. The Taj Mahal
Intercontinental is the modern skyscraper annex,
used by aircraft crews who want to sleep in peace
and by Arabs happy to waive character for car-
peted corridors.

Although all facilities are common to both parts,
the greatest facility is Tata's building. To stay here
in a spacious room overlooking the sea – or better
still in one of the dottier old suites with rooms for

113

the guest's manservants and maids – is to stay at 'The Taj'.

Built to outdo the fashionable and exclusively European Watson's (which no longer survives), it was a roaring success from the start. Sited to welcome with panache the linerloads of visitors, its doors open to all races, it was instantly on a par with Raffle's, Shepheard's and the Peninsula.

Aldous Huxley may have called its style a mixture of 'the South Kensington Natural History Museum with that of an Indian pavilion at the International Exhibition', but high society continues to know it more intimately than its namesake in Agra. Somerset Maugham, the Beatles, Duke Ellington, Gregory Peck and Mohammad Ali have all stayed here. It is the place to be seen, anywhere, any time – even just hanging around the lobby. It has the best art book shop, newsagent, swimming pool and tea lounge and rivals the Oberoi in its health club, beauty salon, plethora of restaurants and quality shopping. The Oberoi has the edge on service but the Taj has a character and smell (cruelly likened to fish by an American-born lady) it is difficult not to get hooked on. See other sections for more.

Oberoi Towers Marine Drive (Netaji Subhash Road), Nariman Point, Bombay 400021
Telephone: 2024343
Telex: 4153/4154 OBBY
Cable: OBHOTEL
Airports 28km
700 rooms, including 48 suites, attached bath.
Single Rs895; double Rs995; suites Rs2,400–4,950
The moddest of mod. cons. plus travel agency, bank, airline offices, business facilities, pool, health club, beauty salon, baby-sitter, massive shopping arcade.

Probably the most efficient hotel in India. Certainly the tallest building in the country when it went up – and possibly still is. (Mr Oberoi was not hampered by such trifles as height restriction, nor was the Maharaja of Gwalior for his skyscraper built on the sea front beyond the racecourse, next to his blue-domed palace.) The Lego-rigid 35-storey block perched on top of a base shaped like a concrete liner.

The block contains the bedrooms, each with identical cleanliness and comfort and most with stunning views over Bombay and the Arabian Sea. The higher the floor, the better – lightning fast lifts avoid long waits. The very modern suites, well decorated using regional Indian crafts, nobble the

best views at the top. The concrete liner contai the facilities. They start at the bottom with t Cellar discotheque (avoid), and rise through good health club, exceptional beauty salon, 7 e ing and drinking haunts (2 more on top of t tower) and a two-storeyed, 200-shop baza attempting to combine Knightsbridge and Oxfc Street, topped by a swimming pool shaped lik clover-leaf. Like the Taj, the Oberoi is a social foc for Bombayites and is already acquiring a disti tive and friendly character rare in a modern hot See other sections for more.

Hotel President 90 Cuffe Parade (Capt. P. Pet Marg), Colaba, Bombay 400002
Telepone: 219141
Telex: 114135 PRES IN
Cable: PREMHOTEL
Airports 32km
300 rooms, including 16 suites, attached ba
Single Rs550; double Rs650; suites Rs1,200–1,40
Facilities include travel counter, bank, busine services, pool, health club, hairdresser, ba sitter, shopping arcade.

Built on the reclaimed land of Back Bay (for nately printed in terra firma orange on the Tou Map but still deep-sea blue on the Latest Road M of Bombay). Modern, non-architectural, 18-sto block in the developing business area. Bet placed for businessman than tourist. Part of the Group, with their solid comfort and good servi Gulzar restaurant its highpoint, see restaurant s tion. Also Italian trattoria, Continental, Chin food.

Ambassador Veer Nariman Road, Churchga Bombay 400020
Telephone: 291131
Telex: 0112918 AMBA IN
Cable: EMBASSY
Airports 28km
125 rooms, including 15 suites, attached ba
Single Rs400–485; double Rs565; suites Rs8 1,550.

Very central, basic shops and offices all n by. The Top revolving restaurant has views, Society has reputation, see restaurant section.

Fariyas 25, off Arthur Bunder Road, Cola Bombay 400006
Telephone: 215911
Telex: 3272
Cable: FARIYAS
Airports 31km
81 rooms, including 2 suites, attached show
Single Rs440; double Rs540.

New, overlooking the harbour. Clean rooms, small pool. Indian/Continental restaurant plus roof-top bar.

Natraj 135 Marine Drive (Netaji Subhash Road, Bombay 400020
Telephone: 294161
Telex: 112302 RAJA IN
Cable: HOTELRAJA
Airports 27km
82 rooms, including 9 suites, attached bath/shower. Single Rs400–430; double Rs500; suite Rs900.

On the plus side are the central site, recent renovation and excellent views in the rooms overlooking the bay. A minus are dreary tri-cuisine food, an ice-cream parlour (it is better to eat out) and general atmosphere.

Ritz 5 Jamshedji Tata Road, Bombay 400020
Telephone: 220141
Telex: 2520 RITZ IN
Cable: RITZ BOMBAY
Airports 28km
73 rooms, including 11 suites, attached bath. Single Rs375; double Rs475; suite Rs650–750.

Old, central hotel with character, newly painted, nice atmosphere. Indian/Italian/Continental food.

Grand 17 Sprott Road, Ballard Estate, Bombay 400038
Telephone: 268211/263558/263559
Cable: GRANDHOTEL
Airports 25km
72 rooms, including 5 suites, attached bath. Single Rs280; double Rs325; suite Rs350.

Old hotel with corridors around central courtyard with potted flowers. Newly green-painted, 3rd and 4th floor rooms have view over harbour, nice gentle atmosphere.

CLUBS

Neither of the two Bombay clubs with good rooms enjoys the social swing of Calcutta clubs. They offer peace, privacy, space and a certain charming refinement.

Royal Bombay Yacht Club Apollo Bunder, Bombay
30 rooms. Single Rs300; double Rs550 plus visiting membership Rs200 for 10 days. To apply for membership and to book, write to The Secretary.
Library, billiards, table tennis, garden.

Stained-glass windows and steel engravings of ships decorate the spacious Yacht Club Chambers. With the room comes a bearer (Rs10 per day) to molly-coddle the guest with breakfast, bedmaking, laundry etc.

Cricket Club of India D Vacha Road, Bombay
Telephone: 220262
40 rooms. Single Rs200; double Rs400. Temporary membership Rs100 for 15 days, open to anyone. To apply for membership and booking, write to Major-Gen. Michigan, Secretary.
Affiliated to the Royal Overseas League, London and the Caledonian Club, Edinburgh.

Cricket, badminton, tennis, pool, squash, table tennis, cards. Huge grounds, very efficient, central and thus popular, so book well in advance. Good restaurant. The Cross Bats, a group of mainly first-class cricketers, fondly nicknamed the Blind Bats, meets here regularly for lunch.

AIRPORT HOTELS

SeaRock Land's End, Bandra, Bombay 400050
Telephone: 535421
Telex: 5460/6990 ROCK IN
Cable: SEAROCK
Airports 8km
430 rooms, including some suites, attached bath. Single Rs550; double Rs650; suite Rs2,200–3,300.
Extensive facilities include travel and airline counter, bank, business services, baby-sitter, health club (sauna, Turkish bath, yoga), beauty salon, shopping arcade, sports (tennis, squash, billiards, gym), 2 pools (adults and children), discotheque, 24-hour room service and restaurant.

Part of the Welcomgroup chain. Superb site, the hotel almost in the sea. Go for a high room and choose it for sunrise or sunset views. Enough amusements, pampering and sports on hand to save the most direly delayed air passenger from boredom. Six small restaurants each serving different cuisines: excellent North West Frontier, seafood, Indian, Continental, Far Eastern (revolving at the top) and 'shudh' vegetarian.

Holiday Inn Balraj Sahni Road, Juhu Beach, Bombay 400049
Telephone: 571425/571435
Telex: 71266/71432
Cable: HOLIDAY INN
Airports 6km
210 rooms, including 16 suites, attached bath. Single Rs525; double Rs600; suite Rs900–2,250.
Facilities include travel desk, health club and beauty salon, shopping arcade, 2 swimming pools (adults and children), discotheque, 4 restaurants, 24-hour room service and coffee shop.

Information and reservations

Maharashtra Tourism Development Corporation, CDO Hutments, Madame Cama Road (tel: 241784/241762/241713). Best on trips out of Bombay, such as booking steamer to Goa or visit to Ajanta and Ellora.

Government of India Tourist Office, 123 M Karve Road, Churchgate (tel: 293144), open Mon.–Sat., 8.30am–5.30pm (closing 12.30pm on the 2nd Sat., of the month and public holidays). Extremely knowledgeable and helpful staff. Issue Liquor Permits, essential for Gujarat (see p. 134). Also have desks at Sahar and Santa Cruz airports (both 24 hours) and at Taj Hotel, Mon.–Sat., 8.30am–3.30pm (closing 12.30pm on the 2nd Sat. of the month and public holidays).

Government of Gujarat Tourist Office, Dhanraj Mahal, C. Shivaji Road (tel: 243866)

Government of Goa, Daman and Diu Tourist Counter, Bombay Central Station (tel: 396288)

Government of Rajasthan Tourist Office, 230 D N Road (tel: 267162)

The Times of India and *The Indian Express* have their headquarters in Bombay. They are the main daily newspapers and are especially good on news and details of cultural events. *The Daily* is for gossip. *The Financial Express* and *Economic Times* are both exclusively Bombay papers. *The Sunday Observer* bears uncanny resemblance to the British *Sunday Times*. The fortnightly semi-glossy, *Bombay*, has a 'briefing' section for films, performing arts, exhibitions, sport. The Government of India Tourist Office publishes *This Fortnight For You!* (free from their office) carrying much the same information in minimal form.

There is no good guide-book to Bombay. The Government of India's free 28-page booklet is a survival kit of names and addresses. Their map is best (although not good). The Latest Road Map of Bombay is hopelessly out of date, even leaving reclaimed land and its buildings under the sea. But excellent journals and books on Bombay have been accumulating since the last century (see Bibliography, p. 142).

TRAVEL AGENTS

American Express, Majithia Chamber, Dadabhoy Naoroji Road (tel: 266361/260629); Indtravel, Neville House, Ballard Estate (tel: 265761); Mackinnon Travel Service, 4 Shoorji Vallabhdas Marg (tel: 268021); Mercury Travel, 70 Dr V B Gandhi Marg, Rampart Row Corner (tel: 273116/

273275) and at Oberoi Towers; SITA World Travel 8 Atlanta Building, Nariman Point (tel: 240666); Thomas Cook, Cooks Building, D N Road (tel: 258556); Trade Wings, 30 K Dubash Marg (tel: 244334); TCI, Chander Mukhi (1st floor), Nariman Point (tel: 231881); Vista Travels, 87 Wodehouse Road, Colaba (tel: 214656/217999).

AIRLINE OFFICES

Indian Airlines, Air-India Building, Nariman Point (tel: 233031). International airlines offices huddle in groups. Those on Veer Nariman Road include Aeroflot (tel: 221743); British Airways (tel: 220888 and Swissair (tel: 293535). In the Taj hotel are Air France and Pan Am (tel: 243366) and Cathay Pacific (tel: 244112). At Nariman Point are Air India (tel: 234142), Japan Airlines (tel: 297492) and Singapore Airlines (tel: 233365), all in the Air-India Building and Lufthansa (tel: 233430) in Express Towers Thai International (tel: 219191/215207) is in the World Trade Centre, Cuffe Parade.

TRAIN RESERVATIONS

Victoria Terminus Station, Bori Bunder (for trains to the east, south and a few north), open 9am–12.30pm, 1–4.30pm. Western Railway Reservation Office (for the west and north), Churchgate, open 8am–1.45pm, 2.45pm–8pm. These are for first class bookings and Indrail Passes, and have Tourist Guide Assistants.

CONSULATES AND EMBASSIES

UK: 2nd floor, Mercantile Bank Building, M Gandhi Road (tel: 274874); USA: Lincoln House Bjhulabhai Desai Road (tel: 823611); France: Mercantile Bank Building, M Gandhi Road (tel: 271528); West Germany: 10th floor, Hoechst House, Nariman Point (tel: 232422). Most countries have representation in Bombay and are listed in the telephone directory. Foreigners Registration Office, Annex 2, Office of the Commissioner of Police, Dadabhoy Naoroji Road, by Mahatma Phule Market (tel: 268111).

Bombay GPO is on Bori Bunder, near Victoria Terminus. The Central Telegraph Office is at Flora Fountain. If illness strikes, the top hotels have doctors on call and the others can find one quickly. There are several hospitals; chemists include Kemp & Co. in the Taj hotel and Wordell on Veer Nariman Road.

The city by day

From Monday to Saturday Bombay is action-packed. Deals are struck. Mountains of rupees are made; more mountains are spent. The streets are full of businessmen scurrying to appointments. Merchants and traders race to keep up supplies in shops and markets. Cars blast their horns. Well-organised beggars – some with devilish charm – earn the family wage at traffic lights. On Sunday, Bombay is silent except for the sound of the cricket bat. The smart spend the day en famille at the Willingdon or Gymkhana clubs, play cricket or golf and go to the races. The less smart play cricket on the maidans and go to museums and parks. It is the best day for seeing the Fort area architecture without getting run over.

Bombay's past and present are business, not culture. Unlike Calcutta and Delhi, there are few museums. And, although immigrants built every sort of temple, mosque and church, it is their secular buildings which are significant. So Bombay is an outdoor city made familiar by wandering the streets of the Fort area, where past tycoons are remembered by their own grand buildings and other people's monuments to them. Bombay's cosmopolitan entrepreneurial spirit is most lively in the huge network of bazaars. Late afternoon is the time to spy on Malabar Hill's grand homes before joining Bombayites for a sunset stroll along Chowpatty Beach or, more spectacular, watching the sun go down and Marine Drive light up from Naaz café opposite the Hanging Gardens.

The MTDC (state) and ITDC (central) tourist offices both run city sight-seeing tours. Neither are worth taking. Some of their stops are without interest, others need more time. The scattered itineraries mean more driving than seeing. Far better to explore one area on foot, moving to the next by public transport. Bombay is swarming with taxis – check the meter works before hopping in. The courageous can take a double-decker bus, but avoid the rush hour. Although roads have old and new names (which get renewed), everyone except government employees uses the old ones.

Apollo Bunder From the opening of the Suez Canal until aeroplanes took over from liners, this is where most arrivals took their first step on Indian soil. Drenched in early morning sunlight, the sparkling Gateway of India and the Taj hotel represent Britain's final imprint on the city and an early monument to the rising influence of the most successful Bombay Parsee tycoons, the Tatas.

Apollo Bunder has always been fashionable. A modest iron gazebo amused 19th century promenaders. All changed in 1911 when King-Emperor George V made the first-ever State visit to India by a reigning monarch. First a hugely decorative white plaster arch, with dome and minarets, was hastily erected for the King and Queen's arrival on December 2. Then, when they had gone, the good idea was made permanent and the visit commemorated with a yellow basalt arch based on Gujarati styles, designed by the Bombay Government architect, George Wittet. It was built in 1927, just 20 years before the final British parade through the arch and out of India. For the Taj building, see Where to Stay section. Inside the hotel, up the grand staircase, is the Sea Lounge for gracious morning coffee and elegant afternoon tea. Around the building are displayed art works collected or commissioned by the Tatas. Early birds can see great activity on Sassoon Dock when the fishermen unload their catch at dawn.

Fort area The area stretching from the remains of Fort St George westwards to the Maidans and from the Prince of Wales Museum north to Victoria Terminus. Fort is a rather loose term for the present core of Bombay which expanded from the original fort and still goes like a fair throughout the day, businessmen, shopworkers and students packing out the restaurants at lunchtime, then leaving en masse for the suburbs at night. Some of Bombay's oldest and finest buildings are here. Two of the oldest stand east of the arcaded Horniman Circle (formerly Elphinstone Circle, now named after an anti-Raj newspaper editor), the classical Mint and Town Hall (behind which are the Fort St George remains, exceedingly difficult to visit, and the old docks). The Mint, with its Ionic Portico, was built on reclaimed land in 1829 (to visit, apply to the Mint Master).

The purer Doric *Town Hall*, designed by Col. Thomas Cowper, fulfilled a double function: municipal building and a home for the Asiatic Society library. It was funded partly by public lottery and took 15 years to build, finishing in 1833. One hitch was the columns sent out from Britain for the 260ft facade: they were too big but fortunately found use in Byculla Church which was then being built. Building and library are open to the public. Inside, men perch at high newspaper racks. Around the grand, book-lined rooms stand statues of Bombay big-wigs: Mountstuart Elphinstone and Sir Charles Forbes, both by Chantrey;

Lord Elphinstone; Sir Bartle Frere and Sir Jamsetji Jeejeebhoy.

Frere was the Governor who brought Bombay architecture up to date. He had James Trubshawe draw up the plan and imported British architects for individual buildings. Frere championed the Gothic Revival, fashionable in Britain, and under him (1862–67) the newly affluent Bombay became, in the words of Gavin Stamp: 'the finest Gothic City in the world with a remarkable concentration of Gothic public buildings'. And it still is.

The grandest are on *K. B. Patel Marg*, past the Cathedral of St Thomas (begun by Aungier in 1672) and across the Piccadilly Circus of Bombay, Hautatma Chowk (formerly Flora, and before that Frere, Fountain). They stand looking across the Maidan, although buildings on the reclaimed land beyond the green now block their sea view – and the consequent impressive land view for arrivals by sea. There is Trubshawe's old GPO (now the Central Telegraph Office); Col. Wilkins's Public Works Office (1869–72); Lt-Col. Fuller's High Court (1871–9); Sir Gilbert Scott's University (1869–78) with the huge Rajabai library clock tower (good views from the top) and Cowasjee Jehangir Hall; and Wilkins's Secretariat (1865–72).

At the north end of the Fort area is Frederick William Stevens's masterpiece, Victoria Terminus (1878–87), showing 'how the Gothic of Scott and Burges could be adapted to India and make a really impressive public building' (Stamp). F. W. Stevens's Municipal Buildings (1893) and Begg's domed GPO (1901) complete this group.

Two other facts account for Gothic Bombay's success: the good local polychrome building stone and the delightful, spirited animal and bird carvings by Indian craftsmen working under the direct stimulus of Lockwood Kipling, Rudyard's father, who was head of sculpture at Bombay School of Art and responsible for carrying William Morris's arts and crafts ideals to India.

Prince of Wales Museum Another building designed by Wittet to commemorate the globe-trotting George V, this time his first visit to India in 1905 before he became king. Shielded from the surrounding roads by a mature garden, the museum was begun in 1905, became official in 1909, took in visitors from 1914, officially began to work in 1921 and was completed in 1937 – a glorious example of the workings of Indian bureaucracy.

The four sections – art, archaeology, natural history, forestry – now form one of the most important collections in India, well displayed and a joy to visit. From the beginning, locals gave generously: the families of Tata, Hydari, Jehangir, Gupta and Latifi. The nucleus of the fabulous art section i the Purshottam Vishram Mawji Collection – don't miss it. The miniature paintings are upstairs. Good guide book, pamphlets and reproductions available. Open Tues.–Sun., 10.15am–5.30pm (July–Sept. to 6pm; March–June to 6.30pm). Closed on public holidays. Jehangir Art Gallery, reached by a different entrance, exhibits what is, sadly, the best in contemporary Indian art, but the Samovar Café is good, and fashionable among the literati.

Markets Concentrated in the area between Victoria Terminus and Maulana Shaukatali (Grant Road. A maze of action and colour in narrow lanes full of temples, mosques and tall, rickety Gujarati style houses, whose carved, projecting balconies almost meet. Actually buying something is an added extra, see shopping section. Beware of pick pockets. Inside *Crawford Market* (bas-reliefs by Lockwood Kipling on the front) are flowers and fruit, piles of pomfret and Bombay duck, and future meals of chickens, goats and birds squawking scampering and hopping around sacks of grain mini temples and astrologers' hide-outs. (Have fresh mango, pineapple or pomegranate juice at the Badshah Cold Drinks House.) Pillow Corner is across the road.

Just north is *Zaveri bazaar*, off Abdul Rahman Street. Here, in mirrored, floodlit caves of gold and silver guarded by electric doors, koli fishing wives jostle with Parsee princesses to hand over fat wad of rupees to even fatter shopkeepers. The brass and copper bazaar (with the up-to-date stainless steel bazaar) is at the top of Kalbadevi Road, by Mumbadevi temple and tank, home of the goddess who gave Bombay her name. To the west is the bangle bazaar on Bhuleshwar.

Further north, centring on Mutton Street, is *Chor Bazaar*, stocking everything from new linen and oil lamps to Staffordshire figures and sandlewood sweetmeat boxes. In the parallel Dhaboo Street is the leather market.

Marine Drive Only claimed from the sea in 1920 hence the austere buildings lining it. But at night it superb sweep from Nariman Point to Malabar Hill twinkles prettily, earning it the cliché: the Queen's necklace. It is the last British contribution to Bombay's town plan, designed as 'Ocean Way' to follow the whole of the west shore, but still in complete. Bombayites promenade here, watching cricket on the green by day, couples bashfull holding hands for sunsets and stars by night. It is a great meeting place.

Chowpatty Beach, at the far end, is the focus for political meetings and festival jollifications as well as daily street entertainment (extra on Sunday), yoga, gossip and snoozing. Sample belpuri, the Bombay snack of murmuras (puffed rice), sev (crisp gram flour strings), onions, herbs and spices made up at stalls according to your taste. The stall-holders are often third generation Uttar Pradesh immigrants, but the ice-cream-wallahs of the stalls behind come from the Punjab. The rich, creamy pineapple and mango ice-cream is delicious. To finish, the paan-wallahs of Chowpatty are famous, their concoctions starting at 50 paise or a simple digestive and rising to Rs500 for an exotic aphrodisiac. The nearby Aquarium is good (open Tues.–Sun., 11am–8pm).

Malabar Hill   Still the smartest place to live, with plenty of elegant old bungalows in leafy gardens, despite the double enticement of the Juhu-Bandra jet-set and developers' cheques. Those who sell out to high-rise builders often get the penthouse apartment as part of the deal. Old Parsee families and former maharajas now have diamond dealers, construction magnates and film-stars for neighbours. On the southern tip, Malabar Point, is Raj Bhavan, a complex of bungalows serving as the seaside Government House until Frere made it the official headquarters in 1885. (It is closed to the public, best seen from Marine Drive.) Nearby is Valkeshwar Temple, where the god Rama stopped overnight en route to save his wife Sita from the evil clutches of Ravana.

On top of the hill are the Parsee *Towers of Silence.* Although they are behind a wall and cannot be visited, they are one of India's most famous tourist monuments. Also here are the Hanging Gardens, reminiscent of municipal gardens at Worthing but with amusing topiary of elephants, ploughmen, camels, etc. The nicer Kamala Nehru Children's Park (named after the first Prime Minister's wife, the current Prime Minister's grandmother), is opposite. The best views of all are from the top terrace of Naaz café next door.

Haji Ali's Tomb   The mausoleum built at the end of a 500-yard long, beggar-lined causeway is supposedly named after a rich Bombayite who, after his pilgrimage (haj) to Mecca, gave away his wealth and lived here. At low tide, when the causeway is not submerged, Muslims come with their servants to pay homage. They exchange rupees for piles of paise with the moneychangers, then run the

gauntlet of the beggars, giving paise to each as the servant ladles home-cooked rice from a cauldron into his metal bowl.

Mahalaxmi Race Course   Named after the goddess of the nearby Hindu temple who, aptly in Bombay, concerns herself with wealth. The British may have brought the racing habit to Bombay but the Parsees have been its strength and are still prominent. It was Dorabji Rustomji who helped establish the original course at Byculla and was an energetic member of the Bombay Turf Club, founded in 1800.

With the expansion of Bombay, the new course opened here in 1878. At the same time, Bombay became well-known for horse-trading, especially in Arab horses. But in 1948 the government banned racing Arab horses in India, thus stimulating the breeding industry which now has more than 70 studs across the country. The Stud Book is kept at the Royal Western India Turf Club in Bombay. The top race of the whole Indian racing calendar is the Derby held in Bombay in February–March.

One of the most successful horse owner/ breeders of Bombay is Ranjit Bhat who, aged 37, already has 4 Derby winners. The 1977 winner, Squanderer, was trained by Rashid Byramji of Bangalore, trainer of the most Derby winners – 10 within the last 12 years. Jagdish, the top prize-winning jockey, rode Squanderer, making this his fourth Derby win. But while Squanderer is considered one of the best ever Indian-bred horses, it is Royal Tern who holds the stakes-earning record, a total of Rs18,52,697. Other big owner/breeders include Y. M. Chaudhry (who taught Sanjay and Rajiv Gandhi at the smart Doon School before devoting himself to the turf), London Pilsner beer baron Noshir Irani, and Bombay industrialist Sunit Khatau (whose Track Lightning won the 1981 Derby and the Invitation Cup).

The course is charming: immaculate flower beds surround the green and white grandstand, where fusty aged colonials and fashionable Bombayites stroll, gossip and lay quite heavy bets. During the season, November to March, meetings are on most Wednesdays and at week-ends.

Victoria and Albert Museum and gardens   Inspired by the other V&A in South Kensington in London and built by public subscription raised by Sir George Birdwood, a physician and authority on Indian crafts who became the first curator, the collection recounts the history of Bombay with prints, maps and charming model groups of trades and crafts. Open Mon., Tues., Fri. and

Sat., 10.30am–5pm; Thurs., 10am–4.45pm; Sun., 8.30am–4.45pm, closed Wed. Outside, the statue of Prince Albert and the clock tower were given by Sir Albert Sassoon. Elephanta Island, in Bombay harbour, was named by the Portuguese after a stone elephant they found there. The elephant now stands to the right of the museum.

There is nothing municipal about the excellent 34-acre Victoria Gardens, a mature and serious horticultural park laid out by Birdwood in the 1850s on drained swamp land. A list of currently blossoming trees and shrubs is chalked up on a blackboard at the entrance. The Minton tiles, terracotta panels and entrance turnstile were all imported from England. Inside, banished from M G Road, is Noble's marble statue of Queen Victoria, mostly paid for by the Gaekwad of Baroda. The zoo is here, with elephant, camel and pony rides for children. Open Thurs.–Tues. 8am–6pm.

Space and peace

Not plentiful in Bombay. The expansive sweep of Marine Drive gives a feeling of space, but little peace. Right in the city, the maidans provide both space and peace in the early morning. Victoria Gardens are green and quiet; the Hanging Gardens are dull and quiet. At Mahalaxmi Temple, on a promontory below Malabar Hill, the air smells sweet and the devotees arriving to perform puja also find a breeze and certain peace. Entree to the Gymkhana or Willingdon Clubs means quantities of space, peace and service. During the afternoon, there are more snores than splashes on the walled lawn of the Taj pool area. All these are jam-packed on Sunday, when the streets and lanes are quiet for architecture addicts.

Keeping fit and beautiful

If the pace of Bombay is not exercise enough, the sports facilities are good and better than in Delhi. The sea surrounding Bombay is definitely not for bathing. If a swim is essential to survival, the best pools, open to residents only, are at the Taj (set in large, walled lawn) and Oberoi (7 floors up, stunning views over bay and city).

Other good pools are at the President and at the big social clubs, which provide more serious sports amid extensive grounds, wicker chairs, and clubhouses with libraries that take *The Times*, *The New Yorker*, *The Illustrated London News*, etc. Clubs usually offer temporary membership to foreigners.

The good hotels can arrange some games fo guests: the Taj manages tennis, golf and sailing the President tennis and golf. Joggers can take o Marine Drive.

Health clubs The body beautiful can be pam pered to an extraordinary level in Bombay. Bot the Taj and Oberoi have scrupulously clean healt clubs and beauty salons housed in a never-endin warren of rooms. The President has reliable bu less extensive facilities. Both Taj and Oberoi healt clubs have all the latest gadgets and facilities including massage, sauna, jacuzzi and Turkis baths, gym and yoga. However, the Oberoi ha only one set of equipment, so women have the firs half of the day, 7am–3pm, and men follow, 3.30pm 10pm, which could be inconvenient. The Taj ha two sets, avoiding the problem. Both beauty salon are excellent and open to non-residents, offerin every sort of hair, face, hand and foot treatment. A the Oberoi men give head and back massage which work wonders on the nerves and rela the whole body. Indians from other cities spen whole days here being rubbed, scrubbed an titivated from head to toe, with food and drin on call.

CLUB CHECK LIST

Bombay Gymkhana, M G Road (tel: 26031 355832/361613). For temporary membership (abou Rs60 per month, maximum 6 months), apply t The Secretary in writing or on arrival, preferabl mentioning a member for proposal (from a firm o hotel). The word gymkhana is a corruption of word meaning ball-house, probably created in th Bombay presidency to describe an essential ingre dient of Raj life: a public place for athletics an sport.

The Bombay Gym was established in 1875 o land in the city centre leased from the government The first Indian test match was played here. The are now held at Wankhede Stadium. Bombay is th centre of cricket in India. Several matches may b played on one green simultaneously, a single play er fielding for two matches – but no accidents t date. The 1,400 members tend to be young or wit families. There is cricket, of course, plus hockey swimming pool, football, tennis (6 courts, 3 floodli for night play), snooker, billiards, squash, an table tennis. The multi-verandahed mock Tudo clubhouse has a relaxed, friendly atmosphere.

Chambur Golf Club, Chambur (tel: 52167). A least an hour out of town, but a nice course. Appl through hotel.

Cricket Club of India, D Vacha Road (tel: 220262). Known as the CCI, see hotel section for membership and facilities. Reliable restaurant. Apply here for details of test matches throughout India and for the two big Indian inter-state competitions: the Duleep Trophy and Ranji Trophy, named after two great Gujarati cricketers. Bombay used to win the competitions regularly. Its team included Sunil Gavaskar, who has achieved the most runs in test cricket. But now Haryana, with Kapel Dev in the team, is stronger.

Maharashtra State Angling Association, c/o Safe Glass Corporation Ltd, 97/99 Dhanji Street (tel: 324395/326247/571641). Contact the Secretary on the last telephone number for temporary membership. Fishing is at Powai Lake outside the city, boat, rod, tackle and bait provided. Possibility of catching katla, rahu, mirgil, kalbos, betki, gorami.

Royal Western India Turf Club, K. Khadye Marg, Mahalaxmi (tel: 377331). Apply to the Secretary for the season's fixtures list. See also p. 119.

United Services Club, Cuffe Parade. Run by the army. Golf and swimming.

Willingdon Sports Club, K Khadye Marg, Tumsivadi (tel: 391754). Apply to the Joint-Secretaries for temporary membership (Rs100 per week, maximum 4 months) and, as with the Bombay Gym, try to acquire a proposer. Founded in 1917 and, notably, open to Britons and Indians from that moment. Those Bombayites not at the Gym on Sunday are probably here. 3,000 members, all believing they belong to the most exclusive club and many passing the week-ends in its extensive grounds, playing golf, tennis, squash and badminton, swimming or just lazing around the gardens and rambling clubhouse. Raj food; stick to drink.

Good eats: Night lights

Eating is a treat here. Bombayites often eat out, especially at lunchtime when workers living in the suburbs can meet their friends. And as each immigrant community brought their own cuisine, here is a huge variety to choose from. It is easy to avoid the awful live European bands in some hotel restaurants, often misleadingly called supper clubs or night clubs.

Cultural entertainment is on a par with Delhi. As well as the avalanche of films, especially classic Bombay talkies, India's top performers in theatre, music and dance fill the concert halls nightly. Moreover, there are pleasant bars for sun-downers and, later on, a choice of discotheques. If this is the

first stop in India, take advantage: the high life doesn't last.

Partial prohibition currently operates in Bombay, meaning that, although there is no dry day and beer is served everywhere, a permit is necessary for buying spirits outside hotel bars and restaurants.

Even in Delhi, where people are loath to admit to Bombay's supremacy in anything, the mention of Bombay restaurants sends hands to stomachs as their owners crow: 'I put on pounds when I go there', 'There's this South Indian place – better than anywhere down south.', 'Ooh, the fish curry from City Kitchen – but they run out if you are late', 'There's a little place near the Metro Cinema . . .'. On and on. And with justification. It is the only city in India with the money and lifestyle to support an extensive network of good restaurants. There is excellent Iranian, Chinese, Continental and Portuguese-Goan food in addition to every cuisine of India, from Bengal to Gujarat, from North-West Frontier to deep South. Although some of the best are in the hotels, here is a chance to choose from hundreds of restaurants in the city and eat fresh, excellent food, even if the decor is basic. The few listed below are just a springboard for gastronomic exploration.

As well as the distinctive cuisines, the Bombay kitchen melting-pot has produced certain dishes associated with the city. Local pomfret, Bombay duck and shellfish (including lobster, but overpriced) are caught off Bombay. Bombay duck is the dried small bummelo fish. The Parsee dish dhansak (meaning open-mouth, so-called for the 24 or so ingredients and spices it contains) is a chicken or lamb dish cooked with lentils and vegetables. It was traditionally eaten for Parsee Sunday lunch but has now entered the general Bombay repertoire (best eaten at Irani cafes). In season (April–June), the west coast Alphonso mangoes, the king of mangoes, are eaten straight or spiced with cardomon, in a dish called aamras. Belpuri (see p. 119, Chowpatty Beach) is the classic Bombay snack.

West Indian food of Maharashtra and Gujarat starts with pudding. A thali of light vegetable dishes follows, served with a constantly replenished variety of freshly baked puris and roti (breads), rather than the rice of the South, and shrikand (thick, sweetened curd flavoured with saffron and nutmeg). Both states produce quantities of milk and make exceptional curd (yoghurt) and exotic fruit ice-creams. The local Aarey Milk Colony and Worli Dairy are much-plugged, over-rated tourist attractions.

Typical Bombay and West Indian dishes are served in the big restaurants.

RESTAURANT SUGGESTIONS

General Indian *Tanjore, Taj*; top of the market, excellent regional dishes, will prepare any others on request. Eat lounging on low sofas entertained by quality Indian dancers and musicians. *Gaylord*, Veer Nariman Road; open 1956, the second in the chain after Delhi, 1952, tables inside and outside (all too rare). *Delhi Durbar*, Falkland Road; in the red-light district, better than its branch at Colaba. Best dishes, biryani and dabba gosh. *Copper Chimney* at Worli; merits the effort to get there, better than its sister branch on K Dubash Road in the city centre. *Oasis*, Colaba; also recommended.

Mughlai Indian *Moghul Room, Oberoi*; setting and atmosphere up to Tanjore (see above), with entertainment of Indian folk dances, classic mughlai dishes with their rich sauces of spices and cream. *Gulzar, President*; again, good traditional decor and entertainment. The Hyderabadi Mughlai and biryani dishes, from the southern Mushal court are recommended.

Gujarati West Indian *The Village, Poonam International Hotel* (near Mahalaxmi Racecourse); set up like a Gujarati village, modelled after Vishalla, outside Ahmedabad, overlooks the sea. Jolly atmosphere, food good. *Samrat*, behind Eros Cinema, off J Tata Road; very Gujarati, heavy thali dish, pudding first. *Thacker's*, corner of M Karve Road and 1st Marine Street; same as Samrat. *Sher-e-Punjab*, Mint Road; pure no-frills Punjabi. Tandoor chicken and the roti (bread) made with maize and spiced spinach recommended. Various cheaper vegetarian 'clubs' in Kalbadeve, open to all, include *Ram Club*, above a sweet shop, opposite the Corn Exchange; supposed to have the best Rajasthani food in town, although the place is not pretty. Try lassi, vegetables, chapattis and rice. Others are *Friends' Union, Joshi Club* and *Thakker's Club*, described by Mala Singh, editor of *India Magazine*, as producing thalis 'out of this world'.

South Indian *New India Coffee Shop*, Kittridge Road, Sassoon Dock; claims to serve the only real Kerala breakfast. *Purohit*, Churchgate. *Woodlands*, Nariman Point; dosa and pongal recommended.

Irani cafés and Parsee food Not many straightforward Parsee restaurants. Even Parsee wedding receptions have foresworn the legendary spreads.

If invited, go to the Parsee club, *The Ripon*. Otherwise, Parsee food, with lots of meat and egg dishes, can be found in the Irani chaikhanas (tea houses), the equivalent of a Parisian café. They are mostly run by Zoroastrians who came to Bombay from Iran early this century. Some have fine interiors of stained glass, mirrors and tiles – and photographs of the Shah of Iran.

Best for breakfast (from 5am, most cafés stock the daily papers), lunch and tea. Eat mawa (cakes) khara (biscuits) or a dibbe wala meal of chicken or mutton covered with thick, spicey soup ladled from a huge witch's cauldron. Dunk in pieces of bun (hard bread), and wash them down with phudina (mint tea made with milk and sugar) or beer. During the 1950s there were about 3,000 cafés in Bombay. Among the few remaining, the best and most beautiful include *Bastani, Kyani* and the *Sassanian Restaurant and Bakery*, all at the north end of M G Road, at Dhobi Talao; *Merwan* on M Shakatal (Grant) Road; the *Bombay A1* (eat Parsee dishes or mutton dhansak, fish patia and sali boti), *Vazir's Pyrkes* at **Flora Fountain** (modern), *Byculla* and *Regal*, both near Byculla railway station, near Victoria Gardens, *Military Café*, Meadows Street Fort area.

Goan *Martin's*, Colaba. *City Kitchen*, Fort Market, lunch best, eat fish curry, pork sorpotel, noon-1.30pm. Very good and cheap. Go early as they tend to run out.

Chinese *Nanking*, Shivaji Marg, Colaba; the best of many, justly lauded in London (by Bernard Levin, among others) and New York, simple, clean, cheap, everything (but especially whole Pomfret Nanking for two) is delicious. *Chop Sticks*, Veer Nariman Road; good food and outside café tables with local paan stall. *The Golden Dragon, Taj* Szechwan, also renowned, but reputation not as high as it was. *Kamling*, Veer Nariman Road; one of the oldest in Bombay, Cantonese, twelve Chinese cooks prepare good, simple food. Packed out for lunch and dinner.

Polynesian *The Outrigger, Oberoi*: So far, the only one in Bombay. Lunch is a buffet.

Continental Can usually be persuaded to serve Indian food too. Worth investigating as they often pinch the best roof-top views. But cooking almost like home and often comes with live European bands. *Roof Top Rendezvous, Taj*; views, French cuisine under the guidance of chefs of Les Trois Frères, London. *The Society, Ambassador hotel*; Bombayites consider it to have the best Continental food, also serves Indian. *Café Royal, Oberoi*; French ood. *Supper Club*, top of Oberoi: views, Continental menu, nightly cabaret and dancing. *The Top, Ambassador hotel*: revolving, best restaurant views in town, Continental food but Indian served on equest.

talian *Trattoria, President hotel*; the hotel's 24-hour coffee shop, reasonable pasta.

Lunch specials Excellent buffet spread at the *Moghul Room, Oberoi* – similar one at the Taj is remarkably bad. More fun are the *Irani cafés* and unchtime haunts of businessmen in the Flora Fountain area which often close at night. Try the *Khyber*, M G road (tandoor); *Vienna Hotel*, near Metro Cinema (ask for fish lunch); *Victory Stall*, Nariman Point (Parsee, eat chicken dhansak for unch on Thursdays, 1–3pm). If by chance you are in Juhu, eat very fresh fish from the small shacks on the beach.

See also SeaRock hotel in Where to Stay section and Chowpatty Beach, in City by Day section.

Sweetmeats *Mathura Dairy*, near the Ambassador hotel; especially for the renowned Bengali concoctions. *Princess Kulfi House*, Samaldas Gandhi Marg (Princess Street); freshly made sweets and ice-creams. *Parsee Dairy*, Princess Street; ice-cream so thick it needs a knife to cut it.

Tea *Sea Lounge, Taj*: the Fortnums of Bombay, deep sofas, the smart meeting between shopping sprees. Tea, sandwiches and cakes. *Gaylord*, Veer Nariman Road; sit outside, café informality, delicious milkshakes, tea, beer and cakes. *Poolside, Taj*: as guests wake from siesta, waiters scurry back and forth delivering trays of tea and fresh lime sodas.

Cocktails *The Ambassador* hotel for best 360 degree views from bar above revolving restaurant. The *Taj's* rooftop bar is good, but the *Oberoi's* has strange windows – it is almost impossible to see out of them. Colonial cocktails in the wicker chairs of clubs have great style.

24-hour coffee shops The big hotels have these rather useful cafés (see p. 57). Needless to say, the *Taj* and *Oberoi* have the best Bombay ones, the Taj exquisitely decorated with appliqué work, the Oberoi looking over the bay.

NIGHT LIFE

Discotheques (Sometimes known as 'night spots' in India.) A discotheque only lives when it is full of people. The Indians have missed this vital point and persist with their elitism, making membership very expensive and exclusive. So several potentially good discotheques playing pacey music are half empty except on Fridays and Saturdays.

The Taj's *Nineteen Hundred* has suffered from this, despite very good design, lighting and music. The best is *Studio 29*, in Bombay International Hotel, at the corner of Marine Drive and D Wacha Road. Rising beautiful film-stars bop with the children of setting film-stars (who inherit star status here). It is run by Sabira Marcharl, a Bombay socialite and TV personality. Foreign visitors gain instant nightly membership at the door.

With Juhu and Bandra the in-places to live, the *Cavern* at the SeaRock hotel attracts the same vivacious crowd yet fails on style and spirit. There are also discotheques at the *Holiday Inn* and *Airport Plaza* hotels. Give the *Oberoi's Cellar* a miss. Entry to hotel night clubs is open to residents for a nominal charge; non-residents should apply to the hotel's Guest Relations Desk.

CULTURE

It cannot be stressed strongly enough that regular opportunities to see the top exponents of classical Indian music and dance-drama are confined to Delhi, Bombay and Calcutta. Notable exceptions are Madras, where there are performances of Bharata Natyam dance, and Cochin for Kathkali dance. See Information section for how to find out what is on where.

Performances are usually at 6.15pm or 7pm. The Taj and President hotels have classical dancing at the earlier time, but it is not very good. Public halls used by visiting artists include Birla Matushri Sabhagar, Tejpal Auditorium, Patkar Hall, Rabindra Natya Mandir, Shivaji Mandir, the huge Shanmukhananda Hall, Lokmanya Talik and the Tata Theatre. The acoustics for the Tata Theatre and the Lincoln Centre in New York are, inappropriately, by the same designer. They are excellent for European chamber music but no good for Indian; it is said that Ravi Shankar and others refuse to play at the Tata Theatre any more.

Theatre The Maharasthrans and Gujaratis have a strong creative thrust, like the Bengalis, but Bombay is a cultural slave to the West and to its Hindi film world. Thus, direct imports such as 'Evita' and 'Death of a Salesman' run for months in packed houses, while traditional Indian plays in Hindi or English fill the remaining theatres. The now highly commercial Parsee theatre, developed from the British touring companies, once full of the literati and an inspiration for early films, produces lightweight comedies. Contemporary Marathi and Gujarati plays, often in English, attract thinner audiences and may only pop up for a day or so

123

before the troupe disappears on tour. They can be found at the National Theatre and the National Centre for the Performing Arts. Folk drama, full of vitality, is sometimes at the Hanuman Theatre, Delisle Road.

After Independence, Indian theatre underwent radical changes and by the 1960s was acquiring a national character. The main exponents were four dramatists: Sombhu Mitra from Bengal, Girish Karnad from Karnataka, Mohan Rakesh who wrote in Hindi, and, perhaps the most important, Vijay Tendulkar, a Maratha. For their texts they went back to Indian classical Sanskrit works or historical events, but they gave their plays a new flexibility, allowing for plenty of music and dance and often incorporating folk traditions. Tendulkar's 'Ghashiram Kotwal', set in a period of Marathi history but injected with contemporary analogies, is one of the most impressive of these plays. Habib Tanvir used folk tunes and techniques to present Hindi versions of Sanskrit texts, so following a play is not difficult.

The lively Marathi theatre continues to evolve at Pune, where both Tendulkar and Mohan Agashe write and direct. A trip to Pune could take in a performance at the Bal Gandharva, Nehru or Tilak Smarak Nidhi theatres. Otherwise, plenty of productions are brought to Bombay.

Contemporary Hindi plays are found at various lively centres. One is the slightly controversial Prithvi theatre, out at Juhu (with adjacent restaurant). The late Jennifer Kendall and her husband Shashi Kapoor were actively involved – they met when they were each acting in their parents' unconventional family theatre companies. Shashi then forsook his family to be with Jennifer in the Kendall's Shakespeareana. Funded by the trust left by his father the great actor Prithviraj Kapoor (which also supports cancer hospitals in Goa and Bombay), Prithvi promotes a national Hindi theatre by putting on its own productions and offering visiting theatre companies low rents.

Cinema Bombay revolves around films. Films are the raison d'être of Bombay social life and a large chunk of its financial life. For a tourist to miss seeing a Hindi film is like missing the theatre on a visit to London. A regular Hindi film is a sophisticated, slick and perfectly timed mixture of heroism, romance and fighting on wildly extravagant sets, interspersed with seductive song and dance (the dancer miming to someone else's voice), all filmed in dazzling hues that give new meaning to 'glorious Technicolor'. They combine the talents of Busby Berkeley, Fred Astaire and Ginger Rogers.

The story is immaterial, although the audience gets completely involved, shouting to warn the hero of an enemy, cheering when a battle is won.

The film is three or four hours of pure escapism and great entertainment, which is why an Indian spends the first part of his wage on the weekly 'philum'. And it is why a humble servant reasoned with his mistress, with astonishing profundity that he should have his wages a day early to pay for his film ticket: 'Because you have everything memsahib, but we have nothing, so we need films for our dreams.'

Naturally there are hundreds of cinemas (some showing Western films), a few surviving from the 1930s–50s, including the Metro on 1st Marine Street, Eros on J Tata Road and M Karve Road, and the very dilapidated but pretty Opera House, in from Chowpatty Beach (with Tea Rooms next door). There are at least three shows a day, at about 3pm, 6pm and 9pm, and some morning shows a 9am and noon. Balcony seats are best. *Bombay* magazine has a round-up of the principal films with criticisms. Newspapers give minimal details The avalanche of film magazines give no details but are almost as entertaining as the films, full of gossip about the gods and goddesses of the film world, and phenomenally bitchy. Among the juiciest are *Ciné Blitz, Star Dust, Star and Style* and *Film World. Screen* is considered the best magazine trade paper.

India produces the most films in the world, about 800 films in 12 languages every year. Bombay is the centre today and Bombay is where it all began. The Lumière Brothers' Cinematographe was first demonstrated here on July 6 1896, just six months after its first showing in Paris. It was advertised as 'The marvel of the century. The wonder of the world. Living photograph pictures.' Success was immediate. There were special zenana shows for women in purdah. And there was no elitism: from the beginning, tickets were cheap, creating the char-anna-wallah (four-anna-bloke) mass audiences, which have determined the rise and fall of the industry's stars and studios ever since.

Dhundiraj Phalke, affectionately known as Dadasahib (daddy-sir), was India's first great director and once observed, with justification: 'I established the film industry in India in 1912.' This was the year his film 'Raja Harishchandra' was released, the first Indian feature, made in Bombay. Script, casting, direction, photography, developing and printing were all done by Phalke, using British equipment, and the titles were in Hindi and English to reach the char-anna-wallahs and their memsahibs. It did so well that two years later he employed 100 people in his studio, the blueprint for future Indian studios. Of his 20 feature films, 'Lanka Dahan' (Burning of Lanka) was such a box-office bonanza that takings had to be hauled away in bullock carts. The film's plot is an episode from the mythological epic, the Ramayana. These myths, together with lives of saints and Muslim romances, have remained sure winners as subjects throughout Indian film history.

The post-World War I industrial boom in Bombay brought fortune seekers and professionalism to films. Studios and actors desperately imitated Hollywood. After the 'Thief of Bagdad''s popularity in 1925, a certain Master Vithal was heralded as India's Douglas Fairbanks. Prithviraj Kapoor (father of Shashi and Raj), who left Calcutta theatre for Bombay films, earned the nick-name 'Errol Flynn of India'.

But Hollywood films reigned supreme, accounting for 85% of films shown in India. Nevertheless, the 1930s and 1940s were the golden age of Bombay film-making. Bombay Talkies, opened in 1934 by Himansu Rai and his wife, was the biggest studio and its Hindi films were the forerunners of today's commercial successes: a careful mixture of glamour, music, melodrama, song and a tiny drop of social consciousness or moral message.

In Pune the energetic Prabhat Studios turned out earthy, imaginative, intelligent films, often in Marathi with the occasional rather uncomfortable Hindi versions aimed at a larger audience. Films were made fast. E. Billimoria, the first Indian cowboy, starred in more than 300 curry-Westerns – with the added feat of avoiding singing and dancing in any.

In March 1931, Ardeshir Irani released the first Indian talkie, 'Alam Ara', just pipping Calcutta's J. F. Madan to the post. It contained 10 songs and first-night tickets changed hands at 20 times their face value. Elsewhere audiences had to be enticed with promises: 'Hear your Gods and Goddesses talk in your own language'. In 1937 Irani produced another first: 'Kisan Kanya' was India's first film in colour.

The smooth changeover to talkies in India, as opposed to the traumas undergone in Hollywood, was because many actors had stage and voice training. But there were hitches. Men could no longer play women's parts. And when Hindi emerged as the most popular language, some non-Hindi-speaking stars bit the dust. One was the 1920s heroine Sulochana, whose salary had exceeded that of the Governor of Bombay. Inspired by Bengal, theatre playwrights were employed to write the dialogues. Film dialogues are still very important and sell as separate records. In the 1970s one film dialogue sold half a million copies.

But film music was even more important and is still the main criterion for a film's success. Music cuts across language barriers, whips up the emotion of a scene and has anyway always been part of traditional Indian theatre, religion, festivals – even politics. Film songs are the chart hits of India. Singer and actor are usually two different people, but no one seems to mind hearing their favourite voice fronted by a succession of fashionable actresses in various films. Lata Mangeshkar, queen of Hindi film singing, has recorded more than 25,000 songs.

The change in power from the studio to the individual star occurred in the late 1930s, when financially tottering studios had to free their actors from the pay-roll and exclusive contracts. Actors then went free-lance and the good ones could – and still do – call the tune. Currently, Amitabh Bachchan is king and can name the craziest price ever demanded by an actor and get it. When he was injured in 1980, visitors to the hospital included the Prime Minister, Mrs Gandhi. On his recovery the hoardings proclaimed: 'God is great: Amitabh lives'.

In Bombay's next boom, after World War II, independent entrepreneurs developed and refined what Bombay Talkies had begun, creating the present-day Hindi masala (mixture of spices) – a film designed to reach the widest possible audience by containing a little bit of everything, from myth and romance to comedy and song. Even now, there is little difference between a social or costume drama and a mythological film. V. Shantaran made the first Indian Technicolor film in 1955, called 'Jhanak Khanak Payal Baaje' (The Jangle of Anklets). It was a dance extravanganza, starring the great Gopal Krishna. Shantaran also made 'Shakuntala', the first Indian film to be commercially released abroad. Mehboob Khan's finest film, 'Mother India' (familiar to Western audiences) was made in 1957. And another Indian classic, 'Gunga Jumna', was made the next year by Nitin Bose, who with Bimal Roy carried social awareness from Calcutta to Bombay. It was Roy's 'Do Bigha Zamin' (Two Acres of Land), about peasants in Bengal, a prize-winner at the 1954 Cannes Film Festival, which really presented an alternative to the Hindi masala.

At the same time, former clapper-boy Raj Kapoor emerged as the first director of the new generation of commercial Hindi film-makers. His 22-year collaboration with script-writer K. A. Abbas began in 1951 with the internationally triumphant 'Awaara' (The Tramp). Raj Kapoor, son of Prithviraj, immensely handsome, good at romance and comedy and an above average tabla player, both directed and starred in this film which established him as a screen idol.

Today the masalas continue to pour out of the studios in what has been described as a crisis of aesthetic bankruptcy, a sterile imitation of former success. Despite huge, alluring advertisements, some in 3-D, and slogans such as 'Titillating Hot Stuff' or 'A Hot Box of Sins', these are empty promises as censorship is strict. But they still make a lot of money. The film-making process is intriguing to an outsider. A visit to a studio can easily be arranged by the tourist office. If luck holds, it will be full of action. And as a dozen studios serve the copious film companies, some work around the clock. Several companies hire various parts of one studio to make entirely different sorts of films. A Western may have a classic myth and a modern romance for neighbours. To add to the confusion, a star may be involved in more than 10 films simultaneously, putting in 4 hours as a whimpering, love-sick princess on one set, then, after a quick change, 3 hours as a destructive goddess two doors along.

Film finance is equally tangled. Armed with a potential film, the producer goes to the big financiers – in Bombay these may be diamond dealers, or the construction industry, Sindhis and Marwaris. They lend a sum of money at a fiendishly high interest rate of 40–60%, subtracting the interest payment out of the money to be lent. The better the stars already signed up, the more favourable the deal may be for the producer. But this only finances a bit of the film. Then another loan must be found to pay off the first loan and finance the next bit.

Naturally, the ball stops rolling sometimes, leaving incomplete films. However, if the stars are big enough at the box office, the distribution rights can be sold before shooting starts, thus financing the whole film. Consequently, there is not much scope for adventurous, experimental, loss-making cinema. The slowly emerging alternative cinema in

Bombay is financed by the Film Finance Corporation. It has a small output, even smaller audience and the majority of screenings are at foreign film festivals.

What to buy where

Bombay and Delhi offer the best shopping. As with the traditional performing arts, crafts from all over India can be found in these cities that are difficult to find as good – if at all – in their place of origin. Both have a big range of Government Emporia (some infinitely better than others) and glorious markets. To know how hard to bargain in the markets, check out the prices in the Emporia. Conversely, to get an idea of the quality and range available, look in the markets.

In addition, Bombay has two hotels with excellent and extensive shopping arcades. Here the latest European-designed clothes, shoes and leather goods are sold for considerably less than their Western prices. Unlike the over-priced equivalent in the West, the shops in the best Indian hotels are good value, reliable, sell high quality goods and – most telling – are full of discerning locals. The Taj shops are scattered down corridors off the main lobby; the Oberoi has a 200-shop, 2-storeyed complex adjoining the hotel. New shops at the World Trade Centre at Cuffe Parade and in the Craft Centre at Nariman Point are not yet as good.

For bazaars, see also p. 118 (City by Day section). **Western India crafts** Gurjari, the Gujarat Government Handicrafts Emporium, is perhaps the best of the state emporia in Bombay. High quality in everything: tie-dye and printed silk and cotton from Ahmedabad; fun appliqué wall hangings and bedspreads in bright colours; muslin and silk from Surat and Khambat; stuffed, embroidered elephants of every size; brasswork and carved wood. For the best Gujarati skills, which are rare now, the manager will arrange for the member of a Patan weaving family living in Bombay to bring in a selection – but skilled craftsmanship is costly: Rs15,000–30,000 a piece. However, the cheaper, but still special, Rajkot weaves are in stock. On the pavement around the rear entrance to the Taj, Gujarati women sell Kutch and Saurastra, some good, mostly old pieces.

Other Indian crafts Central Cottage Industries Emporium, Shivaji Maharaj Marg, just behind the Taj; stocks crafts from the whole of India, used by locals, very efficient staff, shipping quick to range – and arrives safely the other end. Good nge of hand-embroidered Kashmiri furnishing bric (50% of London prices even when shipped), d other goods from Kashmir, Rajasthan and the uth. Quality crafts also found at Jehangir Art allery Shop; Contemporary Arts & Crafts, Jagohandas Marg Road; Craft Centre, Raheja entre, Nariman Point; Khadi Village Industries nporium, D Naoroji Road; Kairali, Nirmal, ariman Point (Kerala crafts); Kashmiri Government Arts Emporium, P Mehta Road; Purbashree, hira Bhavan, Sandhurst Bridge (North-Eastern ates crafts); Fantasia, Oberoi Towers.

ld crafts and antiques See note on legal restrictions, p. 32. Several in the lanes behind the Taj sell allmarked and old Indian silver; more mixed ops include A. K. Essajee, D. Popli & Sons, eermanek and Son, all on Battery Street, and riental Art Museum in Mereweather Road. round the Prince of Wales Museum, Phillips ntiques (no relation to the London auction house) as everything from Raj porcelain to rubbish; atasan, one of the major art dealers in India, has is Bombay branches in the Jehangir Art Gallery omplex and the Taj. Upstairs in the Pundole allery at Flora Fountain plenty of the nice eces are small enough for an already stretched uitcase.

ewellery For gold and diamonds, keep to large ops and there should be no problems. If the averi bazaar ones are too overwhelming, both Taj nd Oberoi have jewellery shops. Indian craftsanship in gold and silverwork and stone-cutting regarded as best of all and is very cheap. Stones re good buys, but gold is quite expensive (ideally, ring your own). Diamonds are 15–20% less than Amsterdam, London and New York and come in wo qualities, deluxe and super-deluxe, each sold vith a certificate and the promise to buy the back the ewellery at any time at the current price (see p. 28). When buying, look out for the four 'Cs': carat, larity, colour and cut. (Diamonds carry special etting restrictions and tourists taking them out of he country require a certificate and must pay in oreign exchange, so check carefully or your diamond may not be forever.) If the designs of the ewellery in stock are no good, any piece can be nade up in about a week. And the customer can ring his own gold or stones. For instance, pearls re very cheap in Hyderabad – a fifth of London rices – but stringing and setting are best in Bombay (for stringing, Hyderabadis go to Rai, ext to the Regal, Colaba). A reliable jeweller is

Tribhovandas Bhimi Zaveri, who has shops in Zaveri Bazaar, the Oberoi and Opera House; and Gazdar in the Taj. For old and new silver, try the silver bazaar at Mumbadevi (especially nos 17, 39 and 47). Check the day's price first as it is sold by weight.

Fabric M Karve Road has the sari shops, which also stock fabric by the metre and jazzy brocading, some wide enough to have elephants, princesses and camels woven in. Customers are expected to take their time. One good shop is Kala Niketan. In the Taj, Indian Textiles has extremely beautiful (but quite expensive) silk, crêpe de chine, brocade and the rare crêpe cotton. Nearby, at Churchgate, Pride sells fabrics that are all Indian made but use European designs and cost less. To have fabric made up, Smart and Hollywood Tailors near the Jehangir Gallery have been tried, tested and praised for copying in a few days a Calvin Klein suit in fabric and an Aquascutum raincoat in soft leather, the fabric and leather bought in the bazaars. (At the time of writing, Handloom House had been gutted by fire and was closed. Should it have re-opened, it is good.) To have fabric embroidered and made up, go to Adity Enterprises, Sea View Terrace, Wodehouse Road.

Books For art and culture, the Taj bookshop is best. If it fails, try Strand Book Stall, off N P Mehta Road, in the lane opposite the HMV shop. Around the university, the second-hand bookstalls sprawling along the streets from Flora Fountain to the General Telegraph Office are a bibliophile's dream – all manner of goodies waiting to be discovered in the tall, wobbling piles. Mr Merchant has his stall outside the New and Second-Hand Book Shop, founded in 1907, which is so full of volumes it is difficult to get in to browse through them. For rare books, prints and maps, go to Jimmy Ollia, 1st floor, Cumballa Chambers, Cumballa Hill Road (tel: 350649)

Leather The instant the designs come out in Milan and Paris, the Indians copy them. And although shops in the two hotels stock a dazzling array of the latest shoes, bags, belts and jackets at a fraction of European prices, Dhaboo Street in the bazaar area has more variety, better quality (suedelinings for bags) and is even cheaper. The Muslim wholesalers' shops are bursting with stock, so search out the best, then bargain hard. Belts start at Rs20, wallets Rs50, handbags Rs65 – the shoe selection is limited. There is also leather by the piece. As recommendation, the Italians come to pick up this year's Guccis, the French their

127

Cardins. Since India does not import either make, their copyrights do not extend here, so the blatant piracy is not illegal. To find the tiny street, get somewhere near, then ask.

See how it's done: Industry and craft

Cinema To visit a film studio (see p. 126), contact the ITDC tourist office.

Cotton mills Much of Bombay's wealth was founded on these. They still smoke and clatter when not on strike. They are straight out of Dickens, labour-intensive, throbbing with huge, out-moded machinery, the air full of cotton fluff and boiling hot. The cotton goes in one end raw and comes out the other as dyed fabric. The tourist offices can arrange a visit.

Diamonds Some of the most famous diamonds were mined and first cut in India – the 410-carat Regent (in the Louvre), the Great Sancy (belonging to the Astor family), the Black Orloff (somewhere in New York) and the Darya-i-Nur (last seen at the late Shah of Iran's coronation in 1967). The Koh-i-Nur (Mountain of Light), weighing 108.93 carats, probably came out of the Golconda mines before the 14th century. In the 16th century, Emperor Babur calculated its value as 'two and a half days' food for the whole world'. Having sparkled on various rulers' heads, the British claimed it from the Lahore treasury as compensation for war losses. It is now part of the Crown jewels and kept in the Tower of London until the next coronation.

Seven centuries later, supremacy in diamond mining has passed to South Africa but India is still a centre of the highly skilled craft of diamond-cutting and polishing, especially small stones. Most is done at Surat in Gujarat, but some in Bombay, the diamond-dealing port. In addition to native diamonds, stones are imported, cut and exported, making India the world centre of the cutting industry. To see the fascinating and intricate process, from bruting the rough stone to the final polish, go to Thakurdwar in central Bombay. Poke into the courtyards to find Gujarati boys aged 16 to 30 working at lathes in tiny rooms.

Awaydays

Bombay is neither claustrophobic nor dull, so the need for a quick escape may not arise. If it does, the worthwhile day trips around the city are few, mostly focused on the abundant cave-temples, so a splash-out teaser is thrown in. The bigger ho make better trips (see next section).

Elephanta Island 10km. For those who ha Bombay and are besotted with rock-cut temple There are four Hindu temples, dated vaguely fro the 4th to the 9th centuries, their beautiful scul tures much damaged by the Portuguese. But to s them involves a grim 10km journey bobbing acro the harbour, fighting fellow tourists up to t caves, getting hit on the head by the football of o of a dozen games being played in and arou them, pestered by shoddy stall-holders, deafen by blaring cassette-players, then the grimmer turn journey. A much nicer outing is to the oth caves (see below) or, better still, fly up to the Ajar and Ellora cave temples for two days on a packa deal (see opposite page).

Beaches For a serious beach, go to *Goa* (see 240). Otherwise, 40km away are *Marve* and *Mano* Go by car to unspoilt Marve (plus nearby fishi village) and on by ferry and horse-drawn tonga Manori. Very romantic, and it is tempting to st overnight at the Manoribel, a clean, simple hotel six cottages right on the beach, but be sure to bo at week-ends. If desperate for a beach, it is 21km dirty Juhu beach (do not swim but do eat fish fro the little huts and have your fortune told). Th smart residents have nothing more to do with than the odd early morning horse-ride and a la night gaze at the moon reflected in the sea.

Sanjay Gandhi National Park 35km. Not one the great wildlife parks, but a big space and plen of trees. Contains a lion safari park and the form Krishnagiri Upavan garden. Beyond them the pa is wilder, with teak woods, blossoming trees, dee interesting birds and the Kanheri caves: 1 Buddhist rock-cut temples and cells hewn from huge circular rock during the 2nd to 9th centurie Biggest cave complex in India, nos 1, 2, 3 and 1 best, not much sculpture, good views.

Bassein 77km. Just across the Ulhas River on th mainland, shortest route by train, then taxi. Rath good ruined city (walls and bits of buildings historically interesting. Built by the Sultan Gujarat but Portuguese from 1534 until 1739 durin which time it was greatly expanded and rose become the 'Court of the North', with cathedra stately homes and the Hildalgos (aristocracy famous for their grandeur and wealth.

Caves day About 250km round trip. Buddhi caves, near *Lonavala*. Best to go entirely by ca stopping off to see one or two of Shivaji's man forts en route, such as Lohagan and Visapur (abov the Bhaja Caves). The *Bhaja Caves*, set in lush greenery, are 2nd-century BC, figurative sculptures in the southernmost cave. The *Bedsa Caves*, slightly later, have jolly carvings on the pillar of the chaitya (prayer hall). Sedan chairs carry visitors up the steep hill to *Karla Cave* (about 80BC), where the chaitya is the biggest in India, with well-preserved, bold carvings of lions, elephants and figures, the 37-pillared hall lit by a sun window.

The other Taj Day trip extravaganza to the Taj Mahal, Agra. Catch an early plane to Delhi (2hrs), drive to Agra (3hrs), ogle the monument to love, swim and eat at the Mughal Sheraton, return – or stay over for the moonlight. A bargain at around Rs3,000. Book through SITA travel agency.

Forays further afield

With its excellent communications, some lesser visited places are accessible from Bombay, particularly in Gujarat. But the pilgrimage to Ajanta and Ellora is first priority. Despite all the coastline, only the Goa beaches are any good (see p. 240). For the nearer places such as Pune (Poona) and the hill stations, trains are worth considering: they go from the city centre, thus avoiding the drive to (and hanging around at) the airport.

The travel agents listed above will advise and book, but try to give them notice for the popular week-end trips to Goa or the caves. There are good off-season deals to Goa, and excellent package deals to the caves which include flight, hotel, coach and guide.

AJANTA AND ELLORA
However short the visit to western India, it is worth squeezing in two days to come here. The caves of Ajanta and Ellora are one of the technical and artistic feats of Buddhist art. Like the Taj, the ruined city of Hampi and the Khajuraho temples, they are one of the wonders of India. There is nothing natural about the caves. They are more than 60 temples cut directly into remote hillsides in the Western Ghats and decorated with sculptures and, at Ajanta, paintings. Since their rediscovery in the 19th century, the air has been fast fading the exquisite wall-paintings, so some caves with paintings may be temporarily closed for conservation.

Indians are as anxious as foreigners to see the caves with paintings before they are closed – or before the paintings fade into obscurity. Good Brahmin parents bring their children to see the pale images they remember with bright hues. So, put

on comfy shoes, take a torch (the lighting is erratic), prepare to join throngs of fellow tourists and catch these treasures while you can. En route to Ellora, the *Boy's Own* medieval fort at *Daulatabad* is an added bonus.

THE HARD FACTS As the monsoon is quite light, it is possible to go to Ajanta and Ellora all the year round, but October–November is best when the post-monsoon lushness and plump cows astound those arriving from the desert of Rajasthan. December–March are pleasant before the work-up to the June rains. There are daily flights from Bombay, Delhi, Jodhpur, Jaipui and Udaipur to Aurangabad (Ellora 30km, Ajanta 106km). Choose between two hotels in Aurangabad, both newish, with mod. cons. (If both are full, go to the Aurangabad Ashok.)

Ajanta Ambassador Hotel (tel: 8211/8367; telex: 0745211; cable: AMBASSADOR); 125 rooms, sensitive service, good pool, sports including tennis, excellent restaurant.

Rama International (tel: 8241/2/3/4; telex: 0745212 RAMA IN; cable: HOTELRAMA); 72 rooms, part of the Welcomgroup chain, next door to the Ambassador and very similar, with same wide range of facilities plus health club, but service and food not as good.

Both hotels can offer an all-in price of breakfast, packed lunch and dinner. Both are slightly out of town but have travel counters for car hire, tour reservations and flight confirmation; both have shopping arcades for more literature on the caves.

OUT AND ABOUT The full day trips run daily by the MTDC and ITDC are excellent value, the guides usually good and the time spent at each spot reasonable. Beware: the bus picks up at around 8am, and it takes a full day trip to see each set of caves. So, passengers on a plane arriving after the bus departs must either hire a car (guides available at each site) or stay an extra day. It does not matter which caves are visited first, even though Ajanta's pre-date those of Ellora. Ajanta caves are open 9.30am–5.30pm; Ellora caves from sunrise to sunset. In Aurangabad, buy himroo (silk and cotton mix) shawls, silk and bidri work.

Ajanta In the 2nd century BC, a community of Buddhist monks came to this remote area and began chipping their retreat out of the semi-circular cliff of a gorge. Over the next 900 years, they carved out 4 chaityas (sanctuaries) and 25 viharas (Buddhist monasteries). Then, in the 7th century, Ajanta was abandoned in favour of a new site, Ellora. It was not until 1819 that a British hunting party, searching out an elusive lion, stumbled upon the pristine caves in the thick forest, then part of the Nizam of Hyderabad's territory. The caves are a pocket history of Buddhist art and thought. In the 2nd century BC a new form of Buddhism broke away from the original exclusive and ascetic Hinayana form which favoured the symbolic and abstract. This new branch, known as Mahayana, went for mass appeal in direct competition with popular Hinduism. It also encouraged the development of a much richer and more realistic art which reached its golden age of maturity under the Gupta dynasty, 320–647. Cave nos 8, 9, 10, 12 and 13 are the simple, Hinayana ones.

Each cave is monolithic. This means the rock has been chipped away from the cliff-face to create the space; nothing has been added. Carving began with the ceiling and worked down, around pillars, monks' beds (with pillow), carvings on capitals, facades and jambs, and huge statues of the Buddha and his consorts in back rooms. The technical feat is mind-boggling. And, in addition, the carving and painting achieves a classical grace. The frescoes of the life of Buddha and the later jatakas (Buddhist fables) are painted in yellow, red, black and a little slate blue, all locally found minerals, with touches of precious, imported lapis lazuli which still retains its brilliance. Benjamin Rowland has observed: 'Nowhere else in Indian art but at Ajanta do we find such a complete statement of indivisible union of . . . sacred and secular art. . . . Here is a turn to a sort of religious romanticism of a really lyric quality, a reflexion of the view that every aspect of life has an equal value in the spiritual sense and as an aspect of the divine.' Best paintings in nos 1, 2, 16, 17 and 19; best sculptures in nos 4, 17, 19 and 26, beautifully lit by the afternoon sun.

Ellora Buddhism was already losing out to the Hindus and Jains when the monks moved to this gentle hillside in the 7th century. So there are caves representing all three faiths: 12 Buddhist (600–800AD); 17 Hindu (around 900AD) and 5 Jain (800–1000AD), the caves numbered in that order. The blasé who have already been to Ajanta will not think much of the Buddhist ones, but note the beginning of Hindu liveliness in nos 11 and 12. The Jain temples, slightly north of the rest, have delicate, highly detailed carvings. But it is the Hindu caves that are spectacular, their profusion of carvings bursting with energy in striking contrast to the static, contemplative Buddhist sculpture.

See especially no. 16, Kailasa Temple, named after Shiva's home in the Himalayas, Mount Kailasa, and built to represent it. A bridge leads through an enclosure to the courtyard where elephants and flagstaffs flank the two-storey temple and Nandi pavilion. Friezes of dynamic carving recount legends of Shiva and episodes from the Ramayana. The complex covers the same area as the Parthenon and every bit is part of the hillside, making it the biggest monolithic structure in the world and one of the greatest monuments of Dravidian art, built at the height of the Rashtrakuta Dynasty in the middle of the 8th century.

Daulatabad Fort Built on a natural pyramid-shaped hill, with everything from anti-elephant multiple doorways and spoof dead-end corridors to steep, slippery, gravelled pathways and a dark spiral tunnel down which defenders dropped hot coals on their attackers. No wonder Mohammed Tughlaq, Sultan of Delhi, could not resist it and decided to move his capital there in 1327, naming it Daulatabad (city of fortune). A few years later he realised his mistake and Delhi's citizens who had not died on the 1,100km walk there had to trek home. Spectacular views from the top.

Aurangabad Named after Aurangzeb. Not attractive. The Ellora-Daulatabad tour bus whizzes around the main sights, which is quite enough. The most amusing is Bibi-ka-Maqbara, a tatty, poor imitation of the Taj built for Aurangzeb's wife in 1679; the most interesting is the Panchakki waterwheel, driven by a natural spring, which finances an orphanage.

HILL STATIONS
Matheran 171km at 800m. The best switch-off near Bombay. In the Sahyadri range, made popular in the 1850s by one Hugh Malet (although Ptolomy went there long before). Bombayites who are not grand enough to have retreats at Ooty come here, to nearby Khandala and to Mahabaleshwar. Season October–May (pre-rain June is misty); avoid the deluge of the rainy season and, if possible, week-ends. Go for shady trees (Matheran means mother forest), orchids, views, walks, riding and peace – no cars; no action.

Take the Pune Express to Neral (2hrs), then change into brightly painted, tiny, narrow-gauge carriages (1st class has pink curtains) for the last 21km (2hrs), full of twists, tunnels and monkeys with black or red faces. The nicest place to stay is

rd's *Central Hotel* (tel: 28; cable: CENTRAL
OTEL), clean, modest, usual tri-cuisine res-
urant. Move around on foot or on horseback –
corts provided if needed. The rickshaws are less
n.
Views of Bombay and sunsets are seen from
onkey, Hart, Echo, Chouk, Porcupine Points
d, best of all, Panorama Point; but go up to
uke's Nose (named after Wellington) on the
eccan Plateau for the most spectacular views. For
outing, the caves around Lonavala.

ahabaleshwar 200km at 1,372m. Highest hill
ation in western India. In Raj days, the fashion-
le place where the British cooled off. Sir John
alcolm initiated the hill station in 1828. Go for
ews, waterfalls, walks, some sport. Season as for
atheran.
The journey is by train or plane to Pune, then
xi, or by car all the way. Stay at the *Mahabaleshwar
ub* (tel: 221), period charm, peace (temporary
embership for foreigners, write to the Secretary);
at the *Fredrick* (tel: 240, cable: FREDRICK), *Dina
* , (tel: 246, cable: DINA MAHABLESHWAR) or
ce View* (tel: 238, cable: RACEVIEW), all modest
ngalow hotels.
Walk through the flower-filled woods (April for
chids and lilies); see Dhobi, Chinaman and
ngmala waterfalls and views of Krishan and
oyna valleys from Raj-named spots such as Wil-
n, Kate, Bombay, Elphinstone and, to make
ots feel at home, Arthur's Seat – one of the best,
ith a sheer drop of 600m. Keep in shape with golf
d tennis at the club, go boating and fishing on
enna Lake. Visit the old village, very holy to
indus (festival, February–March). Take trips to
ree of the best Shivaji forts: *Pratapgarh, Raigadh*
d *Simhagad*. Bee-keepers sell their honey.

JNE (POONA)
urrently most famous – or notorious – not as the
ace where the Maratha leader Shivaji was raised,
or for its fine museums and precocious theatre
d film work, nor even its race course, but for the
i Rajneesh Ashram where Westerners (especially
mericans and Germans) pranced around in their
rthday suits extolling the merits of free love much
the amazement and horror of the locals and, via
ex Guru' articles, the rest of India.
Sri Rajneesh had an annual turnover of £2 mil-
on at the ashram alone, amplified by sales of his
scourses: 33 million words distilled into 336
ooks and 4,000 hours of tape with titles such as
Jinety Nine Names of Nothingness'. Then, quite

suddenly, Sri Rajneesh disappeared, to re-emerge
with a fleet of cuddly Rolls Royces in Oregon,
USA. Meanwhile, the ashram has been rubber-
stamped by the government and is now on the
official Pune tourist bus route.

THE HARD FACTS At 580m. The fresh air of
this pleasant provincial town is especially welcome
during Bombay's sticky months which coincide
with the racing season from July to October. Pune
was the Bombay Government's hide-out during
the monsoon. Get there by the hare or tortoise
routes: the hare takes the daily 30-minute plane
hop between slow road and airport queues; the
tortoise goes by train, enjoying a leisurely breakfast on the Deccan Express (4½hrs, leaves 6.45am)
or tea and toast on the Deccan Queen (3½hrs,
leaves 5.10pm).
The best place to stay is the *Hotel Blue Diamond* in
Koregoan Park (tel: 28735; telex: 0145 369; cable:
BLUEDIAMOND), concrete, good service, mod.
cons, pool, health club, beauty parlour, both tri-
cuisine restaurants quite good. Best information
counter is on the railway station.

OUT AND ABOUT Spend time in the *Raja Kel-
kar Museum* where a selection of Shri Dinkar Kel-
kar's magnificent collection is exhibited in rotation
in an old house. (If interested, ask to see pieces not
on show.) Especially fine miniature paintings,
musical instruments and everyday objects. Dr Kel-
kar intends to open a section devoted entirely to
women. Excellent illustrated catalogues. (Open
Mon.–Sat., 10.30am–4.30pm.) The Bhandarkar
Oriental Institute contains an important collection
of Oriental manuscripts.
Wander around the Shanwarwada Palace remains and the Express Gardens (with zoo and
temple) and Bund Gardens. Go into Pan-
cheleshwar rock-cut temple (8th century) and catch
a good view from the hilltop Parvati Temple. See
the buildings erected under the British: the Council
Hall, Wellesley Bridge, Deccan College (Bhandarkar, Edwin Arnold and Wordsworth's nephew
taught there; Jeejeebhoy founded it). The race
course is in the old parade ground. Film buffs can
visit the National Film and Television Institute.
Theatre-goers can catch one of Agashe's or Tendulkar's plays at the Bal Gandharva, Nehru or Tilak
Smarak Nidhi theatres (several performances
daily). Irani cafés are here too (see p. 122 above).
The best are Café Good Luck and The Lucky, both
near the Deccan Gymkhana.

Central India

The lesser-visited cities of Mandu, Ujjain, Bhopal and Sanchi are quick and easy to reach and the rewards are rich. Moreover, in the high tourist season of November to February they remain, so far, delightfully empty compared to the beaten track.

THE HARD FACTS   The richly forested state of Madhya Pradesh is most pleasant from October to March, with the bonus of constant Hindu festivals. Go by air: daily planes connect Bombay and Delhi with Indore (for Mandu, 38km; Ujjain, 30km) and Bhopal (for Sanchi, 70km; Mandu 83km). It is best to hire a car from the airport or hotel and keep it until the flight out, bargain hard for an all-in price. Hotels are fairly modest, so the fussier must steel themselves. There is no prohibition in Madhya Pradesh at present.

MANDU

Its other name, Shadibad, means 'City of joy'. Former magnificent and courtly capital of the central Indian kingdom of Malwa, now a romantic, ghost city sprawled over a 12 sq km hilltop, remarkably intact. Its atmosphere has been described as 'dormant rather than dead'. There are mango, tamarind and banyan trees. The city is particularly beautiful when emerald green and full of waterfalls immediately post-monsoon.

Wander around some of the 70 or so fine Muslim and Hindu monuments built during its heyday from the 11th to 16th centuries, especially under Mahmud Shah (1436–69) and Ghiasuddin (1469–1500), who was devoted to women – his harem was reputed to hold 15,000 pretty maids. The 500-elephant parade heralding the entry of Jehangir (1605–27) was one of Mandu's last great spectacles. See the palace and pavilion of Baz Bahadur (the last king, defeated by Akbar) and his Rani Rupmati, India's Romeo and Juliet. Baz Bahadur came across the lovely Rajput peasant girl, Rupmati, singing in a forest, fell in love at first sight and brought her to his palace. He erected buildings for her but then had to flee in the face of Mughal defeat. Rupmati, captured for the general's future pleasure, committed suicide by swallowing ground diamonds.

To be right in the city, stay at *Taveli Mahal*, a converted palace or at the ITDC *Travellers Lodge* (tel: 21; cable: TOURISM) or the state's *Tourist Bungalow* (bookable at Indore Tourist Office). To be

more comfortable, stay in Indore. Buy D. R. Pati excellent booklet on Mandu (with map), publishe by the Archaelogical Survey of India.

UJJAIN

The Gupta king Chandragupta II (380–414) forsoc the official capital of Pataliputra to rule here what his poet, Kalidasa, described at 'the tow fallen from heaven to bring heaven to earth'. It w. dogged by political upheavals later on. See th riverside temples and ghats, Maharaja Scindia palace and go out of the city, past yet another of J Singh's observatories, to Kaliadah, the Manc Sultans' pretty pleasure palace. Ujjain is one the seven sacred cities of India, and the trienni Kumbh Mela festival takes place here every years, next one 1995, see p. 253 (festivals list).

INDORE

Major textile centre but good base for Mandu ar Ujjain. Do not miss the museum's major archaeo ogical collection (open Tues.–Sun., 10am–5pm See also the Jain Kanch Mandir (glass temple), or of the more over-the-top giant Jain reliquarie encrusted with mirrors, crystal, beads and mothe of-pearl (open 10am–5pm). Stay at *Suhag Hotel* (te 33270-9; telex: 735 345; cable: SUHAG HOTEL 75 rooms plus 8 suites, all with bath; a: conditioning, travel agent, car rental, beauty salo: Tourist Office (tel: 38888) in the bus station, o, posite the railway station. Tours to Mandu ar Ujjain.

BHOPAL

Capital city of Madhya Pradesh. City of lakes ar gardens, refreshing base for Sanchi. Named afte Raja Bhoj, the 11th-century founder, and the hug lake he built that dominates the city (pal mear dam). An Afghan mercenary from Delhi, Do Mohammed Khan, founded the Bhopal dynasty : the end of the 17th century, a tiny Muslim dot in predominantly Hindu state.

See remains of his fort and walls; his descenda: Shah Jahan Begum's unfinished, pink Taj-u masjid (another mosque claimed to be the bigge in India); the Nawab's palace overlooking the lak the museum (local archaeological findings). Mo: of all, wander in romantically-named gardens suc as Farhatafza Bagh (Enhancer of Joy), catch suns: views of the minareted city from Shamla Hill, ar go evening boating on the lake. Charles Correa new *Bharat Bhavan* building is here. It is one of th leading centres for the performing arts and for th preservation and practice of tribal and folk art.

ie centre is also trying to preserve the dying
issical music form of dhrupad. Well worth visit-
g to see craftsmen during the day and, possibly, a
rformance in the early evening.

The most pleasant place to stay is *Imperial Sabre*,
ilace Grounds (tel: 72738); former palace guest-
iuse, recently refurbished. Run by a charming
inian family. Alternatively, there is *Hotel
imsons International*, Hamidia Road, (tel: 72298;
ble SETHI-BROS); 22 rooms (6 air-conditioned),
iall but good, or the bigger *Rajdoot Hotel*,
amidia Road (tel: 726912; cable: RAJDOOT); 120
oms (30 air-conditioned), travel agent, bank, car
re. Tourist Office at 5, Hamidia Road (tel: 3400),
urs to Sanchi.

iNCHI

illtop site of an imposing collection of magnifi-
nt Buddhist monuments. The buildings span
most the whole range of Indian Buddhist art,
im its birth in the 3rd century BC to its decay in
e 12th century AD. Here are also the best-
eserved stupas (Buddhist relic mounds). All this
very unusual since Sanchi has no connections
ith Buddha's life. The answer lies in the Mauryan
nperor Ashoka (*c* 273–236 BC), a zealous convert
Buddhism who probably built the first stupa and
llar, selecting this spot as peaceful yet close to
osperous Vidisa. (Ashoka, in the tradition of
en converts, built 7 more stupas at Sanchi and an
timated 84,000 throughout India.) Pious mer-
iants of Vidisa then endowed the monastery,
ying the foundation for its energetic and quality
iilding activities. In 1818 General Taylor 'dis-
vered' the deserted ruins, marking the start of
ime tragic destructions (the pillar of Ashok was
ied to build a sugar-cane press), disappearances
id restorations (some of the gateway architraves
e reversed).

If architectural indigestion comes fast, then start
ith the four tornas (gateways), followed by stu-
as no. 1, 2 and 3; temples 17 and 18, temple-
ionastery 45 and monastery 45. Debala Mitra's
ssential guide to Sanchi (plus map), published by
ie Archaeological Survey, should be on sale at the
ioking office. Official guide-lecturers free. Open
iily, sunrise to sunset (small museum 9am–5pm).

iujarat

ujarat State is a contradictory mixture. Success-
il, modern businessmen move their rupees out of
iot of the fiendish state taxes, while democratised

aristocrats of the hundreds of tiny princely states
club together to make extravagant marriage deals
with big-wigs such as the Mysores. There is the
sophistication and enlightenment of the textile millionaire Sarabhai family and the blind ignorance of
men who are still mesmerised by cars and mown
down so often that local newspapers no longer find
it newsworthy. The typical Gujarati has two jobs
and makes a tidy fortune, yet the siesta system
produces a state of total inertia from noon until
4pm. The Gandhi presence is strong, though
sometimes it seems more superficial and self-
rightous than truly austere. So, officially there is
total prohibition – Gandhi's great ally, octogen-
arian Morarji Desai, still a political force in Gujarat,
threatens death by fasting if it is repealed. But
unofficially there is hardly a man who does not
have his tame bootlegger, hardly a 'bash' (party)
without whisky.

Non-Gujaratis derisively call the state 'a village
where they make money and they hoard money'.
Certainly the Gujarati merchants are highly successful at home and abroad, although rarely in the
Marwari and Punjabi big business league. The
Parsees' key into India was the promise of bringing
wealth to Gujarat and they still live in every town,
their flame-topped pillar burning in Sanjan where
they arrived in 745. The money-making Jains concentrate in Gujarat. Their religion has added force
to the state's almost total vegetarianism. The
Kasturbhais are the biggest Jain family, owning 7
textile mills plus dyeing and chemical works. And,
in accordance with Jain piety, they have established educational and religious trusts including a
big one at Mount Abu.

Ahmedabad, thick with relics of its Mughal
grandeur, is the thriving commercial centre of
Gujarat, with fine museums and an enlightened
patronage of contemporary and traditional Indian
arts almost unique in India. Amid the hubbub of
cars, buses and countless bicycles in the fast-
moving city centre, camels obediently plod round
one-way systems and stop at traffic lights. But the
final nonsense in Gujarat is the new town of Gandhinagar, built 30km away from Ahmedabad as
the bureaucratic capital. Ahmedabad workers and
businessmen are forced to lose a day's wages and
make a 64km trip every time they have to collect,
complete or sign a piece of paper – which is often in
India.

At the same time, the rural areas are hardly
industrialised at all. People maintain their traditional dress, skilled crafts (especially weaving)

and village lifestyle. To the north lies the Raan of Kutch. To the south is Saurashtra and the Sasan Gir wildlife sanctuary and Jain pilgrimage centres. To the west are the territories of the fun-loving deity, Krishna, and freedom-fighter Gandhi. To the east lies the palace-filled, cultural centre of Vadodara (Baroda). Around it all, the long coastline is dotted with ports which have brought trading wealth since Harappan times.

THE HARD FACTS Gujarat has interesting buildings (Muslim, Hindu and Jain), villages, museums and wildlife, with very few of the tourist trappings (both the good and the bad ones) found in neighbouring Rajasthan. This is because there are still few Western tourists. Gujarat has yet to catch on. Therefore a warning or so is needed. Most hotels are simple and inexpensive, but their charges are subject to a sliding state luxury tax that can add 30% to the bill. Full prohibition is in force. There is not a bar in the state. If the nightly whisky soda is essential, be sure to go equipped with an All India Liquor Permit (see p. 12 for how to get one). It has to be produced at the liquor store, where the bottle will be subject to a 45% sales tax. Obviously, bootleggers are cheaper, but illegal.

The season is November to February; then it hots up. There is an abundance of festivals and village fairs, especially Krishna-related ones. With so many Gujaratis in Bombay (and perhaps because until 1956 Gujarat was part of Bombay state), there are superb air connections with 8 cities: Ahmedabad, Bhavnagar, Bhuj, Jamnagar, Keshod, Porbandar, Rajkot and Vadodara (Baroda). There are daily flights from Delhi and Jaipur to Ahmedabad. A good mini-tour could start in Ahmedabad, then continue by car for a few days, spending nights in palace hotels and flying out from another city. Below are one or two suggestions of places that might be included. Bombay travel agents can advise and book everything. (Mercury Travels run special Gandhi tours from Bombay.) One of the best things to buy are the superb handloom textiles, avoiding the machine-woven fabrics on which Ahmedabad's 20th-century wealth was founded.

AHMEDABAD

Although a thriving industrial city, much of the town founded by Ahmed Shah in 1411 is still standing and many of the 20th-century buildings are also notable. Peak period was the 16th century, when it was described as 'the greatest town in

Hindustan, perhaps the world'. And Sir Thoma Roe compared it favourably with London in 161 The royals of the textile families are the Sarabhais, brilliant Jain family who became cotton m lionaires in the 19th century and have now dive sified into chemicals and pharmaceuticals. Fami members have become top scientists, dancers an art connoiseurs. They mostly live at The Retreat, leafy compound of art-filled houses surroundir the old Sarabhai mansion. Here is perhaps th most successful of Le Corbusier's private house where house, garden, sculpture and paintings i termingle to make a mature and harmoniou home. The Ambanis are newer to Ahmedaba They came from Aden and built up the man-ma fibres Reliance Textile Group, rags to vast synthet riches in 15 years flat.

THE HARD FACTS Try to coincide with th Navrati festival, September–October, 9 days street dancing and bhavai (lively Gujarati fol theatre), or the Makara Sankranti kite festival o January 14, the biggest of all kite festivals. Kit makers from across Indian show off their vividl coloured masterpieces. Ahmedabad is 8km fro the airport.

Only two good hotels, both central and lookir across the river at Le Corbusier's Mill Owner Association building.
The Ritz, Lal Dawaja (tel: 393637/8/9; cable: RITZ built by a wealthy Muslim in the 18th centur simple but lots of character and atmosphere, we run by knowledgeable Goan, Mr Pereira, whos father started the hotel; lightning-fast room servic by smiling uncle figures who instinctively brin the right newspapers with breakfast; 20 room shower/bath attached, good beauty parlour.
Cama Hotel, Khanpur Road (tel: 25281–5; tele 012377 CAMA IN; Cable: HOTELCAMA): co crete new, very efficient management, keen your staff; 45 rooms, bath attached, car rental, liqu store, beauty parlour, chemist, beaut salon, fast room service yields delicious fres coffee, good restaurant but Gujarati food for lunc only.

Copious information from Tourist Offic Ahmedabad Municipal Corporation, Danapa (tel: 36364) and Tourism Corporation of Gujara H K House, off Ashram Road (tel: 449683). Th TCG run several half-day city tours, worth co sidering as monuments are widely scattered. Ind an Airlines is on Lal Darwaja (tel: 391737). Be travel agents are TCI, near Handloom Hous

shram Road (tel: 77601/78770) and Sherry Tours
d Travels, Lal Darwaja (tel: 26932).

UT AND ABOUT Central Ahmedabad has
me of the best Indo-Saracenic buildings con-
ructed for the Muslim rulers. They are distinctive
r their bold Muslim structure happily married to
tricate Hindu decoration carved by locals. Do not
iss the Rani Sipri tomb and mosque (1514) or
ddi Sayyad's mosque (1515), with extraordinarily
elicate jali (pierced stone) windows – (merits risk-
g death to reach it on a traffic island). Rani
ipmati mosque (1430–40) is worth seeing, as is
e Jami Masjid (1424), where local kids guide
urists up to the women's balcony and then on to
e many-domed roof which resembles a sci-fi
nar landscape. The citadel remains and the Sidi
ishir mosque ('shaking minarets') are not as in-
resting as promised (minarets currently closed
definitely, for restoration).

Also Muslim and unique to Gujarat are the richly
rved, galleried baolis (step-wells) which light-
ied the drudgery of fetching water. See Dada
ari baoli (1435, closed for siesta 1–4pm) in town
id the most beautiful one of all, Adalaj Vav (1499),
km (30 minutes' driving) north of Ahmedabad
lmost the only building that does not close for
esta). Kankaria Lake, south of the city centre, is
here Emperor Jehangir and his beloved Nur
han frolicked. It is still a refreshing area, with
keside cafés and a good zoo. In the south-west
iburb of Sarkhej are the remains of a more Hindu
alace scheme built around 1457 by Mahmud
rgarha, possibly designed by Azam and
lu'azzam whose mausoleum is nearby. In the
evailing aesthetic climate of Gujarat, the chaste
egance extended to every last detail.

Skipping on to the 20th century, visit the river-
de Sabarmati Ashram (designed by Charles
orrea), founded by Mahatma Gandhi (1869–1948)
1915, who moved here 2 years later. This was the
adle of the non-cooperation movement begun in
)20. It was from here that Gandhi began the
andi March in 1930, protesting against the Salt
ax. Of all the institutions associated with Gandhi
India, this is the place that gives the clearest idea
f the Mahatma's strong and charismatic character,
is austere code of living and his mammoth ambi-
on for India's independence and self-reliance,
/mbolised by the spinning wheel. Romain
olland described him as 'A small weak man, with
lean face and tranquil brown eyes and with
read out big ears. This is the man who has stirred

to action three hundred millions of men, shaken
the British Empire and inaugurated in human politics the most powerful moral movement since nearly two thousand years.' Open around the clock.
English sound and light shows on Wed., Fri. and
Sun., at 8.30pm (tel: 866873).

The museums are a treat – if they can be caught
open. Most important is the Sarabhais' Calico
Museum, the only substantial museum in India
devoted entirely to textiles, now housed in the
gardens of the family mansion. Excellent publications (See p. 142) Shauhi Baug Area (tel: 51001),
open Tues.–Sun., 10am–12.30pm; 2.30–5pm. The
mansion itself is to open in 1985 as a centre for
Hindu studies: Jainism, Vishnuism and Shivaism.
On exhibition will be objects from the textile collection and the Sarabhai Foundation Collection.
There are three other not-to-be-missed museums.
N. C. Mehta Museum of Indian miniature paintings
is one of the finest collections, housed in Le Corbusier's Sanskar Kendra Municipal Museum, Paldi
(tel: 78369), open Tues.–Sun., 11am–noon, 3–
5pm. (Next door is the Tagore Hall designed by
B. V. Doshi, a leading Indian architect who worked with Le Corbusier on Ahmedabad and Gandhinagar buildings.) Vechaar is a large collection of rare
Indian utensils, housed in a newly constructed
traditional Gujarati village called Vishalla, on the
outskirts of town, at Vasana (see below) (tel:
79845), open Mon.–Sat., 5–11pm; Sun., 10am
–1pm; 5–10pm (see also food section below).
Another worthwhile museum is the Shreyas Folk
Museum, holding traditional mirrorwork, distinctive tribal clothes and decorations, off Circular
Road, open Thur.–Tues., 9–11am; 4–7pm.

FITNESS, FOOD AND ENTERTAINMENT
Apart from the old centre, Ahmedabad is a flat,
industrialised and unattractive city to wander in.
For pleasant walking, there is the zoo and Kankaria
(with boating) and Chandola Lakes. The clubs'
facilities of tennis, billiards, badminton and swimming are accessible through the good hotels. In
addition, Ahmedabad Gymkhana, Airport Road
has the golf course; the Sports Club of Gujarat,
Sardar Patel Stadium, Navrangpura, has cricket;
Ellisbridge Gymkhana has bowling. All three have
pools. Sherry Tours can organise chikar (hunting)
for partridge, duck and chinkara (one of the deer
family) October–February.

All this and more may be necessary after a
Gujarati thali feast at Vishalla, Sarkhej Road,
Vasana (5km), built as a Gujarati village with

135

museum, crafts, performing arts and restaurant. This is not only the best place to taste the exclusively vegetarian Gujarati cuisine but is one of the most enjoyable restaurants with entertainment in India. On arrival for dinner (not later than 8.30pm), order and pay for 'meal' plus fruit juice before and pudding after (about Rs75 for two). Fruit juices (pineapple, orange, apple, sugar cane, etc.) and entertainment fill the long gap between ordering and being called to eat. People weave, pot and make paan in the village buildings. The excellent museum is open (until 10pm), as is the shop. And outside there are string beds to lounge on, while puppeteers recount legends with huge string puppets, musicians play and dancers perform.

Dinner is an overwhelming feast taken sitting cross-legged on the floor, knees resting on pink-painted wooden leg rests (the stiff-limbed are given chairs). Waiters converge, bearing steaming tin pots and ladle an array of vegetables, pulses and fresh curd on to a platter of leaves sewn together. Millet flour chapati and other hot fresh breads arrive continuously. A dozen or more chutneys and salads are served in separate pottery dishes – onion, lime, green chillies, tomato, coconut. Mugs of buttermilk wash it down. Everything is constantly replenished. Then come the hot, sweet, cardamom-scented, crunchy-and-gooey jalebis (some Gujaratis eat the sweet at the beginning of the meal). Then a rich rice and wheat mixture ladled over with ghi (clarified butter), an irresistable calorie concentrate. Finally, be sure to leave space for creamy, nutty, homemade ice cream. No need to eat again for a week.

In the town centre, eating is a mundane experience by comparison. But *Hotel Saba* (opposite the Cama) and *Hotel Chetna*, next to Krishna Talkies on Relief Road, should produce a good thali. A revolving sky restaurant called *Patang* (kite) opening in 1985 will serve the tri-cuisine plus Gujarati food. Dishes can have odd combinations. Khaman dhokla is a chickpea flour cake; undhyoo is a winter dish of aubergines, broad beans, potato and sweet potato cooked buried (undhyoo) under a fire; srikand, signifying hospitality, is hot savoury puris eaten with sweetened yoghurt flavoured with saffron, cardamom, nuts and candied fruit. The special Surat sweet is gharis (thickened milk, butter and dried fruits), best from *Azad Halwai* sweetmeat shop, Relief Road.

Ice-cream eating in Gujarat is serious business and it is tempting to try some. A good parlour competes with the American Baskin and Robbins

and Dayvilles chains. There is a good parlour every street corner. The aptly-named *Havmor* Relief Road is especially good, where mango a pineapple are in the huge selection of ice crea and strange flavoured milk drinks.

Good drama, dance and music programmes held regularly at the Tagore Theatre, Paldi; Surd Hall, Raikhadi; Sheth Mangaldas Town Hall, Ell bridge; and Paemabhai Hall, Bhadra. It is wo looking out for performances by the local Darp Academy. There may also be some bhavai (Gu rati folk theatre), which is undergoing a reviv The Tourist Office or Sangeet Natak Akade provide information and advice on what is where.

SHOPPING AND CRAFTS Gujarat's rich t dition of high quality weaving, hand-block pri ing and tie-dye fabrics has risen to its form heights under the energetic and watchful eyes Mrs Jaya Jaitly (who runs the Gujarat emporium Delhi) and Mrs Mrinalini Sarabhai, widow of t brilliant scientist, Dr Virkram Sarabhai. M Sarabhai is a dancer by training, runs the Darp Academy of dance and theatre and is Chairman the Gujarat Handicrafts Corporation. Both are ad mant about maintaining the correct colours ar crafts – no bastardisations for a quick sale.

Some women who had left their crafts to ea better money as stone-breakers and road laboure have even been persuaded to return to their v lages to produce good embroidery. The Gurj state emporia in Ahmedabad, Bombay and De are well stocked so, unlike Orissan crafts, Gujar crafts can be bought just before leaving India. Gujarat itself, the good and easy shopping is Ahmedabad. Elsewhere, delve into back streets find nut crackers, silver, wood, brass and oth treasures in tiny, dark shops. But some towns, li Bhavnagar, have nothing.

Fabrics The endless variety of textiles, at prices, are the best buys. There is smooth cre and fine cotton by the metre, screen-printed wi small floral motifs (36" wide, Rs14–16 per metre Pieces of cloth are hand-painted with co centric patterns of deities and flowers (Rs15–8C Bandhana (tie-dye) silk or cotton is first wove then tied and dyed to create the pattern, the be produced at Rajkot, Jamnagar and the Saurasht villages. A special bandhana cotton is the raba abla with appliqué mirror work (worn b shepherds, rabaris).

Saris, 5½m long, can be batik-printed (Rs8C

0), stamp-printed with stars, flowers and man-
es in bright colours on dark ground (Rs80–100)
block-printed with traditional earth tones (Rs130
70). Moving up, silk is grown near Saurat and
tan. The striking silk panetar (wedding sari) is
zzling red and white, often with a crisp checked
sign and elephants around the edge for good
:k (Rs550–1,500); a lagdi patta has a double bor-
r, a thick gold stripe and floral field that is either
nted or richly embroidered.

The zari (gold thread) work loved so much by the
ughals comes from Saurat and is applied to saris,
lvet, evening shoes and handbags. Tanchoi is
e tapestry-thick Saurat brocade. Beware: the
ld' thread is usually metal over a plastic core;
ssibly Gurjari would have a piece with real gold
read.

The queen of textiles is the *patola* sari, kept under
:k and key in the few shops that stock them. It
mands accurate planning and skilled craftsanship. First, the intricate design of rows of
ures, animals and patterning is worked out.
en the threads for the whole sari are tie-dyed
brant colours precisely according to the design.
ially, they are woven, the crispness of the com-
·ted design determining the quality and price –
2,000–Rs18,000 if just the weft is tie-dyed;
15,000–Rs30,000 if both warp and weft, the true
tola.

A few families still practise the true patola weave
Patan. But it is easier to see at the National
hool of Weaving at Rastriya Shala educational
stitution in Rajkot, where patola and other
·aves are being revived.

There is plenty more besides textiles. At San-
eda, near Vadodara, carpenters make and var-
sh highly decorative furniture, achieving their
ep golden lacquers by using juice extracts from
ods. There are glorious swings and rocking
airs which can be shipped or, easier to carry,
ols, mirror frames and candle-holders. Gaily
abroidered, stuffed toy elephants, horses and
mels of all sizes come from Kutch (Rs17–90).
ass and wood pataras (chests) come from
avnagar, woollen shawls from Saurashtra and
ver or brass nut crackers from Kutch. But leave
e new embroidery, beadwork and wood-
rving. Old pieces are better, so hunt around the
anek Chowk area of the old city. This is where
e jewellery market is, where tiny shops sell
eap 'n' cheerful bandhana and where kids sit on
e mosque steps doing wood-block printing, their
ends spinning cotton nearby. And remember to

look up, for here and in Ratan Pole area the houses
are beautifully carved. Each is one room wide but 4
or 5 storeys high, the layers cantilevered out on
supports carved as swans, musicians or gods, the
overhanging balconies carved with rich floral and
geometric friezes.

Find fabrics, furniture and toys at Gurjari,
Ashram Road; fabric only at Handloom House,
Ashram Road. Among the fabric shops lining
Ratan Pole streets, Deepkala has good pieces (ask
to go upstairs to see handloom patola silks, avoid
their synthetics) and is open long hours, Sun.–Fri.,
8.30am–8pm.

Forays into Gujarat

These few suggestions include day trips. The
places further away link up to make trips of a few
days that can end back at Ahmedabad again, or at
one of the several cities with airports, or can lead
on to surrounding states. Outside Ahmedabad,
Gujarat is immediately very rural and made up
of tiny villages. There are blue-eyed shepherds
dressed in baggy white jodhpur and kurta
(waistcoat) and cerise turbans, and cows, sheep
and bullocks with huge curly horns.

HEADING NORTH

GANDHINAGAR
30km. India's second planned town, named after
the Mahatma and designed, like Chandigarh, by
Le Corbusier, assisted by Indian architect B. V.
Doshi. Begun in 1960 as the capital of Gujarat after
it was separated from Maharashtra. The city is
planned as government offices surrounded by 30
residential sectors, each with its own community
facilities, all set in green, blossoming parks beside
the Sabarmati River. Sounds idyllic but not all
inhabitants describe it in such glowing language.

MODHERA
106 km. *Surya Temple*, dedicated to the sun, was
built in 1026 under the Solanki king, Bhimdev I.
Many parallels with the Shiva Temple at Somnath
on the south coast. Both were erected under the
Solankis, whose affluence came from east–west
trade passing through their coastal ports; both
were financed by public subscription and built by
voluntary skilled labour; and both were devastated
by the Muslim iconoclast Mahmud of Ghazni and
then suffered subsequent earthquakes. But the

typical Solanki carving, extremely rich yet very refined, encrusts every remaining surface. Sited above a stepped tank, the sandstone Surya Temple glows appropriately in the late sun.

Dawn rays reach into the temple to the spot where Surya's image was placed. In *Indian Architecture*, Percy Brown goes into ecstacies over this building: 'lit with the living flame of inspiration, . . . an atmosphere of spiritual grace . . . its creator a weaver of dreams'. There is also a two-storey, 11th century baoli.

PATAN

130km. Little remains of the Hindu capital Anhilwara, sacked by Mahmud of Ghazni in 1024, but this quiet provincial town has fine carved wooden houses, 108 Jain temples and some master weavers creating the legendary patola weaves. One of the families still creating Patan patolas is the Salvis, whose home is right in the centre – locals give directions. (To visit weavers, consult with Gurjari in Ahmedabad.) *Ambaji* lies about 120km to the north, just south of Mount Abu in Rajasthan, and the Gujarat folk drama, Bhavai, is often staged in the temple courtyard (consult Tourist Office for dates).

HEADING SOUTH-EAST

VADODARA (BARODA)

120km. Parks, lakes and palace museums still dominate this expanding industrial town, former capital of the Gaekwads (means protector of cows) of Baroda who were so rich last century they had a carpet woven of diamonds and pearls and had canons cast in gold.

See the crazily extravagant *Lakshmi Vilas Palace* with its 500-foot facade, completed in 1890 at a cost of £180,000 to designs by one Major Mant for Maharaja Sayajirao – whose Maharani campaigned against purdah and chaired the first All Indian Women's Conference. Museum of armour and sculpture open at erratic times. This is where the current ex-Maharaja lives. Cambridge-educated, former Member of Parliament and minister, mad keen cricketer and wildlife conservationist, this energetic man is now forming a museum of turbans.

The Baroda Museum and Art Gallery is set in a fine park: good Mughal miniatures and European oils (open Sun.–Fri., 9.30am–4.45pm; Sat., 10am–5.45pm). Not far away is the Maharajah Feteh Singh Museum where Titian and Raphael turn up

in a mixed collection of world-wide goodies (op＊ Tues.–Sun., 9am–noon; 3–6pm except April–Jur＊ 4–7pm). Other places to see include old Bhad＊ plus Nazarbagh and Makarpura; an excellent bao＊ Naulakhi Well; the Islamic Maqbara for filig＊ marble screens; and Sarsagar Lake for boating.

Do seek out the superb Tambekarwada, a fou＊ storey haveli (merchant's town house) whose wa＊ are covered from top to bottom with murals. Op＊ daily, managed by the Archaeological Surv＊ of India, directions available from the Tour＊ Office opposite the railway station. The fine M＊ (Maharaja Sayajirao) University of Vadodara h＊ especially strong music, dance and drama fac＊ ties. Regular evening performances attract t＊ leading artists of India. Vadodara also has a thr＊ ing contemporary art school whose painters e＊ hibit world-wide. Out of town, visit *Champar＊* (1485 Jami Masjid), *Dabhoi* (13th-century Hin＊ fort) and *Sankheda* (centre of lacquered wood＊ furniture-making). Vadodara connects by ro＊ with Indore (5hrs), by air with Delhi and Bomba＊ Stay at *Utsav Hotel*, Professor Manekra Road (t＊ 51415).

HEADING SOUTH

LOTHAL

87km. Archaeological find of major significance:＊ important Harappan port that traded with Egy＊ and Mesopotamia around 2,400–1,500BC, a＊ thus the earliest known urban settlement in t＊ subcontinent. Major known Harappan si＊ are further north, such as Mohenjo-Daro a＊ Harappa. Discovered in 1954 by archaeologist S.＊ Rao. Excavations reveal a sophisticated port usi＊ a scientific understanding of tides; planned stre＊ and bazaar areas, with underground drains; m＊ chants' houses with bath areas and fireplaces; jo＊ burial grounds; dockyards and warehouses; ter＊ cotta seals with Indus valley script; fine gold a＊ faience jewellery and children's toys that includ＊ chess set. Excellent on-site museum.

PALITANA

215km. For Jains, Shatrunjaya is the most sacred＊ their five, temple-covered, sacred hills. Girna＊ near Junagadh, comes second. *Jainism* develop＊ in the 6th century BC and, like Buddhism a centu＊ later, was breaking away from rigid, caste-ridd＊ Hinduism. Like Buddhism too, it was a prince w＊ led. Mahavira (599–527 BC), the 24th and la＊

rthankara (saint), renounced his pampered life
d lived as a naked ascetic for 12 years before
hieving the highest spiritual knowledge. He
en became a jina (conqueror) and his followers
came Jains.

Jains have no god since they believe the universe
as not created but is infinite. However, they do
lieve in reincarnation and in salvation, to be
und through, amongst other efforts, temple
ilding and ahimsa (reverence for all life) which
mands strict vegetarianism. Many wear mouth
asks in case they should swallow an insect. There
e two sects: Digambaras (sky-clad) who have no
ssessions, not even clothes, and Shvetambaras
ho are less strict. Jains concentrate in Gujarat,
mbay and Rajasthan to be close to the sacred
lls as pilgrimage should be on foot. Like the
rsees, they tend to be bright, commercially suc-
ssful and exercise power disproportionate to
eir meagre 3½ million population. Well-known
milies are the Sarabhais and Kasturbais but, in
neral, Jains are self-effacing, neither giving
oney to the community nor spending it ostenta-
usly on themselves, which would contradict
eir tenets.

To visit Palitana, arrive by 7am to climb before
e heat. The route is already full of white-clad
lgrims, the old or sick carried in dolis (string
airs), the rich on gaily caparisoned elephants. It
kes about 1½ hours to climb the 4km of steps up
atrunjaya (place of victory over worldliness) and
rive through a white marble jungle of 863 tem-
es, each in its tuk (enclosure), on to the rooftops,
1m up. If climbing is too much, be carried up in a
li.

Stunning views, air filled with the scent of jas-
ine trees. The biggest temple, Chaumukh, was
ilt by a wealthy banker in 1618 to save his soul.
t the most sacred is dedicated to Shri Adishwara
r Rushbhadav), the first Tirthankara, where the
ithful chant at the image bedecked with gold and
ormous diamonds. Coffers groaning with more
wels stand nearby. A successful Ahmedabad
erchant might well add a diamond necklace to
em. A 'donation' of Rs900 brings the honour of
ening them and dressing up the deity in more
wels. They are no longer on public display.
iests hand a pass to each leaving visitor who,
any steps down and 45 minutes later, exchanges
for a free, reviving breakfast of ladu (a heavy
veetmeat) and brass dishes of steaming, sweet
a. Open 7am–7pm, when even the priests
ave.

BHAVNAGAR

244km from Ahmedabad; 60km from Palitana.
Cotton-exporting port with Gandhi Smitri
(museum and library to the Mahatma) and one
shop, Gandhisamriti. The splendid palace-like
hospital built in the 1930s by Maharaja Takhtsing-
hji was designed so that a patient could ride up to
the operating theatre on his camel.

Stay here to visit Palitana, at **Nilambag Palace
Hotel** (tel: 24340/24422; cable: NILAMBAG
PALACE); Welcomgroup's unpretentious, small,
courtyard palace well-built at the turn of the
century; much polished wood and Maharaja's
furnishings, private house atmosphere. It was
Maharaja Krishnakumarsingh who was the first
maharaja to hand over his state to the Union of
India and who later became Governor of Madras
State (now Tamil Nadu). 14 rooms (suites very
spacious), attached bath, big verandahs on upper
floors, garden, pool, hard tennis court. To escape
the heat, Gujarat's answer to Srinagar is *Mahuva*,
lush with coconut palms, but it is not well developed for western tourists yet. Bhavnagar connects by air with Bombay, by road with Somnath
and Gir.

HEADING WEST

RAJKOT

216km. Former capital of Saurashtra, now associated with Gandhi who passed his childhood here
when his father was diwan (chief minister) to the
Raja. His home can be visited. Other Gandhi connections are the fine Alfred High School where he
was educated and the Rashtriya Shala, founded in
his presence in 1921 (housing the National School
of Weaving). See also Rajkumar College (built 1870
to educate Gujarati princes, with a fine hall) and
Watson Museum (building and contents open
Thurs.–Tues., 9–11.45am; 3–5.45pm). Local
bandhana, patchwork and mirror work are good.
Rajkot is the junction for exploring Saurashtra and
Kutch, flat areas with colourful tribes and walled
kots (village forts), the occasional Kutch one still
locked at night. But stay at Wankaner, 38km away
(see p. 141). Rajkot connects by air with Bombay.

WEST FROM RAJKOT

JAMNAGAR

87km. 16th-century pearl fishing town, the Rajput
Jadeja's capital, whose fame rests as much on

producing the two Indian cricketers Ranji and Duleep as on its bandhana fabrics and its Ayurvedic College and Research Centre. Broad streets and old buildings surround the Ranmal lake, whose island Lakhota Palace now houses a museum of Saurashtran sculpture and pottery (open Thurs.–Tues., 9am–noon; 3–6pm). See also the odd Manekbhai Muktidham, a cremation ground covered in statues of Indian gods, goddesses and saints. Several markets to watch the craftsmen and buy their bandhana, embroidery, silver, nutcrackers – and renowned sweetmeats. Jamnagar connects by air with Bombay.

DWARKA

234km. Krishna's capital, regularly referred to as Dwaravati in the great epics, especially the Mahabharata. Intensely holy, therefore, for Hindus who flock to celebrate his birthday, the Janmashtami festival (August–September). Blue-skinned *Krishna* is believed by many to be the 8th incarnation of Vishnu. He was born into a nomadic cattle-herding family of the Yadeva clan who later migrated here from Mathura (near Agra, see p. 68). He spent a gloriously naughty childhood, a wickedly flirtatious adolescence, had a very sexy romance with Radha, defeated various less fun-loving gods and rulers, and is number-one popular hero. See the fine exterior of Dwarkanath temple with its 5-storey spire, and the 13th-century Bhadkeshwar temple on the shore.

PORBANDAR

178km. Port town of narrow lanes, used by Arab traders since the 8th century. Visit the old house where Mohandas Karamchand Gandhi was born in 1869 and the nearby Kirti Mandir memorial to him which blends architectural elements of all India's religious styles. Gandhi's father and grandfather were diwans (chief ministers) of Porbandar.

Take a stroll along the shore to see the turn-of-the-century Daria Rajmahal palace showing Italian, Gothic and Arab influence (now a training college) and the sprawling 1927 Anut Nivas Khambala shore palace built by the cultured Maharaja Natwarsinghji (now a museum of Gujarat history), Plans to open it as a hotel may be realised by now. Incidentally, Natwarsinghji in 1931 captained the first official Indian cricket team to play in England. Charming 1930s *guest-house* nearby for overnight stays. Porbandar connects by air with Bombay.

SOUTH FROM RAJKOT

JUNAGADH

99km. Archaeological finds push Junagadh back pre-Harappan times. Later, in the 15th century, produced the great poet-saint Narshi Meh whose devotional songs are still sung througho Gujarat. But today, the Jains' sacred Girnar H draws the crowds (although there are Hindu te ples and a mosque too). See notes on Palita above, p. 138. This hill has a mere 2,000 ste rising 600m through a wood to the topmost temp Amba Mata, where couples worship to secure happy marriage. Just below is the biggest a oldest temple, dedicated to the 22nd Tirthankar Neminath, in the 12th century.

En route to the hill, see the epigraphically i portant boulder inscribed by the Mauryan emper Ashoka (3rd century BC), Rudradaman (150AD) a Skandagupta (454AD) (open 9am–noon; 3–6pn Visit the fine old city fort, Uparkot, founded in t 9th century by the Chudasamal Rajputs. Inside t triple gateway are 2 more stepwells, a Rajp palace, Buddhist caves with clever spiral staircas a mosque and Jami Masjid. See also the Maqba (Nawabs' mausolea); Durbar Hall in the pala museum (open Thurs.–Tues., 9–11.45am; 5.45pm, also closed alternate Sats) with tour information next door; the Sakkar Bagh Museu Rupayatan institute for handicrafts and the zoo (f a foretaste of the Gir lions). Find craftsmen wo ing on embroidery and patchwork, sometimes high quality. Junagadh connects by air w Bombay from Keshod airport.

Sasan Gir: (58km). See wildlife section, p. 141

SOMNATH

88km. Although destroyed and rebuilt about dozen times – early ones including the dem Ravana's in silver and Krishna's in wood – t superb 11th-century shore temple has sufficie still standing, either on site or in the museum, testify to its legendary beauty. Best at 7am, noon sunset. See notes to the better preserved Modhe above, p. 137. The Archaeological Museum is Surya Mandir, Patan City Bazaar (closed Wed. a alternate Sats). Krishna is believed to have left mortal incarnation here, at Bhalka Tirth.

NORTH FROM RAJKOT

Not far are *Morvi*, with bulky Venetian Gotl mansion and superbly stylish Art Deco 1931- palace with tubular-framed furniture, su

ranean bedrooms and lift; and *Halvad*, with
autifully carved, lakeside palace.
But the more adventurous should press on north
the salt flats of Kutch and see the Asiatic wild ass
d the largest breeding flamingo area in the
orld; *Bhuj*, a kot (walled town) until recently
ked at night; tiny villages and the port of
ndavi. In Bhuj, hunt in the back streets for some
he very best Gujarat bandhana embroidery and
er. Rewarding, but not for those fussy about
ir comfort. On the roads notice the pallias
ones commemorating poets and warriors). Each
carved with a man on a horse, a woman in a
riot or just a hand denoting death by sati (self-
molation), the sun or moon above recording the
e of the death or act of bravery. Sati was per-
med by husbands, wives and mothers here; one
n watching his wife commit sati in 1805 com-
ined to Sir Alexander Walker 'not from feeling
ret for his loss, but for the expense he was
osed to in his endeavours to procure another
e'.

NKANER
km. The base for west Gujarat. Stay at either the
nd and glorious Ranjitvilas palace or the Purna
andra Bhavan (full-moon house) in the palace
unds, once the royal guest-house.
njitvilas Palace (tel: 363621; cables to Secretary,
vraj Digvijaysinh, Palace, Wankaner); home of
another Rajput family, the Jhalas. Former
haraja Rajsabheb Pratapsinhji now looks after
minions as Member of Parliament and runs his
ace as a country house for paying guests. Set on
ll in 225 acres, it was built 1907–14 to designs of
then Maharaja, Amarsinhji. He ruled for 67
rs, travelled world-wide and threw all his
hitectural experience into the palace: Victorian
work, Gothic arches, Italianate pillars, Dutch
f and colossal, domed central clock-tower. In-
e there is a marble double spiral staircase de-
ned to prevent those ascending from seeing
se descending (useful for night-time corridor
lking); an indoor swimming pool; a 1930s baoli
e of the last to be built) for air-conditioning and
useum.
2 double rooms, attached bath, palace furnish-
s, meals included (picnics provided), chikar
nting) for antelope and small game can be
anged as can visits to rural villages and fairs,
rvi, Halvad and trips to Kutch. Essential to book
etter or cable, indicating time of arrival and first
al needed. The *Purna Chandra Bhavan* in the

palace grounds is booked through the palace and
guests can use the palace facilities.

Wildlife sanctuaries

Only two, but both excellent. However, the
Karnataka and Tamil Nadu reserves in the South
are as near as these and connected by direct flights.
See p. 217.

KANHA, MADHYA PRADESH
Season February–May. Direct flights from Bombay, Delhi and Calcutta to Nagpur, then by road
270km; or fly to Jabalpur, then by road 175km. Stay
at *Kipling Camp*, well-sited, equipped with both
tents and chalets built in local style; bookable
through Bob Wright, Tollygunge Club, Calcutta or
through a travel agent, such as SITA. (Reports say
the camp is nicest when Bob Wright is in residence.) Alternatively, stay at the state-run *Kisli
Hotel*, bookable through MPSTDC, Bhopal or
B. Rekwar, Shakti Travels, Mandla, MP. For local
information and other government accommodation, apply to The Manager, Wildlife Tourism,
MPSTDC, 1494 Wright Town, Jabalpur (tel:
23906). Explore on elephant.
2,200 sq km of very rich faunal land in the Banjar
Valley right in the middle of India and hunted over
until recently. Setting of Kipling's *The Jungle Books*.
Set up in 1955 to save the almost extinct hard-
ground barasingha (the Indian swamp deer), now
numbering about 150. The park is part of Project
Tiger and now provides a near certainty of seeing a
tiger. The first serious research on tigers was done
here by American big-cat expert, George Schaller,
in 1963–65. There are also chital, leopard, hyena,
blackbuck, barking deer, gaur (Indian bison) and
sambhar; plus birds such as crested serpent-eagles
and black ibises.

GIR, GUJARAT
Season October–June. Fly to Keshod, then 90km by
road. Stay at *Sasan Gir Forest Lodge*, Junagadh,
bookable in writing or through ITDC Bombay (tel:
233343); or at *Forest Bungalow*, Junagadh (60km),
bookable direct two weeks in advance or through
the Government of Gujarat Office, Dhanraj Mahal,
Apollo Bunder, Bombay (tel: 257039) or the Gujarat
Information Centre, Baba Kharak Singh Marg,
New Delhi (tel: 343147).
1412 sq km of Gir deciduous and thorn forest
constitutes one of the most important Indian sanc-

tuaries and the largest single tract of land reserved for conservation.

Here the rare Asiatic lion, once found throughout the Middle East and north India, has been saved (although some find them a bit too tame). Not only did it suffer from Raj guns, but also from the famine of 1899–1900. This led the Viceroy Lord Curzon to cancel his shoot and the Nawab of Junagadh to begin protecting the Gir lions. Meanwhile, the lions, short of food, ate 31 people in the state the next year, and made off with countless cattle. Although there has been controlled shooting since then, Gir now has over 200 lions. See them up close, in their natural habitat, sometimes in prides of more than a dozen together. They tend to mate October–November, producing young in January–February. See also wild boar, deer, antelope, hyena, leopard and the Indian chowsingha (antelope) whose buck is the only wild animal to have four horns – the female is hornless. Birds include oriole, rock-grouse, paradise fly catcher and flocks of flamingoes.

Find out more

Buhler, A., and Fischer, E.: *The Patola of Gujarat*, 2 vols, Basle, 1979
Burgess, J.: *The Temples of Palitana in Kathiawad*, Bombay, 1869, reprinted at Gandhinagar, 1976
Burra, R., (ed.): *Looking Back, 1896–1960* (on Indian cinema), New Delhi, 1981
Chittar, S. D.: *The Port of Bombay: a Brief History*, private publication, Bombay, 1973
David, M. D.: *History of Bombay 1661–1708*, Bombay, 1973
Edwardes, S. M.: *The Rise of Bombay*, Times of India Press, 1902
Forster, E. M.: *The Hill of Devi*, London, 1953
Gosh, A., (ed.): *Ajanta Murals*, New Delhi, 1967
'Homage to Indian Textiles', *Marg*, Bombay, nd (in print)
Jackson, Stanley: *The Sassoons*, London, 1968
Jain, J.: *Folk Art and Culture of Gujarat*, Ahmedabad, 1980
Jain, J.: *The Master Weavers*, Bombay, 1982
Karkaria, R. P.: *The Charm of Bombay: an anthology of*

writings in praise of the first city in India, Bomb 1915.
Kulke, Eckehard: *The Parsees in India: a Minority an Agent of Social Change*, India, 1978
Lala, R.M.: *The Creation of Wealth, A Tata Sto* Bombay, 1981
Lala, R. M.: *The Heartbeat of a Trust, Fifty Years of Sir Dorabji Tata Trust*, Bombay, 1984
Maclean, J. M.: *Guide to Bombay*, Bombay, editi published 1875–1902
Singh, M.: *The Cave Paintings of Ajanta*, Lond 1965
Stamp, G.: 'British Architecture in India 18 1947', *Journal of the Royal Society of Arts*, V CXXIX, 1981, pp. 357–377.
Stamp, G.: 'Victorian Bombay: Urbs Prima Indis', *Art and Archaeological Research Papers*, J 1977, pp. 22–27
Tindall, Gillian: *City of Gold, The Biography Bombay*, London 1982
'Treasures of Everyday Art: Raja Dinkar Kel Museum', *Marg*, Bombay, and 'Treasures of Ind Textiles', *Marg*, Bombay, 1980
Yazdani, G., (ed.) *Ajanta Frescoes*, Vols I– Oxford, 1931–46
Yazdani, G.: *Mandu, City of Joy*, London, nd.

FABRIC NOTE
The unrivalled collection at the Calico Museum gradually being covered in substantial volum edited by John Irwin, former Keeper of the Orie Department, Victoria and Albert Muse London. They should be available in good libraries.
Irwin, J., (ed.): *Historic Textiles of India at the Ca Museum*, vols I–IV, Ahmedabad, 1972–81. I, Ir and Hall, M.: *Indian Painted and Printed Fabi* 1972. II, Irwin and Hall: *Indian Embroideries*, 19 III, Talwar, K., and Krishna, K.: *Indian Pign Paintings on Cloth*, 1979. IV, Buhler, A., Fischer, and Nabholz, M.: *Indian Tie-dyed Fabrics*, 1981. V V and VI on costumes and zari brocade are to published soon.
The Chintz, Ahmedabad, 1983: a de luxe, limi edition of colour plates of museum items, p lished with notes and the texts of vols I an above.
The museum also stocks copies of *The Journal Indian Textile History*, ed., J. Irwin, 1955 ad seq.

Heading east:
Calcutta and Varanasi

The temptation to explore the toytown palaces of Rajasthan on the first trip to India, then, next time, climb up into the hills or plunge down south, leaves eastern India out in the cold. And stories of poverty in Calcutta and death in Varanasi (Banares) do not help.

But whereas Calcutta is certainly not for the tourist who demands a time-warp of paintbox palaces, charming markets and romance, nor for the over-sensitive who prefer poverty and death to be kept conveniently out of sight as they are back home, it is a fascinating city for the seasoned traveller. It is rich in good museums and buildings, both the inheritance of the British. Its colonial foundation lives on in social and sporting life. It is the centre of the vibrant contemporary Bengali culture, seen in literature, politics and the visual and performing arts. And it is an excellent springboard for visiting Varanasi, Orissa, the hills of north-east India, Bhutan and Nepal – or escaping to the Andaman and Nicobar Islands.

However, it is not an easy or welcoming place for a first-time visitor. The fabric of Calcutta is decaying. Geoffrey Moorhouse calls Calcutta: 'A permanent exhibition of decaying English Classical Buildings', while Bombay 'still glories in preposterously confident Gothic Revival constructions'. Yet, by peering through the crumbling masonry and dirt, the former colonial grandeur can be found, conjuring up visions of glittering balls and echoes of William Hickey's wicked gossip.

In Indian terms, Calcutta is a new city. In 1690 Job Charnock, an agent for the British East India Company, leased the three tiny villages of Sutanati, Govindpur and Kalikata, on the banks of the Hooghly River, from Emperor Aurangzeb. Six years later the Company built the first Fort William, named after King William III. It was the beginning of the Indian Empire. After various teething troubles – including Clive the trouble-shooter arriving from Madras in the nick of time to recapture the city from the Nawab of Murshidabad in 1757 – Warren Hastings became the first Governor of British India in 1772.

From then until 1911 when the capital was moved to Delhi, Calcutta blossomed. And even when it lost the political throne, it maintained commercial supremacy right until Independence, when the Indian economy changed from being colonial-based to Indian. It was at that moment that the new industries sprang up in Bombay. Until then, Calcutta was the headquarters for all the major British firms, from the traditional Jardine Henderson to the modern ICI. For their raw materials – jute, coal, iron ore and tea – came from Calcutta's rich hinterland.

After Clive's triumph the Fort was rebuilt (costing £2 million) and a huge area of jungle cleared so that the enemy could be seen

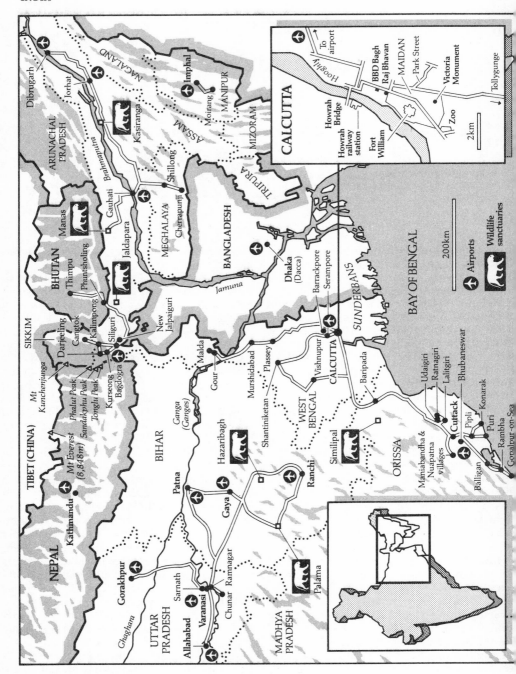

CALCUTTA

To airport

Hooghly

Howrah Bridge

BBD Bagh
Raj Bhavan

Howrah railway station

Fort William

MAIDAN

Park Street

Victoria Monument

Tollygunge

Zoo

2km

Dibrugarh

Jorhat

NAGALAND

Imphal

MANIPUR

Moirang

ARUNACHAL PRADESH

ASSAM

MIZORAM

Kasiranga

Brahmaputra

Gauhati

Shillong

MEGHALAYA

Cherrapunji

TRIPURA

BANGLADESH

Manas

Jaldapara

BHUTAN

Thimpu

Phuntsholing

Dhaka (Dacca)

Jamuna

Barrackpore
Serampore

SUNDERBANS

BAY OF BENGAL

SIKKIM

Darjeeling

Gangtok

Kalimpong

Siliguri

New Jalpaiguri

Jalpaiguri

Mt Kuncheniunga

Phalut Peak

Sandakphu Peak

Torglu Peak

Kurseong

Bagdogra

Malda

Gour

Murshidabad

Plassey

Vishnupur

CALCUTTA

WEST BENGAL

Baripada

Udaigiri

Ratnagiri

Lalitgiri

Bhubaneswar

Konarak

Cuttack

Pipli

Puri

Rambha

Gopalpur-on-Sea

ORISSA

Simlipal

Maniabandha & Nuapatna villages

Balligan

200km

Airports

Wildlife sanctuaries

TIBET (CHINA)

NEPAL

Kathmandu

Mt Everest (8,848m)

Gorakhpur

BIHAR

Patna

Gaya

Ganga (Ganges)

Hazaribagh

Shantiniketan

Ranchi

Palamu

Sarnath

Ramnagar

Chunar

Varanasi

Allahabad

Ghaghara

UTTAR PRADESH

MADHYA PRADESH

approaching and the British could have a clear aim of fire at them. Around this two-mile long Maidan (open space) rose extravagant Regency mansions with columns, pilasters and porticos, built by the newly wealthy jute and opium millionaire merchants, the nabobs, who might keep a hundred servants for a family of four. Government House and Dalhousie Square formed the administrative centre to the north. It was a stuccoed classical city of palaces, likened by contemporaries to St Petersberg and Nash's London, although the climate attacked the buildings very quickly. Crumbling Calcutta is nothing new. Many of the great figures of the period are buried in South Park Street Cemetery, a potted history of colonial Calcutta.

The British left a thriving legacy: many museums, the university, the Asiatic Society, the Botanical Gardens and, above all, the clubs. Colonial Calcutta parallelled the British development of exclusive social clubs with rigid codes of conduct and elaborate ceremonial, providing dignity and privacy for the rising bourgeoisie, the new elite. Calcutta has more clubs than any other Indian city and they are still the focus of social life, from cricket and cocktails to swimming and Sunday lunch. Prettiest among them is the Tollygunge Club in south Calcutta, the perfect country club on the edge of the city. For the Bengalis, the 19th-century cultural renaissance led to an awakening of national identity that culminated in the Bengal Uprising in 1857, which the British, from their side, call the Mutiny. Their intellectual and political precocity produced the liberal thinker Rajah Ram Mohan Roy, the literary Nobel Prize winner Rabindranath Tagore, politician Subas Chandra Bose, film-maker Satyajit Ray and now a far less radical second Communist government.

But they seem to have abandoned all efforts to cope with their city, either conserving the past or looking after the present. The problems are too huge, the finances too small. Its position as commercial, administrative and political capital of the Indian Empire has long gone. Few people put money into Calcutta. The Indian princes and the European lords of commerce have mostly gone, leaving the once dazzling social season a mere shadow, the pleasure palaces either sold off, closed up or used as government offices.

Today the few old families, still using diamonds for buttons on their silk shirts, stylishly dissipate the fortunes amassed by their forefathers, burying their heads in sweet sands of golf, racing and club life rather than quitting Calcutta for the thriving markets of Delhi, Bombay, Bangalore and elsewhere. They are great raconteurs of past family extravagances. One recalled: 'My father had great style. He loved women. At the end of a dinner party, he would give each woman a precious stone to match her dress – emerald, amethyst, etc.'

The most energetic and enterprising of the many immigrants Calcutta has absorbed are the Marwari families from Rajasthan, epitomised by the Birlas. Other big families are the Modis, Goenkas, Singhanias and Podars. Marwaris make up most of the new rich. Having arrived in Calcutta at the end of last century, made several fortunes, often by taking over where the British were pulling out, they now diversify their business interests and their social life throughout India. Their lifestyle tends to emulate anything Western, from French gilt furniture and concrete to jeans and junk-food, rather than offering patronage to the architects and craftsmen working within the Indian tradition. (For more on Marwaris, see p. 90, Shekhavati.)

The Birlas, who are to the Marwari what the Tatas are to the Parsees, are an exception. Amongst much else, they own *The Hindustan Times*. (The Goenkas of Madras own *The Indian Express*.) Although they are amongst the richest Marwari families and thus one of the richest families in India, they are devout and keen on education. The not-so-modestly named Birla temples glitter with rich mosaic, precious stones and metals in Calcutta, dazzle with white marble on a Hyderabad hilltop and add to the 2,000 or so other temples at Varanasi. The Birlas have also set up an institute for technology and science, an education trust, a planetarium and the Birla Academy of Art and Culture in Calcutta. Mahatma Gandhi was a close friend of the family. It was at their home in Delhi that he was assassinated.

In a country where normally well-balanced modest men of all ranks fall into a life-time of debt in order to give an impressive wedding and provide dowry enough to upgrade the status of their daughter (and therefore themselves) or strengthen inter-family bonds (or business bonds), the Marwari wedding is the grandest of all. The most ostentatious are held in the extremely lavish new houses, furnished with ex-Maharaja gilt. Lavish public weddings are held at the flashy grand hotels in December and January when it is worth joining the crowd to gawp at the kilos of diamonds and pearls and gold – after all, they are worn to be noticed. The wedding guests may well be honoured with fruit imported from Harrods and orchids from Thailand.

But the old and new rich are an even tinier minority in Calcutta than in other Indian cities, to be glimpsed at the few fashionable restaurants, the very pucka clubs (more Pall Mall than the real Pall Mall) and the races (in the members' enclosure, of course). What is more immediately apparent on arrival in Calcutta are the sheer numbers of people, like drones of a queen bee, seething and swarming over the pavements and roads. There are millions of them everywhere, put at well over 9 million in 1984.

From the beginning, Calcutta has accepted quantities of immigrants from the Bengal hinterland, from other states and from outside India. It was Job Charnock who invited the Armenians and many others. The Chinese came to do successful business in leather. After Independence, they continued to cure leather and make excellent shoes but they also supplied the best hair cutters and went into the restaurant trade, formerly dominated by the Italians and Swiss. But since Partition the population has swollen to epidemic proportions, increased again during the Indo-Pakistan war of 1965 and the Pakistan-Bangladesh war of 1972. And the numbers continue to grow.

However, for most arrivals Calcutta has not produced her golden egg (unlike Bombay, which has expanded to keep pace with immigration). Overburdened with people the roads are not repaired; the transport system is a disaster; the inadequate water supply has led to the use of polluted water and an increase in water-borne diseases; the sewerage and rubbish collection services cannot cope; and the supply of power is so erratic that, in addition to the hotels and offices, even private flats have their own generators.

There is enormous unemployment and consequent poverty and squalor. A few may be found by Mother Teresa and her Sisters of Mercy who work ceaselessly and selflessly touching just a tiny fraction of the problem with their love and tenderness, always bringing smiles and making the poor feel wanted. Their work is all the more extraordinary because the suffering is on such a huge scale.

Mother Teresa simply calls her work 'doing something beautiful for God'. In his tribute to her, Malcolm Muggeridge writes: 'to (choose), as Mother Teresa did, to live in the slums of Calcutta, amidst all the dirt and disease and misery, signified a spirit so indomitable, a faith so intractable, a love so abounding that I felt abashed'. Since 1948 when she stopped teaching at the Loretto Convent School in Calcutta, with five rupees in her pocket, Mother Teresa and her increasing number of helpers have cared for destitute children, lepers and the dying. For she believes deeply that, even more than food and shelter, the poor need to be wanted.

Even well away from the slums, in the streets off Chowringhee where deprivation is not so acute, the density of slow-moving human bodies winding between the skyscrapers, the decaying old mansions and the bustees (huts) of the poor is stifling. There are bodies everywhere.

On the pavements they lounge, chat, sleep or set up shop. There are dubious, make-shift kitchens, complete with vegetable preparers, cooks, and washing-up sections. They vie for space with leather, tool and fruit vendors, typists, booksellers and beggars. There is no space to walk. There is no space on the roads either, which are full of nose-to-tail, honking, stationary jallopies, over-flowing city buses, cows, rickshaws with jangling brass bells, more people and piles of earth. For those who can afford it, even the shortest journeys are taken by car, to maintain prestige and dignity and to avoid the cluttered, potholed pavements.

The piles of earth are part of the construction of the underground – a misnomer as much of it will run above ground, and apparently parts will even have to be raised. A man who arrived in Calcutta in 1946 remembers wide avenues, elegant vistas, houses with big lawns, streets washed every morning and two new projects: the underground and the fly-over incorporating a second – and much needed – bridge over the Hooghly River. Nearly forty years on, neither is complete. The underground has suffered from a series of foreign engineers advising Indian workmen who did not have the necessary machinery and began work with pick-axes and baskets. The work on the fly-over is halted each time the designers wish to modify the plans.

But the administration and labour of both keeps up employment. And meanwhile the dust fills the heavy, humid air so that by 8am you are ready for your first bath of the day.

It takes at least three days to achieve in Calcutta what takes one day in Bombay or Delhi. Every Calcuttan agrees about that, because communications are so atrocious.

So, the combination of the exhausting humidity, the crowded pavements and the almost standstill traffic means that planning your day is crucial. And Calcutta is big – a city area of 102 sq km: the Metropolitan District 1,380 sq km – and just crossing the centre can easily take an hour by car. Walking the quite large distances between interesting places is by no means a picturesque promenade. A successful itinerary goes for geographical proximity rather than a personal desire to see a number of sites in a specific order.

The traffic is not the only hurdle in Calcutta. The telephone system barely works at all, yet most people have a minimum of three telephone numbers, often more. The solution, even for a businessman, is just to turn up, which is what everyone has come to expect.

But this can be tricky since the confusion of road names is worse here than anywhere else in India. In Calcutta it seems that every road has two names, before and after Independence. 'Before' names are known by everyone: 'after' names are printed on the maps. A few people know both names of a few roads – and they are rarely the taxi drivers or hotel staff. Most people react to both Dalhousie Square and BBD Bagh – although the full works of Benoy-Badal-Dinesh Bagh might baffle. But Lenin Sarani has not caught on for Dharamtala Street, and Ho Chi Minh Street is unlikely to replace Harrington Street, where the US Consulate happens to be sited.

When to go

The intense humidity, due to low altitude and closeness to the sea, may deflate the most energetic. November to February is best: from March, it begins hotting up, reaching a crescendo before the colossal rains which pelt down from the end of June until mid-September, bringing slight relief but also flooding, washing away many homes and most of last year's efforts on the underground.

FESTIVALS European Calcuttans say the Season begins with Durga Puja in September–October and ends with Holi in February–March. 'After that,

Calcutta is hell.' Bengalis take a broader view: 'Baro mase tero parban' (thirteen festivals in twelve months). In fact they have 20 official – and several unofficial – holidays and let their hair down at any excuse, be it Diwali, Christmas, the Muslim Id, a political hero's birthday or the day bank accounts are closed at the end of December. Bengali New Year in April–May is especially fun, if hot. See p. 251 for more on festivals.

Durga Puja is the biggest Calcutta festival, the Bengal version of Dussehra. The goddess Durga, destroyer of evil, is one of the many forms of the great goddess Devi, portrayed as a goddess riding a tiger. (Kali, another form of Devi, is altogether more sinister.) Riotous celebrations last about three weeks. It is a bad time for business as the city hardly functions, but good for spectacle, music, dance and drama. On the final day, elaborate images of Durga are processed through illuminated streets throbbing with loud-speaker music, to be dunked in the Hooghly River at night, with more rejoicing on the Maidan.

SOCIAL CALENDAR Calcutta races are run from early November to late March on Saturdays or mid-week, about six meetings a month. There is the Calcutta Thousand Guineas and Two Thousand Guineas; the Calcutta Oaks, Derby, St Leger and the Governor's Cup. But the climax is the Queen Elizabeth II Cup (end of January). In the Members' Enclosure (entrance Rs30) the best banyan tree in Calcutta gives shelter to ladies in the latest saris, frocks and hats. In the days of the Empire, Christmas race week was a social highpoint when the Viceroy and Vicereine would drive past the fine grandstand with regal formality. For the season's fixtures list contact the Royal Calcutta Turf Club office, 11 Russell Street, Calcutta 700071 (tel: 241103/241105/248053, closed Mon. afternoon and Tues).

ARTS Culturally, Calcutta is one of the most vibrant Indian cities. A musician has not made it until he has performed here. The major music festivals are November–March. The most important are Park Circus (January), Dover Lane Conference and ITC Music Festival, but there are countless high-class performances throughout these months. Calcutta is the home ground of leading Indian musicians such as Ravi Shankar, Ali Akbar Khan and Nikhil Banerjee. The city also has one of the oldest symphony orchestras in Asia.

Getting there: Getting away

The best way to arrive is by train, especially from Delhi. Howrah station, teeming with activity, is just across Howrah Bridge from the centre, whereas Dum Dum airport is an unscenic hour's drive away.

The lightning fast (16hrs) Rajdhani Express, with first-class air-conditioned coupés and three-course meals (Indian or European), leaves New Delhi on Mon., Tues., Fri. and Sat. Or there is the more sedate and traditional Delhi–Howrah Mail (22hrs) and the Air-conditioned Express (24 hrs). From Madras, take the Coromandel Express up the

coast; from Bombay, the Gitanjali Express or the Calcutta Mail. The shorter trip from Varanasi takes about 12hrs.

Sealdah Station on the east side of Calcutta serves the north and north-east, including Darjeeling.

Dum Dum airport (close to the small arms factory where the soft-nosed bullet was invented in 1898) is, ironically, the only clean and efficient international airport in India. Thai Airways, British Airways and Air India have good time-tables for flying in and out. Internally, Indian Airlines connects Calcutta direct with all other major cities including Bombay, Delhi and Madras daily, Bangalore and Hyderabad Tues.–Sun. There are daily flights to Bagdogra (for Darjeeling) and Bhubaneswar (for connections with Varanasi on Tues. Thurs., Sat. and Sun.). A flight to and from Kathmandu goes daily except Tues. and Sat.; the Port Blair flights (for the Andamans) are Tues. and Fri.

Sadly, there is no passenger sea service between Madras, Orissa and Calcutta.

Where to stay

The Indian system of awarding stars to hotels is particularly bizarre in Calcutta. There is only one top quality hotel, the Oberoi Grand, although the Taj group are building a possible rival near the Zoo. The five-star-rated Hotel Hindusthan International and The Park do not provide rooms or services to live up to their ratings and the Great Eastern Hotel has pretentious prices for its entirely faded grandeur. The fact that Kipling stayed there is a somewhat outdated recommendation. If funds do not stretch to the Oberoi and a central location is essential, the New Kenilworth Hotel is good, but there is much more character at the modestly priced family-run Fairlawn. The very pukka Bengal Club has rooms, but introduction must be through a member.

The real alternative to the Oberoi is the Tollygunge Club, set amid huge grounds about forty minutes from the city centre. Rooms and facilities are open to all foreigners and the air is glorious.

As in Bombay, good accommodation is scarce, so book well in advance. Communications within Calcutta may be atrocious, but letters sent in and out of Calcutta have a high success rate.

Oberoi Grand 15 Jawaharlal Nehru Road (Chowringhee), Calcutta 700013
Telephone: 230181

Telex: 7248,7854 OBCL
Cable: OBHOTEL
Airport 16km; railway station 5km
250 rooms, including 29 suites, all with attached
bath. Single Rs775; double Rs875; suites Rs1550–
2750.
All mod. cons, including travel agency, bank,
shopping, hairdresser, in-house astrologer, safe
deposit, baby sitter, business services. A rare combination of old character and style with modern
facilities and high standards. Originally built in the
1890s as the Royal Hotel incorporating the Theatre
Royal and run by a former jeweller, Arrathoon
Stephen. When the theatre burnt down in 1911, he
acquired some adjacent land and expanded.

Since Mohan Singh Oberoi bought it in 1938, it
has become to the Oberoi chain what the Taj Bombay is to the Taj chain. Its efficiency is a daily
miracle in Calcutta. Not only does it have generators for power cuts but the water is purified ten
times before guests receive it and the telephones
work quite often. Corridors are hung with prints of
Calcutta, but the newly decorated rooms have that
anonymous comfort which results in the brain not
knowing which Oberoi hotel it is waking up in. The
large swimming pool is pure joy amid the stifling
air. Health Club excellent (massage, sauna, Turkish bath, gymnasium); hairdresser patronised by
local Europeans. The Chowringhee bar (murals by
Desmond Doig), the Garden Café, the Polynesia
and Moghul restaurants are the best (if not unique)
in town. The Pink Elephant is the best discotheque
in India. See also night life section.

Tollygunge Club 120 Deshapran Sasmal Road,
Calcutta 700033.
Telephone: 467806, 461922, 463141
Airport 23km; railway station 12km.
51 rooms, bathroom attached. Single Rs170;
double Rs200. To book, write to Bob Wright,
secretary.

Set in an estate of over 200 acres, facilities include
riding (open to non-residents), golf, 8 tennis courts
(5 hard, 3 soft), indoor and outdoor swimming
pools, 2 squash courts, badminton, billiards, cards.
Founded in 1895 to 'promote all manner of sports',
Tolly not only offers a beautiful club house, vast
grounds, healthy horses and lungfuls of gloriously
fresh air, but is run by Bob and Anne Wright who
know everyone and everything and share it all
with their guests. In 1788 Richard Johnson built the
club house which later became the residence of the
deposed sons of Tipu Sultan. By the close of the
19th century Tollygunge was already known as

Sahibangicha, 'the garden of the white men',
where Europeans relaxed outside the city. Today,
Calcutta society meets at the club to play sports,
gossip over tea, chocolate cake and later cocktails,
and wander in the grounds with their blossoming
trees, tropical plants and exotic birds. The atmosphere is relaxed, friendly and welcoming.

New Kenilworth 1 & 2 Little Russell Street, Cal-
cutta 700071
Telephone: 441916, 442647
Telex: 3395
Cable: NEWKEN
Airport 18km; railway station 7km
90 rooms, including 6 suites, attached bath. Single
Rs300; double Rs400; suite Rs650.
Spacious garden and all mod. cons.

Good, clean hotel located at the south end of the
Maidan, off Shakespeare Sarani. Stay in the old
wing which has been renovated. Take tea and
dinner in the garden.

Fairlawn 13/a Sudder Street, Calcutta 700016
Telephone: 244460, 241835
Cable: FAIROTEL
Airport 15km; railway station 6km
20 rooms, attached bath. Single Rs230 (non-
airconditioned Rs200); double Rs330 (non-
airconditioned Rs300).
Meals included in room cost.

The Kapoors (Shashi, Jennifer Kendall and
offspring) have been coming to stay with Mr and
Mrs Smith for 29 years and recommend its
'tremendous atmosphere, great ambience'. Mr
Smith is English, his wife Armenian. He goes to
market daily for the hotel provisions. Their spotless, cosy home is stuffed with personal treasures,
all cared for by a dedicated staff.

Bengal Club 1/1Russell Street, Calcutta 700016
Telephone: 299231, 299233, 240752
Airport 18km; railway station 7km
14 beds, attached bath. Double Rs550, including
some meals. Apply for temporary membership
through a member. To book, write to Mr S. V. S.
Naidu, Secretary.
Facilities include an extensive, well-run library.

The oldest survivor of colonial Calcutta's social
clubs still retains its period style, although it is
reduced to a shadow of its former self. It was
established on February 1, 1827, in Esplanade
West. In 1845 the Club moved into the house
on Chowringhee where Thomas Babington
Macaulay, Law Member of the Supreme Council,
had so enjoyed living the decade before. A new
building replaced it in 1909 but with the decline of

149

British society in the 1960s the club retreated into the back of the building.

Each room comes with a bearer. The club has a reserve list of retired bearers, one of whom is hired on your arrival, fired on your departure. Cocktail parties in the grand room spill out on to the lawn which twinkles with fairy lights. Deep green leather sofas in the reading room; peace in the large library; the London *Daily Telegraph* is constantly perused. Upstairs, five-course set luncheon starts with thick soup and sherry, ends with Kalimpong cheese. Bengal food on Wed. Downstairs, the well-run Oriental Room is open to families. It is lively and serves à la carte Indian and Chinese food.

Information and reservations

Government of West Bengal Tourist Bureau, 3/2 BBD Bagh (tel: 238271), open Mon.–Sat., 7am–6pm; Sun., 7am–2pm. Very helpful. Also have desks at the airport and Howrah station.

Government of India Tourist Office, 4 Shakespeare Sarani (tel: 443521, 441402), open Mon.–Sat., 9am–6pm (until 1pm on 2nd Sat. of each month). Extremely helpful; run by knowledgeable locals. Also have desk at airport.

Orissa Tourist Information Centre, 55 Lenin Sarani (tel: 445266). Uttar Pradesh Tourist Information Centre (for Varanasi), 12A Netaji Subhas Road (tel: 226798).

Calcutta is a highly literate city and publishes several English language newspapers including *The Statesman*, *Amrita Bazaar Patrika* and *The Telegraph* which carry reports of the city's current controversies and triumphs and details of the day's events and entertainment. The WBTB produces *Calcutta This Fortnight*, a free leaflet (from their office or the Government of India Tourist Office).

Guide-books are scanty: either the WBTB's *Calcutta*, a booklet with selected lists and opening times, or *Calcutta Briefs* (Rs6), a maze of quotes, facts and pull-out maps. But there are a number of good books on Calcutta, see Find Out More, p. 171.

TRAVEL AGENTS

American Express, 21 Old Court House Street (tel: 236281); Mercury Travels, 46C Jawaharlal Nehru Road (tel: 443555); SITA World Travels, 27B Camac Street (tel: 432610); Speedways International, 3 Chowringhee Square (tel: 276419); Trade Wings (Calcutta), 32 Jawaharlal Nehru Road (tel: 249951); TCI, 46C Jawaharlal Nehru Road (tel: 445469).

AIRLINE OFFICES

Indian Airlines, 39 Chittaranjan Avenue (te 260730). International airline offices are concer trated on and near Jawaharlal Nehru Road. Tho on J N Road include Air India at no.50 (tel: 442356 Air France at no.41 (tel: 240011); British Airway also at no.41 (tel: 248181); Pan Am at no.42 (te 443251); Swissair at no.46C (tel: 444643) and Roy Nepal Airlines, again at no.41 (tel: 243949). Catha Pacific Airways are at 1 Middleton Street (te 447238); Thai International and Scandinavian Ai lines are both at 18 Park Street (tel: 24969€ Aeroflot is at 58 Chowringhee (tel: 449831).

TRAIN RESERVATIONS

Eastern Railway Booking Office, 6 Fairlie Place (te 224356), with Tourist Guide Assistant. Soutl Eastern Railway Booking Office, Esplanac Mansions (tel: 239530, 235074). For Orissa, consu Orissa Tourist Information, 55 Lenin Sarani (te 243653); for Sikkim, 5/2 Russell Street (tel: 247519

CONSULATES AND EMBASSIES

UK: 1 Ho Chi Minh Sarani (tel: 445171); USA: 5 Ho Chi Minh Sarani (tel: 443611); France: 26 Pa Mansions (tel: 240958); West Germany, 1 Hastin₃ Park (tel: 459141); Netherlands, 18A Brabourr Road (tel: 225864).

For trips out of India the following may hel¡ Bhutan: 48 Tivoli Court, Pramothesh Barua Sara (tel: 441301); Burma: 67 Park Street (tel: 21320(Nepal: 19 Woodlands Strandle Road (tel: 454293 Thailand: 18B Mandeville Gardens (tel: 460836). Foreigners Registration Office, 237 A J C Bose Roa (tel: 440549/443301)

Calcutta General Post Office is at BBD Bagh. Lo₁ queues, good poste restante.

For medical assistance, your accommodatic will recommend one of the numerous Englisl speaking doctors. Dey's Medical Stores, on Lin say Street, is a good chemist.

The city by day

The golden rule in Calcutta is 'the earlier the be ter'. As the people and traffic and humidity i₁ crease, so movement and energy slow down. Tl city centre retains the broad streets of its coloni planning but it is easier to appreciate without tl bellowing horns and choked-up traffic.

And there is plenty to do before the ma₁ museums reveal their treasures. Temples ar

urches open early as do the Botanical Gardens
1 the Zoo. At the other end of the day, the
netarium and Birla Museum stay open late,
ly evening strolls are pleasant, most shops stay
en until 7pm or 8pm and the Kali Temple only
ses its doors at 10pm. Almost no two monu-
nts keep the same hours and the relation be-
een the printed hours and actuality depends
on current 'short staffing'. There is no official
sta in Calcutta; Monday is the closed day for
dmarks such as the Victoria Memorial and the
lian Museum, and West Bengal has 20 official
blic holidays when almost everything shuts up.
n addition, the sights are scattered across this
ge, slow-moving city, so a spot of planning,
n by the vaguest tourist, pays dividends.

he WBTB and ITDC (at the Government of
lia Tourist Office) run almost identical full and
f-day introductory sightseeing tours. Go for the
rning ones which cover scattered sights. The
seums in the afternoon trip are better enjoyed
ne. For transport, it is cheaper (and much more
wenient here) to hire a car and driver from
er tourist office for a half or full day rather than
ch taxis. Rickshaws (pulled by wiry, barefoot
n who refused to convert to bicycles) are good
short hops. Buses and trams are only for a
ious game of sardines.

tanical Gardens The finest in India and Cal-
ta's principal lung. Here, amid lakes, lawns and
e trees in 273 acres sprawling along the west
nk of the Hooghly, are the Palmyra palm and
hogany avenues; the palm, orchid, fern and
ti houses; the gigantic banyan tree like a
nplete wood (apparently so-called because the
ndu traders, or banias, sheltered under these
es in the Persian Gulf) and a herbarium of 40,000
cies of dried plant.

he Gardens were laid out in 1786, under Col-
el Kyd, and the plant collection expanded by Dr
xburgh; there are memorials to both. The tea-
ture of Assam and Darjeeling was developed
e. Best in the early morning sunlight and fresh
Go the traditional way, by ferry from Chandpal
Takta Ghats (checking first that the Botanical
rden Ghat will be open); or by car (about 40
ns), being sure to return over the Howrah Bridge
er before the rush hour at 9am – or much later
Cars carrying foreigners may be driven inside
Gardens. Open 7am–5pm.

wrah Bridge and Station A single turmoil of
ving bodies and overloaded vehicles. The loads

carried by humans defy belief: a door balanced on
the head with six trunks on top is quite normal. The
single-span cantilevered bridge built in 1943 is
the only bridge across the Hooghly and carries 2
million people every day. Beneath it, masseurs,
barbers and flower sellers do brisk business.

The station was designed in 1906 by Arts and
Crafts architect, Halsey Ricardo. Its hall throbs
with food-sellers, water-carriers and passengers
arriving and leaving, each with hordes of well-
wishers and luggage carriers. And, of course,
astrologers for the journey, here in the form of
neon-lit weighing machines that punch out a person's weight and consequent fortune. Station plat-
forms are wide enough for the gentry to go directly
from the train into their waiting cars. Over the
platform entrance, a large blue and white neon
sign pompously proclaims: 'Godliness is next to
cleanliness'.

BBD Bagh (Dalhousie Square) Writers' Buildings, constructed in 1780 for the clerical staff of the
East India Company, bear testament to this former
powerhouse of the British. The GPO, built in
1864–8, was designed by Walter Granville, one of
his many Calcutta buildings. It stands on the west
side, on the site of the first fort, indicated with
brass markers. The controversial Black Hole inci-
dent of 1756 was in a guard-room in the sleeping
quarters. The WBTB is on the east side; and nearby
is 2 Brabourne Road where permission to visit the
Marble Palace is obtained. There is a tablet marking
Warren Hastings's house in Mission Row, an old
street to the east. Clive and Philip Frances lived to
the north-west, now the commercial quarter. Lit
up at night, and without the cars and people, the
square gives an idea of what British Calcutta was
like.

Asutosh Museum of Indian Art The first public
museum in an Indian university, founded in 1937
and named after Asutosh Mookerjee, champion of
university Indology studies. The collection concen-
trates on the rich artistic heritage of eastern India,
and includes sculpture, folk-art, textiles and an
excellent group of Kalighat paintings and terracottas. Well displayed. Informative booklet. In Calcutta University, College Street. Open Mon.–Fri.,
10.30am–5pm; Sat., 10.30am–1.30pm. (For books,
see What to Buy section.)

Marble Palace After the ethnic Asutosh collection, here are Rubens, Reynolds and Murillo
paintings, stuffed birds, Chinese porcelain, vast
Venetian gilt mirrors, Belgian chandeliers, a grandfather clock, statues of Pan and the young Queen

Victoria – looking disturbingly seductive – all piled into dusty, half-lit rooms. Rajendra Mullick, at the age of 16 began building and filling his Palladian mansion in 1835, apparently using 148 different kinds of marble, which led the Viceroy, Lord Minto, to dub it Marble Palace on his visit in 1910.

In the grounds are an aviary, a menagerie, the family temple and pelicans swimming round the European fountain. Rajendra never left India: his creation is the product of a hybrid culture developed by the Calcutta nouveaux riches under British influence. The Mullicks still live in a wing of the building and continue Rajenda's tradition of charity, feeding hordes of poor who collect at the palace gates daily at noon. The totally run-down palace next door was built by Rajendra for his relations. 46, Muktaram Babu Street, off Chittaranjan Avenue. Open 10am–4pm (except Mon. and Thur.). To visit, obtain a letter of permission from the WTBT, 2 Brabourne Road.

Rabindra-Bharati Museum The ancestral home of the extraordinarily gifted Tagore family, now devoted to the 19th-century Renaissance Movement of Bengal which involved several Tagores. The poet, philosopher and fervent nationalist Rabindranath Tagore (1861–1941), who won the Nobel prize for literature in 1913, was considered the embodiment of modern Indian culture and India's poet laureate. It was he who composed the anthem 'Jana Gana Mana Adhinayaka' for the Calcutta Congress of 1911 which was adopted as the National Anthem after Independence. 6/4 Dwarkanath Tagore Lane, off Rabindra Sarani. Open Mon.–Fri., 10am–7pm; Sat., 10am–1.30pm; Sun., 11am–2pm.

St John's Church Of the many churches in Calcutta this is especially interesting. Modelled on Gibbs's St Martin in the Fields in London (with the local addition of a palanquin ramp) and consecrated in 1787, it later served as the cathedral 1814–1847, until St Paul's was ready. Inside, pretty wicker-work seating, Zoffany's 'Last Supper' with local residents used as models for the Apostles (given by the artist as the altar-piece, now in the south aisle), and fine marble memorials to distinguished servants of the Empire. In the vestibule, a desk and chair used by Warren Hastings, who headed the building committee and was married here in 1818 to Mrs Marian Imhoff whom he had met on a boat to Madras.

Outside, the churchyard served as the first burial ground of Calcutta, 1690–1767. One of the city's oldest masonry structures is the octagonal

mausoleum of Job Charnock who died in 1692, t years after he founded the city. Nearby is the to of Admiral Charles Watson who helped Clive take the city and died a few months later, in 17. The domed grave belongs to 'Begum' Johnson much-loved Calcutta grande dame who died 1812 aged 87 after an eventful life that includ four marriages, being imprisoned by Suraj- Daula and fuelling local gossip with her wh parties in Clive Street.

Indian Museum Largest museum in Ind founded in 1814, having originated in a collecti accumulated by the Asiatic Society (established Calcutta in 1874). The huge collection is basica divided into art, archaeology, geology, zoolo and industry, arranged in rooms around a gard courtyard. Short-staffing tends to put padlocks several rooms, but this in fact aids decision-maki as everything is worth seeing. Stars to search include the coin collection, textiles and bidri wo Indian miniature paintings and the Sunga a Gandhara carvings. In the zoological section displayed a collection of thick brass bangles fou inside dead, man-eating crocodiles. Excelle general guide book, although staff reluctant admit to the existence of the publications offi Open Tues.–Sun., 10am–4.30pm (March to N until 5pm).

Victoria Memorial George Frampton's statue the Empress of India set between two ornamen lakes welcomes the visitor to this gigantic reliqu of white marble. From the moment Lord Curz conceived of a museum to depict Indian histo especially the Victorian era, the project and res epitomised British Victorian attitudes. Funds w raised by public subscription. Sir William Emers designed a Renaissance building with tok Saracenic features. One Prince of Wales (la George V) laid the foundation stone in 19 Another (later Edward VIII) opened it in 1921. T exterior was faced with Makrana marble fr Jodhpur, the dome surmounted by a figure Victory.

And inside, anyone who was anyone in Briti Indian history is remembered. A Royal Gallery paintings extols the glories of Queen Victori reign. Her writing-desk and piano are in the cen of the room. There is a replica marble statue of L Clive (the original bronze is in London) and Vere chagin's glorious painting of the Prince of Wa (this time the future Edward VII) making his st entry into Jaipur in 1876.

Among the many good paintings by Briti

:ists, it is well worth looking at Burne-Jones's
rtrait of Rudyard Kipling; Thomas and William
iniell's oil paintings (the finest collection of their
ork); and several of Zoffany's best works, includ-
g a portrait of Warren Hastings and his family.
.is last is on the first floor from which there is a
od view over the Maidan. The publications
ice, when open, has a useful catalogue of the
iniells collection and another on the busts and
tuary. Open Tues.–Sun., 10am–4pm (March to
t. until 5pm). Closed on public holidays.
Just outside the magnificent gates there used to
nd the statue of Lord Curzon, replaced by a
ssile-like bronze of Sri Aurobindo Ghosh, the
ltured mystic of Pondicherry (see p. 213).

useum Round-up Calcutta's strong cultural
dition, combined with the legacy of the Vic-
rian passion for systemisation and public edu-
tion, has given birth to more than 30 museums in
e city. Like the Rabindra-Bharati Museum, they
:en concentrate on a single topic. In the selection
low, opening days and times are merely guide-
es: both are very erratic and should be checked
th a tourist office before arriving at closed doors.
The Academy of Fine Arts (contemporary and his-
rical Indian art), Cathedral Road, open Tues.–
.n., 3–8pm. *Birla Academy of Art and Culture*
ontemporary and historical art collection plus
nporary exhibitions), 108–9 Southern Avenue,
en Tues.–Sun., 4–8pm. *Birla Planetarium*
cond only to London's), 96 J Nehru Road, open
es.–Sun., 11.30–8pm, with shows and pro-
ammes in various languages. *Ethnographic
useum*, Tribal Welfare Department, New Secre-
riat Buildings, K S Roy Road, open Mon.–Fri.,
.30am–5pm. *Government Industrial and Commer-
l Museum* (West Bengal handicrafts and cottage
dustries), 45 Ganesh Chandra Avenue, open
on.–Fri., 10.30am–5.30pm; Sat., 11am–1pm.
taji Museum* (Netaji Subhas Chandra Bose's
me), 38/2 Lala Lajpat Rai Sarani, open Mon.–
i., 6–8pm; Sun., 9am–noon. *Nehru Children's
useum*, 94 J Nehru Road, open Tues.–Sun.,
on–8pm. *Regional Handicrafts Centre*, 9–12 Old
urt House Street, open Mon.–Sat., 3–5.30pm.
yal Asiatic Society of Bengal* (fine library of books
d manuscripts; good, but flaking, European
intings), 1 Park Street, open for studying only,
on.–Fri., noon–7pm; Sat., noon–6pm. *State
chaeological Museum*, 33 Chittaranjan Avenue,
en Mon.–Fri., 11am–5.30pm; Sat., 11am–2pm.
In south Calcutta (about an hour from the centre)
ere is the excellent *Gurusaday Museum* (folk art),

Bratacharigram, off Diamond Harbour Road,
Thakurpkur, open Fri.–Tues., 11.30am–4.30pm;
Wed., 11.30am–1.30pm; closed Thur. On the way
down there is *Lok Sanskriti Samgranhasala* (folk culture, an annex of the Archaeological Museum), 1
Satyen Roy Road, off Diamond Harbour Road,
Behala, open Mon.–Fri., 11am–4pm.
Maidan area The Maidan may be a two-by-one-
mile open space, but it is not the refreshing green
park the map promises. Main roads criss-cross the
tired grass, worn down by trade exhibitions,
sportsmen, festival celebrations and the huge,
annual Communist rally in January. The quantities
of colonial statuary have been removed by the
government to Barrackpore. A good time to take
a stroll here is late afternoon while locals play
cricket, yoga, football and tennis or saunter
along Strand Road as the sun sets over the
Hooghly. Boats can be hired for a sunset row.
Looking across the Maidan from the massive walls
of Fort William (still in use, so not open to the
public), little remains of the Esplanade (J. Nehru
Road), once the backdrop of great houses mirror-
ing the wealth and security of imperial power.
    But at the north end *Raj Bhavan* (Government
House) still stands, designed in 1799 for the Mar-
quess of Wellesley by Captain Charles Wyatt of the
Bengal Engineers who, lacking imagination, found
an adequately imposing model in Adam's recently
completed Kedleston Hall, Derbyshire, built for
Lord Curzon. (Now the residence of the Governor
of West Bengal, it is not open to the public.)
    To the left of Raj Bhavan are the pretty Eden
Gardens. To the right, the bizarre Sahid Minar
(Octherlony Monument), with Egyptian base,
Syrian column and Turkish dome, erected to commemorate a man whose enjoyment of everything
Muslim ran to taking thirteen wives who would
ride out together on a string of elephants. For a
superb view from the top of the column, first get
permission to ascend from the Deputy Commissioner of Police, Police HQ, Lal Bazaar. The Victoria Memorial, the excellent Birla Planetarium, St
Paul's Cathedral (unremarkable except for Burne-
Jones's great west window of 1880) and the race
course lie to the south.
    And across Tolly's Nulla (a canal dug from the
silted up Adiganga, the old course of the Ganga, by
Major Tolly in 1775) in Alipore is the spacious,
41-acre zoo opened in 1876, with good collections of
birds, animals, reptiles and fish, and the rare white
tiger of Rewa (open daily, 8am–5pm).
South Park Street Cemetery It is one of the

153

ironies of decaying Calcutta that the only thorough conservation job has been carried out on a colonial Christian cemetery. Flowers and blossoming trees surround the restored obelisks, urns, temples and towers of the classical mausolea erected to Calcutta's notable figures. The cemetery replaced St John's churchyard in 1767. It was then some distance from the British town, along narrow Burial Ground Road (later named Park Street after Sir Elijah Impey's deer park – he lived in Middleton Row). Burials were often by torchlight at night or with military pageantry.

Among them were William Hickey's wife Charlotte Barry; Col. Charles Russell Deare, who died fighting Tipu Sultan; Captain Cooke, who died in a sea fight off Calcutta; Col. Kyd, founder of the Botanical Gardens; the linguist Sir William Jones, founder of the Royal Asiatic Society (his is the tallest monument); Thackeray's father; the Anglo-Indian poet Louis Vivian Derozio; and Sir John D'Oyly, a vivacious gentleman whose love of the hookah finally finished him. People often died young, from the heat, cholera, dysentry, tuberculosis, although the disease was often not recognised. Eating too many pineapples was supposed to have killed one Rose Aylmer. There is a piazza of headstones from the French Cemetery, formerly on the opposite side of Park Street, now replaced by a school. Very good booklet available from the custodian. Open all the time, every day.

St Paul's Cathedral The first Church of England cathedral built in the British Empire. Begun in 1839, designed by Major Forbes, the imposing building was partly funded by the East India Company. Lady Dalhousie, wife of the Viceroy, compared the interior to a railway station in 1840. But it is worth going inside to see the Burne-Jones stained glass west window; Francis Chantrey's statue of Bishop Heber; and Sir Arthur Blomfield's mosaics around the altar.

Kali Temple One of the few buildings apart from the Victoria Memorial that people have heard of before their arrival in Calcutta and one of the city's few landmarks of Indian architecture. Kalighat is an important place of pilgrimage and the temple, built in 1809, is only the latest of several. Kali or Kalika (meaning 'the black') is one of the forms of the goddess Devi. Devi is the wife (and therefore female energy) of Shiva and has two characters – benevolent and malevolent. Each is manifest in several forms, but the nasty ones like Kali and Durga are worshipped most often. When the frenzied Shiva was wandering the cosmos with Devi's corpse, Vishnu cut the body into pieces with Sudarshan wheel (a sort of quoit) and a toe here. Paintings of Kali are sold around the temple the black-skinned goddess shown dripping w blood, snakes and skulls hung around her ne her ten arms wielding a variety of weapons. N Hindus cannot enter the temple. The daily sacrif of a goat or sheep in the courtyard witnessing the destroyer goddess's power gives the crowd surrounding market an ugly atmosphere. Op until 10pm.

Space and peace

The Botanical Gardens, especially in early mo ing, are serene and empty and well worth journey (slightly busier at week-ends). And Tol gunge Club is a haven at any time. In the city cen there are more escape holes than appear at fi South Park Street Cemetery, the well-plan grounds of the zoo, the Agri-Horticultural Garde behind the National Library on Belvedere Rc (where the annual flower show is held – a gr social event), and Rabindra Sarobar lakes and p to the south. Peace and coolness are found the many churches and synagogues scatter throughout the city. Despite the drawbacks of Maidan, Eden Gardens and the Strand are ve pleasant from late afternoon onwards and boats the Hooghly leave from Chandpal ghat.

Keeping fit and beautiful

The humidity of Calcutta may not encourage ex cise, but the Bengal sweets may demand it. T only hotel with a decent swimming pool is Oberoi. The Maidan is good for jogging but horses for hire there should be avoided – go Tollygunge for riding. For quieter exercise, yc and gymnasium centres include North Calcu Yoga Byayam Centre, 9/A Lakshmi Dutta Lar and Paschim Banga Yoga Byayam Society, Ghose Lane. Gentler still, the only hotel with health club is the Oberoi (others claim to be bui ing them): excellent, cheap for residents, w massage, saunas, gym and well-trained staff.

Calcutta is full of wizard Chinese hair-cutters, on a long trip in India, this is the moment for a tri Residents go to Fairy Nook on J. Nehru Road, Ne Ennis and Sunflower on Russell Street, Blue Hav on Park Street, Eve's near New Market and t Oberoi Hotel.

The best sports are found in the lively clu

which perpetuate the colonial combination of social meeting-place, good facilities and great style.
At the top of the club hierarchy are the Calcutta
Club, Tolly, the Royal Calcutta Turf Club, the
Bengal Club and the Royal Calcutta Gold Club.
Any friend or business colleague in Calcutta will
belong to more than one of the 20 or so clubs and
can take guests. Some have reciprocal membership
with overseas clubs. But in any case, temporary
membership is open to bona fide foreign visitors at
most (a notable exception is the Calcutta Swimming Club). If in doubt, contact the Secretaries.

CLUB CHECKLIST
Tollygunge Club See Where to Stay section.
Probably the best all-round facilities. They are
open to foreigners, but telephone or write first.
Bengal Club See Where to Stay section. Billiards.
Bengal Flying Club, 95 Park Street.
Calcutta Club, 241 Acharya J C Bose Road (tel:
443318). The 2,000 members number the most
senior Bengalis – another 4,000 are on the waiting
list. Tennis, swimming, etc.
Calcutta Cricket Club, 19/1 Gurusaday Road (tel:
478721), also tennis. The first cricket match in India
was played on the Maidan. The club is the oldest
existing cricket club outside Britain.
Calcutta Ladies Golf Club, 42B J Nehru Road (tel:
443816)
Calcutta Polo Club, no club house, contact via the
Turf Club, see p. 148. Although it originated in
Persia, polo was introduced into India from Manipur where it had been played since the 16th century by tea-planters. Silchar Polo Club was the first
of its kind, established in 1859; then Calcutta's in
1863. The season is December, the same month as
the Calcutta Horse Show.
Calcutta Rackets Club, by St Paul's Cathedral (tel:
441152). Also tennis.
Calcutta Rowing Club, 15 Rabindra Sarobar (tel:
463343)
Calcutta Swimming Club, 1 Strand Road (tel:
232894)
Lake Club, 29 Rabindra Sarobar (tel: 462538)
Royal Calcutta Golf Club, 33 Tollygunge (tel:
461288): The centre of Indian golfing and the oldest
royal golf club outside Britain. Originally the Dum
Dum Golf Club, founded in 1829. The Amateur
Golf Championship, the oldest (est.1892) and most
important annual golf event in the East, alternates
between Calcutta, Delhi and Bombay (1985
Bombay, 1986, Delhi). Guests can hire caddies and
clubs, playing caddies available.

Royal Calcutta Turf Club See p. 148.
Saturday Club, 7 Wood Street (tel: 445411). Established in 1872 for the juniors of the Raj, still popular
with the young. Very large membership. Good
swimming, tennis, squash and card room.
Mohan Bagan Athletic Club, CFC Ground (tel:
231634)

Good eats: Night lights

Calcuttans are fond of reminiscing about how
sprightly the city was right up to the end of the
1960s. It is not so now. Again, the social centres for
eating – lunch, tea and dinner – are the clubs,
although the food tends to have remained as Raj as
its surroundings. The handful of good restaurants
outside the hotels tend to close by 10pm. Supper
clubs offer mediocre food and raucous live European music. They fold up around midnight and
should be avoided.

Currently, there is partial prohibition in Calcutta. So, jolliest nights are Wednesday, before dry
day on Thursday, and Saturday.

However, the cultural scene is very healthy. As
in Delhi and Bombay, here is a chance to see top
quality theatre, music and dance, and sample the
distinctive Bengali cinema, with a wide choice of
performances each evening.

RESTAURANTS
In Calcutta, even more than Delhi, people eat in. A
Bengali believes his Mum's cooking is best. If a
household cannot cope with guests, there are
caterers galore. Usually, only the famous Bengali
sweets are bought. This is partly tradition and
partly because Bengali dishes must be eaten freshly
cooked as the delicate herbs and the fish do not
wait well. When the smart go out, they want
European, Chinese or north Indian food and their
friends seated at the next table, in common with
the rest of smart India. But moving downmarket,
the Chinese population supply quantities of excellent restaurants.

RESTAURANT SUGGESTIONS
Bengali *Suruchi,* Elliott Road; the only reasonable
restaurant serving typical Bengali dishes – suruchi
means 'good taste'. Fish dishes recommended.
The mustard oil used in Bengali cooking gives it a
distinctive flavour. Try bekti, rui, Bagda and Golda
prawns and hilsa. There is dahi maachh (ileesh or
katla curried in yoghurt, ginger and turmeric),

155

malai curry (prawns and coconut) and prawns cooked in mustard oil with garlic and coriander. All are eaten with a variety of rice dishes or with loochi (deepfired bread, like puri) – the local hilsa fish has lots of bones but good flavour. Finish with a sweeter-than-sweet Bengal sweetmeat or with misthi dohi (sweetened curd with raw jaggery – sugar). Then go off to a paan-wallah and sample Calcutta maghai, one of the most special paan concoctions.

North Indian and Mughlai *Amber*, 11 Waterloo Road; Punjabi food on three floors, patronised by local commercial centre and journalists from *The Statesman* and *Amrita Bazaar Patrika* at lunchtime, crowded, good atmosphere, large menu, good food. *Kwality*, 17 Park Street; one of the best and most reliable of this large chain. *Moghul, Oberoi Grand Hotel*; excellent Mughlai food eaten lounging on low sofas in a marble-lined room, with good live Indian music. *Shan-en-Shah, Great Eastern Hotel*; tandoori dishes recommended, with more live Indian music.

Chinese *The Bengal Club* has very good Chinese food, as does the *Ming Room, Trinca's*, Park Street. Those not at the Amber for lunch are probably here, exchanging gossip across tables. Jolly, get a table in the front room. Extensive menu with stars denoting 'pungent' dishes. *Chinese Restaurant, Great Eastern Hotel*; food recommended, but at the cost of the surroundings. *Jade Room, Park Hotel*; again, good food, flat atmosphere. For less grand Chinese restaurants, try *Kimwah*, 51/a Garcha Road (behind the tram depot on Gariahat Road); chimney soup at *How Hua* on Free School Street; *Chung-Wah*, 7/1 Chittranjan Avenue; *Coley*, Russell Street and any in the Tanga area.

Polynesian *Oberoi Grand Hotel*; amusing, slightly self-conscious ethnic setting, but food alright.

Continental *Sky Room*, Park Street. No alcohol but fashionable, especially with Marwaris, so book.

Bengal sweets One is named after Lady Canning. Ishwar Gupta wrote an ode to another, the rossogolla. Recently, a politician was compared to the same sweet: pure, white, soft, sweet and all too soon finished. That is how serious sweets are in Calcutta. Sample rossogolla, rasmalai, sondesh, gulab jamun, shorbhaja and barfi as *K C Das* (who invented rasmalai) on Esplanade Road East, *Gupta's* on Park Street or *Ganguram's* on J Nehru Road near the Planetarium.

Tea A still thriving Raj ritual, performed on the lawns of Tollygunge Club or Kenilworth Hotel,

beside the Oberoi pool or in a restaurant. At *Flury'* tearoom on Park Street, start a full nursery tea with beans on toast and end with home-made meringues. Recently gone downhill.

Cocktails Nowhere with a view over the city Hotel bars mostly dowdy, except the *Chowringhee* in the Oberoi whose main attraction is the Desmond Doig murals (it is nicer to drink beside their pool). Or, again, head for the club lawns.

Discotheques Several have closed; others are apparently going to open. That leaves one at the moment, the *Pink Elephant* at the Oberoi. Fortunately it is good: well-designed, good music system (both by Juliana's of London) and excellent atmosphere, mainly because it is the only place for the young elite of Calcutta and their pals – from ex-maharajas to the son of the Governor of Communist West Bengal.

Discover what's on offer by consulting the daily *Amrita Bazaar Patrika*, the *Sunday Telegraph* or, to a lesser extent, the *Daily Telegraph*. For extensive listings, *Calcutta This Fortnight* (from the tourist office). Opposite the Calcutta Club on Acharya J C Bose Road is an excellent information centre and box office for the arts. Main halls include Rabindra Sadan, the Academy of Fine Arts, Birla Academy and the Sisir Mancha. Of the traditional theatres centred in north Calcutta, one of the oldest is the Star, with a revolving stage. Another is the Empire. Avoid the awful 'Dances of India' programme at the Oberoi Hotel.

As performances start around 6.30pm when the rush hour is in full swing, allow plenty of time to get to the hall.

Theatre Modern Indian theatre has its roots in Calcutta, where performances began in the late 18th century. Plays were often – and still are – adaptations of novels. At the beginning of this century the actors were just as involved in early cinema as theatre. Mime, exaggerated gesture and interludes of dance or cabaret are still staple ingredients, so language need not be a barrier. Since the 1950s the offshoot of modern developments has been towards a greater realism, especially in Bengal where the politics of the left have led to the characters of Karl Marx and Ho Chi Minh being introduced into the traditional folk form. Bengali writers and directors to look out for: Sombhu Mitra, Badal Sircar and Utpal Dutt.

During the day, lively street theatre still thrives in Calcutta, the ad hoc performances attracting small crowds on street corners.

Dance Performances of the Indian classical dance-dramas are often difficult to find in their places of origin. The top dancers go to the big cities. So it is worth catching whatever is around, be it southern Bharata Natyam or northern Kathak. Closer to Calcutta were developed the strong traditions of Manipuri, Odissi and Chhau – and countless folk dances.

In the lyrical and graceful devotional dances of Manipur the women use delicate steps and gestures for the raas dances, based on the stories of Krishna. But in the pung cholom dance the men leap, whirl and spin as they beat out the rhythm on drums slung from their necks. Look out for top dancers Guru Singhajit Singh and Charu Sija.

The classical Odissi temple dance also favours Krishna, recounting the tales with highly sensuous and lyrical movements of the hips and back, balancing pure dance with story-telling. Leading exponents include Sunjukta Panigrahi, Sonal Mansingh, Madhavi Mudgal, Protima Bedi and Malvika Sarrukai. All these dancers have trained under Guru Kelucharan Mohapatia, who was instrumental in the revival of Odissi and, as a child, was a gotipura (a young male odissi dancer dressed as a woman).

Chhau are the highly expressive folk dances of Bihar, Bengal and Orissa, usually recounting stories from the Mahabharata or the Ramayana. Although some dancers use elaborate clay masks and headdresses, the whole story is told with body movement – no mime or song – as in Kathakali dance.

Cinema Choose between English, Hindi and Bengali. Bigger cinemas advertise in the press, with screening times – three or four a day. The Bengali film industry played a big part in India's film history and is now undergoing a revival, so it is worth trying a Bengali film.

Moving pictures reached Calcutta in 1896. In 1901 the enterprising Hiralal Sen screened films of plays staged at the Classic Theatre as an added attraction, after the stage performance was over. Jamshedji Framjee Madan, the Parsee owner of a successful theatrical company in Calcutta, became the first Indian movie magnate, with cinemas throughout the land. It was Madan Pictures which showed the first foreign talkie in India, 'Melody of Love', and which in 1931 missed producing the first Indian talkie by one month.

With sound came regional language cinema and naturally Bengal was the first to adapt its literary giants to the screen: Tagore, Bankimchandra Chatterjee and, most importantly, Saratchandra Chatterjee, whose plays 'Devdas', 'Parineeta' and 'Swami' have since been made in most regional languages. With sound came songs too, almost 70 on one 1930s film. New Theatres was the big Calcutta studio. From the start it was more political and cultural than the commercially minded Bombay. It bravely pioneered genuine political cinema such as 'Udayar Pathe' 'Awakening', 1944, about the spiralling tension between rich and poor in Calcutta, and Ritwik Ghatak's 'Nagarik' (Citizen), 1952, calling on the working class and refugees not to lose hope after Partition. When the studio broke down, Nitin Bose, Bimal Roy and others went to thriving Bombay, introducing their social awareness into Hindi films.

Since then, despite lack of funding, bad laboratories and constant power cuts, such figures as Satyajit Ray, who made the landmark 'Pather Panchali' in 1955, and the radical Mrinal Sen, have produced an alternative, caring cinema. It is better known in the West than across India, although Ray has a strong cult following in Calcutta. And with the injection of financial support from the government of West Bengal since 1980, a more secure industry is growing, blending the old recipe of colour, action and music with social relevance. Ray's film 'Ghaire Baire' (The Home and the World), released in 1984, is an adaptation of Rabindranath Tagore's novel. It manages to marry the fiercely political theme of the Swadeshi (freedom) movement with a hero and heroine who break into dubbed song.

What to buy where

Shops in Calcutta do not have the variety of quality goods found in Delhi or Bombay. Books, crafts and fabrics are best buys. As one English woman living there said: 'I shop in Delhi'.

New Market (formerly Hogg Market) has the best prices mainly because the shops for each item are grouped together – silver, fabric, etc – so they compete fiercely. It goes like a fair from 9.30am to 8.30pm, and is very pretty lit up in the evening, the air filled with aromas from food-vendors' stalls. Bargain hard here and at Burrabazar around Harrison Road.

Lindsay Street has the chemist, Dey's Medical Stores; the tailor, Gulam Mohammed Bros who

157

will copy shirts and suits in 2 days (there are many more tailors on Madge Lane, a side-street); Handloom House for fabrics and West Bengal Government Emporium. At the north end of J Nehru Road the Central Cottage Industries Emporium stocks reliable quality from all over India. Nearby in Easplanade Road East, weavers from East Pakistan sell their silk and cotton at Refugee Handicrafts. Assam Government Emporium has very good plain silk, and Naga and Manipuri products. In north Calcutta College Street is the Indian Mecca for second-hand books. The Gariahat area in South Calcutta is the traditional quarter for jewellers and handloom saris. Avoid the air-conditioned market: 100% imported goods, down to the last pencil.

Books   Calcutta University awards the most degrees of any university. The Royal Asiatic Society was founded here. The National Library is here. Calcutta gave birth to the 19th-century literary renaissance and India's national and political consciousness, and claims that one in three of its citizens are poets – see them reading their lines on the Maidan at weekends. There are probably more publishers here than anywhere else in India. So there are a lot of books, old and new, many in English. College Street is a book collector's dream: solid shops and stalls that spill down side-streets. Hours of happy browsing – and always the real possibility of falling upon a first edition of Murray's guide to India or a Daniell print. For new books, go to Oxford Book Company on Park Street.

Bengal crafts   Traditional terracotta figures are made in villages throughout the state: a Bengali lady and babu (old man) may come from Jayanagar or Majilpur; models of occupations from Krishnanagar. Rice measuring bowls made of wood inlaid with brass, often in a shell design, are less fragile to pack. So are the brass oil-lamps in the form of figures or horses.

Delicate, cream-coloured pith work is carved from a dried freshwater plant into a horse, an elephant or Krishna and Radha. There is delicate silver jewellery, conch-shell bangles from north Calcutta and carved ivory from Murshidabad. The local children's dolls are made of papier maché or cotton. Give Kalighat paintings a miss: the artists no longer have the talent displayed with such bold assurance in the 19th century. For all these goods go to Bengal Home Industries Association, 57 Chowringhee and West Bengal Government Sales Emporium, Lindsay Street.

Fabric   The huge variety runs from gaily striped cotton through embroidered bedspreads and woollen blankets to the queen of Bengal silk saris, the Baluchari. Striped cotton comes in all weights and is cheap (Rs21 per metre). The fish, tiger, horse and other Bengali motifs embroidered on to bedspreads and table-cloths were originally applied to cotton shawls used by old women or to wrap a baby – one of several successful adaptations of a dying craft to modern use. The more intricate cotton Kantha embroidery quilts are sometimes further enriched with surface embroidery. For silk, fine Murshidabad saris are woven plain, then printed all over with delicate floral designs. From Dacca, formerly a great Muslim weaving centre, the finest cotton saris have very precise geometric designs woven into their borders.

But a *Baluchari* brocade sari is for the collector. The name derives from an extinct village near Berhampur in Murshidabad district. It has been suggested that Gujarati weavers possibly migrated there in the 18th century, bringing with them the brocade weaving tradition. In the 19th century, the aristocratic Bengali lady's showiest sari came from this area and may have taken six months to weave. The great late 19th century Baluchari weaver was Dubraj, who signed some of his creations.

The highly complicated design of floral motifs with a palo (end border) of bands of figures in compartments covered the whole sari. There might be nawabs smoking hookahs, durbar scenes, ladies giving flowers to lovers – even steam engines. Owners of such treasures used a mixture of neem leaves, dried polas flowers and black cumin seed as mothballs.

Today the designs worked at Vishnupur (see below, p. 139) are slightly less sophisticated, although prices start at Rs800. Ask for Baluchari palo. These fun designs are also available much cheaper as prints. Buy fabrics at Handloom House on Lindsay Street and Khadi Gramodyog Bhavan (which stocks much more than khadi) on Chittaranjan Avenue.

See how it's done: Crafts, industry and caring

To see the striped cotton and other fabrics being woven around Calcutta, contact the All Bengal Women's Home, 89 Elliott Road.

Idol-makers   Near the river in the Kumartuli (Potters') area of north Calcutta, off Chitpur Road, the idol-makers prepare images of Kali, Ganesh, Lakshmi, but most of all Durga. They work all year, modelling clay images around straw cores.

The chief kumar gives the goddess her features and expression (often strikingly similar to film star matinée idols). They are then painted in gaudy colours. Traditionally, they are unbaked, terra cruda, because they are for religious use.

Calcutta port The city's wealth was founded on trade and the port is still one of the most important in the East, despite bad silting in the Hooghly. This started when the current in the Ganga altered some years ago, but may be checked when – and if – the Farakka Barrage is completed. To visit, telephone the Port Authority to arrange a permit in advance.

Jute Fortunes were also made in jute which continues to be a major industry. To visit a factory or mill, contact the Jute Museum, Jute Technological Research Laboratories, ICAR, 12 Regent Park (tel: 464541).

Charity Mother Teresa's Missionaries of Charity have been more successful than any government effort in relieving a particle of the mammoth suffering in Calcutta. There are, of course, many other organisations doing similar work. Her headquarters at 54a Lower Circular Road (tel: 247115) may be visited. Donations should be made payable to Mother Teresa Missionaries of Charity and delivered there or, outside India, sent c/o Barclays Bank Ltd, Station Approach, Southall, Middlesex, England. Further information from Mrs Ann Blaikie, Chairman of the International Committee of Co-Workers, Missionaries of Charity, 41 Villiers Road, Southall, Middlesex, England.

Awaydays

Probably essential for anyone spending more than a few days in Calcutta. For a gentle day take a picnic to the Botanical Gardens or cruise up the Hooghly (boats seasonal). For something more ambitious, visit Murshidabad or Vishnupur, both reached by pleasant rural drives. Tourist offices and travel agents carry the latest information on when, where and how to travel. For greater freedom, a hired car is usually better than a tourist bus.

Boating on the Hooghly There are several ghats in central Calcutta, so traffic can be avoided at source. Boats can be hired from the ghats on Strand Road to go down to the Botanical Gardens. Trips up to Serampore and Barrackpore are much longer.

Botanical Gardens 8km. See p. 151.

Sunderbans This is the Ganga delta, an area of forest, creeks and swamps originally stretching from the mouth of the Hooghly inland for about 300km and full of game. Still the largest mangrove forest in India, watered by the daily tides. The best way to go is first by car, then take a launch up the creeks. Good chance of seeing some of the 300 or so Bengal tigers, and deer, crocodiles and wild boar; crocodile farm; Sajnakhali Bird Sanctuary; Lothian and Halliday Island Sanctuaries. To stay overnight, sleep on the launch or in the WBTB Tourist Lodge. The WBTB run tours. To charter a launch, contact the Sunderbans Launch Syndicate, Calcutta.

Barrackpore 24km. After Richard Wellesley had finished his extravagant new Governor's House in the city, he planned to build a country house here, connecting the two with a 14-mile-long avenue. In fact, only the 'bungalow' was built (and that after Wellesley left), a large classical building beside the Hooghly. The landscaped park has suffered but the house, now a hospital, can be visited. Best to go by boat.

Serampore 24km. Facing Barrackpore across the Hooghly, the former Danish colony of Fredericknagore was sold as a job lot with Tranquebar and a bit of Balasore to the East India Company in 1845, for £125,000. Under the Danes it was an important missionary centre. The fine Danish Governor's house, church and college still stand. The college contains an exceptional library of manuscripts and early printed books collected by the Rev. William Carey, including first editions of translations of the Bible into 40 Indian and Asian languages printed in Serampore (open Mon.–Fri., 10am–4pm; Sat., 10am–1pm). The spectacular Car Festival held at Mahesh temple 3km away in June–July is second only to the one in Puri.

Vishnupur 200km. Capital of the Hindu Malla dynasty in the 16th and 17th centuries. The Mallas made Vishnupur a cultural centre of Bengal, then sold it by auction to the Maharaja of Burdwan. It was a centre of sericulture and weaving (see What to Buy section). The dhrupad style of Indian classical music was developed here. And the kings built some outstanding – if odd – terracotta temples, (see especially Shyam Rai and Jore Bangla). In the chowk bazaar and shops see the excellent handicrafts being made and sold: silk, metalware, terracotta horses. It is here that the Baluchari saris are still woven. Vishnupur is also famous for Bengal sweetmeats and flavoured tobacco. At the Jhapan festival in July–August, dedicated to the snake goddess Manasa, the city is full of snake-charmers performing tricks from bullock carts.

Santiniketan 170km. Rabindranath Tagore developed his father's ashram in an open-air school in 1901 (enlarged to a university in 1921). Its aim is to bring man closer to nature – santi means peace, niketan means abode. The Maharani of Jaipur studied there, as did Mrs Gandhi. Worth visiting to see interesting 20th-century art, rare in India. The buildings were designed by Tagore's son, Rathindranath, and the sculptures, frescoes and murals are by Jamini Roy, Ram Kinkar, Nandalal Bose and others. Also Tagore Museum and, during the winter, cultural festivals. Open to visitors Thurs.–Mon. by appointment with the Public Relations Office which the WBTB will arrange.

Murshidabad 220km. Clive described Suraj-ud-Daula's city as 'extensive, populous and rich as the city of London'. What once was the capital of the Nawabs of Bengal, brimful of bustle and grandeur, is now a quiet rural town, living on sericulture and mango cultivation (some connoisseurs say the finest mangoes of all).

But there is plenty to see including the Italianate Nizamat Kila palace built in the 1830s for the Nawab, known as Hazarduari Palace (house of a thousand doors) with armoury, library and Queen Victoria's gift of a gigantic chandelier. There are the ruins of Katra Mosque, modelled on the mosque at Mecca, and the palace of Jagat Sett, one of the richest 18th century financiers. It is nice to take a boat across the river to the Khusbarh (garden of happiness) and see the sunset from Moti Jhil (pearl lake). Local Murshidabad block-printed silk saris and ivory carving can be bought. The road to Murshidabad passes Plassey, site of Clive's triumph in 1757. To see the monuments of Gour and Malda another 120km north, stay overnight at the clean but modest WBTB Tourist Lodge at Murshidabad.

Seaside If desperate, go to Digha (240km) or Bakkhali (132km). Both have good beaches but bad accommodation and week-end crowds. Better to take a longer break and go down to Orissa (p. 167).

Forays further afield

If the power breakdowns, communication failures, congestion and humidity become unendurable, then getting right away from Calcutta is easy. An hour's flight does it: north into the cool Himalayas; west to the pilgrimage city of Varanasi; south to Orissan temples and beaches; and south-east to the Andaman and Nicobar Islands.

Trips to some of these and all the north-eastern states and to Bhutan and Burma require special permits and visas and therefore need advance planning (see p. 11). The travel agencies listed above have the latest information on these more sensitive areas. They will also help plan and book any trip – it is even more uncomfortable and time-wasting queuing in Calcutta than other Indian cities. For Nepal, see p. 232; for the Andamans, see p. 248.

European firms with offices in Calcutta often own houses in Darjeeling, Kalimpong or Puri for use by their employees and guests. Their hospitality can reach Indian heights, so there is no harm in asking what they have got and whether it might be available.

DARJEELING

The British bolt-hole from steamy Calcutta. The cool, fresh air, green vegetation and scenery were irresistible. The inquisitive rushed around recording the flora and fauna, playing sports and creating Surrey gardens. The fruits of their energies contributed to the Botanical Gardens in Calcutta and to Kew Gardens in London. The adventurous nipped up mountains – Edmund Hillary left from Darjeeling with his four 'small, sinewy, smiling' Sherpas on his Gawhal expedition in 1951, two years before the Everest triumph. The entrepreneurs planted tea gardens. The civil servants removed the headquarters of the Bengal Government there for the summer. Today, the jungle may be less dense but little has changed. Flowers, mountains, tea and glorious views abound. The local population is a hotchpotch of Lepchas, Limbus, Tibetans, Nepalese, Bhutias, Kashmiris and Bengalis, often wearing their colourful tribal costumes. Buddism flourishes here, described by John Keay as 'the only place where one is conscious of a living Buddhist ambience'.

THE HARD FACTS Darjeeling lies on a spur of the Ghoom-Senchal Ridge, at an altitude of 2,134m, with spectacular views across to the Himalayan peaks. The climate is best from April to mid-June (for rhododendra, magnolia and other blooms) and mid-September to December (for views). Either side there are mists, the winter air drops to 1°C and the monsoon blots out views and blocks off roads. Most festivals are in January and February.

The journey up is part of the trip. First, fly to Bagdogra or catch the Rocket Service night train (which is fun, but one way might be enough,

turning by air). Then, instead of a taxi, take the
narrow gauge toy train from New Jalpaiguri or
Siliguri to Darjeeling along the two-foot-gauge line
completed in 1881. Seven hours of chugging,
puffing, loops, hair-pin bends and changing
scenery.
Choose between two hotels, both central, with
character and views. The *Hotel Oberoi Mount
Everest*, 29 Gandhi Road (tel: 2616–7–8; cable
OBHOTEL): Red-roofed, cream chateau built by
rrathoon Stephen, (who built the Oberoi Grand,
Calcutta); 70 rooms, facilities include health club,
hairdresser and baby-sitter, stunning views over
the Kanchenjunga range; good food.
Windamere Hotel, Bhanu Sarani (The Mall) (tel:
341/2396; cable: WINDAMERE): 27 rooms. Built
as a house around central garden, fires lit in the
rooms at night, library, badminton court, food
reasonable – children eat at 6pm, adults at 8pm.
Modest prices.
The Tourist office, 1 Nehru Road, is not wonderful; wiser to obtain full briefing from a Calcutta
travel agency, especially for trekking or climbing.
Foreigners Registration Office, Laden La Road (tel:
261), for permits (see permit note below). Indian
Airlines, 1 Nehru Road (tel: 2355).

OUT AND ABOUT Dawn at *Tiger Hill* (at
2,590m, 11km away), the sun rising over Mount
Kunchenjunga – and on a clear day Mount Everest
is truly worth getting up for. Get there by 4am
(one hour's drive), clad in jumpers. Views from
Tonglu, Sandakphu and Phalut good, too, but
further away.
In addition to roaming the hills to see unusual
flowers, there are collections in town: Lloyds Botanical Garden (founded 1865), with extensive hot
houses (open daily, 6am–5pm); Zoo, mixes mountain plants with animals; Natural History Museum
open Fri.–Tues., 10am–4pm; Wed., 10am–1pm).
There is an interesting and well-maintained cemetery of Raj residents. The Himalayan Mountaineering Institute, the only one for training
mountaineers, comes complete with a museum
devoted to the mountains and mountaineering
equipment. And there is even a living exhibit
teaching there: Sherpa Tenzing Norkay, who accompanied Hillary up Everest in 1953.
The Passenger Ropeway (3km), the first one in
India, 8km long, connects Darjeeling with Singla
Bazar. Not for vertigo sufferers. To ensure a seat,
telephone the Officer-in-charge at the ropeway
station (tel: 2731).

FITNESS, FOOD AND ENTERTAINMENT Just
tackling the steps and vertical lanes of this hillside
town keeps the muscles in trim. But if the addi-
tional walking, trekking (on foot or pony) and
mountaineering are not enough, try the Senchal
Golf Club (at 2,484m, one of the highest); tiny
Lebong Race Course (the highest in the world;
spring and autumn seasons) and fishing on the
Rangeet River at Singla (8km) and Teesta River at
Riyand (41km, the District Forest Officer gives
permits). Darjeeling Gymkhana Club, Bhanu Sarani West (tel: 2002/2020); well equipped for indoor
and outdoor games, offers temporary membership
to visitors. Both the Oberoi Mount Everest and
Windamere hotels have beauty salons and health
clubs.
Tibetan food is thoroughly unexciting. The two
hotels mentioned serve the regular Indian,
Chinese and European dishes. Apart from these,
go to *Glenary's* for stylish uniformed waiters and
unstylish food, or to *Chowrasta* for South Indian
food. Kalimpong cheese, rather like Lou Palou, is
one of the few harder cheeses made in India.
Darjeeling faces west, so sunset cocktails are particularly good. Local ethnic groups perform interesting folk dances, especially during festivals.

SHOPPING, CRAFTS AND INDUSTRY **Tea:**
With 78 tea plantations in Darjeeling employing
46,000 people (the bulk Nepalese) and producing
10.5 million kilos of tea annually, tea-growing
takes on a new interest. Although much more tea is
grown in the less accessible Assam, Darjeeling is
considered to be best because of the favourable
climate. It is so expensive that a 'Darjeeling' tea is
usually blended with leaves from other areas. It is
possible to visit the Happy Valley Tea Estate (2km)
to see the orthodox production method, from fresh
green leaf through withering, rolling, pressing,
fermenting and drying to the final grading (open
Tues.–Sat., 8am–noon and 1–4.30pm; Sun., 1–
4.30pm). The best tea to buy is unbroken leaves of
Golden Flowery Orange Pekoe.
Tibetan crafts When the Chinese invaded Tibet,
many refugees came here. At the Tibetan refugee
Self-help Centre, established in 1959, the workshops for weaving and carving, etc., are open to
visitors and the finished goods are on sale: wool-
lens, carpets, leather, wood-carving. Himalayan
crafts: At Hayden Hall in Laden La Road, local
women sell their woollen products. Bargain hard
for good wood carving and local jewellery
(but avoid the mediocre thankas) in touristy

161

Chowrasta, J Nehru Road or the more colourful bazaars off Cart Road. On the road out to Ghoom, Manjusha, the Bengal Government Emporium, stocks Himalayan crafts and Bengal fabrics at fixed prices.

KALIMPONG

(51km from Darjeeling at 1,250m). See permit section. Reached along magnificent scenic route. Hillside market town with glorious views, blossoming flowers throughout the year and colourful markets (Wed. and Sat.) where villagers in local costume sell farm goods and wool. Several monasteries, the best being the newly restored, brightly-painted Thonga Gompa Bhutanese monastery, founded 1692. Kalimpong is a centre for commercial nurseries that export orchids, cacti, ammaryllii, roses, gerbera, dahlias and gladioli. Standard, Sri L. B. Pradhanand and Sri Ganesh Moni Pradhan are among the top nurseries. Arrange a visit to one through the WBTB in Darjeeling. Many good picnic spots with views, especially Durbindras; otherwise go to the Himalayan Hotel or Hotel Maharaja (South Indian food). To stay overnight, the Himalayan Hotel and the WBTB Luxury Tourist Lodge are clean and modest.

Other options: *Kurseong* (36km); or a bigger trip to the *Jaldapara Wildlife Sanctuary* in the Dooars (120km from Siliguri). There are also connections to Bhutan and Sikkim.

Sikkim, Bhutan and the North-East Frontier

Trips to these areas need to be planned in advance. See permit section. Here a good travel agency is essential. Visitors should not expect fancy accommodation nor, in some cases, great freedom of movement. But the scenery, wildlife and trekking opportunities are exceptional.

SIKKIM

Go for the mountains, flowers (500 species of orchid alone), painted houses and monasteries. Season February–May and October–December. Fly to Bagdogra, then use a taxi/bus/train combination. Stay in the capital, **Gangtok**, at the *Nor-Khill Hotel* (tel: 386/720; cable: NORKHILL)) or *Hotel Tashi Dekel* (tel: 361/458/862: cable: TASHIDEKEL). Information: Government of Sikkim Department of Tourism, (tours, car hire, guides); Foreigners Registration Office (visas); Sikkim Himalayan

Adventure, Yak and Yeti Travels a. Snow Lion Treks (essential for trekking). S Tsuklakhang palace, the Institute of Tibetolo Orchid Sanctuary and Chorten Institute of Cotta Industries; views from Enchey Monastery and t deer park. Go out to Bakkim and Dzongri; mon teries at Pemayangtse, Tashiding, Rumtek a Phodang. The monasteries have painted walls a fantasy butter sculptures and are the setting masked dances. There is nice jewellery to buy.

BHUTAN

Go for the mountains and more painted house palaces and monasteries. Season March a September–November. Fly to Bagdogra, then it 380km of bumpy road to the capital, **Thimp** Currently all visits are a fixed package, payable advance, with high prices for rather basic acco modation. A more comfortable hotel is *Ho Drunk*, in the foothills at the border town of Phu sholing. Built and run by the Welcomgroup, it h a distinctly Bhutanese character. Informatic Director of Tourism, Ministry of Finance, Tach hho Dzang, Thimpu; (see also permit section).

NORTH-EAST FRONTIER

Consists of two Union territories, Mizoram a Arunachal Pradesh, and five states, Assa Manipur, Meghalaya, Nagaland and Tripu Go for the wildlife (especially Kaziranga Natu Reserve), countryside, rich tribal cultures and th constant festivals of song and dance, tea plan tions – and the lack of tourists. As it is close China, the whole area is politically sensitive. Son parts may be closed; in others, movement may restricted. But reports testify to every effort bein well rewarded. Indian Airlines run a full servi from Calcutta and connect Bagdogra with Gauha Again, advanced planning is necessary (at least weeks), and a good travel agent essential.

ASSAM

Season October–May. For wildlife see p. 171.
Gauhati Stay at *Hotel Nandan*, G S Road (t 31281; cable: NANDAN), new, central, garde travel agent, airline counter. Information: thr tourist offices, on B K Kakati Road, Ulubari ar Station Road. See Assam State Zoo (one-horn Indian and two-horned African rhinos), Umana da and Kamakshya temples, sunset over th Brahmaputra River and the anthropology, fo estry, crafts and State museums. Visit Sualkashi see silk-weaving in every house; buy Endi, Mu

d Pat silks. If it is operating, take the steamer up Dibrugarh. Visit Manas wildlife sanctuary.

hat Stay at the ITDC *Kasiranga Forest Lodge* in sanctuary (tel: 785109; cable: RHINO ALK). En route, see the Jay Sagar temples and mpse a bush or so of the 60% of India's tea crop wn in Assam, and visit a tea garden. To the east s Nagaland, where the tribesmen's culture is der government protection. Intrepid travellers ll find the Nagas living in tiny villages and see eir impressive war dances.

GHALAYA
ason all the year round, except the monsoon d May to mid-August); Shillong's annual rain-l is 241cm. Nearby Cherrapunji's is 1,150cm, the ghest in the world.

illong: Pretty, sporty hill station at 1,496m alti-de. Stay at *Hotel Pinewood* (tel: 3116, 3765, 4176; ble: PINEWOOD), modest. Arrive via Gauhati port. Information: four tourist offices, all on lice Bazaar. See waterfalls, streams, pinegroves, wers (such as on road to Cherrapunji) d Khasi tribal dancing (at Smits and ngkrem). Sports include good 18-hole golf urse and fishing on Uniam Lake and at Ranikor d Dawki.

ANIPUR
l the women and most of the men spend hours ncing. When not dancing, they weave. Land of oded hills and lakes, with a surprising number Christians among the many tribes.

aphal Go for the dance, especially Rash Lila stival (October–November). Fly to Imphal. commodation basic, best at *Hotel Ranjit*, Thangal zaar (tel: 382) or *Tourist Lodge* (reserve by letter to rector of Tourism). See temples, museum. Visit oirang (folk–culture). Buy weaving and crafts in e large Khwairamband bazaar.

RMITS AND VISAS
ovided that some of these areas are open to sitors, foreign nationals will need a separate per-it for each state and a visa for Bhutan. The permit ay define that only part of the state can be en-red. Validity is often short. Only a few can be tended at the destination. Some states require fferent permits for different districts. Some go rther: To go to Darjeeling by air requires no rmit, but to go by train or road does. Finally, any gulations are apt to change.

The moral is to get the latest information from your Indian mission (see p. 15) before leaving home and try to obtain all the necessary papers. Apply as early as possible – some states require twelve weeks notice. Then check again at the city of entry into India. If booking the trip in India, go to any Foreigners Registration Office. In Calcutta there is also the Home Political Department, 1st floor, Writers' Building, BBD Bagh. Alternatively, the recommended travel agencies will do all the hustling and paperwork for a very small fee.

It would be extremely annoying to arrive at a frontier or airport and be refused entry. However, should a difficulty arise, as usual in India knowing the right person works miracles and, short of that, just going straight to the top gets miracles started.

For the most accurate information consult the Deputy Secretary, Ministry of Home Affairs, Government of India, (F–1), North Block, New Delhi 110001.

Varanasi (Banaras)

(Banaras is a British corruption of a Mughal version of the old Hindu name. This original name was revived after Independence.)

The holiest Hindu city in India and one of the oldest living cities in the world, contemporary with Thebes, Babylon and Nineveh. For the devout Hindu the 2,000 odd temples piled on to the bank of the sacred Ganga make up Kasha (divine light) and must be visited at least once in a lifetime to wash away sins, and, preferably, be visited again shortly before death. To die here is to have the greatest hope for the next life.

Varanasi may be the centre of Hindu culture with fine music and a good museum, but its daily trade is pilgrims, India's most important tourists. Here, every facet of Hinduism is to be seen, from great purity and holiness to the depths of degradation and squalor – and certainly some confidence tricks. An extraordinary quality of light permeates it all.

The maze of filthy, clattering, cow-filled, narrow city gullies (alleys) swarms with pilgrims, rich and poor, old and young, gurus and pupils, straight and eccentric, sane and batty, whole and limbless, sighted and blind, healthy and sick. Between temple visits they buy puja items (religious offerings) of flowers and spices from tiny peephole shops set high in the street walls. They also buy tourist mementoes of green, plastic, hopping frogs. There are noisy processions following a celebrated priest or a marriage, and quieter ones for the dead who, wrapped in white silk or cotton, are borne to Jalsain Ghat on stretchers, bicycles, rickshaws or horses.

Everyone heads for the Ganga, the goal of every pilgrim. On the 5km of ghats (waterside steps) leading down to the sacred water they give discourses or listen to discourses – the fat Brahmins sit beneath tatty straw umbrellas. They perform puja. They wash and attend scrupulously to their toilet or live in abject squalor. They read, practise contorting yoga or lounge vacantly and sleep. They beg or give alms, and quite often they die. The less devout gossip, smoke various intoxicants and talk twaddle. There are priests, yogis, widows and philosophers. And there are barbers to shave heads before taking the purifying waters. More secular entertainment comes from akhara (pit) wrestlers and acrobats who climb the mal kham (smooth wooden pole).

Local children entice tourists on to their boats grinning 'Best time see burning bodies' (untrue: they are burnt around the clock). Bigger children propose a 'massage'. And music and chants blare out from a very loud loud-speaker.

In the sacred water the faithful wash, perform Hindu rites, pumice-stone their feet, lather up their hair, have a pee, clean their teeth and wash their dhotis. The city sewers empty out nearby. They also drink the water and, extraordinarily, do not suffer. As Eric Newby writes in *Slowly Down the Ganges*: 'At Banaras, thousands drink the water every day . . . My wife and I have both drunk the water unboiled in the 50-mile stretch of the river where it first enters the Indian Plain . . . without any unfortunate effects. Yet when we left the river we invariably became ill.' Visitors would not be wise to follow his example.

Both river and ghats are saturated with a serene and holy light. Under this, human activity stirs into prayer at the first glimmer of the pure and magical dawn, gains momentum through the morning, then slumps into a stupour under the glowing, almost tangibly thick, afternoon sunlight before rousing itself for more prayers and night-time temple visits.

Although the word Varanasi is a compound of the two small rivers it lies between, the Varuna and the Asi, its whole raison d'être is the river Ganga whose powers of cleansing can bring salvation. The Ganga rises near Gangotri, at an altitude of 4,000m in the Himalayas, irrigates the north-east plains of India (sometimes with terrible flooding

and devastation) and empties into the Bay of Be gal 2,000km later, through a huge delta stretchi from Calcutta to Dacca. Most of the temples Varanasi are dedicated to Shiva. For, when t water goddess Ganga was told to save great sou Shiva caught her in his thick, tangled hair to pr vent her flooding the world. Thus, Ganga's wat trickled out over the souls, freeing them to go heaven.

Varanasi was already thriving 2,500 years ag when Buddha passed by. It was at Sarnath, 10k away, that he delivered his first sermon after r ceiving enlightenment, making it as important Buddhists as Varanasi is to Hindus. From the 11 century, Muslims periodically ravaged Varana and its temples, the worst case being Aurangze who converted the most famous temple into mosque. But the city survived. Temples are st being added – the rather flashy Birla one (Tul Manasmunda) has just been completed – and creative and cultural heritage is unbroken. T philosopher Kabir was born here, as was the fre dom fighter Rani Laxmi Bai. The thumri melody Indian song originates here.

Today, Varanasi produces many of the top m cians, including Ravi Shankar, and some of t best tabla players. The city has always been centre of Sanskrit and classical Hindu studie Now it is also a centre of modern Hindu studie focused at the Banaras Hindu University whi was founded by the nationalist Madan Moha Malviya. It is enthusiastically patronised by t present ex-Maharaja.

Around the city schools of gurus continue dedicate their lives to interpreting the Hindu epic the Mahabharata and Ramayana. Each has his p subject and holds saptahs (weekly sessions) whe he sits on a plinth and expounds and elaborate with great oratorical skill on a single stanza fro the text. Crowds of thousands may gather to hear good speaker such as Dr Shri Vats. Smaller saptal are held indoors (as they are throughout India mostly attended by older women who take alor the younger members of the family to learn th scriptures. Some temples specialise: gurus at th Krishna temple, Gopal Mandir (run by a woma Sharad Ballabha Betijee), concentrate on the Bh gavad Gita, a philosophical discussion betwee Krishna and Arjuna before the big Mahabhara battle.

There is little of the Swami cult here that h attracted Westerners to India since the 1960s. Th Maharishi Mahesh Yogi's ashram is far upstream

Hardwar. It was there that the Beatles went and
here Mia Farrow's younger sister meditated non-
op for 96 hours. Swami Shivananda, founder of
e Divine Life Society, is not here either. The
vami, apparelled in ochre, would give lectures on
he Exploration of Inner Space' and then pass
und chocolate biscuits to eat. Afro-haired Satya
i Baba seems to have little time for holy Varanasi.
e gave a special audience to Delhi diplomats and
rformed his miracle of making 'sacred ash'
aterialise between his thumb and forefinger be-
re their cynical eyes. This yoga cult attracts more
estern devotees than Indian. Only a small frac-
on of India's Hindus know of its existence. The
ajority follow the old traditions seen here at
aranasi.

IE HARD FACTS Varanasi perpetually over-
ows with pilgrims, but the weather is best Octo-
r–March; it rains mid-June to September. The
am Lila festival (the northern version of Dussehra)
September–October is even more spectacular
re than in Delhi: some 30 days of plays and music
honour of Rama, each night a different venue,
iding with a massive procession. The ex-
aharaja of Varanasi is patron of the whole event.
here are no regular concerts, so music festivals are a
re chance to hear some of the great Varanasi
lents. They include: Lalit Sangit Parishad, Dec-
nber; Rimpa (started by Ravi Shankar), January;
hrupad Mela, last week of February; music dedi-
ted to Hanuman, played at Sankat Mochan Tem-
e, first week of April; music dedicated to Durga,
id-August.
There are flights to and from Calcutta on Tues.,
hurs., Sat. and Sun.; connections with Delhi,
gra, Khajuraho and Kathmandu daily. Taxis are
appy to take more than one customer into town
5km), halving the fare.
There are only two good hotels and this is tourist
rritory, so book. The better one is **Clarks Varana-**
, The Mall (tel: 62021; telex: 0545-204; cable:
LARKOTEL); the first of the Clarks chain, a
)th-century building with lots of character
lthough there is a threat to 'modernise' the lob-
/), started by the Clarks who sold out to the local
rothers Gupta in the 1930s. 120 rooms, attached
ath. Garden rooms in the old block are nicest,
ith 1930s furniture, huge bathrooms, and views
ver the garden. Back rooms look across fields to
ie Varuna river. Shopping, bank, post office,
avel agent, health club, yoga classes, pool. Res-
urant decor dreary but food has best reputation

in town and includes Mughlai and Lucknowi dishes and a full Chinese menu (with Chinese chef).
There are lunchtime poolside barbecues with live
Indian music; fresh Mysore coffee if you ask for it;
instant coffee if you don't.
Taj Ganges, Nadesar Palace Grounds, Raja Bazar
Road, (tel: 54385/54395/56125; telex: 0545-219
TAJG IN). New building, opened 1981, with all
the Taj chain comforts but lacking the usual polish.
80 rooms, attached bath. A high storey is best, for
views over fine, well-tended hotel garden to one of
the Maharaja's palaces (where the Queen and
Prince Philip stayed in 1955). Fair shopping, travel
agent, excellent big pool, tennis, tiny golf course,
restaurant nice with good food (including some
rich Lucknowi Mughlai dishes) and a garden buffet
dinner.
Uttar Pradesh Government Tourist Bureau,
Parade Kothi, Cantonment (tel: 55415) is superb,
run by a knowledgeable team of locals headed by
Mr D. K. Burman, a trained archaeologist. It will
arrange good guides for Sarnath (not the easiest
place to visit unaided), and special music and
dance performances. It provides reliable advice on
the ghats, shopping and tours (city, Ramnagar
Fort, Sarnath). For news and entertainment guide,
see the Northern India Patrika newspaper. Best
guide books: Glimpses of Varanasi by K. Jaycees or
Banaras by S. N. Mishra. The Survey of India map
of Varanasi is, surprisingly, currently in print. Best
book shops: Motilal at Banarsidas in Chowk and
New Metrex International, in front of the UPGTB.
Partial prohibition currently in force: the 1st and
7th of each month are dry days.

OUT AND ABOUT **The ghats**: One 4am start is
essential – sleep off the shock around the pool
later. As dawn breaks, the notes of the shehna
(reed instrument) played by the great Bismillah
Khan on the terrace of Shiva (or Shanka) Temple
echo across the Ganga. The dawn light on the
Ganga is unique. In the half-dark, you take a little
boat from Dasaswanadh Ghat and go first up river
to Asi Ghat, then back and on at least to Panchganga Ghat. (To feel the atmosphere and peace,
avoid going with a group.)
Pilgrims can be seen on the shore, rousing themselves on the ghats beneath the palaces of the
maharajas of Varanasi, Jaipur, Udaipur, Gwalior,
Mysore. They needed salvation too, but in comfort. Some are occupied by squatters now. Boatmen dump the odd corpse in the river, an honour
permitted only to a Sadhu (holy man) and those

who die of small-pox, because they are possessed by Sitala, goddess of fever diseases who might be injured by cremation. Every year, the remains of the other 35,000 or so bodies are thrown into the water after cremation.

As the sun rises, the faithful flow down to the holy water, washing begins and the city comes alive. Of the 80 or so ghats, each with a Shiva lingum (phallic emblem), five (the panchtirath) are especially sacred and should be visited by a pilgrim in one day, in this order: Asi, Dasaswanadh (where Brahma sacrificed 10 horses), Barnasangam, Panchganga (where the four other sacred rivers of India are said to mingle) and Manikarnika (the most sacred, where Mahadeo dug the tank to find Parvati's earring; also the principal burning ghat, where the most privileged families are burnt on the Charanpaduka slab marked with the imprint of Vishnu's feet). Other ghats have their own importance and are interesting to visit strolling under the rich, late afternoon sunlight, having slept off the morning's effort.

Starting in the south, Asi Ghat is where pilgrims bathe in the confluence of the Asi and Ganga waters. Next comes Tulsi Ghat commemorating the poet Gosain Tulsi Das who translated the Ramayana and died here in 1623. The sewage pumps out under Janki Ghat. Bachhraj Ghat is Jain. Shivala (or Kali) Ghat has a splendid Shiva lingum and is owned by the Maharaja of Varanasi, who is an accomplished musician and an active force in the city. As a devout Brahmin, he bathes in the holy water daily. Hanuman Ghat is popular with devotees of the monkey-god. Nearby, the Dandi Paths (a cult of ascetics) use Dandi Ghat. Harish Chandra (or Smashan) Ghat, named after a Hindu drama hero who worked on this ghat, is one of two burning ghats (the other is Manikarnika). Kedar Ghat has fine lingums and temple. Mansarowar Ghat is named after a lake just inside Tibet which is near the Ganga's source and at the foot of Kailash Mountain where Shiva lives.

At Someswar Ghat, meaning 'moon-lord', the diseased are cured. Ahalya Bai's Ghat was built by the able Mahratta princess who governed Indore 1767–95. Man Mandir Ghat is beside yet another of Jai Singh's observatories (also at Jaipur, Delhi, Ujjain). Lalita Ghat leads to the Nepalese Temple full of erotic paintings, and further inland to the Golden Temple. The famous burning ghat with a heap of temples is Jalsain (photography forbidden), named after Vishnu's form of Jalsai (sleeper on the ocean). Dattatreya Ghat is named

after a Brahmin teacher-saint believed to be incarnated with the Trinity: Brahma, Vishnu and Shiva. Finally, the Trilochan Ghat is where pilgrims bathe in the specially sacred water between its two turrets. The akhara wrestling and malkham acrobatic are staged near here.

In the city the most interesting thing to do is to wander in the gullies and peep into the temples especially around the Golden Temple (which is no open to non-Hindus, only partially visible from th balcony opposite and not worth it). If you peep int the dilapidated palaces you will see the carve wood, marble and brass of former grandeur. Paa shops sell the special Varanasi patta, relishe throughout India and second only to the Calcutt maghai. There are also bhang (hashish) shops o every corner, selling all sorts of varieties prepare by different rituals – sometimes even in sweet meats and drinks. To the south is the red-staine Durga (Monkey) Temple next to the Tulsi Mana Temple which has the Ramayana told in relie inside. Beyond is the Banaras Hindu Universit (known as BHU). Here is the Bharat Kala Bhavan one of the finest museums in India, with a mag nificent collection of Indian miniature painting and sculptures (open Mon.–Sat., 11am–4pm).

From here, the ferry sets off across the river t the 18th century *Ramnagar Fort* where the ex Maharaja of Varanasi still lives, complete with pe elephant, vintage Cadillac, court ceremonial an audiences. (Fort and museum open daily, rough1 10am–noon; 2–5pm.) The archaeological digs her have revealed evidence of Varanasi's existence i the 9th century BC.

To eat in town, both the *Diamond Hotel* at Belupu and the *Chinese Win-Fa* at Lahurabir are reliable Varanasi vies with Calcutta in sweetmeat fame taste kheer mohan, pista burfi, the delicious chum chum (oval-shaped, coated with dessicated coco nut and sometimes stuffed with mallai-cream) an rasgulla at Kamdhenu, Luxa in Guruduara Marke or Ram Bhandar at Thatheri Bazaar in the Chow1 area. An excellent snack is pati (also called chiky), sort of sweet bar of jaggery (raw sugar) and nuts.

SHOPPING AND CRAFTS There is no Hand loom House in Varanasi, nor good governmen emporia, except a huge Kashmiri one (with high prices) opposite the Taj hotel. Shopping is done i the bazaars: Satti bazaar for saris; Thetary bazaa for silver and traditional Varanasi or Moradaba brass (the pinker the better, showing high coppe content); Gadolia and the whole central Chow1 area for everything (especially toys).

Fabrics But the hand-woven, sumptuous Varanasi silk brocades are the best buy. These were the finest fabrics of the 16th century Mughal court, although at that time Varanasi was famous for its muslins and zari cloth (like cloth of gold) rather than *kinkhabs* (brocades of metal threads worked on a silk ground). Varanasi brocades are still the flashiest today. Gold, silver and silk threads are woven into heavy, textured saris and stoles, with an all-over design of small motifs. Some can be bought by the metre. The guldasta kinkhab (flower bouquet gold cloth) is so thick it can only be draped as a shawl; a gyasar has Buddhist motifs; a latifa has rows of buti (flowers); a badal me phul has a free pattern of clouds and flowers.

These are classics, so expect to pay for a work of art, a combination of top quality materials (Karnataka silk, real silver and gold-polished silver thread) and master weavers' skills. The finest cost up to Rs20,000, but there are perfectly beautiful cheaper ones. Beware: ignore young men who ask, usually in a single breath: 'Please may I practice my English would you like to come for a cup of tea and see my uncle's silk factory?'.

Find the best fabrics at Brij Raman Das (in a beautiful old house) and Ushnak Malmulchan (also branches in Delhi and Madras), where discerning Indian women shop. Mohan Lal Kishan Chan keeps the Bombay film actresses swathed in metres of top quality brocade. More modest spending is at Ram Bhaj Rosham Lal at Chowk and Bhagwan Lila Exports, Sundunagar. If you ask to see the fabric for export, you may be taken across town to the warehouse and have a much better selection. Find cheap saris (about Rs220) at Satti bazaar, woven in the surrounding villages. To see silk weaving, go to the Lohata suburb, Bari bazaar in the Adampira area and the Rewari Talab area. The hardest work is done November to February; there is no weaving in July and August.

The classic, tightly knotted carpets from Mirzapur and Bandoli are very big buys and should be undertaken with great care (see p. 61).

AWAYDAYS
SARNATH

11km. Visit for archaeological remains and historical-religious importance. Here, on a July full moon around 528BC, Buddha preached his first sermon, after he had received enlightenment. Called 'Setting in Motion the Wheel of Righteousness', it set out life's problem and its solution, advocated mod-

eration (the Middle Way) and became the essence of Buddhist teaching. Before this, Buddha was a royal prince, Gotama Siddhartha, probably born around 563BC, who renounced his family and went in search of peace and an end to suffering. It is thought he was about 35 years old when, after years of meditation at Gaya in Bihar (now called Bodhgaya), he attained enlightenment and began his mission to impart it to others, emphasising dhamma (religion), sangha (monasticism) and bodhi (enlightenment), but no extremes. He seems to have lived into old age, perhaps until 80, but his biography was not written until much later, when history and legend were already fused.

Sarnath became a thriving monastic centre. Emperor Ashoka (c 273–236BC), the great Buddhist convert, built stupas and a pillar. But the 3rd century decline in Buddhism and subsequent Muslim destruction have left little. The capital of the Ashoka pillar, carved with back-to-back lions, is now the official symbol of India and is preserved in the excellent (but badly labelled) museum, together with fine Gupta sculptures (open Sat.–Thurs., 10am–5pm). Essential guide book to Sarnath by V. S. Agrawala available at the ticket office. Buddha Purnima festival celebrates Buddha's birth with a big fair and procession on the day of the full moon in May.

CHUNAR

15km. West of Ramnagar, excellent for space, fresh air and a picnic. The old fort on the hill was taken by Humayun in the 16th century. There are fine Mughal tombs and a very interesting British cemetery. Until 1860, soldiers who had married Indian women, and therefore wanted to retire in India instead of going home, could take half their pension and come to live at Chunar. Many are buried here.

ASHRAMS

For health in mind and body. There are several around Varanasi, on the whole reputable and not the Swiss bank account variety. Two recommended are *Matha Anan Mayi Ashram* and *Vharat Sev Sangh Ashram*.

Orissa

A green, fertile and almost entirely agricultural state strewn with densely-carved, beehive-shaped temples and tiny villages of red houses, the exteriors exquisitely decorated with white rice-flour paintings. There is even fresh air, good beaches and a traditional seaside hotel. It is the complete antithesis of Calcutta's stifling, seedy splendour and overcrowding. Indeed, Orissa is so unindustrialised that rural Bhubaneswar hardly seems fit to be the capital of its 25 million Oriyans. Many of the great monuments from Orissa's days of glory are here. Most important are the group of temples built at the height of Oriyan Hindu culture between the 7th and 15th centuries. Through paddy fields and villages lies the Sun Temple at Konarak built in the shape of a huge chariot and covered in carvings.

The seaside resort of Puri is just down the road, where the Jagganath temple's huge and magnificent festival chariot gave its name to the ugly, thunderous juggernaut lorries of Europe. The June–July *Rath Yatra* festival is one of the most spectacular of all Indian festivals, when Puri is over-run with pilgrims. To commemorate Krishna's journey from Gokul to Mathura, the images of Jagganath and his brother and sister are hauled through Puri on vast raths (chariots), so heavy they need the strength of 4,000 temple inmates to pull them. The gods are then left at the Gundicha Mandir (garden house) for their annual week's holiday before being dragged back home. Then, with healthy religious entrepreneurship, the raths are broken up and sold as instant relics.

THE HARD FACTS Inland, the best season is September–March. But Puri is a popular breather for Calcuttans all the year round. Either studiously head for or absolutely avoid the Rath Yatra festival. Other popular times are the October Durga Puja festival, and May to September when Calcutta is unbearable, the courts close and the legal profession along with everyone else head for the sea or the hills. The pre-monsoon breakers (May–June) produce the best surf. Puri or Bhubaneswar (61km apart) make good bases; Gopalpur-on-sea is a bit far away and best used as a pure beach resort.

From Calcutta, daily flights go to Bhubaneswar. There are direct flights from Hyderabad (Tues., Thurs., Sat.) and Varanasi (Tues., Thurs. Sat., Sun.). Overnight train to Puri is more fun, at least one way. The Howrah–Puri Express leaves Calcutta at 8.50pm, arriving 8.35am; the Puri–Howrah Express leaves Puri at 6.05pm, arriving 5.30am. For Gopalpur-on-sea, the Howrah–Madras Mail leaves Calcutta 8pm, arriving Berhampur 6.42am; the reverse journey leaves at 10.20pm and arrives 6.16am. Hire a car on arrival or through the hotel,

bargaining hard for an all-in flat price until your departure.

In **Bhubaneswar**, choose from three hotels, all in the new town but not far from the temples. Best is the *Hotel Kalinga Ashok*, Gautam Nagar (tel: 53318; telex: 0675 282; cable: TOURISM). Clean, pleasant, well-run and a restaurant that serves some local dishes – every quality delightfully surprising in one of the ITDC government chain of hotels. 36 rooms, attached bath, car rental, mod. cons.
Hotel Konarak, 86A-1 Gautam Nagar (tel: 53330/ 54382; cable: SWAGATAM); 64 rooms, attached bath, every mod. con., travel counter, car rental, health club, small swimming pool, bad restaurant but pretty 24-hour coffee shop.
Hotel Swosti, 103 Janpath (tel: 54178/50365; cable SWOSTI). New but looks promising. 53 rooms, attached bath, mod. cons, restaurant includes local dishes. The big Oberoi chain is building a hotel here. Avoid Hotel Prachi.

Sparse information from the Tourist Bungalow on Phanta Nivas, who sometimes run day trips to Konarak; ask here to see training classes at the Odissi Dance Academy or the College of Dance and Music. Indian Airlines is on Rajpath.

In **Puri**, stay at the *South Eastern Railway Hotel*, Chakratirtha Road (tel: 63; cable: SURF); built as the home of Lady Ashworth, bought by the Bengal–Nagpur Railway with land going right down to the sea. Opened as a hotel in 1925. Still known affectionately as 'the BNR' by Calcuttans, although the BNR was taken over by the SER some 30 years ago. Puri was the Brighton of India, frequented by both Raj and maharajas and, later, ambassadors. J. K. Galbraith came when he was ambassador to India and loved it (the hotel built him an extra long bed): 'I am not what you might call a beach man . . . with the single exception of Puri in India where the main attraction is an excellent hotel set well back from the sand.'

It is still excellent, and guests and staff are as pucka as can be, like a cast from an Agatha Christie thriller. 37 spacious and spotless rooms, 1st floor with sea view best. Spacious verandahs with green and red cane chairs overlook well-kept lawns and bright flower-beds. Sedate staff give traditional service. Huge Raj nursery meals (saved by the very fresh fish course – they will try to get lobster, if asked) are included in room price – porridge for breakfast, fruit cake for tea.

One is expected to take a siesta: notices upstairs

read: 'silence please, 2–4pm and 10.30pm–7.30am'. There are billiards, table tennis and books but no longer a tennis court. A charming, elderly life-saver escorts swimmers to the beach where passing traders arrive like gannets, offering shells, garnets, etc. However, away from the front of the hotel, the beach is quieter and more interesting, with fishermen and the occasional little bazaar. Note: payment is by travellers' cheques or cash. No credit cards.

There are two other beach hotels if the 'BNR' is full. At the other end of Puri, right on the beach, is the *Prachi Sun and Beach Hotel* (tel: 638; cable: PRACHI). 37 double rooms, attached bath, car rental, very new but promising, some Oriyan furniture and decoration. Ground-floor rooms have small verandah and then sand. Three hours down the coast the Oberoi chain have a hotel at **Gopalpur-on-Sea**, *Hotel Oberoi Palm Beach* (tel: 23; cable: OBHOTEL); 172km from Bhubaneswar, 16km from Berhampur railway station. 20 rooms, attached bath, car rental, badminton, tennis, baby sitter. 100 metres from the sea. Arrangements made for riding, sailing and fishing.

BHUBANESWAR

OUT AND ABOUT Known as Ekamrakshetra during the medieval period when it was one of five religious centres in Orissa. There was keen temple building in the 7th century to secure a place in heaven and show off to fellow mortals, which maintained its vigour under a succession of kings until the 15th century. Some 7,000 sandstone temples were built around the main tank alone (glorious at sunset), of which about 500 partly or wholly survived the Mughal conquest of the 16th century.

The temple design was governed by strict mathematical rules down to the tiniest detail. But basically each temple had an entrance (jagamohan) and a sanctum for the deity (deul) which had the bee-hive tower (sikhara) above. Endless extras could be added, from dancing halls to sub-temples and shrines. The earlier small, squat shrines developed into large, ostentatious temples of increasingly slender proportions. Every outside surface was carved with geometric designs, flowers, animals and cavorting or loving gods and humans. Carvings are modest and story-telling at first, cut in shallow relief. Later, there are more single female figures, cut in high relief and given increasing delicacy and seductive charms. They reach their height of joyful sensuality at the Rajarani and

Brahmesvara temples and at Konarak on the Sun Temple. The interiors were usually left plain.

Note: the Lingaraja temple, considered by Hindu experts to be the finest, is not open to non-Hindus, who may peer at it from a platform but can see little. Better to see some of the other good ones and look closely at the special Oriyan temple architecture and its decoration: Parasuramesvara, 7th century, tiny, lavishly carved; Vaital Deul, slightly later, carving freer and more elegant; Muktesvara, almost perfect proportions covered with vibrant, delicate carving; Rajarani, spirited and vibrant carvings, especially the nayikas (females); Ananta-Vasudeva, the form almost a mini-Lingaraja temple, the carving rich and profuse.

Visit also the state museum, with well-displayed archaeological and crafts departments (open Tues.–Sun., 10am–5pm). Just outside the town are the part-excavated ruins of *Sisupalgarh*, occupied from the 3rd century BC to the 4th century AD, thick with pottery shards (best reached on foot across the fields from Brahmesvara Temple).

At *Dhauli* (8km) are a set of edicts by the Mauryan emperor Ashoka (c 273–236BC), one of the earliest inscribed records in India (with an English translation set up nearby). Ashoka was India's Constantine, a fierce, warring tyrant who, after winning the Kalinga wars near here, suddenly turned to Buddha and became all sweetness and light. In these edicts he states: 'All men are my children'. The elephant boldly carved out of the rock above the edicts symbolises Buddha, 'best of elephants', and is the earliest known sculpture in Orissa.

A little further is *Pipli*, which once produced good appliqué work: now tourist junk fills the main street – quality work is sold in Bhubaneswar. The caves in the *Udayagiri* and *Khandagir* hills (5km) are best visited at sunset for good views over the surrounding plain. Further out of town, head north-east to Lalitgiri, Udaigiri and Ratnagiri for Buddhist relics; north-west to the Buddhist weaving villages of Maniabhanda and Nuapatna. Further inland live Orissa's 60 or so tribal groups. *Chilka Lake* (100km), on the coast between Puri and Gopalpur-on-sea, is a shallow, salt-water lake with good bird life (migratory birds October–January), best seen at sunrise by taking a boat out from Balligan or Rambha.

For eating, Oriyan food is similar to Bengali. There is plenty of fish: bekti, rui and sometimes lobster, prawns and crab; an Oriyan thali has puris, pappa, white rice, fish, vegetable (perhaps kara saag, spinach) and sweet. The Oriyan speciality is chena purda patha, meaning cheese-burnt-sweet, and is just like caramel custard – very settling for the stomach.

SHOPPING AND CRAFTS It is important to buy the superb fabrics and crafts of Orissa now, in Bhubaneswar; a few are available in Delhi, Calcutta and Varanasi; almost none in Bombay. (Puri has a good bazaar-like town centre; Konarak has just the temple.) There is a riot of choice: good appliqué work (including glorious sun umbrellas), terracotta toys, bold papier mâché masks (elephant, lion, etc., originally used for the epic dramas), playing cards, bell-metal bowls and plates, brass dhokra work (cast by the lost wax method) from Mayur-bhanj and Barapali, patta chitra (Puri paintings) on muslin, wood carving using the almost grainless white gumbhari tree and tarkashi (silver filigree) from Cuttack, still showing the flat, intricate Isla-mic designs brought by the Mughals.

Fabrics The finest cotton or silk weave of Orissa is the *double ikat*. For this, the warp and weft threads for the whole sari are first tie-dyed accord-ing to the pattern, then woven together – a techni-cal and artistic triumph. The different designs of each area are still very distinct, unlike Andra Pradesh where they are losing their individuality. Maniabandha saris often have a pink field; Sambal-puri saris have very clear designs and often a brocade effect in the weaving; but top notch is a Sonepur silk sari woven with rows of clear, small figures, elephants, flowers and fish.

Crafts and some fabrics can be found at Orissa Co-operative Handicraft Corporation, Hall No. 1, East Market Building (where Mr Burma will give directions for seeing craftsmen at work). The best fabrics are at Handloom Weavers' Co-operative, Hall No.2, West Market Building (open Mon.–Sat., 9am–noon; 4–9pm). Gauri Handicrafts in the old town has a good selection. Modern Book Depart-ment, New Market stocks books on Orissa. In principle, everything closes for a siesta, noon–4pm, and all day Thurs. Note: Very few credit cards are accepted in Orissa shops. Master weavers can be seen at Maniabhanda and Nuapatna, 70km.

KONARAK 64km from Bhubaneswar; 30km from Puri on the new coast road. Here is one of the finest temples in India which must be clambered over to enjoy the carving. (The inside is filled with sand, to prevent it collapsing.) First stop, however, should be at the small but good museum which stocks Debala Mitra's guide to Konarak (closed Fri.).

The temple was probably built in the 13th cen-tury to celebrate a ruler's war victory and marks the peak of Orissan architecture. It symbolises Surya, the sun-god, and looks like a vast stone chariot with 12 pairs of wheels, drawn by 7 galloping horses, every facet richly carved, some very deli-cate, some equally bold, with scenes of love, royal hunts and military processions and huge, free-standing elephants and beasts.

PURI A quiet, slightly has-been resort, full of charm. The stylish Bengali villas are now a bit dilapidated. But it has a lovely seaside atmosphere and feels as if ice-cream and candy-floss should be on sale. A good place to relax and swim. Old Puri town should be visited at sunset. The Jagganath temple, the focus of the town, is not open to non-Hindus, but can be seen by going to Ragunan-dan library which is on the first floor of the market square opposite the temple. The librarian will show you on to the roof (and supply a stick for warding off the monkeys). The sun setting behind the temple is beautiful. A donation to the library is expected afterwards. It has a good collection of 16th–18th century Pali manuscripts available on request Mon.–Sat., 9 am–noon; 4–8pm).

As darkness falls, the whole town twinkles with the lights of shops and stalls and the air is filled with chattering, shouting and and delicious smells as the huge bazaar rumbles into action for the whole evening. Holy men take up their positions near the temple. Some sit inside a thorn bush, only the begging hands poking out. In dark side-streets old people queue at the bars of now illegal opium shops that were once so common.

Wildlife sanctuaries

Eastern India is rich in wildlife sanctuaries. Here some of the most important research is being car-ried out on how best to save endangered species and increase their numbers. The gharial crocodile is one current subject. Notable success stories are the great Indian one-horned rhinoceros – called the 'hideous' unicorn by Marco Polo – and the wild buffalo, both to be seen in the uniquely unspoilt tracts of Assam in Kaziranga and Manas. If permits are being issued for either sanctuary, then go if at all possible.

Kanha, Madhya Pradesh: see p. 141.

KASIRANGA, ASSAM

Season February–May. Fly to Jorhat, then 96km by road. Advance booking (rooms and elephants) and permit essential. Three weeks before your intended departure either go to a travel agent or apply direct to the Divisional Forest Office, Sibsagar Division, Jorhat. If short of time, cable the Officer in Charge, Kohara Tourist Lodge. Stay at ITDC *Kasiranga Forest Lodge* (see p. 163), and ask for a room with balcony and view, good facilities, occasional dance programmes. Explore by elephant, car and boat.

430 sq km of forest, swamps, plain and the totally wild Baguri area. The park was established in 1908 when poachers had reduced the rhino count to a mere dozen. The Chinese pay high prices for the blood, skin, urine and bones, believing them to have medicinal and magical properties. But they pay highest for the horn which is believed to have aphrodisiac powers. Today about 900 rhinos roam the sanctuary. There are also 800 wild elephants and 700 wild buffalo, along with swamp deer, hog deer, tiger and Himalayan bear. Around the jheels (swampy lakes) are blacknecked stork and ring-tailed fishing-eagles.

MANAS, ASSAM

Season January–March, with fishing November–December. Fly to Gauhati, then 176km by road. Best is to stay at the *Forestry Department bungalow*, bookable through the Division Forest Officer, Wildlife Division, Sarania, Gauhati; or at the *Manas Tourist Lodge*. Explore by elephant and boat.

270 sq km of outstanding sub-Himalayan riverine forest on the south bank of the River Manas which divides India from Bhutan. There are morning and afternoon flights of great pied hornbills; rare waterfowl include white-capped redstart, mergansers, ruddy shelduck and large cormorants. Also to be spotted are elephant, rhino, buffalo and tiger.

ALDAPARA, WEST BENGAL

Season February–May. Fly to Bagdogra, then 153km by road; or by Jamair to Hashimara airstrip 5km away. Trains stop at Hashimara. The place to stay is the pretty *Madarihat Forest Lodge* just outside the sanctuary or the *Holong Forest Bungalow* inside. Information: Forest Utilisation Officer, 6 Lyons Range, Calcutta. Explore by elephant. Just below Bhutan, 100 sq km of sub-Himalayan forest and savannah harbouring elephant, rhino, rhesus, hog deer, pig, tiger and leopard and rich birdlife (including lesser florican, great stone plover, red junglefowl).

HAZARIBAGH AND PALAMAU
SANCTUARIES, BIHAR

Season February–March. Fly to Ranchi, then by road, 100km to Hazaribagh, 150km to Palamau. Accommodation at *Dak Bungalow* or *Forest Lodge* at each.

Hazaribagh Sanctuary is in undulating hill forests in the Damodar valley, abounding in big, healthy sambhar. These are best seen by car at night, as are the nilgai, muntjac, chital and occasional tiger and leopard.

Chital, tiger, leopard, jungle cat, elephant, gaur, langur and the rare wolf live in the dry deciduous Palamau Sanctuary and there is also rich bird life.

SIMLIPAL, ORISSA

Season November–June. About 300km by road from Calcutta or Bhubaneswar. Nearest railway station Baripada. Visitors stay in modest forest bungalows.

The park is part of Project Tiger. So there are tiger to be seen, as well as leopard, elephant, chital and sambhar. They roam over 2,750 sq km of the Simlipal Hills, with waterfalls and streams in the forest clearings. See Barhepani and Jaranda waterfalls. Good hill birds.

Sunderbans, West Bengal: See p. 159

Find out more

Anand, M. R.: 'Konarak', *Marg*, Bombay, 1968
Archer, M.: *Early Views of India, The Picturesque Journeys of Thomas and William Daniell 1786–1794*, London, 1980
Archer, M.: *Indian and British portraiture, 1770–1825*, London, 1979
Banerjee, Samik: *Calcutta 200 Years, A Tollygunge Club Perspective*, Calcutta 1981
Bose, Nirmal Kumar: *Calcutta; a Social Survey*, 1968
Busteed, H. E.: *Echoes from Old Calcutta*, 1st published Calcutta 1882, reprinted by Shannon, 1972
Doig, Desmond: *Calcutta; an artist's impressions*, Calcutta 1969
Eck, Diana: *Banares the City of Light*, London, 1984
Ganguly, N.: *The Calcutta Cricket Club, its origins and development*, Calcutta 1936
Ghosh, J. C.: *The Bengali Renaissance*, London, 1948
Griffiths, P.: *History of the Indian Tea Industry*, London, 1967

Hickey, William: *Memoirs*, ed. Peter Quennell, London 1960

London, J.: *Calcutta and Its Neighbourhood*, Calcutta, 1974

Marshall, P. J.: *East Indian Fortunes: The British in Bengal in the Eighteenth Century*, Oxford, 1976

Mehta, R. J.: *Konarak, The Sun-temple of Love*, Bombay, 1969

Mitra, D.: *Bhubaneswar*, New Delhi, 1978

Mitra, D.: *Konorak*, New Delhi, 1976

Mohanty, B. C.: *Applique Crafts of Orissa*, Ahmedabad, 1980

Mohanty, B. C.: *Patachitras of Orissa*, Ahmedabad, 1980

Mohanty, B. C. and Krishna, K.: *Ikat Fabrics of Orissa and Andhra*

Moorhouse, Geoffrey: *Calcutta, The City Revealed*, London, 1983

Muggeridge, M.: *Like It Was: The Diaries of Malcolm Muggeridge*, London, 1981

Muggeridge, M.: *Something Beautiful For God*, London, 1972

Nakamura, H. and Maruyama, I.: *The World Buddha*, Gakken publishers, Japan

Newby, E.: *Slowly Down the Ganges*, London, 198

Newby, E. and Singh, Raghubir: *Ganga, Sac River of India*, Hong Kong, 1974

Patnaik, D. N.: *Odissi Dance*, Orissa, 1971

Shellim, Maurice: *Patchwork to the Great Pagoda (Thomas and William Daniells)*, Calcutta, 1973

Skelton, R. and Francis, M. (eds): *Arts of Beng* London 1979

Spear, P.: *Master of Bengal – an Illustrated Life Clive*, London, 1975

Spear, P.: *The Nabobs – the Social Life of the English 18th Century India*, London, 1932

Stamp, G.: 'British Architecture in India 185 1947', *Journal of the Royal Society of Arts*, vol. CXXI 1981, pp. 357–77

Welch, S. C.: *Room for Wonder: Indian Painting d ing the British Period 1760–1880*, New York, 1978

Woodruff, Philip: *The Men Who Ruled India*, Ca, 1953

The sizzling South:
silk, spices and cities of faded splendour

uth India is an exotic land. Weddings, stivals and political meetings are celebrated th gusto and with lashings of tinsel, music, iety and fireworks. The Hindu faithful eeten their temple precincts with perumes of coconut, camphor, incense and garnds of flowers. The temple elephant saunrs off for his bath, bucket in trunk, and the nple musicians beat drums and blow trumts to signal puja (worship). Finest silks of prant colours are cultured and woven in ud huts. Pricy spices are nurtured on the lgiri Hills and artfully displayed on large atters in the bazaars. Wildlife parks abound th rare animals, birds and flora.

Everywhere there are flowers: the rickaw boy constantly renews his jasmine garnds; women wear white and orange blosms woven with tinsel in their hair; heaps of lkless flowers, sold by weight or strung o garlands, fill the air of flower bazaars th a heady, intoxicating perfume. Bullocks' rns are painted in red and green stripes d bells are fixed to the tips. A scarecrow is ven a big, glossy, red and black face.

Even the languages sound exotic, from the egant Urdu in Hyderabad to the gobbledyok Tamil and Malayalam of the deep South at sounds like someone practising a ngue-twister based on double '11s'. Words ve Germanic multi-syllable length, names e unpronounceable and familiar gods acire local names, like Padmanabha for Vish-

nu. And the whole peninsular is encased in the band of coconut palms and white beaches that form the Coromandel coast of Tamil Nadu and the Malabar coast of Kerala.

The South Indian film industry pervades all. The tiniest village boasts a magnificent Art Deco cinema, proudly lettered 'Tirumalai Talkies 1940'. Massive, garish 3-D movie hoardings are tarted up with tinsel and gold. Podgy wooden arms and legs are added to the poster images of the gods and heroes to make them burst out beyond their huge frames. A 20 metre-high Roger Moore, fattened up to appeal to local taste, brandishes an outsize 007 revolver in a Bangalore street.

Cinema neon lights inspire a Kerala coffinmaker to have as his shop sign a remarkably tasteless, blood red, flashing neon coffin. The splashes of crimson, saffron, lapis and deep pink found in Rajasthan make way for the harsh celluloid clashes of gaudy mauve, icecream pink, yellow, orange, sky blue and peppermint green. The centuries-old temples, with their riot of leaping gods, are being 'restored' with this same palette, using weather-wearing hard gloss paint, which is causing a great debate among the art historians. And, most telling of all, three out of the four southern states have at some time elected film stars as their Chief Ministers of State: Tamil Nadu, Karnataka and Andhra Pradesh.

Scene changes are dramatic. Muslim

173

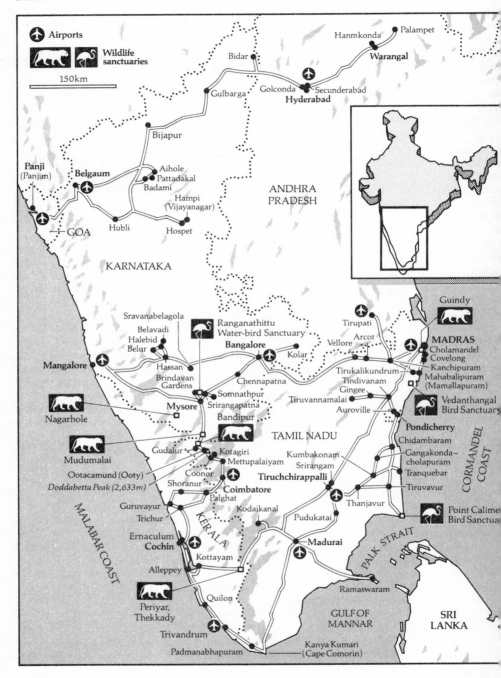

✈ Airports

🐅 🦩 Wildlife sanctuaries

150km

Palampet
Hanmkonda
Warangal
Bidar
✈ Golconda Secunderabad
Gulbarga Hyderabad
Bijapur
ANDHRA PRADESH
Panji (Panjim)
Belgaum Aihole
Pattadakal
Badami
Hampi (Vijayanagar)
✈
GOA Hubli Hospet
KARNATAKA
Sravanabelagola
Belavadi
Halebid
Belur
Ranganathittu Water-bird Sanctuary
Tirupati
Bangalore Arcot
Vellore MADRAS
Cholamandel
Mangalore ✈ Hassan Kolar Covelong
Brindavan Tirukalikundrum Kanchipuram
Gardens Chennapatna Tindivanam Mahabalipuram (Mamallapuram)
Somnathpur Gingee
Mysore Srirangapatna Tiruvannamalai
Nagarhole Bandipur Auroville Vedanthangal Bird Sanctuary
TAMIL NADU Pondicherry
Gudalur Kotagiri Chidambaram
Mudumalai Mettupalaiyam Kumbakonam Gangakonda–cholapuram
Ootacamund (Ooty) Coonor Srirangam Tranquebar
Doddabetta Peak (2,633m) Shoranur Tiruchchirappalli Tiruvavur
Guruvayur Palghat Coimbatore
Trichur Kodaikanal Thanjavur Point Calimere Bird Sanctuary
Ernaculum KERALA Pudukatai
Cochin Madurai
Kottayam PALK STRAIT
Alleppey CORMANDEL COAST
MALABAR COAST Ramaswaram SRI LANKA
Periyar, Thekkady Quilon GULF OF MANNAR
Trivandrum
Padmanabhapuram Kanya Kumari (Cape Comorin)

174

derabad, city of the lucrative pearl trade
d decaying palaces, sits on the arid Deccan
teau. Moving off south-west, parched, flat
dhra Pradesh and Karnataka are dotted
:h piles of giant-sized boulders like Barbara
pworth sculptures. Magnificent forgotten
es of the wealthy Mughal, Chalukyan,
egu and Hoysala kingdoms are now back-
ter towns or totally deserted. Passengers
agging through on steam trains are con-
nted with huge advertisements, beautiful-
painted directly on to boulders, exhorting
·m to buy Campa Cola or Charminar
arettes (named after Hyderabad's land-
rk). Coconut sellers squat at road-
e oases ready to slash their wares and
er fresh, soothing milk to dusty throats.
rther south, the plains are brightened by
ilberry bushes for silk and flowers
.ich will eventually be sold in Bangalore
rket.

Through the wildlife sanctuaries beyond
·sore lie the Nilgiri Hills, covered with an
ongruous mixture of valuable spice
ests, coffee bushes, monkeys and water-
s, topped with tea plantations and mossy,
ling hills like those found in the English
ke District.

Here are Ooty and her sister hill stations.
ere are sights which seem familiar to
glish eyes. There are timber-frame houses
those in a South of England county like
rrey. There are horses, hounds and pink-
ted huntsmen chasing after a fox, as if
oss a farmer's fields in Lincolnshire. These
st side by side with run-down princes'
aces and local Indian shacks. The inhabits and visitors are a strong cocktail of
ialite Indian honeymooners (even the
vly-wed Jaipurs, with the world their oys-
. came here), flashy Bombay and Banga-
e film-stars, the primitive Tonda tribe and
-over colonials who cast disapproving
nces from horn-rimmed spectacles as they
reading old copies of *The Daily Telegraph*.

Plunging further south there are the two
tes that form the tip of India. The viridian
en paddy fields of Tamil Nadu, known as
rice-bowl of India, are littered with life-
e, brightly painted, terracotta horses, gods

and elephants that look like giants' toys.
Here are the great temple cities of the Pallava
and Chola kings, with pyramid gopura (gateways) alive with wrestling, dancing and
fighting deities and demons.

Across the Cardamom Hills is wealthy
Kerala, a narrow, verdant, west coast strip
whose backwaters, paddy, rubber and coconuts (Kera means coconut) provide a lush,
fluorescent green backdrop for toytown
Christian churches, mosques and houses.
They are all of crazy designs, looking spick
and span and boldly painted in gleaming
candy pink, sky blue, mustard, mauve and
apple green. Sometimes, whole walls are
striped or checked, with some sculpture
thrown in as well.

Kerala is very different from the rest of
India. It has a tradition of home ownership
and distribution of wealth. You rarely see a
beggar in Kerala. The state consumes more
soap powder than any other. Here, the
Christian Church is as politically influential
as the film industry. Here also is India's highest literacy (60%, twice the national average)
and lowest birthrate.

There is a political awareness to rival that of
Bengal. It is so intense that no-one dares start
an industry without the prior consent of the
trade unions. It is difficult to know if there are
more strikes than festivals – they both look
much the same and pop up everywhere.
Kerala was only created in 1956 (out of Travancore, Cochin and Malabar) and promptly
voted in India's – and the world's – first freely
elected Communist government the following year.

Her wealth from exporting coconuts, rubber and the Nilgiris' produce, which accounts
for some 25% of all India's cash crops, is
now further boosted. Kerala supplies most
of the labour for Middle East construction,
the workers returning annually laden with
outsize videos, cassette recorders and the
latest gadgets. In response to all this com-
parative literacy and wealth, small bookshops advertise 'school books and bank
guides'.

In this mixture of rural simplicity and celluloid crassness, natural beauty and architec-

tural marvels, three modern and energetic cities have grown up around colonial Madras, the Nizam's courtly Hyderabad and the cool bolt-hole bungalows of Bangalore. Each threatens to throttle its fine old buildings with pollution and planning. Conservation is ignored in a blind destructive rush for modernism. The Urban Ceiling Act, which applies throughout India and restricts the amount of undeveloped land a man may own within the inner city, seems to have contributed to the damage. Land that has to be sold naturally fetches a better price if it has planning permission. And up go the sky-scrapers.

The provincial cities, in contrast, tuck their industry away, leaving Mysore still looking and feeling like the Maharaja's private city of palaces. The temple city of Madurai is as seething with pilgrims as Vatican City during a Holy Year. In Trivandrum, the older people still go to the main street every morning to

doff their caps to the Maharaja as he rid from his palace to the temple for morni puja.

There is a myth that south India consi solely of dreary temple ruins. It is an ug slander. The deserted temples are in fa splendid remains of whole temple cities. A the living temples vibrate with commun life – bazaars, smells, colour, music a worship. The South also has a variety scenery, monuments, peoples and traditio to rival anything the North can offer. And benefits from the added charms of an ev more open-hearted people than those in t North, less touched by Western commerci ism and ideology. This is the luxury of Sou India. And the way to find it is to brave t heat and dust and hie off into the countr side, stopping overnight in a Mysore pala or an old British Residency or a simple Circ House, then cooling off in the hills or relaxi on empty silver beaches.

When to go

Apart from the hills, the South is hot or very hot. The season for the Deccan and Tamil Nadu is November–February when winter days resemble a European mid-summer heatwave and nights bring little freshness. From March, the mercury rises to boiling point. Even the locals faint, break out in prickly heat and get sunstroke. The beaches are difficult to enjoy when it gets really hot. Then, with luck, come the monsoons between May and October, depending on the area (see Weather chart, p. 2).

Kerala sun is less ferocious (monsoon from May until October). The hills experience a much softer climate: November–February bring misty mornings, warm sunshine days and cold nights; March –June and September–October are delightfully warm, with spring flowers and then autumn colours; June is windy, July–September wet.

FESTIVALS Amid the constant stream of festivals, there are some worth planning an itinerary around. *Pongal* (called Sankranti in Karnataka), is harvest festival and the most important festival of all. It is celebrated across the South but best in Tamil Nadu. After a successful harvest, crucial

to rural India, the land, sun and animals are thanked.

Four days of holiday celebrations begin on first day of the Tamil month of Thai (usua January 13 or 14). The first day is Bhogi, on eve of Pongal, when evil spirits are driven out homes by removing old pots and clothes and bu ing them on a village bonfire. Houses are spri cleaned, whitewashed, some re-thatched and decorated. Women draw exquisite kolams (r gious patterns, see p. 181) with moistened flour pots, stove, front doorsteps and the place wh the special offering will be cooked.

On Pongal day, families have baths, massa each other and put on new clothes. Then the ne harvested rice, sugar-cane and turmeric (and ot ingredients) are boiled up in the new pots. Wh the froth is pongu (boiling over, the more it sp the better the year ahead), some is offered to Sur the sun god.

Day three is Maattu (cattle) Pongal, when t cows and bullocks, so valuable to the farmer, lovingly washed and sprinkled with turmeric ward off evil. Their foreheads are anointed w red powder, their long horns polished and brigh painted. Bells and beads are fastened to the t d heavy garlands of coconut and mango leaves, gar-cane, palmyra shoots and flowers are hung und their necks. More Pongal rice is offered to em before they are paraded around the village. en come the very competitive games, including e manja virattu (chase for turmeric) and the jalli ttu, a sort of American rodeo where the young en chase bulls to wrench off bundles of cloth tied und the horns or necks. The winner keeps the ntents, of cane, vegetables or even jewellery and oney.

Of the big all-India Hindu religious festivals, ussehra (September/October) and Diwali (Octo-r–November) have southern versions. Dussehra best in Mysore (where it is called Dassera) and lebrates the triumph of good over evil in the ddess Chamundeswari's triumph over the de-on Mahishasura. (In the North it is Rama's umph over Ravana.) Ten days of medieval geantry come to a climax with Vijayadashami, a mptuous procession of caparisoned elephants, rses and cavalry and garish and garlanded ities (often with faces similar to the latest film-r). The parade ends with fireworks, symbolising ditionally auspicious days when major projects re embarked upon, such as buildings or wars. A lebration of the goddess of learning, Saraswati, is own in at the same time, so there is a good tural programme of yakshagana dance-drama, arata Natyam classical dance and huthuri folk nce held in the splendid palace Durbar Hall and ounds.

Diwali follows the North in worshipping Lak-mi, goddess of wealth, but not in celebrating ma's return to Sita. Here it is the triumph of ishna and Satyabhama over the demon Naraka-ra, who had got too big for his boots and ducted some gods' pretty daughters and even bbed the mother goddess, Aditi, of her earrings. e demon was slain at dawn, when the celebra-ns are held: coloured kolams decorate the uses, effigies of Narakasura are burnt in every lage, sweetmeats exchanged, oil baths taken and w clothes donned.

The Muslim festivals of Muharram, Id-ul-Fitr at e end of Ramadan and Id-ul-Zuha (or Bakr-Id) e best seen in old Hyderabad (see pp. 39 and 49 : more on these).

Apart from Pongal festival, there are other uthern specialities but they mostly happen in e place only. Madurai has two big ones. The epam (float) festival (January–February) cel-rates the birthday of the 17th century ruler,

Tirumala Nayak. Temple gods are dresed up in silk, bejewelled and garlanded and processed to the big tank. They are dragged round on a huge barge, with music and chanting, the tank lit by thousands of oil lamps in built-in niches. *Meenakshi Kalyanam* (April–May), held at the thronged Meenakshi temple that constitutes most of Mad-urai city, celebrates the marriage of Meenakshi to Shiva. Ten days of jollity lead up to the procession of the deities on a huge chariot that rivals the raths of Puri (see p. 168).

The most spectacular Kerala temple festival is the *Pooram* at Trichur (April–May), just south of the Nilgiris. It is described by Kerala temple expert Pepita Noble as having 'breathtaking' sights, 'gigantic' crowds and 'stunning, earsplitting, glorious' music. 'Everything about it is on a grand scale.' Two goddesses, Paramekkavu and Thiruvambady, and eight other deities are hon-oured. Fairs are set up as crowds flood in. Vantage points on shop roofs are sold for Rs250. Cars are forbidden as the streets are decorated with coconut leaves, pendants and oil lamps.

The 30 elephants, chosen for their size and beauty of trunk, tail, ears and tusks, arrive on the eve, together with their food – lorryloads of pana-patta (palm leaves). On Pooram morning, they are dressed up in nattipattams (like gold-plated chain mail) and Brahmins sit on top of them to hold the symbolic deity, silk parasols, vencharmanrams (whisks) and alavattoms (peacock feather fans). Then the whole party sets off on a slow, glorious day-long procession and ritual, with constant music, cheered along by the faithful with offerings of rice and flowers.

The whole thing is repeated after sunset with different music and flaming torches, ending with a massive firework display which lasts until dawn. At 8am, the elephants assemble again, there is three hours of drumming, then more fireworks.

At Irinjalakuda (30km south of Trichur) there is nightly Kathakali and Karnatic music for 11 days, starting on the second night of Trichur Pooram.

Onam lasts for a week, leading up to full moon day in Chingom (August–September), and is Kera-la's harvest festival and new year. Feasting, new clothes, washed houses and dancing greet the annual visit of the legendary king, Mahabali, who was famous for his prosperous reign. The snake boat races held on the backwaters at Kottayam, Aranmula and Payipad are the climax. Long, low, dug-out boats, with highly decorated beak-shaped or kite-tailed sterns, compete for the Nehru Cup,

177

when up to 100 rowers race in boats along the palm-fringed backwaters.

SOCIAL CALENDAR Dominated by horse racing. Bangalore and Bombay have the main stud farms in India and Bangalore's racing season is May–July and October–February, with meetings most Fridays, Saturdays and Sundays. Ooty's season is April–June, with meetings on Saturdays and Sundays, but mid-May is the climax when the Ooty dog show and flower show are also held. Madras meetings are in December; Hyderabad's July–September and November–February.

Getting there: Getting away

The South has an efficient network of a dozen airports, making it very easy to fly into one, take a short trip by car, then take a second plane hop and another trip. Indian Airlines encourage this with their 30% discount South India Excursion Fare (see p. 8). Airports also connect directly to the best beaches (Madras, Goa, Maldives, Sri Lanka) for a pre- or post-sightseeing rest (see p. 237).

The principal direct connections are as follows. Daily between Bangalore and Delhi, Bombay, Cochin, Coimbatore, Dabolim (for Goa), Hyderabad, Madras, Madurai; between Hyderabad and Bangalore, Bombay, Delhi and Madras; between Madras and Bangalore, Bombay, Calcutta, Delhi, Hyderabad, Madurai, Tiruchirapalli and Trivandrum; between Madurai and Madras via Bangalore; between Trivandrum and Bombay, Madras and Tiruchirapalli. Hyderabad and Bangalore connect with Calcutta via Bhubaneswar (Tues., Thurs., Sat.) or via Nagpur (Wed., Fri., Sun.). For Sri Lanka, there are flights to Colombo from Madras (daily, except Fri.), Tiruchirapalli (Tues., Sat.), Trivandrum (Wed., Sun.). For the Maldives, fly from Trivandrum to Male (Mon., Thurs.).

Some train journeys are excellent for seeing the countryside and often fill a gap where there is no air connection. They chug along the lush coastline or cut across valleys, rubber plantations and the Cardamom and Nilgiri Hills. Good ones include the overnight Madras-Cochin Express (departs 7.20pm, arrives 9.40am); the Madras–Madurai–Quilon Mail (departs 7.05pm, arrives Madurai 6.40am; departs 6.55am, arrives Quilon 2.50pm); the Parasuram Express from Quilon to Trivandrum (departs 4.55pm, arrives 6.25pm). The Madras–Bangalore train journey is not particularly pretty.

But the train up to Ooty is a collector's item spectacular views from little yellow and blue ca riages as they slowly climb the narrow-gauge line locking into special teeth for the steeper slopes. three-part journey: first to Coimbatore by air, tra or road; then from Coimbatore to Mettupalaiya on the Nilgiri Express (depart 6.30am, arrive Me tupalaiyam 7.30am); then to Ooty on the narro gauge (depart 8am, arrive 12.30pm). Take the 2p train down from Ooty (only 3½hrs) to connect ba to Coimbatore.

The best way to travel in Kerala is by ferry on th backwaters (see p. 204). Sadly, considering th beautiful coastline, there is no ferry service b tween ports.

Information and reservations

The best way to set up a trip in the South aft arriving in India is to go to the recommended trav agents in Delhi, Bombay or Calcutta (see pp. 4 116, 150), choosing one with offices in the South go to one of the big southern cities and bo everything from there.

The big, reliable chains are found in the South follows. Mercury Travels are at 71/1 Infantry Roa Bangalore (tel: 576355); 5-9-101 Public Gard Road, Hyderabad (tel: 34411) and 191 Mount Roa Madras (tel: 83521). SITA are at 47 St Mark's Roa Bangalore (tel: 578091); Tharakan Building, M Road, Cochin (tel: 34634); 3-5-874 Hydergud Hyderabad (tel: 223628) and 26 Commander-i Chief Road, Madras (tel: 88861). TCI are at 9 Re dency Mount, Bangalore (tel: 573326); 1st floo Telstar Building, M G Road, Cochin (tel: 3164 Khushru Jung House, 6-1-34 Secretariat Roa Hyderabad (tel: 220578); 734 Anna Salai, Madr (tel: 88915); Hotel Amritha, Thycaud, Trivandru (tel: 66858) plus operating through other agen in Belgaum, Bijapur, Coimbatore, Madurai a Tiruchirapalli. Trade Wings are at 752 Anna Sal Madras (tel: 89461) and have other southe branches.

Many of the hotels are modest and simple, b they often have great charm and, because of t heat, hygiene standards in the South are conside ably higher than in the North. This applies to t preparation and consumption of food, too. Nigh life ranges from limited to non-existent, but it worth making every effort to see the exception classical dance found almost every night in Madr and Cochin and also worth going to a South Indi film (see p. 181). Shopping is best in Bangalore, Hyderabad and Madras.

The state and government sightseeing tours in the big southern cities are very good, some say better than in the North, but the southern accents can be rather heavy. Local 'approved guides' at remote spots are usually awful, reeling off lists of multi-syllabled gods, interspersed with useless facts, and using archaic phrasing in broken English.

South Indian food

Many dishes are hotter than northern ones, but that does not mean they have to frizzle up the taste buds and bring on a sweat. Indeed, combined with lots of rice, soothing fresh dahi (curd) and coconut, they are pleasantly light to eat in the heat and easy to digest. The southern cuisine is less rich than the northern and therefore less likely to give tummy trouble. The vegetarian diet can be supplemented with delicious freshwater or sea fish.

It is best to avoid meat, except to enjoy the superb Mughlai food in Muslim Hyderabad and at the top hotel restaurants of Madras, Bangalore and Madurai. Those desperate for a steak will find beef in Kerala where the population has a high Muslim and Christian content. The trading Chettinand tribe of Tamil Nadu have given a spicy chicken dish to the southern repertoire. Cocktail titbits are delicious: fresh, hot cashew nuts, fried prawns and crunchy banana chips.

The South is almost totally vegetarian, as is Gujarat, and many north Indians eat vegetarian at least one day a week – when they often use their abstemiousness as an excuse for a whacking great sweetmeat or rice-based pudding after the vegetables. Thus, the Indian vegetarian cuisine is highly developed, with an almost infinite variety of vegetable combinations cooked with different – and often very gentle – spices.

It is quite possible to eat a different dhal (pulses) dish every day. Sambar is a dhal cooked with several seasonal vegetables. The most common basic ingredients include brinjal (aubergine), okra (lady's fingers), sag (any green leaf vegetable), palak (spinach), mattar (peas), sarson ka sag (mustard leaves), pyazi (onion), aloo (potato), tomato and many others, each turned into a delicious and distinctive dish. Plain boiled potatoes are an abhorrence to Indians, who consider most Western food dreary and unimaginative.

The easiest way to order is to ask for a *thali* (large,

circular tin platter). It is delivered with six or so katoris (little dishes), each containing a different vegetable or pulse dish and one katori with dahi (fresh curd, sometimes seasoned and mixed with onion and tomato to make pachadi), one with chutney and one with mithai (sweet pudding). They are usually arranged in order, so you work round the different, complementary flavours, often beginning with rasam (clear lentil soup, later anglicised into mulliga-tanni, meaning pepper-soup, at the Madras Club) and ending with payasham (rice pudding with almonds, raisins and cardamom seeds).

More chutneys and pickles are put on the table, together with salad and possibly a side dish of pakoras (fried vegetables, known as bhajias in the North). Mango pickles can be fire hot, like kadu manga and thokku, or cool, like vadu manga. The substance of the meal arrives separately: a pile of steaming, boiled rice ladled from a big tureen into the middle of the thali dish, replenished as it goes down. The rice comes in many forms: flavoured with lemon or tamerind, cooked with curry patta (leaves) or with coconut.

Those with bigger appetites can also have a constant stream of hot, freshly baked breads and other treats, such as crispy thin poppads (small poppadums, the big ones are known as Punjab poppadums) or a dozen varieties of dosa (paper thin rice pancake a metre in diameter). Other breads are appam (soft-centred, crisp rice and coconut pancake), adais (thick, spicy lentil and rice pancake), murka (deep-fried rice, peanuts and cashewnuts), vadas (a crunchy, doughnut-shaped, deep-fried mixture of dhals and spices) and uppama (seasoned semolina).

But these are really better ordered as a light meal in themselves, the huge dosa often served wrapped around a dryish potato filling, then called masala dosa, and served with some freshly ground coconut and chutney. The typical south Indian idlies (steamed cakes made from fermented rice flour), a breakfast favourite, need ghi (clarified butter) or a more liquid sambar (potato, peas, mustard seed and other spices). And there is no fear of lacking the protein of a thick steak: the mixture of cereals and pulses provides it all.

Fish is especially good in the South. The white, flakey bekti is cooked with coconut milk to make fish curry, called molee in Kerala when the coconut milk is spiced with ginger, green chilli and herbs. There is pomfret, lobster, mussels, oysters, prawns, crab and small sharks. Fried mackerel and sardines are excellent. Pickled fish is considered a delicacy. Karimeen, a freshwater fish found in Kerala, is cooked in a fiery sauce of onions, green chillies and spices.

Every restaurant, even the tiniest roadside café, has somewhere to wash your hands and is used by everyone on arrival. (There is often no towel, so shake your hands dry or take one with you.) Then, when the steaming food arrives, however smart the restaurant, get stuck in with your fingers (right hand only), mixing sauces with rice, dunking breads, scooping up chutneys and dahi with bread and finger tips, drinking up the rest of the sauces and generally enjoying it all with abandon. Indians claim that to eat with cutlery is as unsatisfactory as to make love through an interpreter.

Wash it down with the very refreshing fresh coconut milk or lassi (yoghurt drink). Other drinks available are fresh fruit juices such as mango, orange, pineapple or guava; nimbu sodas or fizzy bottled drinks (Fanta, Campa Cola, Limca, etc.). If the spices are still tingling, have a kulfi (ice-cream flavoured with saffron and pistachio nuts) or, in September, fresh custard-apple ice-cream (found especially in Hyderabad). Fruits include the southern mangoe varieties of romani or malgoa and several varieties of banana: the small yellow and the big pink both have strong, delicious flavours. Try also jackfruit kernels and fresh toddy, best cut fresh in the market or on the roadside.

See how it's done: Crafts and customs

As with Rajasthan in the North, the essence of enjoying South India is to be adventurous and get out into the countryside. Many of the best historical sights are separated by long, dusty drives, cutting across state frontiers. They are worth every effort to reach but, to repeat, the South is not just temples and monuments. There is masses to see on the way. Trains go slowly, passing right beside rural villages. Buses stop in villages and towns for the driver and passengers to stretch their legs, eat and drink.

But the most versatile way to travel is by car, asking the driver to stop for anything that catches the eye. It is a good idea to set out very early, before sunrise, while it is cool, then stop for breakfast. Here are just a few things to look out for, in towns, villages and along the roads. Take a tip from the Indians and carry plenty of drinks on a trip – the sun gets very hot.

Small restaurants Unlike in the North, thes modest cafés that pop up on roadsides and in sid streets of towns are very hygienic. There is no nee to take boring hotel picnics. The cafés are known a udipis, vihars, meals, tiffin houses, etc. Some c the best dosas and idlies of all are found where th big lorries stop (just as it is often where the be breakfasts are to be found in England).

For something more substantial, order 'meal' c 'special meal'. Watch the food being cooked wit acrobatic speed and efficiency. Then, with luck, will be served on beautiful fresh banana leave although the patron is liable to proudly honour hi Western visitor with cutlery and crockery. Th mountain of rice will be replenished up to fou times, under the assumption that a whole pile wi be gobbled up with each of the four sauces: gh sambar, rasam and finally thayyur (thick curd).

Don't drink the water, which is delivered aut matically. Instead, stick to bottled drinks such a Limca or tea or coffee (both well boiled). Coffee served piping hot in a stainless steel beaker set in dish (the two together called a davara). This equip ment cools and froths up the sweet, milky liquic You pour it from as high as possible from beaker t dish and back again – a serious ritual known a 'coffee by the yard'.

Rice Miles and miles of green paddy fields ar dotted with the vibrant coloured backsides c women bent double planting and transplantin paddy. The Chola dynasty's wealth was founde on the Tamil Nadu rice bowl and rice is still th principal southern crop, with two annual harvest (Three near the Cauvery and other large rivers There are many varieties. The small nellore grair are grown in Andhra Pradesh. The up-market basmati rice is grown here but Dehra Dun basma grown in the North is the queen of rice. Basmati low yield makes it twice as expensive as the regula white rice usually served. Red rice (with re streaks) is the cheapest and has a better flavour bu has to be asked for specially. Hotels usually serve to their staff, not their clients. Harvesting method vary. In Bengal, sela is rice that is harvested, pa boiled in the fields and then dried until needed.

But rice is not just the staple diet; it is a fu damental part of social and religious life. A baby' first food is always rice, symbolising the hope tha it will never go hungry. There is a rice ceremony Saraswati, goddess of learning, before a child goe to school to learn the alphabet by drawing wit fingers on a tray of rice. At the sacred threa eremony, when a Brahmin boy enters adulthood, ie begs for rice from his family.

A new bride tips over the bowl of rice placed on the threshold of her house, spilling it into the home o bring fertility and prosperity. A pregnant voman is given presents of rice. Rice is a medicine or the eyes, is part of every festival, in Andhra 'radesh is fed to crows (the incarnation of people's ncestors), and is meant to ward off evil. In Tamil Jadu it is showered on brides as a blessing and, nixed with turmeric powder to make akshintulu, howered on children and offered to the gods. 'inally, at the sradh ceremony after death, rice alls are offered to help the spirit find peace.

Kolam More rice, this time the ritual decoration f the floor with muggu (rice powder), carried to a ine art in the South (as are the alpanas of Bengal nd rangolis in Gujarat, mandanas in Rajasthan nd sanjhnis in Uttar Pradesh). The southern voman makes the kolam every morning, after weeping her home. With great dexterity and years f practice, she skilfully lays a very beautiful and ntricate geometric design of dots outside the iouse to bring prosperity and happiness – and to ncourage the plagues of black ants (favourites of he elephant-faced god, Ganesh) to gorge them-elves and not bother to come inside.

In Margazhi month (mid-December to mid-anuary) the kolams are especially huge and intri-ate. For the January festival of Ratha Saptami, vhen the sun god steers his chariot towards the 'ropic of Cancer, she makes a stylised chariot .olam. For big occasions (festivals and weddings) nuggu is mixed to a paste so that it lasts longer, nd kaavi (red mud) is used as a border. In Kerala, he glorious kolams around the Onam festival (see). 177) are composed of petals of all the seasonal lowers. Places of worship have specific designs for lifferent areas: the padman is a stylised lotus .olam made where the ceremonial lamp is placed. .olams can be spotted on roadsides in the early norning.

Cinema Tamil is the most influential Indian cine-na after Hindi. What is more, Madras is second mly to Bombay in sound film production. And, vith three out of the four southern states voting ctors as their Chief Ministers, with hoardings that utdo Hollywood, and with film gossip flooding he papers, economic journals and conversation, it night be interesting to sample a southern celluloid tunner and get an insight into this obsession. icreenings are around 10am, 1.30pm, 6.30pm and '.30pm, and the smarter cinemas are air-

conditioned, so it makes for cool, relaxed sight-seeing.

Two-star rated films are considered tops, and the current favourite two-star Kanada actor is Rajkumar, who threatens to follow southern form and enter politics. Half the cinemas of India are in the South, the biggest choice being in Bangalore, where 40 of its 150 cinemas line Kempe Gowda Road. They mostly show films in Kanada and Tamil, but it is the turned-up Technicolor, outlandish sets and incongruous singing and danc-ing that matter, not the plot or dialogue. (The thriving serious cinema of the 1970s and 1980s is more difficult to find and to understand and English sub-titles are rare.) If curiosity is aroused, the Tourist Office can set up visits to film studios in Bangalore, Madras and Trivandrum.

The political and technical strength of southern film-making began early. With the coming of talkies to the South in the mid-1930s, the Madras studios were hit hard: the four southern languages – Tamil, Telegu, Kanada and Malayalam – belong to the Dravidian family, quite different from the Indo-Aryan Hindi, Bengali and Marathi of the North. So the South went its own way, de-veloping a flourishing, flamboyant cinema at such Madras studios as Gemini, Modern Theatres, AVM and Vauhini, and perfecting dubbing tech-niques into the four main languages – hence their sound supremacy now. By the late 1950s, half the Indian cinemas were in the South, and half the Indian films were made in the four southern lan-guages.

Above all, Tamil films exercised a social, political and cultural influence stronger than anywhere else. Politics stepped in quickly, in the shape of the Dravida Munnetra Kazhagam (DMK) party which stood for southern nationalism and the revival of Dravidian culture. They were anti-Hindi and anti-North and their rising sun symbol can be seen on many walls. They used films to reach the mass public, in the way Bengal had done during the Independence struggle, and they introduced crude rising sun symbolism.

The campaign was a winner. The Congress Party was destroyed and DMK came to power. Its first three Chief Ministers were all from the film world, the third being M. G. Ramachandran, elected in 1977 as the first real superstar Chief Minister. MGR (as he is known) was a matinée idol for 30 years. Now he has broken away from the DMK to form his own party.

Silk and cotton dyeing The splashes of cherry

red, deep green, punk pink, lilac and seaside blue that catch the eye on rooftops, among cows and bullocks in back gardens, along alleys and on road-sides are skeins of newly dyed cotton. Somewhere nearby is the dark dyeing room. Here, cotton is boiled hard to render it good for absorbing dye. Then it is hung from poles across a large stone tank, heated by a wood fire underneath, containing the warm water in which the dye is dissolved. After rinsing and squeezing the cloth in a wooden mangle, it is put out to dry.

To dye silk is slightly more complicated. Raw silk contains 30% sorocom (silk gum) which is removed by boiling in soda ash, soap and water in big copper pans, again heated with wood fires. (Fires bypass the constant electricity cuts that plague even big cities and prevent the necessarily precise timing.) Then the silk is dyed like cotton, ending with a wash in cold, diluted acid, termed scrumping, which gives the silk its lustre and crispness and is also a fixative. Unlike cotton, silk is dried in the shade. As in most areas of India, the dyes are now chemical. Even indigo, once so vital to Indian trade, is now only grown in the Cuddapah district of Andhra Pradesh.

Cotton lunghi weaving Lunghis, worn by men in the South, are the coloured, usually check, versions of the northern white dhotis. The clue to finding weavers' houses is the loud clatter of shuttles flying to and fro as the weaver works at amazing speed on looms set up over a pit. He controls the shuttle and movement of warp threads with foot pedals. Several weavers, both men and women, may work together under a palmyra leaf awning, their ages ranging from eight to very old age.

An adept weaver turns out two 2-metre lunghis a day, his family usually sticking to one colour and check size. Quality, and thus price, is determined by the number of weft threads, the coarsest with only about 20, the finest up to 100. You can buy direct from the weavers, having looked at prices in government shops (which also give an idea of the range available). Sometimes 4-metre pieces are available, the weaver having done a two-in-one job. Some lunghi weavers also make cotton towels with pretty fish motifs on the borders.

Handloom silk sari weaving Altogether more sedate than the frantic clack-clacking of lunghi weaving, and with a tradition stretching back, possibly even to the 3rd century BC. The heavy, lustrous and richly brocaded Kanchipuram sari, developed for temple rituals under the patronage of the 4th-century Pallava kings, is every souther belle's dream, her equivalent of a Zandra Rhode ball gown and well on a par with the weaves Varanasi, Orissa and Gujarat.

These exquisite, dazzling silks are woven dark, modest rooms down narrow alleys or in litt white-washed houses with palmyra roofs, ofte near dyers. Weaving is a family affair, with plen of variations of method. For instance, the man ma sit on the floor spinning silk on to shuttles whi the children sort the threads for the palo (patterne end). The mother will be weaving the main sa (5–7 metres) with an older child, worked on th reverse side before changing the warp threads f the metre of palo.

It takes two weavers working on a loom 15–ː days to complete a good silk sari, plus a week prepare the silks and tie the threads on to the loo The bundle of knotted threads that dangle from th loom mysteriously contain the elaborate pattern the border and palo. The weaver can tug a kn between rows to alter the arrangement of we threads. The shuttle is thrown from end to en between the two weavers. The senior weaver w sit on the border side to check the pattern f mistakes and to control the valuable zari threads gold and silver. Each row is tightened with a com and threads often have to be unmuddled betwee rows.

If there is a mistake in an important piece, su as a flashy, reversible wedding sari heavy wi gold zari work, the weaver takes it to a mast craftsman who, after negotiations over price, c rects the barely visible error overnight. It is pai staking craftsmanship, provided at ridiculous low prices.

Some weavers abandon the bundle of knots revolving cards of wood, which automatica create the pattern, and use the pedals-in-pit syste of throwing the shuttles, completing an inferi sari in three days. Others weave sari lengths an palo without changing warps, and add a metre the end, to be cut off and made into the matchi chola (tight-fitting bodice). Weavers of cotton sa are even speedier, tossing off one a day.

Weavers are especially easy to find in an around all southern towns – Hyderabad, Mysor Bangalore, Madras, Madurai, Thanjavur, Triva drum, etc. There are about 20,000 silk weavers an 10,000 cotton weavers in Kanchipuram alon Weavers are always thrilled, and a little abashed, that people should be interested in the work.

To order special pieces to be woven by a master raftsman, and to see methods and designs, conult the Weavers' Service Centres in Madras and anchipuram or ask at the Tourist Office. lthough it is nice to buy a sari direct from the eaver, it is best to buy them in big city shops, here choice is wide and the prices are reliable.

NDHRA PRADESH AND KARNATAKA

anjaras The colourful gypsy tribe, also known s Lambadis and Sugalis. They originally came om Rajasthan, where they traded salt and reared attle. Now the largest tribe in India, numbering bout 10 million and concentrated in Madhya radesh, Maharasthra, Andhra Pradesh and arnataka. They came to the Deccan as baggage arriers for the 17th-century Mughal armies, but ow follow their original occupation of cattle rear- ag.

They live in close-knit tandas (settlements) and peak their own language, gor boli. It is the family f a Banjara bridegroom, not the bride, that gives ae marriage dowry. Banjaras celebrate any event rith wild singing and dancing.

Their dress and jewellery is magnificently bold nd colourful. Women wear a bright, patchwork nga (full gathered skirt) of pink, mustard, emer- d green and piercing blue. They also wear a chola olouse) and an odni (shawl) edged with coins. ach has areas of beautiful embroidery which they ork themselves, sewing from bottom to top to aow the progress from earth to sky up the ladder f life, adding mirrors to ward off wild animals. Ieavy silver jewellery – up to four kilos on a voman – adorns ears, arms, nose, neck and nkles. Ivory and bone bangles stretch up to the rmpits. Tassels and ornaments are tied on to hair vorn in ringlets. The most characteristic elements f a Banjara woman's appearance are the huge, ngling, chandelier-like earrings and zig-zag ank- ts.

They move about the country in bullock carts ecorated like the caravans of European gypsies, to vhom they may be distantly related. They are aostly seen in the markets, and along the roads of orth Karnataka and around Hyderabad and, in- ongruously, working on road and construction tes. Pieces of their embroidery work and their wellery can be found in markets.

idri ware A technique of decorated metalwork nique to India, developed under the Mughals and amed after Bidar, in north Karnataka, where it is aought to have originated. Dishes, hookah bases,

boxes, ewers and other pieces are cast from an alloy of zinc, a little copper and tin, and sometimes lead. Each piece is then decorated with very fine arabes- ques, flowers, geometric patterns and sometimes scripts, the designs inlaid in silver, brass and, in the past, gold. The piece is coated with a paste of mud and sal ammoniac which, when later re- moved, reveals the metal, now a rich, matt black, the perfect foil to the gleaming inlay. Craftsmen work in the alleys around Charminar in Hyderabad and in Bider. However, pieces can be bought throughout India.

Pearls Adored by the Nizams, who ate them powdered, rubbed them over their bodies for good health and draped great chains of them around their necks. Hyderabad is still the pearl market of India, concentrated in a row of shops on Pertherghatty Road, near the Charminar. Here thousands of pearls arrive from Japan between December and March (the Gulf supplies have dried up).

Sorters divide this kachcha mal (raw stock) of unlustrous blobs according to size, shape and col- our (white, pink, blue, brown, etc.). A decision is taken whether to pierce the pearl horizontally or vertically. It is then clamped on to wood, drilled with a sharp needle using a very basic bow-and- string drill (pearls split easily), then cleaned in a solution of hydrogen peroxide and dried in the sunlight, inducing a chemical reaction which whitens it even more; the length of soaking and drying can vary between 15 and 50 days. The pearls are then washed, sorted, graded (according to shape, shine and colour) and strung on silk.

The sorting and grading is done in the shops, where women from all over India come to buy this year's pearls. Prices are a fifth of British prices: a two-string, classic necklace is around Rs1,200 –1,400; four strings of tiny pearls are Rs700–800; cluster earrings Rs100–200. Pearls can be bought by weight (enough for strings and matching ear- rings, bracelets and rings) as the best stringing and clasps are found in Bombay (see p. 127). Natural pearls are a better buy than cultured as they do not taint. Old pearls can be traded for new.

Sericulture According to some figures, 80% of Indian silk is grown in Karnataka, with Bangalore the centre of the sericulture market for India and for export. Special farms for breeding and rearing the silkworms are fascinating to see and open to visitors.

Japanese male moths are mated with local Mysore females for the best strains. (Tops of cocoons are merrily snipped off to demonstrate the aristocratic orange pupa.) After mating, the female is put on squared paper, covered with a conical hat (she is too shy to lay eggs in the light) and left for 24–30 hours, by which time she will have laid 400–600 eggs. She is then crushed, examined under a microscope and, if diseased, the eggs are destroyed. If not, they hatch after 10 days and are sold to the mulberry bush owner for 30 paise. He rears them to the cocoon stage, then sells them to the reeler, the person who twists the yarn and winds it on to reels.

Rearing is merely a question of satisfying the insatiable appetite of the worms for their 26–28 days of solid eating, during which time they moult four times and become 10–15cm long. They live entirely on freshly picked leaves from mulberry bushes which produce six crops a year, just about keeping pace with their hunger. Then the worms turn from white to yellow and furiously spin their cocoons for the next three or four days. In fact, they are discharging a viscous solution which dries to form fine fibres, each cocoon unravelling to 1,200 metres or so of silk yarn. The cycle is then complete. Of the several farms along the Bangalore–Mysore road, Tippu Silk Farm, founded 1912, is the oldest in Karnataka. It both breeds and rears and is open to visitors at all times of the day.

Reelers often live and work in the dyeing and weaving area of Bangalore. A taxi driver can always find one (several of his brothers and cousins will inevitably work in silk). The reeler's workers reel, double and twist the silk on thundering machinery in a boiling hot room – the heat increases the crispness of the silk. The reeler also prepares the warp threads for saris on a huge wooden wheel frame. Then the silk thread is steamed in a hot dustbin to prevent it untwisting. Reelers sell through the Government of Karnataka silk auctions. The weavers buy the silk and take it to their favourite dyers. As well as at the independent firms, all the processes can be seen at the Government of Karnataka Department of Sericulture in Bangalore.

THE NILGIRI HILLS

Spices A masala (blend of spices and herbs) is essential to every Indian dish and gives it the basic flavour. The meat and vegetables are added later, then the liquid. And India's spices, which improved food world-wide, were traded like gold with Greeks, Romans, Arabs and Chinese, then Portuguese, Dutch, French and British. It was the stranglehold on spices by the Arabs and the Venetian middlemen that inspired Vasco da Gama discovery of the sea route around the Cape of Good Hope (1498), Christopher Columbus's attempt th other way – when he bumped into America – an Magellan's maiden circumnavigation of the worl

The spices come from the South, mostly betwee the Kerala coast and the Nilgiris. Indeed, the wor curry is derived from kari, Tamil for a thin, spic sauce which enlivens the bland diet of rice. Pepp was, and is, the king of spices, grown on Kera homesteads and offered to the goddess of Kodu gallur Temple with bawdy songs and a big feast.

Cardamom, a member of the ginger famil grows in big, broad-leafed bushes in evergree mountain forest. The seeds sprout from the ba and are picked by women, dried and often used aphrodisiacs. Ginger and haldi (turmeric) are bo rhizomes. Ginger is used as a digestive. Haldi used as an antiseptic and by women to soften th skin. With those properties, 98% of the 100,00 tons of haldi produced in India annually is co sumed by the home market. Cinnamon looks li cassia (found in the north) and is the inner bark the lateral shoots of pruned trees, sold in tight curled quills.

Nutmeg and mace come from one tree, for th mace is the soft outer membrane of the nut whos kernel is the nutmeg. A pinch of nutmeg in teaspoon of honey should cure an upset stomac The best cashewnuts are grown in the Nilgiris ar along the west coast, right up to Goa.

Chillies, grown in Andhra Pradesh, and som other states, come in all sizes. The big ones a eaten as vegetables and called capsicums (probab introduced into India by the Portuguese). Mi paprika is crushed red capsicum. Red pepper stronger. Chilli powder is next up in strength ar whole chillies have the most fire. Most of these ca be seen growing in Kerala and on the Cardamo and Nilgiri slopes. Chillies are also seen in Andh Pradesh. All can be bought in the bazaars.

Coffee Traditionally believed to have been intr duced from Moka, the Arabian coffee centre, Mysore by an Arab Muslim saint, Haji Budan Bab to keep sufi mystics awake during all-night whi ing sessions. It was certainly here and in Kerala b the 1720s. Both climate and terrain proved perfe for growing coffee and ports such as Cochin ar Alleppey were already trading with Arabian ar Red Sea ports.

There are two main species of coffee bus arabica and robusta. Each has many differe arieties of bean such as Billigiris, Bababudans, hevaroys, Pulneys, Nilgiris, Malabar-Wynaad nd Naidubattam. The beans grow in pairs but if ere is a freak single bean it is called a Peaberry nd prized by connoisseurs. Although India only roduces 2.3% of the world market, Indian beans e highly sought after. Most beans are grown in arnataka, Kerala and Tamil Nadu.

The lush, green foliage of coffee bushes first roduces starry white flowers in March, then ber-es, which are picked by women. They are then ried for seven days, either with their husk, as herries', or without, as 'parchment'. Then they e cured, hand-sorted by specialists, graded, sted and finally marketed through the Coffee oard at Bangalore. Coffee bushes can be seen on wer hillsides (700–2,000m).

South Indians grind their beans fresh and make ery strong coffee, adding lots of hot milk and 1gar to make a sort of rich cappuccino. Small staurants serve good coffee, as do the string of idian Coffee Houses in Kerala. In big hotels, you ould be sure to ask for fresh Mysore coffee herwise instant coffee, which is now, sadly, con-dered more fashionable, is served automatically.

odas A small tribe living on the west slopes of e Nilgiris, who claim descent as the chosen peo-le of their creator, Aanu, and whose handsome en and women wander through and around oty, draped in toga-like puthukulis (shawls) and lver jewellery. Their lives revolve around tending eir sacred horned buffalo and maintaining a tall, onical temple that functions like a dairy. The ected temple priest, like a dairyman, puts the uffalo out to graze in the morning, brings them in night and is responsible for the milking and for aking butter and buttermilk. The tattooed Toda omen are not allowed near the temple-dairy or e buffalo, yet, rarely in India, they can choose eir own husbands, and even take several. While e men tend the buffalo and collect firewood, the omen gossip, wash their hair in buttermilk and ind it round bamboo to make long ringlets. And ey embroider their puthukulis in striking red, lue and black. The Todas live entirely on dairy roducts, berries and roots and they keep bees for oney. They are vegetarian but consider agricul-ire beneath the dignity of the chosen people, so ey come into Ooty to buy grains and rice in the arket.

ea Grown in the Nilgiris. It is neither of the uantity nor the quality of that in Darjeeling and orth-east India, but enough of the hills are covered in squat bushes to encourage curiosity and an explanatory visit to a tea estate.

Women pluck tea leaves in the morning, deliver full baskets about nine o'clock, and then go out again in the afternoon. The leaves are withered, rolled, sifted, fermented, dried, sorted and graded. The bigger the leaf, the better the flavour. Tea dust is the dregs. Visitors to a tea estate soon become tea snobs. To them, cheap teabags full of dust are dismissed as a thing of the past. Glen Morgan Tea Estate at Paikara, near Ooty, is one of the few where the owners, Mr and Mrs Vadera, still live on the estate, in an enchanting ginger-bread bungalow. Tea-maker Mr Sadanand is happy to explain every process of the Indian and Japanese teas grown there. He also has some leaf liquor for visitors to taste. Open 9am–3pm, best before 10am for action.

KERALA

African Moss The enemy waterweed which is threatening to throttle beautiful Kuttanadu, the 260 sq km area of backwaters, paddy fields and coconuts palms between Alleppey, Kottayam and Quilon. The velvety leaf and its cushion of inter-twined fibrous roots have spread at an alarming rate over the last 15 years, with a drastic effect on locals' lives. It has so polluted the water that it cannot be used for drinking or washing. By pre-venting the sun's rays penetrating the water, aqua-tic life and fish have died. It has blocked up rivulets and canals so that boats, often the only means of transport, cannot get through. And no-one has devised a means of controlling it.

Kerala temple festivals Every temple holds a festival for its deity between late December and early June, so it is possible to bump into one every day. Each is a local variation of a set form of ritual combined with a ceremonial procession, the big-gest being Trichur's Pooram. The deity, symbol-ised by a golden shield, is paraded down the middle of a main road on the gaily caparisoned back of the biggest and tallest elephant, escorted by other suitably dressed elephants (usually four or six) and entertained with loud drums, cymbals and horns and trumpets.

Toddy Fermented liquor made from the sap of coconut palm, collected just before the palm blos-soms. (It will not then produce fruits.) Toddy men can be seen shinning up the tall palms before sunrise and after sunset, knives in teeth, earthen-ware bowls around their necks. They slash the trunk just beneath the leaves and collect the sap.

Drunk fresh, it is sweet, refreshing and very good for the stomach. After fermenting with sugar for a few hours, it is like beer. After a few more hours it is a bitter, intoxicating liquor. Toddy shops are little dens. If encouraged to taste, beware of adulterated liquor.

Chinese fishing nets Weird contraptions made up of large, delicate teak frames and nets perched above the water like giant praying spiders. They are an efficient and effective way of fishing the backwaters from Cochin right down to Quilon. They were possibly introduced by Chinese traders, like much else in Kerala – deep roofs of houses, temple architecture, conical fishermen's hats and Chinese paper and porcelain.

The structure is simple but expensive to set up and costs about Rs5,000. A combination of cords, pulleys and weights is attached to the two strong poles that soar into the air from the platform. From their tops hang four wooden talons, the netting suspended between their tips. It takes four men to operate the seemingly fragile gadget, working the weights and pulleys to swing the net down into the water. Perhaps 15 minutes afterwards, they haul up the catch – sardines, mullet, crab, lobster and fresh-water fish. Like everything else in Kerala, the fishermen have their own union to protect themselves from the net owners or, as they put it, the 'stranglehold clutches of exploitation'.

Kathakali Literally, story-play. The most important of the classical dance–drama styles, derived from a form of yoga and revived from almost extinction about 40 years ago. Dancers with weird, elaborate and brightly coloured make-up and costumes perform a religious pantomime dance to recount stories from the great epics. Originally the ritual lasted throughout the night. A dancer (always a man) trains for about 20 years, starting in early childhood. He is kept in peak condition with special aryavaidya massages.

The performance is worship which begins with a good four hours of preparation. The make-up to assume the stylised character is in the strictly traditional colours, head-dress and costume. All make-up and costume is prepared especially for the dancer, using minerals, vegetables and woods. It is all highly symbolic and applied in a fixed order. A green face denotes the pacha character, the hero king or a god such as Krishna, who wears a crown and a white frill from ear to ear. Thadi (beard) is a demon character, whose face is black, with a red beard, and who wears an outsized crown, false nose and a big frill. He is also a comic character.

The actor is dressed by assistants in a gathered skirt like a tutu, a jacket, jewellery and head-dress. He slips a seed from the cunlappuvu plant inside the lower lid of each eye to turn the white a flaming red.

The actual dance, lit by a brass lamp and accompanied by musicians, is as formal as the preparation, yet highly dramatic. It takes years to learn and demands extraordinary muscle control to contort the face and eyes into exaggerated, caricature expressions and to perform sudden leaps, spins and freeze-balances.

Leading exponents to look out for include Guru Gopinath and Chatunni Paniker. The easiest place to see a kathakali performance, including the make-up, is Cochin, where there are daily shows with explanation and narration, at Art Kerala, Menon & Krishnan Annexe, in a lane off Chitter Road (tel: 39471); performances 6pm make-up, 7pm dance, and at Kathakali Theatre, Cochin Cultural Centre, Durbar Hall Ground (6.30pm).

Krishnayattam, a precursor of Kathakali, is performed at Guruvayur temple, outside Trichur, every clear night from October to April, starting around 10pm. Mohiniattam, meaning dance of the enchantress, is suitably graceful, fluid and seductive. It is found in programmes of Kathakali and Bharata Natyam (see p. 187).

TAMIL NADU

Ayyanars Huge, brightly painted, heraldic terracotta figures of equestrian deities with their horses and elephants, found on village outskirts throughout Tamil Nadu, always with a tiny shrine. They protect the villages from all calamities such as plagues, hauntings and hurricanes. They make barren land fertile, cure illness and act as village watchmen at night – hence the horse, elephant or dog for the deity. A priest looks after each group, performing puja at noon and accepting offerings on behalf of the deities: milk, coconuts, fabric, silver, even prized cattle. Extra money is offered for special requests, followed by thanks when they are granted: either a celebration at the shrine, penitent fire-walking, even more penitent swinging on a hook driven through the shoulder muscle (neither ordeal seems to leave scars) or the offering of another horse. Especially prolific between Madras and Madurai.

The most sensational ayyanar sanctuary is near Pudukatai, outside Tiruchchirapalli, at Namur Samdran: hundreds of horses, often three deep, form a half-km avenue through a deserted wood.

ome are old and rotting, others are newer. They re increased each year when the nearby villagers ake a new horse, paint it pink, green, yellow and lue, and offer it to the earth.

tone-carving Practised on the local granite roughout the state but especially at Thanjavur Tanjore) and Mahabalipuram. The government is nding the revival of the craft, setting up centres hich now attract top carvers who make sculp- res for Hindu temples world-wide. All the la- orious processes are done in one compound, from ipping smooth the granite block and drawing the esign in red chalk, to cutting, chipping, rubbing nd polishing the shape – just polishing a capital ith emery takes two to three weeks. There is even resident blacksmith to sharpen tools.

harata Natyam Probably the oldest classical dian dance form, performed for centuries by evadasis (girls dedicated to south Indian tem- les), following religious texts. It suffered con- derably after the British passed the Devadas Act utlawing the devadasi practice. However, the ance was revived early this century.

It is performed solo, by a woman, who begins ith alarippu, a dance symbolising the body un- lding as an offering to the gods. She then com- ines nritta, pure dance, with nritya, emotions escribed with bold face and hand expressions, to escribe the many moods of a young girl's love, as counted in the poems. The poems are sung by e nattuvanar (conductor), and accompanied by usicians.

The dancer's face may be by turn hurt, laughing, ensive, perturbed or solemn; her hands tell of the oon, anticipation of a love letter, lotus flowers or bee collecting pollen. Strong rhythms are crucial, eightened by the dancer jingling her ankle bells fast and strong, often stamping, footsteps, to ittily answer the nattuvanar or musicians.

The centre of Bharata Natyam is Madras. Lead- g dancers include Leela Samson, Sonal Mansing, harati Shivaji, Alarmel Valli, S. Kanaka, Yamini rishnamurti, Shanta Rao, Indranai Rehman, yjayantimala and Kamla and Padma Subraman- am. Balasaraswati, the last of the great devadasi xponents (see p. 214), died in 1984.

There are daily performances at the Kalakshetra entre, Museum Theatre, Music Academy, Raja nnamalai Hall and elsewhere (the Tourist Office dvises on which dancer to see). There are also egular performances in Bombay (Kala Mandir) nd Delhi (Triveni Kala Sangam).

Related to Bharata Natyam are the Tamil Nadu

Bhagavata Mela dance–drama and Kuravanji dance–opera and the Andhra Pradesh Kuchipudi.

The cities: Where to stay; out and about

Few southern cities offer enough diversity for a long stay. Even Madras and Bangalore, the fourth and fifth largest cities in India, are unlikely to hold the tourist for more than two or three days. In addition, the South has few hotels with pampered palace luxury, service and facilities of the sort found in the North. And the really interesting places are often far enough from big cities to merit an overnight stay in a modest hotel. This way, travelling is much more comfortable, allowing you to avoid retracing your journey at the end of a hot day. So, the key to the South is Out and About, not Where to Stay.

The Deccan: Andhra Pradesh

HYDERABAD

Former capital of the Croesus-rich Nizams who maintained their isolated, Muslim, extravagant court life right up until the 1950s (officially stop- ping in 1947). They ruled a land bigger than France, whose population was (and is) mainly Hindu and very poor. Today, Hyderabad is the sprawling, crowded and decaying sixth largest city in India and twin capital (with ugly Secunderabad) of Andhra Pradesh, a huge state that takes in most of the Nizam's land plus the Telegu-speaking part of Madras state to the east. The artist Andrew Logan likened it to a great city which has been flattened. Historically, power in Andhra Pradesh moved from Buddhist Ashok to the Hindu Chaulukyas and Cholas before the Muslims arrived in the 14th century.

Hyderabad was laid out on the banks of the Musi River in 1591 by Mohammed Quli (ruled 1580– 1612), when the water supply of Golconda city-fort became inadequate. It was a strict grid plan of two broad intersecting streets with a big arch at the crossing (the Charminar), some 14,000 shops, schools, mosques, baths and caravanserais lining the streets. In 1652, the traveller Tavernier com- pared it to Orleans, 'well built and opened out' and by 1672 Abbé Carré found it 'the centre of all trade in the East'. Mohammed Quli was fourth of the Qutb Shahi dynasty (1512–1687) which finally lost out to Mughal Emperor Aurangzeb.

After Aurangzeb's death in 1707, the Mughal empire collapsed and in 1713 the Mughal-appointed viceroy of Hyderabad, Mir Kamruddin Khan, given the title Nizam-ul-Mulk (Regulator of the Land), declared independence and initiated the Asaf Jahn dynasty. Their riches, from land and gifts, made them some of the wealthiest individuals in the world. Gold bricks were piled in stacks and chests overflowed with diamonds and pearls.

Stories, some apocryphal, abounded. When the tenth and last Nizam, who ruled 1911–1950, was offered an egg-sized diamond by a jeweller, he pondered for a moment on how to use it, then asked for six more, to make a set of buttons. A 280-carat diamond was used as a paperweight. He was rumoured to be a miserly host yet he presented the Royal Air Force with a complete squadron of Hurricane fighters on the outbreak of the Second World War. The nobility lived in eccentric style: a Minister of Justice was reputed to rise at 4.30am, exercise with dumb-bells, swallow two huge pills of opium, go riding, then return for a hearty tumbler of chicken soup.

As the main Muslim court of India after the collapse of the Mughal Empire, Muslim nobles and merchants from the North as well as Muslim immigrants came south to cocoon themselves in their traditions, cuisine, dress and culture – an introverted Muslim refuge in the Hindu South. Old Hyderabad still has a 19th-century, courtly air about it. But it may not exist much longer: the Andhra Pradesh Government want to put a bulldozer through the lot to 'modernise' the only part of their capital left with any character.

THE HARD FACTS   Airport 7km from Hyderabad centre. Two nice hotels, and Oberoi have one under construction. For service and efficiency, stay at the *Banjara Hotel*, Banjara Hills (tel: 221616; telex: 0155-329 CAR IN; cable: WELCOTEL); concrete, lakeside building, under redecoration, run by the Welcomgroup, recently vastly improved under new staff; 132 rooms, the best overlook the lake. All mod. cons include a good pool, doctor, shopping arcade, travel desk and beauty salon. Excellent food in coffee shop, restaurant, on terrace and beside lake. It includes nightly barbecues and the best Hyderabadi Mughlai cooking in town – heavily patronised by discerning locals and government ministers.

For character, go to the *Ritz Hotel*, Hillfort Palace (tel: 33571; telex: 0155 215; cable: RITZ); an ex-palace built in Scottish baronial style for Princess Nilouphar, daughter-in-law of the Nizam. It has been run as a hotel for 30 years by the Ritz chain formerly associated with the Veeraswamy's Indian restaurant in London. It has 36 rooms, only some with individually controlled air-conditioning. Car rental, hard tennis court and a large lawn and pool grounds nice for tea and drinks. Locals report food has deteriorated. The problems of converting a small palace manifest themselves in the rooms. Some are poky with new dreary decor. The ground floor of the main section is best, in particular nos 9 and 24 which are large and lofty-ceilinged with old fittings. The two pavilions are nice too.

The *Rock Castle Hotel*, Road No.6, Banjara Hill (tel: 33541/2/3; cable: ROCKCASTLE) was a favourite with the Raj and still has a loyal clientele and strong character, but it is rather far from the city centre. 22 rooms, extensive gardens.

Tourist information is scanty but best from the ITDC office, 3-6-150 Lidcap Building, Himayat Nagar (tel: 220730). They run unsatisfactory day-long tours of the city (8am–6.30pm) which give a fleeting look at Golconda Fort and waste time at the gardens and the zoo. Good guides are rented from the Information Bureau, Lidcap House (tel: 223384/5). The best news and entertainments information is found in *The Deccan Chronicle* (performing arts are at Ravindra Bharati). There is no good guide book. The bookshop A. A. Hussain, on Abid (also known as M G) Road, is an essential stopping-point for stocking up on information if travelling south through Karnataka.

The Banjara will arrange sailing on Husain Sagar Lake and, for the desperate, golf is available on very brown greens. Indira Park is pleasant and has rowing. There is a lot of local publicity for dreary lakes, dams and reservoirs. Quite naturally, the Indians get very excited about water; Europeans usually get quite enough back home.

OUT AND ABOUT   The best way to see Hyderabad's buildings is to start by going out to the earlier city of Golconda (11.5km, see below). Back in town, **Charminar** is the central landmark of the old city, a carved, marble triumphal arch with upstairs mosque and minarets, built in 1591. (There are excellent views from the top.)

Surrounding it is one of the best bazaars in India and certainly the most interesting and colourful in the South. There are old chemists with wooden boxes of spices, herbs, powders and scales; walls of rainbow-coloured bangles; piles of lunghis; Banjara women jangling their goblet-sized earrings; huge coloured tassels for decorating the hair; Muslim women jostling to buy bangles, silver and thick brocades; smart ladies buying pearls; and antique shops selling off courtiers' clothes and trinkets. In the tiny alleys, craftsmen work on fine silver filigree and bidri ware.

Nearby is the huge Mecca Masjid (1614–87), the Nizams' tombs in a row on the left of the courtyard, and the Asar Khana (relic house), with beautiful tiles. Few of the old city palaces in the surrounding streets can be visited. However, to see the huge, extravagant and immaculate Falaknuma Palace, built in 1872 by a noble and after 1911 occasionally used as a guest-house by the Nizam, apply to the Chief of Protocol, Secretariat, Secretariat Road.

For an idea of the opulent, nawabi taste, the extraordinary **Salar Jung museum** displays the vast collection formed by Nawab Mir Yousuf Ali Khan Salar Jung III (1889–1949) and his ancestors, whose family produced five of the Nizams' prime ministers. Originally housed in Salar Jung's palace, the Diwan Deori, it was moved in 1968 (and reportedly much pillaged) to fill 38 galleries of a dull, pink, concrete box with some 40,000 objects. Salar Jung travelled in Europe and the Middle East for 40 years, box of gold in hand, to buy whatever tickled his well-trained eye, be it fine Indian jade, French ormolu furniture or high Victorian oil-paintings.

Particularly impressive are the ground-floor rooms containing family heirlooms, the textiles, lacquer, sculpture, decorative arts and miniature paintings. Upstairs are rooms of jade, bidri ware and armour. And just a fraction is on view. The corridor storage cupboards are stacked from floor to ceiling. Café, reference library, good publications. Open Sat.–Thurs., 10am–5pm.

The Government Archaeological Museum in the Public Gardens has sculpture, bidri ware, coins, arms and armour and textiles (open Tues.–Sun., 10.30am–5pm). The fine British Residency, like a vast British stately home, was built by the Nizam for James Achilles Kirkpatrick to designs by John Russell in 1803. (It is now a college, but can be visited.) Kirkpatrick was so popular with the Nizam that he was adopted as a son and became the only person to represent the British and the Nizam simultaneously; but his marriage to a beautiful Hyderabadi aristocrat alarmed the Governor General, Lord Wellesley, so much that he

narrowly escaped a public inquiry. Sunsets are best seen from the Birla Mandir, the modern, dazzling white hilltop temple which was built by the Birla Foundation in 1966–76 of Rajasthan marble, decorated with reliefs of the Ramayana and surrounded by statue-studded, lush gardens.

RESTAURANTS Best Hyderabadi food is at the *Banjara*; then at two restaurants on Basheer Bagh: *Mughal Durbar* and *Nilgara*. The best biryani can be found at *Hotel Medina*, near the Charminar. Cheap and crammed with locals. Haleen (lamb cooked with wheat) is a special Hyderabadi dish. (For more on Mughlai food, see Delhi eating section, pp. 55–6). Special local sweetmeats are ashrafi (gold coin), with a Mughal stamp on each one, and badam ki jali (almond nest).

The adventurous should try one of the many Irani cafés for nihari, the sustaining traditional breakfast. Try the *Rainbow Restaurant* on Abid Road (also called M G Road) and order paya (chicken soup), ladled from a huge cauldron, shirman (bread) and pauna (rich tea made with milk), served 5–8am (see also Bombay eating, p. 122). The really brave polish it off with a digestive paan from across the road. Good south Indian food is found at the several branches of *Kamat*, the best one being at Ravandrapati. Locals patronise the *Blue Diamond* Chinese restaurant.

SHOPPING AND CRAFTS The bazaar has everything to buy, as well as the pearl market, bidri work and silversmithing to watch. Lepakshi Handicrafts Emporium at Gun Foundry (top of Abid Road, good packaging and shipping) has good bidri ware, including cuff links, dishes and boxes. There are kondapalli (sandalwood toys); Andhra Pradesh fabrics such as ikat weaves from Pochhampalli or Koyyalagudam; striped and checked silk from Dharmavaram; dark fabrics from Narayanpet; the broad double-stripe palos of Madhavream saris; and himru (cotton and silk mixtures), worn by Muslim women who are not permitted to wear pure silk.

The assistants at Lepakshi Handicrafts can put visitors in touch with the AP Weavers Cooperative and can advise on which weaving villages to visit. For instance, Pochhampalli is 60km; Koyyalagudam 80km. The big Handloom House is on Mukharam Jahi (Salar Jung) Road. There are more fabric shops on Nampali Road. Jamma Raat flea market is held early Thursday morning near the Charminar.

GOLCONDA

11.5km from Hyderabad. A magnificent, deserted fort-city of the Qutb Shahi kings, built on a steep, granite hill. In the 14th century the Hindu Kakatiya kings of Warangal gave the modest hill fort to the Muslim Bahmani kings whose capitals were Gulbarga, then Bidar (see below).) The Bahmani kingdom was divided between five governors who each declared independence at the turn of the 15th century, initiating the dynasties of Bidar, Berar, Ahmadnagar, Bijapur and Golconda.

Sultan Quli Qutb Shah (1512–43), the first of seven Qutb Shahi rulers, and his two successors, the brothers Jamshed Quli (1543–50) and Ibrahim Quli (1550–80), built the fort which was lost to Emperor Aurangzeb after his long siege of 1687. It followed the pattern of Gulbarga and Bidar fortifications but was larger and more impregnable. The legendary diamond bazaars (supplied from mines at Parteal and Kolur, 130km away) lined the road up to the Fateh Darwaza (double gateway) guarded by Abyssinians. A curtain wall across the gateway made it difficult for enemy elephants to gather momentum.

Inside, enough buildings remain to reconstruct in the mind's eye the complete layout and lifestyle of the rich and wealthy state. There is a sophisticated Persian wheel water system; hot and cold water pipes; Turkish baths; bazaars; a ministers' hall with built-in shelves for the files; massive weights for measuring out elephant food; ingenious acoustics between gateway and citadel; royal palaces with scented gardens; a swimming pool and secret hide-outs for the watchful eunuch guards of the zenana; a people's complaints room; natural air-conditioning and roof-gardens in the hilltop citadel; and even fragments of a celadon china dinner service.

Nearby are the more complete and just as impressive domed tombs of the royals, silhouetted against the clear blue Deccan sky and set in a beautiful garden of blossoming trees and clouds of bougainvillea. They are based on the tombs at Bidar but are much more flamboyant and baroque, with stucco ornament, fancy pinnacles and blown-up, bulbous domes. A ruler would have his tomb built during his lifetime, often with a small mosque for the last rites beside it; then it was furnished with carpets, chandeliers, gold brocades, silver censers and manuscripts. Good little guide-book. Small museum nearby. The Fort and tombs are best visited for a long morning, taking a guide. Exposed and hot, so take a hat.

WARANGAL AND HANMKONDA

157km north-east of Hyderabad. Definitely a challenging day trip from Hyderabad for architecture buffs. It is also worthwhile for those going south to see the wonderful Chalukyan temples at Aihole, Badami and Pattadakal. The journey passes paddy fields, piles of perilously balanced giant boulders, old forts and every sort of people from bejewelled Banjaras to rats-tail-coiffed fakirs (religious men).

The Kakatiyas ruled from their mud-brick fort at Warangal from the 12th to the 14th centuries, until conquered by the Tughlaqs of Delhi. They took the Chalukyans' architectural style to new heights, seen in the *Hanmkonda temple*, built in 1163 by King Rudra Deva. The lowroofed, carved building has a massive, monolithic Nandi bull in front of it and a hall of elaborately carved columns, giving it the nickname 'Thousand-pillar Temple'. (South Indian temples often have a 'Thousand-pillar Temple' but few have anywhere near that number of columns.) Badrakali temple is on a hillock between Hanmkonda and Warangal. The *fort* at Warangal is spectacular, with massive walls and a free-standing gateway. The interior of the fort is strewn with quantities of black stone sculpture.

The really keen travellers go on to the elaborately carved Ramappa Temple (1234) at *Palampet* (77km further north-east), one of the finest pieces of Deccan architecture. It is best to go by car or bus. There is a good ITDC trip (excluding Palampet) in a fast, air-conditioned bus, but they need some persuasion to admit that it exists.

The Deccan: Karnataka

BIDAR

110km north-west of Hyderabad, 40 km north-east of Gulbarga. Described by historian Simon Digby as 'a sensational stone fort built on a natural bluff rising from the plain'. Bidar was the capital of the Bahmani kingdom 1428–c 89, then of the Barid Shahis until Ibrahim Adil Shah II of Bijapur annexed it in 1619. Besieged by Aurangzeb in 1656 and under a series of Mughal governors until 1724 when it was swallowed up by the Nizams. The *tombs* on the plains outside the town are magnificent. There are eight fine Bahmani ones at Ashtur, their interiors decorated with calligraphic and floral designs in gold and bright colours. A watchman opens them and supplies mirror to reflect the light into the tombs (open daily, 8am–

pm). The lesser Baridi tombs are to the west, on the Nanded road.

Inside the walls, the old town of Bidar surrounds the soaring, green and yellow tiled Madrasa (University), founded in 1472 by Mohammad Gawan, merchant traveller and scholar. He equipped it with a library of 3,000 manuscripts and made it a centre for scholars from throughout the Muslim world. You can see bidri work being done in the narrow lanes.

The *Inner Fort*, mostly built by Mohammad Shah 1482–1518), is entered through a massive double gateway. Inside, there is a complete city fort. Inside the entrance, on the left, is the Rangin Mahal (Colourful Palace), whose rooms are exquisitely decorated with tiles, inlaid mother-of-pearl, carved granite and carved wooden pillars. If locked, the museum curator has a key. Good views from roof. There are also baths, a mosque, palaces, audience halls and pavilions, many with coloured tiles, paintings and carving intact. The little museum in the middle is excellent (open daily, 8am–5pm).

To stay overnight, the best place is the State-run *Barid Shahi* (tel: 571); or *Habshi Kot Guest House* (apply to Executive Engineer, Bidar).

GULBARGA

110km from Bidar; 145km from Bijapur, along a road that descends through rolling hills of wheat fields, with rather wild-looking locals clad only in a loin-cloth. It was the Bahmani capital from 1347 until the move to Bidar in 1428. Ala-ud-din Hasan Bahman Shah, a Persian adventurer from the Delhi court, established the Bahmani dynasty after he left the service of mad Mohammad Tughlaq, the Delhi Sultan who in 1327 forced the Delhi populace to move to a new capital at Daulatabad in the northern Deccan (see p. 46). The architecture of Gulbarga, Bidar and Golconda has a distinct style, merging Persian and Delhi Sultanate elements.

There are four interesting things to see, all to the north of the modern, industrial town. Bullocks with incredibly long, red-painted horns loaf about in the wide, muddy moat around the *fort* which now contains only the citadel, some of the towers and the Jami Masjid (1367) – very unusual in being a pillared hall entirely domed over, lacking an open courtyard. (Local legend attributes its design to a Spaniard.) Nearby are five big, black, domed cubes which are royal *tombs*.

Two more are at the end of a bazaar street, beside a dazzling white *Dargah* (Shrine) of the Muslim Chishti saint, Gesudaraz (1321–1422), who migrated here from Nizamuddin in Delhi. Its plastered exterior is a foil to the riot of lace-like red, yellow and silver arabesques covering the interior walls. (Women have to peep through the doorway.) The tomb of his favourite wife, opposite, is also covered in murals.

In the town, the historic *covered bazaar* and side-streets are packed with activity for the Saturday market. Peasants flock in from the surrounding plains, bringing their bullocks, carts and wares, exchanging gossip, buying supplies and having a good time. To stay overnight, or just to eat, go to *Hotel Pariwar*, Station Road (tel: 1422/1522), spotlessly clean, south Indian food only.

BIJAPUR

145km from Gulbarga; 120km from Badami; about 250km from Hampi, through dusty roads, past Banjara women in all their red, blue and saffron finery, limbs sparkling with ivory; past men with deep saffron or dazzling pink turbans. Bijapur is a perfect provincial city, a pre-industrial time-warp. Life here ambles along gently, in the fabulous walled Muslim city of broad streets, majestic buildings, lawns, ex-palaces, old houses with carved balconies, ruins and mosques. Transport is by bicycle rickshaw or by tongas with jingling bells, driven by children who constantly honk-honk their squeezy horns. There is hardly a car. Banjara gypsies, processions of white bullocks doused with pink water, an antique palanquin, and pipers and drummers add splashes of colour to the bustling evening bazaars.

The Chalukyans ruled Bijapur until 1198 when their kingdom was divided between the Hoysalas in the south and the Yadavas in the north. The city was annexed to Ala-ud-din Khilji's Delhi Sultanate in 1318 with his son as Governor. Then, when the Tughlaqs took over Delhi and Sultanate power in the South waned, two kingdoms rose in this area, divided by the River Krishna: Bahmani (capital Gulbarga, then Bidar) in the north and Vijayanagar (capital Vijayanagar, or Hampi) in the south. In 1489 Yusuf Adil Khan, Governor of Bijapur for the Bahmanis, declared independence, founding the Adil Shahi dynasty, which lasted until 1686. The four other governors did the same sooner or later, at Bidar, Berar, Ahmadnagar and Golconda – only once joining forces to crush the mighty Vijayanagars at the Battle of Talikota in 1565.

The reign of Ali Adil Shah I (1557–79) marked Bijapur's rise. He expanded and consolidated the kingdom, laid Bijapur's waterworks, built the central moated *citadel* of halls, palaces, pavilions and gardens, encouraged the arts and built the *Jami Masjid* to commemorate the Talikota victory. (See the painted mihrab behind a black curtain.) Under his successor, Ibrahim Adil Shah II (1580–1626), Bijapur reached its political, cultural and territorial zenith. The kingdom stretched right to Mysore. Mark Zebrowski compares Ibrahim to Akbar and calls him 'the greatest patron of the arts the Deccan produced'. *Ibrahim Rauza*, the exquisite walled tomb and mosque of the ruler and his family, is just one of the sublime buildings he constructed. The exterior is covered with faded floral murals and carved Arabic calligraphy.

Then began the decline. His son, Mohammad Adil Shah (1626–56), built the huge-domed, ponderous *Gol Gumbaz* for his mausoleum. The dome is thought to be second in size only to St Peter's, Rome. (Exceptional views from the roof outside the whispering gallery.) It is set in a pretty garden, with a gatehouse now housing the museum which has old Bijapur carpets and paintings upstairs (open Sat.–Thurs., 10am–5pm). Then came over-stretched extravagance at the end: the soaring arches of the *Bara Kaman*, Ali Adil Shah II's even bigger tomb (wonderful at sunrise), which was still unfinished when the dynasty fell to the Mughal, then Nizam, overlords.

It is best to allow at least two days to see the many fine buildings, hiring as transport a rickshaw boy who will wait at each building. Most are open constantly; a few 8am–5.30pm. Stay at the Karnataka state-run *Hotel Adil Shahi* (tel: 934); simple, clean rooms around a central garden courtyard with cascades of bougainvillea. The bad food can be supplemented with fruit and sweetmeats from the market. Otherwise, eat at the *Hotel Tourist* or the *Hotel Midland*. Adil Shahi is the only hotel that is not smelly and dirty, so book. If desperate, the ITDC hotel is opposite the Adil Shahi. Helpful Tourist Office in the Adil Shahi (open Mon.–Sat., 10.30am–1.30pm; 2.15–5.30pm). As at Gulbarga and Bidar, there is no good guide book or book shop, so arrive prepared.

AIHOLE, PATTADAKAL AND BADAMI:

The three sites are very close to one another and lie 120km from Bijapur; 100km from Hubli; 150km from Hampi. Here is to be found some of the earliest Hindu architecture and the foundation of the achievements that followed: three clusters of glorious, well-preserved *Chalukyan caves and temples*. They are all cleaned and maintained within spick and span lawns and blossoming trees. Round about are peaceful rural farms. The bullocks' horns are decorated with big pompoms and bells. And there are delightful children (who, for once, do not ask for coins or pens), itinerant musicians and the occasional overflowing cartload of villagers full of festive gaiety.

The early Chalukya kings, sworn enemies of the Pallavas, became powerful rulers in the central Deccan from the 4th to the 8th centuries. Aihole was their first capital, replaced by Badami from the reign of Pulakesin I (543–44) (who marked his accession by a horse sacrifice) until 757 when the dynasty was overthrown by the Rashtrakutas. Pattadakal's importance was as the second capital, religious centre and coronation city from the 7th to 9th centuries.

Aihole Aihole is 46km from Badami, 32km from Pattadakal. Here, the earlier temples are simple and squat, with heavy, flat roofs. Yet they are decorated with pierced stone windows and columns crisp as if turned on a vast lathe. There are sculptured images of loving couples, rosettes and friezes. Lad Khan Temple is probably the earliest. Meguti, Kontigudi and the circular Durg are progressively more complex until they acquire a tower over the shrine. The last to be built has stunning reliefs on the ambulatory and a developed shikara (tower). This looks forward to the northern, Indo-Aryan Hindu architecture. To stay overnight in this delightful, remote setting, go to the *Tourist Bungalow*; clean and simple. They will prepare meals for passing visitors. Order on arrival so that then it is ready when you have finished seeing the temples.

Pattadakal Badami 14km; Aihole 32km. The buildings are now higher and more complex; sculpture has taken off. Most impressive are: the large Lokeshwari (or Virupaksha) Temple, covered in lively sculptures recounting the major battles of the great Mahabharata and Ramayana epics and depicting Chalukya social life; and the Mallikarjuna Temple (*c* 740), whose carvings concentrate on the Bhagavata Purana, the story of Krishna. There are also many carvings of gently swaying, loving couples. Both temples are built in a nascent Dravidian style, which was already being developed under the Pallava dynasty (5th–8th centuries) in Tamil Nadu (known then as Dravidadesh). Others are in the Indo-Aryan style of the North, such as Papanath Temple (*c* 680). About 1km from the temple compound, in the

adami direction, is a Jain temple with two beauti-
ul stone elephants. There is no accommodation.

adami Badami is 46km from Aiole, 14km from-
attadakal. The only lively town of the three. The
ap-bashing of women washing clothes in the tank
nan-made lake) and their gossip and singing echo
ll round the sheer cliffs rising high either side.
eside the water, bullocks, orange rickshaws and
hildren squeeze between the tightly-packed,
hite-washed houses, which have exterior stairs
ading to the roof.

The five large rock-cut cave temples in the south-
vest cliff have magnificent sculptures of giant-
ized gods, so vivacious they seem about to leap
ut for a dance. After the second cave, at the top of
erilously steep steps, is a ruined fort area with
ncredible views. (Try to avoid the unofficial cave
uides.) On the other side of the tank lie the
ristine and fascinating museum and the water-
ide Bhutanath Temples. There are more temples
nd ruins up the cliff, which is topped by Malegitti
hivalaya Temple. To stay overnight, the nicest
laces are the *Tourist Bungalow*, clean but only two
uites, so be sure to book; or there is the state-run
halukkya Hotel next door, also clean. Here it is
mportant to make a fuss over being given boiled
vater to drink and, if you ask, they will make fresh,
trong morning coffee. There is reasonable local
ood at *Laxmi Vilas* restaurant, next to the tonga
tand. The Archaeological Department and Tourist
)ffice are both useless, so arrive prepared.

IAMPI (VIJAYANAGAR)

50km from Badami; 350km from Bangalore.
'alatial capital of the Vijayanagars, the largest
mpire in India's history. At its height under
<rishnadevaraya (1509–29), the city rivalled Rome
n splendour and controlled almost all of India
outh of the Krishna and Tungabhadra Rivers. The
/ijayanagars rose at the same time as the Bahma-
is. While fighting in the Deccan, the Sultanate
rmy took two local Telegu princes prisoner,
rought them to Delhi, converted them to Islam
nd sent them back south to restore Sultanate
uthority.

Once that was done, the princes, Harihara and
3ukka, broke loose to establish their own kingdom
n 1336 – and reverted to Hinduism. In 1346 their
victory over the Hoysalas made them pre-eminent
n the South. Harihara planned and built the
magnificent new city of Vijayanagar (City of
Victory), which became the capital in 1343.

The city was vast: 33 sq km within seven concen-

tric lines of fortifications, sustaining a population
of about half a million and alive with international
bazaars that impressed European travellers and
were reputed to sparkle with, literally, piles of
gold. Modest sized buildings were embellished
with profuse and sumptuous carvings, described
by the architectural historian, Percy Brown, as 'a
range of ideals, sensations, emotions, prodi-
galities, abnormalities, of forms and formlessness,
and even eccentricities, that only a super-
imaginative mind could create . . .' He compares it
to the Baroque period in Europe as the 'supremely
passionate flowering of the Dravidian style'.

Wealth came in from controlling the spice trade
to the south, the cotton trade to the south-east,
clearing surrounding forests for agriculture, elaborate hydraulic engineering for irrigation and, of
course, the levying of a land-tax. And wealth went
out on imported horses for the cavalry and a
mercenary army of a million (many of whom were
Turks). Tragedy struck in 1565 when four of the
five independent Deccan Sultans that had split up
the Bahmani kingdom finally joined forces to win a
crushing victory at the Battle of Talikota. (It was a
short-lived victory as the Mughals in Delhi already
had their eye on the South.)

Today, the deserted buildings of the ruined city
straddle the barren hillocks piled with huge Karnataka boulders, all glowing fiery orange at sunset.
Down beside the Tungabhadra River is *Hampi
bazaar*, worth visiting first. In the bazaar is the
bookshop, Aspiration Stores. It is run by the helpful Guthi brothers and stocks A. H. Longhurst's
good guide, *Hampi Ruins*, lots of other useful
books, post-cards and, by 1985, will have a decent,
detailed map of the ruins. Hampi Tourist Counter,
on the same side, supplies useless guides and a
joke map and is to be avoided. Here also is the main
temple complex.

After this, it is best to set off on foot, bicycle or by
car, to seek out the Hajari Rama Temple which has
wonderful carvings of dancing girls and scenes
from the Ramayana. The palace throne platform is
coated in exuberant carving. There are majestic
elephant stables, the queens' bath house and much
more. It is worth going up through the banana
groves to the Vitthala Temple, with its richly
carved animal columns, for sunset.

The most pleasant place to stay is *Hampi Power
Station Guest House*, 3km from Kamalapuram. Book
in writing to the Superintending Engineer, HES,
Tungabhadra Board, Tungabhadra Dam, Hospet
(tel: 8272), ordering meals if you want them.

Nearer the ruins is the PWD Inspection Bungalow, opposite the Archaeological Office at Kamalapuram. At *Hospet* (10km), there is a very helpful Tourist Office on Patel Road, near the very good Shanbhag restaurant at the corner of College Road and Taluk Office Circle. *Malligi Tourist Home,* off Hampi Road (tel: 8377), is the best hotel but, according to locals, to be outshone by a hotel being built in Railway Station Road. From Hampi or Badami the road west to Goa, via Belgaum, is a glorious drive up over the hills, then plunging down among the lush green palms to the sea. The road down to Bangalore is rigidly straight and punctuated with vast boulders.

BANGALORE
350km from Hampi; 140km from Mysore; 185km from Hasan. An excellent and efficient base for booking up, resting up, shopping and equipping oneself before setting off north, west or south. This is the capital of Karnataka state and India's fastest-growing and fifth largest city (recently jumping ahead of Hyderabad). It is also the seventh fastest-growing city in the world; between 1970 and 1980, its population increased by 75%, much of it caused by the influx of science-based industries. Its epithets of being a garden city and a naturally air-conditioned city are almost entirely inappropriate today.

Countless blossoming trees have been axed. The Preservation of Trees Act, imposing a hefty fine or imprisonment for illegally felling a tree, has had little effect. Concrete mixers worked over-time. And smog has arrived. However, the more traditional occupations of coffee-trading, sericulture, stud farms, horse-racing and film-making still thrive. There are more cinema seats per capita (with heavy competition from Trivandrum) and a wider linguistic range of films than in any other Indian city. And there are big parks, wide avenues, plenty of trees with hydrangea-sized blooms. And some elegant bungalows survive – just.

It was Kempe Gowda, a feudal lord of the Vijayanagar kingdom, who built a mud fort here in 1537, enlarged and rebuilt in stone by Tipu Sultan's father, Hyder Ali. After being the subject of numerous diplomatic gifts and sales, Bangalore became a British garrison town in 1809, in place of unhealthy Srirangapatna. The British constructed wide avenues for their troops; built pretty Gothic and Classic bungalows for their families set in gardens with roses, tennis courts, croquet lawns and aviaries; and they erected churches, museums and colleges. They even built the little Russe Market to protect the memsahibs, following a scan dal when a money-lender assisted a lady to pa for an abortion and then demanded her favou himself.

In 1937, Winston Churchill wrote from Banga lore that he and two chums, Reginald Barnes an Hugo Baring, had taken over a 'palatial bungalov from a friend. The columns of its deep verandah were 'wreathed in purple bougainvillea'. They ha two acres of land, 150 roses, kept about 30 horse and devoted themselves to 'the serious purpose (life . . . polo'.

THE HARD FACTS There are good air conne tions north and south, including direct flights t Goa and Mangalore for beaches (see p. 237) Airpo 7km from city centre. There are two special fest vals in addition to the regulars: Karaga, symboli ing strength of mind, when people balance ta piles of pots on their heads; and Kadaleskay (Groundnut Fair), held at the Bull Temple t appease the great bull who might destroy the crop Bangalore still blossoms with jacaranda, labu num, cassia, pride of India, peacock glory an camel foot in April–July and bougainvillea, jasmine honeysuckle and other creepers from Decembe onwards. It is always busy with busines men, supplemented at week-ends by race-goer (May–July; October–February) so book we ahead. There are two excellent hotels near th golf course, each with a distinct character, and runner-up plus an emergency if the first three ar full.

West End Hotel, Race Course Road (tel: 2928 telex: 337; cable: WESTEND); Bangalore's oldes hotel. It is elegant, traditional and spacious, wit great style and decorum, the verandahs and mai rooms arranged on three sides of a spacious lawn There are more immaculate gardens and annexe behind, covering 20 acres in all. There are whit cane chairs, flowers and pot plants everywhere. Si Alec Guinness, Dame Peggy Ashcroft, Sir Davi Lean et al. stayed here happily while shooting ' Passage to India'. Definitely the place to be stayin during the races.

145 rooms. Mod. cons include a good poo herbal clinic, beauty salon, car rental, busines services. Tea or candle-lit cocktails on the lawns ar delightful. The food is reasonable.

Windsor Manor, 25 Sankey Road (tel: 28033/4/5 telex: 0845–8209 WIND IN; cable: WELCOTEL) This is a new, gloriously kitsch and successfu

ke-off of a Raj Regency hotel, with a circular
marble lobby, detailed right down to the uniforms
the bell-hops, English wood-panelled bar,
nglish prints, chintz curtains, deep sofas for tea
d dainty cakes. The interior was designed by
ran Patki. It is run by the Welcomgroup. 140
oms. Mod. cons include a large swimming pool
d terraces, health club (which should be ready in
85), beauty salon, travel counter, business ser-
ces; golf by arrangement; restaurants and pool-
le barbecue excellent.

j Residency, 14 Mahatma Gandhi Road (tel:
8888; telex: 0845–8367 TNLR IN; cable: RESI-
ENT); gleaming white marble lobby with tinkling
untain characteristic of Taj group style, opened
84. 180 rooms. Mod. cons include good health
ib, gym and beauty centre; pool; car
ntal; business services. The coffee shop empha-
es south Indian food. Elsewhere the theme is
inese or American.

The ITDC's classy-looking **Hotel Ashok**,
mara Krupe, High Grounds (tel: 79411; telex:
3; cable: TOURISM), has the slowest staff and
e murkiest swimming pool water imaginable –
it it does have a tennis court, large grounds and
e Indian music in its restaurant.

A plethora of tourist offices. Best are Karnataka
urist Office at 19 St Mark's Road, 10/4 Kasturba
ad, Queen's Circle (tel: 578753), and on the 1st
or of 52 Shrungar Shopping Centre (tel: 579139),
circular complex at the corner of Brigade Road
d M G Road. The Government of India Tourist
ffice is in Church Road. Tours from the Kasturba
ad office take six hours to see the few city sights
t they also do good 13hr day trips to Mysore and
irangapatna or to the Hoysala temples. In ad-
tion to the recommended travel agencies,
luljee's Car Rental, 101 Brigade Road (tel: 51248)
most reliable. Now is the moment to book up for
agarhole wildlife sanctuary, through Jungle
dges and Resorts, 348/9 Brooklands, 13th Main,
ijmahal Vilas Extension (tel: 31020). *The Deccan
rald* gives good news coverage and entertain-
ents (i.e. cinema) guide. Good bookshops are
igginbotham, Gangarams, and The Book Cellar,
. on M G Road. Best guide-books are the TTK
ngalore Guide and Morris's *Guide To Bangalore*.

The golf course is in the town centre, between
e West End and the Windsor Manor hotels. Both
n arrange a game. Bangalore United Services
ub has swimming, tennis, billiards, squash and
dminton. Access is via a member (ask your hotel
anagement to fix it). At Kempe Gowda Road, the

Santosh Cinema is said to get the latest releases
and is air-conditioned. Performances of Karnataka's strong dance and music (especially lively
in March and April) tend not to be advertised
so, if interested, ask at Chowdiah Memorial Hall,
Sankey Road; the Bharatiya Vidya Bhavan; or
call up Indu Sridhar at the Windsor Manor (tel:
366233). Bangalore takes a serious siesta 1–4pm,
after which markets and shops stay open until
8pm.

OUT AND ABOUT   Bangalore is not crammed
with sights. In the **city centre**, public buildings
surround the 300-acre central Cubbon Park (1864),
stocked with benches and shady trees. Here are the
Gothic public Library, High Court, the obligatory
statue of Queen Victoria and three museums. The
excellent Government Museum (1887) houses 18
sections, its treasures including the fine Atukar
stone (c 950), the Hero stone (c 890) and finds from
the great Harrapan site at Mohenjodhao in Sind,
excavated in 1922; some good miniature paintings
and plenty of pasty, fleshy faces of the Tanjore and
Mysore rulers (open Thurs.–Tues., 9am–5pm).
The Venkatappa Art Gallery, housing the painters'
turn-of-the-century work for the court, is in the
museum building. The Technological Museum is
next door (open Tues.–Sun., 10am–5pm).

The massive grey granite wedding cake on the
north side of the park is Vidhana Soudha (Secretariat and State Legislature) built in flamboyant neo-
Dravidian style in 1956. It is open to visitors after
5.30pm, apply to Under Secretary (Protocol), Dept.
Social and Administrative Reforms, Vidhana
Soudha (tel: 79401).

Kempe Gowda Fort is currently closed to the
public (with no immediate prospect of re-opening),
but the remains of **Tipu's palace** are open, their
walls, ceilings and niches painted Pompeian red,
blue and yellow with floral designs and trellices,
the black columns outlined in gold (open daily,
8am–10pm). The fine Bangalore palace of the Mysore rulers is open for the week that includes
November 1.

Lalbagh Botanical Gardens, laid out by Hyder Ali
in 1760, has delightful 19th century pavilions,
lamps and halls set in 240 acres of well-planted
avenues and flower-beds, pleasant for an early
morning or sundown stroll. (Flower shows the
week of Jan. 26 and Aug. 15.) Tipu Sultan introduced many new species brought by ambassadors
from Kabul, Persia, Mauritius and France. He also
made an unsuccessful attempt to introduce mul-

berry bushes and a silk industry. Mysore only became the silk-growing centre of India after his death.

On the hill beyond is the Bull Temple, built by Kempe Gowda, its monolith bull claimed by locals to grow in size each year. The immaculate and charming race-course should not be missed, whether the races are on or not. South of it lies cinema-lined Kempe Gowda Road and the scented city market, piled high with flowers. There are pretty Gothic bungalows with monkey windows surviving in Langford Town, their painted green, red, mustard and white houses and gardens well-maintained by Bangalore's new rich.

RESTAURANTS Quite a good choice. Smartest of all is the immensely plush *Prince's Restaurant*, 9 Brigade Road (tel: 578787, best to book), with the top food, clientele and service (including good steaks). Its adjacent *Knock Out Disco* is the only one available. It is free to restaurant clients Tues.–Thurs., otherwise about Rs40 per couple (who have to be one of each sex – singles not admitted). There are a few seedy places elsewhere, to be avoided. All food at the *Windsor Manor* is good – they can even serve Indian sweetmeats. There is an airy coffee shop, with beautiful Chinoiserie murals. There are lunch and evening poolside barbecues (North-west Frontier food). In the main restaurant, the delicious food (South Indian chicken Chettinand and cheese-stuffed kulcha recommended) is blighted in the evening by live European music.

The poolside barbecue of the *West End* is good. The inside restaurant is not. For spicy Andhra food eaten off a banana leaf, go to the popular *R&R Restaurant*, Church Street. *Blue Fox*, M G Road (including fish and meat), and *Chalukya* (vegetarian, near the West End), have good south Indian food. The *North Indian Tandoor* on M G Road is excellent. Chinese food is good at the *Ashok's Mandarin* and at *Chinese Hut*, 45 Palace Road. *Mavalli Tiffin Room* on Lalbagh Road has excellent south Indian breakfast. Best before 7am.

SHOPPING AND CRAFTS The best shopping in the South is here and in Madras. Fine **silk** is the best value, woven into crepe de chine, georgette, chiffon, soft silk and spun silk, all priced by weight. (There is often a 10% discount for payment in foreign currency.) Traditional Mysore silks are in deep blue, mustard yellow, turquoise, chestnut and burgundy. Georgettes are often woven with

checks. Top of the range and quality is found Vijayalakshmi, M G Road; Karnataka Silk Indu tries Corporation (KSIC), Gupta Market, Kemp Gowda Road; Imor, 49 Victoria Layout (selectiv closed Wed.) and Janardhana Silk House, Uni Building, J C Road. KSIC also has thick rugs mad of the waste silk, in plain colours, all sizes.

Kaveri (Karnataka emporium), on M G Roa has a fair range of sandalwood, inlaid ivory, etc and Poompuhar (Tamil Nadu's) on Brigade Roa has quite a good stock. Both will be overshadowe by the excellent Cottage Industries Emporiu (based in Delhi), to open on M G Road (1985 1986).

On Commercial Street, there is quality **silve smithing** and fair prices at C. Krishniah Chet and Sons, whose shop sign proudly announc '1869–1984, A Glorious 115 Years'; old silve brass, wood etc. at Asia Arts and Crafts; and, ju before it, a little lane of tiny jewellers who ha regular stock and will alter and copy pieces.

In Langford Town area is Artworks, in Kana Bank Building on O'Shaughnessey Road, stockir well-made goods from all over India. The on shop of this range and quality and with reasonab prices. The reliable Natesan's Antiquarts is at M G Road (smaller showrooms at the West En and Ashok). On and around Avenue Road, the are lanes of gold and silver smiths, and the bac lanes sell spices and agarbathi (incense sticks).

To see all **sericulture** processes (see p. 183) ask taxi driver, the KSIC shop manager, go to th government Department of Sericulture or to th Weavers' Centre upstairs in the Life Insuran Building on Kempe Gowda Road. On the Bang lore–Mysore road, silk-growing farms along th roadside can be visited, or make a small detour Chennapatna and Ramalangram villages.

The various heavily promoted picnic spots ar waterfalls are not that attractive. Howeve *Whitefield* (16km) is interesting for its few old bu galows around the church and for Brindava ashram, the head quarters of Sri Satya Sai Bab who, as the literature puts it, 'draws thousands visitors all the year round searching for pea and the healing touch'. Rather more down earth, indeed right below the earth, are *Kol Gold Fields* (100km), with some of the deepe shafts in the world, going down to 3,000n To visit, apply to the Secretary, Kolar Go Mining Undertakings (Central Administration Oorgaum PO (tel: 77).

SRIRANGAPATNA

25km from Bangalore; 15km from Mysore. An island fortress town synonymous with Tipu Sultan, whose tiger-mania and hatred of the English are summed up in Tipu's Tiger, his musical box toy of a tiger devouring an Englishman that would growl and shriek when wound up. It is now to be seen in the Victoria and Albert Museum, London. After the fall of Vijayanagar, Mysore became independent under the Wadiyars. In 1759 Hyder Ali, a self-made, illiterate but politically brilliant Muslim, deposed Chikka Krishna Raj Wadiyar and ruled until his death in 1782. His son, Tipu (1750–1799), also an outstanding leader, ruled until British sieges of his capital, Srirangapatna, in 1792 (when he surrendered half his territories and two sons) and then 1799, led to his death. (The fifth generation of descendants lives in Calcutta.) Lord Wellesley then put a five-year-old Wadiyar on the throne and kept a watchful eye while getting on with British expansion in the South.

Tipu was highly cultivated, unlike his father, and a democratic ruler, yet he was obsessed with the destruction of kaffirs (non-Muslims). Even in his dreams he played the role of royal tiger chosen by God to devour his enemies. He surrounded himself with tigers, real and false; tiger-head cannons; sitting-tiger mortars; tiger-head sword handles; and had tiger symbols on his soldiers' uniforms.

The fort at Srirangapatna was mostly destroyed by the British, but Daria Daulat Bagh, Tipu's beautifully painted summer palace, remains, set in a very lovely garden, as does Gumbaz, the family mausoleum. Wall-paintings surround the main rooms of the mostly teak palace, both fine decorative arabesques and pictures of Tipu's battles. Spot in the pictures the clean-shaven British, the moustachioed French (Tipu's allies), and the Nizam of Hyderabad, shown as a cow and then a boar after he double-crossed Tipu. (To keep up supplies of money for his wars, Tipu had twelve mints.) The excellent museum in the small upstairs balconied rooms includes fine drawings of Tipu's sons. (Open daily until 5pm; good guides.) Dovecotes at the garden entrance were for pigeon post. It is possible to picnic among the roses, mango trees and lawns before going to see the dazzling white Gumbaz (1784). The rosewood doors are inlaid in ivory with delicate floral designs.

SOMNATHPUR, BELUR, HALEBID AND BELAVADI
Rural drives past paddy fields, bullock carts, tiny villages and brick kilns lead to temples built at the climax of the culturally precocious and dynamic Hoysala dynasty (1006–1310). With those at Bhubaneswar, Konarak and Khajuraho, these mark another peak in Hindu architecture.

The Hoysalas rose from brigand hill chieftains of the Western Ghats to rulers of the plains, where they extracted rich revenues and taxes as well as political allegiance from their conquests. But it was Vishnuvardhana (also called Bittideva), ruling from Belur (1108–42) who finally broke away from his Chalukya overlords to establish the Hoysala kingdom. He converted from Jainism, the Chalukyas' faith, to Vishnuism – hence his change of name. His grandson, Ballala II (1173–1220), extended the empire to cover the south Deccan and called himself Maharajadhiraja (King of Kings). A century later, the third attack by the Muslim army of the Delhi Sultanate crushed the Hoysalas in 1310.

With great patrons of poetry, music, painting, dance, architecture and literature for rulers, temple art reached new heights. The buildings, based on Dravidian architecture, are quite squat and usually star-shaped. Some still have their shikara (tower) and are raised on a big platform. The material is a blue-grey soapstone that is easy to carve when newly quarried but hardens under exposure – hence its crispness today.

The sculptures covering the buildings are vibrant animals and human figures who dance, play music, make love, make war and trot along in timeless processions. The recesses and projections of the star shape offered the optimum amount of surface for decoration. As at Khajuraho, the carvings are very easy to look at. The architecture helps by highlighting some parts while throwing others into almost black shade. The layout of the carvings helps by contrasting strong horizontal bands of friezes with tall single figures. It also offsets complicated narrative scenes from the epics with a simple running floral motif. And areas are divided with deep cuttings that resemble solid black lines.

Somnathpur 137km from Bangalore; 45km from Mysore; 25km from Srirangapatna. The temple, built in 1268 and dedicated to Keshava, is the easiest to reach and perhaps the most sublime and perfect of all the Hoysala temples. It is set in a cloister courtyard. (Steps at the far end on to the roof.) The building is complete, finely proportioned and the sculpture is glorious, especially the six horizontal friezes running round the temple base: hamsas (geese), yalis (hippogryphs), cavalry, guardian elephants and a floral band flank stories from the epics, each story ending with a closed or half-closed door. The temple guardian should have copies of P. K. Mishra's guide, *The Hoysalas*. He certainly has the key to a very clean lavatory. No refreshments.

Hasan 185km from Bangalore; 90km from Mysore; 40km from Belur; 32km from Halebid. Worth starting very early from either big city and stopping here for a South Indian breakfast en route to Belur – Hotel Sathyaprakash is clean and good. To stay overnight, go to ITDC's *Ashok* (tel: 8330/8731); Tourist Office almost opposite.

Belur 225km from Bangalore; 130km from Mysore. When Vishnuvardhana (1108–42) defeated the Cholas at Talkad in 1116, he commemorated his victory by building the Channekashava Temple in a spacious, walled complex. As well as countless elephants running round the base and story scenes, there are delightful figures of women putting on make-up (especially on the brackets under the eaves), playing with a pet parrot, removing a thorn from the foot. Some are signed by the sculptor. There are also wonderful guardian beasts and lots of internal decoration. This is a living temple, so a drummer and piper summon the faithful every now and then, a huge gold and red lion, elephant and horse are stored in the cloisters for festivals and the temple chariot sits outside the gateway. The two subsidiary temples are Channigariaya and Viranarayana. Good guides are available.

Halebid 32km from Hasan; 15km from Belur. Capital of the Hoysalas for three centuries and known as Darasamudra. There is a large complex and open-air museum (which sells postcards), set in a beautifully kept garden with shady, flowering trees, beside a lake (a nice picnic spot). The double Hoysaleswara Temple, designed and begun by Kedaroja for the ruler Narasimhal (1141–82), was still incomplete after 86 years of chiselling. Here the riot of flamboyant carving is even more Baroque and extravagant than at Belur, particularly on the south-west side, and is considered by many to be the peak of Hoysala carving. Just beyond the complex is another, less visited temple. The whole site is run by the Archaeological Department. There are good guides.

Belavadi 12.8km north of Halebid, on the Banavar-Belur road. Worth catching this little-visited nearby temple in a tiny village. Built around 1116, its overall effect is even more horizontal than the other temples. There is less decoration, but the columns are very sharply chiselled and the deities

in the three shrines are especially fine. (To see them, the villagers will call the priest, who unlock the doors and then performs puja. Visitors shoul give an offering.)

SHRAVANABELGOLA
52km from Hasan; 158km from Bangalore; 90km from Mysore. Jain pilgrims flock here to the 17 metre high image of *Lord Gomateshvara* (Bahubali) carved into the rock of Indragiri hill and visibl from 25km. Jainism was introduced to the South b Chandra Gupta Maurya and held powerful swa until the Hoysala conversion and Jain interna disputes. Every 12–14 years the Mahamasta kabhisheka ceremony is held here (last one 1981) when Jains pour in to witness the anointing of th deity. Water, ghi (clarified butter), dates, almonds poppy seeds, coconut milk, bananas, jagger (sugar-cane), sandalwood, flowers and even gold silver and precious stones are poured over th head and cascade down the huge body.

MYSORE
140km from Bangalore; 90km from Hasan; 150km from Ooty. A pretty, slow-paced, palace-filled rural town, rich in craftsmen and fortunately left in peace by busy Bangalore. Beloved by R. K Narayan, who uses it as the inspiration for hi Malgudi novels and writes of it: 'The atmosphere i placid and poetic, and one is constantly tempted t enjoy the moment, setting aside all othe thoughts.' The Wadiyar family were the Maharaja from the 14th century until Hyder Ali's takeover in 1759, and were then restored by the British in 179 when the five-year-old Krishnaraja was installed.

Left with nothing much to do, the 19th century maharajas earned a reputation for superb hospital ity and spectacle, political stability and progress Mysore Week became the Raj's Ascot Week, it highlight the massive khedda (a round-up of wil elephants for training), when the Maharaja mir aculously produced electricity, running water an an orchestra in the depths of the jungle.

Their building had the same flamboyan approach: a Scottish baronial mansion at Ooty, South Indian Windsor Castle at Bangalore, Italian ate Rajendra Vilas and then, after a fire in 1897, th new city palace. There were five palaces and 1 mansions in Mysore alone. The many peppermin green, pink and yellow buildings with turrets pavilions and domes were mostly built by th stylish and powerful rulers, giving Mysore th feudal atmosphere found in many Rajasthan cities he ex-Maharaja, in his thirties, lives in a corner of he gigantic, fairytale Amba Vilas city palace floodlit on Sundays, 7–8pm) where he runs his tud farm. Two of his former palaces are now .otels.

HE HARD FACTS A pleasant and comfortable ase for visiting the Hoysala temples and Sriranga-atna. Dussehra festival (September–October) s worth seeing (see p. 177). Nearest airport angalore. Stay at one of two palaces, both ood on character but weak on service and pam-ering, or a charming colonial hotel in the city entre.

alitha Mahal Palace Hotel (tel: 23650; telex: 846–217; cable: TOURISM) is huge, overlooking ne city. It was built in 1931 for foreign visitors, so nat they could be served meat – the Maharaja was trictly vegetarian. It has a gloriously grand pale ellow and green hall with huge chandeliers, weeping staircase and Italian marble balustrade. Original furnishings include Heath Robinson free-tanding baths whose dial taps provide bath, hower or an onslaught of sprays from every side. : is managed by the government Ashok chain which seems bent on destroying the gracious tmosphere. 54 rooms (including pale-blue royal uite) behind cool, deep verandahs. It is essential o be in the old building and overlooking the city. Mod, cons include pool (dirty), tennis, billiards, able tennis, extensive and well-maintained gar-ens, cavernous dining hall with bad food, slow ervice but some charming elderly ex-royal ser-ants.

Rajendra Vilas Palace (tel: 22050/22900; telex: 846–231 HRV–IN) is a small, Italianate villa built a 1939 on steep Chamundi Hill outside the city so nat His Highness could get a spot of peace during ne Dussehra festivities; HH now runs both this nd his Fernhill Palace at Ooty and is to open the oka Ranjan Mahal (in 1985 or 1986), the women's ummer palace in the centre of Mysore. Rajendra Vilas has original furniture and fittings – and orig-nal royal staff, full of smiles and eager to please but bit amateur at hotel service. 29 rooms, tennis ourt (should be ready by 1985), golf by arrange-nent. The small garden needs attention. There are retty pavilions outside the first floor drawing oom. Reasonable food is served in the red velvet-ned dining room. It is essential to have a car if taying here.

Hotel Metropole, 5 Jhansi Lakshmi Bai Road (tel: 0681; telex: 0846–214; cable: METROPOLE). 18 rooms, only four air-conditioned, each in the colo-nial tradition of bedroom, dressing room and bath-room. Spacious lawns, excellent food and exten-sive Indian menu.

State Tourist Office, 2 Jhansi Lakshmi Bai Road (tel: 23652); very helpful, run tours around and outside Mysore. News and events can be found in the *Deccan Herald* and *Mofussil Diary*; books at the well-stocked Geetha Book House, K R Circle. To book up for wildlife parks, for Bandipur go to Project Tiger, Government House (tel: 20901) and for Nagahole go to Assistant Conservator of Forests, Wildlife Preservation, Chamarajendra Circle, Vanivilas Road (tel: 21159). But bookings for a trip with Tiger Tops are made through Jungle Lodges in Bangalore (see p. 195). Racing season is August–October (Sat., Sun.), when the Bangalore smart set come across. Mysore connects with Mangalore for a beach (220km by road, see p. 244). The coast road from Mangalore down into Kerala has been described as 'like the Côte d'Azure before it was discovered'.

OUT AND ABOUT **Amber Vilas**, the city palace, is the unmissable attraction. Designed by an En-glishman named Irwin, it incorporates everything that is grand, huge and fun: glorious stained glass with peacocks and flowers; avenues of carved pil-lars; huge inlaid doors; walls coated in gold and red arabesques; and marble floors polished to mirror-brightness. Open daily, 10.30am–5.30pm, no guide book, guide or postcards.

There are several other things worth seeing: Devaraja market, alleys perfumed with piles of flowers, spices and everything else, full of colour and action; the town centre Zoo; Sri Chamarajen-dra Art Galley, Jaganmohan Palace, for Indian miniature paintings, musical instruments (open Fri.–Wed., 8am–5pm); and Sri Chamundeswari Temple, a healthy climb up Chamundi Hill (4km of steps – or 13km by car), passing the huge monolith Nandi bull (cafés at the top).

Brindavan Gardens (19km) are undoubtedly the local sunset spot and, despite the crowds, are very beautiful: gardens with cascading fountains beside the Krishnaraj Sagara, courting couples take snaps of each other and, as the sun sets, pretty illumi-nations are switched on to oohs and aahs. Tea or cocktails can be taken on the semi-circular hotel verandah, which is another ex-royal guest-house.

RESTAURANTS If palatial surroundings do not make up for the food, try the *Metropole, Ridge* and *Hoysala hotels*, *RRR* at Gandhi Square, *Gun House Imperial* and the *Punjabi Bombay Juice Centre*, Dhanvantri Road.

SHOPPING AND CRAFTS Shop at Kaveri Arts and Crafts Emporium, Sayaji Rao Road (closed Thurs.) for local sandalwood, rosewood, teak, inlay (wood and ivory), silks and agarbathi (incense). Sandalwood is quite expensive. If it is offered cheap, it is likely to be another wood, with added scent. For safety, buy at government-approved shops. Sri Lakshmi Fine Arts and Crafts, opposite the Zoo, has a very good range of goods; their factory of craftsmen at 2226 Sawday Road, Mandi Mohalla, Mysore is open to visitors and sells stock.

Karnataka Silk Industries Corporation factory shop, Mananthody Road, has the best range of quality handloom and machine silks, with an informative sales officer, Mr Gupta. The on-site weaving is by machine, not handloom (open Mon.–Sat., 7.30–11.30am; 12.30–4.30pm). The other KSIC silk shop is in town, Visweswaraiah Bhavan, R K R Circle.

At the Government *Sandalwood Oil Factory* (which produces 60% of the Indian production), see the basic distilling process and how incense is made, then buy goods (open Mon.–Sat., 9–11am; 2–4pm). In the back lanes find craftsmen working with bamboo, wood, inlay work and weaving. Mysore is also the centre for *incense sticks*. In many homes, adept women and children furiously turn out up to 10,000 sticks a day. They roll sandalwood putty on to slivers of bamboo, then dip them into powdered perfume before drying them in the shade.

The Nilgiri Hills

OOTACAMUND (OOTY), TAMIL NADU
159km from Mysore; 86km from Coimbatore, 280km from Cochin. Altitude 2,268m. A wonderful journey, whichever way is chosen. It can be approached from Mysore through banyan avenues and wildlife sanctuaries with scampering mongoose and strolling elephant, or from the palms and pineapples of Trichur. Or it can be reached by train. The rise is through thick forests of creeper-filled trees, scratching monkeys (road notices announce they have right of way) and spice bushes, emerging among fat cows, rolling Nilgiris (blue hills) like Cumbria in England, spongy hillside carpets of tea bushes, wild arum lilies, twittering birds and air scented with pine and eucalyptus.

Ooty is known by local Tamils as Udagamanda lam. Ootacamund (meaning village of huts) i where the smart come to cool off. John Sullivar Collector of Coimbatore, took a fancy to Ooty i 1819, was the first European to build a house ther and had the lake built in 1823. The British, quic to sniff out anything cool in India, were hot o Sullivan's heels, followed by the maharajas.

By 1821 the mountain pass was in use. Th British built Surrey-style houses, planted garden and founded the glorious Botanical Garden funded by public subscription in 1840. Both R and rajas enjoyed pucka British pastimes: riding golf, tennis, hunting, racing and polo. There wa full social season, complete with flower shows an dog shows. Snooty Ooty it most certainly wa And, from 1869, it became the summer headquar ters of the Government of Madras. The Duke Buckingham built a hills edition of Governmer House in 1877 with a pillared portico copied fro his seat at Stowe in Buckinghamshire.

Today film-stars and foreign firms maintain th houses – still a status symbol – smart honeymoo couples flock here in the winter (if they do not go t Kashmir), and the flower show, dog show an hunt, pink coat 'n' all, continue. But with a slight hollow ring. The palaces are rarely opened, th club is kept pristine for a handful of aged member staying on because 'it's like Devonshire with bett blooming roses and three servants'. Smart Ooty rather run-down. What thrives is an Indian hi town producing eucalyptus oil, making cinem film, building hydro-electric schemes and mark gardening, set amid charming scenery and a pe fect climate.

Ooty may be low on Raj nostalgia but the d scription by Lord Lytton, Viceroy 1876–80, sti holds good: 'It far surpasses all that its most e thusiastic admirers and devoted lovers have sai to us about it. . . . Imagine Hertfordshire lane Devonshire Downs, Westmoreland lakes, Scot trout streams and Lusitanian views!'

THE HARD FACTS Driving up or down b tween Mysore and Ooty, there are two routes: v Gudalur–Naduvattam–Pykara or, steeper but eve more beautiful, via Masinagudi–Kathati. Comin up from the South, the train is a must (see p. 178 The usual options for hotels: efficiency or romant character. Tariffs operate for high season Septem ber–October and March–June; all other months a low season, with possible reductions.

The Savoy, Club Road (tel: 2572/2463; telex: 85

40; cable: SAVOY) is efficient, established and
ery pucka, opened in 1841 as Dawson's Hotel by
Mr H. Royal Dawson. The main part is built
round a cottage (now Garden Cottage), using
eams dragged up by elephants from Tipu's palace
t Srirangapatna. It is managed by the Savoy
roup. 50 rooms; some in the main building,
thers built as charming cottages, each with a
erandah (and full room service). Good garden,
wood fires and hot water bottles if needed. Good
ndian and European food served in a dining room
anelled with Karnataka rosewood. But it lacks
ublic rooms. Efficient Gordon at the front desk
an arrange anything from riding and golf to visits
o tea plantations. Tea and Britannia biscuits can be
aken on the lawn.

ernhill Palace, Fern Hill (tel: 2055; telex: 853 246
FERN IN; cable: FERNIMP). HH the (ex-) Mahar-
ja of Mysore's hilltop pad – he keeps a cottage in
ae grounds to stay in during May. Deep pink
cottish-baronial building with magnificent views
est across the valley, with a pavilion and Indian
ouble swing on the lawn, from which to watch the
our-long, flaming red sunsets. HH's furniture is
ll there, including books, pictures and low-watt
ght bulbs; awash with character and the sleepi-
ess of a rundown country house. 74 rooms vary
om pokey box-room to vast, multi-roomed suite,
pread over the palace and outbuildings (cottages
01–4 have good views). The service is disastrous.
he food is bad but served in the seedy splendour
one candle in a three-hole candelabra) of the fine
wo-storey baronial hall with plasterwork ceiling,
he balconies furnished with beautiful billiard and
ard tables. Recreation facilities include squash,
adminton, table tennis. The gardens are under
estoration.

The Tourist Office is useless. Higginbotham's
ookshop has guides. Racing is April–June, en-
vened in May by: a visit from the hunt, belonging
o Conoor Staff College; the two-day flower show
n the Botanical Gardens, around the 14th; the dog
how and, at the end of the month, Founder's
Veek at the smart Lawrence School at Lovedale.
his is Tamil Nadu state, where total prohibition is
fficially in force. It is wiser not to carry drink
round. The bars of both hotels serve liquor with-
ut demanding permits.

OUT AND ABOUT Ooty is a doing, not seeing,
lace. However, a stroll around town reveals some
ed-tiled Raj villas, the private Nilgiri Library and
ne parish church of St Stephen, designed by one

Captain John Underwood in 1829. It is Gothic
outside, Tuscan inside, with more teak from Tipu's
palace for the roof. If possible, visit the very fine
Club, built as a villa in 1831–2 by the Hyderabad
merchant Sir William Rumbold, and rented by
Lord William Bentinck when Governor-General. It
then became the social centre for tea planters and
the military, where an English subaltern invented
snooker in 1875. (Write to or ring The Secretary for
admittance.) The terraced Botanical Gardens below Raj Bhavan (Government House) cover 51
acres, boast 650 plant varieties and incorporate
Sullivan's lake. There are orchids, ornamental and
medicinal plants, rock plants, ferns and mature
trees. The knowledgeable Curator of the Nilgiri
Agri-Horticultural Society is found here.

SHOPPING Silver and embroidered shawls are
sold at the Toda show-room at Charing Cross (see
p. 185 for more about the Todas). The jewellery,
actually made by another tribe and sold to the
Todas, can also be found at silversmiths in the old
bazaar. Mrs Evan Piljain Weidemann also sells
Toda shawls. At Spencer's there is local honey, and
Kathleen Carter's Cheddar and Wensleydale
cheeses. Also distilled eucalyptus, geranium,
lemon-grass and camphor oils. There is a belief that
eucalyptus oil keeps mosquitoes away; it does not.

KEEPING FIT Riding is easy and cheap: horses
are brought to the hotel or found at the Boat House,
to be hired with or without escort. Boating is on
Ooty Lake (1.5km, 8am–6pm). To fish for trout at
Avalanche, a licence and hired tackle may be
obtained from the Assistant Director of Fisheries,
Fishdale, Ooty. The Hon. Secretary, Nilgiri Game
Association, Ooty, should be contacted for chikar
(hunting). There are good walks out in the hills.
Wenlock Downs (8km) are about 60sqkm of undulating grassland and shola forest (hotels provide
picnics). A car will deliver walkers and collect
several hours later. Alternatively, local buses make
a similar journey. Nearer the centre, the view from
the top of Dodabatta ridge, which rises behind the
Botanical Gardens and is the highest in Tamil
Nadu, is superb on a clear day. A pathway above
the gardens leads to a Toda village (see p. 185).
Hotels can arrange golf.

AWAYDAYS Several interesting places to visit,
driving through the unspoilt hills. The nearest tea
estate is *Glen Morgan* (see p. 185). *Kotagiri* (23km) is
a lower station, discovered by the British before

Ooty but now a quiet backwater surrounded by thick forests and a golf course; nearby are *Catherine Falls* (8km), *Elk Falls* (8km) and *Kodanad View Point* (16km, stunning view down to plains). *Coonor* (13km) is lower again, with tea plantations and nice walks (stay overnight at Hampton Manor on Church Road, run by Mr and Mrs Dass).

To visit *Mudumalai Wild Life Sanctuary* (64km), contact the District Forest Officer, Nilgiris North Division, Ooty for information and accommodation. At Lovedale, the John Lawrence Memorial Asylum (Lawrence School), built by the British in the 1860s in memory of Lawrence of the Punjab, is a caricature of an English boarding school, full of pucka Indian boys: monastic Romanesque buildings in a lovely setting where every pupil dreams of escaping to the smoky city.

Kerala

TRICHUR

200km from Ooty, via Mettupalaiyam, Coimbatore and Palghat; 80km from Cochin. Through dazzling green paddy, coconuts, pineapples and blue cacti, studded with the odd pink cinema and toddy shop, to an attractive and prosperous town with large, sparkling, brightly-painted houses. The great *Trichur Pooram* is held here, in the town centre (see p. 177). There is also the beautiful Vadakkunnathan Temple complex of wooden, steep-roofed buildings, some open to non-Hindus. Guruvayur (29km west, on the coast) is where the night-time Krishnayattam temple dance is performed, but only for Hindus (see p. 186). To see this, it is best to stay in the *Tourist Bungalow*. Kerala Kalamandalam (Arts Academy) at Shoranur (29km north) is where Kathakali dance has undergone its renaissance, under the stimulus of the poet Vallathol, and is the principal training centre (see p. 186). Training can be seen in the early morning. Performances are at night. It is possible to stay overnight at the nearby PWD Rest House.

COCHIN AND ERNAKULUM

80km from Trichur; 67km from Kottayam; 63km from Alleppey; 210km from Kodaikanal; 280km from Ooty. Ernakulum is the undistinguished mainland town which has the Kathakali dance halls (see p. 186) and is connected with Cochin over the narrow bridge. Cochin is its picturesque harbour with islands, backwaters, pretty buildings and a rich history. There seems to be more water

than land here. Cochin is also one of India's busies ports and has one of Kerala's two airports, bu neither encroach on its beauty.

Some say the Jews arrived in Kerala over 2,00 years ago, as refugees from Jerusalem when it fe to Nebuchadnezzar in 587BC. Certainly, they hav been a strong community in Cochin for the la 1,000 years, although now the lure of Israel ha reduced their numbers to about 30 – not one chil The Portuguese (arrived 1500), Dutch (arrive 1602, pushed out the Portuguese 1663) and Britis followed, all hungry for spices, and all leaving the mark.

THE HARD FACTS Both nice hotels are o Willingdon Island, a man-made island named afte the Viceroy, Lord Willingdon and constructed by Mr Bristow in the 1920s and 1930s out of wast when the harbour was dug deeper. For efficiency stay at **Casino Hotel**, (tel: 6821; telex: 0885-31 SAFE IN; cable: CASINO). Sadly, it is sited we back from the water. It was begun in the 1950s an restaurant opposite the terminus of the big trains t South India – after this the line was single-trac only. 47 rooms including one suite with beautifu Keralan decor. The old part is the nicest. There is spacious garden, motor launch and a good re taurant. (Ask for fresh fish, prawns and lobste South Indian dishes on request.) One drawback the live Western music, nightly. The staff efficient.

For location, stay at **Malabar Hotel**, (tel: 681 telex: 885 281 JOHR IN; cable: COMFORT Maintenance work is urgently needed on the buil ing. However, it is a glorious setting: right on th tip of the island with lawns to the water's edge an a jetty, looking on to little fishing boats and cat marans laden with coir (coconut fibre) and with th boatman's hut on top. Big ships pass by too. Th views look across to Mattancherry, some old Bri ish trading buildings and some Chinese fishin nets. 37 rooms, best of which are on the first floc with a balcony for views (nos 6, 7, 14 and 15). The is a clean pool, motor launch, rowing boats, beaut salon. Breakfast, snacks, tea and star-lit cocktai are served on the lawns. It is delightful to take night-time row from the jetty. The food is ba They cannot even manage freshly ground coffe and the dreaded live Western music is playe nightly. However, the staff are quite efficient.

The lovely **Bolgatty Palace Hotel** on Bolgatt Island (tel: 35003), was built by the Dutch in 174 and used as the British Residency. It is state-run (

ther, not run) and in such a sad state of dilapida-
on that it is only worth being rowed across (from
ne High Court Jetty in Ernakulam) to catch its
eeting beauty before it tumbles down. An exem-
lary Government of India Tourist Office is in the
nnex of the Malabar hotel, run by Mr V. Lakshmi-
arayanan. There is not much literature but good
dvice on the whole area. The Cochin tour (Wed.–
Ion., 9am and 2pm) includes Mattancherry and
undu island to see coir factory. There is no guide
ook.

UT AND ABOUT It is quite tricky to move
oout, so it is best to shop and sightsee at once. The
rry system is obscure. It is better to hire a boat
nd a rower. When negotiated away from the
otels, the prices reduce from Rs50 per hour to
s20 per hour. Exploring Mattancherry and Fort
ochin is most fun by bicycle, hired from any
icycle shop. Otherwise, use a car.

There is not a lot to see on Willingdon Island.
Over the bridge to **Mattancherry** the old docks and
nerchants' houses lie to the right, and beyond
hem the Jewtown: horizontal striped warehouses,
lue-shuttered houses, two good handicraft and
ntique shops called Athena Arts and Indian Arts
nd Curios (bargain hard for painted jewellery and
noney boxes, nut-crackers, masks, ivory bracelets
nd spice boxes, both open daily, 9am–6pm)
nd a fine synagogue. It was built in 1567 and re-
uilt after destruction by the Portuguese in 1662,
vith an upstairs gallery for women, Chinese
villow-pattern floor tiles, 19th century Belgian
handeliers and beautiful interlocking benches
open daily 10am–noon:3–5pm, knowledgeable
ustodian).

Nearby is the so-called **Dutch Palace**, set in a
valled garden backing on to mango trees, built by
ne Portuguese in 1557. It was then diplomatically
iven to the Cochin Raja, Veera Kerala Varma
1537–61) and repaired by the Dutch. Upstairs, the
eautiful rooms have remarkable Hindu wall-
aintings illustrating the Mahabharata (Raja's bed-
oom, left) and Ramayana (stair room, right), with
arved teak ceilings and a vast teak Indian swing in
ne Rest Room (open daily, 9am–5pm).

At the tip of the isthmus is **Fort Cochin**, a parody
f an English country village. Here the British coir
nerchants lived in fine houses and gardens sur-
ounding the church and green, where Sunday
ricketers watched from shady trees. It looks just
ne same today. The church, dedicated to St Fran-
is, was the first European church to be built in

India. It was built in 1503 by Franciscan friars who
accompanied the Portuguese admiral, Albuquerque. Vasco Da Gama established a factory here in
1502 and returned to Cochin as Portuguese Viceroy
in 1510, to die here in 1524. His tombstone can be
found at the east end of the church, on the right.
Many other Cochin colonial notables are also
buried here, including John Christie of Pierce
Leslie and Co. whose handsome building can be
seen from the Malabar. The church was successive-
ly Protestant Dutch, Anglican and is now Church
of South India. It is packed on Sundays, when the
punga is still operated. This is a manual air-
conditioning system. Men pull strings to move the
large fans which are suspended from the ceiling.
South of St Francis's Church lies the jolly Santa
Cruz Cathedral (1557), its interior painted from top
to toe with provincial mock marble, tiling, arcad-
ing, garlands and the stages of the Cross on the
ceiling. The whole east wall is a riot of pink, blue
and yellow.

Up on the shore facing Vypeen Island stand the
incongruous Chinese fishing nets, looking like
pop-art sculptures, best seen in action from 5pm
onwards (see p. 186). Across the water, on tiny
Gundu island, is the coir (coconut fibre) factory
where doormats are made. They can be made to
order, all colours and patterns, even incorporating
a 'welcome home' or more personal message; then
shipped home.

Ernakulum does not have much besides the fascinating Kathakali performances. Cochin Museum,
opposite Indian Airlines, houses Cochin raja
memorabilia. Tea, spices and cashewnuts are sold
in the market. The freshly roasted cashews are sold
according to size: jumbo, full, half or broken, costing about Rs70 per kilo. At Curio Palace on M G
Road, there is old and new carved rosewood and
walnut, masks and other kathakali props and
jewellery.

For eating in Ernakulum, *Ceylon Bake House*,
opposite Woodlands on M G Road, has good
Kerala food, open noon until 2am; *Jancy Café* on
Shanmugam Road serves good South Indian food
(appam and puttu recommended); the roof-
top *Chinese restaurant* of the *Sealord Hotel*, Shanmugam Road, has splendid views and a terrace; and
Ernakulum ice-creams are delicious, including fig,
pineapple and mango flavours.

At the north end of Shanmugan Road is High
Court Jetty, for hiring a boat and rower to go to
Bolgatty Island or to explore the backwaters. This
can take a few glorious hours – or even a day.

KUTTANADU

The area stretching from Cochin to Quilon, known as the backwaters, where life is lived on, beside and often in the water (see p. 185). On the water people fish, go to school or to work, punt their narrow dug-out boats along with a tall pole, which is plunged into the water, pushed and then whipped out just before disappearing beneath the surface. Other boatmen paddle furiously, skimming along the canals. Lazy ones tag on to motor ferries. Artistic ones carve the wooden prow. Others put up sails. Boatmen of bigger dug-outs, carrying loads of coir, copra (dried coconut meat) and cashews, have small palmyra leaf huts to live in.

Beside the water, women wash clothes and pots and pans. Brightly painted houses and thatched huts are built on narrow walkways, often seeming to float on nothing. They jostle for space with tailors and fruit shops and with jackfruit trees (good wood for house-building), mauve flowering creepers, coconut palms, cows, pigs, chickens, ducks, banana palms, red and white flowering trees, pineapple palms and, of course, Chinese fishing nets. On the other side of the walkway are fields of wheat, to be harvested before the monsoon when the whole area is flooded.

The only way to see this area is on the water, hiring a boat to explore up creeks and taking ferries from town to town with the local commuters. Towns are bases for exploration and are very incidental. Ferry timetables have their own logic: the Quilon–Alleppey boat was out of service for well over a year. If you are travelling through Kerala by car, the driver will drop you at, say, Kottayam ferry, then drive furiously to meet you at Alleppey while you gently chug through the green fields of African moss, past coconuts. It is much further for him. Barring strikes, there should be ferry services between the following: Kottayam–Alleppey (2½hrs); Quilon–Alleppey (8½hrs); Quilon–Kapapuzha; Quilon–Guhanandapuram. Your hotel will check.

KOTTAYAM

By road, 68km from Ernakulum; 37km from Alleppey; 117km from Thekkady Wildlife Sanctuary. It is a busy town, full of churches, the headquarters of Kerala's several newspapers and a major centre for the Kerala Syrian Christians. St Thomas is believed to have landed at Cranganore in 52AD and converted a few Namboodiri (Brahmini) families to Christianity. Their descendants are still very aware of their importance and careful about whom they

marry. Syrian Christians were certainly in India 190AD and, although slightly battered by t Portuguese in the 16th century, have thrived commerce, culture, politics and numbers. 25% Keralans are Christians, their churches a glorio mish-mash of Portuguese, Dutch and Briti church architecture. Syrian Christian events ha pily mix religion with pageantry and politics, sta ing lavish fireworks displays attended by 'big-sh ministers from Delhi. In Kottayam, it is best to st at the *Anjali Hotel* (tel: 3661; telex: 888–212; cab ANJALI). It is clean and comfortable. Ask the ch to prepare the local freshwater fish, karimeen, the Keralan way.

ALLEPPEY

By road, 37km from Kottayam; 63km from Ernak lum; 85km from Quilon; but nicest by far by fer from Kottayam. A quiet market town, trading ba of coir rope, and piles of sacking and green bar nas along its canals. Split coconuts can be se drying in the sun. The essential black umbrell carried by every Keralan are sold at Coch Umbrella Mart on the high street. To eat, drink relax, go to the Indian Coffee House, opposite t Hindu temple. It has a Parisian café atmosphe with excellent coffee and food in charming a spotless rooms. It is run by a co-operative, with other branches in Kerala. Alleppey bursts in action in high summer for Onam (see p. 177). T nearby beaches are beautiful. Stay overnight at *George's Lodge* or the *Government Rest House*. Bo are modest.

QUILON

By road, 85km from Alleppey; 71km from Triva drum; 198km from Thekkady Wildlife Sanctuary is one of the oldest ports on the Malabar Coa After the Phoenicians, Persians, Greeks, Roma and Arabs, the Chinese established a busy tradi port here from the 7th to 10th centuries, ev exchanging envoys under the 13th-century rule Kubla Khan. Today, it is an unimportant, rath sprawling market town, with wooden hous overhanging the winding back streets. To st overnight, Quilon has one of the most delight places in Kerala, the *Tourist Bungalow*, which w built as the British Residency. It is set in extensi gardens maintained by three gardeners, with jetty on to Ashtamudi Lake, next to a park on t outskirts of the town. It is spotless and well-run Kerala state, and has simple rooms with Kera wood-framed chairs, all with shower, tub and h

ter. Pilastered first-floor drawing room is fur-
shed with prints of Warren Hastings' victories,
rd tables, flower stands and wine-coolers. It is
pular, so book in writing, requesting air-
nditioned room (only 3). There is boating on the
ke (if no boats at hotel, hire one in town) and the
nds of Thangasseri beach are 3km away. Forget
e nearby over-rated Portuguese, Dutch and
tish ruins.

Along the roads, look out for the occasional
osque. The Malabar Muslims, known as Mappil-
, arrived as Arab traders in the 8th century and
ere given land and religious tolerance. They are
thing to do with the destructive invaders of
orth India and preferred trading with their clients
converting them to Islam.

IVANDRUM

km from Kovalam; 71km from Quilon; 87km
om Kanya Kumari (Cape Comorin); 154km from
ekkady; 307km from Madurai. An attractive,
ly town whose real name is Thiru-Vananta-
ram (Abode of the Serpent), but the British
uld not cope with that. Raja Marthanda Varma
'29–58) transferred his capital here from
dmanabhapuram in 1750, dedicating the whole
te of Travancore to Sri Padmanabha (Vishnu).
yal succession is matriarchal, through the eldest
ter's eldest son. The ruler is not supposed to
rry in case his love is diverted from his state to
s children. The present ex-Raja continues to be
ry devout, crossing the town from his palace
ery morning, at about 7.30am, to worship at the
dmanabhaswamy Temple. But his city is now
e Communist capital of Kerala, stocked with all
at that implies: government buildings, informa-
n, shops, bazaars, museums and, of course, a
nstant parade of strikers outside the Secretariat.
he site is so popular that unions have to book up
eir demonstration space months in advance.)
e one drawback is that it lacks any metropolitan
nosphere.

IE HARD FACTS Trivandrum has one of
rala's two airports (3km from the centre), so it
nnects into the spider's web of Indian Airlines
d serves the Maldives (Male) and Sri Lanka
olombo). To stay in town, go to the efficient
otel Luciya Continental (tel: 3443; telex: 0844-330
JCY IN; cable: LUCIYA); 104 rooms including
n suites in Arabic, Chinese and Kerala styles.
ere is a beauty parlour and the best coffee and
od in town (especially South Indian). One dis-

advantage: it costs Rs50 to the beach and back, so it
is best used as an overnight stop en route to the
Maldives or Sri Lanka. To stay on the beach, go to
the magnificent **Kovalam Beach Resort**, if you can
tolerate the poor service (see p. 244 on beaches).

There is a superb Kerala government Tourist
Office at Park View (tel: 61132), conveniently opposite the gateway to the zoo, gardens and museums complex. Kerala Tourist Office, Thampa-
nur, near Central Bus Station (tel: 2643) runs tours
around the city, to Padmanabhapuram Palace and
Kanya Kumari (Cape Cormorin), and to Thekkady
Wildlife Sanctuary. There is a Government of India
Tourist Office at the airport. On M G Road, there
are book shops, Natesan's and other antique shops
and the government emporia. Everything of interest closes on Mondays.

OUT AND ABOUT At the centre of the old fort
area is **Padmanabhaswamy Temple**, with nice old
houses built around its tank and back streets. It is
worth a peek for the goporam (pyramid gateway),
the carved columns and the daily temple procession, at about 12.30pm. The two temple festivals
are in March–April and October–November, each
lasting 10 days, with a big procession down to the
sea. Although it is closed to non-Hindus, much can
be seen from the outside. Keralans use their temples in a different way from Tamils: they go there to
pray, then leave, whereas Tamils make the temple
the centre of social, cultural and commercial life,
full of banter, music, shops and open to all and
sundry.

The other interesting area is the 64-acre **Zoo and
Botanical Gardens**, containing the museums (zoo
and gardens open daily, museums open Tues.
and Thurs.–Sun., 8am–6pm; Wed. 2–6pm). R. F.
Chisholm designed the new, gaily painted, hilltop
Napier Museum (1874–80) for the Governor of
Madras, touring south India to study its architecture before embarking on the project. When the
collection originally opened in 1857, the only other
museums in India were at Madras, Calcutta and
Karachi. The museum was not a success, so the
gardens and zoo were laid out two years later to try
to attract visitors. Inside are fine Chola bronzes,
stone carvings, masks, puppets, gold jewellery,
musical instruments and raja's nicknacks (good
guide book). The other museums house natural
history, contemporary paintings, a gallery for Ravi
Varmar, and a good collection of miniature paintings (firmly locked up at the moment, but worth
trying to see).

205

PADMANABHAPURAM PALACE, KERALA

55km from Trivandrum; 45km from Kovalam; 32km from Kanya Kumari. One of the finest buildings in Kerala. Splendid palace of the former capital (dating from 1550), built of teak with deep, overhanging roofs, elaborately carved, and furnished with rosewood, all probably Chinese-influenced as a result of trading both commodities and craftsmen. See especially the carved open hall where the king addressed his people; the richly carved ceiling of the hall behind; the upstairs council chamber with broad-seated chairs for ministers to sit on cross-legged and an ingenious air-conditioning system; the dance hall, pool, temple, women's quarters, guard rooms and the wonderful tower whose topmost room is reserved for the god, complete with bed and murals for his comfort – the raja took the room below it.

There are good guides, but no guide-book. Open Tues.–Sun., 7am–9pm. If going by bus or train, get down at Thakkalai. On the Trivandrum–Padmanabhapuram road is *Balaramapuram*, a centre for cottage industries where almost every family dyes and weaves. Warps of 50 metres or so are prepared and combed out on rickety trestles under jackfruit trees.

KANYA KUMARI (CAPE CORMORIN),
TAMIL NADU

32km from Padmanabhapuram; 87km from Trivandrum; 300km to Madurai. The Land's End of India. This is where the waters of the Arabian Sea, Indian Ocean and Bay of Bengal mingle. It is of enormous importance to Hindus who believe that to bathe in the waters is to be fully cleansed. This is because the goddess Parvati did penance here in order to marry the god Shiva. The ghats are especially lively just before sunset. Sunrise and sunset here are sensational; even more so on full moon nights when the moon rises as the sun sets. Be there by 5.45am for the first beams of light at sunrise, then the ball of fire around 6.15am. Sunset is 6–6.30pm. To see both, arrive for sunset and stay at the TTDC *Cape Hotel*.

Tamil Nadu

MADRAS

45km from Mahabalipuram; 62km from Kanchipuram; 145km from Vellore; 300km from Tiruchchirapalli. The seaside capital of Tamil Nadu and India's fourth largest city, Madras is a major p and a centre for the textile, leather, and mc industries and for engineering factories. world's top fashion designers employ work from Madras; Zandra Rhodes has the beadwor her creations stitched here. Yet, spread over a 80 sq km or so, its elegant colonial centre sprink with gardens, palms and a broad esplanade alc the shore, it actually feels airy, especially a Bombay or Calcutta. The luxury of space has sulted in sufficiently few tall buildings for a loca proudly point out to a visitor the Weimer buildi 'Fourteen floors, memsahib, all in one bu ing'.

While the rest of Tamil Nadu is dominated the monuments of the great Pallava, Chola Pandya empires, central Madras is dominated its Fort, decaying classical houses plastered white chunam and soaring Gothic public bu ings. For it was here that the East India Comp got its first foothold on the east coast. (It already established a factory at Surat, north Bombay, in 1612.)

The Company arrived in 1639, was given land the friendly Raja of Chandragiri, built Fort George in 1641, had between three and four h dred weavers working there and started export cloth back home. Twin towns developed: For George for the Europeans; Madraspatnam or Bl Town for the Indians, confusingly renan Georgetown in 1911, when King George V vis Madras. In 1688 James II granted a munic charter, the first in India. By 1740, British trad India represented 10% of all Britain's public venue. Madras was the chief British settlemen position maintained until Calcutta stole the li light in 1772. Many of the early British her passed through Madras before moving up coast – Clive, Hastings, Wellesley and the r who was to found Calcutta in 1690, Job Charn who had the local Pallavaram granite named a him as Charnockite.

Various periods of trouble with the French lowed: they occupied Madras 1746–9 but the young Clive finally defeated them and their lea Dupleix, at the battle of Arcot in 1751. Meanwh south of the Fort, the spacious garden house residential Madras continued to expand fur and further into the countryside, making relaxed garden city punctuated with clubs churches instead of a tight-knit Imperial pov house, to be cruelly described by Kipling a 'withered beldame brooding on ancient fame'.

A late flowering in the 1870s and 1880s embel-
·hed the classical city with grand Victorian Gothic
ιblic buildings designed by R. F. Chisholm and
·enry Irwin. And an elderly leather merchant,
ith a twinkle in his eye, recalls life in Madras even
·the 1940s as 'glorious fun, like an overgrown
ιiversity, and always that cooling sea breeze'.
Today, the clubs are less amusing and many of
·e great studios are devoted to sound processing,
·t film-making. However, M. G. Ramachandran
·lds a touch of glamour. The former matinée idol,
·ho played Robin Hood roles in the Errol Flynn
·d Douglas Fairbanks tradition, continued to
·ake films while he was an MP, only reluctantly
·pping when he became Chief Minister of Tamil
·adu.

·IE HARD FACTS   The air is clearest Decem-
·r–January, but tree and flower blooms are best in
·arch. There is a *dance and arts festival* mid-
·ecember to early January, a marathon of perform-
·ices daily from 2pm to late at night in several
·cations. It is well worth aiming to be in Madras to
·e it (see p. 187). Madras is a busy commercial city,
·there are good flight connections within India
·d to Sri Lanka and the Andamans. Airport 14km
··m city centre. Here is a good opportunity to take
··interesting train journey across the South (see
·ove, p. 178) but remember there are two stations:
·more serves the south, Central the rest of India.
·e more adventurous can take a boat to the
·aches of the Andamans (see p. 249), booking
·rough K P V Shaikh Mohammed Rowther & Co,
·2 Linghi Chetty Street (tel: 25756/7/8), but the
·rvice is irregular and the journey not very excit-
·g – better to do the Goa–Bombay trip.
Madras hotels cater for the businessman, not the
·urist, and are neither centres for the local social
·e nor full of character. The two recommended
·ith a spare third) are exceptions, so book in
·vance. For more congenial hotel life, stay down
·e coast at one of the beach hotels, 30 to 60
·inutes out of town (see p. 243), and come in to
·op and see the sights and dancing.
·*j Coromandel,* 17 Nungambakkam High Road
·l: 848888; telex: 041-7194 TAJM IN; cable:
·OTEL ORIENT). A concrete tower with rooms
·singularly dreary anonymity, compensated by
·od views from higher floors (they go up to 7).
·ficient Taj group service, exceptional food and
·od Indian classical dance performances. 225
·oms including 27 suites. All mod. cons include
·vel agent, car rental, excellent extensive health

club and beauty salon, pool and lawn, large shopping arcade. There is a poolside coffee shop,
pleasant bar (rare in India), both the Chinese and
Indian restaurants are excellent, and the Indian
one has three good Bharat Natyam dance programmes nightly.
Connemara Hotel, Binnay Road (tel: 810051/83161;
telex: 041-486 CH IN; cable: CONNEMARA).
Formerly a spacious town house of the Nawabs of
Wallajah, it has large rooms, fountains, courtyard
gardens and stables. It was bought and converted
into a hotel in the 1930s by the immensely successful Spencer & Co, the shop that started in Madras
in the 1860s, then opened branches throughout
British India to supply the Raj memsahibs with
everything from Ovaltine and paraffin to furniture
and its famous Spencer's Torpedo No. 1 Cooking
Range. (Spencer's also run the West End Hotel,
Bangalore and the Savoy, Ooty). The whole interior has recently been refurbished.

145 rooms including 8 suites. It is important to be
in the old part and at the back for large rooms and
peace. All mod. cons include travel desk, car
rental, beauty salon, courtyard pool, squash court.
There is an extensive shopping arcade patronised
by discerning locals. The food is good in the restaurant, barbecue and coffee shop.

If both these hotels are full, go to the *Chola
Sheraton* (tel: 82091; telex: 041 7200; cable: HOTEL
CHOLA). It was built 1975 by the Welcomgroup,
and is rather soulless but central. 129 rooms
attempting a south Indian character with carvings
and pictures. Mod. cons include travel desk, car
rental, pokey swimming pool. The food is fair,
with the bonus of a roof-top Chinese restaurant
(but live Western music).

Like Bombay and Calcutta, Madras has the pre-
and post-Independence street name problem, the
most important being Anna Salai, still known as
Mount Road (good for shopping), and Netaji
Subhash Bose Road, still called Parry's Corner
(commercial area). The Government of India Tourist Office, 145 Anna Salai (open Mon.–Sat., 9am–
5pm) is excellent, stocking the city map and lea-
flets including information on dance. It will
advise on which is the best of the many good
current dance performances. (Go clutching copy of
'*The Hindu*'.) But, beware, dance performances
tend to start early, around 6pm. It will also organise visits to film studios (such as Vauhini). It runs
daily tours of the Fort and museums, 2–6pm
plus day trips to Kanchipuram–Thirukkalikun-
dram–Mahabalipuram and to Tirupati. And it

stocks the free monthly booklet, 'Hello Madras', containing a mass of useful information. Tamil Nadu Tourist Office is at 143 Anna Salai (tel: 88806).

News and complete listings of dance and cinema can be found in *The Hindu*. The best guide-book is S. Muthiah's *Madras Discovered*. Best bookshops are Pai & Co (found by turning left out of the Government of India Tourist Office) and Higginbotham's, both on Anna Salai, and Giggles Book Boutique in the Connemara hotel. The Archaeological Survey of South India is in the Fort, behind St Mary's Church, and provides information on temple sites right across the state.

Officially, there is currently total prohibition in Tamil Nadu: foreigners need a liquor permit (obtainable at the Tourist Office) for buying alcohol from shops, but not for drinking in the recommended hotel bars and restaurants. Shops are mostly open 9am–8pm, without a siesta. There are several high commissions and consulates here, including those of the UK, 24 Anderson Road (tel: 83136) and the USA, Gemini Circle, Anna Salai (tel: 83041). The British Council, extremely informative, is at Local Library Authority Building, 150A Anna Salai.

OUT AND ABOUT There are two interesting areas, the compact Fort and the buildings scattered in the former residential area, now the city centre. **The fort and north Madras** Although the bastions of the *Fort* were completed in 1642, there were several rebuildings, the last being when the French left in 1749. There are several interesting buildings inside. St Mary's Church (1678–80, rebuilt 1759), the first Anglican church in India, was originally designed by Chief Gunner William Dixon with walls 4ft thick and a roof 2ft thick to withstand attack. There are windows with pretty stained glass, elegant cane seating, walls covered in memorial tablets and a graveyard with some of the oldest British tombstones in India.

Elihu Yale was the first to be married here (1689). He arrived in Madras in 1672, aged 24, rose in 15 years from Company Writer to Governor (1687–92). He stayed in Madras to augment his fortune and gave £560 worth of books and pictures to the Collegiate School in Connecticut, where his father had emigrated, which led to the university being named after him. Charnock's children were baptised here and, in 1853, Clive was married here.

Behind St Mary's is Clive House (next to the Archaeological Survey office) and the dilapidate Wellesley House. To the north are the mighti grand Governor's House (now the Secretaria with black pillared portico, Cornwallis Cupola ar the Officers' Mess (1780–90), now a good museu of Madras history. It has everything from prints terrified Europeans landing through the surf on the beach to portraits of Major Stringer Lawrenc Queen Victoria (by Sir George Hayter) and Edwa VII (open Sat.–Thurs., 10am–5pm).

Just north of the Fort are the lighthouse and t *High Court*, the second largest judicial building the world, after London, and considered the fine Indo-Saracenic building in India. Designed Henry Irwin and J. H. Stephens in 1892, it is d scribed by Jan Morris and Simon Winchester 'one of the most romantically exciting of the Briti buildings in India'; its interior 'spectacular . . . li a Piranese jail in its contrapuntal and crypt-li surprise – court after court, staircase after staircas warrens of arcaded and vaulted corridors, ha hidden alcoves where the lawyers gossipped, hu verandahs thronged with litigants, cool gallerie . . . a palatial porte-couchere, . . . and on top of t building . . . a bulbous and eccentric tower, . really a lighthouse'. Certainly worth a wander.

North again, overlooking the man-made ha bour, are two more magnificent buildings: t Southern Headquarters of the State Bank of Ind and the General Post Office. West of here, passi the Indo-Saracenic Central Station and Moo Market (both by Irwin), lie the Connemara Libra (1896, Irwin again) and Museum and the Nation Art Gallery. The first houses superb Dravidi sculptures and bronzes and is well worth a vis despite bad labelling and a lack of guide boo (both open Sat.–Thurs., 8am–5pm but bron gallery only opens at 10am).

Central Madras Crossing the Cooum Riv something much more Indian can be found: the 8 century *Parthasarathy Temple* on Triplicane Hi Road and, down in Mylapore, *Kapaliswarar Tem* off R K Mutt Road, its gopuram painted up wi Rowney colours. And, from late afternoon o wards, there is music from drums and doub pipes, puja, women exchanging horoscopes a hawkers selling ribbons and jasmine. (The festiv of Sixty-three Saints of Shaivism, held in Marc April, is very spectacular.) Right on the shore *San Tomé Cathedral*, where the remains of Thomas are buried. The 1504 structure was rebu in 1893. St Thomas is thought to have arriv at Crahganore in Kerala in 52AD, then travell

ound the coast to Madras where he died a few
ears later.

Throughout this part of the city there are elegant
hite villas and a few old garden houses, sur-
ounding pristine garden squares which are often
wned by private firms who compete to produce
e best blooms.

The hugely wide sandy **beach**, nearly 13km
ong, is glorious for a walk (not glorious for swim-
ing), with the domes of Mohammed Ali Walla-
h's Chepauk Palace (1768), Chisholm's Presiden-
College (1864) and his Madras University along
e front. Bullocks and people share the sands, and
oats bob on the water. Fishermen launch their
atamarans (from the Tamil, meaning tied logs) at
-5am, returning 2–5pm with their catch of pom-
et, bekti, small sharks, lobster and prawns. Then
ey lay out their nets on the beach.

The headquarters of the **Theosophical Society**
e just across the Adayar River, in a gloriously
afy and serenely peaceful 270-acre garden which
ould not be missed. The Society, whose adher-
ts advocate the essentially spiritual nature of
an, was founded in the USA in 1875 by Madame
avatsky who came to Madras two years later. Its
lendid library contains some 17,000 manuscripts
pen daily 9–10am; 2–4pm). (Open Tues.–Sat.,
30–10.30am; 2–4.30pm; Sun., 2.30–4.30pm. Gar-
en open daily, sunrise to sunset). It is best to
ombine a visit to the gardens with a dance per-
rmance at the nearby Kalakshetra School of
dian classical dance.

Some of the most beautiful of the old colonial
ouses are scattered around **Adayar area**, such as
e current home of the Madras Club on Chamiers
oad where mulligatawny, the Raj version of the
mil pepper soup, was created. The Club was
uilt as a house by Robert Moubray in 1771, and
as gardens down to the river. (Apply to the
ecretary for a visit, tel: 440121.) Ramalayam on
attice Bridge Road, the Maharaja of Travancore's
ome, is now a children's school. And, in *Guindy*
eer Park and Snake Park, the Raj Bhavan, built as
e Governor's house, is open to visitors. The park
a rare treat: some 300 acres of natural forest right
the city, stocked with corkscrew-antlered black
ck, chital and monkeys. Here too are a reptilium
d India's first snake farm, set up by conserva-
onist Romulus Whitaker and stocked with the 200
arieties of Indian snake, only five of them poison-
s, living in pits. Remember not to arrive carrying
snakeskin handbag, or you will be very unpopu-
r. (Open daily, 9am–6.30pm).

SPORTS   The colonial tradition provides quite a
good selection of sports. At Guindy, south of the
Adayar River, there is the charming race-course
(November–March). Temporary membership is
available (tel: 421171). And a rather sandy, 18-hole
golf course (beware of hitting the park's deer),
open to visitors by applying to the Cosmopolitan
Golf Club, Mount Road (tel: 441840). The Boat Club
offers instant guest membership. Apply in writing
to the Secretary of the Madras Gymkhana, housed
in an elegant colonial house on Anna Salai, beside
the river, for tennis, squash, pool, billiards, table
tennis and beautiful gardens. The MCC (Madras
Cricket Club) has, naturally, cricket, as well as
tennis, squash and billiards.

RESTAURANTS   Excellent Indian food and
good dance is at the *Taj's Mysore* – a good way of
seeing some dance if the early evening performances do not easily fit into your schedule. (Try local
fresh fish, special fish curry, chicken Chettinand
and Hyderabadi dishes, or a thali.)

Other good hotel restaurants are the *Connemara*,
Chola and *Adayar Gate*. For Chinese food, there is
the only roof-top restaurant in Madras, *the Sagari* at
the Chola Hotel, or there is the *Taj's Gold Dragon*.
Apart from hotels, try the excellent *Buhari* on Anna
Salai and the restaurant next door where clients
pack out three floors with a good atmosphere, and
where food is ordered by number. The more
adventurous find good food in tiny places such as
Café Amin, next to the Police Station in the Roya-
pettah area or *Velu Military Hotel* in Eldams Road.
Amaravati restaurant, on Cathedral Road, does a
superb biryani (and sweetmeats) as does *Queen's*
on Nungambakam High Road. For south Indian
food, *Woodlands* drive-in on Cathedral Road is the
best of their several branches. *Desaprakesh Hotel* has
a roof garden restaurant.

The Madras evening highlight is without doubt a
performance of Bharata Natyam dance (see p. 187).
To sample south India films, good cinemas include
Sathyan, Devi and Safire. And that's it. As a couple
of jet-set students at the university complained:
'After 10pm, Madras is dead'.

SHOPPING   Madras is the best place to shop in
Tamil Nadu, so don't only rely on the good hotel
arcades. **Fabrics:** Silk and cotton are the most obvious things to buy. Co-Optrex, at Kuvalagan on
N S C Bose Road, is a five-storey, air-conditioned
building next to the museum, and the headquar-

ters of the South Indian handloom goods. It stocks everything from dress to upholstery fabrics, sold by sari or metre length. Conran, Habitat and FabIndia (of Delhi) all buy here.

Rasi Silk Shop has quality south Indian silks and is behind Kapalishwara Temple, where lots of tiny, traditional Brahman shops sell oils, scented powders for the bath and Indian make-up (Rasi has a second, smaller branch on M G Road.) More good silk can be found at Nalli's and Kumaran's, both at Panagal Park, Mambalam.

On **Anna Salai** there is the classic Raj department store, Spencer's, whose wonderfully period stock includes Merritt treddle sewing machines and a good chemist. Also on Anna Salai are the state emporia of which Kaveri (for Karnataka state), Kairali (for Kerala), Poompuhar (for Tamil Nadu) and the Victoria Technical Institute (VTI) are the best.

VTI has the jazzy cotton appliqué lanterns used to decorate temple chariots for southern festivals. (See them dangling from the Valluvar Kottam, a stone chariot memorial to the poet-saint Thiruvalluvar, in the Nungambakkam area.) They also stock useful and beautiful picnic baskets at Rs20–52 and wonderful canework laundry baskets the shape and size of baby elephants, at Rs1,500. (These are apparently worth shipping if you fill up the body with other purchases.) Poompuhar has nice lanterns, cane mats, small stone elephants and good bronzes and wood carving. Much comes from their workshop at Kallakkurchi village near Tiruneliveli, outside Madurai.

Good antique sculpture, paintings and brass can be found at the Aparna Art Gallery, near the Connemara. With all the **leather** tanning and export, Madras has hopped on the bandwagon of copying the latest European designs, and the prices are even cheaper than in Bombay and Delhi. Find up-to-the-minute leather jerkins, suede coats, luggage, bags and shoes in the Taj and Connemara arcades and the excellent emporium opposite the Taj (open daily 9am–10pm). Italian shoe designs can be found at Vasson's, 829 Anna Salai Road. Madras bazaars are not as colourful or good as elsewhere.

Moore Market, next to Central Station, has everything from pink plastic elephants to black wigs and piles of second-hand books. Beware of pick-pockets in China Bazaar and Evening Bazaar where it is almost impossible to resist such bargain offers as 'buy your teeth here' and 'sex specialist, come and look'.

TIRUPATI, ANDHRA PRADESH

Round trip about 340km. A fascinating trip for th hardy and curious, for this is a very sacred Hind pilgrimage centre and one of the few where no Hindus are permitted to enter the holy of holi and thus see, feel and understand a little mo about the spirituality and strength of Hinduism The best way to go is on an ITDC or TNTDC da trip, leaving Madras 6am, returning 9pm. (Part the ticket price goes to the temple.) 98% of th fellow passengers will be pilgrims. The faithf make for Tirupati all the year round. The temp complex is built on the peak of Tirumala hill in th Seshachalam range, surrounded by mango, tam ind and sandal trees. With the Chola, Pandya an Vijayanagar rulers endowing it, and its continui importance, the temple is immensely wealthy.

At Tirupati town, there is a technicolour clust of painted houses and temples at the foot of t hill. Worldly pilgrims change buses for a terri ing trip up 20km of hair-pin bends (fine views). T stunt driving demanded of the bus-driver is equ ly breath-taking. Ominous signs offer 'space f sick vehicles'. A serious pilgrim climbs the hill part of the pilgrimage, the sadhus (holy men) wi painted faces carrying a suitcase or bedding their heads and black umbrellas.

At the top, the pilgrim's first job is to have h head shaved – men, women and children alike – part of the cleansing process. The temple baza has a variety of goods on sale including long-ear pink plastic rabbits (pilgrims are like any oth tourist) and scented offerings of marigolds, ca phor, coconuts and sugar (a symbol of wealth). T milk of broken coconuts scents the air. The coac load queue-jumps past the chanting faithful w wait their turn for hours, sometimes days. Th chanting reaches fever pitch as they near the sar tum sanctorum. Inside, the incense-filled air intoxicating and the holy atmosphere drives ma into a state of spiritual ecstasy – some even collap – followed by physical and emotional exhausti when they emerge into the temple precinct, sn ing with a deep, spiritual serenity.

KANCHIPURAM

70km from Madras; 65km from Mahabalipuram is an amusing drive, along palm-fringed roa busy with bullocks dragging loads of long bamb There are travelling salesmen with red and gre plastic pails, which they sell for old clothes, r money. And workers thrash grain in the middle the tarmac road so that passing car wheels he with the work. As usual, there are many tanks where women are washing saris and adding splashes of vibrant colour as they put them out to dry. Bathing people share the water with bullocks cooling off.

Kanchipuram (Golden City), is one of the oldest towns of India and one of its Seven Sacred Cities. It is, unusually, dedicated to both Shiva and Vishnu – the other six cities are dedicated to one or the other (see p. 260). It is an exceptionally pleasant rural town of broad streets, full to the brim with exquisite temples and master weavers. And, in the January wedding season, halls are dressed up with canopies of banana leaves, tinsel and garlands of marigold and jasmine. Musicians strum outside.

The town's monuments and weaving tradition date from when it was the capital of the *Pallava* and Chola empires, the two successive political forces in Tamil Nadu after the Guptas. The later Vijayanagar occupants added buildings too. The Pallavas were at their most powerful from the 5th to 8th centuries and often at loggerheads with the contemporary empires of the Chalukyas of Badami in the Deccan and the Pandyas of Madurai in south Tamil Nadu. The rulers believed in their divine right, tracing their ancestry straight back to Brahma, the first of the Hindu trinity.

Although this ancestry might be contested, they certainly rose from local ruling dynasty to wealthy empire, extending their influence right up to Badami and promoting agriculture to increase both produce and taxes. In addition to rice, the main crop and bartering unit, there were coconuts, mangoes, plantains and oil extracted from cotton and gingelly. Tanks, so essential for water, were built by the whole village, lined with stone or brick and strictly managed by a committee. The tax system became all-pervading, like Britain's VAT, touching toddy-men, letter-carriers and even marriage parties. Only weavers to the royal court were exempted.

Political power and cultural patronage leapt forward under Mahendravarman I (600–630). He was a dramatist and poet who was converted from Jainism to Shaivism by the saint Appar, and he ended Jain influence in Tamil Nadu – hence many Pallava temples are dedicated to Shiva or Vishnu. During his reign, some of the rock-cut temples were chiselled at the Pallava port of Mahabalipuram. It was under the Pallavas that Dravidian – the Pallava name for Tamil Nadu – literature, applied arts and architecture developed a distinct and influential character that contributed substantially to Indian civilization.

The *Dravidian* temple follows a basic format whether big or small, and is usually full of life and colour. Gopura (gate-houses with soaring, pyramid towers) pierce the high walls of the complex. The tops of the walls are crammed with multi-limbed gods. The lowest caste, the Hariyans, were not permitted to enter the temples until after Independence, so they worshipped their deities outside the gopura, looking at the sculptures.

Inside, various courtyards, subsidiary temples and a tank surround the central shrine, which is entered through mandapams (hall-like porches) and surmounted by a vimana (pyramid tower). Gopura, temples, mandapams and vimana are all smothered in a riotous confusion of writhing, leaping, fighting and dancing deities. Many have recently been painted up in vivid hues using gloss, not the original matt, paints. This preserves the stonework but gives heart attacks to archaeologists.

The temple was the centre of all village or town life. It was built by the locals, for the locals; for their trading, meetings, worship and enjoyment. Here lived their gods, who loved, fought, married, had birthdays and went on holidays – and still do today. A village without a temple is likened to a man without a soul. The temple was also the background to the intense devotional cult of Tamil Hinduism which stimulated hymns, music, dance and gifts of silk. The choreography of temple dancing developed from the jigs of simple folk to the sophisticated Bharata Natyam, performed by girls living in the temples. Combined attacks by the Pandyas of Madurai and the Cholas of Thanjavur brought down Pallava power in the 9th century (see p. 214).

Of some thousand temples in and around Kanchipuram, several are especially worth a look. *Kailasanatha Temple* (*c.* 725) is one of the earliest and finest in architecture, sculpture and murals, its only later addition being the front built by Mohendra-varman III. It is simple, small-scale, with one of the first examples of a gopura and mandapam. There are beautiful sculptures of gods (Parvati in particular) and yalis (hippogryphs) and there are also vestiges of wall-paintings in the miniature wall shrines. The 7th century *Vaikuntaperumal Temple* has lion-pillar cloisters, precursors of the so-called 1,000-pillar halls of later temple complexes.

The typical Dravidian complex of the large *Ekam-*

bareshwara Temple, with delicate carvings on the 1,000-pillar temple, is an amalgam of Pallava, Chola and Vijayanagar work. (It is worth asking to get on top of the buildings for a splendid view. The custodian's office is behind the 1,000-pillar temple.) *Kamakshiamman Temple* is where the principal chariot festival happens (February–March); their elaborately carved wooden chariot is stored in the high street for the rest of the year.

The pleasantest way to visit the temples is to hire a bicycle for the day – there are no hills here. And, en route, it is good to stop off to see cotton dyeing, lunghi weaving and silk master weavers behind almost every door (see pp. 181–3). Living temples close noon–4pm. There is no tourist office but further information can be obtained from the Archaeological Survey, opposite Kailasanatha Temple (often closed). The Weavers' Service Centre, 20 Railway Station Road (tel: 2530), has a selection of silk for sale and can also advise on where to see weavers. During April, the south Indian New Year, every temple gives its god a procession and there is street theatre in the evening. If necessary, stay overnight at ITDC *Traveller's Lodge*, Kamakshi Amman, Sannathi Street (tel: 2561). It prepares safe, dreary food – but it is much nicer to stay on the coast (see beaches, p. 243).

VELLORE
145km from Madras, via Kanchipuram and Arcot (120km direct from Madras); 180km from Bangalore. It is the site of the 16th century *Vijayanagar fort* and, within it, the Jalakanteshwara Temple (fine carving), both in good condition. The fort, a perfect *Boy's Own* piece of military architecture with a moat, round towers and underground water supply, was probably built by Vijayanagar vassal Sinna Bommi Nayak. It then had a succession of occupants: Mortaza Ali, who claimed the Arcot throne; the Bijapur Sultans; the Marathas; Daud Khan of Delhi and finally the British, who imprisoned Tipu's family here after the fall of Srirangapatna. *Arcot* is also worth pausing at to see the ruined fort, Clive's room above the gate, the ruined palace of the Nawabs of the Carnatic and the tomb of the saint, Tipu Auliya, after whom Tipu Sultan was named.

CHOLAMANDEL
10km south of Madras. A seaside village where a genuine community of artists live and work. There is a permanent exhibition of works for sale and visitors are welcome to meet the artists. The more creative visitors can attend workshops for painting, fabric printing, sculpture, etc., and stay in the pleasant, simply furnished Artists' *Guest-House* close to the beach (tel: 412892). (Apply in writing.

TIRUVIDAVENTHAI
37km south of Madras, just beyond Covelong. It i a temple village in the perfect, unspoilt setting of small valley.

MAHABALIPURAM (MAMALLAPURAM)
45km from Madras; 20km from Covelong; 65kr from Kanchipuram. The Pallavas' second city an port for their capital, Kanchipuram, was already famous port in the 1st century, known to Gree traders. It is now a village sitting quietly among i fabulous rock-cut temples, friezes and shor temples. Starting at the beginning, the *Fiv Rathas* (named after the Pancha Pandavas, the fiv hero brothers of the Mahabharata) are 7th centur embryos of the future Dravidian temples, each on a single block of stone carved as a temple chariot i the shape of a miniature temple, with a huge ston elephant in the middle.

Right in the village centre, the huge and gloriou *frieze* is cut on to a flat granite rock-face, 28m lon and 12m high. It was produced under Narasimha varman I (*c* 630–70). A mass of animals and figure recount the Mahabharata episode of Arjuna penance: after Krishna persuaded him to figh Arjuna did penance to Shiva for the guilt h felt in killing fellow humans. On the right, th Ganga River flows from Shiva's matted hair.

The hillside is scattered with eight *mandapan* (wall-like temple porches cut into the rock) wit bold figure sculptures inside, one with Krishn raising Mount Govardhan to protect his peopl from the wrath of the rain-god, Indra, another wit elephants pouring water over Lakshmi. There also a huge, balanced boulder, known as Krishna' butter (the cave above is his kitchen).

The sole surviving *shore temple* – archaeologist are hunting under the sea for the others – was bui by Rajasimha (690–715). A row of Nandi bulls is o guard on the surrounding walls. The carving of cow being sacrificed is right beside the actual sacr ficial stone, serving as a perpetual sacrifice t appease the gods.

There is a nice open-air museum. Stone-mason and sculptors work in the town centre (see p. 187 The village is best enjoyed by simply wanderin about for a few hours at sunset and sunrise. Fishe men launch their catamarans at daybreak, fir

ffering a little prayer. Other locals fish from the
hore using a short net. *Silver Sands Hotel* is good
or seafood (grilled lobster delicious) and swim-
ing. Accommodation is here at this or one of the
ther beach hotels (see p. 243).

IRUKALIKUNDRAM
5km from Mahabalipuram; 50km from Kanchi-
uram. There are two fine temples, both worth
eeing, one down in the village and one on the
ummit of a tall hill. It is a steep climb, but a good
iew at the top,

ONDICHERRY
60km from Madras; 60km from Chidambaram;
80km from Tiruchchirappalli (Trichy). If you are
oming from Madras, it is worth starting very early
o have time to detour inland at Tindivanan to the
emple town of *Tiruvannamalai* pausing en route at
ingee, the huge Vijayanagar fortress encompas-
ing three hills, built in 1442. (Entry is on the north
ide.)
Pondicherry was capital of the French settle-
ents in India right up until November 1, 1954. It
as founded by François Martin in 1674 and rebuilt
y Jean Law 1756–77. It is now an eerie ghost town
ith closed colonial shutters keeping out the de-
erted streets of Law's tidy White Town, near
here the Governor's elegant house looks out to
ea. Across the canal is the Black Town, with all the
appings of a perky Indian rural town.
To add to the incongruity, the headquarters
f the not altogether convincing *Sri Aurobindo
shram* and movement are here, on Marine Street.
ri Aurobindo Ghosh (1872–1950) was born in
alcutta, got a first-class classics degree at Cam-
ridge, worked for the Maharaja of Baroda, re-
urned to Bengal briefly for the Independence
truggle, then retired here to practise the spiritual
iscipline of yoga.
His principal disciple was a Parisian, known as
he Mother (1878–1973), who established the
shram and education centre. In 1968, she founded
he nearby futuristic and optimistic town of
uroville, designed by the French architect
oger Anger, for people of all religions, politics
nd cultures to live together. It is still unfinished.
pparently things have not been the same since
er death. (Open to visitors 8am–noon; 2–5.30pm;
ining room and several guest houses; quantities
f literature and nice hand-made marbled paper for
ale.)

CHIDAMBARAM
120km from Tiruchchirappalli; 60km from Pondicherry, along a narrow, very rural road, with
water and islands of coconut palms on either side.
If the temples of Thanjavur and Tiruchchirappalli
excite you at all, then this trip is a must. But be
warned: the temple closes noon–4pm and there is
nothing much else here.
A Chola city from 907 to 1310, the exquisite early
shrine at Chidambaram was embellished with
many fine buildings and became a repository of
dance and literature. Two high walls surround the
32-acre temple complex, pierced by four mighty
gopura. The exquisite relief panels of women on
the walls of the gopura porches, each in a different
pose, are a catalogue of the 108 positions for
classical Bharata Natyam as laid down in the
Natyashastra, the Sanskrit treatise on Indian
dance and drama.
Through the main gopura from the village, the
main shrine is straight ahead. Every column inside
is carved but see especially the corner on the right
of the entrance where the Parvati Temple, roofed
in copper gilt, contains both a beautiful image of
Shiva Nataraja (Lord of Dance) and a tiny shrine.
The oldest part of the complex is designed in the
form of a temple chariot with wheels and horses.
Its 56 pillars were praised by the architectural
historian, J. Fergusson as 'most delicately carved,
. . . ornamented with dancing figures, more graceful and more elegantly executed than any others of
their class, so far as I know'.
The large temple tank is behind the main shrine,
with temples to Parvati (again) and Subrahmanya.
Diagonally across from the temples, huge reliefs of
elephants decorate the exterior walls of another
temple. To stay overnight, there is a very modest
state Tourist Lodge.

TRANQUEBAR
40km down the coast from Chidambaram. It was a
Danish settlement (1616–1845) built by the Danish
East India Company, with a fort, several old
Christian mission churches, charming Dutch colonial houses lining King and Queen Street and a
fine Collector's House beside the sea. To stay
overnight, there is a very modest Travellers'
Bungalow in the fort.

KUMBAKONAM
70km from Chidambaram; 40km from Thanjavur.
It is a centre for gold and silver-smithing as well as
for growing the much sought after betel, used to

make paan. Here are some 18 shrines, four of particular merit, all covered in fine sculpture (see especially the Hall of Pillars in Ramaswami Temple). The largest, with an 11-storey gopuram, is second only to Meenakshi Temple at Madurai. Every 12 years the Ganga is believed to flow into the Mahamakham Tank; pilgrims flock to bathe and the water level rises, either with Ganga water or the extra bodies. (The next time it is due is in 1992.)

GANGAKONDACHOLAPURAM

About 30km from Kumbakonam. This little-visited tongue-twister even draws a 'well worth a visit' recommendation from the cool-tempered Murray's Guide. Its Germanic name means 'Ganga brought by Chola king city', and it was built by Rajendra I (1002–44) to commemorate his trip up to the sacred Ganga and the water he brought back. It is a vast building, modelled on his father's Brihadeshwara Temple in Thanjavur. There are fine sculptures and a huge tank where the Chola vassal rulers brought more Ganga water when they visited the king's court. And there are soaring gopura visible for miles around.

THANJAVUR (TANJORE)

50km from Tiruchchirappalli; 158km from Madurai. To understand the importance of Thanjavur, it is important, first, to understand the importance of the *Cholas*. If Dravidian arts and culture developed under the Pallavas, they flourished and crystallised under the Cholas. The historian, Romesh Thapar, considers 'the standards established during this period were regarded as classical and came to dominate the pattern of living in the south, and to influence and modify at certain levels the patterns existing elsewhere in the peninsula'. The huge temples in the Chola capital, Thanjavur, and its surrounding cities, can be seen from miles around and were the social, cultural and economic focus of Chola life.

The Cholas were mere chieftains in Tamil Nadu from the 1st to 8th centuries. Then one leader conquered Thanjavur, declared it a state and quickly claimed descent from the sun. Real expansion and consolidation of power came under Rajaraja I (985–1014) and his son Rajendra (1012–44) – they ruled jointly for two years. Campaigns from Kerala to Sri Lanka and from the Maldives up through Orissa to the Ganga brought most of the Indian peninsula south of Bombay and Puri under Chola control along with parts of Sri Lanka,

Malaysia and Sumatra. Strong and lucrative trading links were established with South-east Asia, China, Persia and Arabia. Then, in the 12th century, the Deccan empires, especially the Hoysala, expanded from the North, while in the South the Pandyas of Madurai saw their chance and took in becoming the dominant power in Tamil Nadu.

The Chola kings ran lavish royal households and were great art patrons. They encouraged the god king cult through image–worship of past rulers and by building temples as monuments to dead kings and symbols of royal grandeur, emphasised when the raja-guru (king's priest) became the king's confidant and adviser for things both temporal and spiritual. Officials, chosen for their caste (the Cholas became very caste-conscious), birth connections and qualifications, oversaw an administration that was divided into village units, each with a committee for everything from taxes to gardens and, of course, the valuable tanks. In this way, central government kept in close contact with the farmers, whose efficiency brought in two or three crops of paddy a year, the biggest export earner. And there were plenty of other trading goods, including textiles, spices, drugs, jewels, ivory, horn, ebony, sandalwood, perfume and camphor. The major imports were the fabulous and expensive Arab horses which the Indians never learnt how to breed. Trade was controlled by merchants and guilds who, naturally, became rich enough to buy whole villages and donate them to a temple. Likewise, the villagers were encouraged to gain spiritual and social respect by giving most of their earnings to the temple – to a lesser degree still true today.

Indeed, the temple was the centre of all. The main building was paid for by the king or a rich merchant, keeping to the same basic form as the Pallava temples at Kanchipuram (see p. 211) although the gopura (gate-houses) gradually became as big as the vimana (tower over the shrine). This employed hundreds of local artisans, often for several years. And when built, it was the locals who maintained the temple, went to school in it (where their formal education was in Sanskrit) and were on the committees and assemblies held in it.

They even gave their women to it. A daughter could be dedicated to the temple at birth or when very young, to become a *devadasi* (female slave of the gods), thus averting calamity for her family. Her life was devoted to giving herself in worship to the gods, for which some underwent the tough discipline of learning Bharata Natyam dance owever, the system was abused, the priests' arnal appetites satisfied and the devadasis often ecame little more than caged prostitutes. The evadasi cult continues today, often unhappily. In elgaum, young children are annually 'married' to ie god, while devadasis reaching puberty are hisked off to stock Bombay brothels. In an effort • counter this, the Karnataka government is cur- ently offering Rs3,000 to any man who will marry, id thus save, a devadasi. Surprisingly, since the rls are considered impure, several marriages ave been arranged, and reported with much fuss the press.

rihadeshwara Temple at Thanjavur was, naturally, ie biggest and richest of them all. Built by Rajaraja '85–1014) as a temple-fort and dedicated to Shiva, s moat is now used by the giggling and chatting omen as they do their laundry. A huge Nandi ill guards the gopuram. The vimana is 64m high. ll the richly detailed carving is of the highest uality; the podgy white faces of frescoes around ie inner courtyard walls and ceilings are still fresh id there is a portrait of Rajaraja with his guru, arur Thevar. There is a small but informative rchaeological Museum off the inner urtyard. Under the Cholas, the temple's im- ense annual income included 500lb of gold, 250lb precious stones and 600lb of silver, made up om donations, contributions and revenue from s hundreds of villages. The huge Seppunaikam ink is beyond the temple.

About 1km away is the palace of the Naiks of Iadurai, built around 1550. There are beautiful alls and a garden courtyard, one section now ousing a very fine collection of Chola bronzes and atues. The Saraswati Mahal Library has a remark- ole collection, tragically suffering from worms id rot. (Palace open Thurs.–Tues., 10am– ,30pm). The Protestant missionaries headed for iis area of India first, and nearby is the missionary . F. Schwartz's church (1777), a marble by the nglish sculptor, Flaxman, inside.

In Thanjavur town, it is worth seeking out one or vo of the other 70 or so temples. Craftsmen can be een working at stone-carving, wood-carving and i brass and bronze. Copper inlaid with brass and lver is the characteristic work of the city, as is the epoussé work (tapping a design into relief from ehind). There are silk weavers, musical instru- ient makers and a pretty bazaar. To buy crafts, the tate emporium, Poompuhar, on Gandhi Road tocks new goods as well as attractive bits of last ear's discarded carved wooden temple chariots.

To stay overnight, go to the ITDC Traveller's Lodge, Vallam Road (tel: 365), with gardens and a res- taurant open to non-residents (exceptionally slow service). Or stay at the TNTDC Tourist Bungalow, Gandhiji Road (tel: 601), which also has maps of the town.

In addition to those at Kumbakonam and Ganga- kondacholapuram, there are more Chola temples at Thirukaniyur (10km north), Thiruvaiyaru (13km, music festival in January) and Thiruvarur (55km east), and all make pleasant rural trips.

TIRUCHCHIRAPPALLI (TRICHINOPOLY)
53km from Thanjavur; 130km from Madurai; 310km from Madras; and is serviced by an airport. This tongue-twister means City of the Three- headed Demon, more commonly known by its British nickname, Trichy. The former, much fought over, citadel switched around between the Cholas, Pallavas and Pandyas. Right in the centre, visible for miles around, is the Rock Fort Temple, reached by climbing up a tunnel of 437 steps to the top where there is the reward of a splendid view, especially of Raghunathanswami Temple at Srirangam and, to the right of it, the smaller Sri Jambukeswar Temple – the real reasons for coming here.

Srirangam temple complex, dedicated to Vishnu, is vast, one of the biggest in India. It was built over a number of centuries: 250 hectares spread over an island in the Cauvery River, whose irrigating waters are so essential to the paddy crop. Its seven concentric walls and 21 gopura contain colourful bazaars in the first layer and Brahmins' houses in the second.

The temple proper is at the centre. There are painted ceilings and remarkable carving, much of it newly painted. Two unpainted parts are especially beautiful. One is the small 10th century section on the left after passing through the last but one gopuram, with sublimely delicate female figures (a shy maiden awaiting her lover, another putting on jewellery, another standing with a parrot at her feet). The other is across the main courtyard to the right, where the sensational row of pillars on the Narayana Temple are carved into men on rearing horses spearing tigers, each pillar a monolith (probably 15th century). The 10-day Vaikunta- Ekadasi temple festival, beginning December 24, is worth attending. The central temple is open 6.15am–1pm; 3.15–8.45pm.

The temple of Sri Jambukeswar, dedicated to Shiva – south Indian temples often come in pairs, dedicated to Vishnu and Shiva – has a mere five enclosing walls and seven gopura, which have nice carvings and painted ceilings, open 6am–1pm; 4–9.30pm. To stay overnight in Trichy, try the *Sangam Hotel*, Collector's Office Road (tel: 25202). The Tourist Office is in TNTDC Tourist Bungalow (open 8.30–10am; 5–8.30pm).

MADURAI

130km from Tiruchchirappalli; 158km from Thanjavur; 307km from Trivandrum; 440km from Madras. It is also serviced by an airport and good trains. Madurai is a temple town throbbing with life and teeming with pilgrims and industries to serve them, just like all the temples used to be. This is the one place in the South where a temple continues to live, almost unchanged, as it has done for hundreds of years, attracting pilgrims the year round but particularly during its two big festivals, celebrating the birthday of king Tirumala Nayak and the marriage of Meenakshi to Shiva (see p. 177).

The *temple, dedicated to Meenakshi*, constitutes most of the city. Its bazaars sell everything from temple offerings, spices and garlands of jasmine to bangles, strip-cartoon comics recounting the gods' escapades and plastic green frogs that hop. It has granaries, kitchens, store rooms and so on. Every facet of Hindu ritual is practised. The faithful cleanse themselves in its tanks, sit chatting, loll about, pray, meditate, perform puja, visit the museum or climb to the top of a gopuram, where there is a superb view. Here, the gopura (gateways) are tallest of all, dwarfing the vimana (central shrine).

From dawn until late at night, its avenues of carved deities, courtyards and temples are seething with trumpeting musicians and drummers. Processions escort a deity on the move (Meenakshi has plenty of companions living in the temple), the temple elephant takes a stroll, there are meetings, gossips, readings and the odd snoozing body. The wealthy give substantial donations into a large safe beside the holy of holies, and are rewarded with a sliding scale of processions – Rs1001 buys the golden chariot procession which keeps the donor well in with the deities and impresses the neighbours.

If this is your first Tamil Nadu temple, a good dose of temple life can be found here, both by day and evening. None other is as colourful as this. If you have toured down from Madras, stopping to see the Pallava and Chola temples, this is wh(?) they were all about.

The Pandyas ruled from Madurai until t(?) Cholas ousted them in the 10th century, b(?) returned for the 12th and 13th centuries when th(?) were the strongest local power. After the tempo(?) ary yoke of the Delhi Sultanate and the Vija(?) anagars, the Nayaks took over and ruled from 15(?) to 1781, when the British arrived. Althoug(?) Meenakshi temple had been established for centu(?) ies, and was the centre of Sangam (ancient confe(?) ences to promote Tamil literature), the bulk of t(?) buildings now standing were erected under Tir(?) malai Nayak (1623–55).

Meenakshi, daughter of a Pandyan ruler, w(?) born with three breasts, one of which was to di(?) appear when she met her Romeo, neatly fulfill(?) when she saw Shiva on Mount Kailas. They m(?) back in Madurai eight days later to marry, Shi(?) doing so in the form of Lord Sundareshwara. T(?) temple has nine gopura, with writhing figures a(?) two slender, gold vimanas. Beside the tank, just(?) front of a mural of Meenakshi and Shiva's we(?) ding, there are two monolith sculptures, su(?) posedly of the 12th century king who began t(?) temple and his Chief Minister.

The best way to see the temple is simply(?) wander around. Good music is played mo(?) nights, 6–7.30pm and 9–10pm. The south-faci(?) gopuram can be climbed. The whole inner temp(?) opens 5am–12.30pm; 4–10pm. Photography(?) only permitted 12.30–4pm but there are excelle(?) large black and white photographs sold at lo(?) prices in the bazaar and hotel.

THE HARD FACTS Two or three nights c(?) easily be spent at the very pleasant **Pandyan Hot(?)** Race Course Road (tel: 26671; telex: 0445–2(?) COSY IN; cable: TEMPLECITY). It is run by t(?) Taj group. All mod. cons include a travel agent, c(?) rental, bank, doctor, beauty salon, shoppi(?) arcade, a restaurant (offering good South Indi(?) food) and extremely well-nurtured garden. The(?) is a good Tourist Office at 180 West Veli Street.

OUT AND ABOUT Apart from the temp(?) there are a few other places to see. Tirumalai Nay(?) Palace (1636), restored by Lord Napier, is no(?) partly a mediocre museum, with dance-drama a(?) concerts performed in the courtyard (daily, 8a(?) 5pm). Mariamman Teppakkulam Tank (1646) ha(?) central island for cool royal picnics. This tank(?) where the great Teepam (Float) festival is hel(?)

ere is another Gandhi Museum here, this one
ell laid out and housing, along with much else,
e khadi dhoti the Mahatma was assassinated in
d his glasses (open Thurs.–Tues. 10am–
30pm). And there are, of course, more temples
attered around as well as dyeing, cotton lunghi
eaving and silk weaving down almost every
ley.
About 10km out of town, the *Tiruparankumdram
ck-cut temple* is very lively, although much smaller
an Meenakshi Temple. There is a facade of huge
ue and yellow dragons. Inside, there is a maze of
rk rooms filled with multi-limbed sculptures,
d neon lights marking up which god is which in
ng strips of Tamil, flickering oil lamps, a bazaar,
e temple elephant wandering about and people
orshipping, jostling, gossiping and lounging
ound.

HOPPING In the shops and bazaars of the
mple there is fun, out-size costume jewellery –
ostly of little value. In the emporia and neigh-
uring shops there are good fabrics, brass trays
d figures, wood-carving, stone-carving and the
ightly coloured, appliqué cotton lanterns that are
ed to decorate temple chariots. The Pandyan
otel shops sometimes have very beautiful chess
ts of Tamils, an elephant for a Knight, made by
phans living locally at Tirumanagalum (if not on
ow, ask the Manager).

AMASWARAM
0km from Madurai. A trip for temple-addicts.
nown as the Varanasi of the South but it lacks its
agic and its light. The *Ramanathaswamy Temple* is
uge and impressive, with seemingly endless
rved corridors. But it is easiest to see en route to
i Lanka – and even then, this is the nastiest way
getting there. As one hardened, round-the-
orld traveller said: 'Ramaswaram is one of the
w real pits. And never take the ferry to Sri Lanka
nless you are keen on character building.'

DDAIKANAL
0km from Madurai; 150km from Thekkady Wild-
e Sanctuary; 210km from Cochin; 150km from
oimbatore. Apart from Thekkady Wildlife Sanc-
ary, this is the nearest place to get cool from
amil Nadu or Kerala. It is a charming, peaceful
ackwater hill station reached by a beautiful drive
ross the plains and up into the woods and water-
lls of the Palani range which branch off north-
st from the Cardamom Hills. Unlike Ooty,

Kodaikanal is mercifully forgotten by smart
Indians, tourists, seekers of Raj nostalgia and
modern industry. It has a slightly warmer climate
too, free from cold spells.

The town clusters around the lake where ginger-
bread Raj houses nestle in well-tended gardens
along the shore. There are boats to row and horses
for appetising rides before a hearty breakfast.
There are good rambles on the surrounding hills.
The Flora and Fauna Museum at nearby Shemba-
ganur is rich in orchids and has an observatory
(open daily March, April and June, 10am–12.30pm;
7–9pm; otherwise only Fridays, 10am–noon). Stay
at the old *Carlton Hotel*, Lake Road (tel: 252),
modest, period hotel with character, overlooking
lake.

Wildlife sanctuaries

The South is stocked with good National Parks,
mostly concentrated in Tamil Nadu and near its
borders. They are substantially easier to get to than
many parks elsewhere. The distances are often
short, the roads are good and the scenery en route
is stunning, especially up to Thekkady from Kottayam or Madurai. Many sanctuaries lie conveniently between two interesting places and
easily fit into an itinerary. And the Madras Snake
Park, the Crocodile Farm and Vedanthangal Water
Bird Sanctuary are right on the doorstep for visitors
to Madras and the beaches south of it. To stay in
these parks, be sure to book accommodation and
jeeps in advance.

BANDIPUR, KARNATAKA
October–June and September–October best,
although good all the year round. It lies on the
Mysore-Ooty road. Fly to Bangalore, then by road
219km; train to Mysore, then by road 80km; from
Ooty 80km by road. It is all right to stay in any of
the Forest Lodges or Guest Houses, the Wooden
Cottages (3, each sleeps 12) or Swiss Cottage Tents
(4, each sleeps two). Book the room and in-park
transport (essential) from the Divisional Forest
Officer, Mysore or Field Director, Project Tiger,
Government House Complex, Mysore (tel: 20901).
Explore on the good network of roads by elephant,
or observe from machans (tree-platforms) at water-
holes.

There are 400 sq km of mixed deciduous forest,
the original sanctuary of the larger Venugopal
National Park. Currently being expanded under
Project Tiger, it is lush and well-stocked with game

217

and was the first South Indian park to be included in Project Tiger. It adjoins Mudumalai sanctuary (across the River Moyar) and Wynad sanctuaries. Game moves freely between them. It is possible to see gaur (Indian bison), chital (they come near the Lodges at night), tiger, leopard, sambhar and herds of the famous Karnataka elephant (the best for war) at water pools. There is good bird life, too.

MUDUMALAI, TAMIL NADU

December–June. On the Mysore–Ooty road. Arrive as for Bandipur (see above). The distances by road are 97km from Mysore, 64km from Ooty. There is lots of accommodation, including *Mountainia Rest House* at Masinagudi Village (a collection of cottages, the de-luxe ones are best, with good food plus bar) and *Sylvan Lodge* at Theppakadu Village (4 suites, good food). You can book a room and in-park transport through the District Forest Officer, Ooty; Safari Travels, Ooty (tel: 3141); or State Wildlife Officer, Forest Department Block III, Administrative Buildings, 81 Mount Road, Madras (tel: 440174). But by far the nicest place to stay is *Bamboo Banks*, with charming and informed Parsee owners (book through Mysore or Ooty tourist-office). Explore remoter areas by jeep and thick jungle by elephant.

400 sq km of thick, mixed deciduous hill forest in the Nilgiris, adjoining Bandipur and Wynad sanctuaries. It is rich in wildlife near the villages but well worth exploring further afield. It is possible to spot leopard, giant squirrel, tiger, elephant, gaur (especially around Theppakkadu's teak forest), sambhar, chital, mouse-deer, pig and two types of monkey, the bonnet and common langur. Spring and summer are good times for visibility, with blossoming and fruiting trees and rich bird life (Great Black woodpeckers, barbets, Malabar Grey hornbill, etc). Autumn is good for lush, tall grass, herds of gaur and elephant and exceptionally large herds of mature, antlered chital (spotted deer) around the Masinagudi-Moyar area. The park also contains an Elephant Camp where the huge beasts are trained to help with logging, acting as mobile cranes to lift huge sandal tree trunks on to lorries.

NAGARHOLE, KARNATAKA

October–May. Travel as for Bandipur, then 224km by road from Bangalore, 94km south-west of Mysore. Stay at Tiger Tops' beautiful new riverside *Kabini River Lodge* just outside the park, incorporating the restored Maharaja of Mysore's Hunting Lodge and Viceroy's Bungalow. 36 beds, bar an good food (open mid-September to mid-June Book through Jungle Lodges and Resorts, 348 Brooklands, 13th Main, Rajmahal Vilas Ext, Bang lore (tel: 31020). Explore by jeep, buffalo, corac (hide boats) and observe from machans.

284 sq km of tropical deciduous trees, swamp and streams, densely inhabited by elephant, tige leopard, gaur (Indian bison), several species deer, crocodile, water fowl and rich bird life. Som fishing, especially for mahseer, a powerful fightin fish of the carp family, growing up to 150lb weight. Some of the biggest are found in the Cau ery River and a special fishing camp is run b Jungle Lodges and Resorts, best January–March The government Elephant Camp for trainin elephants can be visited.

RANGANATHITTU WATER-BIRD SANCTUARY, KARNATAKA

June–September. As for Bandipur, then 133km b road from Bangalore, 20km north-east of Mysore 2km from Srirangapatna. No accommodation. beautiful island in the Cauvery River, rich in bir life, includes a mixed heronry, red wattled lap wing, white ibis, spoonbill, open bill stork, egre darter, cormorant and river tern. Boats for hir Observation point.

PERIYAR, THEKKADY, KERALA

February–May. Fly to Cochin, then by road 208km fly to Madurai, then by road 160km; 119km by roa from Kottayam, 258km from Trivandrum. It is be at dawn and dusk, when there are wonderful nigh noises. So, it is worth spending a night or so her rather than going for the day. Stay at the smartis and newish *Aranya Nivas Hotel* (tel: 23, cabl ARANYANIVAS), overlooking the lake. It comfortable, with mod. cons but bad food. It is als well placed for forest walks. However, there a two much nicer alternatives, with character. Th first is *Hotel Lake Palace* (tel: 24; cable: ARANYAN VAS), an old bungalow on an island, with prett garden. Of the six rooms, nos 44 and 66 best f views. This is a good place for viewing game Stipulate Indian cooking when booking to avoi dreary Raj food. The second is the charming, three roomed *Government Rest House* in the forest. Boo direct; information from the Wildlife Preservatio Officer, Thekkady. Explore forest on foot, lake b boat and observe from machans.

Over 700 sq km of hilltop sholas surrounding vast artificial lake built by the British in 1895 f rigation (old tree trunks stand sentry in the lake), p in the Cardamom Hills near the border of Tamil Nadu and Kerala. It is one of the largest sanctuaries n India, was established in 1934, is part of Project Tiger and is the best place to watch wild elephant. t is best to take the 7am boat up the lake between ills with the shapes and colours of the Scottish Highlands. Mist rises from the water, game stirs nd elephants come to drink – they even swim in he lake sometimes. And there is gaur, pig, dhole (wild dogs), otters and freshwater tortoise. Bird fe is rich: herons, kingfishers, egrets on the vater; hornbills and fishowls in the dense forests f spices, blossoming trees and creepers. When is hot, the tiger and gaur come down to the vater.

Two new sanctuaries in the Cardamom Hills are he *Mundanthurai Tiger Sanctuary*, to the south of Periyar, and the *Anamalai Tiger Sanctuary*, north of t. Both are for the keen wildlife spotter, rich in nimals but as yet not very organised for tourists, ven by the standards of Indian wildlife sanc- uaries. Further information from Tamil Nadu or Government of India Tourist Offices.

VEDANTHANGAL WATER BIRD SANCTUARY, AMIL NADU

October–March but busiest December–January. By road, 80km south of Madras. It is nicest to stay t a seaside hotel nearby (see p. 243). Further nformation from Chief Conservator of Forests, Madras. This is a major breeding sanctuary for migrating birds and the South's equivalent to Bhar- atpur outside Agra (see p. 67). The best times of day are early morning, as the birds wake, and 3–6pm, when they return. Flocks can be of several housand, including several varieties of heron, gret, stork, pelican and ibis.

POINT CALIMERE, TAMIL NADU

November–January. By road, 150km from Than- avur to the north coast point of Palk Bay. Accom- modation is available at the very basic *Forest Rest House*, or in Thanjavur, which is preferable. Fur- her information from the Chief Conservator of Forests, Madras. Although there are black buck and wild pig to see, this is really a place for ornitho- ogists. The tidal mud flats attract thick flocks of migratory water fowl to swell the rich local water owl population. First come teals, sandpipers, hanks, herons and thousand upon thousand of lamingoes which rise up in pink clouds. Then, in pring, see mynas and barbets, etc.

CROCODILE BANK, TAMIL NADU

Season all the year round. Between Covelong and Mahabalipuram, 42km south of Madras by road. No accommodation. Open daily, 8am–6pm.

This is a farm for breeding crocodiles which are endangered as a result of hunters. It is highly successful and is now helping to repopulate Indian wildlife sanctuaries. In a somewhat sinister way, it is a fascinating place to visit. Guides show visitors eggs, newly hatched babies and fully grown croco- diles. The different types live in seemingly over- crowded groups in disarmingly low-walled pits and the guides take delight in demonstrating feed- ing time to visitors, teasing enormous beasts with a dangling dead rat before hurling it among them to be fought over.

For **Madras Snake Park**, Tamil Nadu, see p. 209.

Find out more

Archer, M.: *Tipoo's Tiger*, London, 1959
Balasubrahmanyam, S. P.: *Later Chola Temples (AD1070–1280)*, India, 1979, 4th and final volume of the series
Census of India, 1961, vol.IX, part 7a, no.1, *Silkweav- ing at Kanchipuram, Madras*
Chowdhury, A. R.: *Bidri Ware (Salar Jang Museum illustrated catalogue)*, Hyderabad, 1961
Cousens, H.: *Notes on the buildings and other anti- quarian remains at Bijapur*, Bombay. 1890
Cousens, H.: *Bijapur and its architectural remains*, Bombay, 1916
Irwin, H.: *Garlands Galore: Recollections of an Oil Merchant in the East*, London, 1983
Khokar, M.: *Bharata Natyam*, Bombay, 1979
Lutyens, M.: *Krishnamurti: the Years of Awakening*, London, 1975
Meister, W., (ed.): *Encyclopedia of Indian Temple Architecture, South Indian Lower Dravidesa*, vols I & II, Delhi, 1983
Menon, A. S.: *Cultural Heritage of Kerala, An Intro- duction*, Cochin, 1978
Merklinger, E. S.: *Indian Islamic Architecture, The Deccan 1347–1686*, UK, 1981
Murphy, Dervla: *On a Shoe-string to Coorg: An Ex- perience of South India*, London, 1976
Narayan, R. K.: *Swami and Friends*, 1935, the first of many delightful novels set in fictional Malgudi, inspired by Mysore, many available in Penguin paperbacks; the latest is called *A Tiger for Malgudi*
Panter-Downes, M.: *Ooty Preserved*, London, 1967
Ramaswami, N. S.: *Mamallapuram, An Anotated*

Bibliography, Madras, 1980 (quotes the relevant passages from all books on the subject)
Sarabhai, M.: *The Sacred Dance of India*, Bombay, 1979
Sarkar, H.: *Monuments of Kerala*, Delhi, 1978
Sewell, R.: *A Forgotten Empire*, Delhi, 1982
Sivaramamurti, C.: *South Indian Paintings*, Delhi, 1968
Soundara Rajan, K. V.: *Invitation to Indian Architecture*, India, 1984

Wiles, J.: *Delhi Is Far Away, a Journey Through India*, London, 1974
Woodcock, G.: *Kerala: Portrait of the Malabar Coast*, London, 1967
Yazdani, G.: *Bidar: Its History and Monuments*, Oxford, 1947
Zebrowski, M.: *Deccani Painting*, London, 1983
Zebrowski, M.: 'Bidri: metalware from the Islami courts of India', *Art East*, 1982, no.1

The hills and Nepal:
Playtime paradise

Apart from playing at politics, Delhi is not hot on recreation. But the Himalayas, a plane-hop away, are one big, beautiful amusement park with an abundant choice of games between the green Simla slopes and the snowy Nepal peaks. The whole region is as fashionable now as when the Governor-General, Lord William Bentinck, initiated the British habit of abandoning Calcutta's cloying summers for Simla in 1832.

From 1865 until Independence the Viceroy and his entire government decamped there from Calcutta, and later Delhi, in trainloads of trunks, papers and officials. They went all the way up in March to rule India from a castle, a country mansion, mock-Tudor houses and red-roofed chalets amid the serious business of gardening, racing, polo, cricket and amateur theatricals at The Gaiety. Baden Powell, Kitchener and Kipling played there. Lord Lytton, while Viceroy, directed his own play in 1876. In October, they came all the way down again.

When Lutyens saw it in 1912 he wrote: 'It is inconceivable, and consequently very British! – to have a capital as Simla is entirely of tin roofs . . . if one was told the monkeys had built it all one could only say "what clever monkeys – they must be shot in case they do it again".' Simla is now a pure Raj time-warp amusement arcade, where ex-colonials join the smartest Indians in roast chicken and rice pudding. Between them lie the flower-strewn valleys of Kulu, Kangra and Manali for walks and gentle treks.

The joys of the Kashmir Valley were discovered much earlier, by the Mughals. Akbar, the romantic couple Jehangir and his Nur Jehan, and Shah Jahan were all crazy about it, cooing 'happy valley', 'paradise on earth', 'only Kashmir'. Kashmir is still mainly Muslim.

Nehru, himself a Kashmiri, wrote in 1940: 'Sometimes the sheer loveliness of it all was overpowering. How can they who have fallen under its spell release themselves from its enchantment?' (Huxley was less keen in *Jesting Pilates*, accusing the Kashmiris of having a 'genius for filthiness'.) Srinagar is still sublimely romantic, perfect for wandering the gardens and drifting about aimlessly in a shikara on the lakes. And the pampering in the carved, wooden houseboats surpasses the attentions Cleopatra received.

The hills have good sports facilities, too. There is water skiing, winter skiing, golf on the highest course in the world at Gulmarg, trekking on stocky ponies, fishing at Pahalgam and luxurious camping beneath the cliffs of the Leh monasteries.

Big-time trekking in the Nepal mountains is more challenging. Penelope Chetwode (Sir John Betjeman's widow) leads some parties. Roman Polanski also goes there 'to get as far away as possible . . . ever higher through glorious rhododendron forests, heading for

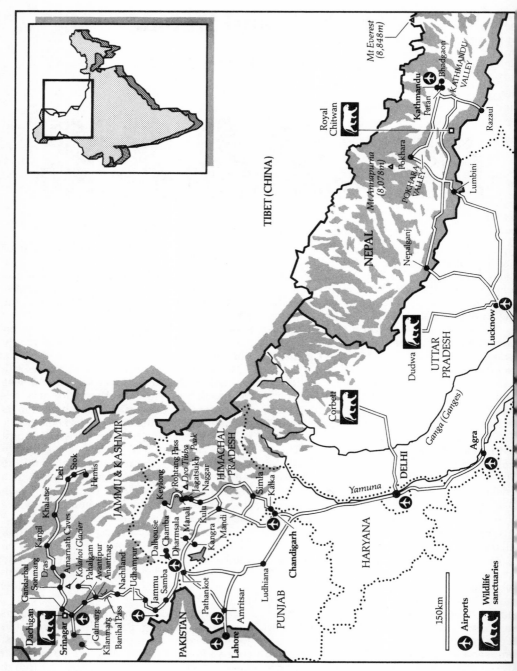

ie snow line . . . the extraordinary Hima-
iyan panorama, with its plunging valleys
ind soaring mountain ranges . . . I'd seldom
elt happier.'

There is river-rafting, game-spotting from
lephants and, the ultimate joy ride, a dawn
ight over Mount Everest – the easy way to
ee the roof of the world that Sir Edmund

Hillary and 111 others have seen the hard
way (including 5 women – Miss Pal was the
first Indian woman to reach the top, in May
1984).

Amidst all this frolicking and frivolity live
the hill peoples with their own distinctive
customs, crafts, architecture and festivals
and fairs full of folk dancing and music.

The hard facts

WHEN TO GO Each area has an optimum
eason (see below). While the rest of India puts up
imbrellas against the June–September monsoon,
Kashmir is fresh and sunny. In HP (Himachal
Pradesh), weather is very localised. There will be
ine views in one area and downpours and mist in
nother. For flowers, head for the foothills in
March–April, higher up in June–July. Lotus blos-
oms cover the Srinagar lakes in August. Autumn
olours in Kulu are blinding. Nepal is in blossom
April–June, but February and October have the
est weather. So check carefully, according to your
aste. It is also worth coinciding with the better
estivals and fairs, such as those at Leh, Kulu,
Rampur, Mandi, Chamba and Renuka.

GETTING THERE: GETTING AWAY In most
ases it is best to fly up to an area, often with
stunning views from the plane (see p. 39 – Delhi
travel info.), although there are some collectors'
train journeys. The drive up from Delhi is not
especially pretty. Once there, you can use one
place as a base for sport, relaxation and the occasional foray. Alternatively, you can walk/trek/drive
for a few days, flying out from another airport.
There are some exceptionally splendid drives, such
as from Jammu to Srinagar, and memorable flights,
such as from Srinagar up to Leh. See sections
below for more.

WHERE TO STAY While a few hotels offer
European facilities, the luxury tends to lie in
character and in charming, caring, old-fashioned
service that is sadly disappearing from Delhi
hotels. A whole family attends to 2 guests on a
houseboat. Fishermen have the flies put on their
hooks. Trekkers may have a staff ratio of 10 to 1,
with people to carry belongings, pitch the tent,
cook full meals and tend to every need.

Remember the altitude when packing: summer
evenings get distinctly chilly and winter brings
snow. On the whole, the food is not exciting and
the Raj nursery influence persists to make it difficult even to sample local food, especially in Kashmir. Nor does the night life thrive, apart from local
folk dancing.

WALKING AND TREKKING: Little exercise
preparation is needed for those keeping below
11,000 feet. Those going above may need more.
Trekking varies from a gentle amble to serious
climbing. It is essential to check exactly what is
involved. One London City businessman's view is
that: 'Days spent in the Kulu Valley are one of the
most stunning things to do in India. Serious trekking is uncomfortable, unsexy, sordid and shakes
some people rigid. The food is crummy. You don't
change clothes for 10 days. But there's no other
experience so glorious. Nothing in the Alps to
match it.'

There is no age limit for trekkers, but they should
be fit, do a bit of walking to get into shape and, if in
any doubt, have a medical check-up. There will not
be room service and baths but, as one trekker
addict put it: 'There is an extraordinariness about
being in such mountains that words cannot con-
vey. I cannot go a year without this sort of experience.' Trekking can be quite challenging, but, with
a good Sherpa, no trekker is ever pushed to do
more than he feels able to.

ExplorAsia produce an excellent booklet, Trekking Information, covering everything from what to
pack, and how to pack it, to the daily trekking
routine, how to take photographs and how to have
a pee at 8,000 feet. Christina Noble and Kranti
Singh of West Himalayan Holidays brief their
clients in London before going out to lead the
walks and treks. (For addresses, see p. 6) Always
hire a guide, porters and ponies to carry supplies
and tents. Walking may sound unluxurious, but

the scenery, views, flora and nurse-maid service are luxurious beyond doubt. Remember to pack insect repellant, suntan lotion (thin air equals scorching sun) and plenty of camera film.

If the trip is not already planned from home, the Delhi travel agencies recommended on p. 44 should give reliable advice, make up an itinerary exactly suited to your interests and sportiness and then book the lot for you.

SIMLA

The setting for Kipling's *Plain Tales from the Hills*. A thick Raj atmosphere persists in this former summer capital of British India, now capital of Himachal Pradesh. The air is pine-scented. The pace is slow. There are no bicycles, no rickshaws; just strolling people, many of them tourists.

THE HARD FACTS Set at 2,213m in the Shivalik hills of pine forests, the best months are April–June when hyacinths and lilies fill the meadows; monsoon comes in July; September–October are pleasant again before snow December–March. Get there by first taking the daily 6.15am flight to Chandigarh, arriving 7.25am. It is then 110km by bus. But much more fun is to take the Himalayan Queen on the narrow gauge railway built 1903–4, leaving Kalka (a 14km taxi drive away) at 8.20am, arriving Simla 2.35pm. This will not suit architecture buffs. Spacious Chandigarh, India's first planned city, was conceived by Le Corbusier and Maxwell Fry as capital for the Punjab state (shared with Haryana). It is now 30 years old, with mature trees and gardens. For a good nose around, stay overnight at the Hotel President (tel: 40840; cable: COMFORTS), central, clean, food OK, car rental.

In Simla, there are two hotels of the Oberoi chain, both with plenty of character and stunning views. *Oberoi Clarkes*, The Mall (tel: 6091-5; cable: OBHOTEL); turn-of-the-century, centrally sited, mock-Tudor building acquired by Mohan Singh Oberoi in 1935, the first of his chain that now has 26 hotels. Oberoi, born 1900, arrived in Simla in 1922 with 25 rupees and got a job as a front desk clerk in the Cecil Hotel. 12 years later he mortgaged his assets and his wife's jewellery to buy the nearby Clarkes. Four years later he bought the Oberoi Grand in Calcutta. By the mid-1950s he had 14 hotels, often formerly run by British or Swiss families who traditionally ran hotels. He opened the first School of Hotel Management in India, led the considerable rise in Indian hotel standards, served

as a Member of Parliament in both houses and, a Chairman of the Oberoi empire, now lives on farm near Delhi.

Clarkes has 48 rooms, including 8 suites attached bath. Facilities include car rental, excur sion advice, picnics, baby sitter, safe but wel cooked food served indoors or in the garden.
Hotel Cecil, The Mall (tel: 2073/6041-4; cable OBCECIL); only open May and June, right on th edge of town but with splendid colonial grandeu from its days as finest hotel in north India. 3 spacious rooms including 21 suites, with attache bath. Car rental, excursion advice, picnics, soli Raj food served in the garden or indoors.

Helpful Tourist Office, The Mall (tel: 3311). The run pleasant tours into the surrounding hills. Goo guide-book from Maria bookshop (which stock old and new books and prints) on The Mall.

OUT AND ABOUT The Mall is the main stree on the crescent-shaped ridge covered by the town It is the hub of Simla and nice to stroll along. Yor can pause for refreshment, and to watch the worlc go by, in one of the many cafés and restaurants There are a number of Indian Coffee Houses They are South Indian and therefore tend to be clean and serve good Mysore coffee. Davies ha a Raj club style. Next door is a good Indian res taurant.

Just near Clarkes Hotel, on the corner, is the sit of Mr Isaacs' shop. Kipling based Lurgan Sahib who trained Kim to spy, on Mr Isaacs. On and nea The Mall there are stylish houses built by Britisl sahibs and called 'Strawberry Hill' and 'The Grot to'. Kennedy Cottage there is the first British house at Simla, built 1822. Then there are some grande British buildings: the Gothic Christ Church (1857) the Municipal Buildings combining Scottish baro nial with Swiss chalet, the mock-Tudor public lib rary next door, the Scottish baronial Viceregal palace and mock-Tudor Barnes Court.

The bazaar is as mixed as the architecture. There are local tribes, stocky hill people and tall Punjabis. Himachal State Museum has Pahari miniature paintings, an unusually good collection of Pahari sculpture and other treasures (open Tues.–Sun., 10am–5pm). You can follow the visit with tea at the Cecil, opposite. For the best view of Simla, go to the top of Jakko hill – beware of monkeys at Hanu man temple; for afternoon promenades, go along the Ridge. Buy Kulu shawls.

SPORTS There is golf and tennis (arranged by the

otel). In the summer take picnics and go for orious walks in the pine-scented air in every irection. In January–February, ski at Kufri 6km), equipment for hire. Go to Naldera for golf; hail for bird-watching and to see the world's ighest cricket ground; Hatkoti for trout fishing.

HE KULU VALLEY
etween 200 and 4,000m. Kulu town is at 1,200m. he narrow valley runs north from Mandi, past ulu and Manali to the Rohtang Pass. The Beas iver flows through this fertile, terraced valley, the ost accessible one in the area. Excellent for long alks and treks in flower-covered valleys and up rough pine and cedar forest. The agrarian eoples are hard-working, honest, deeply re-gious – there are about 6,000 temples – and love a arty.

HE HARD FACTS   Go April–May for blossom-g trees and flowers, September–October for azzling autumn colours, local fruits (especially pples), clear air and light. There are dancing and irs at any excuse. Every village has its own god ho is taken to visit related gods, given a bath, ven has a birthday – all with much merriment, ressing up, processions and plenty of the local hang (rice or barley-based liquor).

The whole of Mandi is decorated for *Shivarati* fair ebruary–March), when deities are brought on alanquins and chariots. There is folk dance, dra-a and music played on the hill instruments such s karnal, dhol, narsinghas and drum. But best of ll is *Dussehra* (September–October), 10 days of olid celebration beginning on Vijaya Dashmi, the ay it ends in the rest of India. It commemorates ot so much Rama's victory over Ravana as an idol f Ragunathji in Kulu, to which some 200 gods om the surrounding villages are brought to pay omage, followed by nightly folk dance compe-tions.

Flights go to nearby Bhuntar airport March–eptember. Otherwise, fly to Chandigarh, then by oad 270km to Kulu, 310km to Simla – long but very retty rides. In Kulu, stay at *Kulu Valley Resort*, rranged in cottages, restaurant with superb iews. Or both Kulu and Manali have good Ashok *ravellers Lodges* (tel: Kulu 79; Manali 31). Tourist ffice by the maidan in Kulu (tel: 7), in the main treet of Manali (tel: 25), both with advice on walks. he Himalayan Mountaineering Institute is for nore ambitious climbs, has equipment for hire and herpas to guide; the most exciting climb is up

Hanuman Tibba, 5,929m (2 days). The impressive Rohtang Pass trek, which begins at Kothi, is easier (4,000m).

OUT AND ABOUT   In the villages, especially Vashist, see the carved temples and houses of the agrarian locals who are quite wealthy (compared to Nepal and Kashmir) and often landowners. Crops are maize, rice, wheat, barley, potatoes, pulses and, of course, apples.

Peep inside houses – almost every one has a loom for weaving tartan or striped tweeds and the very fine pashmina wool, made from the under-coat that a high altitude goat grows. The goats are kept by the nomadic Gaddis. Fabrics, shawls and Tibetan jewellery (lots of refugees here) can be bought in Manali, as well as new tankas and car-pets with a cut pile. Prices are absolutely fixed here and no credit cards taken.

Do not miss *Old Manali Village* (2km) nor the old wooden *Hadimba Devi Temple* (c 14th–16th cen-turies) among the cedars (3km). Himachal State Museum is at Kulu. There are also two former Kulu capitals: *Naggar*, with castle (now a rest house) and fort, and *Jagatsukh*, the earlier capital, with old temples. At *Mandi*, Triloknath Temple and Rewal-sar both merit a look. There is trout fishing on the Beas at Raison, Katrain and Kasel, March–October, licences through the Tourist Office from the Director of Fisheries, Dehra Gopipur.

There are also treks up the Malana, Parbati, Solang and Seraj Valleys and up Deo Tibba (6,000m). The *Kangra Valley*, with the impressive Kangra fort, starts near Mandi and is lower than Kulu and subsequently hotter, with a short July–August monsoon. Beyond the valley lies the hill station of Dharamsala whence the Dalai Lama fled, now full of Tibetan refugees and western hippies.

JAMMU
At 305m. Thriving, bustling capital of Jammu and Kashmir with some of its old character. It was the Maharaja of Kashmir who bought a Rolls Royce, signed the usual agreement that the car could only be driven and repaired by a Rolls Royce-trained chauffeur and then remembered his position. He was a maharaja; they were merely tradesmen. So, he sacked the chauffeur. Rolls Royce took him to court, won and sold the car second-hand in Bombay.

Jammu was formerly the cultural centre for the fine miniature paintings produced at the courts of the hill states during the 18th and 19th centuries.

Worth pausing here to see two excellent collections of paintings, both open the year round.

THE HARD FACTS Flights connect Jammu with Delhi, Chandigarh, Srinagar and Amritsar. Stay at either Hotel *Jammu Ashok* (tel: 42084; telex: 377227; cable: TOURISM), right opposite the Amar Mahal Museum; or the Welcomgroup's *Asia Jammu-Tawi*, (tel: 47373; cable: WELCOMOTEL), better facilities include travel counter, beauty salon, health club, pool. J & K Tourist Office, Vir Marg (tel: 5324). Fishing the Tawi river for the plentiful mahseer, seeng and mali only possible with a permit from the Tourist Office in Srinagar and own fishing equipment.

OUT AND ABOUT First stop is Dogra Art Gallery, Gandhi Bhavan, facing the New Secretariat. It was set up in 1954. There are some 600 paintings as well as terracottas, arms, sculptures, manuscripts and murals. They include the outstanding illustrations to the Rasmanajari (Posies of Delight), a 14th century Hindu text by the poet Bhanu Datta, describing the behaviour and feelings of lovers. They were painted for Raja Sangram Pal and his half-brother Hindal Pal (1660–70) by the finest Basohli court artists who use bold designs and flat areas of vivid colour, further enriched with green beetle wing. Only some paintings on view; try asking to see more. (Open Tues.–Sun., 7.30am–1pm in summer; 11am–5pm in winter).

Amar Mahal Museum is also worth visiting. Dr Karan Singh's collection is exhibited in a French-designed palace complete with furnishings, built on a bluff overlooking the Tawi River in 1907 by Dr Singh's grandfather, Raja Amar Singh; hall hung with 47 illustrations to the Nala-Damayanti (part of the epic Mahabharata) recounting Nala and Damayanti's marriage, followed by Nala gambling his kingdom away, then recovering it; painted at Kangra, 1800–1810, with soft tones, in a lyrical detailed style striving for realism. (Open Tues.–Sat., 5–7pm; Sun., 8am–noon, closed holidays).

Honey, dried fruits and pretty wicker baskets with yellow and red painted decoration are the things to buy.

Around Jammu are good hill forts (Samba, Bahr), temples (Purmandal, Basohli). There is a very picturesque narrow-gauge railway trip from Jammu to *Dalhousie* (2,035m), a backwater Simla developed for those who could not afford the real thing. Its mock-Tudor houses are still furnished with commodes and fitted with beautiful fire places. *Aroma-n-Claire* (tel: 99) is one of man slightly run-down Raj hotels. Beyond Dalhousie through a beautiful forest, you descend to *Chamb* (926m), a very pretty hilltop town with fine views There is riding, trekking and the Raja Bhuri Sing Museum (more exquisite paintings). The colourfu Minjar festival is in July–August. Hotel *Akhnaa chandi* (tel: 171) is very modest but the best.

SRINAGAR

At 1,768m. Mughal-designed gardens; British designed holiday houseboat cottages; Kashmir hills; lakes bordered by tall chinar (oriental plan trees); flowers and pampering. A perfect combina tion for romantic relaxation. And, if you stay on houseboat, it is as near to privacy as is possible i India. Days slip away deliciously on the house boats on Nagin or Dal lake. Deep 1930s sofas invit a good read or a snooze. The electric wireless wit big tuning knobs (definitely not a 'radio') bring music and All India news read by a lady with twin-set-and-pearls voice. From the sun-trap boa roof or the carved porch there is the gentle li of the lake to watch. An electric blue kingfishe dives for its dinner. The wily Kashmiris glide pas on laden boats, crying out their wares: 'floot minlalal water, fledge' (fruit, mineral wate fudge).

Afternoons are for outings taken lounging on th canopied, floral double bed of a shikara boat (with names like 'Queen of Sheba'), being paddled t Mughal gardens or through the backwaters o Srinagar. Tea of scones, lotus-blossom honey an fresh macaroons at 4pm prompt, whether on a boa or shikara. Mr Bulbul, the flowerman, appears ou of the sky-drenching, hour-long sunset to presen gladioli picked from his floating florist shop o zinnias, marigolds and carnations. A moonli paddle. Candlelit dinner.

It all seems a dream. It is difficult – and no particularly necessary – to do much else. Indulger laziness is the key. States of advanced sloth ar easy. There is even a floating post office for card and stamps. The odd sightseeing and splurge o Kashmiri crafts in Srinagar, perhaps. Possibly trip to Gulmarg or Pahalgam. Or a spot of fishing pony-trekking, swimming, water-skiing or walk ing. However, if relaxation means social action, d it in style at the Maharaja of Kashmir's palace And, on leaving this paradise country, the Kash miris quite rightly ask if sahib and memsahib ar going to India next.

THE HILLS AND NEPAL: PLAYTIME PARADISE

THE HARD FACTS Go April–September.
Spring for almond, walnut, pear and apple blossom and flowers; August for big lotus flowers which grow on sturdy stalks above their huge pancake leaves, covering the lakes. It gets chilly towards the end of September. Daily flights up from Delhi and Jammu. 18km into town. From Jammu the 8-hour drive through the beautiful Kashmir Valley is best. Choose between staying on a houseboat or at the palace run by Oberoi (see below).

J & K Government Tourist Reception Centre, off Sherwani Road (tel: 72449/77303/73648/77305) (also airport). It is not good but supplies houseboat information, permits for going into Hari Parbat fort and temporary membership for the excellent Kashmir Golf Club and the rather run-down Nagin and Srinagar clubs. Here are also the director of fisheries (tel: 72862) for fishing permits and hiring rod and tackle, game warden, Indian Airlines (tel: 73538/73270), post office and bank. To arrange trips out of Srinagar, use SITA World Travel in Hotel Broadway, Maulana Azad Road (tel: 77186); Mercury Travels in the Oberoi (tel: 78786) and Mountain Travel, Houseboat Zanzibar, by Zero Bridge, Jhelum River (tel: 77757; postal address: PO Box 36, Srinagar). Harkar and Sunshine are both good chemists on Sherwani Road.

Beware: whether booking a houseboat or shikara ride, buying a carpet or a piece of lacquer, check on quality and every detail and bargain very hard. Many Kashmiris are smiling rogues making a tidy fortune from tourists. Their hard-luck stories are rot.

Houseboats When the British finally discovered Kashmir, the Maharaja of Kashmir forbade European building on his land. So the ever resourceful island race 'improved' the lakes and took to boats. The first charming, carved houseboat was built around 1875. Many now date from the 1930s and, even if they are rebuilt, keep the original furnishings and evocative names, such as 'New Happy Life', 'Prince of Bombay' and 'Nur Jehan'. Boats are no longer moved, as in the days of Paul Scott's Lady Manning being pointedly left alone, but are built on a static raft. This means being stuck with the neighbours, so change boats if their life-style intrudes.

Houseboats come in all sizes, for a couple up to a large party. At the back are the bedrooms with adjoining bathrooms, then a dining and sitting room and front verandah with steps down to the water. The roof deck, with tables, chairs and

umbrellas, spans all the rooms. Most have their own shikara and paddle boat. There is a well-stocked fridge and fruit-bowl.

The Kashmiri owner and offspring (who live in another boat or on land) rush on and off attending to everything from morning 'bed tea' and laundry to bath water and beer, and serve four very square, very nursery meals a day, all included in the daily rate (but delicious fresh yoghurt is made on request). They also stop the floating shopkeepers from becoming a pest. Take out a contract with a floating florist to fill a dozen vases on alternate days. It is essential not to share a boat with anyone outside your party. But, if staying a few days, take a boat that sleeps more than your number – slightly more expensive but much less cramped.

Some areas of the lakes are definitely more pleasant than others. For optimum peace, beauty and a cleaner lake, go for the east bank of Nagin Lake (boats therefore face west). The east-facing bank of Dal Lake, behind Nehru Park, is good (see sunsets from the roof). Avoid the hugger-mugger crush at the south-west corner of Dal Lake (known as Boulevard) and the west side of Nagin Lake which is in shadow for the afternoon and misses the ritual sunset.

Obviously, personal recommendation is best, like any holiday retreat. One perfect houseboat is Mr Major's 'Peony' (sleeps 4, very luxurious for 2), his 'New Peony' (sleeps 6) and cosy 'Young Peony' (for 2), all on Nagin Lake. To book, write or cable Gulam Mohammad Major, PO Box 101, Nagin Lake, Srinagar (tel: 74850). Otherwise, good travel agents who arrange houseboats should have checked them out thoroughly (Welcomgroup have some. Several of the British travel agents recommended on p. 6 will book good houseboats).

On arrival, if someone says your booked boat is occupied and how about their boat instead, don't believe a word of it. If booking on the spot, go the Tourist Office, ask for a de luxe category boat (Rs350 per double room per day, all in), and go and see it before taking it.

Hotel Oberoi Palace (tel: 75641/75642/75643; telex: 0375 201 LXSR; cable: OBHOTEL); former palace of Maharaja Hari Singh of Kashmir, built in the 1930s. Magnificent views; set in 20 acres of gardens leading down to Dal Lake. Srinagar was the summer capital for the Maharaja (winter was spent in Jammu).

105 rooms (including 20 suites) furnished with local crafts, attached bath, central heating, travel desk, car rental, beauty salon, shopping arcade;

spacious facilities include 6-hole golf course, putting green, tennis, pool, 2 drawing rooms, 2 good bars overlooking lake. Restaurant and garden snacks and buffets have the usual tri-cuisine plus Kashmiri dishes on request. A room with lake view, preferably on the 1st floor, is nicest.

The recently discovered cache of astounding royal jewels are to be fought over by royal descendant Dr Karan Singh (ex-cabinet minister, formed Jammu museum) and central Government – Singh has employed both the brilliant lawyer S. K. Kandhari (who won back the Jaipur emeralds claimed by the Government in 1977) and eminent jurist and defence lawyer Nani Palkhivala to argue the case in court, so perhaps the riches will stay in Kashmir.

The Centaur Lake View Hotel (tel: 73175/77601; telex: 375205; cable: CENTAUR); brand new hotel at the foot of the hills on the shores of Dal Lake. 285 rooms (including 27 suites); facilities include travel desk, air-conditioning (in summer) and central heating (in winter); restaurants, tennis court, swimming pool (an indoor pool is also planned) and private jetty.

OUT AND ABOUT   Do as much as possible by boat. Go up the *backwaters* of Srinagar, founded in the 6th century by Raja Pravarasen II, the canals crossed by rickety wooden bridges and overhung with multi-storied wooden houses. Locals shop by boat at tiny stores like packing cases on stilts. Life is lived mostly on the water. Vegetables are grown on the floating gardens (called rads and dheems), built on heel, a water weed, and willow saplings. The mass of lotuses between them are merely fillers. Locals nip about on narrow dugga boats. Some collect water chestnut leaves or heel; others deliver vegetables, fish for carp or tend their waterside vineyards. If you get up early (about 5am), you can catch the magic early light and boat down to the vegetable market which seethes with activity, the haggling often progressing to fisticuffs.

Nagin Lake, the Bod and Lokut parts of *Dal Lake* (each with a tiny picnic island) and the floating gardens are all fed by springs. By exploring them by boat, you can stop off to stroll in the formal, terraced *Mughal gardens*, following the footsteps of Nehru who 'loitered . . . and lived for a while in their scented past' (all open sunrise-sunset). Shalimar Bagh (Garden of Love) is the most sophisticated, with fountains and cascade, built by Jehangir for Nur Jehan in 1616, the top terrace for courtesans only (ITDC son et lumière in English,

9pm, quite picturesque). Nishat Bagh (Garden Bliss), in a similar form but bigger and steepe with better views and fewer tourists, was laid c in 1633 by Nur Jehan's brother, Asaf Khan.

Sadly, the oldest garden, Nasim Bagh (Garden the Morning Breeze), laid out by Akbar in 1586, h gone to seed. Chashma Shahi (the Royal Spring) the smallest garden, begun by Jehangir, complete by Shah Jahan in 1632, now restored. Above Parimahal was the home of a 15th century astro omer and a Sufi college. The ruins are now tl highest of all gardens, glorious for sunset – best pay off the boat and then walk down to the Ober for cocktails.

BOAT TRIPS   A delightful shikara day trip through the bird sanctuary on the north-west si of Nagin Lake, then through Anchar Lake to Ga darbal. Joanna Lumley described it as 'the mc blissful scenery, rather non-Indian except for tl mountain backdrop. There are acres and acres lotuses. A glorious, peaceful day.' What bett recommendation? (5–6hrs there, shore-side picni 3hrs back). A longer but utterly blissful two-and-half day shikara trip goes up to Manabel Lake. Y sleep on the banks in tents (there is even a lavato tent with a seat on stilts). Cooks prepare meals th are eaten off china. Manabel Lake is surrounded l mountains that are reflected in the clear wate perfect for swimming. To stay there longer, there a very up-market, pretty *Dak Bungalow* with te raced gardens down to the lake (bookable throug Srinagar Tourist Office).

In town, apart from seeing the wooden Ja Masjid and wandering the lanes behind the canal there is the good *Sri Pratap Singh Museum*, house in an old palace: everything from 4th–12th centu: stone sculpture to a 17th century tapestry m; of Srinagar, textiles, stuffed animals shot by tl British, coins and an Englishman's stamp c lection (open Thurs.–Tues., 10am–5pm, close holidays).

SPORTS   To keep fit and enjoy the finest view go up Sharika Hill to the 18th century Hari Parb Fort, surrounded by almond orchards and Akbar wall; or sprint up Takh-i-Sulaiman (Throne Solomon, now officially Shankaracharya Hill). Sa ing, swimming and good water-skiing on Nag Lake. Good golf on Srinagar Golf Links (apply the Secretary, or through Tourist Office). Fisl ing in the surrounding rivers for rainbow tro April–September, mahseer August–Septembe easant exercise is to hire a bicycle (from Boule-rd shops) and go around the north ends of Dal nd Nagin lakes.

OOD AND RESTAURANTS Houseboat oks can be a bit dull. But real Kashmiri cuisine is od. It is still heavily Persian influenced and rich. me houseboat cooks can be persuaded to pre-re some of the 17 meat courses that make up a azwan (royal dinner) feast. Dishes might include shtaba (meatballs cooked in yoghurt and ices), tabakmaz (shin of mutton cooked in shewnut, poppyseed and onions), kebabs and ryanis. The Oberoi hotel will prepare these and her Kashmiri dishes (roghan josh, mutton oked with yoghurt and ginger, originated in ashmir).

Restaurants in Srinagar include *Lhasa's*, off ulevard, with a beautiful back garden. It is run Tibetan refugees who make excellent Chinese od, and is packed every night. *Ahoo's* is not as od as promised. Try Kashmiri tea, kahwa, very veet, flavoured with saffron, cardamom and monds.

Apart from gazing at the moon and stars, eve-ng entertainment is minimal. It is possible to find assical Sufiana Kalam music in town. Some ouseboat owners can advise, including Abdul azac who is to be found on Aristotle Houseboat, al Lake (opposite Boulevard).

HOPPING AND CRAFTS Often in the same lace here. A **carpet factory** has areas devoted to ch process of carpet-making. In one a man is boriously drawing designs on graph paper which e then translated into book form; after that, omen duplicate them by hand. In the weaving om, whole families, excluding the women, sit at e looms, their fingers speedily twitching the ool and silk into tight knots – the nimble fingers f the young boys are released for half-day school-g. After the grand tour, it is sale-room time: undreds of carpets of every size and colour are rown down before the boggling eyes of the client ho is oiled with cold drinks or tea. If buying, keep the big factories and bargain hard; carpets can be ipped home (see p. 61).

In **papier mâché** factories a hotch-potch of dis-rded paper is soaked, dried in a mould, then ainted by men and boys who fortunately still void chemical colours. They grind coral for red, pis for blue, quartz for white, charcoal for black, rdamom for yellow and gold leaf mixed with salt for gold. There are grades of papier maché: the top one is rarely exported and uses real gold. In all grades many of the patterns are more delicate than those exported. The varnished boxes, eggs and paper-holders are easy to carry; bigger trays and lamps are best bought at the last city before flying out of India. Kashmiri walnut bowls, with their knarled knots, are a very good buy. So, too, are the walnuts and walnut oil.

The Kashmiri **crewel-work fabric** with bold, meandering tree-of-life. The Muslim women sit together in their dark houses, dressed in kaftan-like wool pherons, slipping kangris (willow wicker baskets of hot charcoals) underneath them during the winter. As they gossip, they chainstitch over designs drawn out by the men on coarsely woven cloth. The piece is usually 57m long, about 130cm wide and, unless it is a special commission, no two bales are identical in colour or design. So here is a chance to buy unique, hand-embroidered fur-nishing fabric relatively cheaply – about Rs80–120 per metre which, even after shipping, is half London prices. Of course, it can also be bought made up as cushion covers and bedspreads.

Fur coats are comparatively cheap. There is limited government control on jackai, jungle cat, fox (com-mon, hill and red) and toddy cat but no control on sheepskin. Coats are put in the shops unfinished, to be altered, lined and tidied up as the buyer wishes. Prices are according to the fur and the size of pieces but roughly Rs2,000–12,000 full length; Rs1,500–5,000 half length, plus Rs300 for lining and a small UK import tax (it must be declared). There is also good silver and gem-studded jewellery.

Then there are the **Kashmir shawls**. The craft was possibly introduced to Kashmir from Persia ('shal' is Persian for woven fabric) by Sultan Zain-ul-Abdin (1423–74), together with paper-making, sericulture (silk growing) and fruit trees. After a period of decline, the emperors revived the art and stocked their wardrobes with shawls, since when they have remained expensive and much sought after. Shahtus shawls were the finest of all, and today's lower-grade version is still pricy. They are woven from pashmina (known in the West as cashmere, from the country of its origin), the inner, soft fleece grown by mountain goats in the winter and shed in spring. An even finer wool from the throat of the ibex was used to make the legendary shawls that can be passed through a ring, very rare today.

Originally, a dozen or so specialists worked on a

shawl. Up to 300 colours were prepared and a shawl took several months to complete. Weaving, hereditary and restricted to men, was the most skilled operation, yet the designer got the highest salary and the shawl-broker, who acted as middle-man between the ustad (master weaver) and foreign merchant, made the serious profit.

The floral designs of the 17th century tightened up in the 18th century into stylised butas (floral motifs) and by the 19th century into the familiar stylised kairi (mango) known as Paisley, even by Indians. By around 1800, those who could not afford the woven shawls could buy embroidered ones which expertly imitated the woven effect.

Akbar initiated the practice of stitching two together so that there was no 'wrong' side showing. He also gave shawls to foreign dignitaries, a tradition that persists. Shawls had enough value to be part of the East India Company's bribing equipment. Then, as 19th century trade with Europe increased, standards went down to satisfy first British, then French demand. Napoleon's gift of a shawl to Josephine set off a shawl rage amongst the Empire aristocracy – Josephine had 300–400.

Wild prices were paid but the weavers could not keep up, so Norwich and Paisley manufacturers stepped in. When Lion & Paisley's imitation wool and silk shawls costing next to nothing flooded the market around 1835 – hence the term Paisley – the Kashmiri market was severely reduced. Now the weaving is being revived, and shawls of all qualities are made.

It is best not to buy crafts from the boatmen. And beware of small Srinagar shops, too. Either be sure of what you are buying and barter hard, or go to a fixed price government emporium of which there are many. Kashmir Government Art Emporium, Residency Road, and Government Central Market, Exhibition Ground, are both good. Bigger spending should be done at these. Their shipping should be reliable too.

The **tailors** in Kashmir are excellent. To have a Kashmiri suit of pyjamas (baggy trousers, from the Hindi) and straight shirt made, choose one of the many tailors who all sit cross-legged working at Singer hand sewing machines. He will say how much material to buy and where, measure obscure distances all over the body very quickly without writing anything down, and produce a perfectly fitting suit the following day. Ideal for hot travelling down on the plains.

GULMARG

38km from Srinagar, at 2,730m. Spring in th valley of the Pir Panjal range is almost unrivall (only Yusmarg, south-east of here, is supposed beat it). It is so spectacular that Sultan Yusuf Sha changed its name from Gaurimarg (after Shiva wife) to Gul (flower) marg (meadow) in 158 Jehangir, whose albums are full of flower illu trations, once collected 21 different varieties her When the Maharaja of Kashmir moved to Srinag for the summer, the British Resident nipped u here with his pals. Apart from glorious walks, tre and riding, there is the highest natural golf cour in the world (2,650m) and, in winter, the be skiing in India (but do not expect Gstaad or Moritz standards).

THE HARD FACTS Season mid-May to Mi October (May–June for best flowers); mi December to mid-March for decent skiing. Fly Srinagar, then by bus or taxi along a road lined wi poplar trees. It is fun to do the last stretch throug the pines from Tangmarg by pony – especially the road is rather treacherous for cars whi apparently fall off occasionally.

Three nice places to stay, all with good atmo phere, character, pretty settings and breath-takin views. Best is *Highlands Park* (tel 30/50; cab HIGHLANDS); closed Nov. 15–Dec. 10. 37 room (including 10 suites), car rental, fine building, goo gardens, social style. Then there is *Nedou's* (tel: 2 closed November–March, 50 rooms; or *Woodlan* (tel: 60/21). The Government Tourist Huts a charming, red-painted, wooden chalets, wi linen, hot water bottles and a sort of central hea ing, bookable through Srinagar Tourist Office travel agents.

For ski instruction, mountaineering and tre king, contact the Indian Institute of Skii and Mountaineering, Gulmarg (tel: 46, 47; cab SKISCHOOL GULMARG).

OUT AND ABOUT Good walks, treks and rid include the Outer Circular Walk (11km) encircli Gulmarg, with stunning views right down to Sr nagar and up to Nanga Parbat (8,137m), the fif highest mountain in the world, especially good sunset. Khilanmarg is good for flowers (nice café 6km); Alpatha Lake, a good ride (13km). The there is Tosha Maidan (50km) begun from Fero pore Nallah, trout fishing (permit from Srinagar In spring, drive to Yusmarg and wander amid th blooms.

Gulmarg's 18-hole Golf Course, with small wooden club house (temporary membership immediate, Rs2 per day, clubs for hire), is up to international standards (tournaments held here and at Srinagar) but has various hazards. Many streams criss-cross the course, so walk it first for a serious game. Being so high (2,650m), the air is thinner, so the ball flies further. Kites are apt to swoop down to pinch the balls, believing them to be eggs – the ball-boy's sole function is to stop them. Local professionals (handicap about 6) will partner visitors first time, lending shoes and clubs.

Skiing will seem rather quaint to Europeans, but is the smartest and best in India. There are a few ski-lifts, runs up to 10km and nursery slopes. Ski equipment and toboggans can be hired – plus porters to carry everything around, up and down. There is also an ice-skating rink, with skates for hire. Night life is sitting beside log fires in the winter, evening strolls in the summer.

PAHALGAM

98km from Srinagar, at 2,130m. Excellent treks and fishing in the Liddar Valley. The town, originally a shepherds' village, lies at the junction of the fast-flowing Lidder and Shashnag Rivers below blossoming alpine meadows full of sheep and mountains thick with pines and firs, populated by berry-eating brown bears.

THE HARD FACTS Go mid-April to mid-November, climate cooler than Srinagar, warmer than Gulmarg. Fly to Srinagar, then by car – best done over an entire day, stopping en route at various places. Pampore is the Kashmir centre for tricky – and therefore expensive – saffron production. Sangram is where many of India's essential tools, cricket bats, are made. Avantipur has two 9th century Hindu temples. There is a short detour after Rnuntnag to Achabal and Kokarnag to see Mughal gardens before going up to Pahalgam.

The hearty stay in tents, complete with electricity, equipment hired from one of the dozen agencies here (or booked at Srinagar Tourist Office). Others go for comfort at the two rather expensive hotels, both overlooking the river: Pahalgam (tel: 26/52/78; cable: PAHALGAM-HOTEL). In the bazaar area, 41 rooms (including no less than 16 suites). Insist upon a river view. Facilities include car rental, health club, pool, meals included in room price, picnics provided, log stoves at night. Alternatively, the Woodstock (tel:

27; cable: WOODSTOCK); slightly nearer the river, 34 rooms, ensure river view, car rental. Trekkers get equipment through the Tourist Office. Fishermen need to pay for permit, beat and gillie at Srinagar Tourist Office; rod and tackle for hire locally.

OUT AND ABOUT Good walks and treks in every direction range from gentle strolls to 5-day treks. They include Mamaleswara, just opposite, across rickety bridges and Tulian Lake (16km), excellent views at 3,353m, usually surrounded by snow-covered slopes, reached via Baisaran meadow (5km). Amarnath Cave (47km, at 3,962m) is a longer trip, done on foot or by pony. It is believed to be Shiva's home, an ice Shiva lingum is fed through the limestone roof. Pilgrims flock for Yatra festival on full moon of July-August. More ambitious trips are to Kolahoi Glacier (36km), camping at the glacier base, 3,352m, and to Sonmarg (74km), the name means meadow of gold, very beautiful and also a good base for further treks.

Fishermen can hook plenty of trout June-September and mahseer August-September (Spring water is too cold). For June trout fly-fishing, drive up beside the Lidder for about 3 hours. The golf course has more stunning views (temporary membership immediate).

LEH

434km from Srinagar, at 3,505m. This tiny, barren, remote town high in the pink granite Karakoram range of mountains in the Indus Valley is the capital of Ladakh. It has only been open to foreigners for a decade. Its past importance was as a junction on the silk route (where roads met from Sinkiang, the Indian plains and the Middle East) and as a centre of Tibetan Tantric Buddhism, although Buddhism was possibly first brought to Ladakh by emissaries of Ashoka in the 3rd century BC.

The friendly Ladakhis ingeniously irrigate fields to grow barley and preserve their Tibetan culture and religion which is now hard to find in Tibet. Buddhism still thrives: there are over 50,000 lamas residing in the lamaserais of Ladakh. The perilous, cliff-top gompas (Buddhist monasteries) newly restored with profits from tourism are the sights to see, glorious in the thin, bright sunlight under a dark blue sky. They pay good dividends for the adventurous, determined people who get to them.

231

THE HARD FACTS   A trip to Leh is governed by the weather. In theory the road from Srinagar is open mid-May to mid-November, but snow may shorten the period considerably. Worth coinciding with Hemis festival in June–July, three days of constant celebrations plus masked dances. Either fly up from Delhi (Mon. and Thurs.) or Srinagar (Wed., Fri. and Sun.), sensational views of the Himalayas; or go 434km by road from Srinagar (reasonably exhausting but stunning scenery). Best is to go up one way, down the other. As the weather is capricious, flights are often cancelled, and there are often two planeloads fighting for one set of seats. So make friends in very high places and allow an extra day to get back, just in case.

The journey up by road, slightly hair-raising at moments, crosses Zoji La (3,529m), Namika La (3,718m) and Fatu La (4.094m) Passes and takes two days of 10-hour drives, overnight at Kargil. (Stay at the *Highlands* or *D'Zokila* hotels – all others are dirty. Highlands is run by the Welcomgroup chain.) Six-seat jeep is better than Class A bus as it gives freedom to stop and peek at mosques, monasteries and views, most especially at Lamayuru gompa, the first of many and formerly very grand, with 400 monks.

On finally reaching Leh, there are various rum hotels, of which the best bets are: *Kang-Lha-Cheu* and *Lha Lha-Ri-Mo*, both central. Far better and more peaceful (Leh attracts a surprising number of European bus-loads) is to stay at Mountain Travel's *Ladakh Serai* (11km), a camp of beautiful, comfortable tents (far removed from Girl Guide days), adapted from the yurts used by Central Asian nomads, pitched amid willow trees, near the village of Stok. Ideal base for visits to the monasteries, short treks and for river rafting. Bookable through London, Delhi or Srinagar offices (see pp. 6, 44 and 227). The same firm organises reliable trekking and climbing.

Tourist Office in the Dak Bungalow, for information on monasteries, map and advice on trekking and the current half and whole day rates for jeep-taxis to see the scattered gompas. Indian Airlines is next door.

OUT AND ABOUT   Navigate steep lanes in and around Leh to see outsides and insides of gompas at very odd times. In town, climb up to the 16th century Leh Khar Palace, fine view of the Zanskar mountains across the Indus River (open 6–9am;

after 5pm); then go on up to Leh Gompa (Re Gompa), more views, built 1430 and find goo Buddha inside (open 7–9am; 5–7pm). Then t Shanka Gompa to see gold statues (2km).

It takes a few days to see the important gompa out of town using a jeep-taxi, but each journey different, with good walks and scenery (take pic nics). They include *Spituk Gompa*, with a goo collection of masks, the seat of the head lam (10km). There is *Phiyang Gompa* (red sect of Buddh ists) and village (20km), *Thiksey Gompa*, 12th cer tury, 12-storey hilltop gompa with 10 temples, a full of statues, tankas (paintings on cloth), wal paintings and a huge engraved pillar, views dow into green Indus Valley (17km). *Hemis Gompa* is th largest and most important, with wall-paintings statues and a superb collection of tankas includin possibly the biggest one in existence, exhibite every 11 years (next time 1991) (49km).

Stok Palace (16km), where the royal family live now and the 15th century ruined Shey palace (15km) where they used to live, reached through flowe strewn Choglamsar, are also worth visiting.

Tibetan food is not very good, mostly noodles Give shopping a miss: what little is sold here can b found cheaper elsewhere. But do see if there is game of local polo. It is played at Leh on probabl the highest, and certainly the most spectacular polo ground in the world.

Nepal

Out of India and up into the highest kingdom of al ruled by King Birendra Bir Bikram Shah Dev Arriving at the capital, Kathmandu, is like walkin into a Brueghel painting, with wooden houses flags and flowers, men and women quietly prepa ing food. In India, there are no casinos, so Kath mandu is the nearest place where the Indian ric can nip out for a quick night's gambling. Lookin out from the city, the drama begins. 25% of Nepa is above 3,000m. The greatest Himalayan peaks c Everest, Kunchenjunga, Lohotse, Makalu, Ch Oyu, Dhaulagiri, Manaslu and Annapurna touc the sky at well over 8,000m. This is a land of soarin mountains, rivers rushing through deep gorges tiger-inhabited lowland jungles and whole valley of rhododendrons, peopled by tribes with a ric variety of customs and languages.

Buddha was born here, at Lumbini. But nov Nepal is officially 90% Hindu and the only Hind kingdom in the world. However, in practice

eligion mixes both – many Nepalese profess
uddhism and Hinduism at once, with fervour.
he country is thick with beautiful temples and
vayside shrines, proportionately more than any
ther country. And there are possibly even more
estivals than in India.

As well as wandering in the colourful villages
nd markets, there is game-spotting, river-rafting
nd, of course, trekking. Nepal is the home of the
ourageous, stocky Gurkhas and the mountaineer-
ng Sherpas. It is not obligatory to scale Everest
3,848m), affectionately known as Chomolungma
Goddess Mother of the World) by the Sherpas of
.humba, but it is certainly true that the most
nteresting scenery and peoples of Nepal can only
e reached by trekking. But do not fear. Nepal is
ne of the safest places for a trek. It can be tailored
o extreme gentleness and resemble a pleasant
valk, free from all cares, with frequent stops,
noughtful Sherpas, cooks and porters.

To see game, the Royal Chitwan National Park is
ne of the finest wildlife sanctuaries in Asia – and
ne of the trendiest. The World Elephant Polo
.hampionships, Nepal's answer to Ascot, are
taged here. In season there is usually a spattering
f the world's royals mingling with showbiz royals
ke Goldie Hawn, Robert Redford and Michael
ork and sporty royal Bjorn Borg. However, jet-set
ourists and hippies alike are beginning to affect
nese friendly, unindustrialised people, so it is
vorth going soon. A week of trekking, game-
arking or valley-hopping in Nepal easily slips into
trip to north India.

HE HARD FACTS   If Nepal is on the itinerary
efore leaving home, buy and read the weighty
nsight Guide to Nepal. Season is October–April;
)ctober–November for harvest festivals, clear air
nd trekking; February–March for high altitude
ower spotting; April–May for trekking, river-
afting and spotting game in Chitwan NP; July–
eptember is monsoon. Best blooms, including
ouble jasmine and orchids, are April–June, sadly
idden sometimes in the heat mist. Worth aiming
or the concentration of festivals after the rice har-
est (August–October), Dasain with plenty of
nimal sacrifice (October, Nepal's version of Durga
uja), Tihar in honour of Lakshmi (October), the
(ing's birthday with processions and fireworks
December 28), Baisakha Purnima celebrating
uddha's birthday (April–May) and many more.

Fly up to **Kathmandu**: good connections by
ndian Airlines from Delhi and Varanasi (daily),

Calcutta (Mon., Wed., Thurs., Fri. and Sun.) and
Patna (Tues., Sat.); and other airlines, including
Royal Nepal Airlines and Thai International. All
fares are expensive compared to internal Indian
flights and package trips do not reduce them
much, so it is better to spend several nights in
Nepal, if possible. Going by train or bus is hard
work, although there is the stunning mountain
highway drive along Tribuvan Rajpath to Kathmandu after the Calcutta train ends (after several
changes) at Razaul, and a bus connection from
Darjeeling (special permit needed).

Busy time at the airport: tourist information
desk, hotel counter, foreign exchange counter (for
Nepal Rupees, which, like the Indian version, may
not be imported or exported). The 7-day visa can be
bought here, NR134, renewable up to 3 months (or
produce a 30-day visa obtained from a Nepalese
embassy or consulate back home or in Delhi or
Calcutta). Special trekking permits for off-beat
areas are obtained from the Immigration Department in Kathmandu, at Maiti Devi (tel: 12336) or in
Pokhara.

Increased tourism and a short season means
booking a hotel in advance or working down the
list until there is a room. Check the taxes; they can
increase a bill by 22%.

Top is **Soaltee Oberoi** (tel: 11211; telex: NP203;
cable: SOALTEE, OBHOTEL); 300 rooms (including 18 suites), ensure one with the panoramic
views; every facility including bank, travel counter, fully equipped health club, pool, tennis,
mini-golf, casino, 4 good restaurants including
Himalchuli which is decorated with local
hangings, serves Nepalese dishes and has nightly
Nepalese folk song and dance; single disadvantage
is being 5km from town centre. With SITA travel
agency, the hotel sometimes runs a package deal
from India which includes '3 nights of luxury and
excitement and Rs900 in free casino coupons'.

Other, less flashy hotels, include the following:
Hotel Yak and Yeti (tel: 16255; telex: NP237; cable:
YAKN YETI); 110 rooms, tennis, pool, good food
in much older restaurant, central.
Hotel de l'Annapurna (tel: 11711; telex: NP205;
cable: ANNAPURNA); 155 rooms (including 8
suites), pool, much more central.
Hotel Malla (tel: 15320; cable: MALLOTEL); 75
rooms (including 8 suites), tennis, garden, new but
built with local character, quite central, friendly.

Then two cheaper hotels, both clean, one for
character, the second for position.
Shankar (tel: 12973; telex: 230NP; cable:

SHANKAR), 135 rooms, stylish former palace of the Rana set in large gardens on town edge.
Crystal (tel: 12630; cable: CRYSTAL); 53 rooms, fine views from roof garden, good food, sited just off Ganga Path.

In Kathmandu, the Government Tourist Office is on Ganga Path (tel: 11203), for brochures, maps and even film shows; Indian Airlines, Durbar Marg (tel: 11196). Best of many travel agencies for tours and individual arrangements are: Everest Travel, Basantapur Square (tel: 11121); Kathmandu Tours and Travel, Dharma Path (tel: 14446); Yeti Travels, (tel: 12329/11234) and Gorkha Travels (tel: 14895), both on Durbar Marg.

For rewarding trekking and mountaineering, book well in advance. By far the best, safest and most reliable agent is Mountain Travels, PO Box 170, (tel: 12808); founded in 1964 by Colonel Jimmy Roberts, British explorer and mountaineer, employing 170 Sherpas and responsible for assisting Chris Bonnington to be first up the south-west face of Everest and helping Habeler to be first to the top without oxygen (see pp. 6–7 for worldwide addresses). For river-rafting, pay high prices but you will get a good time with Himalayan River Exploration, Durbar Marg (tel: 212455; postal address: PO Box 170). To book up for Royal Chitwan National Park (p. 235) go to Tiger Tops' office, next to the Annapurna hotel in Durban Marg (tel: 12706; postal address: PO Box 242).

Transport within Nepal is by Royal Nepal Airlines, New Road (tel: 14511), taxi or bicycle – excellent for the Kathmandu Valley, find newish ones with working brakes in the bazaar. Saturday is considered dangerous by locals, so everything is closed. Sunday goes like a fair. Alcohol is very expensive, so take rations.

OUT AND ABOUT   This is a country with immense variety. The travel agents listed above can cater to every taste. Books listed in the bibliography should also help. But, on a first visit, wrench yourself out of bed to see the sunrise over Everest and also to take the morning Mountain Flight. Also, see something of Kathmandu Valley and its three cities: Kathmandu, Patan (Lalitpur) and Bhadgaon (Bhaktapur). Before unification in the late 18th century, each was an independent kingdom of great culture and affluence, fed by the trade route traffic.
The two early rises The dawn trip to Nagarkot Hill (45mins, leave 5am wearing several jumpers)

to see sunrise over the Himalayas is unforgettab (or see it as a mini-trek, sleeping out overnight then warming breakfast (including delicious loc curd) in nearby Bhadgaon (see below) at the chale like café next to the tallest temple. The fine 5th 12th century art of Changunarayan temple a pleasant 2-hour walk from here and Thim where the big, brightly-painted, papier mâch dance masks are made, is on the road back Kathmandu.

The early morning Mountain View flight cos NR655 but is well worth the cost (book throug Royal Nepal Airlines, check visibility). In the thi fresh sunlight at 6,000m, the plane flies along th mountain range, past the 10 highest peaks in th world and back again. Passengers are given check-list plan of the peaks before and a certif cate of their momentous, breath-taking journe after.

In **Kathmandu**, in the old market place ar around Durbar Square there are exquisitely carve buildings and both the Old Royal Palace ar Kumari Devi (House of the Living Goddess). Th Kumari is carefully and ruthlessly selected at abou five years of age and remains goddess un puberty, when she loses deity status and another chosen.

Across the Bagmati river lies *Patan*, the mo Buddhist of the three towns. It is the place to se beautiful temples and 17th century buildings and around its Durbar Square and to buy hig quality bronze and carved wood. *Bhadgaon*, at th other end of the valley, is the most unspoilt ar medieval. The tiny cobbled streets are lined wi beautifully carved old black and white houses ar temples. There are no cars, the pace is slow, fa mers and millers amble about and potters thro beautiful pots on huge turning stones.

In the valley around Kathmandu, see the hillto *Swayambhunath Temple*, with its watchful eyes Buddha; *Pashpatinath Temple* and Bodnath stup beyond it; and *Kirtipur*, a medieval town busy wi dyeing and weaving. Go north to see one of th largest sculptures of sleeping Vishnu at *Budhan kantha*. For rewarding day walks in the valley to se the rural villages, hire a Sherpa who directs the ta where to drop him and his wards and where collect them at the end of the day.

Further afield, the stunningly beautiful *Pokha Valley*, with its backdrop of the Annapurna rang is worth seeing. In the jungle, try three days ar two nights of white-water rafting on Sun Kos Trisuli or Gandaki Rivers: some paddling, som

lashes and lots of fun (fastest flowing in October
d spring). You can also do the classic trek to
rerest Base Camp; encircle Annapurna Massif, or
into the heart of Nepal to Langtang Valley. You
n also combine rafting and trekking, or go to the
yal Chitwan National Park by raft. In the spring,
ere are treks devoted to seeing the blossoms, not
ly hillsides of rhododendrons (whose blooms
t stronger the lower they are) but orchids,
ntians, azaleas, daphne and viburnum.

JOOD, ENTERTAINMENT AND SHOPPING
le food in Kathmandu is better than anywhere
se in the hills. As well as the inevitable Tibetan
d Nepalese, tourists can sit in the highest king-
m and go on a disorientating world tour of
vours, picking up bortsch and brownies,
ateaubriand and chow mien. Sample the meat
es from Pie Street (full of hippies and known
cally as Freak Street).
At the *Everest Cultural Society* or the *Oberoi's
machuli* (both with Nepalese dancing), there is
od Nepalese food: soups (alu tama, thukpa
ndruk), then rice, vegetables, millet bread and
hani (yoghurt pudding) washed down with
her raksi, a rice-based liquor, or chang, the local
er made with rice, millet or barley. The *Yak and
ti Chimney Room* offers food and atmosphere
rge open fire in old palace hall). *Boris's*, on the
tskirts, has Russian food, ambience and Boris,
rmerly a Russian ballet dancer but since the 1950s
excellent hotelier and restaurateur. There is
od Indian food amid Pahari paintings and Indian
usicians and ghazel singers at *Kabad-e-ghar*, near
otel de l'Annapurna.
Nepalese dance and music can be found at the
ational Theatre, Everest Cultural Society (7pm,
ghtly) and, for a good setting, at the Sweta
achendranath temple near Indrachowk. Night-
e does exist – just. Either win or lose a fortune at
e Oberoi Casino where play is in Indian Rupees
US dollars and there is no restriction on taking
nnings out of the country (free buses there from
her hotels; free drinks to encourage players). The
o and Down disco in town uses the Indian ploy of
elcoming Westerners and making the Nepalese
y high membership fees (closed Friday).
Shopping is good but now very tourist-
lentated, as in Kashmir, so bargain very hard or
to fixed price Government emporia. Good buys
e the jolly masks from Thimi; brass from Patan
ist by the rare lost wax method, as in Orissa),
ukris (the short, lethal, Nepalese daggers),

jewellery and wood carving and some of the fine
pieces of dhaka woven cloth from the Kosi hills.

Wildlife sanctuaries

ROYAL CHITWAN NATIONAL PARK, NEPAL
Season mid-September to mid-June; best April–
May for seeing game when the grass is short. Fly to
Kathmandu, then 130km south by road or another
flight to Megauli, near the park; lodge collects
guests by elephant during the cool season. But the
most exciting way to arrive is by a three-day river
trip starting from near Kathmandu.
There are various places to stay: Tiger Tops'
Jungle Lodge, the *Tented Camp* or *Tharu Village*. All
are bookable at Durbar Marg, PO Box 242,
Kathmandu (tel: 12706; telex: NP 216 TIGTOP;
cable: TIGERTOPS. See also Delhi and London
addresses, p. 6 and p. 44. The treetop Jungle
Lodge is built of the local hardwood, sal; 20 rooms,
attached bath (hot water), log fires, quite social,
very comfortable. Tharu Village is a longhouse
with central communal area, adapted from the
local Tharu people's villages and built and decorated by them; 8 rooms, modern plumbing separate, local food and dance and visits to Tharu
villages.
The Tented Camp is sited on an island of the
Narayani River, the large safari tents (16 beds, hot
water and showers) pitched around the campfire,
good jungle atmosphere and peace and quiet. Each
is efficiently run by one management, so guests
can spend a few nights at one and then move on
(package tours available).
Each has a restaurant and bar and expert guides
day and night who also give evening talks, the
team trained by naturalist and tiger expert
Dr Charles McDougal, led by the lodge manager,
K. K. Gurung. Safaris conducted on elephant.
Tiger Tops are opening a new camp in the undeveloped Royal Bardia Wildlife Reserve in western
Nepal in 1985. Details from Tiger Tops or Mountain
Travel, see addresses above.
Lying in the Rapti Valley of floodplain jungle
and elephant grass only 150m above sea level, this
fine park was established in 1962 as a rhinoceros
preserve. The 932 sq km of forest and rivers can be
explored by elephant or Land Rover to see one of
the 300 great Indian one-horned rhinoceri. There
are now fewer than 1,500 in the wild and the largest
numbers are here and at Kasiranga National Park
in Assam (see p. 171). There are also leopard, wild

boar, buffalo, sloth bear, deer and monkeys. And, by staying at Tiger Tops, there is a serious possibility of seeing one of the 30 Bengal tigers from a specially built blind. The rivers contain freshwater dolphin and the gharial crocodile (now being saved from threatened extinction).

For sports, there is canoeing, fishing (mahseer), bird-watching (some 400 species) and nature walks. The gharial crocodile conservation farm can also be visited. The crocodiles are bred in captivity and then released into the wild. Of all Asian wildlife parks, this has the best accommodation and guides, reportedly praised by Sir Peter Scott as the best wildlife lodge of all.

DACHIGAM, KASHMIR

Season June–July. Fly to Srinagar, then by road 22km, then trek on foot or pony. Camp or stay in Srinagar (see above). Information and permits from the Game Warden, Srinagar Tourist Office. Former royal game reserve of sub-Himalayan forest, notable for the hangul (Kashmir stag, related to the Scottish red deer) and the Himalayan black bear and brown bear. Down in the Lower Dachigam there is an excellent heronry along the river.

Find out more

Ali, Salim: *The Book of Indian Birds*, Bombay, 1979

Anderson, J. G., (ed.): *Nepal, Insight Guide*, APA Productions, London 1983

Archer, W. G.: *Indian Paintings from the Punjab Hills*, vols 1 & 2, London, New York and Delhi, 1973

Armington, S.: *Trekking in the Himalayas*, Lonely Planet Guide, South Yarra, Australia, 1979

Bezruchka, S.: *A Guide to Trekking in Nepal*, London, 1981

Blunt, W.: *The Art of Botanical Illustration*, London 1950

Cleare, J.: *Collins Guide to Mountains and Mountaineering*, London 1979

Crowe, S. et al.: *The Gardens of Mughal India*, London, 1972

Dunsmore, S.: *Weaving in Nepal*, British Museum 1983

Fleming, R. and R. and Bangdel, L. S.: *Birds of Nepal*, Kathmandu, 1979

Fleming, R. and R. and Bangdel, L. S.: *Kathmandu Valley*, Kathmandu, 1978

Gurung, K. K.: *Heart of the Jungle*, London, 1984

Hagen, T.: *Nepal*, Kummerley and Frey, 1961

Irwin, J.: *The Kashmir Shawl*, London, 1984

Keay, J.: *The Gilgit Game: The Explorers of the Western Himalayas 1865–95*, London, 1979

Keay, J.: *When Men and Mountains Meet: The Explorers of the Western Himalayas 1820–75*, London, 19

Kipling, R.: *Kim*. 1901 and *Plain Tales from the Hills* 1886, are among much his writing set in the hills

McDougal, C.: *The Face of the Tiger*, London, 197

Mierow, D. and Shrestha, T. B.: *Himalayan Flowers and Trees*, Kathmandu, 1973

Prater, S. H.: *The Book of Indian Animals*, Bombay 1980

Raj, P.: *Kathmandu and The Kingdom of Nepal*, Lonely Planet Guide, South Yarra, Australia, 1982

Schettler, R., and M.: *Kashmir, Ladakh and Zanskar*, Lonely Planet Guide, South Yarra, Australia, 19

Scott, P.: *The Raj Quartet*, London, 1966–75

Scott, P.: *Staying On*, London, 1977

Stainston, J. D. A.: *The Forests of Nepal*, London 1972

Woodcock, M.: *Collins Handguide to the Birds of Indian Sub-Continent*, London, 1980

Sun, sand and switch off

wever glorious the Mughal monuments
d the Tamil temples, the palaces and forts,
e hills and exotic wildlife, however fasci-
ting the Indian peoples and their traditions
d crafts, it is always good to spend a few
ys simply flopping. Swimming, sunbath-
g, sleeping and eating are a magical com-
ation for unwinding from the worries of
ork at home on arrival in India, before
ting off to do sight-seeing. And it is just as
od at the end of a tour to soak up the sun
a while before returning to a cold climate.
dia has 6,000km of coastline. It should be a
radise of beaches, but it is not. This is
inly because there is no seaside holiday
dition among Indians. The rich usually
ad for the cool hills; the less rich might visit
nily or go on a pilgrimage; the poor do not
ve holidays. Few Indians swim and none is
search of a suntan. Quite the opposite. The
e in India is: the paler the skin, the better.
e pale skin of a young girl is a major
mmodity and increases her value to would-
suitors and it is included in the match-
king advertisements of each Sunday's
nes of India. An occasional gaggle of Indian
ls may go wave-jumping, in full saris,
id yelps and screams of delight, but most
lians think the Western habit of toasting
e body and dancing in the waves is quite
id.
The horse-shoe of almost continuous sil-
r, palm-fringed coast encasing the Indian

peninsula is therefore hardly developed.
Where beach hotels exist, only a few satisfy
the demands of the sophisticated Western
beach-hopper. The only two serious resort
areas are Goa, south of Bombay on the
west, and the coast south of Madras on the
east. It is all very well foregoing some
creature comforts to see and experience a
few of India's great attractions, but when it
comes to looking for pure relaxation, the
demands for a quality environment, good
facilities and efficiency are usually stepped
up.

Without question, Goa supplies the best of
everything, making it tops for pure beach
enjoyment. There are good hotels, good
food, good beaches and good water and
sports. But, for someone who gets itchy feet
after a few hours lolling in the sun, the Portuguese sights of Goa do not compare with the
Hindu glories on the east coast of Tamil
Nadu. Here, the Coromandel coast just south
of Madras has a slightly lower quality of
hotels, beaches and facilities, but fascinating
nearby sights.

Across on the west coast, in Kerala, the
very beautiful Malabar coast is just beginning
to be exploited for tourists, although hippies
have been there for some years. The award-
winning architecture of the Kovalam Beach
Resort is stunning and the facilities are good.
It should be the perfect place to switch off
after driving through the South but, sadly,

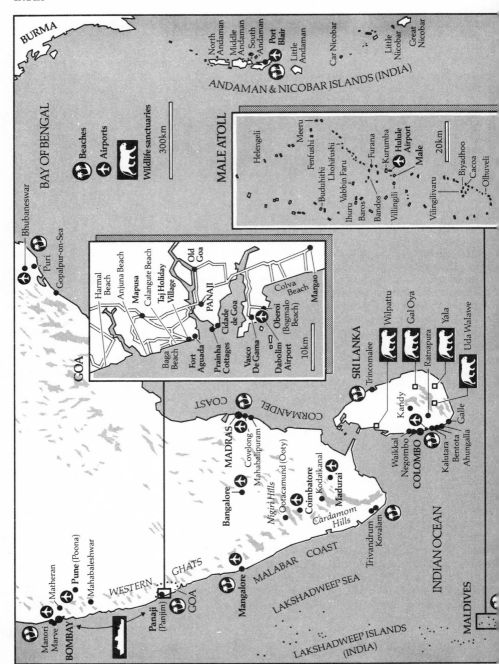

BURMA

BAY OF BENGAL

North Andaman
Middle Andaman
South Andaman
Port Blair
Little Andaman
Car Nicobar
Little Nicobar
Great Nicobar

ANDAMAN & NICOBAR ISLANDS (INDIA)

Beaches
Airports
Wildlife sanctuaries

300km

MALE ATOLL

Helengeli
Meeru
Fenfushi
Buduhithi
Lhohifushi
Ihuru
Vabbin Faru
Baros
Bandos
Furana
Kurumba
Hulule Airport
Male
Villingili
Vilingilivaru
Biyadhoo
Cacoa
Olhuveli

20km

Bhubaneswar
Puri
Gopalpur-on-Sea

GOA

Harmal Beach
Anjuna Beach
Mapusa
Calangute Beach
Taj Holiday Village
Old Goa
PANAJI
Cidade de Goa
Colva Beach
Margao
Baga Beach
Fort Aguada
Prainha Cottages
Vasco De Gama
Oberoi (Bogmalo Beach)
Dabolim Airport

10km

SRI LANKA
Trincomalee

Wilpattu
Gal Oya
Ratnapura
Yala
Uda Walawe

Kandy
Waikkal
Negombo
COLOMBO
Kalutara
Bentota
Ahungalla
Galle

MADRAS
Covelong
Mahabalipuram
CORMANDEL COAST

Bangalore
Nigiri Hills
Ootacamund (Ooty)
Kodaikanal
Coimbatore
Madurai
Cardamom Hills

Trivandrum
Kovalam

Manori
Marve
BOMBAY
Matheran
Pune (Poona)
Mahabaleshwar
WESTERN GHATS
Panaji (Panjim)
GOA
Mangalore
MALABAR COAST
LAKSHADWEEP SEA

INDIAN OCEAN

MALDIVES

LAKSHADWEEP ISLANDS (INDIA)

e abysmal service is likely to aggravate
ther than relax.

Elsewhere in India, there are one or two
uick escape routes to the seaside from the
g cities. From Calcutta, it is easy to nip
own to Puri or Gopalpur-on-Sea (see pp.
57–70). From Bombay, go up to Marve and
lanori if there is no time to get to Goa (see p.
28). From Mysore (no airport) and Banga-
re in southern Karnataka, the quiet sands of
angalore are an alternative option to Goa.
uring India's summer, when it is too
veltering to go to the coast, romantic Srina-
ar is the best bet (see p. 226) with its sunny
kes covered with pink, blossoming lotuses.

Apart from these mainland spots, sun
ekers must hop across to the islands. Most
ovious and best equipped is Sri Lanka
Ceylon), off the southern tip, in the Indian
cean. The large island is becoming in-
easingly like one big, up-market holiday
sort for Westerners escaping from their de-
ressing winter climates. Gita Mehta even
oes so far as to damn it as looking 'like the
osta del Sol'. But its hotels, beaches and
cilities are extremely good. Quite the oppo-
te is found on the newly accessible Anda-
an and Nicobar Islands in the Andaman
ea, across the Bay of Bengal.

For pure paradise and total escape, the tiny
lands of the Maldives are worth visiting for
week. There is sun, sand, wonderful
arine life, very simple living and nothing
uch else. You may even have an island
ntirely to yourself.

If switching off for you means also cooling
f, then it is best to head for the fresh air of
e Himalayas, stretching from Gulmarg and
inagar in the west right across Nepal to
arjeeling. Here are autumn colours, snowy
inters and spring and summer flowers. In
ajasthan, the nearest relief from the desert
eat is Mount Abu. Near Bombay, there are
atheran, Mahabeleshwar, and Pune hill
ations. In the South, the Nilgiris and Cardamom Hills offer cool, refreshing peace at the
Ooty and Kodaikanal hill stations and in the
richly forested wildlife parks.

THE HARD FACTS Hotels should be
booked well in advance for the peak season,
November–February.

Beware of the sun: it is very powerful. Pack
the full quota of full-strength suntan lotions,
after-sun lotions and sun-burn lotions. Even
Goa fails to overcome import problems to
have good brands on sale. Indian beaches are
usually very clean but take some antiseptic to
put on any cuts. One or two hotels have
in-house doctors who supply soothing camo-
mile lotion for sunburn and prickly heat.

A Sony Walkman and a few tapes is good
for relaxing music and a tiny radio can pick
up All-India Radio, the BBC World Service or
blasts of the latest local Indian film music (see
p. 14). Remember to pack plenty of batteries
for both. You will have to take a supply of
reading matter, so stock up in the big cities.
Beach hotel bookshops, where they exist, are
not good.

Newspapers, weeklies and glossy magazines are luxuries and eyed greedily on your
arrival. Eventually a fellow guest will ask to
borrow them. Even Goa, an hour's plane-hop
from international Bombay, can easily get 12
days behind with *The Times* of London.

Despite the miles and miles of glistening
white sands on the Coromandel and Malabar
coasts, it is wiser by far to stick to the hotel
area for scantily clad sun bathing, to avoid
offending locals. It is not considered quite the
thing to scamper across Madras sea front or
Bombay's Chowpatty beach in a bikini. And
it is best to be sensitive to local approval or
disapproval on the quieter, but irresistible,
stretches of sand. And beware of the under-
current in some places, which can be quite
strong, so check with the hotel or local fishermen before taking a dip (see p. 28).

Goa

THE HARD FACTS   It is possible to go all the year round as Goa is very beautiful during the monsoon (June–September), but certainly best November–February. The pre-Advent Carnival at Panaji (February–March) is a pale shadow of the former colourful and exotic spectacle, and locals do not hold out hope for its improvement, whatever the tourist literature might say. Getting to and from Goa is easy and straightforward. Daily flights from Bombay and Bangalore serve Dabolim, Goa's airport. The steamer trip between Panaji in Goa and Bombay is glorious, best taken in the Goa–Bombay direction (operated by Mogul Lines, bookable in Panaji at V. S. Dempo & Co. (tel: 3842) or through hotel (see Bombay chapter, p. 113 for more on this). Car drives are especially beautiful across the Western Ghats from Hampi or, harder work, along the unspoilt coast down from Bombay or up from Mangalore. Train journeys to Bangalore and Bombay take over 20 hours (to Delhi about 46 hours), but it is cheap and the scenery is beautiful.

Tourist Information is found in Panaji. The Government of India Tourist Office is at Communidada Building, Church Square (tel: 3412), and is very good. Goa Tourist Office, Rua Afonso de Albuquerque, is hopeless. Goa Tours and MGM International Travels (tel: 2150) are both reliable. Good bookshops are Singbal Book Depot, Sarmalker Book Depot and those in hotels recommended below.

THE BEACHES   Over 100km of some of the most beautiful, palm-fringed beaches in the world. Certainly the best in India. So there is no need to stick to the hotel's silver sands. If it is at all possible to grade these glimpses of Paradise into beautiful and more beautiful, then the 40km of Colva comes tops: sparkling sand, coconut palms, calm clean sea and hardly a soul. Baga, north of Calangute, also rates very high. John Lucas, who has been in Goa for a decade, runs a wind-surfing school here, but it only takes up a tiny corner of the beach. At the moment, the smiling hippy population centres on Anjuna, Chapora and Calangute villages, attracting good little markets and restaurants, but their presence definitely discounts them from the Paradise stakes. The nicest way to move beaches is by boat and hotels with motor boats will zoom you a few km up the coast and collect you by boat or car later. Alternatively, use bicycles or taxis.

WHERE TO STAY
There are dozens of hotels in Goa, but only a fe are good. The following are the crème de la crèm for their setting, the hotel buildings, quality service, food, beach and range of facilities.

Fort Aguada Beach Resort, Sinquerim, Bardez
Telephone: 3401
Telex: 194-206 TAJ IN
Cable: FORTAGUADA, GOA
Airport: 45km; Panaji port: 10km; railway stati 48km
120 rooms, including 32 cottages, attached bath; sea-facing. Single: Rs360; double Rs425; Janua and February supplement of Rs50–65 per roo per night; December flat rate tariff of Rs550 single or double; rooms with terrace cost Rs1 extra; cottages: Rs1,500–2,000.

First-class facilities include pool, extensive a mature gardens with hammocks, car rental, bu ness services, post office, bookshop, chemi shopping arcade, beauty salon, masseur, bab sitter, doctor, fishing (salmon and mackerel), cla pigeon shooting, scuba-diving, Beach Buggy a bicycles available, indoor restaurant, poolside b becue and bar, beach café. Room service 7 –10pm only.

Sports and Fitness Complex: water skiing, sa ing, para sailing, wind surfing (9am–6pm); 2 ten courts (one floodlit), badminton, squash, v leyball, basket ball, full gymnasium, hydrothera (steam and sauna rooms, whirlpool), beauty p lour (men and women), billiards.

The best beach hotel in India, built and run the Taj Group, managed by a Goan, Mrs As Rishi. Sited next door to the Taj Holiday Villa (see below). Guests can use the facilities of b and can easily book to stay a few nights at one, th a few nights at the other. The Fort Aguada h extremely beautiful, low-lying architecture th sprawls up the hillside from seemingly endle Calangute Beach. The site incorporates the ruins the 17th century Portuguese Fort of Aguada. T hotel was opened in 1974 and extensively enlarg for the Commonwealth heads of state and th entourages to come and switch off after their me ing in 1983. One cottage is now named after M Thatcher. Rooms of the main block spread arou lawns, hammock-strung trees and the pool. T cottages are further up the hill (up to five minut walk), making for slow room service. It is ve worthwhile taking a room in the main block wit large terrace. Plenty of local Goan furnitu throughout. Dolphins play in the early morni

a. There are hammocks for afternoon siestas.
here is a gloriously long beach and sunsets from
e fort ramparts are sensational. Good food in-
udes barbecued lobster and giant prawns, Goan
shes, Goan wines and local feni.

he Taj Holiday Village, Sinquerim, Bardez
elephone, telex, cable and access from airport and
ort: as for Fort Aguada.

 non-airconditioned rooms arranged in cottages
leep 2–6), attached bath. Single Cottage Rs250–
0; 2-Room Villa (sleeps four) Rs600; Cottage
uites (sleeps three-four) Rs550; Family Unit
leeps 6) Rs925; supplements during January–
bruary, higher supplements for December.
Facilities include car rental, baby-sitter, pool,
iddling pool, leisure centre (library, reading
om, card tables, chess), free coach to Panaji once
day; Beach House serves Goan and Portuguese
untry cooking; room service limited to breakfast
impers, tea hampers and cocktail hampers; each
ttage has a fan, telephone and sitting-out area.
l the shopping, restaurant and beach facilities of
ort Aguada and the Sports and Fitness Complex
ee above) are available.
The Village is made up of charming cottages
signed in the style of Goan homes, right on the
ach, next door to Fort Aguada. It has a very
laxed atmosphere, quite unlike a hotel. Each
ttage is separate, providing a great degree of
ivacy and peace. Perfect for a romantic escape.

otel Oberoi Bogmalo Beach, Bogmalo, Dabolim
lephone: 2191
lex: 0191-297
ble: OBHOTEL
rport 2km; Panaji port 30km; railway station 7km
6 rooms on 8 floors, all with sea view, small
lconies and attached bath. Single Rs400; double
475; both carry Rs100 and Rs125 supplements
ecember 16–January 31; substantial reduc-
ns May 1–September 31 make singles Rs225,
ubles Rs275; enquire about week-end package
als.
Excellent facilities include travel desk, business
rvices, baby-sitter, shopping arcade, beauty
lon, video room, large pool with children's sec-
n, fully equipped gymnasium and health club
auna, Turkish bath, aryavaidya oil massage),
nnis, volley-ball, 9-hole golf course, wind-
rfing, para-sailing, water-skiing, scuba-diving,
ater polo, yoga classes; arrangements for speed-
at and river cruises, fishing, bicycles, treks to
arby villages; good Goan dishes and local sea-
d served at indoor restaurant; poolside bar-

becue, snacks and bar (daily live music); beach
barbecues; full 24-hour room service.
It is built right on a secluded beach near a tiny
Goan fishing village, about 10 minutes from the
airport. The beach is good but small by Goan
standards; the pool area quite small and lacks
lawns. However, beach sports and water sports are
excellent here. Health fanatics rave over the gymnasium's exercise machines and the health club's
massages. And Colva Beach, one of the most sensational in all Goa, is very near.

Cidade de Goa, Vainguinim Beach, Dona Paula
Telephone: 3604/3606/2136/2555
Telex: 0194-257 DONA-IN
Cable: CIDADE
Airport 26km; Panaji port 7km; railway station
45km
101 rooms including 4 suites, all sea-facing, with
balcony and bath. Single Rs350; double Rs400;
December 20–January 31 all rooms a flat Rs450;
suites from Rs1,050. Run by the Welcomgroup.
Excellent facilities include travel counter, business services, shopping arcade, book shop, beauty
salon, health club (sauna, massage), Yoga club,
two swimming pools (freshwater and saltwater),
video films and games, tennis, table tennis, indoor
games, wind-surfing, water polo, fishing, motor
launch excursions; bicycles, motor bikes and cars
for hire; arrangements for hiking, trekking, shooting and frog-catching (a Goan rainy season pas-
time); restaurant serves very good Goan, Portuguese and Mughlai dishes, coffee shop extends on
to poolside terrace, bar (local musicians), poolside
buffet.
Another piece of Charles Correa architecture
(see Kovalam, below), this time with clear, crisp
lines, rooms opening on to courtyards and terraces
down to the sea, described by Correa as 'Moorish
casbah concept' but approved by guests as 'very
beautiful, like a Portuguese fishing village; lovely
landscaping'. Rooms designed in three styles using local furniture: Gujarati, Portuguese and the
Goan Damao; restaurant decoration by the Indian
cartoonist, Mario, a Goan whose drawings are
found in almost every Indian glossy magazine.

Prainha Cottages, Dona Paula; information and
booking address: Palmar Beach Resorts, 1st Floor,
Glendela, Rua de Ormuz, Panaji
Telephone: 4004
Cable: PRAINHA
Airport 26km, Panaji port 7km
13 cottages linked together, each with attached
shower and verandah. Single or double Rs180;

241

December 15–January 15 Rs200; mid-June – mid–September Rs90.

No air-conditioning, communal dining-room, laundry service, babysitter, car/motorbike/bicycle rental. This is perfect for a quiet time, away from the jet set. These simple cottages are patronised by discerning diplomats and other old India hands. They are set on a very secluded beach on a rocky part of the coast, well run, spotlessly clean and serve good food. It is all under the supervision of Aires Dias, whose brother runs the excellent O Pescador restaurant about 50m away. Unfortunately, the sand is black, but a bicycle or car gets you to endless empty beach in minutes.

OUT AND ABOUT   Goa is very un-Indian. Its history stretches back to the Mauryan Empire of the 3rd century BC. Then followed a string of distant rulers such as the Chalukyas, Vijayanagars, Bahmanis and the Adil Shahis of Bijapur. But its character today was determined by the Portuguese rule from 1510 to 1961. There is a strong Portuguese flavour about everything, from the Konkan language to the pretty floral dresses worn by locals. And the interesting sights are Portuguese too, including some fine churches.

Panaji has pretty narrow streets, attractive buildings and cafés. Old Goa has Se Cathedral, the Basilica of Bom Jesus and the Convent and Church of St Francis of Assisi, which has beautiful murals and an excellent museum round the back (selling S. Rajagopalan's good booklet, *Old Goa*). Slightly separate from this group is the Baroque Church of St Cajetan, built by Italian friars. The nicest way of getting from Panaji to Old Goa is by ferry: breakfast in a Panaji café, lunch on board, Old Goa sights early evening before taxi back to the hotel or on to a restaurant. Most of the other ferry rides are equally pretty. It does not really matter where they go: there is always a nice walk, a nearby beach or a village taverna the other end.

Margao town, in the south, still smells strongly of the Portuguese. Some of the most beautiful of the large, old Portugese houses are here, lived in by the descendants of those who built them 400 years ago, their very fine interiors a mixture of Portuguese, Indian and Chinese skills. The exceedingly hospitable owners patronise the hotels for dinner, and often invite foreign tourists back to these wonders.

One of the most exciting things to do is to go out with the fishermen. Your hotel room boy normally has at least one relative who is a fisherman and he will fix it up. The long day starts early, but you a usually given some of the catch at the end.

RESTAURANTS   It is tempting to stick to exotic diet of superbly cooked seafood – lobste giant prawns, oysters, crabs, mussels, shrimp etc. Local Indianised Portuguese dishes are a delicious, such as chourisso (Goan sausage), s potel (pig's liver) and suckling pig. All the hote mentioned above have good indoor and outdo restaurants. They will also cook anything bough or caught – oneself. In the hotels, an evening at t rustic *Taj Village* is especially nice; the *Bogmalo* ha special female chef for Goan dishes. Across t bridge from Panaji, the *O Coqueiro* at Porvorim the best of all for unusual Goan dishes.

The current best seafood restaurants are *La* and *Zuari Hotel*, both at Vasco, and *O Pescador* Dona Paula (see Prainha Cottages hotel, abov On Colva Beach, the *Dolphin* Restaurant and *Ma Baiai do Sol* are the best of several. Sadly, t much-loved *El Gazella* has closed down.

Local Goan wines are much cheaper than t Indian Golconda and Bosca, but local *feni* is t thing to try. There used to be whole villages d voted to making it, such as Bogmalo village, whe every house had a distillery. Feni is made fro either the cashew apple or the coconut palm a usually sold after the first distillation. But in t Bogmala tavernas, double distilled feni is serve the second distillation flavoured with cumin, g ger, etc., and producing a smooth liqueur. T asking for cumin seed palm feni or sasaparilla pa feni, made from a medicinal root.

SHOPPING   The traditional Portuguese work malachite with gold filigree is cheap and prett often sold in sets of necklace, earrings and ring Platinum beads set in gold are typical Goan Chr tian jewellery and the fisherwomen still buy chai of it as a form of security, to prevent their m getting at the savings. Another Christian traditi is to make roses out of coral. Find all these, of go quality, at Sirsat Jewellers, Panaji. For shoppir and colour, the Friday market at Mapusa is e cellent: every sort of fish, spice, sausage, flow and vegetable for sale, as well as delicious fre cashew nuts and quantities of appliqué work i cluding Banjara tribal work, and Gujarati weddir hangings.

FIND OUT MORE
'Goa', *Marg* special publication, Bombay, 1981

Golden Goa', *Marg* special publication, Bombay, 1983
Hutt, A.: *Goa: Rome of the Orient*, London, 1985
Mario: *Goa with love*, Goa, 1974
Richards, J. M.: *Goa*, Delhi, 1982

Coromandel Coast

THE HARD FACTS These sparkling beaches, where the fishermen launch their catamarans at dawn, are on the east coast of Tamil Nadu state, south of Madras, at Covelong and Mahabalipuram. All three recommended hotels have huge, empty beaches one side and the good coastal road behind them, providing the perfect combination of relaxing on the beach with sight-seeing to some of the real wonders of India. No other Indian resort has this combination.

Best season is November–February, when fair skin still turns lobster red in less than an hour. After then, the really sizzling heat begins and there are liable to be water shortages. Beware of the east coast undertow of the Bay of Bengal and always check before swimming. As a result of this danger, a hotel swimming pool is an important asset but, if possible, check near the time of arrival that it is filled – there have been cases of empty seaside pools in November. Very easy access to the main three resort hotels: fly or train to Madras (see p. 78), then drive south for about an hour. Madras is the base for information, entertainment (Bharata Natyam dance) and shopping (see p. 206–10).

WHERE TO STAY
The Fisherman's Cove, Covelong Beach, Chingleput District, Tamil Nadu
Telephone: 268/269
Telex: 041-7194 TAJM IN
Cable: FISHCOVE
Airport 36km; railway station 35km; central Madras 30km
70 rooms including 28 cottages, all with attached bath. Rooms: single Rs325, double Rs375; cottages: single Rs375, double Rs425.

All mod. cons include business services, doctor, car hire, shopping arcade, swimming pool, spacious lawns, tennis, table tennis, chess, children's playground, fishing, boating, rowing, horse riding, daily video films; restaurant with outside terrace, bar, poolside snacks. Room service limited to drinks and snacks.

Three-storey hotel built in 1974 by the Taj Group, well decorated with local cane chairs and roll-up blinds, all providing local and restful atmosphere. The circular cottages are right on the beach, at the bottom of the hotel lawns, their verandahs looking directly on to dazzling white sand and sea. The pool, set amid a mature garden, is a major advantage when it is dangerous to swim (occasionally emptied), check at any Taj office on arrival in India. Glorious walks along the totally empty beach; starlit cocktails on the lawns. Food varies but can be very good, especially seafood.

Silversands Fun Resort, Mahabalipuram, Tamil Nadu
Telephone: 28/83/84
Telex: 041-7707
Cable: VEECUMSEES
Airport 60km; railway station 58km; central Mahabalipuram 2km
65 rooms, bath attached; 55 rooms have air-conditioning. Single Rs240–350, double Rs250–450.

Facilities include car rental, three restaurants, bar and coffee shop.

A good, simple, seaside hotel, not flush with facilities but excellent food, its restaurants patronised by the Madrasi cognoscenti. Apart from the lauded grilled lobster, they serve the usual tri-cuisine of Indian-Continental-Chinese as well as Rajasthan and Gujarati dishes.

VGP Golden Beach Resort, Injambakkam Village, Madras
Telephone: 412893/412884
Cable: VIGIPI
Airport 25km; railway station 20km; central Madras 10km
78 rooms, including 3 suites, bath attached. Single Rs200, double Rs250, suite Rs350; some rooms do not have air-conditioning and are about 40% cheaper.

Facilities include car rental, travel agent, beauty salon, camel and horse fun rides; restaurant and coffee shop.

Very well placed for nipping into Madras and sited on another very quiet stretch of beautiful beach, some rooms arranged as cottages on stilts. Again, a hotel enjoyed by the Madrasis for its food.

OUT AND ABOUT A huge quantity of fascinating things on the doorstep. Early morning or sunset visits to Mahabalipuram are magical. Tirukalikundram lies en route to the temple and the silk city of Kanchipuram. The artists' colony of Cholamandel is near the Beach hotel. And many of the interesting parts of Madras are at the south end of the city – the Theosophical Gardens, Guindy Deer and Snake Park and the Kalakshetra School of Indian classical dance. Madras is also near enough for a wide choice of restaurants, some amusing south Indian cinema and very good shopping. For longer forays, there are trips inland to Vellore, Gingee, Pondicherry and Chidambaram.

Malabar Coast

Kovalam, kerala

THE HARD FACTS   There are just two isolated beach resorts in the 1,000km of western coastline between Goa and Kanya Kumari. Kovalam is on the Malabar Coast near the tip of India, just outside Trivandrum and on the Kerala-Tamil Nadu border. Mangalore, the other, is very new (see below). Kovalam experiences the Malabar climate, softer than the Coromandel's. Its season stretches September–April; monsoon and humidity last from May to August. Access is easy: plane or train to Trivandrum; it is also a good finishing point for a drive through Kerala or Tamil Nadu. Information, shopping and museums are in Trivandrum (see p. 205).

WHERE TO STAY
Kovalam Ashok Beach Resort, Kovalam, Trivandrum
Telephone: 3031-10/3331-7
Telex: TV-216
Cable: TOURISM VIZHINJAM
Airport 19km; railway station 14km; central Trivandrum 13km
72 rooms, including 2 suites, plus *Halcyon Castle*, 42 cottages and 16 detached units, all with bathroom attached. Hotel: single Rs450, double Rs500, suite Rs675; Halcyon Castle de-luxe suite Rs450; cottage or unit: single Rs450, double Rs500.

Good facilities include travel desk, car rental, shopping arcade, large pool, tennis courts, table tennis, chess, excellent and extensive yoga and massage centre, water sports (water-skiing, motor boats, paddle boats, etc.); restaurant, poolside service from coffee shop, bar. Disadvantages: no individual control of the air-conditioning (one guest shivered in socks and jumpers in February); only the double rooms have a bath tub, singles have just a shower; Halcyon Castle has no room service; poolside barbecue Sat. evenings only.

This is the showpiece for the Ashok Group, th government-run hotel chain. It has a glorious sit and a fine building, but is abominably run. Charle Correa's beautiful design won him an award from the Royal Institute of British Architects. The lobb and public rooms, including the swimming poc and a large terrace which faces out west over th sheer cliff, are at the top of the hillside site. Th view is remarkable at all times, especially sunse The rooms drop down the hillside to the beach each room with its own very large balcony (whic cannot be overlooked), good views and local coi and cane furnishings. Halcyon Castle is above th hotel: no room service, and peace would be dis turbed since business conferences are held here Kovalam Grove is a cluster of self-contained cot tages right down on the beach, each with terrace refrigerator (room service for breakfast and te only), surrounding another swimming pool an snack bar.

There is a long beach where fishermen launc their catamarans 7am, returning 4–5pm and other fish from the shore using huge nets. The beach are near the hotel is cordoned off from hawkers an furnished with life guards (take advice from the on sea current; they can also fix up trips wit fishermen – the hotel will cook any lobster an crabs caught); changing huts and bar for drink and Indian snacks.

However, all this beauty is marred by servic which is consistently slow and slack. The food i almost inedible, menus lacking local dishes (a loc; lobster dish has to be ordered a day in advance the room furnishings are not being maintained (th coir is already fraying) and white clothes can retur from the laundry with pink blotches.

If the advantages do not outweigh the disadvar tages, there is the brand new, state-run *Samutr hotel* and numerous very simple hotels in the ba south of Kovalam.

OUT AND ABOUT   For the sights of Trivar drum, Padmanabhapuram and Kanya Kumari, se pp. 205–6. In the next bay south live hippies attracting numerous good and cheap restaurant serving delicious fresh crab.

Mangalore, Karnataka

THE HARD FACTS   The Konkal coast of Karna taka is still almost entirely free of tourists. Bes season September–May. Certainly, the nicest wa

arrive is along the beautiful coast road from
[B]angalore north to Goa (about 370km) or south to
[C]ochin (about 450km), which was compared to the
[C]ôte d'Azur before it was exploited. And the drive
[a]cross from the glorious Hoysala temples (Belur,
[H]alebid, Hasan, about 150km), Mysore (220km) or
[B]angalore (320km) is pretty too. Alternatively,
[th]ere are direct flights to Mangalore from Bombay
[an]d Bangalore.

HERE TO STAY

[S]ummer Sands Beach Resort, Chotamangalore,
[U]lal, Mangalore
[T]elephone: 6253/6284
[C]able: SUMMERSAND
[A]irport 30km; railway station 12km; central
[M]angalore 10km

[9]8 rooms, including 64 suites, arranged in 42
[c]ottages, bungalows and family houses, all with
[b]ath attached. Single Rs110; double Rs155; suite
[R]s190. Only 29 units have air-conditioning; rates
[ab]out 30% cheaper without air-conditioning. 30%
[o]ff-season discount.

Facilities include car rental, good swimming
[p]ool, deep sea fishing, sailing by arrangement,
[m]ini golf, tennis court, health club (massage, hyd-
[ra]ulic bath); poolside and beach restaurants, gar-
[d]en and seaside bar-cafés.

The cottages, bungalows and houses are built in
[th]e local architectural style amid coconut groves,
[o]verlooking the Arabian Sea; larger units have
[si]tting room and terrace. Good pool and excellent,
[e]mpty beach (patrolled to preserve privacy). Res-
[ta]urant lit by lanterns serves well-prepared local
[K]onkan dishes including seafood (fish, prawns,
[so]metimes lobster), and the toddy and feni liquors;
[lo]cal sweetmeats are sugar-coated cashew nuts
[an]d banana halwa.

[O]UT AND ABOUT The Hoysala glories of Belur
[an]d Halebid are not far (see pp. 197–8) nor are the
[Ja]in statues at Karkala and Venus (53km). Local
[fi]shermen of Ullal will take hotels guests out for the
[d]ay. The hotel will advise on finding the local
[Y]ayalata-Yakshagana (local song and dance), Kori-
[k]atta (cock-fighting) and Thalim (martial arts using
[d]aggers and firebrands). In Mangalore, shopping
[is] best at Hampankatta for local crafts using coir,
[ju]te, banana and pineapple, as well as feni and
[fr]esh cashew nuts and coffee.

Sri Lanka (Ceylon)

Apart from Goa, the most sophisticated and best
equipped beach resort hotels for India holiday-
makers are here. Sri Lanka means Resplendent
Land and is a far cry from the Robinson Crusoe
escapism of the Maldives. It is highly accessible.
Planeloads of socialites arrive from all over the
world to escape winter and pep up their tans. A
few days of flopping on a Sri Lankan beach can
easily be tagged on to the front or back of an Indian
holiday. Sri Lanka's beaches are magnificent but
there is much more – a people, language, history
and culture that are all outside the orbit of this
book. There is plenty to see for a complete holiday,
without ever crossing the waters to India.

THE HARD FACTS There are no formalities or
visas for holders of European or United States
passports for stays less than 30 days. To avoid
the monsoon, head for the south-west coast
December–March and the north-east coast April–
September. Access is easy: direct to Colombo on
international flights; direct connections with India
between Colombo and Madras (daily except Fri.),
Bombay (Tues., Thurs., Sat.), Tiruchchirapalli
(Tues., Sat.) and Trivandrum (Wed., Sun.). The
airport has a good tourist desk, car rental (average
price about SLR450 per day), hotel reservations
desk and bank for buying Sri Lankan rupees (Indian rupees should be left in India).

To find out more, the best guide books are *Insight
Guide to Sri Lanka* and *Sri Lanka – a travel survival
kit* (see bibliography). For full information, contact the
Ceylon (Sri Lanka) Tourist Board at Suite 433, High
Holborn House, 52 High Holborn, London WC1
(tel: 405 1194/5); North American Office, Suite 308,
609 Fifth Avenue, New York, NY 10017 (tel:
212.935 0369); Office de Tourisme de Ceylan, 11–13
Rue Gaillon, 75002 Paris (tel: 331.742 9457).

For all its social sophistication, the basics still
cannot be bought in Sri Lanka. When packing, the
same rule applies for Sri Lanka as for India: Anything that is sold in Boots in Britain is unavailable in
Sri Lanka; even the soap is grim. So, all lotions,
cosmetics, perfume, lots of anti-mosquito preparations (absolutely essential, sticks better than
aerosol, Autan is a good brand), cotton clothes and
socks and a jumper for going up into the hills need
to be thrown into the suitcase.

WHERE TO STAY

The coast of Sri Lanka is bursting with hotels. They came in all sizes, characters and qualities. As in Goa, off-season prices plummet from May to October. The five chosen below are recommended on their merits as beach hotels alone: good beach, swimming, facilities, food and service. When making reservations, it is best to confirm that the hotel will arrange collection from the airport. Except for the Moonlight Beach Hotel, they are all on the south-west coast and thus good December–March. Moonlight Beach Hotel, for the April–September months, is on the north-east coast where the beaches are, if anything, even more beautiful. But the resorts are less developed and there is a drive of about seven hours from the airport.

Triton Hotel, Ahungalla
Telephone: 97.228/218
Telex: 21142
Cable: AITKEN Airport
2½hrs by road
125 rooms, including suites, bath attached. Single SLR1345, double SLR1660. May 1–Oct. 30: off-season tariff.

Facilities include tours desk, beauty salon, health club, shopping arcade, and exceptionally good pool, tennis, badminton, billiards, indoor games; several restaurants and bars indoors and outdoors, barbecues.

Sri Lanka's current top hotel, a bold design by Geoffrey Bawa who was also architect for the new parliament complex in Colombo. Buildings open direct on to the long beach, with no buildings either side.

Tangerine Beach Hotel, Kalutara
Telephone: 42.2640/2295
Telex: 211889
Airport 2hrs by road
167 rooms, including 7 suites, bath attached. Single SLR1100, double SLR1200. Off-season, May 1–Oct. 30: single SLR500, double SLR600. Facilities include travel counter, shopping arcade, large pool, 2 tennis courts, water gardens; restaurants and bars include a supper club and coffee shop.

Well-designed hotel with particularly nice rooms and pool area, set amid the palms of a 12-acre, landscaped coconut property. Faces on to a wide, clean, 500m-long beach protected from the quite rough sea of the south-west coast by a coral reef.

Bentota Beach Hotel, Bentota
Telephone: 48.5176/5266
Telex: 21104

Cable: HOLIDAY COLOMBO
Airport 2hrs by road
135 rooms, attached bath. Single SLR1,100–1,56
double SLR1,180–1,660. Off-season, May 1–Oc
30: single SLR840–1,200, double SLR920–1,200

Facilities include shopping arcade, beauty salo
gymnasium, health club, pool, water-skiing, boa
ing, river cruises up the lagoon, mini-golf, tenni
good restaurants and bars with well-stocked cella

A slightly older hotel built on the site of a Port
guese fort, with beautiful views over the lagoon
one side and the sea on the other. Just near t
hotel is Brief, the home of the elderly landscap
artist, Bevis Bawa, open to the public. His house
a museum of antique furniture and contempora
works of art, set in a most lovely garden.

The Dolphin, On The Beach, Waikkal
Telephone: 031.3129
Telex: 21601 STAMCO CE
Cable: HONDAGENT
Managed by the Indian hotel chain, Welcomgrou
so bookable through their offices in India, s
p. 11.
Airport 30mins by road
76 rooms, all with balcony or patio and bathroor
Single or double SLR780; May 1–Oct. 30 SLR500

Facilities include shopping arcade, travel cou
ter, beauty salon (health club planned), enormo
pool, sailing, boating, wind-surfing, wate
scooters, water-skiing, deep sea fishing, 8-ho
golf course, 2 tennis courts, billiards, squash, tak
tennis; indoor and outdoor restaurants and ba
include Sri Lankan cuisine.

New hotel conveniently near the airport for
short stay, the buildings arranged in four cluste
amid 8 acres of landscaped gardens reaching dov
to the private beach. Boasts one of the biggest poc
in Asia: five linked pools along the facade, t
central one with water jets, making a total of 25,0
sq ft.

Moonlight Beach Hotel, Nilaveli, Trincomalee
Telephone: Nilaveli 22/23
Telex: 21115
Cable: SUNTRAVELS
Airport 6–7hrs by road
70 rooms, only some air-conditioned. Apri
September, single or double SLR625; Octobe
March, SLR300. Facilities include shoppir
arcade, pool, tennis, sailing, windsurfing, ski
diving.

An older and slightly less luxurious hotel tha
the others recommended, but lots of charm and s
in beautiful gardens that stretch down to a love

ach. For a gentle journey from the airport, stop vernight at The Lodge, Habarana Village, right in ne middle of the island. The Moonlight will book it hen you make your reservation with them. The onsoon is short, November–January, and so the inter months, when the tariff is much lower, are orth considering for a quieter beach.

UT AND ABOUT A car plus driver is even neaper than in India, but it is important to estab- sh the price and the overnight and meals rates efore leaving base. Colombo has everything a pital should have and is worth a visit: fort, har- our, bazaars, National Museum, churches, new arliament buildings, good shopping and old otels to take sustenance in, such as the *Galle Face* uilt 1856) and the *Taprobane* (at the port, good ews from fourth floor restaurant). Good res- urants in Colombo include *Cosmopolite, Alfred ouse Gardens, Colombo 5*, run by a French–Viet- amese couple; *Renuka* in Galle Road and *Galle Face otel* (both for curry).

There is plenty to buy, above all the gems from atnapura. The cheaper moonstones, quartz (all olours, lemon, smoky, rose, brown), garnets and ne more pricy sapphires, star rubies, cat's eyes nd aquamarines are all best bought at the hotel nops, not in the back streets. The State Gem orporation at 24 York Street, Colombo, is reliable nd has several branches including one at Bentota each Resort. All their gems are guaranteed and ney will also inspect gems you may be wishing to ny from other shops, to confirm they are what ney purport to be.

Pretty sarongs for the beach are very cheap, as e local masks, batik work, basketry and clutch ngs woven in all colours, all found in Laksala, the ri Lanka government emporium. Tailors are very neap and good and will copy clothes, but the ndian fabric is better than the rather coarse nhalese cotton. Barbara Sansoni's excellent Bare- ot shop in Galle Road, Colombo (another branch the Intercontinental Hotel, Colombo) can range a tailor if it proves tricky to find one.

North from Colombo lies *Negombo* fishing vil- ge, past a Dutch canal, Portuguese churches and alms. South is *Galle*, with a big Dutch fort, the narming *New Oriental Hotel* (tel: 1684) for refresh- nent and, inland, the Sinharaja, the last primeval ainforest left in Sri Lanka. Southeast is the gem- ining capital, *Ratnapura*, with three gem nuseums and the gateway to the pilgrimage up the 243m Adam's Peak. Up into the hills, *Kandy* is a

very pretty provincial town and former capital with a most beautiful nature reserve and glorious bot- anical gardens, very well maintained and con- sidered one of the most important in the world. Stay at the colonial *Queen's* or *Swisse hotels*. (Queen's is run by the Indian hotel chain, Oberoi, and can easily be booked in India.)

For wildlife, there are four *national parks*: Yala, Walawe, Wilpattu and Gal Oya, each with a better chance of seeing animals if you stay overnight.

FIND OUT MORE
Brohier, R. L.: *Seeing Ceylon*, Colombo, 1965
Brohier, R. L.: *Discovering Ceylon*, Colombo, 1981
Insight Guide to Sri Lanka, APA Productions, Hong Kong, 1983
Raven-Hart, R.: *Ceylong: History in Stone*, Colombo, 1964
Sri Lanka – A Travel Survival Kit, A Lonely Planet Guide, South Yarra, Australia, 1982

Republic of Maldives

A paradise of more than twelve hundred tiny coral islands off the south-west tip of India. Most islands are uninhabited but where there are natives they are Muslim, proud and friendly. The islands that are open to tourists are all similar. Their size varies from small, about three sq km, to tiny, about 700m by 120m. Each has simple cottage accommodation, swaying palm trees, the finest white coral sand and is surrounded by crystal clear water, ideal for skin diving and snorkelling.

Visitors find the marine life superior even to Thailand's and the Maldive government intend to keep it that way, strictly prohibiting hunting fish and collecting shells. Above the water activities are wind-surfing, some sailing and water-skiing, ex- ploring uninhabited islands by boat and some fishing excursions. There is no night life, little jolly camaraderie and the simple food consists of a large dose of fish. People come here for total peace and privacy. The smaller the island, the greater the isolated paradise quietude and the simplicity of life.

THE HARD FACTS There are no formalities or visas required to visit the Maldives. Season November–April; showers but not heavy monsoon May–September. Access is by air to Hulule Airport at Male from Trivandrum (current service Mon. and Thurs. only), and from Colombo (Mon., Tues., Thurs., Sat. and Sun.); then boat to the island you are staying on (2–7hrs) – so it is better to go for a week, or more.

The easiest and most reliable way to book a hotel is through a tour operator who will also coordinate the plane and boat connections. Alternatively, book up with the Taj hotel group, the only big chain operating in the Maldives so far, who have two island resorts. It is definitely better to book than just to turn up.

Pack a complete supply of reading, music, drawing, painting, games (chess, cards, etc.) and other pastimes, plus pre- and post-sun lotions, beach towels and a rubber face-mask and tube – although underwater equipment is available for hire, the water is so clear it is hardly necessary. And pack a bathing costume – nudity is frowned upon. The best things to buy there are sarongs, flip-flop sandals and the very special black coral. There is a spirit licence for tourist islands but the rest of the Maldives are dry, so it is best not to have bottles in the suitcase. The most useful currency is US dollars, although a local Maldive rupee currency exists.

WHERE TO STAY
All the accommodation is arranged as cottage-bungalows strung along the beaches. The choice of island depends upon how remote you want to be from Male and how often you want to bump into fellow humans. Here is a short selection to choose from. Rooms range from US$50 to $120 and always include full board.

Villi Varu Island Resort, Vilingilivaru
and
Bi Ya Doo Island Resort, Biyadhoo
The two Taj group resorts, both bookable c/o Prabhalaji Enterprises Ltd, H Maagala, 2 Amir Ahmed Magu, Male; or through Taj Central Reservations (see Bombay, p. 11)
Telephone: Male 2717
Telex: 66021 BALAJI MF
Airport 32km

Villi Varu has 60 rooms, no air-conditioning, single US$53, double US56; Bi Ya Doo has 96 rooms, full air-conditioning, single US$70, double US$73. Rooms at both resorts have hot and cold water and a refrigerator in every room. Each resort has a swimming pool, diving base, wind-surfing, snorkelling and boat excursions; each has an air-conditioned restaurant and bar. The Bi Ya Doo is the plusher of the two, but both are considered the most luxurious of what is available. Elsewhere,

facilities tend to be very minimal – but that mig be just what you are looking for. It is even possib to camp on an uninhabited island.
OTHER ISLANDS
Bandos: airport 15km; 210 rooms
Baros: airport 20km; 10 rooms
Buduhithi Coral Islands: airport 40km; 110 room
Cacoa; airport 22km; 8 rooms, unusually good foc
Forykolhufushi: airport 5km; 124 rooms. Pea somewhat disturbed by the Male Club Medite ranée
Furana: airport 10km; 124 rooms
Helengeli: airport 60km; 48 rooms
Ihuru: airport 22km; 74 rooms
Kuramathi: airport 45km (2½ hours by boat); rooms, particularly rich in coral and fish life; Bar kuda of Hamburg run the island's diving school
Kurumba: airport 5km; 130 rooms
Lhohifushi: airport 35km; 120 rooms
Meeru and Fenfushi: airport 45km; 260 rooms
Olhuveli: airport 45km; 100 rooms
Vabbin Faru: airport 20km; 50 rooms
Villingili: airport 5km; 220 rooms

Andaman and Nicobar Islands (India)

A string of more than 300 almost virgin islands quietly in the Andaman Sea, east of the Bay Bengal, hardly touched by modern civilisatio These are for the traveller who wants to pla explorer between swims and snorkels, the unde water fanatic who thought the Maldives were goc but wants to be more impressed, and the trav snob who enjoyed the beauties of Goa and t other resorts before the rest of the world kne where they were on the map. James Camerc called the archipelago 'about the most tranquil ar beguiling place I ever visited. Golden, warm ar empty beaches between unpolluted turquoi bays. There are very few remaining places bo wholly lovely and wholly unspoilt. And this is o of them.'

The northern islands are the Andamans, wi Port Blair as capital and a mixed population aborigines, Burmese and Indians. The southe islands are the less accessible Nicobars, almo entirely inhabited by tribes. Thickly forested hi of teak, mahogany and rosewood stretch rig down to the soft white sand that twinkles wi finely shredded shells. Under the indigo blue ar crystal clear sea, the coral and marine life a stunning.

As in the Maldives, the islands inhabited by the ᵖrotected tribes are out of bounds to tourists. In the ᴬndamans and Nicobars, this leaves only a dozen ˢᵒ that are regularly open to visitors, plus others ᵧ arrangement. It is worth arriving with the ᵖecial permits needed to visit these. On her recent ᵗᵖ there, Josceline Dimbleby found the Anda-ᵃns 'much more beautiful than Goa but very ᵃckward and not ready for tourists. There was a ᵗrange and wonderful atmosphere, as if we were ᵉghteenth century explorers.'

ᵀHE HARD FACTS In theory, formalities for ᵛˢitors have been considerably relaxed and it is ᵖossible, but difficult, to collect a permit on arrival ᵃᵗ Port Blair airport or port. In practice, to avoid any ᵖossible delays, apply for a permit from your Indi-ᵃn Embassy or Consulate before leaving home. The ᵖermit is limited to two weeks. The completed ᵗᵒrms, including requests to visit restricted areas, ᵗᵃke only 48 hours to process if delivered personal-ᵎʸ and about two weeks by post. If an Andamans ᵗrip is decided upon in India, apply to the Fore-ᵍners' Registration Office in Bombay, Calcutta, ᴺew Delhi or Madras for a regular two-week per-ᵐᵢt, but to the Ministry of Home Affairs, New ᵖelhi for restricted areas.

Season is December–April, with monsoon May–ᴼctober. A soft breeze cools the tropical climate ˢᵢghtly. Access is by air or sea. Flights connect Port ᴮlair with Madras (Wed., Sun.) and Calcutta ᵀues., Fri.). The sea trip from Madras or Calcutta ᵗᵃkes three days but it is not very picturesque, the ᵇoat is very hot and the water is often choppy. In ᵃddition, there is no fixed timetable. However, to ᵻnd out the next sailings and to book, contact The ᵖhipping Corporation of India, 13 Strand Road, ᶜalcutta or their Madras agents, K P V Sheikh ᴹohammed Rowther & Co., 202 Linghi Chetty ˢtreet, Madras. The SCI also have an office in ᴮombay, at 229–232 Madame Cama Road.

The easiest way of going is with TCI, a most ᵣeliable Indian travel agent, who set up individual ᵗᵒurs to the Andamans, using the Andaman Beach ᵣesort (see below) where they also have their ᴬndamans office (tel: 2599/2781; cable: TRAVEL-ᴬIDS). TCI's other offices are in all major cities. As ᵥith the Maldives, it is wiser to pack everything – ᵍerman and Italian visitors are known to bring ᵉven their cooking utensils and a small Calorgas ˢtove so that they can cook their fishing catch on ᵗhe beach. Collecting coral is strictly forbidden.

WHERE TO STAY
Andaman Beach Resort, Corbyn's Cove, Port Blair
Telephone: 231881
Telex: 2366
Airport 2km; city centre 4km
32 rooms, all with balcony and bathroom. Single Rs215, double Rs240.

Facilities include travel desk, shops, library, wind-surfing, water-skiing, sailing, scuba-diving, snorkelling, fishing, tennis court, croquet, volley ball, table tennis, restaurant and bar.

A new hotel with modern furnishing, likened by one visitor to a government high school building. Views through a row of palms on to the crescent-shaped beach of Corbyn's Cove.

Bay Island, Marine Hill, Port Blair
Telephone: 209
Cable: WELCOTEL
Airport 5km; city centre 2km
50 air-conditioned rooms, including suites, attached bath. Single Rs275, double Rs375, suite Rs500.

Facilities include transport counter, beauty salon, health club, doctor on call, sea-water pool, fishing, snorkelling, scuba diving, indoor games, video, restaurant.

Lavish new building, using local architectural traditions and furnishings, with pretty views over-looking Phoenix Bay. Restaurant serves good local fish dishes as well as Indian and Burmese food. The disadvantage: no beach by the hotel.

OUT AND ABOUT The archipelago has been called 'Paradise plus'. The plus stands for the flora and birds in the rich jungle. The Maldives are simply 'Paradise'. Early mornings are magical, as the mist lifts off the water and the islands come into focus while dolphins play in the water. In Port Blair there are interesting Anthropological and Marine museums, a bazaar and the Cottage Industries Emporium (shells, wood-carving). Hiring a boat can be tricky as there are not enough to supply the few tourists' needs.

To avoid the problems of finding a boat and getting permission to visit other islands, the Anda-man Beach Resort runs a variety of excursions, by road and boat, and the TCI desk will try to arrange any others. They include one to Chiriya Tapu at the southern tip of South Andamans where there is good fishing in the creeks, interesting bird life, mango groves and lovely beaches. Another trip goes to Wandoor Beach, where the sea is excep-tionally rich for snorkellers and divers.

Boat trips include a day spent on uninhabited forest islands of Grub, Snob, Red Skin and Jolly Boy, all surrounded by beaches and excellent snorkelling and scuba-diving to see coral, tropical fish, shells and turtles in the clear waters. And fishermen can have their catch grilled on the beach. Another trip is to Cinque Island, actually a group of islands, where you can camp overnight. Again, exceptionally clear water and rich marine life make ideal diving; the lush forested islands are rich in bird life and flora; and the fishing is good.

There are now just a few tribal groups left and, despite protection, the Indian government's current encouragement to immigrant farmers ma mean they have little peace to look forward to. Th gentle Onghies with naked, painted bodies live o Little Andaman. The more savage Jarwas live o the west coast of South Andaman, the Nicobaris o Car Nicobar and the Shompens on Great Nicoba All these areas are worth trying to get permits fo as is Ross Island in Port Blair harbour, where th beautiful Raj buildings are being throttled by ram pant vegetation and trees.

Calendar of Indian festivals

Thousands of festivals are held in India every year. The religious and national ones are celebrated with great gaiety. The cultural ones attract some of the many great Indian performers. Hardly a day passes in India without a festival taking place somewhere near where you are. They range from small, one-day village or temple celebrations to a fortnight of high quality arts performances or religious ritual. However, only a few have fixed dates. Hindu festivals follow the lunar calendar and their dates are only decided upon during the previous year. Some festivals are local to one area or one town. Even the national ones are best seen in certain cities, as indicated below. Most cultural festivals are held during the winter months.

By October of each year, your nearest Government of India Tourist Office will have available a list of the major festivals together with their dates for the following year.

Below are listed a few of the more colourful and interesting festivals, with their approximate dates, the best places to witness them and page references to further information. For Nepalese festivals see p. 233.

January
International Film Festival Delhi on odd years (1987, etc.); another major city on even years (p. 39).
Park Circus arts festival Calcutta
Tyagaraja music festival Thiruvaiyaru, near Thanjavur
Pongal (Sankranti): begins January 14 or 15. South India, especially Tamil Nadu (Madurai and Tiruchchirapalli, p. 176)
Kite Festival January 14. North India, especially Gujarat (p. 134) and Rajasthan
Lori mid-January. Punjabi festival celebrating the height of winter
Rimpa music festival Varanasi
Republic Day January 26. Across India in state capitals but best in Delhi (p. 38)
Folk Dance Festival January 27–28. Delhi (p. 38)
Beating Retreat January 28/29. Delhi (p. 38)

January–February
Teepam (Floating Festival): Madurai (p. 177)
Desert Festival Jaisalmer (p. 104)
The livestock fair Nagaur, near Jodhpur (p. 103)
Vasant Panchami Across India but especially in the north (where it marks the first day of spring) and in Bengal (where it honours the goddess of learning, Saraswati)

February
Carnival Goa (p. 240)
Tansen music festival February in Delhi; December in Gwalior (p. 69)
Lucknow arts festival Lucknow (p. 72)
Dhrupad music festival Delhi
Maharaj Kalka Bindadi Kathak dance festival Delhi
Dhrupad music festival last week of month. Varanasi

February–March

Shankar Lal music festival   Delhi
Shivarati   February–March. Shaivites throughout India spend the whole night worshipping Shiva. Best at Mandi (p. 225), Chidambaram, Khajuraho and Varanasi
Holi   Across northern India but best in Rajasthan (p. 80) and especially in Mathura and surrounding villages (p. 68)

March

Khajuraho dance festival   Early March. Khajuraho (p. 70)
Jamshed Navroz   New Year's Day for Parsees following the Falsi calendar, best witnessed in Maharashtra and Gujarat

March–April

Gangaur (Gauri Tritiya)   Rajasthan, especially Udaipur and Jaipur (p. 80), Bengal and Orissa (where it is called Doljatra)
Mahavir Jayanti   A Jain festival dedicated to Mahavira, 24th Tirthandara, best seen at Jain centres in Gujarat (pp. 138 and 140)
Ramanavami   Celebrations of the god Rama's birthday are held in temples throughout India

April–May

Pooram   Trichur (p. 177)
Meenakshi Kalyanam   Madurai (p. 177)
Spring Festival   Celebrations in the orchards of almond blossom at Srinagar in Kashmir.
Baisakhi   Across northern India and in Tamil Nadu, celebrating the Hindu solar New Year. Best seen in the Mughal gardens of Srinagar and in the Punjab where Sikhs celebrate Guru Gobind Singh's formation of Sikhs into the Khalso (the pure one) in 1689

May–June

Buddha Purnima   On full moon night, Buddha's birth, enlightenment and his attainment of nirvana are celebrated at all Buddhist centres, such as Sarnath (p. 167)

June–July

Rath Yatra   Puri (p. 168)
Car Festival   Serempore (p. 159)

July–August

Minjar   Chamba
Teej   Rajasthan, especially Jaipur (p. 80)
Nag Panchami   Jodhpur (p. 81)

Amarnath Yatra   On full moon, at Amarnath, near Pahalgam (p. 231)
Jhapan   Vishnupur, near Calcutta (p. 159)
Raksha Bandhan   Across northern and western India, where girls tie rakhi (tinsel and silk amulets) around the wrists of men in memory of the god Indra's triumph in battle after his consort gave him a rakhi

August

Vishnu Digambar music festival   Delhi
Independence Day   August 15. Across India but best in Delhi (p. 35)

August–September

Janmashtami (Krishna's birthday)   Celebrated across India; best seen in Mathura (p. 68), Dwark (p. 140), Agra, Delhi and Bombay
Onam   Throughout Kerala but best at Kottayam (p. 177)

September

Ganapati (Ganesh Chaturthi)   Bombay (p. 112)
Bhatkande music festival   Lucknow

September–October

Navrati   Ahmedabad (p. 134)
Dussehra   One of the most colourful of all festivals, celebrated across India. Best in Varanasi and Delhi (called Ram Lila in both, pp. 165 and 39), in Calcutta (called Durga Puja, p. 147) in Mysore (called Dassera, p. 177) and in the Kulu Valley (where it begins the day it ends in the rest of India (p. 225)

October

Sadarang music festival   Calcutta
Gandhi Jayanti (Mahatma Gandhi's Birthday)   October 2. Across India
Karwa Chauth   In Delhi, after a day of fasting, Hindu women dress up in wedding saris and make offerings to their mothers-in-law

October–November

Diwali   Across India but best in Delhi and the North (pp. 39, 80 and 177)

November

Govardhana Puja   Hindus throughout India worship the cows, their sacred animals
Sonepur fair   The largest cattle fair in the world, lasting a month, is held at Sonepur in Bihar, on the banks of the Ganga

Sangeet Sammelan music festival   Delhi
Sir-Singar music festival   Bombay
Lavi fair   second week of November. Rampur
Nanak Jayanti   The birthday of Guru Nayak,
founder of the Sikh religion, is celebrated by
Sikhs; best seen at Amritsar and Patna
Children's Day   November 14, Jawaharlal Nehru's
birthday, is celebrated by children throughout
India (p. 53)

November–December
Pushkar cattle fair   November–December.
Pushkar (p. 93)

December
Lalit Sangit Parishad music festival   Varanasi
Feast of St Francis Xavier   December 3. Goa.
Tansen music festival   Gwalior (p. 69)
Paus Mela arts festival   Santiniketan, Bengal
(p. 160)
Christmas Day   December 25. Across India but
best in Delhi, Bombay, Goa and Calcutta
Shanmukhananda arts festival   Bombay

December–January
Madras dance and arts festival   mid December–early
January. Madras (p. 207)

Kumbh Mela is the huge religious and commercial
fair held every three years consecutively in one of
four places: Allahabad (Uttar Pradesh), Nasik
(Maharashtra), Ujjain (Madhya Pradesh), and
Hardwar (Uttar Pradesh). Hindu pilgrims and
every variety of Hindu holy man gather from all
over India to cleanse themselves in holy water.
The huge fair provides endless food, markets and
entertainers. The next Kumbh Mela is at Hardwar
in 1986.

Muslim festival dates move right around the year,
following the lunar calendar. The best places to
witness them are the old Muslim centres of
Lucknow, Old Delhi, Hyderabad and
Ahmedabad. The principal ones are:

Ramadan (30 days of fasting, p. 49)
Id-ul-Fitr (also called Ramzan-Id, celebrating the
end of Ramadan, p. 49)
Id-ul-Zuhar (also called Bakr-Id, commemorating
Abraham's attempted sacrifice of Ishmael p. 39)
Muharram (10 days long, commemorating the
martyrdom of Mohammed's grandson, Imam
Hussain, p. 39)
Urs (best at Ajmer (p. 92) or Nizamuddin in Delhi,
p. 39)

Key dates in India's history

BC	
c 324	Rise of Maurya dynasty
c 273–236	Reign of Emperor Ashoka
AD	
320–647	Gupta dynasty
4th–8th centuries	Early Chalukya dynasty in the Deccan
5th–8th centuries	Pallava dynasty of South India at its most powerful (capital Kanchipuram)
8th–12th centuries	Chola dynasty of South India at its most powerful (capital Thanjavur)
950–1002	Reign of Chandella king Danga (built temples at Khajuraho)
985–1014	Reign of Chola ruler Rajaraja I from Thanjavur
1013–44	Reign of Chola ruler Rajendra from Thanjavur (joint rule 1013–14)
1006–1310	Hoysala dynasty of South India at its most powerful (capitals at Belur and Halebid)
12th and 13th centuries	Pandya dynasty of Tamil Nadu at its most powerful (capital Madurai)
1191–1246	Slave dynasty (capital Delhi)
1206–1526	Sultanate period (capitals Delhi and Agra)
1290–1320	Khilji dynasty (capital Delhi)
1320–1413	Tughlaq dynasty (capitals Delhi and Daulatabad)
1336–1565	Vijayanagar empire in South India (capital Vijayanagar)
1347–c 1489	Bahmani kingdom of the Deccan (capital Gulbarga, then Bidar)
1414–51	Sayyid dynasty (capital Delhi)
1451–1526	Lodi dynasty (capital Delhi)
1489–1686	Adil Shahi dynasty (capital Bijapur)
1502–1648	Capital removed from Delhi to Agra
1512–1687	Qutb Shahi dynasty (capital Golconda, then Hyderabad)
1526	Battle of Panipat: Babur defeats Ibrahim Lodi, initiating the Mughal Empire
1526–1707	Great Mughal period (capitals Agra and Delhi)
1526–1530	Reign of Mughal emperor Babur (lived 1483–1530)
1530–1556	Reign of Mughal emperor Humayun (lived 1508–1556)
1556–1605	Reign of Mughal emperor Akbar (lived 1542–1605)
1565	Battle of Talikota: The Muslim dynasties of the Deccan ally themselves and defeat the Vijayanagars
1568	Maharana Udai Singh moves the capital of Mewar to Udaipur after the third sack of Chittaugarh
1600	East India Company receives its trading Charter from Elizabeth I
1605–1627	Reign of Mughal emperor Jehangir (lived 1569–1627)
1612	British establish their first factory in India, at Surat
1627–1658	Reign of Mughal emperor Shah Jahan (lived 1592–1666)
1648	Triumphal entry of Shah Jahan into newly built Shahjahanabad (Old Delhi)

632–1653	Shah Jahan builds the Taj Mahal at Agra
639	East Indian Company establish a trading post at Madras
661	Mumbadevi, the largest Bombay island, is part of Catherine of Braganza's dowry when she marries Charles II
658–1707	Reign of Mughal emperor Aurangzeb (lived 1618–1707)
690	Job Charnock founds Calcutta
699–1744	Reign of Maharaja Jai Singh II of Jaipur (laid out Jaipur in 1728)
719–1748	Reign of Mughal emperor Mohammad Shah
751	Battle of Arcot: The British, under Clive, defeat the French, under Dupleix
757	Battle of Plassey: The British, under Clive, recapture Calcutta from the Nawab of Murshidabad
759	Hyder Ali (died 1782) deposes Chikka Krishna Raj Wadiyar of Mysore
772	Warren Hastings becomes first Governor of British India
775–1797	Reign of Asaf-ud-Daula, Nawab of Lucknow
782–1799	Tipu Sultan rules Mysore kingdom until the second British siege during which he is killed
798–1814	Reign of Sa'adat Ali Khan, Nawab of Lucknow
837–1858	Reign of Mughal emperor Bahadur Shah II
857	Bengal Uprising (which the British, from their side, call the Mutiny)
858	November 1. British India placed under direct government of the Crown
862–67	Sir Bartle Frere is Governor of Bombay
869	Suez Canal opens
875	Prince of Wales (later Edward VII) visits India
877	Queen Victoria becomes Empress of India
889	Second visit of the Prince of Wales
899	Lord Curzon becomes Governor-General
911	December 12. George V, King and Emperor, announces at Delhi the transfer of the capital from Calcutta to Delhi
920	The Non-Co-operation Movement begins
921	Prince of Wales (later Edward VIII) visits India
930	Mahatma Gandhi leads Dandi march from Ahmedabad, protesting against the Salt Tax
931	February 9. Inauguration of New Delhi
935	New Government of India Act
947	August 15. India Independence Act
948	January 30. Assassination of Mahatma Gandhi
949	November 26. Constitution adopted and signed
950	January 26. Constitution of India comes into force
965	Hindi proclaimed the national language
1966–77	Indira Gandhi is Prime Minister of India
973	Project Tiger launched by the World Wildlife Fund
975	June 25. The President declares a State of Emergency
977	March. General Election. Morarji Desai (Janata Party) becomes Prime Minister (March 24). The President revokes the State of Emergency
1980	January. Indira Gandhi returns as Prime Minister of India
1982	The Asiad Games
1983	Non-Aligned Meeting (known as NAM)
	Commonwealth Heads of Government Meeting (known as CHOGM)
1984	October 31. Assassination of Indira Gandhi in the garden of her home, no. 1, Safdarjang Road, New Delhi. President Zail Singh swears in her son, Rajiv, as Prime Minister of India at Rashtrapati Bhavan.
	November 3. Indira Gandhi cremated at Shanti Vana, beside the River Yamuna in Delhi, witnessed by more than 100 world leaders.
	November 13. Rajiv Gandhi calls a general election for December 24.

Glossary

Although English is the connecting language of India and you do not need a Hindi phrase book, there are some words in Hindi and other Indian languages that it might be useful to know. In addition, some English word carry an unfamiliar meaning in India. Amic the vast plethora of Hindu gods, the ones yo will encounter most often are also included.

a-c: air-conditioning; a room may be 'a-c' or 'non a-c'

ahimsa: non-violence, reverence for life

atcha: OK

afion: opium

air-cooled: system of cooling a room by fans or an electric machine fitted into the window

agarbathi: incense

apsaras: beautiful nymphs who seduce men and are consorts to gods

ashram: spiritual retreat; centre for practicing yoga and meditation

attar: perfume

avatar: incarnation of a god

ayah: nanny/nurse for children

ayyanar: large, painted terracotta figures of deities

baba: religious master; also used in a broader context to denote respect

bagh: garden

baksheesh: gift in the form of a bribe to get service, a tip to reward service or a direct gift to a beggar

Balarama: brother of the god **Krishna** (q.v.)

bandhana: tie-dye method of printing fabric

baoli: step-well, often elaborately decorated

bash: party

bazaar: market, market-place

bearer: similar to a butler

beedi: small, hand-rolled cigar

Bhagavata Purana: epic chronicle of the god **Vishnu** (q.v.) and his incarnations; books 10 and 11, about **Krishna** (q.v.), are especially popular

Bhagvad Gita: Song of the Lord, a glory of Sanskrit literature and part of the epic **Mahabharata** (q.v.); **Krishna**, as Arjuna's charioteer, reveals himself as god incarnate and expounds on the human struggle for love, light and love

bhang: hashish (north India)

Bharata Natyam: classical dance of Tamil Nadu

bhavan: big building, big house

bhisti: water carrier

bhopa: folk balladiers of Rajasthan

big-shot: important person, VIP

biryani: Mughlai dish of meat and rice

Bodhisattva: near **Buddha**, that is, a follower of Buddha capable of attaining **nirvana** (q.v.) who postpones it to show others the way

Brahma: Creator of the universe; head of the Hindu Trinity of Brahma, **Vishnu** (The Preserver) and **Shiva** (The Destroyer), collectively known as Trimurti; sometimes **Saraswati** (q.v.) is his daughter or consort; his vehicle is Hamsa, the goose

Brahmin: highest of the four Hindu **castes** (q.v.)

Buddha: The Enlightened One, from the word buddhi, meaning intellect; The Buddha was a prince, Gotama Siddhartha, who lived in the 6th to 5th centuries BC

cantonment: military and administrative area of a town, built and used by the British during the **Raj** (q.v.)

caste: station of life into which a Hindu is born. There are four: Brahmins (priests and religious teachers); Kshatriyas (kings, warriors, aristocrats); Vaisyas (traders, merchants, professionals) and Shudras (cultivators, servants, etc, formerly called Untouchables). See also **Harijan**

chai: tea

chappals: sandals

chappati: fried, unleavened bread

chat: snack

chaukidar: doorman, watchman

chauri: fly whisk

chhatri: mausoleum, tomb, cenotaph

shikar: hunt (sporting)

choli: tight-fitting blouse worn under a sari

chowk: market place

chunam: polished lime plaster

Congress (I): a division of the political Congress Party formed in 1969 by Indira Gandhi – hence (I)

crore: ten million, written 1,00,00,000

curd: yoghurt; also known as **dahi**

dacoit: armed robber, bandit

dargah: shrine of a Muslim saint

devi: a goddess; **Devi** (or Mahadevi) is another name for **Parvati** (q.v.)

dhal: pulses (lentil, split pea, etc)

dharma: Buddhist teachings

dhobi: clothes washer

dhoti: white cloth worn by men

dhurrie: flat-weave rug

Diwan-i-Am: public audience hall

Diwan-i-Khas: private audience hall

dosa: paper-thin rice pancake

durbar: court audience or government meeting

Durga: a malevolent aspect of the goddess **Parvati**

Dravidian: South Indian architectural style, derived from Dravidadesh (country of the Dravidians), the old name for the area covered by Tamil Nadu state

emporium: shop, often large and selling local crafts

fakir: Muslim holy man who has taken the vow of poverty; also applied to Hindu ascetics

feni: cashew or coconut-based spirit drink made in Goa

Ganesh: elephant-headed god of learning and good fortune, son of **Shiva** (q.v.) and **Parvati** (q.v.); also known as Ganapati

Ganga: goddess or personification of the Ganges, the sacred river of the Hindus; name by which the river is referred to by Hindus

ganja: hashish (eastern India)

Garuda: eagle or mythical sunbird, vehicle of the god **Vishnu**

ghat: steps down to a river, lake or tank; can also mean mountain

ghazel: light Urdu songs

ghi: clarified butter

gompa: Tibetan-Buddhist monastery

gopi: cowgirl, milkmaid; especially befriended by the god Krishna

gopuram: temple gate-house with soaring, pyramid tower (South India)

gulli/galli/gali: alley, lane

guru: spiritual teacher, holy man; his pupils/followers are called **chelas**

gymkhana: social club, usually run on traditional colonial lines, with pleasant club house, spacious grounds and good sports facilities

ha: yes

handloom cloth: mill-spun yarn that is woven by hand

Hanuman: the monkey god, Rama's ally in the **Ramayana** (q.v.)

Harijan: Children of God, the name coined by Mahatma Gandhi to describe the Shudra caste (Untouchables)

haveli: courtyard town mansion

hookah: hubble-bubble pipe in which the tobacco smoke is cooled by passing through water

howdah: elaborate seat on top of an elephant

idli: rice cakes

imam: Muslim leader

Indra: god of rain and thunder

ITDC: India Tourism Development Corporation; if the first initial is replaced by another, it usually refers to the state-run equivalent, such as K for Kerala

Jalebi: a sweet of rings of deep fried batter soaked in warm syrup

jali: carved stone or marble screens

jharokah: projecting balcony

ji: suffix used as mark of respect, as in Gandhiji, daddyji

johar: mass suicide by fire, committed by women to save themselves from a conqueror

Kali: The Black, the fearsome goddess of death and destruction who is one aspect of the goddess **Parvati** (q.v.); also known as Chamunda

Kaliya: serpent demon whom **Krishna** subdued

kama: desire, physical love, worldly pleasure; one of the four goals of life in Hindu philosophy; Kama is the god of love

karma: the idea that deeds in previous existences dictate the favourable, or less favourable, form of man's present and future incarnations

Kartikeya: god of war, son of **Shiva** (q.v.); also known as Subrahmanya

kathak: classical dance of northern India, from katha (story)

kathakali: story play; also used to describe the classical dance-drama of Kerala

kathputli: puppeteering

kebab: marinated meat, fish or vegetables cooked on a skewer

khadi: cloth that is spun, dyed, woven and printed by hand

Krishna: blue-skinned god of human form, considered by some to be the 8th incarnation of the god **Vishnu** (q.v.) but worshipped by many in his own right; protagonist of the **Bhagavad Gita** (q.v.); the gopi, Radha, is his lover and consort

kulfi: traditional Indian ice-cream, flavoured with pistachios and cardamoms

lakh: a hundred thousand, written 1,00,000

Lakshmi: goddess of wealth and good fortune, consort of **Vishnu** (q.v.); also known as Shri

lassi: thin yoghurt drink

lingum: phallic emblem of the god **Shiva** (q.v.), representing energy

liquor: spirits/alcohol, thus liquor store, liquor permit

Lok Sabha: House of the People; this and the **Rajya Sabha** (Council of States) are the Lower and Upper Houses of the Indian Parliament

lunghi: coloured version of a **dhoti** (q.v.), worn in the South

machan: watchtower in a wildlife park

Mahabharata: epic poem recounting the civil war between the Pandavas (of whom Arjuna was one) and Kurus over the right of succession, whose hero is Arjuna, with countless subsidiary stories. About 90,000 couplets long, passed on by oral tradition and probably first written down 4th to 2nd century BC

mahal: palace, queen

maharaja: great ruler, thus king

Mahatma: great soul, thus Mahatma Gandhi

mahout: elephant keeper/rider

maidan: open grass space in a city/town

mali: gardener

mandapam: hall-like porch of a temple

mandir: temple

marg: road, as in M G Marg; meadow, as in gulmarg (meadow of flowers)

masala: mixture of spices and herbs used in cooking; also used broadly to describe any mixture, such as the commercial Hindi films

masjid: mosque, thus Jami Masjid (Friday Mosque), the principal mosque of a town

meenakari: enamelling

mela: fair

memsahib: Western married woman; used broadly as a term of respect to all women, as 'madame' is used in French

mendhi: myrtle leaves whose orange dye is principally used to decorate the hands and feet of women

mihrab: prayer niche of a mosque, containing the *qibla* (indicator) for the direction of Mecca

mithuna: amorous couple, as found in temple sculpture

mojadi: leather slippers

moksha: enlightenment, release from worldly

...sitence; one of the goals of life in Hindu ...ilosophy

...onsoon:** rainy season, the period varies in ...ngth but usually falls sometime between June ...d October

...uezzin:** Muslim who calls the faithful to prayer, ...ually from a minaret of the mosque

...ughals:** Muslim dynasty ruling large tracts of ...rthern and central India from the 16th to 18th ...nturies

...ughlai:** cuisine of the Mughals, Persian in origin

...ullah:** Muslim priest

...urg:** chicken

...hin:** no

...maste:** a word of respectful greeting when ...ople meet or depart, accompanied by the ...sture of putting hands together, fingers ...inting upwards

...n:** baked leavened bread

...andi:** bull; vehicle of the god **Shiva** (q.v.)

...wab:** local ruler

...mbu paani:** refreshing drink of fresh lime juice ...d soda water; also called nimbu soda or fresh ...ne soda

...rvana:** in Buddhist philosophy, the state of ...lease from the cycle of rebirth and thus the ...hievement of total peace; the term is also used ...Hindus

...vas:** house, accommodation

...an:** betel nut mixed with condiments, chewed ...a digestive

...kora:** a meat or vegetable snack fried in ...am-flour batter

...llia:** commemorative stone, seen along the ...adside, often carved

...lo:** decorated end of a sari

...ratha:** a bread layered with butter, sometimes ...uffed with meat or vegetables

...rvati:** Daughter of the Mountains, goddess of ...ace and beauty; the female energy of the gods, ...so known as **Devi**, who also has a destructive ...ower manifest in various forms such as **Kali** ...v.) and **Durga**; consort of **Shiva**

...chwai:** painting on cloth

...etra dura:** stone (often marble) inlaid with ...loured stones or gems to form patterns

...ol:** gate

poppadum: thin, crisp lentil pancake, often eaten as an appetiser

pucka: correct, in the colonial sense; genuine

puja: worship, prayer, religious offering

pundit: teacher, professor (of scriptures, music, etc)

Puranas: 18 collections of traditional Hindi myths and legends

purdah: curtain behind which Muslim women live, screened from men and strangers; the practice of women living in purdah spread to Hindus

pyjama: baggy trousers, usually worn with a kurta (long shirt)

qawwali: mystical poems set to music, sung in chorus

qila: citadel, fort

Raj: rule, usually referring to the British rule in India

raja: ruler, prince

Rajput: Hindu rulers of Rajasthan and the Punjab

Rama: 7th avatar of the god **Vishnu** (q.v.), the human hero of the epic **Ramayana** (q.v.), brother of Bharata and Lakshmana; his wife is Sita

Ramayana: epic poem recounting the story of good king **Rama** (q.v.) who, aided by monkey and bear allies, rescues his wife Sita from abduction by Ravana, the multi-headed demon king of Lanka (Sri Lanka); about 24,000 couplets, with an oral tradition until it was written down around 4th to 2nd century BC

raga: the musical mode providing the framework for improvisation by the musician; there are ragas for all times of day and all moods; they inspired the development of a complex iconography in Indian miniature painting

rath: temple chariot or car, often of carved wood, on which temple deities are paraded at festivals; monolithic Pallava shrine

rickshaw: mode of transport: a bicycle rickshaw is a small, two-wheeled cart pulled by a bicycle; an auto-rickshaw is a covered, three-wheeled vehicle powered by a motorbike; in Calcutta, some rickshaws are still pulled by men or boys

sadhu: a Hindu ascetic

sagar: ocean, large lake

sahib: lord, master; broadly used as a term of respect, as 'sir' is used in English

sampsa: a meat or vegetable snack wrapped in short-crust pastry and deep-fried

Saraswati: goddess of knowledge, music and the arts; sometimes daughter or consort of Brahma

sari: long length of fabric worn by women

sati: a widow's honourable self-immolation, often on her husband's funeral pyre; outlawed by the British under the Regulation XVII Act of 1829 but continued for many years after this

Seven Sacred Cities: Varanasi, Hardwar, Ujjain, Mathura, Ajodhya, Dwarka and Kanchipuram are sacred pilgrimage centres for Hindus. Each city is dedicated to **Shiva** (q.v.) or **Vishnu** (q.v.) except Kanchipuram which is dedicated to both

Shaivite: worshipper or **Shiva** (q.v.)

shakti: life force, spiritual energy

Sherpa: a Nepalese people renowned as high-altitude porters and mountain guides

Shesha: the serpent on whom **Vishnu** (q.v.) reclines on the Cosmic Ocean

shikara: in boating, a luxurious gondola-like boat on which people are paddled around the lakes of Srinagar; in architecture, a beehive-shaped tower on a temple (also written as sikhara)

Shiva (or Siva): The Auspicious, third member of the Hindu Trinity; symbol of destructive and creative energy manifested in many forms such as Nataraja (Lord of the Dance); his consort is **Parvati** (q.v.); his sons are **Ganesh** (q.v.) and **Kartikeya** (q.v.); his vehicle is Nandi, the bull; his emblem is the **lingum** (q.v.)

Sita: wife of **Rama** (q.v.)

sitar: stringed musical instrument

sof: aniseed seeds, a digestive chewed after eating, often delivered gratis in restaurants

stupa: Buddhist relic mound

supper-club: restaurant, usually with live Western music and dance floor and not restricted to members

Surya: god of the sun; Aruna, symbol of dawn, is his charioteer

tabla: small drum

tandoor: clay oven

tank: water reservoir, artificial lake

tatti: grass matting, often soaked in water and hung across windows to cool the air during the hot season

thali: circular platter on which a vegetarian meal served in **katories** (small dishes)

thik hai: OK (eastern India), like atcha

tiffin: light lunch

tikka: dot of paste, often red, worn by Hindus (the dot worn by married Hindu women is called *suhag*); in cooking, tikka is meat or fish marinade and then cooked in a tandoor oven

Tirthankaras: the 24 Jain teachers

Tonga: mode of transport: a cart drawn by a pony

tri-cuisine: restaurant menu offering Indian, Chinese and Continental dishes

toddy: spirit drink made from coconut palm sap

Untouchable: see Harijan

utsav: festival

Vaishnavite: worshipper of **Vishnu** (q.v.)

vimana: principal temple or central shrine, including sanctuary and porches, of a Hindu temple complex; also used to refer to the tower surmounting this building

vina: the primary stringed instrument of classical Indian music

Vishnu: The Preserver, second member of the Hindu Trinity (cf. **Brahma**); symbol of the creation and preservation that maintains the balance of the forces which sustain the universe. His ten principal incarnations (avatars) include Matsya (1st, the fish); Kurma (2nd, the turtle); Varaha (3rd, the boar); Narasimha (4th, the man-lion); **Rama** (7th, hero of the **Ramayana**, q.v.); **Krishna** (q.v.) or Balarama, his brother (8th, both in human form but opinions vary as to which is an avatar). His consort is **Lakshmi** (q.v.); his vehicle is **Garuda** (q.v.)

wallah: fellow, thus rickshaw-wallah, dhobi-wallah

yali: a mythical composite animal made up of a lion, horse and elephant, often carved on temples

yoga: phsycho-physical discipline involving the practice of meditation, exercise positions and breathing control to achieve spiritual peace

zari: gold or silver metal thread used in weaving brocades, now often applied to imitation thread

zenana: women's quarters of a household

Index

261

59 KP